FORENSIC ACCOUNTING

We work with leading authors to develop the
strongest educational materials in accountancy,
bringing cutting-edge thinking and best
learning practice to a global market.

Under a range of well-known imprints, including
Financial Times Prentice Hall we craft high-quality print and
electronic publications which help readers to understand
and apply their content, whether studying or at work.

To find out more about the complete range of our
publishing, please visit us on the World Wide Web at:
www.pearsoned.co.uk.

FORENSIC ACCOUNTING

John Taylor

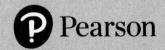 **Pearson**

Harlow, England • London • New York • Boston • San Francisco • Toronto • Sydney • Dubai • Singapore • Hong Kong
Tokyo • Seoul • Taipei • New Delhi • Cape Town • São Paulo • Mexico City • Madrid • Amsterdam • Munich • Paris • Milan

Pearson Education Limited
Edinburgh Gate
Harlow
Essex CM20 2JE
England

and Associated Companies throughout the world

Visit us on the World Wide Web at:
www.pearsoned.co.uk

First published 2011

ISBN: 978-0-273-72296-0

British Library Cataloguing-in-Publication Data
A catalogue record for this book is available from the British Library

Library of Congress Cataloging-in-Publication Data
Taylor, John.
 Forensic accounting / John Taylor. — 1st ed.
  p. cm.
 Includes bibliographical references and index.
 ISBN 978-0-273-72296-0
 1. Fraud investigation—Great Britain. 2. Forensic accounting—Great Britain.
3. Corporate governance—Law and legislation--Great Britain. 4. Auditing, Internal—
Law and legislation—Great Britain. I. Title.
 HV8079.F7T39 2011
 363.25'9360941—dc22

                                                                    2010030525

10 9 8 7 6 5 4 3 2 1
13 12 11 10

Typeset in 9/12pt Stone Serif by 73
Printed and bound in Great Britain by Ashford Colour Press Ltd, Gosport, Hampshire

Brief contents

Contents

Part 2   THE ROLE OF THE ORGANISATION AND THE PSYCHOLOGY OF FRAUD

Part 4 CARRYING OUT A FRAUD INVESTIGATION

Frauds 459

Glossary 464
Index 473

Author acknowledgements

Many people have assisted me in the preparation of this book, some unconsciously through their writings and lectures, others voluntarily.

Wherever possible credit has been given for those whose written work has been used in the writing of this book and any omissions will be corrected at the earliest opportunity.

Of those who helped voluntarily I would particularly like to thank Chris Clements and Amie Taal of Grant Thornton who bailed me out at a time of crisis, Vivien Osborne and Claire Marshall of KPMG in Leeds for their input and Anthony Forde and Steph Dixon of Leeds Metropolitan University for valuable and very useful reviews of areas I knew little about then but know more now.

The content of this book is entirely the responsibility of the author and no endorsement should be imputed to any firm or individual who assisted in its preparation.

Lots of valuable support also came from Lindsey Dunbar to whom this book is dedicated.

John R. Taylor

Publisher acknowledgements

We are grateful to the following for permission to reproduce copyright material:

Figures

Figure 6.1 from 'The Uniform Occupational Fraud Classification', *Report to the Nation on Occupational Fraud and Abuse*, p. 10 (2004), Association of Certified Fraud Examiners, USA, http://www.acfe.com/documents/2004RttN.pdf.

Text

Extract on page 33 from ISA 200 'Objective and General Principles Governing an Audit of Financial Statements', p. 2; extract on page 35 from ISA 240 'The Auditor's Responsibility to Discover Fraud in an Audit of Financial Statements', p. 8; extracts on page 40 from ISA 320 'Materiality in Planning and Performing an Audit', p. 2; Exhibit 2.1 from *Learning from Fraudsters*, Protiviti Ltd (Gill, M. 2005) p. 40, copyright © 2005 Protiviti Ltd; extracts on pages 54, 56, 59, 60 and 62 from Fraud Act, 2006, Crown Copyright material is reproduced with the permission of the Controller, Office of Public Sector Information (OPSI); Exhibit 3.3 adapted from 'Second Life world may be a haven for terrorists', *The Daily Telegraph*, 13/05/2007 (Leapman, B.), http://www.telegraph.co.uk/news/uknews/1551423/Second-Life-world-may-be-haven-for-terrorists.html, copyright © Telegraph Media Group Limited 2007; Exhibit 3.4 from 'Sacked whistleblowers win £1m payout from council', *Yorkshire Post*, 14/08/2007 (Waugh, R.), http://www.yorkshirepost.co.uk/news?articleid=3107592, copyright Ross Parry; Exhibit 4.4 adapted from 'Grieving father took revenge by stealing £875,000', *Mail Online*, 09/10/2007, http://www.dailymail.co.uk/news/article-486447/Grieving-father-took-revenge-stealing-875-000.html; Example on page 137 from *Learning from Fraudsters*, Protiviti Ltd (Gill, M. 2005) p. 20, copyright © 2005 Protiviti Ltd; Exhibit 5.2 from 'Prison sentence for book keeper who stole £1m from food firm', *Mail Online*, 28/07/2006 (Tozer, J.), http://www.dailymail.co.uk/news/article-398142/Prison-sentence-book-keeper-stole-1m-food-firm.html; Exhibit 6.1 adapted from 'Jailed – Council executive who stole £617,000 of public money for fake children's home', *Mail Online*, 13/03/2009 (Narain, J.), http://www.dailymail.co.uk/news/article-1161770/Jailed-Council-executive-stole-617-000-public-money-fake-childrens-home.html; Exhibit 7.1 from 'Anti-fraud policy statement – a sample', www.fraudadvisorypanel.org, © Fraud Advisory Panel 2010; Exhibit 7.2 after *Fraud Risk Management – A Guide to Good Practice*, CIMA, London (2008) pp. 62–3, © CIMA 2008; extract on page 216 from Auditing Practices Board Glossary of Terms (2009) – Internal Control, p. 13; extract on page 233 adapted from *The Invisible Crime – a business survey*, British Chambers of Commerce (2008) pp. 12–13; extract on page 237 adapted from CobiT 4.1

© 1996–2007 ITGI, all rights reserved, used by permission; extract on page 241 adapted from http://www.iso.org/iso/catalogue_detail?csnumber=42103, with permission of British Standards Institution; extract on page 241 adapted from http://www.iso27001security.com, © IsecT Ltd 2010; Exhibit 11.1 adapted from 'KPMG accountant jailed for £550,000 expenses fiddle that paid for "wife's lifestyle"', *The Daily Telegraph*, 16/09/2009 (Hough, A.), http://www.telegraph. co.uk/news/uknews/crime/6194567/KPMG-accountant-jailed-for-550000-expenses-fiddle-that-paid-for-wifes-lifestyle.html, copyright © Telegraph Media Group Limited 2009; Exhibit 11.5 adapted from 'Car parks cashier stole £½ m to fund Elvis obsession', *The Daily Telegraph*, 21/10/2005 (Britten, N.), http://www.telegraph.co. uk/news/1501100/Car-parks-cashier-stole-m-to-fund-Elvis-obsession.html, copyright © Telegraph Media Group Limited 2005; Exhibit 11.6 adapted from 'Disgraced ex-UKIP MEP Tom Wise jailed for two years for expenses fraud', *The Daily Telegraph*, 11/11/2009 (Bingham, J.), http://www.telegraph.co.uk/news/newstopics/politics/6545334/Disgraced-ex-Ukip-MEP-Tom-Wise-jailed-for-two-years-for-expenses-fraud. html, copyright © Telegraph Media Group Limited 2009; Exhibit 11.7 adapted from 'NHS wages fraudster is jailed for four years', *The Daily Telegraph*, 25/02/2006 (Martin, N.), http://www.telegraph.co.uk/news/uknews/1511412/NHS-wages-fraudster-is-jailed-for-four-years.html, copyright © Telegraph Media Group Limited 2006; extract on page 317 from ISA 580 'Written Representations', p. 4; extract on page 317 from ISA 580 'Written Representations', p. 3; Exhibit 12.1 adapted from 'SFO Historic cases – Independent Insurance', http://www.sfo.gov.uk/our-work/our-cases/historic-cases/independent-insurance.aspx, © Crown Copyright; Exhibit 12.3 adapted from SFO Transtec plc press release 07/04/2006, http://www.sfo.gov.uk/press-room/latest-press-releases/press-releases-2006/transtec-plc.aspx, © Crown Copyright; Exhibit 12.5 adapted from 'Parmalat: All you need to know about the collapse of the Italian dairy giant', *Guardian*, 06/10/2004 (Tran, M. and Jay, A.), http://www.guardian.co.uk/business/2004/oct/06/corporatefraud.businessqandas, copyright Guardian News & Media Ltd 2004; Exhibit 12.8 adapted from 'SFO Historic cases – Mabey and Johnson: Overseas corruption', http://www.sfo.gov.uk/our-work/our-cases/historic-cases/mabey–johnson–overseas-corruption-.aspx, © Crown Copyright; Exhibit 12.9 adapted from 'Celebrities lose out in "British Bernie Madoff Ponzi fraud"', *The Daily Telegraph*, 20/07/2009 (Moore, M.), http://www. telegraph.co.uk/news/newstopics/celebritynews/5864913/Celebrities-lose-out-in-British-Bernie-Madoff-Ponzi-fraud.html, copyright © Telegraph Media Group Limited 2009; Exhibit 13.2 adapted from SFO press release 27/06/2003 'Three sentenced in international advance fee fraud', http://www.sfo.gov.uk/press-room/latest-press-releases/press-releases-2003/three-sentenced-in-international-advance-fee-fraud.aspx, © Crown Copyright; Exhibit 13.7 adapted from '"Robin Hood" bank manager took £7m to give to poor', *The Daily Telegraph*, 17/09/2008 (Khan, U.), http://www.telegraph.co.uk/news/uknews/2974376/Robin-hood-bank-manager-took-7m-to-give-to-poor.html, copyright © Telegraph Media Group Limited 2008; Appendix on page 455 from http://www.businesslink.gov.uk/bdotg/action/detail?itemId=1076142205&type=RESOURCES, © Crown copyright 2010 Accessed July 2010; Appendix on page 457 from http://www.businesslink.gov.uk/bdotg/action/detail? itemId=1076142227&type=RESOURCES, © Crown copyright 2010 Accessed July 2010; Appendix on page 463 from *Fraud Risk Management – A Guide to Good Practice*, CIMA, London (2008) p. 59, © CIMA 2008.

In some instances we have been unable to trace the owners of copyright material, and we would appreciate any information that would enable us to do so.

Introduction

These days the word 'forensic' carries with it connotations of the seedy glamour of the world of crime, the sexy *CSI*, the magical forensics whose painstaking investigation of the minutiae of the crime scene will unearth that small but vital piece of evidence which will, in an unfeasibly short space of time, unmask the criminal.

Add 'forensic' to 'accountant' and even the dull bespectacled figure who is only invited to parties so people can get free tax advice is suddenly suffused with an aura of mystery – what is this forensic accountant, how can such a boring job as being an accountant suddenly be transformed into something, dare we say it, rather exciting?

Forensic accountants are the new kids on the block – the investigators, the seekers after truth who do, indeed, sift the minutiae of financial information in search of the evidence which may convict a fraudster, win a claim or settle a dispute.

The word 'forensic' comes from the Latin *'forensis'*. The dictionary definition describes it as 'public' or 'of a forum' and it relates to public discussion or argument or arguments appropriate to a court of law. What it has come to mean, in this century, is the gathering of facts to support an argument, providing facts or evidence in a court of law.

Forensic accountants gather facts and information and use what they have gathered as evidence to support a case, be it a commercial case for compensation or evidence to convict a fraudster. Their work has to be painstaking and meticulous, capable of being challenged and of withstanding that challenge, carried out with skill and not a little imagination.

Forensic accountants, generally, are qualified, experienced individuals, mostly working in professional accounting firms or for specialised consultancies. It is not so much the professional accountancy qualification that matters in the world of forensic analysis (although having a sound technical knowledge helps), it is the years of experience which the investigators or analysts can bring to bear on the task confronting them. Because their role integrates investigative, accounting and auditing skills many forensic accountants have paid their dues on the road as auditors, learning the craft of analysing company records, testing and checking and making judgements about people and their words and actions. The job of the forensic accountant has some broad similarities with that of the auditor, analysing, interpreting, summarising and presenting often complex financial data in a way which is comprehensible to the lay person and properly supported by sufficient, appropriate evidence.

In recent years the increase in white-collar crime, particularly fraud and corruption, has seen the forensic accountants move more into centre stage as their skills are recognised as being valuable in the settlement of disputes and claims, whether for compensation or matrimonial, and this, in turn has helped to emphasise the need for a more thorough approach to accounting and auditing.

The work of the forensic accountant is complex and varied and requires a range of skills and experience to meet the challenges they face in their day-to-day activities.

Forensic accounting can, broadly, be divided into two areas of specialisation – fraud investigatory work or accounting and litigation support. Clearly the glamour-end of the forensic accounting business is fraud detection.

This can involve:

- investigating and analysing financial evidence
- advising on defensive systems and the methods whereby organisations can detect frauds, hopefully at an early stage
- developing computerised applications to assist in the analysis and presentation of financial evidence
- communicating their findings in the form of reports, exhibits and collections of documents, or
- assisting in legal proceedings, including testifying in court as an expert witness and preparing visual aids to support trial evidence.

Where the case involves prosecution the forensic accountant is usually a key part of the legal team, assisting the prosecuting authorities, including the Police Economic Crime Unit, with the investigation and providing them with any findings as part of their case.

However, forensic accounting isn't just about fraud, although this is often seen as the exciting end of the job, and the techniques of forensic investigators can be brought to bear in a variety of situations including, but not limited to:

- business valuations
- divorce proceedings and matrimonial disputes
- asset tracing
- personal injury and fatal accident claims
- insurance claims for loss recovery
- partnership and corporate disputes
- challenging Confiscation Orders, or
- civil and criminal actions concerning fraud and financial irregularities.

Of course in their everyday work forensic accountants are more likely to get involved in these less exciting activities but they can be called into any situation where information has to be gathered, sorted, assembled and processed into a coherent and understandable format.

Most of the textbooks on fraud detection and forensic accounting, which you will find listed on Amazon and at all good booksellers, are written in the USA by American accountants or academics and deal with the American way of doing things. Whilst much of what they contain may be pertinent to the UK-based investigator, many aspects of the way we do business in the UK are significantly different to business practice in the USA. For example the use of electronic banking for day-to-day transactions is considerably more prevalent in the UK than in the USA, so far, and many US-based textbooks deal with cheque payments in a way that is no longer appropriate in the UK. Clearly the taxation and legal systems are also rather different as is their entire approach to corporate governance.

In the USA they tend to adopt a rules-based approach to regulation and the resultant checklist and 'tickbox' culture has provided many a corporate lawyer with a splendid income in advising corporations on compliance and interpretations of the rules. Having said that, the Association of Certified Fraud Examiners in the USA has pioneered many of the fraud detection techniques in use today and this book is indebted to their pioneering spirit and approach to fraud detection if not, necessarily, the details of their approach.

This book is written from a UK perspective – it deals with our way of doing business under our systems and our rules. Some of the lessons already learned in the USA have been incorporated where appropriate but most of this book is what we can establish as best practice in the UK.

Part 1 sets the scene and describes the corporate governance background which is a necessary part of the management of all good companies. In it we look at the roles of the management and the auditors and the parts they play not only as part of fraud detection and prevention but also as part of corporate culture. We also look at the legal background to fraud. The law is predominantly the Fraud Act 2006 and we look at this in some detail, as the forensic accountant should of course have some familiarity with the legal basis of their work. In addition to the Fraud Act we also look at money laundering regulations, the law surrounding whistle-blowing, anti-corruption rules and at the various fiendish court orders forensic investigators can use to freeze assets, compel disclosures and search for information.

In Part 2 we also look at the organisation and how dysfunctional organisations can create a culture of fraud and corruption which employees involved in it can come to accept as if not totally morally acceptable, at least justifiable in the circumstances. We also look at the psychology and motivation of the individual. This is not an academic tome, as such, so it does not attempt to analyse the whole basis of criminological theory underlying white-collar crime, but it does set out the basic concepts and also deals with some of the underlying crime, such as rationalisation. We also look at one personality disorder, narcissism, which may have encouraged, if not actually driven, the perpetrating of some extremely big and bold enterprises which have descended into crime.

The roots of fraud behaviour are in the psychology of the organisation and the motivations of the individual, so in Part 2 we give these factors the same weight as we do the features of a strong internal control environment outlined in Part 3.

In Part 3 we look at the principles of fraud prevention. This is not a book on auditing, and, although an understanding of basic audit techniques and the principles of internal control will be a help, as it would be in real life, it is not necessary to understand auditing in all its glory in order to follow the principles in this book. This Part includes not only the basic principles of risk management and internal control from a systems perspective but also, and equally importantly, incorporates aspects of organisational psychology and the psychology of the fraudster explained earlier in Part 2.

Forensic accountants are often called in to advise clients and to review organisational systems with a view to improving defences against fraudsters, and those who seek to damage businesses through unauthorised intrusions from the outside. The more the forensic accountant can do to raise awareness of fraud activity by convincing directors and managers to create the right culture in their organisation and to commit resources to business improvement in this direction the less damage will be done by those who seek to take from businesses and give nothing back.

Part 4 deals with the practical aspects of carrying out a fraud investigation by conventional means. Clearly every investigation is different so, in this book, we can only deal in principles and techniques, but careful study will equip the student or trainee with a toolkit of techniques and hopefully even the most hard-bitten and experienced professional will find something new in it. We look at particular types of fraud rather than fraud in particular situations or industries. This Part deals not only with frauds perpetrated against the organisation by managers or employees, but also with fraud committed by the organisation, where directors seek to 'improve' their reporting, either for personal gain or simply to keep the business afloat against the odds.

We include here the arcane world of computer-based investigation and step gingerly into the world of data mining and data analysis. This is not a specialised computer book and the author is not a specialist either, so this Part is written very much for the lay reader. It deals in concepts and principles, hopefully in an understandable way, and those students who wish to expand their knowledge of computer-based forensics will find resources for further study.

Part 5 deals with the non-fraud work of the forensic accountant. Frequently their forensic skills are needed to assist in settling marital disputes by valuing assets, or by tracing assets one party is trying to hide from the other. Forensic accountants haven't forgotten their key skills, and commercial dispute resolution through establishing the quantum of loss or damages claims is an important feature of what they do. This Part contains up-to-date information as to the approach to this kind of work.

This book is not aimed at the experienced professionals – after all they should know most of this stuff but – as we said earlier, there may be some things even they can learn! It is really aimed at:

- the student who wishes to specialise in this area or who is seeking to widen their skills base from the mainstream of the examination syllabus
- the accountant, whether in practice or not, who wishes to learn the skills and techniques of the forensic accountant to increase their skills base, and
- the corporate accountant looking to combat fraud in their organisation by using some of the techniques illustrated here.

The text is illustrated with examples of real frauds and case histories to emphasise the points made in the text.

Each chapter concludes with a summary and a case study relevant to the chapter content which students can use to practice their skills.

Part 1

CORPORATE GOVERNANCE, THE ROLE OF THE AUDITORS AND THE LEGAL CONTEXT

Chapter 1

The development of corporate governance

Chapter contents

- Introduction
- Background to corporate activity
- Agency theory
- Corporate governance
- The Combined Code on Corporate Governance 2003
- The role of the board
- Directors
- The audit committee
- The Turnbull Report
- Sarbanes–Oxley 2002

Learning objectives

After studying this chapter you should be able to:

- Understand the foundations of the modern company
- Understand and explain the outline development of company law
- Appreciate the implications of the theory of agency
- Understand the implications of the growth of executive power and the diversity of ownership
- Understand what corporate governance is and the need for it
- Recognise the relevance of the Sarbanes–Oxley legislation in the USA
- Detail the provisions of the Combined Code in the UK as to the role of directors and the structure of boards
- Understand the audit committee, its composition and role

Introduction

All practising accountants should be familiar with the principles described in this chapter, and may feel that to include a chapter setting out a brief history of the development of the joint stock company and the growth of corporate governance simply constitutes an attempt at irrelevant padding by the author, who is merely trying to bulk out his book in order to make it look a more impressive volume on the bookshelf. 'Old familiar territory to be glossed over,' they will murmur wearily and flick through to the chapter on computer forensic investigations.

Students of accountancy may also feel that they know all about this stuff from their readings in corporate law, entrepreneurial finance or even auditing so, like the jaded practitioner, they too may be tempted to skip this bit and get into the practicalities of fraud investigation techniques.

This would be wrong.

The reason is this. There are fundamental structural principles which lie at the heart of some of the biggest corporate scandals in history and these principles must be clearly understood. It is important for forensic accountants to understand the context within which they have to work and it is equally important for them to have an understanding of the underlying causes of dysfunctional behaviour, and the inherent conflict between the psychology of managers and the aspirations of shareholders.

The modern world of corporate reporting encourages disclosure and openness as it moves inexorably towards embracing the principles encompassed within corporate social responsibility (CSR) and the enhanced disclosures envisaged by its promoters. Moral and ethical behaviour by directors and employees is a part of good corporate governance and is also a significant component of CSR. Understanding behaviour, both at the organisation level and at the level of the individual within the entity, is, as we will see, fundamental to the work of the forensic accountants in whatever work they are engaged, be it a fraud investigation, tracing and valuing assets in separation cases or quantifying damages claims.

It is also important for reporting investigators not only to know what has happened and where they, or more accurately their clients, are in ethical and moral terms but also just how far standards of behaviour may have fallen from the ideal.

The cynical may well ask how corporate governance initiatives, whether enforced by statute or as part of a semi-voluntary code, have prevented fraud and corruption: after all, we continue to see instances of corrupt and dysfunctional behaviour by corporations and an ever-increasing level of fraudulent activity by individuals. The answer is: we don't know. We don't know how bad it might have been, we only know what we have discovered.

What we do know is that there has to be a standard, a benchmark by which behaviour can be judged, and forensic accountants must know what that standard is. As we will see from succeeding chapters dysfunctional behaviour tends to flourish where corporate morality breaks down, either at the organisational or at the individual level. In this and later chapters we take time to consider what is right, which, we submit, is just as significant as discovering what is wrong.

Background to corporate activity

To understand the development of forensic accounting it is first necessary to consider a little history. This is important because forensic accounting, in many ways, derives from the role of the auditor, that unfashionable but critical spectre at the feast hosted by investors and enjoyed by managers. The external auditor has become one of the planks of sound corporate governance, one part of the critical checks and balances that help encourage companies towards levels of transparency and accountability which are hitherto unsurpassed in corporate reporting in the UK.

Once the corporation had finally developed as a legal entity in its own right, resulting in the mass ownership of shares becoming firmly separated from the management and control of the organisation's activities on a day-to-day basis, the stage was set for the role of the auditor as arbitrator and judge. That role becomes increasingly significant where standards of corporate morality are or are seen to be declining. The corporate scandals in the USA and Europe in recent years involving misrepresentation, corruption and theft on a huge scale have increased the demand from both investors and regulators for auditors to be more efficient and more demanding of their clients in terms of their visible adherence to ethical principles and practical internal control systems.

Throughout history there have always been thieves and deceivers. There have always been those who seek to profit at the expense of others. At one level then, auditors and managers are on the same side as they seek to protect the organisation's assets or to catch the offenders and, hopefully, see them punished. Where auditors and managers part company is where it is the managers who seek to enrich themselves at the organisation's expense in a way that the auditor would expose as illegal or immoral because, in that case, it is depriving the owners of the business of what is rightfully theirs.

When managers distort the financial statements so that their share options sell out at a good price, where they create fictitious assets to hide their own depredations, where they stick their noses so far into the trough that their feet leave the ground – this is where the external auditor steps in to expose this bad behaviour, this immorality, this betrayal of trust.

The problem is that external auditors have signally failed to do this over many years.

It has been said that not one major fraud, at least in the modern era, has been exposed by the external audit. Illegal or immoral behaviour has come to light because of whistle-blowers, because of internal auditors, because the house of cards the fraudsters have built is blown down by the cold winds of reality. When that happens, the post-mortem frequently reveals not only the greed and corruption of those who perpetrated the fraud but also the weakness of the external auditors and their apparent willingness to accede to the demands of the directors or, in other cases, the sheer ineptness of their actions.

In 1992, partly as a result of Robert Maxwell's depredation of Mirror Group Newspapers and the scandal of BCCI, the Cadbury Report was published. In his report Sir Adrian Cadbury wrote 'The central issue is to ensure that an appropriate relationship exists between the auditors and the management whose financial statements they are auditing.'

We will look in more detail at the role of both external and internal auditors later, but for now, it is sufficient to say that when alarms go off it is more likely to be the forensic accountant who is called in to sort through the stories and statements to try to ascertain the truth.

The forensic accountant's role in the corporate world is to unpick the detail, unravel the complex schemes of fraudsters, reveal the clandestine behaviour of those who would steal the assets of someone else's business, track down the money, reveal the corrupt and explain where it all went wrong so that lessons can be learned and it won't happen again – until the next time.

It is the separation of ownership from control which is at the heart of corporate misbehaviour and it is this separation which has led to the development of what has come to be known as corporate governance, and with it the role of the forensic accountant. We need to understand how we got where we are before we can see where we might go, so we need to consider a little history.

The history of the modern company

Before the middle of the nineteenth century any entrepreneurs in the West wishing to risk their capital in a commercial venture had few choices. They could risk their own money and pledge their assets to secure further borrowings, rather as small business people do to this day, or they could go into partnership with other like-minded souls and so spread the risk, assuming they could find enough people to assist in financing the venture, which required a deal of trust and no little faith that all would turn out well.

Samuel Smiles expressed it inimitably:

> The implicit trust which merchants are accustomed to confide in distant agents, separated from them perhaps by half the globe – often consigning vast wealth to persons, recommended only by their character, whom perhaps they have never seen – is probably the finest homage which men can render to one another.
>
> (Smiles, 1982)

Much of medieval trading was regulated by Guilds whose role was to oversee the regulation of various craft trades, but the growing development of international trade required more formal structures out of which evolved regulated companies. Members of these companies could trade their in own shares or stock, subject to the rules of the company, although they did not have limited liability for their members; legally they were akin to partnerships.

A company trades at law as a legal person, a single entity which comprises the investments of its members. The Crown has always had the right to grant charters of incorporation and such companies had, prior to 1844, to be set up either by Act of Parliament or by Royal Charter. The would-be entrepreneur had to have both friends in high places and a lot of capital in order to establish any serious business venture, particularly one involving any form of international trade, but the great advantage was that the granting of the charter conferred a legal personality on the company and, with it, limited liability for its members.

Despite the bureaucratic difficulties many very successful companies were set up in this way. Perhaps the most famous were:

- The *Honourable East India Company* granted exclusive trading rights in the East Indies by Royal Charter in 1600 and, arguably, inadvertent founder of the British Empire.

- The *Governor and Company of Adventurers of England trading into Hudson's Bay* formed by Royal Charter in 1670. Later known as the Hudson's Bay Company and famous for opening up Canada and stimulating the market for fur.
- The infamous *Company of Merchants of Great Britain trading in the South Seas* – the *South Sea Company*, formed in 1711, legendary stock operator, creator of the South Sea Bubble, and harbinger of things to come. It is estimated that, at its height, the total value invested in the South Sea Company reached £500m, at eighteenth-century prices – twice the value of all the land in England at that time.

Of all of these it was the South Sea Company which was to have the most profound effect on the corporate governance of the day. A huge speculation in the affairs of the company, fuelled by claims which later proved to be fraudulent, led to a massive investing frenzy which, as all such frenzies do, ended catastrophically. The company crashed and many speculators were ruined. It was the Enron of its day, and just as Enron prompted the Sarbanes–Oxley legislation in the USA in the twenty-first century, in the eighteenth century the government of the day passed, in 1720, the so-called 'Bubble Act' in order, it said, to prevent further fraudulent activity.

This Act provided that all commercial undertakings (both corporations and partnerships) 'tending to the common grievance, prejudice and inconvenience of His Majesty's subjects' would be illegal and void. The Act also banned speculative buying and selling of shares and outlawed stockbroking in such shares. Between 1720 and 1825, when the Bubble Act was repealed, shares could only legally be sold to persons genuinely taking over a role in running the corporation or partnership. The problem was, however, that whilst the Act suppressed unincorporated quasi-companies it did nothing to provide any alternative form of legal structure which could be used as a vehicle for trade.

Between 1720 and 1844 new businesses which might previously have been incorporated were operated, effectively, as partnerships based on an elaborate Deed of Settlement. In law these were classed as partnerships and the partners were, accordingly, jointly and severally liable for the debts of the business.

However, as the eighteenth century progressed and the industrial economy grew rapidly, driven by technological advances in textiles and the smelting of iron, there developed a need for expansion of transport links, which took the form of canals and waterways, to move goods and raw materials to the new manufacturing centres and markets of England. The problem was that, because of the Bubble Act, financiers were not prepared to put their hands in their pockets and put up the money if it meant that they might ultimately be responsible for all debts and liabilities of the business if it failed. The risks were often seen as too high to outweigh the possibility of reward. The governments of the day either could not or would not finance these much needed developments so many of these very early transport infrastructure projects were funded by wealthy landowning individuals.

An answer was needed and the corporate form appeared ideal. Parliament began to approve specific corporations to be created by Act of Parliament ('Statutory Corporations'). An Act of Parliament would authorise the creation of a corporation for a specific and narrow purpose and allow it to bring and defend legal actions in its own name (so protecting the financiers from personal responsibility should the corporation fail).

The general view at the time was that corporations should only be created for very specific purposes. Adam Smith, author of the seminal tome *The Wealth of*

Nations and father of much of modern capitalist thinking, believed it was contrary to the public interest for any businesses or trades to be incorporated and that all should be run as partnerships. He believed in the ultimate aspect of laissez-faire economics – that all speculators should bear their own risk.

It was the rapid expansion of the railways and the increasing demand for what were then high-speed transport links which revolutionised the corporation. The huge sums needed to construct railways on an unprecedented scale, opening up the country for trade and pleasure, virtually compelled the creation of the modern joint stock company in the UK. Adam Smith's vision was fulfilled, at least in part, as companies were formed to build railways across the country, many of which were doomed to failure at the start, but all of which were funded by private capital by speculators who took a risk.

In 1844, with the passing of the Act for the Registration, Incorporation and Regulation of Joint Stock Companies, the facility was given to the public to form joint stock companies by a simple act of registration. This did not permit limited liability but it did ease the difficulties in setting up corporations, and the stage was set for 1855 when the passing of the Limited Liability Act finally allowed shareholders to quantify their risk when investing in new business ventures using the new form of a limited liability company.

As companies grew in size, responding to increasing industrialisation and the growth of markets, the ownership and control of companies became increasingly separated. In particular in the UK and USA, with the protection given to minority shareholders, the shareholder base became much more diverse. This, incidentally, is not necessarily true of companies in countries which do not have a system of common law like that of the UK which relies on precedent and an independent judiciary. The most common form of ownership around the world is the family firm or controlling shareholders.

However, in the UK, and the USA, the growth in share ownership has seen a trend towards both institutional ownership of large blocks of shares and widely dispersed ownership by large numbers of individual shareholders, what has been called 'ownership without power'. Institutions which hold shares as investments are coming under increasing pressure to adopt some of the rights of ownership, particularly in curbing what has been seen, in some cases, as excessive remuneration voted to directors. This has reinforced calls for improved transparency in reporting to correct the imbalance in financial reporting. Directors have lots of information, shareholders relatively little, which will, in the longer term, enable shareholders to assume more of the responsibilities of ownership and make boards of directors more accountable.

The growth of disclosure

After 1855 shareholders were protected from risk, other than the risk to the sum invested, and anyone could set up a company – and did. Students of Victorian business history will discover that new companies were set up for all sorts of reasons and individuals were encouraged to speculate in the new companies. Many investors, of course, lost their money due to fraud, incompetence or over-ambition but many companies succeeded due to the Victorians' penchant for persistence, hard work and ingenuity.

Initially there was a distinct lack of accountability by these companies. The Act of 1844 had required the production of accounts and some attempt at auditing them, but these requirements were repealed by the Act of 1855. Arguments advanced at the time against financial disclosure included the following, rather wonderful, propositions:

- As there is no totally reliable way of accounting for the success or otherwise of a business it is best not to attempt it.
- The books could easily be manipulated by dishonest directors (although quite why this was an argument against even attempting disclosure is hard to see).
- Disclosure would prejudice commercial secrecy and operators of companies would not like their operations to be known – even by their own shareholders.
- Too much disclosure would create a false sense of security among investors.

That is not to say there was no accountability at all, but it was rather selective. Put simply, as the financially astute, the 'insiders', were very much of the same social class or milieu and moved in the same circles they didn't need publicly available information, in fact they tended to rather discourage the idea. 'Outside' shareholders, those not in the know, were simply seen as passive investors who took the risk of losing their investment if the business failed.

Accountability really began in 1900 with the requirement to publish an audited balance sheet. The audit itself was first introduced in 1879 when banking companies were required to have an audit, a concept which was not generally extended until 1900. A balance sheet was not required to be submitted to the Registrar of Companies until 1908, following the passing of the 1907 Companies Act, and private companies were exempted from this requirement. The 1929 Act required a balance sheet and profit and loss account to be presented to the shareholders annually but it was the 1948 Act, following the recommendations of the Cohen Report, that required greatly increased disclosure of the company's financial affairs and the actions of directors.

A key aspect of the Companies Act 1948 was that, for the first time, auditors were required to have a professional qualification and it was that Act which laid the foundations of the modern auditing profession.

Various Companies Acts have followed since then. In turn each one made its mark by:

- tightening the legal restrictions on directors and on the company itself
- setting rules concerning the issues of shares and the payment of dividends
- setting the rules for minimum capital requirements for public companies, and
- most pertinent to our purpose, regulating the content of accounts, increasing accounting disclosure, the requirements for accounts preparation and the records to be kept.

The expansion of legislation has increased the level of compliance required and the consequent need for companies to create financial systems to both gather and present the information legally required and to control its internal financial procedures.

Legislation has continued to this day, culminating in the mammoth Companies Act 2006, the largest piece of legislation ever passed in the UK.

Scotland

In Scotland the legal position for companies was different from that in England. Both regulated and joint stock companies existed there from about the end of the seventeenth century. Scotland's legal system is heavily based in common law which is, broadly, law set by cases and precedent rather than by statute. The common law in Scotland allowed the formation of joint stock companies with transferable shares under the management of directors. It was recognised that a company was a legal person and had a personality separate from that of the directors who managed it and its owners. Scottish common law companies had a lot in common with English 'deed of settlement' companies.

Nowadays, of course, statutory company law applies throughout the United Kingdom.

Agency theory

Although political and even cultural influences have a bearing, it is arguable that the legal status of the entity through which business is conducted is perhaps the biggest influence on the need for strong corporate governance.

History shows that the need for funding business expansion, and the consequent rise of the publicly owned joint stock company, had the effect of slowly separating the ownership of the business from its day-to-day control. When merchant adventurers risked most of their own capital on a venture they tended to watch closely over it, indeed many merchants travelled with their goods to oversee operations themselves or they appointed agents whose honesty and reliability were tried and tested and who relied upon their reputation to stay in business. Partners watched each other; if only because of the danger that a defaulting or defrauding partner could disappear leaving the remaining partners liable for the debts of the business. There was, inevitably, a large element of trust in their dealings.

Even with companies the size of, say, the East India Company, which at its height maintained its own army and navy, the Court of Directors in London received regular reports from a network of agents and they were accountable to the monarch and to Parliament.

However, the introduction of limited liability and the consequent opening up of share ownership to the wider public dramatically widened this gap between ownership and control.

The managers or directors of the business (defined here as 'agents') were given the freedom to run the business without the day-to-day involvement of the owners, the providers of the capital (defined here as 'principals'). They were entrusted with the principals' money and their role, it was hoped, was:

- to use that investment to create profits which the principals could receive by way of dividend, and
- to expand that initial capital on behalf of owners so increasing the value of their investment.

Their primary role as agents was, and still is, the preservation of the assets of the business and to act always in the best interests of their principals, the shareholders.

In return the agents should receive suitable remuneration, concomitant with their status and their level of success in making money for their principals. Thus everybody should get something out of the arrangement – or so it seems. In fact things don't always work out quite as well as might be anticipated because, as usual, human nature gets in the way.

Table 1.1 Agency theory

Party	Objective
Principal	• Safe investment • Regular dividends • Long-term capital growth • Maintenance of value
Agent	• Salary and benefits • Maximum bonus • Share options • Personal success of successful business measured by share price

It is this that lies behind the concept known as agency theory.

Agency theory holds that agents do not, necessarily, take decisions in the best interests of their principals. It states that the objectives or goals of principals and agents mostly conflict and, where they do, agents will, naturally, make the choice which benefits themselves the most, choices which may not be the most beneficial decision for the principals. This is summarised quite simply in Table 1.1.

Agency theory is a relatively simple principle to grasp, but its ramifications are extensive and have important implications for how organisations conduct themselves and what their operational culture might be.

The Institute of Chartered Accountants in England and Wales, in November 2006, put it this way:

> In principle the agency model assumes that no agents are trustworthy and if they can make themselves richer at the expense of their principals they will. The poor principal, so the argument goes, has no alternative but to compensate the agent well for their endeavours so that they will not be tempted to go into business for themselves using the principal's assets to do so.
>
> The origin of auditing goes back to times scarcely less remote than that of accounting . . . Whenever the advance of civilization brought about the necessity of one man being entrusted to some extent with the property of another the advisability of some kind of check upon the fidelity of the former would become apparent.

Clearly this is not universally true, but the extent to which principals don't trust their agents will tend to govern the level of the monitoring mechanisms principals need to create for the overview of their agents' activities and also to decide the extent to which agents' compensation levels are considered to be acceptable by the agent, even if they are considered to be excessive by the principal.

Upon this principle rests the foundation of the modern auditing profession and, in the latter part of the twentieth century and the early part of the twenty-first, the establishment of modern corporate governance.

One of the differences between principals and agents tends to arise because of the different views of the time horizon each party holds. Research indicates that, broadly, principals – individual investors (as opposed to speculators) – tend to view their investment as relatively long term. They require their money to be secure, first of all, and then they will look for steady growth and, possibly a regular dividend. Research also indicates that investors, generally, are more influenced by the prospect of capital growth than a regular income. Dividend returns on capital invested tend to be fairly low: many investors could receive a greater level of income from investment in bonds or some other forms of investment such as property, however they would not achieve the same levels (hopefully) of capital growth.

Agents and managers, on the other hand, tend to want short-term gains such as bonuses, perks or share options which can be cashed in relatively quickly to make a low taxed profit. This encourages short-term decision making or decision making designed to protect or increase the share price rather than the more long-term strategic approach required by investors. It is for this reason, of course, that managers can be tempted to 'improve' results when reporting.

Another factor which has increased the power and control of managers and which, it has been argued, is also culpable in fostering short-term decision making, is the investment community itself, which is often looking to gain short-term profits from portfolio management investment rather than for strategic approaches centred on strategies which stress the need for:

(a) survival, and
(b) long-term growth.

In the modern era we have seen the rise of private hedge funds which use huge amounts of borrowed money to purchase businesses which they then 'improve' so as to maximise their return. These businesses are often sold on after a few years, hopefully repaying the borrowed funds and realising a capital profit. Clearly the return on investment has to be substantial to make the deals attractive so management emphasis is on cost reduction, heavy marketing and operational efficiencies. Hedge funds are about managers, not about owners. What is not at a premium in these companies is research leading to product development or long-term investment in corporate infrastructures.

In the modern world the increasing size of corporations has resulted in the fragmentation of share ownership. In many cases large investors are not individual shareholders but are themselves institutions which are looking for a commercial return on their investment. The private individual shareholder prepared to hold their investment in a single company, as opposed to some sort of composite investment fund, over the longer term and to accept moderate levels of growth in return for security of their investment is now very much a minority shareholder. It can thus be argued that today it is largely managers who now control shares in companies run by other managers. The agents have control, as demonstrated by Berle and Means (Exhibit 1.1) as long ago as 1932.

All of these factors have combined to give managers of big companies extraordinary power, to the extent that major multinationals are bigger than some countries and decisions made in their boardrooms can have an effect on national economies. The recent banking crisis created by the decisions of major international banks to abandon risk management in favour of huge but illusory gains is a striking example of this. It took the combined economies of most of the developed countries of the world to avoid a global collapse of the entire banking system – such is the power, or destructive potential, of company managers.

The separation of ownership from control and the increasing power of company managers in large corporations encourages them to do two things:

● Take risks in order to maximise short-term advantage. This might mean an aggressive acquisition programme funded by short-term borrowing, overseas expansion into foreign markets, or aggressive marketing of products to drive up market share in the short term.

> ## Exhibit 1.1   The modern corporation – Berle and Means
>
> Adolf Berle and Gardiner Means published their seminal work *The Modern Corporation and Private Property* in 1932. In it they stated that as corporations grew, the financing requirements made it increasingly difficult for individuals to maintain majority shareholdings, which meant shareholding became divided and fragmented among larger and larger numbers of individuals and other investing bodies.
>
> As shareholding became more diverse and diffuse the one constant in the company was the management: *de facto* power thereby devolved upon them.
>
> As companies grew in size and power a relatively large amount of total corporate wealth became concentrated into relatively few huge corporations. Managers in these corporations were able to disburse company resources in the way that primarily suited them, i.e. through reinvestment or even enhanced pay, rather than as dividends.
>
> These companies had an impact on society as they were able to open or close factories and branches, thus influencing the lives of millions of people without any real form of democratic accountability.
>
> *Source:* Berle and Means (1932)

- Adopt aggressive accounting practices which may, in extreme cases, amount to fraudulent manipulation of the figures. The classic cases in recent years of this are the cases in the USA of Enron and WorldCom where managers actively colluded in misleading investors in order to maintain an otherwise unsustainable share price, enriching themselves in the process.

Agency theory is the structural framework on which the principles of corporate governance are based and what follows from it. As we will see it can be argued that workplace malfeasance, involving employees at all levels in the organisation, starts from this divorcing of ownership from control and the consequent need for strong corporate governance. As we will see, where corporate governance is weak that weakness forms the context for much of the bad behaviour of managers within organisations and, consequently, following their lead, also by their staff.

Corporate governance

The UK's business community has always prided itself on its long tradition of fair dealing and low-key regulation in contrast to the heavy-handed enforcement favoured by its brasher, more strident commercial cousin on the other side of the Atlantic. The UK, business people like to think, has a long tradition of gentlemanly fair dealing and incorruptibility.

For many years, prior to the 1990s, the system of company regulation was broadly structured around the various Companies Acts 1948 to 1989, bits of which were in force, and life for the auditors and company directors was one uncluttered by the need for excessive compliance because there was relatively little they had to comply with.

The auditing profession had belatedly woken up to the idea of Auditing Standards, previously the province of the individual professional bodies such as the Institute of Chartered Accountants in England and Wales (ICAEW), which issued 'Guidance to Members'. During the 1980s the then Auditing Practices Committee issued about ten standards which governed the carrying out of routine audit work. The business community required an occasional intervention by what was then known as the Board of Trade when a particularly egregious scandal emerged but otherwise the surface of the corporate lake remained relatively placid and unruffled.

Then, in the latter part of the 1980s, the UK suffered a series of corporate scandals which began to undermine the trust investors had in the gentlemanly approach.

The biggest and most notorious scandal was that involving the larger than life Robert Maxwell whose empire, based around his Maxwell Communications Corporation (MCC) finally exploded. It took with it not only suppliers and lenders but also the assets amounting to some £700m belonging to the Mirror Group newspapers pension scheme which Maxwell had 'borrowed' in a desperate attempt to prop up the ailing MCC. Maxwell was a physically imposing and domineering individual who ran his companies as his personal fiefdom, acting as both chairman and chief executive. The non-executive directors on the MCC board, reputable people all, did little apart from lend MCC an aura of respectability. To make matters worse the auditors signally failed to pick up the transfers Maxwell was making from the Mirror Group pension scheme, even though they were in a position to do so.

Maxwell's shenanigans, whilst undoubtedly the most shocking, were only one of several cases of corporate failure around that time which worried both investors and regulators alike and prompted vociferous calls in the media for action. Other legendary exploits included:

- Polly Peck – run by rogue businessman Asil Nadir who decamped to the Turkish Republic of Northern Cyprus, where he remains to this day under threat of arrest, should he leave, on charges of fraud and theft of £34m. He also was responsible for the downfall of then Northern Ireland minister Michael Mates when it was revealed he had paid Mates to ask questions in the House of Commons.
- The Bank of Credit and Commerce International which proved to be a haven for money launderers and drug smugglers, closed down in 1991 by legislators worldwide.
- Coloroll under the management of media golden boy John Ashcroft, which collapsed in 1990 with debts of around £400m created largely by an aggressive but injudicious acquisitions programme.

The prevailing mood was 'something must be done' and so the City, alarmed both by the loss of investor confidence and the prospect of government regulation, reacted quickly and commissioned Sir Adrian Cadbury to come up with some good practice proposals which would:

- reinforce the responsibilities of executive directors
- separate the role of chairman and chief executive
- strengthen the role of the non-executive director
- make the case for audit committees of the board
- restate the principal responsibilities of auditors, and
- reinforce the links between shareholders, boards and auditors.

This Cadbury duly did and his report (imaginatively entitled The Cadbury Report) issued in 1992 formed the foundation of what was to become the Combined Code, a part of the Stock Exchange listing agreement to which all companies wishing to have their shares listed on the London Stock Exchange must comply.

It was Cadbury who first defined what we know today as corporate governance. The definition of corporate governance most often quoted, at least in auditing textbooks, is the one contained in the Cadbury Report 'the system by which companies are directed and controlled'.

This definition was all very well for the time, but as various reports post-Cadbury have refined and enhanced his initial concepts so the definition of what corporate governance actually is has also been refined. In research carried out in 2000 among UK institutional investors the definition which found the most favour was 'the process of supervision and control intended to ensure that the company's management acts in accordance with the interests of shareholders' (Parkinson, 1994).

This, as you see, goes right to the heart of the problems of agency theory outlined above.

The principles of Cadbury and its successors have not been enforced by legislation on companies listed either on the London Stock Exchange or on any other. Instead listed companies are required to abide by what is known as the Combined Code on Corporate Governance, or to state in their accounts why they don't comply, the so-called 'comply or explain' basis (see Table 1.2).

This leaves open the door to non-compliance by listed companies, which may only have to suffer a note in the auditors' report and perhaps a stern word from the Stock Exchange for a first offence, and of course it has no effect at all, other than a persuasive one, on unlisted companies.

Interestingly the Companies Act 2006 does incorporate within it specific duties for directors. Among other things S172 of the Act lays down a specific duty on a company director to:

act in the way he considers, in good faith, would be most likely to promote the success of the company for the benefit of its members as a whole and to have regard to

- the interests of the company's employees
- the need to foster the company's business relationships with suppliers, customers and others
- the desirability of the company maintaining a reputation for high standards of business conduct.

(Note: UK legislation generally uses 'he' throughout although supposedly this has no gender implications and applies equally to women)

Table 1.2 Corporate governance reports after Cadbury

Report	Key feature
Greenbury (1995)	Looked at the question of directors pay. This was partly in response to the 'Cedric the Pig' protest campaign at the 1994 AGM for newly privatised British Gas when the then chairman, Cedric Brown, was looking for a 75% pay rise for doing the same job as he was doing pre-privatisation
Hampel (1998)	Reinforced points made in the original Cadbury Report, in particular the separation of the roles of chairman and managing director and the balance of the composition of the board between executive and non-executive directors
Turnbull (1999)	The role of internal audit
Higgs (2003)	Reinforcing the role of non-executive directors
Tyson (2003)	Additional guidance on recruitment and training of non-executive directors
Smith (2003)	The relationship between the auditors and the audit committee and the role of the audit committee

For the first time there is a specific legal provision for a specified class of individuals to have regard for the interests, not only of those who have invested in the company over which they have day-to-day control, but also of those of the other stakeholders, employees, customers, suppliers and indeed – in its injunction to maintain a high standard of conduct – anyone the business comes into contact with in the course of its business.

It legislates for a moral code, something which companies appear to have seen, until recently, as a useful part of human relations policy, but not as a creed to live by.

The Combined Code on Corporate Governance 2003

The Financial Reporting Council (FRC) drew up guidelines that were published in July 2003 as part of its Combined Code on Corporate Governance.

The Code incorporates the key good governance provisions of the Cadbury Report and the subsequent reports detailed above and is underpinned by a Financial Services Authority rule that requires companies listed on the London Stock Exchange to state, in their annual report, how they have complied with its provisions or to explain why they have not done so. This is known as the 'comply or explain' basis and differs from the purely regulatory approach adopted in other countries, particularly the USA.

Listed companies are supposed to abide by the Combined Code, but it is good practice for all companies to abide by as many of these principles as are practicable.

We will look at the main provisions of the Code, insofar as they are relevant to our subject. In this case we will concentrate on the role of the board of directors and the audit committee.

The role of the board

As part of the background we need to consider the role played by the board of directors. They have many tasks but as this is not a book on management we will confine ourselves to a consideration of the role they have in maintaining good corporate governance and, in particular and most relevant to our purpose, their role in creating and maintaining good systems of control within the business.

There are two fundamental principles underlying good corporate governance practice:

- Accountability – directors and the organisation they control must be accountable to the various stakeholders involved in the business, which will include not only the shareholders but also employees, suppliers, customers and lenders.
- Transparency – not only being accountable but being seen to be accountable to those stakeholders.

This requires the directors to ensure that they report regularly and efficiently to the various stakeholders they have identified. This task is now seen as somewhat wider than a grudging acceptance that they have to prepare and circulate a set of annual accounts with a minimal level of disclosure. Modern corporate governance best practice requires a regular and accessible flow of information using all modern means, including the Internet.

The board of directors is also responsible for the company's system of internal control. This is the system of checks and balances within the organisation designed to ensure that the financial information it produces is free from significant error or misstatement. We will return to the principles of internal control later in Part 3.

The board's role in internal control is to create a suitable internal control environment. This involves:

- setting appropriate policies
- communicating these to staff, and
- seeking regular assurance that will enable it to satisfy itself that the system is functioning effectively.

It does this through its own efforts in understanding and monitoring risks and the control systems designed to deal with those risks through engagement with staff and senior managers on a regular basis. Ideally the directors will institute a system of internal audit, if the organisation is of sufficient size, perhaps reporting to an audit committee of non-executive directors (see later) and of course through the external audit process.

What the board must not be is passive, simply trusting that all is well in the absence of information to the contrary, or trusting solely to the annual audit to expose any defects in their control systems. It must, instead, be proactive in ensuring that the system of internal control is effective in managing business risks in the manner it has approved. Note that, according to best practice, there is no budgetary limitation to managing risk; using budgets as an excuse for poor risk management is dangerous short termism and is likely to lead to problems in the future.

It is the role of line management, below director level, to implement board policies on risk and control. In fulfilling its responsibilities, line management should identify and evaluate the risks faced by the company for consideration by the board and design, operate and monitor a suitable system of internal control which implements the policies adopted by the board. We will look at this in more detail in Chapter 8.

Earlier in this chapter we looked at the broad concept of agency theory, the idea that agents (managers) will tend to make decisions in their own interests rather than in the interests of principals (shareholders).

In Britain the development of a strong code of corporate governance, following on from the Cadbury Report, has possibly sheltered the UK corporate world from the worst kind of corporate scandals epitomised in America by Enron and WorldCom.

The application of framework-based UK codes, reinforced perhaps by the new directors' provisions in S172 of the Companies Act, 2006 have, commentators state smugly, prevented directors indulging in the same kind of blatant manipulations and frauds that rocked corporate America.

Other countries which imposed strong corporate governance regimes have also been largely unaffected by Enron-style shenanigans. This is not to say there has not been some poor practice, evidenced by the collapse of Barings Bank in 1995 and the activities of a lone SocGen trader which caused the major French bank some heartache in 2007. Arguably these cases are somewhat different, being perpetrated by single individuals, not motivated by the desire to steal but by a desire to make a name for themselves, aggravated by corporate systems failure. They were not, after all, corporate frauds designed and led by some or all of the board of directors.

Detractors from this view will, of course, point to such cases as Parmalat in Italy where some of the directors, who also had shares in the business, indulged in large-scale fraud but this case, again, was one which appears to involve theft motivated by simple greed on the part of a few senior individuals rather than institutionalised dysfunctional behaviour as happened at Enron. There will always be corrupt managers and opportunists and these make both entertaining headlines and money for the legal profession when the plots are revealed. They also, at some level, cause personal tragedies.

It should not be forgotten that institutionalised corruption strikes at the very heart of the confidence the financial world needs if it is to function. Loss of investor confidence in the audit profession, in the probity of directors and in the soundness of banks can and, as we have seen, does wreak havoc not only in the financial world but in the economies of those countries which support those corrupt institutions.

The standards of personal morality and the ethical climate established and maintained in an organisation by those who govern it are crucial to successful corporate governance and consequently to reliable financial information and to the security of the organisation's assets. The newest corporate scandals in the USA and the old ones in the UK showed that, when senior management goes bad, the organisation, as the proverb puts it, like fish, rots from the head. The influence of a corrupt senior manager can have a hugely deleterious effect on their subordinates who are forced into an invidious position. They either have to:

- comply – go along with the deception by either turning a blind eye to it if they are able or actively assisting it, or
- deny – by leaving the organisation, getting transferred or blowing the whistle.

This applies irrespective of the level of management involved, whether it be a canteen supervisor stealing food or a managing director falsifying profits to improve a share price. They cannot and do not act alone. Only the lone fraudster covertly siphoning value out of the business acts in this way – all other forms of corporate malpractice are, at some level, team efforts.

It is the responsibility of the board, as part of strong corporate governance, to use their best endeavours to create the climate where fraud and malpractice not only cannot flourish but where any green shoots of fraud are rooted out and dealt with appropriately.

Directors

The rules which derive from the Combined Code insofar as they affect the directors are, broadly, as follows. Suitably adapted these can, of course, be applied to any organisation whether it be a public sector body or charity – the principles are what matter. We will, however, refer to companies and directors throughout for convenience.

- Every company should be headed by an effective board, which is *collectively* responsible for the success of the company.
- There should be a clear division of responsibilities at the head of the company between the running of the board and the executive responsibility for the running of the company's business. No one individual should have unfettered powers of decision. What this means, in practice, is that the chairman of the board should not be the same individual as the managing director or chief executive officer.
- The chairman is basically responsible for running the board and ensuring that it functions as a board and that its members are suitably qualified and competent. This includes taking responsibility for non-executive directors. The chief executive is responsible for the business activities and the actions of executive directors.
- The board should include a balance of executive and non-executive directors (and, in particular, independent non-executive directors) such that no individual or small group of individuals can dominate the board's decision taking.

- There should be a formal, rigorous and transparent procedure for the appointment of new directors to the board.
- The board should be supplied in a timely manner with information in a form and of a quality appropriate to enable it to discharge its duties. This is a requirement to produce good-quality management information, both financial and non-financial, in a form the directors can understand and in a timely manner.
- All directors should receive induction on joining the board and should regularly update and refresh their skills and knowledge.
- The board should undertake a formal and rigorous annual evaluation of its own performance and that of its committees and individual directors.
- All directors should be submitted for re-election at regular intervals, subject to continued satisfactory performance. The board should ensure planned and progressive refreshing of the board.

Director's report on internal controls

We will look at internal controls in more detail later; at this stage it is only necessary to know that this relates to the internal accounting and financial procedures within the organisation which are designed to detect errors and misstatements, and of course frauds, which it is the responsibility of the directors to maintain.

Listed companies have to include, in their financial statements, a narrative report from the directors which:

- identifies the organisation's business objectives
- identifies and assesses risks which threaten achievement of those objectives
- reports on the design and operation of controls to manage those risks, and
- reports on the process of monitoring and reviewing those controls to ensure they are operating correctly.

Directors' remuneration

This is relevant for the purposes of forensic accountancy because the remuneration of directors is often a very political issue in companies. In addition there have been several cases where directors have sought excessive remuneration by falsifying results or distorting performance. An understanding of the principles is therefore appropriate.

- Levels of remuneration should be sufficient to attract, retain and motivate directors of the quality required to run the company successfully.
- A company should avoid paying more than is necessary for this purpose.
- A significant proportion of executive directors' remuneration should be structured so as to link rewards to corporate and individual performance, i.e. incentive-based pay such as bonuses.
- There should be a formal and transparent procedure for developing policy on executive remuneration and for fixing the remuneration packages of individual directors. No directors should be involved in deciding their own remuneration. In practice this usually takes the form of a Remuneration Committee of non-executive directors as recommended by Greenbury (see above).

Accountability and audit

- The board should present a balanced and understandable assessment of the company's position and prospects.

- The board should maintain a sound system of internal control to safeguard shareholders' investment and the company's assets.
- The board should establish formal and transparent arrangements for considering how they should apply the financial reporting and internal control principles and for maintaining an appropriate relationship with the company's auditors. This is should be carried out by an audit committee, comprising at least three non-executive directors.

The key point about good corporate governance is that its requirements should be met in the spirit of good governance and not just by observing the letter of the Code. 'Box ticking' should not be a substitute for clear thought and fair exposition.

It is the responsibility of the directors to produce financial statements which truly and fairly reflect the financial position of the organisation and which make them accountable for the results of the financial period. Figure 1.1 illustrates the process.

Figure 1.1 The financial audit process

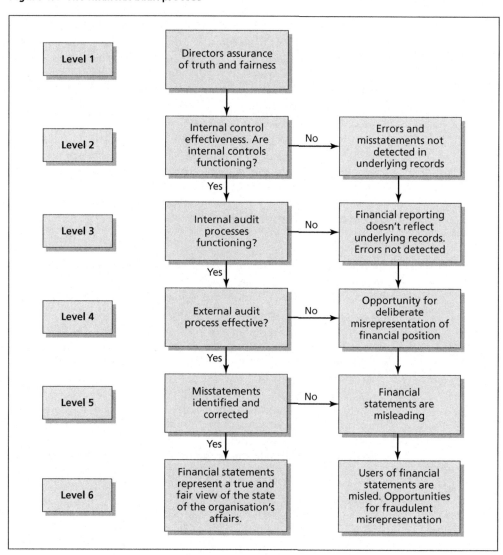

The audit committee

The Combined Code requires that all listed companies set up an audit committee as a subcommittee of the main board.

Ideally:

- it should comprise at least three non-executive directors who are independent of management
- the members should have a wide range of business and professional skills
- the members should have a good understanding of the business yet should have had no recent involvement with direct management of the business, and
- the committee should have clear written terms of reference setting out its authority and its duties.

Clearly this can sometimes be difficult to achieve. However, the object is to create a committee which is competent to carry out its role, is independent and is free from bias.

The key objectives associated with the setting up of audit committees, from the point of view of Corporate Governance generally, are:

- to increase public confidence in the credibility and objectivity of published financial information
- to assist the directors in carrying out their responsibilities for financial reporting, and
- to strengthen the position of the external auditors by providing a channel of communication at board level without the constraint of any executive bias.

There are advantages to having an audit committee. These are:

- It can improve the quality of management accounting as they are able to criticise internal reporting, which is not necessarily the responsibility of the external auditors.
- It can facilitate communication between the directors, internal and external auditors and management.
- It can help minimise any conflicts between management and the auditors.
- It can facilitate the independence of the internal audit role if the internal auditors report to the audit committee directly.

However, there are some disadvantages which the members of the audit committee have to avoid:

- It can be seen that their purpose is to criticise or 'catch out' executive management.
- It can result in the perception, if not the reality, of a two-tier board.
- The non-executives can become too embroiled in detail and start to act like executive directors, thus losing their independence.

In detail, the role of the audit committee can be summarised as:

- to review internal control procedures and processes
- to review the internal audit function and act as a channel of communication to executive management
- to review current accounting policies and the impact of any possible changes
- to review the usefulness and effectiveness of current management information

- to review the financial information presented to shareholders and other information issued by the company such as profit forecasts etc.
- to liaise with external auditors, consider their reports to management and any issues arising from the audit and ensure any audit recommendations are dealt with by executive management
- to review the effectiveness and efficiency of the external audit
- to consider the independence of the auditors from executive management; this can be particularly important where the audit firm is supplying substantial additional services to the client in addition to their role as external auditors
- to recommend the nomination of external auditors and also to deal with their remuneration for carrying out the audit work, and
- to review compliance with the Combined Code on Corporate Governance.

In essence the audit committee is designed to act as an independent voice on the board of directors with regard to audit and corporate governance issues and can be a valuable asset, particularly with respect to maintaining the independence and integrity of the internal audit function which is relevant to any consideration by forensic accountants of the strength or otherwise of internal control systems.

The audit committee is also of practical value to the forensic accountant as it can be the conduit through which the results of any information are passed to the board. It may be that when an investigation is being conducted (Part 4) the link between the forensic investigator and the company is through the audit committee.

One of the reports which followed Cadbury, and built on its foundations, was the Turnbull Report which looked specifically at the issue of the internal controls that should be implemented within the financial management system of an organisation, to minimise the risk of errors or serious misstatements occurring in the processing and recording of financial information.

 **The Turnbull Report**

In October 2005 the Institute of Chartered Accountants in England and Wales (ICAEW) published what has become known as the Turnbull Report (see Exhibit 1.2). The document forms the guiding principles whereby UK-listed companies can meet their responsibility to implement the internal controls required by the Combined Code on Corporate Governance. We will examine precisely what controls should be implemented in Chapter 8, but for now we will simply look at the principles underlying their implementation.

According to the Turnbull Report the company's internal control system should:

- be embedded within its operations and not be treated as a separate exercise
- be able to respond to changing risks within and outside the organisation, and
- enable each organisation to apply it in an appropriate manner related to its key risks.

We will look at the main provisions of the Combined Code, which form the context for the more detailed consideration of the practical implementation of internal controls described in Chapter 8.

According to Turnbull the main principles of a sound system in internal control are:

- that the governing body acknowledges responsibility for the system of internal control
- that a process is in place for identifying, evaluating and managing significant business risks
- that the effectiveness of the system of internal control is reviewed at least annually by the directors or senior managers and that procedures are in place for this, and
- that there is a process to deal with the internal control aspects of any significant problems arising from the audit of the financial statements reported by the auditors.

In assessing what constitutes a sound system of internal control the directors should consider:

- the nature and extent of the risks facing the organisation
- the extent and categories of risk that are regarded as acceptable
- the probability of the identified risks materialising, and
- the ability of the organisation to mitigate the impact of identified risks should they materialise.

We will look in detail at the principles and processes behind this sort of risk management activity in Chapter 7.

With regard to the system of internal control, it should:

- be embedded in the operations of the organisation and form part of its culture
- be capable of responding quickly to evolving risks, and
- include procedures for reporting any significant control failings immediately to appropriate levels of management.

These principles, which form a part of good governance practice, involve all aspects of internal control from systems design to internal audit, and this forms the backdrop against which we will be reviewing both defensive procedures and active investigation techniques later in this book.

Exhibit 1.2   Internal control – the Turnbull Report

A company's system of internal control has a key role in the management of risks that are significant to the fulfilment of its business objectives. A sound system of internal control contributes to safeguarding the shareholders' investment and the company's assets.

Internal control facilitates the effectiveness and efficiency of operations, helps ensure the reliability of internal and external reporting and assists compliance with laws and regulations.

Effective financial controls, including the maintenance of proper accounting records, are an important element of internal control. They help ensure that the company is not unnecessarily exposed to avoidable financial risks and that financial information used within the business and for publication is reliable. They also contribute to the safeguarding of assets, including the prevention and detection of fraud.

Source: The Turnbull Report

Sarbanes–Oxley 2002

The question of the effectiveness of the then approaches to corporate governance was brought sharply into focus by the financial scandals of the early part of the twenty-first century in the USA surrounding, in particular, Enron and the lesser but no less shocking events involving WorldCom, Tyco International, Global Crossing and many others. All of the major accounting firms had clients who were caught up in these scandals, the apotheosis being the destruction of the worldwide accounting firm of Arthur Andersen.

In 2002 this resulted in the USA passing the legislation known as the Sarbanes–Oxley Act (often shortened to 'Sarbox'), which does not affect UK companies unless they are subsidiaries of US firms or are listed on any US stock exchanges.

The Act is designed to enforce corporate accountability through new requirements, backed by stiff penalties. Under the Act, chief executives and chief financial officers must personally certify the accuracy of financial statements, with a maximum penalty of 20 years in jail and a $5m fine for false statements. In addition, and of great significance to auditors, under Section 404 of the Act, executives have to certify and demonstrate that they have established and are maintaining an adequate internal control structure and procedures for financial reporting. This requires them to ensure that all the financial reporting systems, including ancillary systems such as procurement and HR, are functioning in such a way as to prevent material misstatements appearing in the financial accounts. It is a personal liability.

This legislation, which was passed in haste, is slowly being reassessed in the current climate as being too prescriptive and too inhibiting for US business freedoms. There may be further changes to come!

Summary

- The development of the joint stock company separated ownership from control.
- Agency theory holds that agents (managers) will tend to make decisions in their own best interests at the expense of their principals (shareholders).
- Research by Berle and Means (1932) demonstrated the increasing power of directors of large corporations.
- Auditors are required to evaluate the financial statements produced by agents to account for their activities and report to the shareholders on their truth and fairness.
- Full disclosure of financial results is a relatively recent phenomenon but has grown rapidly since the Companies Act 1948.
- The Companies Act 2006 is the current legislation for the running of companies and the rights and duties of directors and external auditors.
- The UK has a framework approach to corporate governance.
- The Cadbury Report established standards of corporate governance following a series of financial scandals in the UK.

- This was reinforced by the Combined Code and later reports.
- Standards have been established for the conduct and activities of directors and the running of corporate boards.
- The board has specific responsibilities with regard to internal control and the preparation of financial statements.
- This has encouraged greater involvement of non-executive directors in companies.
- An audit committee forms a link between the audit function and the board.
- The Turnbull Report defined the role of the internal audit function and helped strengthen its influence.
- The USA passed the Sarbanes–Oxley Act to enforce standards of behaviour by directors and auditors.

Case study

You are the audit manager of Tickitt and Run, a medium-sized firm of accountants. You have recently taken on a new client, Megablast Limited, a privately owned company which is now seeking a listing on the Stock Exchange.

The company has asked for your advice regarding any changes necessary in Megablast to achieve appropriate compliance with corporate governance codes.

This extract is from the company's financial statement regarding corporate governance:

> Megablast is a family company owned by the Blast family but has expanded rapidly in recent years: the expansion has been funded by loans and other forms of finance. They are looking for a flotation to refinance the business. The business is profitable and cash positive.
>
> Mr Blast is the chief executive officer and board chairman of Megablast. He appoints and maintains a board of five executive directors, none of whom is a family member, and one non-executive director, his father, who is a major shareholder but who is no longer active in the company.
>
> While the board sets performance targets for the senior managers in the company, no formal targets or review of board policies is carried out. Board salaries are therefore set by Mr Blast based on his assessment of all the board members, including himself, and not their actual performance. Mr Blast sets his own remuneration following discussion with the non-executive director.
>
> Internal controls in the company are monitored by the senior accountant, although a detailed review is assumed to be carried out by the external auditors. Megablast does not have an internal audit department.
>
> Annual financial statements are produced providing detailed information on historical performance, but no other information is provided to investors.

Required

- Does Megablast fulfil the principles of good corporate governance? If not, why not?
- What would Megablast need to do to comply with good practice?
- In what way might Megablast be affected by continuing non-compliance?

Bibliography

Bentham, J. (1789) *An Introduction to the Principles of Morals and Legislation.* Dover Publications, Mineola, New York.

Berle, A. and Means, G. (1932) *The Modern Corporation and Private Property* (revised edition 1991). Transaction Publishers, Piscataway, NJ.

Cadbury, Sir A. (1992) *Financial Aspects of Corporate Governance.* Gee and Co., London.

Companies Act 2006. HMSO, London.

Frankel, T. (2006) *Trust and Honesty – America's Business Culture at a Crossroad.* Oxford University Press, Oxford.

ICSA (2007) *Companies Act Handbook,* Walmsley, K. (ed.). ICSA, London.

Millichamp, A. and Taylor, J.R. (2008) *Auditing.* Cengage Learning EMEA, London.

Parkinson, J.E. (1994) *Corporate Power and Responsibility.* Oxford University Press, Oxford.

Razaee, Z. (2008) *Corporate Governance and Ethics.* John Wiley and Sons, Chichester.

Slapper, G. and Tombs, S. (1999) *Corporate Crime.* Pearson, Harlow.

Smiles, S. (1882) *Self Help.* John Murray, London.

Solomon, J. (2007) *Corporate Governance and Accountability.* John Wiley and Sons, Chichester.

The Sarbanes–Oxley Act (2002) H.R. Rep. 107–610, 25 July, 2002. US Government Printing Office, Washington, DC.

Turnbull, N. (2005) *Internal Control – Revised Guidance for Directors on the Combined Code.* FRC, London.

Websites

www.frc.org.uk

www.icaew.com

www.icgn.org

www.iod.com

www.opsi.gov.uk

Chapter 2

The role of the auditors

Chapter contents

- Introduction
- The expectation gap
- The role of the external auditor
- Auditing standards and fraud
- External auditors and their clients
- External auditors and fraud
- Materiality
- The external auditor and the forensic accountant
- The role of internal audit
- Internal auditors and fraud
- Internal audit and the forensic accountant

Learning objectives

After studying this chapter you should be able to:

- Understand the role of the external and internal auditor and the differences between them
- Understand the role professional standards play
- Understand what is meant by the 'expectation gap'
- Be able to define 'materiality'
- Understand the role external auditors play in relation to fraud investigation
- Understand the role of internal audit in fraud investigations
- Appreciate the relationship between both internal and external auditors and the forensic accountant

Introduction

As the limited liability company became the vehicle of choice for business activities and the gap between owners and managers increased so the role of the auditors achieved a greater prominence. As we have seen in Chapter 1, there was at first reluctance to compel companies to disclose their results publicly, but it rapidly became obvious that this was an untenable position and from 1900 the role of the independent arbitrator of truth and fairness, the external auditor, was established and enshrined in law.

Auditors were, and still are, expected to have both the highest standards of professional probity and to be competent to carry out the complex task of reviewing a set of financial statements and forming an opinion on their veracity. What was required of them was established early on in two classic cases, where judgment was given before the Companies Act 1900 firmly established their role. The position was summed by Lord Justice Lopes in the legendary case, which all auditors know, re Kingston Cotton Mill Co No 2 (1896), 2 Ch 279, p. 288.

Lopes had sat in an earlier case, In re London and General Bank (1895 2 Ch 16) where the duties of capabilities of the auditor was also considered by the court and he used the Kingston Cotton Mill judgment to summarise the position. The key words have been underlined:

> But in determining whether any misfeasance or breach of duty has been committed, it is essential to consider what the duties of an auditor are. They are very fully described in In re London and General Bank [FN19] (1895), to which judgment I was a party. Shortly they may be stated thus: <u>It is the duty of an auditor to bring to bear on the work he has to perform that skill, care, and caution which a reasonably competent, careful, and cautious auditor would use.</u> What is reasonable skill, care, and caution must depend on the particular circumstances of each case. An auditor is not bound to be a detective, or, as was said, to approach his work with suspicion or with a foregone conclusion that there is something wrong. <u>He is a watchdog, but not a bloodhound.</u>

These words have resonated with the audit profession for over 100 years and are still relevant today, despite the volume of regulation and several other major cases against audit firms since they were spoken. The expression 'he is a watchdog but not a bloodhound' is cited constantly, even in the opening years of the twenty-first century, to explain to the layman why the external auditors are not expected to detect fraud.

As we saw in Chapter 1, it is arguable that the role of the external auditor is a critical one in reassuring stakeholders in organisations generally, and shareholders in particular, that the financial statements produced by their agents, the management, bear some relationship to the true financial position of the business at one point in time. However, apart from this broad fact, the uninformed public generally has a hazy idea of precisely what auditors do or how they go about doing it. This is known as the expectation gap.

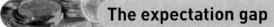

The expectation gap

What auditors call the expectation gap is summarised as 'the difference between what the auditors actually do and what the public think they do'.

The general public and the uninformed, which often, sadly, includes financial journalists who should know better, often labour under the delusion that one of the primary functions of auditors is to detect fraud. For example, when questioned ordinary members of the public think that auditors check all the transactions in the books, or prepare the accounts; they have little understanding of risk-based audit techniques or systems-based approaches to auditing – and who can blame them?

They are under the impression that, as these expert accountants examine a company's books every year, they should have the ability to spot the delinquent fraudster and have them handed over to the Fraud Squad without further ado. The public may concede that fraudsters are often cunning and attempt to hide their tracks, but the confidence of the investing public in the auditing profession, fortunately, remains strong and their faith in the profession's ability to spring on the unsuspecting embezzler, like Sherlock Holmes unmasking the villain, is hard to shake.

The truth is that research shows that external audit is very poor at catching fraudsters and, as we will see in Chapter 5, there is research to show that it is a weak deterrent to fraud. After every corporate scandal commentators who should know better often enquire as to why the external auditors didn't detect the egregious fraud or the bad behaviour of company directors. Of course occasionally this is because they were incompetent or negligent and, if this is the case their inability is often punished by the courts or through an out of court settlement involving large amounts of compensation (which is kept quiet).

The forensic investigator must not fall into that trap and needs a sound understanding of the role of the external auditor and how the investigator may be able to benefit from their presence.

The role of the external auditor

The Auditing Practices Board (APB), which is the body responsible in the UK for issuing Auditing Standards (ISAs) and guidelines, states:

> The objective of an audit of financial statements is to enable the auditor to express an opinion whether the financial statements are prepared, in all material respects, in accordance with an applicable financial reporting framework. The phrases used to express an auditor's opinion are 'give a true and fair view' or 'present fairly in all material respects' which are equivalent terms.
>
> The 'applicable financial reporting framework' comprises those requirements of accounting standards, law and regulations applicable to the entity to determine the form and content of its financial statements.

In the UK the financial reporting framework is the Companies Act 2006 together with all the associated accounting standards etc. which comprise UK Generally Accepted Accounting Practice (UK GAAP).

'Entity' is a general term embracing all types of business, enterprise or undertaking including companies, charities, local authorities, government agencies etc. Some are profit-oriented and some are not.

'Present fairly' instead of 'true and fair' applies mainly to local authorities. A particular point is made of the fact that responsibility for the *preparation* of the financial statements and the presentation of the information included therein rests with the management of the organisation (in the case of a company, the directors). The auditor's primary responsibility is only to *report* on the financial statements as presented by management.

The auditors should be an independent firm appointed to investigate the organisation, its records, and the financial statements prepared from them. External auditors have to be accredited by what are known as Recognised Supervisory Bodies (RSBs) which:

- establish the ethical standards expected of members
- control admission and the standards of technical ability expected of members
- reinforce behaviour through a disciplinary code, and
- provide advice and support for members.

In the UK there are four such bodies:

- The Institute of Chartered Accountants in England and Wales (ICAEW).
- The Institute of Chartered Accountants in Scotland (ICAS).
- The Institute of Chartered Accountants in Ireland (ICAI).
- Association of Chartered Certified Accountants (ACCA).

whose members, suitably accredited by their RSB, are empowered by the Companies Act 2006 to carry out statutory audits. These individuals are known as Registered Auditors.

The role of the auditor is to gather sufficient evidence so as to be able to form an opinion on the truth and fairness of the financial statements. The primary aim of an audit is to enable the auditors to say 'these accounts show a true and fair view' or, of course, to say that they do not. Note they are not certified as being 'accurate', because they include assumptions and estimates, nor are they certified as being 'correct' for the same reason.

The emphasis of the auditor's work is, of course, on the financial statements, their truth and fairness. Any consideration of fraud or deliberate misstatement of the accounts is a secondary, but nonetheless important, issue.

Auditing standards and fraud

Auditors are bound to carry out their auditing activities in accordance with International Standards on Auditing (ISAs) issued by the Auditing Practices Board. The relevant ones in the areas we are interested in are:

- ISA 240 *The Auditor's Responsibilities Relating to Fraud in an Audit of Financial Statements*

- ISA 315 *Identifying and Assessing the Risks of a Material Misstatement through Understanding the Entity and its Environment,* and
- ISA 330 *The Auditors' Responses to Assessed Risks.*

ISA 315 and ISA 330 broadly require auditors to carry out a form of risk assessment based on a review of the internal controls of their client.

Incorporated in this risk assessment will be such issues as:

- the attitude of the organisation towards good corporate governance
- the experience, competence and effectiveness of management at all levels
- the pressures affecting the business such as competition, financing, product life etc.
- the effectiveness of the internal management information systems
- the effectiveness of the internal control systems, and
- the history of audit issues with the client.

As outlined above this review is aimed specifically at the primary task – that of forming an opinion on the financial statements – so consideration of:

- weaknesses in internal controls
- failures of management with regard to implementation of policies and procedures, and
- the possibility of fraud

are secondary to this primary task.

International Standard on Auditing 240 The *Auditor's Responsibilities Relating to Fraud in an Audit of Financial Statements* places the responsibility squarely on the shoulders of management:

> The primary responsibility for the prevention and detection of fraud rests with both those charged with governance of the entity and with management. It is important that management, with the oversight of those charged with governance, place a strong emphasis on fraud prevention, which may reduce opportunities for fraud to take place, and fraud deterrence, which could persuade individuals not to commit fraud because of the likelihood of detection and punishment.

The standard emphasises the management's role in instituting sound systems of internal control and the importance of them placing a 'strong emphasis' on fraud prevention.

The standard goes on to explain that the primary role of the auditor is to express an opinion as to the truth and fairness of the financial statements and that consequently fraud detection must come a poor second. There are reasons why the auditors may not detect fraud which the standard is at pains to spell out. Among these are:

- Fraud may involve sophisticated and carefully organised schemes designed to conceal it such as forgery, deliberate failure to record transactions and intentional misrepresentations designed to conceal it.
- There may be collusion which may cause the auditor to believe that evidence is persuasive when, in fact, it is not.
- Management fraud may be even more difficult to detect than employee fraud because managers are in a stronger position to directly or indirectly manipulate accounting records and present fraudulent financial information. Management is able to override controls or instruct employees to do so whether innocently or not.

Auditors should therefore adopt an attitude of *professional scepticism*, recognising the possibility that a material misstatement due to fraud could exist, notwithstanding the fact that in previous years the client may have been considered honest and trustworthy.

External auditors and their clients

Following the series of accounting scandals in the USA in recent years one of the concerns of the auditing profession has been that the investing public will lose faith in the auditing profession and that the imprimatur that auditors place on a set of financial statements will become devalued, perhaps to the point of worthlessness.

The recent scandals involving Bernard Madoff's Ponzi scheme and Alan Stanford's banking activities have done little to improve the image of the profession in the USA. The activities of both those dubious individuals appeared to have been audited by what were, in effect, tame audit firms; small under-equipped firms for which the considerable fees paid by Madoff or Stanford's companies were perhaps the main part of their income.

As we have seen, it is acknowledged that external auditors have no direct responsibility for the detection of fraud but it is still part of the public perception that this is one of their principal functions. Thus the success of the audit profession in detecting or deterring Madoffs and Stanfords is highly relevant to the overall impression the investing public has of business probity.

In the UK these problems have not yet arisen. The structure of the profession and its mode of enforcement are completely different to those in the USA. Audit firms in the UK, for example, cannot have one significant client. Ethical rules forbid them to have any one client comprising more than 15 per cent (10 per cent in the case of listed companies) of their total fee income. Indeed clients which comprise more than 5–10 per cent of fee income would be likely to encourage firms to maintain a careful watch on firm–client relationships to eliminate any likelihood of unethical practice.

The approach in the UK is that of a non-regulatory framework, a Code of Practice which the profession feels is best policed by itself, a gentlemanly way of conducting affairs, moderated at the bar of professional and personal reputation rather than in the courtroom. The alternative to this honourable approach, which has after all served us well for many years, is to have – as profession points out wincing painfully – a situation where a jackbooted regulator crashes in stamping all over the delicate porcelain of the relationship between an audit firm and its client.

Yet there is a larger problem, one with which the audit profession has wrestled from time to time and one which it has come to the conclusion is best left alone. That problem is the inherent conflict of interest between:

(a) the auditor who acts for the shareholders as the guardian of its investment and the wielder of the stamp of approval of their agent's reports, and
(b) that very same auditor whose fees are paid by the directors and who is able to solicit non-audit work from those very same individuals.

The problem is this. Audit firms are able to garner considerable sums in fees from carrying out a whole range of non-audit consultancy-type work from their clients. Of course there are safeguards to ensure ethical behaviour which firms should scrupulously observe – Chinese walls, use of different teams etc. etc. – but the fact remains that, at the accounting firm level, these audit clients are valuable generators of large amounts of income.

There was a time, in the 1980s, when auditing was very much seen as a loss leader, as a way in to potential clients, and although hotly denied, the practice of 'lowballing' (charging an uneconomic fee to get the audit which would be later recovered by charging prodigious amounts of consultancy fees) was, if not rife, certainly evident. Those days may well be at an end, or may at least be less obvious, but the potential of a client to generate fees in addition to the basic audit fee is a paramount consideration among partners seeking to acquire new clients.

This is the elephant in the room which audit regulators hate to acknowledge. This conflict of interest which can ultimately place seen or unseen pressure on an audit partner to perhaps accept an accounting treatment, which bends the rules rather further than good practice would indicate, or to accept directors' explanations a little more readily and with a little less corroboration than a more prudent auditor might.

This duality of auditor/adviser is what destroyed Arthur Andersen in the Enron case and is what has tainted the profession's purity throughout its existence. In the USA audit firms are now banned under the Sarbanes–Oxley rules from carrying out non-audit services for precisely this reason; in the UK the framework still holds and, as far as we know, has not been broken by an Enron-sized scandal – yet.

Audit firms, and individual partners, must strike a balance between the lure of large fees and the consequences of any revelation of what might amount, at best, to sharp practice and at worst to a criminal activity (see Figure 2.1).

Auditors come back to their clients every year; they have an ongoing relationship with them and these kinds of decisions may have to be faced more than once. However, there is time, the auditor does not have to make a snap decision. The cost–benefit analysis and risk–reward equation is a carefully considered rational choice.

The argument the profession uses for maintaining self-regulation is this. The consequences of being thought of as being so venal that the standards of the profession are compromised or betrayed are likely, in practice, to amount to financial penalties which the large firms may be able to well afford, but the greater loss is that of reputation. Ultimately the transgressing individuals may have sanctions against them, have their audit licence taken away, perhaps even their professional qualification if their crimes are egregious enough, but the cost of the loss of reputation to the firm as a whole can be immense – as the fate of Arthur Andersen now bears mute witness.

The loss of clients, the scorn of the financial press, even the opprobrium of the public can be far more damaging than mere loss of money. The whole firm can be

Figure 2.1 The auditor's conflict

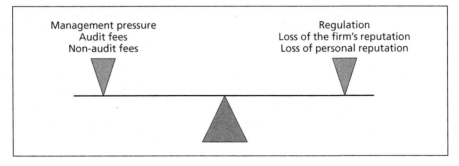

damaged by the actions of a few so, generally, it pays for firms to maintain the standards of the profession and to maintain a clear objective independent line with their client no matter what the temptation.

What, realistically, is the danger to the firm of something going wrong? If a major fraud is discovered two minutes after the audit report is signed off the auditors might look silly for a while, but they can draw their comfort from ISA 240 and the words of Lord Justice Lopes that discovering fraud was never their job in the first place.

 ## External auditors and fraud

The truth is that, whatever the size of the organisation, external audit is terribly bad at fraud detection. A recent survey by PricewaterhouseCoopers showed that perhaps only about 2 per cent of frauds were detected through external audit.

The forensic accountant should bear in mind that however good the external auditor's procedures are:

- They don't, generally, know the company or its staff as well as internal audit would – which is not surprising as they're not present all the time. Audit staff, certainly below audit manager level, are continually rotated and there is a recommendation that audit partners should be rotated after five years. Quite often relatively junior audit staff on the ground are:
  - remarkably ignorant about the entity and its operations
  - carrying out an audit according to a preset audit programme devised by the audit manager
  - under pressure to complete the job quickly and, consequently,
  - effectively, ticking boxes.
- As we have seen, audit firms can be faced with a conflict of interest when put under pressure by management to accept a certain level of what might be called 'financial engineering' which may fall short of fraud, but may also fall short of best practice.
- They are bound by their ethical roles to remain independent and objective as auditors so they should not be developing close friendships with staff members – friendships which might stimulate whistle-blowing. In practice most audit staff below manager level will have very little contact with client staff other than on a formal basis.
- Auditors' objectives are different – they are there to validate a set of financial statements, not to uncover frauds within the organisation. ISA 240 doesn't require them to hunt for frauds but it does require that the auditor adopt a sceptical approach and follow up any indicators of fraud, particularly where the client may have a history of fraud or be in a position where fraud might be likely.
- They carry out their work on the basis of samples of transactions looking to test a positive, i.e. that a control is working. Inherent in the audit approach is the possibility that not all frauds, errors or misstatements will be detected even if they are material. There is a practical temptation for audit staff on the ground to ignore audit evidence which disproves the positive and to find alternative evidence which bears out the findings they wish to achieve.
- Auditors are under considerable time pressure. Audit staff are expensive and audit costs mount rapidly. Staff are therefore more likely to take a risk-based

approach to the audit, perhaps to the extent of relying on very flimsy evidence or extremely limited testing in areas they regard as low risk. This can be a very fruitful area for the fraudster to exploit.

- Management, particularly senior management, have the capacity to hide fraud from the auditors. Quite often it is the management whom the auditors rely on for explanations. It is relatively easy for a senior manager who is engaged in fraudulent practice to mislead an auditor who is not very familiar with the business or its systems or who is inexperienced in dealing with audit issues. The fraud may involve sophisticated and carefully organised schemes designed to conceal it including collusion, forgery, deliberate non-recording of transactions as well as intentional misrepresentations made to the auditor at a senior level.

One area in which the auditors should be competent is to uncover or reveal fraudulent reporting, deliberate misreporting of financial information. However, worldwide, most of the most outrageous and spectacular frauds of this nature have sailed through external audit year after year. One need only whisper the names Enron, WorldCom and Parmalat to set audit partners on the defensive.

To be fair nothing of the size of those cases has appeared in the UK to date, which may be a reflection of our flexible and effective corporate governance regime and the relative honesty of the UK's senior management or may, equally, be a consequence of ineffective audit practices. For the moment the former view prevails.

In the event of a fraud or deliberate misrepresentation of the financial statements being uncovered external auditors can then, justifiably, cry that they were duped along with everyone else. Providing they have some working papers which evidence:

- that they took the possibility of fraud or misrepresentation into account when they carried out the audit planning
- that they asked pertinent questions and carried out sample tests and basic balance sheet verification checks and, most importantly,
- that they got the directors to sign a Letter of Representation stating that there were no material frauds in the organisation, even if it was subsequently proved that those same directors were lying through their teeth.

the auditors can be more or less off the hook (Exhibit 2.1). The victims of the fraud would have to prove gross negligence in court – and good luck to them!

Exhibit 2.1 Fraud example: Eric

Eric was the owner/manager of a property development company who defrauded the business of which he was the majority shareholder. When questioned about his activities and the risk of being detected by the audit he said:

> Accountants can only work on the figures they have got, audit the same. Auditors came to see me and I just lied to them and gave them false pieces of paper and that was that. The checking process was abysmal I was not worried because I have twenty years experience of auditors . . . the lack of attention to detail, the lack of knowledge in auditing and accounting . . . there was no interrogation from audit and that was good for me.

Source: Gill (2005)

 **Materiality**

The work external auditors might carry out is primarily concerned with two types of fraud:

- misappropriation of assets and consequent misstatements arising from that, i.e. a 'cover up' involving the alteration of the accounting records to disguise the theft, and
- misstatements arising from fraudulent financial reporting.

Audit procedures, even when adopting a risk-based approach, are more likely to detect frauds by the organisation, the fraudulent manipulation of the accounts themselves rather than the underlying records, than they are to detect employee frauds within the organisation. Auditors rely on the organisation's own internal control systems to detect or prevent material misstatements, which include fraud, as, of course, do the directors.

One of the key issues which probably affects the external audit approach more than that of internal audit is the issue of materiality.

ISA 320, *Materiality in Planning and Performing an Audit* states:

> Misstatements, including omissions, are considered to be material if they, individually or in the aggregate, could reasonably be expected to influence the economic decisions of users taken on the basis of the financial statements . . . The auditor's determination of materiality is a matter of professional judgment.

In other words, materiality equates to the significance of a transaction or group of transactions. It is perfectly possible for a fraud to be a material item in the context of the financial statements. Materiality has a direct relationship with the assessment of audit risk, that is the risk that the auditors will give an incorrect report, and auditors will take some care in setting materiality levels, revising them as the audit proceeds as necessary.

Over time auditors have derived some 'rule of thumb' quantitative indicators of materiality, defining it as a percentage of some aspect of the accounts such as gross profit or net assets or, in some cases, as an absolute amount. ISA 320 outlines how this can be done. The reason for this is easily apparent insofar as the auditor's primary task is to report on the truth and fairness, or otherwise, of the financial statements so that items which are immaterial are unlikely to be of much interest. The increasing use of risk-based audit techniques and the new requirements of ISA 320 regarding what is known as 'performance materiality', which we don't need to consider here, has perhaps sharpened the overall consideration of materiality but has served to reduce the amount of actual testing carried out by the auditors as they rely on the strength of the organisation's own internal control environment (Chapter 8) to keep them out of court.

Let's look at an example of how materiality works. Suppose there is an internal fraud amounting to say £100,000, one which has been going on at this rate for three years so, overall, some £300,000 of company assets has been stolen over that time.

If the company concerned is, say, Huge Plc with turnover and profits in hundreds of millions of pounds, £100,000 may be well below the external auditor's materiality level. Their procedures would be most unlikely to detect such a fraud unless they stumbled across it by accident or were told about it by a whistle-blower. They would be looking at the risks around considerably larger transactions as only these would have the potential to adversely affect the results of the entity in a significant way.

Clearly however a similar-sized fraud in Small Ltd, with turnover of millions and profits in hundreds of thousands, would be material to the financial statements so one might have a greater expectation that, even if the internal control system had missed it or been bypassed in some way, the auditor's procedures would detect the possibility of an anomaly or an indication which might indicate fraudulent behaviour or the need for further investigation.

Auditors, in their testing procedures, particularly of balance sheet items, can give away indications of materiality levels to organisation staff with statements such as 'Please provide us with an analysis of every Payables balance over £5,000.'

This can give the fraudster an indicator of the levels of materiality the audit team might be utilising, an indication which they might seek to confirm by close observation of the audit testing procedures. If they survive the first year's audit, unless they do something foolish, they have a good chance of surviving subsequent years. Errors uncovered by the audit can often be ignored because they appear to be trivial or not material, unless the cumulative value becomes material, when, in fact, they may be signifiers of a deeper malaise.

The external auditor and the forensic accountant

The forensic investigator will be likely to ask for input from the external auditor early in the investigation. The external auditors should have carried out extensive client assessment procedures, following the precepts of ISA 315 and ISA 330 outlined above, including:

- Gaining an understanding of the client and its operating environment, including its internal control systems, sufficient to identify and assess the risks of a material misstatement due to fraud or error.
- An assessment of the risks of a material misstatement due to fraud or error by considering:
  - The nature of the business, its services and its products which may be susceptible to misappropriation. For example, businesses which involve cash takings (for example, retailers) or easily portable and valuable assets (for example, jewellers) are particularly vulnerable as are organisations where assets are held in a fiduciary capacity (for example, solicitors who hold client's monies before handing them on to the appropriate persons). Also vulnerable are areas where payment is made on the basis of an opinion, i.e. the value of work certified in the construction industry or the value of extras to contract. This may involve corrupt practices such as bribery of a quantity surveyor.
  - Pressures on the business including circumstances which may induce management to overstate profits (or understate losses) in order to:
    - retain the confidence of investors, bankers or creditors
    - meet profit forecasts
    - increase profit-related remuneration
    - stave off the threat of insolvency proceedings, and
    - maintain the share price where management have shares or share options.

- The known strength, quality and effectiveness of management.
- The internal control environment including the degree of management involvement and supervision and the degree of segregation of duties, and where there is excessive authority vested in a senior manager.
- The ability of the management to override otherwise effective controls.
- The existence and effectiveness of internal audit.

Discussions with the external auditors and examination of audit files and audit risk assessments can give the forensic investigator a flying start.

Clearly this will require a formal access letter from the client as the external auditors are bound by the rules of client confidentiality, but this should be a mere formality.

Should a forensic accounting investigation be evaluating the extent of a financial statement fraud, then clearly co-operation with external auditors is going to be difficult. There may be the possibility of legal action hanging over the auditors as well as potential investigations by the regulatory body so they will be extremely conscious of the need to be seen to co-operate whilst, at the same time, trying to avoid making any statements or giving away any information, over and above that required and obtainable by the investigators, which may be prejudicial to any future legal case.

Forensic investigators should therefore proceed accompanied by sound legal advice.

It may be that the forensic accounting team will come from within the external audit firm, which has some advantages to the client not least in terms of access to information and audit experience and expertise, but also has some clear disadvantages centring around issues of independence and conflict of interests within the audit firm.

In any case, even where no blame attaches to the auditors, or even where some does, they have a right to know the nature and extent of what has been uncovered by the investigation. The outcome may well have a bearing on their audit of the financial statements and any adjustment which may be required in respect of prior year figures.

If the investigation has arisen during the course of an audit additional time may be needed for the audit partner to fully evaluate the results of the investigation and the effect it may have on the auditors' report.

Again there are likely to be questions of confidentiality so disclosures should only be made with the benefit of legal advice. External auditors may, for example, wish to know if any information is being withheld from them concerning a fraud investigation and they may seek assurance that such information will not be likely to be prejudicial to any audit opinion they may issue. External auditors have statutory rights to information granted to them under S499 Companies Act, 2006 in connection with their audit of the organisation's financial statements, so it could place the organisation in a difficult position should they refuse to disclose information which may be pertinent to the audit.

Forensic investigators from an independent firm would require their client's permission to disclose information to the external auditors, and even an investigation team from the same firm as the auditors would be well advised to take legal advice before they disclosed confidential information concerning an investigation to their audit colleagues without the specific permission of their client.

Each case has to be considered on its own merits and it is outside the scope of this book to discuss the legal technicalities of this situation any further.

The role of internal audit

The role and function of internal audit is defined by their trade body, the Institute of Internal Auditors (IIA) as:

> an independent, objective assurance and consulting activity designed to add value and improve an organisation's operations. It helps an organisation accomplish its objectives by bringing a systematic, disciplined approach to evaluate and improve the effectiveness of risk management, control, and governance processes.

For internal auditors the IIA bases its professional standards on the *Code of Ethics and International Standards for the Professional Practice of Internal Auditing.* This sets out the key requirements for the effective functioning of an internal audit role and the standards which individual members of the institute must abide by. In carrying out their day-to-day work internal auditors will also, of course, pay due attention to the ISAs issued by the Auditing Practices Board as these set a benchmark of good practice in many areas.

Internal audit's role is thus primarily managerial. The IIA speaks of internal audit as having its primary purpose as being the organisation's 'critical friend' to:

- challenge current practice
- champion best practice, and
- be a catalyst for improvement.

in order to assist the organisation to achieve its strategic objectives. Internal audit is likely to cover issues in some detail which the external auditors would not necessarily review such as:

- Risk management
  - review of procedures
  - monitoring risk-assessment processes, and
  - reviewing risk exposure.
- Operational issues
  - quality systems
  - tendering and procurement procedures
  - supplier selection and performance
  - cost recording and budget monitoring
  - control and monitoring of expenditure
  - asset usage
  - achievement against internal key performance indicators, and
  - control of outsourced operations.
- Sales and marketing
  - customer complaints
  - credit control procedures
  - pricing and sales volumes, and
  - control of sales staff.
- Human resources
  - recruitment and selection procedures, and
  - training.

- Computer systems
  - systems control
  - use of computer-assisted auditing techniques (CAATs), and
  - systems development.
- Compliance with legal and regulatory requirements.
- Value for money issues – economy, efficiency, effectiveness.

The definition of internal audit places it firmly in the risk-management role. They are there to 'improve operations' and 'improve the effectiveness of risk management control and governance processes'. This then would lead one to assume that fraud prevention and detection was a risk they would gladly seek to engage with.

Internal auditors and fraud

In April 2003 the IIA issued its *Fraud Position Statement*, which made it quite clear where responsibility lay:

> The primary responsibility for prevention, detection and investigation of fraud rests with management which also has the responsibility to manage the risk of fraud. Many organisations now have a dedicated in-house 'security' function with responsibility to manage fraud investigations. This function may be assisted by internal audit.

This is as expected. Within the organisation management is primarily responsible for everything and cannot delegate that responsibility to anyone else. The IIA goes on to say, reinforcing this point, that 'it is not a primary role of internal audit to detect fraud'.

They recognise that most people, and perhaps that includes the management of their organisation, probably think that fraud detection is, at least, one of their primary roles. There is another expectation gap here that has to be managed.

Consequently internal audit's official role in connection with fraud is defined by the IIA as being:

- investigating the causes of fraud – (presumably post-detection)
- reviewing fraud prevention controls and detection processes put in place by management
- making recommendations to improve those processes
- advising the audit committee on what, if any, legal advice should be sought if a criminal investigation is to proceed
- bringing in any specialist knowledge and skills to assist in fraud investigations, or leading investigations where appropriate and as requested by management
- liaising with the investigation team
- responding to whistle-blowers
- considering fraud risk in every audit
- having sufficient knowledge to identify the indicators of fraud, and
- facilitating corporate learning about fraud.

What this means in reality is that the internal audit function should be well placed to uncover fraudulent behaviour, far better placed, in fact, than external auditors. The reason for this is simple enough – they know the business and they are not confined to simply testing the accounting entries sufficiently well so as to gather evidence to validate a set of accounts.

Internal audit is well placed to consider the possibility of money laundering and following up reports from whistle-blowers – something we will look at later.

Internal audit and the forensic accountant

The forensic accountant therefore should have an ally in the internal audit function, but before placing any reliance upon that person three things must be considered:

1 Is the internal audit function in the organisation a proper function or does it carry out a box-ticking exercise to satisfy the audit committee? What this boils down to is:
   * Is the head of internal audit a senior figure in the management team?
   * Does internal audit report to the audit committee or in a way which divorces them from the CFO or the CEO?
   * Is internal audit truly independent of line management?
   * Do they have a budget and resources sufficient to enable them to carry out their work effectively?
   * Can they set their own schedule of work or is this devised for them by management?
2 Are the members of the internal audit team qualified and experienced auditors who can be relied on to carry out their work effectively and efficiently? Do they have enquiring minds and a willingness to implement new procedures or are they simply going through the motions in a fairly dispirited way?
3 Does the executive management actively encourage internal audit by responding to its reports and recommendations and by allowing it access to all areas of the business without let or hindrance?

If a forensic accountant is called in to carry out an investigation it is likely to be in circumstances:

* where internal audit has uncovered a fraud or the preliminary indications of one and is bringing in a specialist
* where internal audit have found nothing but the management is not satisfied, or
* where a whistle-blower or other unsubstantiated report has indicated the possibility of fraud or other malfeasance.

In each case the forensic accountant will have to work with internal audit at some level. If the assessment of internal audit is that their direct involvement may be less than helpful because of, say, a lack of skills or some form of bias the decision is a simple one. However, if internal audit is likely to be a useful adjunct to the investigation team the forensic accountant can use them for their:

* Knowledge of the company and systems – in particular how anomalies are likely to evidence themselves.
* Assessments of individuals and departments, systems and procedures. In addition to their official reports they will have, or should have, gathered a mass of unofficial information, unsubstantiated rumour and gossip. They will have their personal opinions of managers and staff, which they certainly could not broadcast but could reveal to a forensic investigator. Whilst much of this may be discounted, the thoughts of experienced local auditors should never be entirely ignored.

They can assist in the actual investigation work by:

- Collecting and collating information and documentation, using core audit skills to carry out tests and analysing data under supervision.
- Using their skills in project management such as planning, scheduling, document management, looking at issue resolution and follow-up and recording and communication of results.

The internal auditors can bring their knowledge of the organisation to bear in terms of providing background information. They can also be a useful resource in collecting data, advising the forensic investigators on their approach and in helping them avoid traps and pitfalls.

Working with a good team of internal auditors saves a lot of time and effort. However, care must be taken not to jump to conclusions or to make false assumptions based on unproven 'knowledge' or supposition – or by reacting inappropriately to malicious rumour or gossip.

There are of course two provisos:

- Internal audit must realise that what they are taking part in is an investigation which may result in legal proceedings. They therefore have to recognise the forensic accountant's responsibility to preserve evidence and the 'chain of evidence' to avoid inadvertently compromising any possible criminal case.
- Normal audit rules don't apply – announcing visits or submitting requests for documentation is simply inappropriate during the course of an investigation. It is the forensic accountant who makes the rules and they have to agree to abide by them.

The ultimate responsibility for the investigation will lie with the organisation – possibly embodied in the form of the audit committee. It may well decide that it is inappropriate for the internal auditors to be involved, in which case they become simply a passive resource, a source of information for the forensic accountant but no more than that.

Summary

- There is a gap between what external auditors actually do and what the public think they do, known as the expectation gap.
- An early legal case described an auditor as a watchdog not a bloodhound, so auditors do not have a prima facie duty to detect fraud.
- The role of external audit is primarily to sign off a set of financial statements in a prescribed format, however they should adopt an attitude of professional scepticism in an audit of financial statements.
- International Standards on Auditing (ISAs) place no requirement of external auditors to uncover fraud.
- External auditors may be conflicted as they often carry out consultancy work for clients in addition to their role as auditors.
- Materiality limits set by external auditors often rule out reviewing smaller transactions and can be an indicator of audit limits to fraudsters.
- External auditors may not review whole areas of an organisation if they are not directly relevant to the financial systems.
- Internal audit is a management function with a remit to improve operational and financial functions.

- The Institute of Internal Auditors places the responsibility for fraud prevention and detection on management.
- The internal audit department must have status and independence within the organisation otherwise its role and function may be compromised.
- Forensic accountants may have to work with both internal and external audit in carrying out their investigations.

Case study

Megachem plc is a multinational agri-business dealing in the import and export of agricultural produce, the manufacture and sale of fertilisers and pesticides and the sale of agricultural machinery worldwide.

The external auditors have placed reliance on the work of internal audit insofar as they have relied on the checking work of internal audit of the purchasing, sales and salaries system. However, during the course of the audit the external audit team discover the following:

(a) The head of internal audit (HIA) is the brother-in law of the financial director. They trained with the same firm and the HIA was appointed after leaving his last job very suddenly without any form of reference.

(b) The HIA had instructed his internal audit team not to query any overseas transactions with certain countries but to refer any questions to him.

(c) External audit was accidentally handed a file containing several delivery notes for 'agricultural machinery' recording deliveries of crates of what are described as 'machinery parts' to several countries in the world where there are local conflicts. These delivery notes had been kept in a separate file in the CEO's office and marked 'confidential' and the auditors had been given it by the CEO's secretary, by accident, when requesting information about another, unrelated, issue. No other documentation appears to exist in respect of the client's names recorded on the delivery notes and they do not appear in the receivables ledger.

(d) The company recorded the receipt of substantial bank transfers from accounts in Switzerland and Panama. These were recorded as 'consultancy fees' but there are no other records relating to these transactions and the actual client's name is not recorded.

(e) The firm appears to be employing consultants in various countries in the Balkans and the Far East as 'commissions' are being paid to them but it is unclear precisely what services these individuals provide. When asked the financial director refused to divulge any information, citing confidentiality.

(f) Visits to one of the manufacturing plants revealed that workers appeared to be handling what looked like dangerous chemicals without proper protective gear. The factory manager said that the gear was provided but the workers refused to wear it on the grounds that it made them hot and impeded movement.

(g) There is an article on an environmental news website stating that a pipe at one of the company's plants is discharging chemicals into the adjacent river. The company says the effluent is treated and that they have a licence to do this but can't show it to the auditors as they claim they have lost it.

Required

Discuss the implications of these discoveries for:

- the external and internal auditors
- the company, and
- the financial statements.

Bibliography

Albrecht, W.S. (1984) *Deterring Fraud – The Internal Auditor's Perspective.* Institute of Internal Auditors Research Foundation, Maitland, FL.

Auditing Practices Board (2009) ISA 200 *Overall Objectives of the Independent Auditor and the Conduct of an Audit in Accordance with International Standards on Auditing.* Auditing Practices Board, London.

Auditing Practices Board (2009) ISA 240 *The Auditor's Responsibilities Relating to Fraud in an Audit of Financial Statements.* Auditing Practices Board, London.

Auditing Practices Board (2009) ISA 315 *Identifying and Assessing the Risks of a Material Misstatement through Understanding the Entity and its Environment.* Auditing Practices Board, London.

Auditing Practices Board (2009) ISA 320 *Materiality in Planning and Performing an Audit.* Auditing Practices Board, London.

Auditing Practices Board (2009) ISA 330 *The Auditors' Responses to Assessed Risks.* Auditing Practices Board, London.

Institute of Internal Auditors (2006) *Code of Ethics and International Standards for the Professional Practice of Internal Auditing.* Institute of Internal Auditors, London.

Institute of Internal Auditors (2003) *Working with Internal Audit.* Institute of Internal Auditors, London.

Institute of Internal Auditors (2003) *Fraud Position Paper.* Institute of Internal Auditors, London.

Gill, M. (2005.) *Learning from Fraudsters.* Protoviti, London.

Hillison, W., Pacini, C. and Sinason, S. (1999) The internal auditor as fraud buster. *Managerial Auditing Journal*, 14, 7, 351–363.

ICAEW (2003) *Fraud – Meeting the Challenge though External Audit.* ICAEW, London.

In re Kingston Cotton Mill (No2) FN12 [1896] 1 Ch. 331. *The Law Times*, LXXIV, Court of Appeal, 11 July 1896.

Millichamp, A. and Taylor, J. (2008) *Auditing.* Cengage, London.

Turnbull, N. (1999*) Internal Control: Guidance for Directors on the Combined Code.* FRC, London.

Websites

http://oxcheps.new.ox.ac.uk

www.icaew.com

www.iia.org.uk

www.frc.org/combinedcode

www.frc.org.uk/apb

Chapter 3

The legal context

Chapter contents

Learning objectives

After studying this chapter you should be able to:

- Understand the composition of a crime and how it differs from an error or mistake
- Appreciate the differences in the evidence requirements between civil and criminal proceedings
- Have a basic knowledge of the main provisions of the key legislation relating to fraud, the Fraud Act 2006
- Understand the difference between the law in England and Wales and the law in Scotland relating to fraud
- Understand the law relating to bribery and corruption

- Understand the money laundering rules and an outline of the intentions of the Proceeds of Crime Act 2002
- Understand the law relating to the protection of whistle-blowers
- Understand the prohibitions against obtaining electronic evidence illegally
- Appreciate the importance of preservation of evidence in a manner suitable for admission in legal proceedings
- Learn the do's and don'ts when interviewing suspects
- Develop a knowledge of the Court orders used by fraud investigators and how they are applied to assist a fraud investigation
- Understand the position with regard to taxation

Introduction

Some of what follows may seem secondary or irrelevant to the forensic investigator, who might well consider it to be the province of their colleagues in the legal profession as, of course, fundamentally it is.

No forensic investigator should embark on a fraud investigation which may result in criminal or civil proceedings without a handy lawyer at the ready to advise them, so what follows is not intended to be comprehensive legal advice. However, it is important that the forensic investigator has a working knowledge of some of the legal principles involved and understands some of the basic rules, if only to avoid making some fundamental error which fatally undermines a prosecution.

Thus we consider the legal principles underpinning the definition of criminal behaviour and look at the relevant statutes, including, of course, the main one, the Fraud Act 2006.

In addition there are sections on two very important features of the law which all forensic investigators should be aware of. These are:

- the rules of evidence, and
- the use of various court orders to support an investigation.

Obeying the principal rules of evidence is absolutely crucial: more than one prosecution has failed because the rules weren't followed during the course of the investigation, thus allowing the defence to claim that the evidence may have been tampered with and enabling the perpetrator to walk away. We also need to consider some of the limits of the investigator's role and what they may or may not do legally.

Learning how to use court orders in an investigation can be a big help in building a case and forensic investigators should be aware of what can be done – even if they have to leave the details to the lawyers.

In Part 5 we look at the work of the forensic accountant in areas other than fraud such as dispute resolution, asset valuation, matrimonial work and asset tracing. This chapter and much of what follows in this book is concerned with criminal actions such as fraud, corruption and money laundering. We believe that the forensic investigator should have a working knowledge of the rules so we will confine the rest of this chapter to what we might loosely describe as aspects of the criminal law, evidence and procedure.

 ## Civil versus criminal

It is important to understand, at the outset, the difference in approach between a civil case and a criminal case insofar as this might affect the work of the forensic accountant.

The most obvious difference is the standard of proof which is required to make the case. In criminal law cases the standard of proof is, quite rightly, considerably greater than that required to obtain a civil judgment or to win a case at, say, an employment tribunal.

Civil cases

In civil cases, for example, actions for damages or restitution, matrimonial cases or employment law cases, the court or tribunal maintains neutrality between the parties. Whilst one party must prove their case, what is known as the burden of proof, the standard of proof required is much lower than in a criminal case: in essence the case turns on the balance of probabilities, i.e. it is 'likely' that the defendant did what they are alleged to have done.

As far as the claimant is concerned, if they fail to prove any essential element in their case judgment is given to the defendant. The claimant has the burden of proving their claim and the defendant may simply deny it. If the defence puts up anything other than a stout denial of the facts as advanced by the claimant they assume a burden of proof and must advance evidence to prove their case. This will take the form of evidence which does not form part of the claimant's case.

The rule in civil cases therefore is, broadly, that both sides must prove their own case. The court will then decide which case is more probable than not. The court is not looking to decide whether the claimant's case is more probable than the defendant's; the test is whether the case is more probably true than not true. Whilst in the generality of civil claims this does result in a lower standard of proof being required for the claimant to prove their claim there is evidence that, in fraud cases, the courts are tending to look for a much greater standard of proof almost analogous to that required in criminal cases.

Criminal cases

In a criminal case the burden of proving every element of the case, from beginning to end, lies with the prosecution. The presumption of innocence is a fundamental attribute of fairness and due process and every individual has the fundamental right to be considered innocent until proven guilty in a criminal case. This has been enshrined in Article 6(2) of the Human Rights Act 1998 which states that: 'Everyone charged with a criminal offence shall be presumed innocent until proved guilty according to law.'

What this means is that the defendant is under no obligation to prove any alternative explanation of the facts, it is for the prosecution to prove that the explanation advanced by the defendant does not hold water. There is a burden on the prosecution to prove the guilt of the defendant, there is no such burden on the defendent to prove their innocence and it is sufficient for them to raise a doubt as to their guilt. They do not have to satisfy the jury of their innocence.

The onus is on the prosecution to demonstrate that a criminal act was committed by the accused beyond reasonable doubt. This does not require an absolute or scientific certainty but equates to a high degree of probability.

In certain circumstances such as a plea of insanity or diminished responsibility there is an evidential burden on the defendant which is unlikely in fraud trials but not perhaps impossible. If the defendant is perhaps trying to establish some sort of alibi they must advance a prima facie case for the alibi and it is up to the prosecution to advance evidence to disprove it. So if the defendant was, for example, trying to claim that false entries in the accounting records could not have been made by them because they were on holiday in Spain at the time the entries were made they will have to produce some prima facie evidence of fact and it would be up to the prosecution to demonstrate that, despite this denial, the accused nonetheless did make the entries or cause them to be made in some way. The burden of proof on the defendant here is thus only sufficient to make a prima facie case because it effectively constitutes a denial of the prosecution case rather than an attempt to make an alternative case.

Where a statute imposes a burden of proof on a defendant the standard of proof required is akin to that required in a civil case which, as we have seen, is the 'balance of probability'. It is not necessary for the defendant to prove their case 'beyond reasonable doubt' in such a situation. This was established in a case in 1943, (Carr–Briant (1943) 2All ER 156) which dealt with a case brought under the Prevention of Corruption Act 1916. Further discussion of this type of situation is beyond the scope of this book; however, this position might apply in corruption cases (see later).

The relevance of this for the forensic accountant is that they must prepare their reports to the highest possible standard even if the client has stated that they do not wish to pursue a criminal prosecution. It should always be assumed by the investigator that their report will end up in a criminal trial where it may be dissected and challenged, so the report must be robust and any conclusions within it supported by sufficient reliable evidence which is capable of withstanding a challenge. The nature of the forensic accountant's work is such that some form of legal action is always a possibility, even if that may not have been in the minds of the parties initially. Nor is it simply a matter of doing good work only in fraud cases; what may start as an amicable separation agreement dividing marital assets can end up as a vicious courtroom battle with expert witnesses on both sides alleging all sorts of wrongdoings or sharp practice. The message is clear from the outset.

Always assume your report is going to be questioned in court and always carry out your work to the highest standard.

Having looked at the standard forensic investigators must work to it is necessary to review some fundamental legal concepts as to what actually constitutes a crime.

Crime

It may be a little strange to the reader at this point for us to say that before we become engrossed in the details of the criminal law and, later in the book, in the methodology of investigating possible crimes, it might be useful to be able to decide if a crime has actually been committed in the first place.

Sherlock Holmes identified this at an early stage in his career when called to assist Sir Henry Baskerville: 'There are two questions waiting for us at the outset.

The one is whether any crime has been committed at all; the other is what is the crime and how was it committed,' which, if you think about it, is actually three questions – nevertheless, Holmes has summed it up succinctly.

It should be stated at the outset, and will be repeated later, that the role of the forensic investigator is to establish what has happened, to establish the facts as they stand. It is *not* to build a case against any individual or to support some sort of claim. Any report prepared should be an objective and dispassionate report with facts that are supported by evidence and conclusions and recommendations which flow from those facts. The strength or otherwise of a criminal case is something the lawyers must decide but, again, it is useful for the forensic accountant to have a working knowledge of the key principles, if only so that they can understand fully what the lawyers are talking about!

Accordingly we need to explain two legal concepts which underlie the commission of a crime. These need not delay us unduly but they are fundamental to an understanding of the process of criminal law. The forensic accountant needs to know what they are and what their legal significance is.

Actus reus and *mens rea*

In law, a person may not be convicted of a crime unless:

(a) the individual is proven, beyond reasonable doubt, to have caused the event (i.e. the crime) or has created a state of affairs which is forbidden by criminal law. In law this is known as the *actus reus,* and

(b) the individual had a defined state of mind in relation to the causing of the event or the creation of the state of affairs. In law this state of mind is called *mens rea* and, for our purpose, we can ally it closely with intent, i.e. the accused intended to commit the crime for which they have been charged.

These concepts are complex and there are multitudinous legal nuances surrounding the establishment of the *actus reus* and any associated *mens rea* where an individual is accused of a crime. As this is not, primarily, a law textbook these concepts have necessarily been somewhat simplified. Nevertheless they are very important because the forensic investigator has to understand that evidence needs to be gathered to support the contentions that:

- a crime has been committed within the terms of common law or statute which defines the *actus reus* of the crime, and
- the accused person intended to commit it and, by their actions, actually did commit it.

Key to the establishment of these two premises is the question of intent – did the accused intend to commit a crime or were they simply foolish, incompetent or both? It will be necessary to establish that the actions of the individual were not simply caused through error or as a result of a mistake but by the intention to commit a crime. For example, false entries in the books of account may be evidence of a deliberate attempt to cover up a fraud or they may have been made to cover up some sort of initial error, thus compounding the mistake rather than mitigating it.

There are several factors to be considered. Clearly there must be some sort of action or conduct by the accused, they must actually do something or, for some offences, refrain from doing something which creates the offence. For some crimes there must be 'circumstances' which create the offence so, for example, in a deception offence there must be 'property belonging to another'. If the property belonged to no one, perhaps because it had been abandoned, the fact that the accused appropriated it is not sufficient to constitute the *actus reus* of theft, however dishonest that action might appear to be, simply because an essential element of the crime is missing.

In some cases, there must be a consequence arising out of the actions of the accused, although this is not the case with theft or fraud where it is simply intention which has to be demonstrated.

Clearly merely doing something may not constitute a crime, there has to be the mental element as well. So an individual must act, or fail to act, with the intention of achieving some sort of result and that intention must be dishonest.

For example Section 2 of the Fraud Act 2006, which we look at in more detail below, states:

> A person is in breach of Section 2 if he:
> (a) dishonestly make a false representation, and
> (b) intend, by making the representation—
> (i) to make a gain for himself or another, or
> (ii) to cause loss to another or to expose another to a risk of loss.

For a case to succeed under this section the prosecution must prove firstly an action and an intent. The action, the making of the false representation, is the *actus reus* of the crime and the *mens rea*, the guilty mind of the accused, is satisfied by proof that they knew the representation was or might be false and that they acted dishonestly with intent to cause gain or loss.

It should also be borne in mind that omitting to do something might be sufficient to create an offence, i.e. might be the *actus reus*. Clearly omitting to file a VAT return is an offence, as is dishonestly failing to disclose information when under a legal duty to do so under S3 of the Fraud Act 2006.

The question of intent is a complex one which we are not going to fully explore here. Simply put, a result of an act is intended when it is the actor's purpose to cause it. Intention can also be inferred by a jury in situations where something has happened which it was not the actor's purpose to cause but the result was a virtually certain consequence of their actions and the actor knew it was a virtually certain consequence, in other words the result could have been foreseen by any reasonable person. So the simple act of making a representation which was known to be false can only have the intent to deceive, it is capable of no other explanation. The question of whether or not the defendant acted dishonestly is, one for a jury to decide.

Note that carrying out criminal acts whilst drunk or under the influence of drugs will not normally create a defence of involuntary behaviour. This is an attempt by an accused person to counter this question of deliberate intent. Statements such as 'I was drunk – I did not mean to do it', 'I was under stress and on medication' are unlikely to succeed as a defence because, broadly, the individual, presumably voluntarily, has put themselves in that state initially. The law takes the view that, generally, by putting themselves in a situation where their normal inhibitions were overcome or their normally impeccable moral standards were abandoned, the individual created the conditions where they may have committed an offence and had done so voluntarily.

The forensic investigator's role is to gather evidence to explain clearly what happened so that a jury can decide whether or not a crime was committed, whether the defendant intended to commit it and did, in fact, do so.

Fraud

There was, surprisingly, no statutory offence of fraud until the passing of the Fraud Act 2006. Prior to that, offences such as conspiracy to defraud or fraudulent trading were the main charging offences but neither constituted a general offence of fraud. One curious consequence was that, until the Fraud Act, there was no attempt to arrive at a definition of what constitutes fraud as fraud, rather than as theft, deception or a conspiracy.

It should be pointed out that the Fraud Act itself doesn't actually provide a general definition of fraud either, however commentators feel that, by dint of listing all the various fraudulent actions, it does define it in practical terms.

The Fraud Act 2006 – main provisions

The Fraud Act 2006 ('the Act') applies in England, Wales and Northern Ireland but not in Scotland. We will look at the law in Scotland separately later in this chapter.

The Act repeals all the deception offences in the Theft Acts of 1968 and 1978 and replaces them with a single offence of fraud, defined in Section 1, which can be committed in three different ways by:

- false representation (Section 2)
- failure to disclose information when there is a legal duty to do so (Section 3), or
- abuse of position (Section 4).

The Act also creates new offences of possession (Section 6) and making or supplying articles for use in frauds (Section7).

The offence of fraudulent trading (Section 993 of the Companies Act 2006) is extended to also apply to sole traders (Section 9).

Obtaining services by deception is replaced by a new offence of obtaining services dishonestly (Section 11).

We will look at Sections 1–4 in some detail as we think that it is important for forensic investigators to appreciate the relevant law, if only to help them make sure that the evidence they gather is sufficient to prove their case.

Section 1 of the Fraud Act 2006

Section 1 creates a new general offence of fraud and introduces the three possible ways of committing it. The three ways, set out in Sections 2, 3 and 4 of the Act, are fraud by:

- false representation (Section 2)
- failure to disclose information when there is a legal duty to do so (Section 3), and
- abuse of position (Section 4).

In each case what must be evidenced is that:

- the defendant's conduct was dishonest, and
- their intention was to make a gain, or cause a loss or the risk of a loss to another.

Crucially, no gain or loss needs actually to have been made.

The maximum sentence is 10 years imprisonment.

Fraud by false representation (Section 2)

This is one of the main charging provisions of the Act, and we are going to look at it in some detail so that the precise meaning of some of the words is made clear.

Please also note that, in law, statutes invariably refer to 'he'. This is not meant to be sexist, although it undoubtedly is, but is a universal if regrettable convention on the part of legal draftspersons.

Section 2 states:

> (1) A person is in breach of Section 2 if he
>   (a) dishonestly make a false representation, and
>   (b) intend, by making the representation—
>   (i) to make a gain for himself or another, or
>   (ii) to cause loss to another or to expose another to a risk of loss.
> (2) A representation is false if—
>   (a) it is untrue or misleading, and
>   (b) the person making it knows that it is, or might be, untrue or misleading.
> (3) For the purpose of the Act 'Representation' means any representation as to fact or law, including a representation as to the state of mind of—
>   (a) the person making the representation, or
>   (b) any other person.
> (4) A representation may be express or implied.
> (5) For the purposes of this section a representation may be regarded as made if it (or anything implying it) is submitted in any form to any system or device designed to receive, convey or respond to communications (with or without human intervention).

We need now to consider some of the specific words and phrases used in this section so the underlying principles can be made clear.

Actions and the form of representations

What does the Act mean by 'false representations'?

The offence focuses entirely on the actions of the perpetrator and is committed as soon as they make a dishonest representation with a dishonest intent.

For this reason it is immaterial:

- whether or not anyone is actually deceived, or
- whether any gain is made by the perpetrator, or
- whether loss is actually incurred by another party.

It is the making of the representation whch is the offence.

Making a false representation is not confined to telling lies about status or to submitting false documents, nor is it confined to statements made or words expressed; it can also be implied by conduct and, as we have seen, there is no limitation on how the representation is transmitted or expressed. So, for example, the misrepresentation could be:

- written
- spoken
- posted on a phishing website
- included in a fax, or
- sent by e-mail.

A representation is implied by conduct when a person uses a credit card dishonestly because by tendering the card, they are falsely representing that they have the authority to use it for that transaction.

A representation can be made through something as simple as body language – a nod of the head or presence in a restricted area implying the right to be there (including presence within a secure computer system).

Being dressed or wearing identification that implies a certain status or right to be present is a form of representation, so wearing a name badge in order to gain access, say, to an office in order to gain access to a computer system is an offence under the Act. Using a false identity in order to open a bank account is an obvious form of representation which is a clear offence under this section.

One area which forensic accountants sometimes encounter when looking at the actions of fraudsters is that of representations by omission – for example, an individual who omits to mention previous convictions on a job application form. That person is representing themselves as being of good character or financial probity when the opposite might be the case.

A representation can be made to a machine (Section 2 (5)), for example, where a person enters a number into a chip and pin machine or a bank ATM. Providing false credit card details to the voice-activated software on the cinema telephone line is the same as providing false credit card details to the person who works in the ticket office. Similarly, providing false credit card details to a supermarket website to obtain groceries is the same as giving false details to the assistant at the till.

'False representation . . . knows that it was, or might be, untrue or misleading'

Section 2 (2) defines the meaning of 'false' and Section 2 (3) defines the meaning of 'representation'.

A representation is defined as 'false' if it is untrue or misleading and, crucially, the person making it knows that it is, or might be, untrue or misleading. The important thing here is that the indivdual making the statement must have actual knowledge that the statement is untrue or misleading – it does not imply any element of recklessness. This is because of the principle of *mens rea* outlined above – there has to be the guilty mind behind the making of the false statement.

Thus the opening of a bank account using a false name and false identification is such a representation under the Act.

Dishonestly

What, precisely, is meant by 'dishonestly'? Lawyers of course have many avenues of argument as to whether the actions of a defendant were 'dishonest' under the provisions of the Act or whether the accused is guilty of mere error or misunderstanding.

For our purpose the current state of the law was established by the Court of Appeal in R v Ghosh (1982 QB 1053, (1982) 2 All ER 689). In that case it was established that the test for dishonesty is:

- Was what was done dishonest by the ordinary standards of reasonable and honest people?
- Did the person realise that what they were doing was, by those standards, dishonest?

It is not relevent, under this test, whether or not the individual *believed* they had an absolute moral right to carry out their actions for themselves: the test is did the person committing the offence realise that their actions would be considered dishonest by standards of, broadly, ordinary reasonable people.

For example, frauds are sometimes committed by individuals as an act of revenge for some real or imagined slight committed against them by their employer. They may feel they have some sort of moral right in their favour to justify their actions, but what they have done is dishonest by any ordinary and reasonable standard so they are guilty of a crime.

The question of dishonesty is ultimately one for the jury to decide.

'Intends to make a gain for himself or another, to cause loss to another or to expose another to risk of loss'

Surprisingly the definitions of 'gain' and 'loss' are not quite as straightforward as accountants would define them – probably because they were drafted by lawyers! It is important that the forensic investigator appreciates the subtleties of these definitions. Again it is the *intent* to make the gain or cause a loss which matters, not whether one was actually incurred by any party.

Gain and loss extends only to gain and loss in money or other property (Section 5 (2) (a)) whether temporary or permanent (Section 5 (2) (b)), and means any property whether real or personal including things in action and other intangible property (Section 5 (2) (b)). 'Things in action' are rights that can only be enforced by taking legal action. The definitions are important:

- 'Gain' includes a gain by keeping what one has, as well as a gain by getting what one does not have (Section 5 (3)).
- 'Loss' includes a loss by not getting what one might get as well as a loss by parting with what one has (Section 5 (4)).

The perpetrator must intend to make the gain or cause the loss by means of the false representation.

For example, if an individual obtains some information, say bank details, by creating a false website purporting to be that of a genuine bank, intending ultimately to make a gain or cause a loss within the meaning of Section 5, by doing so they will have committed a Section 2 offence.

Exhibit 3.1 **The business manager and the trusting employer**

An employee who developed a cocaine habit ended up stealing more than £70,000 from the engineering firm where she worked. Charlotte Fielding, 32, wrote 153 company cheques to pay her bills and also to buy clothes and other items.

The court heard how Fielding was the business manager of a small engineering company called Micro Tec at the Bersham Enterprise Centre near Wrexham. She admitted fraud between January 2007 and July 2008 in which she got away with £57,869 but she also asked for a further fraud involving £15,310 dating back to May 2006 to be taken into consideration.

Fielding was the business administrator and was so trusted that directors would provide her with blank signed cheques to pay the bills, but she took advantage of the system and used some of the cheques to pay her own utility bills and other money went into her own account.

Fielding was jailed for 14 months after admitting fraud. The judge said it was a gross breach of trust and Fielding had simply made out the cheques for her own benefit.

Source: Western Mail (2009)

Fraud by failing to disclose information (Section 3)

A person is in breach of this section if he—
(a) dishonestly fails to disclose to another person information which he is under a legal duty to disclose, and
(b) intends, by failing to disclose the information—
   (i) to make a gain for himself or another, or
   (ii) to cause loss to another or to expose another to a risk of loss.

Again, as with Section 2 offences outlined above, this offence is entirely offender-focused. It is complete as soon as the perpetrator fails to disclose information if they were under a legal duty to do so, and they did so with the necessary dishonest intent. Again it differs from deception offences under the Theft Acts in that it is immaterial whether or not any one was actually deceived or any property was actually gained or lost.

Again, let us look at the detail.

'Fails to disclose information'

Failure to reveal information is tantamount to fraud by conduct or omission and in some cases there will be an overlap with Section 2 offences.

There is no requirement that the failure to disclose must relate to 'material' or 'relevant' information, nor is there any *de minimis* provision. If an individual disclosed, say, 90 per cent of what they were under a legal duty to disclose but failed to disclose the remaining 10 per cent, the *actus reus* of the offence could be complete.

In order for there not to be successful conviction under the Act, therefore, the perpetrator would have to rely on the absence of dishonesty. Simply not passing on information which they are legally liable to disclose is not, of itself, an offence under the Act, but it is when coupled with a dishonest motive.

It is no defence that the perpetrator was ignorant of the existence of the duty, neither is it a defence in itself to claim inadvertence or incompetence, the offence is one of strict liability.

'Which he was under a legal duty to disclose'

A legal duty to disclose information can arise as a result of a contract between two parties or because of the existence of a particular type of professional relationship between them; for example, the relationship between a company director and an auditor.

The explanatory notes to the Fraud Act provide the following examples of a breach of a legal duty:

- The failure of a solicitor to share vital information with a client in order to perpetrate a fraud upon that client.
- A person who intentionally failed to disclose information relating to their heart condition when making an application for life insurance.

Fraud by abuse of position (Section 4)

(1) A person is in breach of this section if he—
 (a) occupies a position in which he is expected to safeguard, or not to act against, the financial interests of another person,
 (b) dishonestly abuses that position, and
 (c) intends, by means of the abuse of that position—
 (i) to make a gain for himself or another, or
 (ii) to cause loss to another or to expose another to a risk of loss.
(2) A person may be regarded as having abused his position even though his conduct consisted of an omission rather than an act.

Like the other two offences, Section 4 is entirely offender-focused. It is complete once the perpetrator carries out the act that is the abuse of their position. It is immaterial whether or not they are successful in their enterprise or whether or not any gain or loss is actually made. In many instances it may be the fact of the gain or loss that could prove dishonesty beyond reasonable doubt.

The terms 'financial interests' and 'abuse' are not defined in the Act and should be taken to have their ordinary meanings.

'A position in which he was expected to safeguard, or not to act against, the financial interests of another person'

The Law Commission has clarified the meaning of 'position'.

The 'position' in Section 4 is a position of trust but falls short of one where there is a legal duty or an entitlement to single-minded loyalty. It is something more than a moral obligation.

The Crown Prosecution Service guidelines on the Fraud Act 2006 provide these examples of offences under Section 4:

- an employee of a software company who uses his position to clone software products with the intention of selling the products on his own behalf

Exhibit 3.2 The 'helpful' solicitor

Thomas McGoldrick, a 59-year-old solicitor from Cheshire, was sentenced to ten years imprisonment in April 2008 for expropriating over £1m from one of his clients. His client had been severely injured in a road accident and had been awarded £1.8m in compensation won for him by McGoldrick's firm. After the award was made McGoldrick forged a letter from his client 'gifting' him half of the money. McGoldrick went on to take about £1.2m. He was convicted on 59 counts including false accounting, money laundering, forgery and obtaining pecuniary advantage by deception.

McGoldrick used the money to fund an extravagant lifestyle and to clear his firm's debts. He was caught when his client had only £200 left and the Law Society called in the police to investigate.

McGoldrick also created false accounts for his firm, which grossly exaggerated profits so that he could borrow money through thirteen credit cards and thirty-three loans.

The police described him as 'shameless, selfish, greedy and calculating, and motivated entirely by greed.'

Source: Telegraph (2008); Jenkins (2008)

- where a person is employed to care for an elderly or disabled person and has access to that person's bank account but abuses that position by removing funds for their own personal use (this may also be theft)
- a solicitor who removes money from a client's accounts for their own use; the Power of Attorney allows them to do so but when excessive this will be capable of being an offence under Section 4
- an employee who fails to take up the chance of a crucial contract in order that an associate or rival company can take it up instead
- an employee who abuses their position in order to grant contracts or discounts to friends, relatives and associates
- a waiter who sells their own bottles of wine passing them off as belonging to the restaurant
- a tradesman who helps an elderly person with odd jobs, gains influence over that person and removes money from that person's account (this may also be theft), or
- the person entrusted to purchase lottery tickets on behalf of others and misappropriates the money – again, this will probably be theft as well.

One interesting point is that the Act refers to an individual who *occupies* a position. If they no longer occupy that position at the time they use information dishonestly, information which they legally obtained whilst they were in a post, they do not commit a Section 4 offence. However, if they breach a contractual post-employment obligation such as a confidentiality clause, or if they plan to take the information and use it dishonestly once they have left their job, then an offence is committed.

Again, the Crown Prosecution Service provide an example:

- An employee who transferred sensitive commercial information from their office laptop to their home computer while in employment and used it after that employment had ended will commit the offence. At that stage they will no longer be 'occupying a position . . .' but they were when the offence was committed (transferring the information intending to make a gain or cause a loss) and so can be prosecuted.

Possession of articles for use in fraud (Section 6)

(1) A person is guilty of an offence if he has in his possession or under his control any article for use in the course of or in connection with any fraud.

This is a widely drawn provision and is intended to catch those in possession of items which they could use themselves, or which they construct for others to use. Thus the person who writes software for use in a fraud but does not so use it themselves is still guilty of an offence.

'Property' caught under this section could, for example, include computer software or material stored on a computer, such as a forged document, which is retained by the individual for the purposes of committing a fraud.

Items stored in such a way are considered to be in the 'possession' of an individual if it is accessible by them (R v Porter (2006) EWCA Crim 560). However, if the software or material had been deleted so that the individual could not retrieve it or gain access to it they could claim not to be 'in possession' of it. Mere possession of the hard disk would not be sufficient to constitute 'possession' under this section of the Act.

In cases where the prosecution will rely on evidence of material stored on computers, it will be necessary to obtain expert evidence using the sorts of forensic techniques used, for example, in cases involving indecent images. This section is important when considering charging provisions in cases where individuals submit fictitious invoices which they have created, say, on their personal home computer for the purpose of committing a fraud on an organisation.

'Article' has its ordinary meaning and is extremely widely drawn covering anything from pen and paper to blank credit cards, credit card numbers and computer software.

There is no defence of 'reasonable excuse'. Those who are in possession of or involved in the development of computer software or other items for use to test the security of computer or security systems must rely on their lack of intention that the items or programs are 'for use in the course of or in connection with any fraud'.

Making or supplying articles for use in frauds (Section 7)

A person is guilty of an offence if he makes, adapts, supplies or offers to supply any article—
    (a) knowing that it is designed or adapted for use in the course of or in connection with fraud, or
    (b) intending it to be used to commit, or assist in the commission of, fraud.

The reference to knowledge is a *mens rea* requirement, there has to be an element of knowing, so even if there is no actual knowledge that the person, say, to whom such items are supplied intends to commit fraud knowledge of the fact that such articles *could* be used to commit fraud is sufficient to create an offence.

Examples of such articles could be:

- the kits that are attached to ATM machines to capture card details
- forged credit cards or the equipment for making them

- lists of credit card numbers
- software for use in a phishing website or for phishing e-mail, and
- counterfeit goods presented as genuine.

The manufacturer of articles that are capable of being used in or in connection with fraud but have other innocent uses will not fall foul of this section unless they *intend* that it should be used in a dishonest way; for example, a manufacturer of credit card readers is not guilty of an offence under this section in the absence of any intent to commit fraud.

Participation in fraudulent business carried on by sole trader (Section 9)

This is a new offence which brings non-corporate fraudulent traders within the ambit of an offence which, for companies, is outlawed by Section 993 of the Companies Act 2006.

It covers sole traders, partnerships, trusts and companies registered overseas.

A defendant will commit an offence under Section 9 (2) (b) in the following ways:

- knowingly being party to the carrying on of a company's business with intent to defraud creditors of any person, or
- for any other fraudulent purpose.

The phrase 'to defraud creditors of any person' covers the situation where creditors are creditors of the business, but the business is not a legal person (i.e. a company). The creditors could be creditors of individuals or of other related companies.

A 'fraudulent purpose' implies the intent to create a dishonest business rather than an honest business. However, a business which commenced originally for bona fide trading reasons but which subsequently trades in a dishonest way could also be caught by this section.

It is designed to capture the so-called 'long-firm' frauds.

'Long-firm' frauds arise when perpetrators set up what purports to be a genuine business which proceeds to trade in a normal way. It purchases and pays for goods, building up a trusted relationship with a range of suppliers. Suddenly, after having ostensibly purchased a considerable quantity of goods for which credit terms have been extended to them, the business and the owners disappear with the proceeds of sale of the unpaid for goods leaving the suppliers out of pocket.

Theft Act 1968

Despite the passing of the Fraud Act several offences under older legislation still remain relevant to a consideration of the overall legal position surrounding fraud.

In many cases the Fraud Act contains sufficient charging provisions to bring a prosecution but it is useful to be aware of these other pieces of still current regulation. These are not covered in great detail so interested students of the law will have to refer to a relevant legal textbook for the detail.

False accounting

Section 17 of the Theft Act 1968 provides that:

(1) Where a person dishonestly, with a view to gain for himself or another or with intent to cause loss to another,—
    (a) destroys, defaces, conceals or falsifies any account or any record or document made or required for any accounting purpose; or
    (b) in furnishing information for any purpose produces or makes use of any account, or any such record or document as aforesaid, which to his knowledge is or may be misleading, false or deceptive in a material particular;
    he shall, on conviction on indictment, be liable to imprisonment for a term not exceeding seven years.
(2) For purposes of this section a person who makes or concurs in making in an account or other document an entry which is or may be misleading, false or deceptive in a material particular, or who omits or concurs in omitting a material particular from an account or other document, is to be treated as falsifying the account or document.

This section of the Act overlaps with other offences including forgery and offences under the Fraud Act 2006 detailed above. The offence under S17 is wider than forgery as not every false statement is a forgery but is narrower than the general offence of fraud because it is restricted to falsity in relation to accounts.

In most cases charges are likely to be brought under the provisions of the Fraud Act as this carries a higher sentence (ten years) and the does not require the prosecution to prove that the offence related to an accounting record.

False statements by company directors, etc.

Section 19 states:

(1) Where an officer of a body corporate or unincorporated association (or person purporting to act as such), with intent to deceive members or creditors of the body corporate or association about its affairs, publishes or concurs in publishing a written statement or account which to his knowledge is or may be misleading, false or deceptive in a material particular, he shall on conviction on indictment be liable to imprisonment for a term not exceeding seven years.
(2) For purposes of this section a person who has entered into a security for the benefit of a body corporate or association is to be treated as a creditor of it.
(3) Where the affairs of a body corporate or association are managed by its members, this section shall apply to any statement which a member publishes or concurs in publishing in connection with his functions of management as if he were an officer of the body corporate or association.

This offence is designed to deal with cases where directors publish a false document, such as a prospectus, in an attempt to induce investment. The offence is quite narrow as it can only be committed by an officer of the company (director, secretary or manager) and applies only to documents sent to members or creditors.

It is much narrower in scope than Section 2 of the Fraud Act. However, it does apply to any *written* statement of account that *may be* misleading. It does not require proof of any intent to cause a loss or make a gain: mere recklessness is sufficient to prove the offence. There is of course the intent to deceive.

In cases prosecuted under this provision it may be that expert evidence is required from a forensic accountant as to whether the accounts were misleading, or it may be that the offence consists of a misleading statement to the effect that certain individuals were backing the venture or that additional supporting finance was more available than in fact was the case.

Cheating the public revenue

This is an incredibly widely drawn offence as it arises out of common law. The offence of 'cheating' was abolished by S32 (1) of the Theft Act but only 'except as regards offences relating to the public revenue'.

It has been defined as 'deceitful practices in defrauding or endeavouring to defraud another of his own right by means of some artful device, contrary to the plain rules of common honesty'.

This offence is widely used by government agencies in connection with frauds against HM Revenue and Customs such as VAT fraud, e.g. carousel fraud, tax fraud and even social security frauds. Courts have held that cheating does not require a positive act such as a deception, mere omission is sufficient. The act or the omission must be intended to cheat HMRC or the Department of Work and Pensions. It cannot be used in connection with local authorities or, perhaps, the EU.

There is no requirement to prove deception or evidence of an actual loss to the public revenue or conversely a gain to the individuals involved.

Practical offences include:

- failing to account for VAT
- withholding PAYE and National Insurance, and
- failing to register for VAT or failing to disclose income.

This is a particularly useful offence when it comes to carousel frauds (see Chapter 12) where the element of conspiracy can also be added. Very often the only real issue is that of dishonesty.

Where offences involve considerable loss, i.e. in excess of £1m, sentences can be substantially in excess of the maximum of seven years available under the statutes.

Fraud law in Scotland

Whilst Scotland shares much of its legislation with England, Wales and Northern Ireland, when it comes to aspects of the criminal law it has its own unique legislation.

The Fraud Act 2006 does not apply in Scotland so there is no statutory offence of fraud. Instead Scotland treats fraud as a common law crime which is committed when someone achieves a practical result (i.e. makes a gain) by means of a *false pretence*. However, this does not necessarily rule out a prosecution under the Fraud Act for events which may have originated in Scotland. For example, if a false representation takes place in Scotland resulting from a call made to a call centre in India which ultimately results in a loss from a bank account in Birmingham, under the Criminal Justice Act 1993 there is jurisdiction to prosecute under the Fraud Act. Remember the perpetrator does not have to have been physically present in England and Wales at the time of the committing of the offence, nor do they have to be a British citizen, so it may be possible in certain circumstances to prosecute Scottish fraudsters under English law.

In Scotland individuals are prosecuted for causing prejudice to another, e.g. a pecuniary loss, by means of a false pretence. For a prosecution to succeed there must be what is known as 'proximity', in other words there must be connection between a false pretence made and a prejudicial result to the victim of the false pretence. There is no requirement that the person making the false pretence profited by it, there merely has to be a prejudicial result to another person.

There is no time limit for prosecution of these offences as they are committed under what is known as 'common law' which means, in practice, that law is made through precedent, i.e. previous case law.

Scotland also has a crime of *uttering*, in which a forged item is presented which is falsely represented as being authenticated by another person. An article, usually a document, is passed off as genuine in order to deceive another person. In this case the crime is not the forgery, it is the presentation or 'uttering' of it. The forgery may be an entire document or just a signature. Again there has to have been a prejudicial result and intent must be proved.

For the crime of embezzlement to be proven under Scottish law the individual has to have appropriated money or goods which are due to another person, without their consent.

- The goods or money must be in the possession of the accused, i.e. must have been entrusted to them.
- The accused must have the right to receive the goods and the obligation to account for them to another.
- The accused must have had the right to possess, use or deal in the goods and embarked on a course of dealing with them.

An example of this kind of situation might be client monies entrusted to a solicitor or monies invested through a broker who implies they are investing on the client's behalf. The point is that the accused had the right to receive the money or goods in the first place, which is the difference between embezzlement and theft. A thief has no right to the money or goods at any time.

Embezzlement is a pure crime of dishonesty and, to be charged with embezzlement, the accused has to have received the goods honestly, for example in the normal course of their employment, and then, only later, formed the intention to steal them.

In addition to acts by individuals Scottish law also deals with conspiracies or collusion by means of provisions known as 'art and part'. Fundamentally the rule is that a group is responsible for the actions of a group. Consequently if a group decides to commit a fraud or theft, even if only a few members actully commit the criminal actions, then, providing the rest of the group were aware of their actions, all are guilty.

Thus a group who are involved in corrupt acts, for example, missrepresenting goods for sale, or bribery and corruption, are all guilty 'art and part' even if only a few of them did the actual bribing or misselling. There has to be proximity, of course, but relatively inactive participants who may have merely rendered advice or provided resources to the others are nonetheless equally guilty. To avoid being charged in this way an individual must have taken demonstrable steps to stop or expose the crimes.

There also exists the crime of conspiracy where two or more persons conspire to effect a criminal purpose. Conspiracy is proved when there is agreement between them, and is not cancelled even if the crime they contemplate is impossible.

Other forms of fraud may be classified as theft and dealt with accordingly.

There has been criticism that the lack of suitable statutory offences has resulted in convicted fraudsters receiving lower sentences in Scotland than they might do for an equivalent offence in the rest of the UK.

There does not appear to be any publicly available information as to whether perpetrators have escaped prosecution as a result of a lack of a suitable charging provision, so the law may work well enough in practice even if individual prosecutions may be more complex and more difficult to prove under the Scottish system than under the Fraud Act.

Some of what follows also applies in Scotland and various enabling provisions have been enacted to ensure that, in particular, the provisions of the Proceeds of Crime Act 2002 and the money laundering regulations apply there.

Proceeds of Crime Act 2002 (POCA)

This Act, which came into force on 31 July 2002, amended the power of the courts to recover the ill-gotten gains of convicted individuals. Prior to this Act the process had been rather old-fashioned as, basically, confiscations were enforced through magistrates courts, as if they were a fine, or a Receiver was appointed by the High Court to find and realise any assets.

The amounts recovered were felt to be insufficient and there was a feeling, generally, in the population that criminals should not be freed to enjoy the fruits of their illegal endeavours.

The government's view was stated in their Asset Recovery Action Plan issued by the Home Office in May 2007:

> Asset recovery prevents criminal proceeds being reinvested in other forms of crime. By reducing the rewards of crime, it begins to affect the balance of risk and reward, and the prospect of losing profits may deter some from crime. Fundamentally it serves justice, in that nobody should be allowed to continue to profit from crime. The long term purpose of recovering the proceeds of crime is to reduce harm. Our performance regime has tended to measure success in terms of value recovered. There probably is a broad relationship between value and harm reduction – clearly the more extracted, the bigger the deterrence and crime prevention impact is likely to be. But asset recovery can also be powerful against lower level offenders who are damaging role models in communities. Visibly depriving these negative role models of their property can have an impact out of all proportion to the value of the goods recovered.
>
> Home office (2007)

The Serious Organised Crime Agency (SOCA) undertakes civil recovery of criminal property and tax investigations in England and Wales and Northern Ireland.

Criminal property

To prove that property is 'criminal property' (i.e. the proceeds of crime) it is necessary to prove that:

- The property constitutes benefit from criminal conduct or that it represents such a benefit (in whole or part and whether directly or indirectly).

- The alleged offender knows or suspects that it constitutes or represents such a benefit. The property which may comprise the benefit from criminal conduct is widely defined and includes:
  - money
  - all forms of property or real estate, and
  - things in action and other intangible or incorporeal property.

There is no distinction here between the proceeds of a defendant's own crimes and of crimes committed by others, nor is it necessary to prove that particular assets relate to specific crimes.

Money laundering

Forensic accountants should be familiar with the provisions of the money laundering regulations, but for students we will review the main provisions here.

These regulations were introduced by POCA to prevent individuals disposing of criminal property by concealing or disguising it or transferring it out of the jurisdiction of the Court. The term 'laundering' refers to the principle of 'washing' dirty or criminal money to make it appear legitimate.

For example, individuals involved in organised crime may also own what appear to be legitimate businesses, particularly those dealing in cash such as bars, restaurants, clubs or companies operating in areas where record keeping may be somewhat 'flexible' – parts of construction or the darker fringes of waste disposal. Criminal proceeds are 'washed' through the business bank accounts and the criminals can enjoy a lifestyle based on the apparent 'profits' of these businesses.

Money laundering has three phases.

Placement

Cash generated from crime is placed in the financial system. This is the point when proceeds of crime are most apparent and at risk of detection. Banks and financial institutions have developed extensive anti-money-laundering procedures in an attempt to detect this phase.

Layering

Once proceeds of crime are in the financial system, layering obscures their origins by passing the money through complex transactions. These often involve different entities like companies and trusts and can take place in multiple jurisdictions.

Integration

Once the origin of the funds has been obscured, the criminal is able to make the funds reappear as legitimate funds or assets. They will invest funds in legitimate businesses or other forms of investment, often using bona fide individuals such as solicitors or property agents to buy a property, set up a trust, acquire a company, or even settle litigation, among other activities. This is the most difficult stage of money laundering to detect.

The three principal money laundering offences are contained in Sections 327, 328 and 329 of the Act and there are three main offences.

Section 327 relates to the concealment of criminal property:

(1) A person commits an offence if he—
 (a) conceals criminal property;
 (b) disguises criminal property;
 (c) converts criminal property;
 (d) transfers criminal property;
 (e) removes criminal property from England and Wales or from Scotland or from Northern Ireland.

There is a defence in the section which is repeated in Sections 328 and 329. We will look at it here and not repeat it:

(2) But a person does not commit such an offence if—
 (a) he makes an authorised disclosure under section 338 and (if the disclosure is made before he does the act mentioned in subsection (1)) he has the appropriate consent;
 (b) he intended to make such a disclosure but had a reasonable excuse for not doing so;
 (c) the act he does is done in carrying out a function he has relating to the enforcement of any provision of this Act or of any other enactment relating to criminal conduct or benefit from criminal conduct.
(3) Concealing or disguising criminal property includes concealing or disguising its nature, source, location, disposition, movement or ownership or any rights with respect to it.

Section 328 is another very broad offence which relates to the making of an arrangement:

(1) A person commits an offence if he enters into or becomes concerned in an arrangement which he knows or suspects facilitates (by whatever means) the acquisition, retention, use or control of criminal property by or on behalf of another person.

Section 329 creates three offences of acquisition use and possession of criminal property:

(1) A person commits an offence if he—
 (a) acquires criminal property;
 (b) uses criminal property;
 (c) has possession of criminal property.

Subsection 2 is the defence for Section 329:

(3) For the purposes of this section—
 (a) a person acquires property for inadequate consideration if the value of the consideration is significantly less than the value of the property;
 (b) a person uses or has possession of property for inadequate consideration if the value of the consideration is significantly less than the value of the use or possession;
 (c) the provision by a person of goods or services which he knows or suspects may help another to carry out criminal conduct is not a consideration.

All three of the principal money laundering offences contain certain defences. In the case of each of these offences it is a defence to have made an authorised disclosure to, and obtain appropriate consent from, the authorities before doing the act which would constitute the offence.

Money Laundering Regulations 2007

These Regulations apply to most UK financial and credit businesses including banks, building societies, money transmitters, bureaux de change, cheque cashers, pawnbrokers, savings and investment firms.

In addition the Regulations cover independent legal professionals (when undertaking certain financial and property transactions) accountants, tax advisers, auditors, insolvency practitioners, estate agents, casinos, high value dealers (when taking cash of €15,000 or more) and trust or company service providers.

It is outside the scope of this book to detail the regulations regarding how businesses should comply with the appropriate regulations. However, briefly the Regulations require relevant businesses to:

- put in place checks, controls and procedures in order to anticipate and prevent money laundering or terrorist financing
- train staff in those procedures and in the law relating to money laundering and terrorist financing
- appoint a nominated officer or Money Laundering Reporting Officer (MLRO) to receive and consider internal disclosures and to make suspicious activity reports to SOCA [where the business is a sole trader with no employees, the proprietor will be the person responsible for making the reports], and
- put in place procedures to identify customers and verify the customer's identity before entering into a business relationship or transaction and to obtain information on the purpose or nature of the business relationship.

These procedures are known in the regulations as 'customer due diligence' and also require businesses to conduct ongoing monitoring of the business relationship as appropriate. The regulations specify circumstances in which businesses are not required to undertake customer due diligence measures or must undertake enhanced measures.

It is a criminal offence not to report any dealing that is suspected, or ought to be suspected, of involving the proceeds of crime. The report should be made to SOCA via a MLRO. In most cases this will be *after* the transaction has taken place. Where the organisation has advance notice of the transaction, it is protected against an allegation of 'assistance' if it gets consent, or 'deemed' consent, from SOCA before it carries out the transaction.

SOCA is deemed to have consented if the transaction is reported to it, and it:

- does not refuse consent within seven working days of the report, or
- *does* refuse consent within seven working days of the report, but does not obtain a 'restraint order' within 31 days of refusing consent.

This creates a problem for the organisation when they have to delay processing a transaction. Experienced money launderers may well recognise that a report has been or is about to be made if any delay extends towards the 7- or 31-day period.

Exhibit 3.3   Examples: money laundering and proceeds of crime

Peter and Donna Davis from Birmingham sold their £150,000 house for £43,000 which was just enough to clear the mortgage, to local estate agent, Leslie John Pattison, in an attempt to prevent the property being considered as an asset in a proceeds of crime hearing.

Pattison instructed 45-year-old conveyancing solicitor Philip John Griffith, according to whom Pattison had explained that he was purchasing the property to help out friends who were having trouble paying their mortgage.

Pattison and Mr and Mrs Davis were all convicted of money laundering and Griffith, while he was cleared of being concerned in the actual arrangement, was convicted of failing to disclose a suspicious transaction. The court stated that he had closed his eyes to the obvious and he was sentenced to 15 months' imprisonment.

Source: Scottish Law Agents Society

A virtual crime?

A report drawn up for Britain's Fraud Advisory Panel (FAP) is calling on the government to extend real-world financial regulation into Second Life and similar games. The study warns that players can transfer large sums of money across national borders without restriction and with little risk of being detected.

The FAP, a watchdog established by the Institute of Chartered Accountants in England and Wales, says that criminal or terrorist gangs could use the game to move funds and avoid surveillance. Other risks, it says, include credit card fraud, identity theft, money laundering and tax evasion.

Players create on-screen characters known as 'avatars' who can mingle with others anywhere in the world. Using a pretend currency called 'Linden dollars', they can buy and sell virtual items from clothes to homes, for fun or to impress. Characters can even start up businesses. Crucially, Linden dollars can be freely exchanged for real American dollars. On an average day, about £750,000 changes hands.

The report describes Second Life as 'a parallel universe with almost no external rule of law, no enforced banking regulations or compliance, no policing and no governmental oversight'.

Source: Telegraph UK online

Care has to be taken in any dealings with the suspicious client that there is no element of disclosure which might create an offence of 'tipping off'.

'Tipping off'

'Tipping off' is exactly what it says it is.

It is a criminal offence for anyone to do or say anything that might 'tip-off' someone else that they are under suspicion of acquiring, retaining, using or controlling proceeds of crime. That applies whether or not any report has been made to SOCA.

The fact that a transaction was notified to SOCA, but they did not refuse consent within seven working days, or did not obtain a restraint order, does not alter the position so far as 'tipping-off' is concerned.

This means that an organisation cannot, at the time or later (unless SOCA agrees), tell a customer that a transaction is being delayed because a report has been made under the Proceeds of Crime Act.

Whistle-blowing: The Public Interest Disclosure Act 1998

The Act protects most workers in the public, private and voluntary sectors but does not apply to genuinely self-employed professionals (other than in the NHS) or voluntary workers (including charity trustees and charity volunteers).

The Act refers to the making of 'protected disclosures' involving the revelation of malpractice or corrupt behaviour to an employer, a regulator or to the wider public or police.

Though the Act does not require organisations to set up or promote any particular whistle-blowing policies, they are strongly recommended as part of the organisation's anti-fraud strategy. An example of such a policy is included in Chapter 7.

Protected disclosures

For a disclosure to be protected by the Act's provisions it must relate to matters that qualify for protection under the Act. These are known as 'qualifying disclosures'. Qualifying disclosures are those which the worker reasonably believes tends to show that one or more of the following is either happening now, took place in the past, or is likely to happen in the future:

- a criminal offence
- the breach of a legal obligation
- a miscarriage of justice
- a danger to the health and safety of any individual
- damage to the environment, or

deliberate concealment of information tending to show any of these five matters.

A disclosure made in good faith to the employer (be it a manager or director) will be protected if the whistle-blower has a reasonable belief the information tends to show that the malpractice:

- has occurred
- is occurring, or
- is likely to occur.

Where a third party or person is responsible for the malpractice, e.g. a contractor or other party who is not the employer or an employee, this same test applies to disclosures made to them, or rather their management. The same test also applies where someone in a public body whose leaders are appointed by ministers (e.g. the NHS and many quangos) blows the whistle direct to the sponsoring government department.

The Act protects workers in a number of ways, for example:

- If an employee is dismissed because they have made a 'protected disclosure', that will automatically be treated as unfair dismissal.
- Workers are given the right not to be subjected to any 'detriment', i.e. to be treated badly or unfairly by their employers, because they have made a protected disclosure, and the worker can make a complaint to an employment tribunal if they have suffered detriment as a result of making a protected disclosure.

To be protected, most disclosures must be made in good faith. Essentially this means the disclosure is made honestly so that the concern can be addressed rather than maliciously or dishonestly with intent to injure or damage another person in any way, i.e. to influence the perception of an individual's reputation by an employer.

In other words, unfair or malicious allegations made about one employee by another will not be protected under the Act, nor will unsupported allegations about an employer or individuals made to a third party such as a regulator or the media.

Notice that the test here is one of reasonableness. This is hard to define but should be taken, in this context, as a belief which a normal person might reasonably hold, which ultimately might be for a tribunal to decide. It is a test which will discourage supposition on the part of a reporting individual as much as it will prevent them approaching the wilder shores of fantasy.

The Act makes special provision for disclosures to specific bodies including regulators such as the Health and Safety Executive, HMRC and the Financial Services Authority. Such disclosures are protected where the whistle-blower meets the tests for internal disclosures outlined above and, additionally, reasonably believes that the information and any allegations in it are substantially true and relevant to that regulator.

Wider disclosures (e.g. to the police, the media, MPs, consumers and non-prescribed regulators) are protected if, in addition to the tests for regulatory disclosures, they are reasonable in all the circumstances, are not made for personal gain and:

- the whistle-blower reasonably believed they would be victimised if they had raised the matter internally or with a prescribed regulator, or
- there was no prescribed regulator and they reasonably believed the evidence was likely to be concealed or destroyed, or
- the concern had already been raised with the employer or a prescribed regulator, or
- the concern was of an exceptionally serious nature.

Gagging clauses in employment contracts and severance agreements are void insofar as they conflict with the Act's protection.

Exhibit 3.4   Whistle-blowing – how not to handle it

Six care workers sacked for revealing a shocking catalogue of mismanagement in children's homes won a £1m settlement from Wakefield Council.

The whistle-blowers' victory represents a vindication of their decision to speak out about a series of serious management failures in local authority homes which were damaging the lives of some of the most vulnerable children in the region. Following their dismissal the residential care workers, all of whom had previously unblemished employment records, launched an Employment Tribunal case under the terms of the Public Interest Disclosure Act.

Wakefield Council opted for an out-of-court settlement. Neither the council nor the whistle-blowers would comment on the amount involved but the overall cost to the local authority is estimated to be around £1m.

The bulk has gone to the sacked staff, but the council has also built up a substantial legal bill over the last 18 months as it sought to defend the case.

Source: Yorkshire Post News (2007)

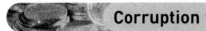

Corruption

Prior to the passing of the Bribery Act in April 2010 UK companies were generally able to escape legal actions for bribery and corruption as it was difficult to prove that their 'directing mind', i.e. the board of directors, intended an employee or agent to pay a bribe. In practice it would have been necessary to find evidence of authorisation to pay a bribe.

The new Bribery Act has clarified the law, sweeping away the old Prevention of Corruption Acts 1889–1916 and the various common law offences which served to fill in gaps in the inadequate legislation and were thus fragmented and unwieldy. The new Act codifies and clarifies the legal position and makes it clear to organisations what they have to do to avoid being caught up in its provisions.

The Act had been heavily trailed so organisations should already have begun to put policies and controls in place. Those which have not, particularly those who trade or operate overseas, could run the risk of being caught by the Act unintentionally. The Act applies to all organisations, including charities, which means that practices which may have applied in the past may no longer be appropriate.

This is not a legal textbook so we will consider the practical impact this has on organisations. Note that this legislation affects those individuals or organisations based in the UK and those which are overseas-based but doing business in the UK and it relates to offences committed anywhere in the world – so it is very far reaching.

The Act contains two general offences of 'active' and 'passive' bribery. This is the offence of 'Offering' and consists of:

- Active bribery, broadly, means giving a bribe or offering or promising to do so.
- Passive bribery in requesting, agreeing to receive, or accepting a bribe.

A person, which for the purpose of the Act includes individuals, incorporated organisations (i.e. companies) and unincorporated associations (e.g. partnerships), can be guilty of these offences whether the act of giving or receiving is done directly by themselves or through a third party, i.e. a local manager or agent. This has implications for international companies or other organisations such as charities or aid bodies who employ agents or representatives overseas, particularly in areas where bribery and corruption is endemic. These agents may carry out what they consider to be the perfectly normal business practice of bribing local company executives or local government officials in order to obtain work, or to facilitate the movement of goods, something head office in the UK knows nothing about, only to create an immense problem for the company because this process contravenes the Act. Companies are responsible for these agents and must train them in appropriate procedures.

As we will see below, there is a defence under the Act for the organisation to have adequate procedures in place to prevent corrupt acts, which is an area where the forensic accountant can become involved.

There is a new and specific offence of bribing a foreign public official. The giver must have the intention of influencing the recipient in their performance of public duties.

This means that such things euphemistically known as 'facilitation payments' or 'commissions' are outlawed by the new legislation unless the payments are permitted or required under the law of the relevant country or are legitimately due under a contract. Facilitation payments, small payments designed to expedite routine activities, are permissible under US law but will continue to be considered to be bribes under UK law.

Corporate hospitality

It will not be possible to substitute facilitation payments with excessive corporate hospitality as the Serious Fraud Office, whose role it will be to pursue bribery offences, has indicated that if they consider this has been done to create an advantage, it will constitute an offence under the Act. Routine and inexpensive hospitality, they say, would be most unlikely to lead to an expectation of improper conduct. They do not define what they consider to be 'routine and inexpensive' and it may be the opinion of a prosecutor which is the determining factor.

The company would have to justify its level of hospitality as routine in the context of the organisation and the question of expense may be subjective.

Acquiring liability

Where an organisation acquires another company or organisation it assumes responsibility for any corrupt activity which may have occurred within the acquired entity. Thus the process of due diligence will have to encompass this aspect with immediate effect, and this is another area for forensic accountants to consider.

Failing to prevent

The most important change under the Act is the introduction of a new corporate offence of negligently failing to prevent the giving of bribes by its employees or agents.

It is a defence if the business can show that it had adequate procedures in place to prevent bribery taking place, albeit that those systems have failed in the individual instance. Importantly, this defence is *not* available if the negligence is the fault of a senior official within the business. There is not, at the moment, any guidance on what will constitute 'adequate procedures'.

This new offence is designed to encourage business to take anti-corruption more seriously and to put in place appropriate measures to stamp out unethical business practices.

The Anti-Corruption Domain of the Serious Fraud Office (SFO) will be responsible for policing this area. For the new corporate offence the Act makes no provision as to the size of the penalty which will be a fine. For individuals the fines are limited to the 'statutory maximum', currently £5,000, but for what is known as a Section 7 offence, i.e. failing to prevent the giving of bribes, it has been proposed that fines will be unlimited. The current view is that the level of fines might be referable to the global turnover of the business in appropriate cases – which could have huge implications in the case of large multinational businesses.

For individuals, including directors or senior management who 'consent or connive' to the giving of a bribe, the maximum sentence is 10 years imprisonment or a fine, or both.

There will be various enabling measures before the Act is fully operational. Organisations and their advisers who consider themselves to be potentially at risk should keep abreast of current legal advice. The new corporate offence introduces an indirect form of corporate liability that should encourage businesses to take positive action to prevent corruption. If they negligently fail to do so, they may face prosecution. The SFO will doubtless be looking for a high-profile scalp to reinforce the anti-corruption message. In assessing the negligence or otherwise of a business under this new law, the courts will consider the adequacy of the anti- corruption and corporate governance systems in place. This will be directly linked to the business sector and risk level of the market in which the business operates. The notes which accompanied the original Bill suggested that the size of the organisation will also be taken into account.

All businesses should therefore review their systems and take a step back to consider whether they would be viewed as adequate if they came under the scrutiny of the court. For some, a basic anti-corruption policy may suffice. For others, a more sophisticated training and awareness programme will be required together with checks and balances built into procurement and tendering processes and systems.

The SFO have recently issued guidelines in connection with cases of overseas corruption. They are, broadly, encouraging corporate bodies to self-report cases of overseas corruption with a view to limiting the possibility of a criminal action by the SFO. Cases of corruption which are self-reported will be more likely to have a civil outcome, unless the corrupt acts are perpetrated at board level.

The implications of a criminal conviction are:

- fines
- confiscations of any unlawful property, and
- automatic debarment from tendering under Article 45 of the EU Public Sector Procurement Directive 2004.

This latter sanction could have serious implications for companies in areas such as construction, arms, pharmaceuticals and service supply where significant levels of business are with public bodies.

The SFO would investigate self-reported cases and, of course, gives no assurances that a prosecution would be thus avoided. However, their expressed intention is to work towards a mutually agreed outcome which would include demonstrable efforts by the organisation to change its culture away from one where corruption is deemed to be acceptable business practice.

The SFO would expect to see a genuine effort at culture change involving a commitment, at a senior level in the organisation, to a change programme involving training and enforcement of anti-corruption policies. They would also, where appropriate, require organisations to make public disclosures of their actions and the efforts made towards restitution of their reputation. They would also be pursuing settlement globally where corrupt acts have been carried out in other jurisdictions.

They would, of course, be expecting full co-operation in any investigation, provision of appropriate evidence and full disclosure of all pertinent matters. This could very well involve the work of a forensic accountant acting for the organisation in gathering evidence and presenting it to the SFO as part of any disclosure.

 ## Foreign and Corrupt Practices Act 1977 (FCPA)

This is a piece of US legislation which probably only has significance to forensic accountants who act for multinational clients. These provisions will apply to subsidiaries of US companies and to US citizens and, whilst they may not be part of the day-to-day routine for most forensic accountants, they are nevertheless important provisions which they should be aware of.

The anti-bribery provisions of the FCPA make it unlawful for a US person, and certain foreign issuers of securities, to make a corrupt payment to a foreign official for the purpose of obtaining or retaining business for or with, or directing business to, any person. Since 1998, they also apply to foreign firms and persons who take any act in furtherance of such a corrupt payment while in the United States.

A 'foreign official' means any officer or employee of a foreign government, a public international organisation, or any department or agency thereof, or any person acting in an official capacity.

The FCPA only prohibits payments made in order to assist the firm in obtaining or retaining business for or with, or directing business to, any person. The US Department of Justice interprets 'obtaining or retaining business' broadly, such that the term encompasses more than the mere award or renewal of a contract. The FCPA does not, however, outlaw 'facilitation payments' made after the business has been obtained.

The FCPA potentially applies to any individual, firm, officer, director, employee, or agent of a firm and any stockholder acting on behalf of a firm. Individuals and firms may also be penalised if they order, authorise, or assist someone else to violate the anti-bribery provisions or if they conspire to violate those provisions.

The FCPA also prohibits corrupt payments through intermediaries.

A US company or national may be held liable for a corrupt payment authorised by employees or agents operating entirely outside the United States, using money from foreign bank accounts, and without any involvement by personnel located within the United States. US parent corporations may be held liable for the acts of their foreign subsidiaries where the parent authorised, directed, or controlled the activity in question, as can US citizens or residents who were employed by or acting on behalf of such foreign-incorporated subsidiaries.

The person making or authorising the payment must have a corrupt intent, and the payment must be intended to induce the recipient to misuse their official position to direct business wrongfully to the payer or to any other person. Note that the FCPA does not require that a corrupt act succeed in its purpose and the offer or promise of a corrupt payment can constitute a violation of the statute.

Exhibit 3.5	Foreign and Corrupt Practices Act – the Siemens case

The US Security and Exchange Commission (SEC) alleged that between 12 March 2001 and 30 September 2007, Siemens Aktiengesellschaft, a German company whose shares were listed on the New York Stock Exchange, violated the FCPA by engaging in a widespread and systematic practice of paying bribes to foreign government officials to obtain business.

Siemans was charged with violations of the anti-bribery, books and records and internal control provisions of the FCPA. The SEC alleged that the German controlling board had failed to implement sufficiently rigorous controls to deter corrupt payments.

Siemens created elaborate payment schemes to conceal the nature of its corrupt payments, and the company's inadequate internal controls allowed the conduct to flourish. The misconduct involved employees at all levels, including former senior management, and revealed a corporate culture long at odds with the FCPA. The SEC's complaint alleged that despite the company's knowledge of bribery at two of its largest groups – Communications and Power Generation – the tone at the top at

▶

Siemens created a corporate culture in which bribery was tolerated and even rewarded at the highest levels of the company.

Siemens has offered to pay a total of $1.6 billion in disgorgement and fines, which is the largest amount a company has ever paid to resolve corruption-related charges, and has agreed to pay $350 million in disgorgement of profits to the SEC. In related actions, Siemens will pay a $450 million criminal fine to the US Department of Justice and a fine of €395 million (approximately $569 million) to the Office of the Prosecutor General in Munich, Germany. Siemens previously paid a fine of €201 million (approximately $285 million) to the Munich Prosecutor in October 2007.

The fines were considerably below the maximum chargeable because of the extensive co-operation received from the company.

This is the first case where the charges related not to bribery but to failure to maintain proper and effective internal controls.

Source: Securities and Exchange Commission (2008)

Regulation of Investigatory Powers Act 2000 (RIPA)

This is an act which investigators should be aware of but which they may come across in practice only rarely.

Under the Act it is an offence for any individual to intercept any communication, which includes letters, phone calls and e-mails, in the course of transmission without consent.

The intention underpinning the RIPA legislation is to regulate the use by public bodies of covert surveillance techniques. This covers covert activities such as photographing people, bugging, informants and undercover work, accessing and intercepting communications such as e-mails or phone traffic.

There is a huge list of public bodies where RIPA might be relevant, one of which is SOCA.

One of the problems of the RIPA legislation has been the use by local authorities of surveillance governed by RIPA against individuals to check if they lived in a particular school catchment area or for the illegal harvesting of cockles and mussels. These have been represented as human rights infringements and a threat to civil liberties.

Investigators must therefore not engage in bugging or interception techniques without legal advice as they may fall foul of this legislation and the Computer Misuse Act 1990 which prohibits unauthorised access to computers.

Exhibit 3.6   E-mail spying

Clifford Stanford and investigator George Liddell were prosecuted for an unlawful interception of electronic communications under RIPA.

The two of them arranged for e-mails of John Porter, son of Dame Shirley Porter, to be copied into an account set up by Liddell. Their object was to gather evidence or information to enable Stanford to oust John Porter from the board of Redbus and install himself in Porter's place. Stanford had previously resigned from Redbus after a dispute.

▶

The e-mails revealed the hidden wealth of Dame Shirley and were passed to the media and Westminster City Council – she was the former leader of that council. She had been surcharged £42m in a homes for votes scandal but had claimed to have assets of only £300,000. Following the revelations arising accidentally from these illegal intercepts she handed over £12.3m.

Stanford and Liddell had uncovered a vast amount of private information including bank details and family details contrary to the Act. They were fined and received a suspended sentence.

Source: ZD Net (2005)

Police and Criminal Evidence Act 1984 (PACE)

Investigators should have regard to the provisions of the Police and Criminal Evidence Act 1984 particularly in relation to evidence obtained through interview. PACE is, of course, primarily designed to regulate police powers and most of it has no direct relevance to the fraud investigator. However, its provisions are the benchmark for the admissibility of evidence and should therefore be followed closely.

It should be noted that PACE does not apply in Scotland, which has a different legal process. However, we refer in this section to principles which represent good practice and, if followed, will not interfere with any judicial process in Scotland. As always, legal advice should be taken before any of the procedures in this section, particularly those relating to the interviewing of suspects, are undertaken.

The provisions of Section 69 PACE are directly relevant to the fraud investigator. This deals with computer evidence and, in particular, scanned images as evidence in criminal cases. Any submission of a scanned image as evidence must be accompanied by a S69 certificate from the person responsible for the computer system. This basically certifies that the system was working properly or that any defect would not alter the accuracy of the record. The point is that the court requires to be assured that the computer system faithfully recorded the document and processed and stored it in such a way that it can be faithfully retrieved without amendment or alteration of the original image.

Similar considerations must be given where documents are stored on microfilm.

Admissibility of evidence

Later in this chapter we will look at the admissibility of evidence obtained through interview, so here will look briefly at the basic rules governing the admissibility of documentary or other evidence. For legal purposes the term 'document' is quite widely drawn and will, broadly, encompass not simply paper records but also microfiche or scanned images.

There is a difference between civil and criminal cases. In civil cases there are, generally, no prior requirements which need to be met before a document, which would include a scanned image, can be admitted in evidence. Broadly the documents proposed to be admitted are shown to the other side before proceedings commence (known as 'discovery') and agreement is reached that the items are authentic.

An important point in civil cases is that the records of a business or public authority are automatically admissible without further proof of authenticity. This is presumably broadly because there is generally little doubt about their authenticity. If there is a dispute then proof of authenticity will be required.

Civil actions for recovery would therefore, technically, require a lower standard of evidence preservation than would a criminal action, however investigators are reminded of the ideal of best practice set out earlier: that it should always be assumed that there will be criminal proceedings so best practice should be observed at all times.

In criminal cases the fundamental rule is that there must always be an audit trail. What this means is that, from the moment of discovery to the moment that the item is presented as evidence in court, the entire process of handling evidence must be documented.

It should go without saying, but we'll say it anyway, that *in no circumstances* should an original document be altered, amended, written on, defaced or otherwise tampered with by any of the investigating team, or anyone else involved in the investigation. This includes referencing the document, numbering it or otherwise identifying it. Instead it should be preserved intact and untouched and any reference attached to it without altering the document. This would include stapling anything to it, for example, let alone writing on it!

There are some particularly important, and complex, rules which affect the preservation of computer evidence, especially where disks have been imaged to preserve the original disk and to enable investigators to work on an identical copy. In these cases the court must be assured that what is presented to it has not been affected or tampered with in any way during the course of the investigation.

We deal with electronic evidence in Chapter 13.

As far as documentary evidence is concerned there are two issues:

- preservation and recording of original documents, and
- use of 'imaged' documents as evidence.

Authentication of evidence involves proving to the court that a document is what it purports to be. Accordingly the 'chain of evidence' must be preserved. In practice where any document is transferred out of the control of the original discoverer and recorder the transfer should be recorded by means of a signature and date.

Investigators must take great pains to ensure that there is no possibility of a challenge to vital evidence due to poor document control.

 ## Interviewing suspects

At some point it may be necessary to interview a suspect.

It may be that enough evidence can be gathered to incriminate the suspect and build a prima facie case against them which can be handed to the Economic Crime Unit of the police. If the prosecution is to be conducted by the police then criminal interviews under caution can, of course, be carried out by them and neither officers of the organisation nor the forensic accountant need be directly involved.

As stated above, the law regarding criminal acts and procedure is different in Scotland and the mechanisms of prosecution work differently. However, the differences are confined to police and legal actions and not the actions of any pre-prosecution investigations being carried out privately. These principles constitute good practice generally and so should be followed in private investigations whether in Scotland or elsewhere in the UK.

This type of interview should not be confused with a disciplinary interview for employment purposes. There is no requirement for a prosecution to have been completed before a suspect individual is made the subject of disciplinary proceedings under their contract of employment and, in accordance with proper procedure, interviewed with a view to disciplinary action being taken. We will look at that separately.

These are interviews in connection with the prosecution of a criminal case. One word of caution at the outset:

It is extremely foolish for anyone, even an experienced HR practitioner, to conduct these interviews without legal advice – in fact without a lawyer present.

These are murky waters for the unwary and there is a very strong possibility that any evidence revealed may be inadmissible in any future legal action if the interviews are conducted otherwise than in accordance with the rules set out in PACE, as amended.

However, it is considered important that forensic accountants are aware of these rules, if only to avoid the pitfalls, so guidelines are set out here to explain the key points.

Speaking to the suspects – disciplinary versus criminal interviews

At some point in an investigation it will usually be necessary to speak to any suspected individuals. At this stage the investigation is clearly overt and the individuals concerned may well be suspended pending disciplinary proceedings.

It is important that these two things are not confused: internal disciplinary procedures should be handled by a different team to the one carrying out any investigation. Clearly there will be an overlap insofar as the offences allegedly committed are what has triggered the HR procedures in the first place; however, for a disciplinary meeting, all that is needed is information sufficient to justify disciplinary action. An example of such grounds might be, for example, a breach of company procedures in connection with accessing information where the perpetrator has confidential company information they should not be privy to. There is no need at such a meeting to reveal the full extent of any possible charges which might ultimately be brought under criminal proceedings.

An individual might be made subject to disciplinary proceedings without being made aware of the discovery of their involvement in a possible fraud. In this way the individual could be suspended from duties, on full pay, leaving the field clear for the investigation to continue. Of course by this time the investigation will become known to the staff, which may result in additional information being forthcoming as staff who may have knowledge of the perpetrator's activities, or even a peripheral involvement in the fraud, rush to protect themselves.

Where a person is to be asked questions about their suspected involvement in a criminal offence, the questioning should always be in the form of a formal interview under caution. A formal interview under caution, known as a PACE interview, must be carefully handled and all the procedures must be fully observed otherwise any information gathered or evidence obtained may become inadmissible in any criminal proceedings.

In the unusual event of the offender being an organisation, for instance in a case of corruption, this will include interviewing a nominated representative of the organisation.

It is not practical or advisable to set down hard and fast rules as to when a suspect should be interviewed. It may seem logical to interview them towards the end of an investigation, when a lot of evidence gathering work has been done – the 'what have you got to say about that?' approach. On the other hand it may save a lot of time and effort to interview earlier, once grounds for suspicion have been established. 'Grounds for suspicion' are more than vague unsubstantiated feelings or suppositions; they require some basis in fact, but this can be somewhat less than evidence supportive of a prima facie case.

It may be that the suspect will attempt to make a deal, i.e. full disclosure in return for an immunity to prosecution and being allowed to resign quietly. (Some have even been known to ask for a reference!)

The timing depends on:

- the circumstances of the case
- what evidence is available and, most importantly,
- the anticipated reaction of the suspect based on an evaluation of their character and the extent of their criminality.

Bridges should not be burned too early. It may be necessary, at any stage in the investigation, to go back to individuals interviewed earlier and put to them documents or comments that have been uncovered subsequent to the initial interview.

PACE interviews

The Police and Criminal Evidence Act 1984 (PACE) is primarily concerned with the powers and duties of the police, the rights of suspects and the admissibility of evidence. Seven Codes of Practice have been adopted under this Act, including Code C for the Detention, Treatment and Questioning of Persons by Police Officers, and Code E on the audio recording of interviews with suspects.

Section 67(9) of PACE places a duty on persons other than police officers 'who are charged with the duty of investigating offences or charging offenders' to have regard to any relevant provisions of the Codes of Practice. Investigators should therefore be familiar with the provisions of the Codes, and follow them when questioning suspects.

It is desirable that persons who are suspected of committing offences are interviewed under caution because:

- the interview may provide important evidence against the suspect, which the investigator would otherwise be unable to obtain
- the interview may provide important information revealing further lines of inquiry
- the interview may provide relevant information to be considered in any prosecution decision, or
- it is fair and proper to allow a potential defendant an opportunity to answer the allegations and give their own account.

Remember that any accused person has the right not to incriminate themselves. They do not have to attend an interview and, if they do attend, they do not have to say anything. They may simply attend in order to discover the strength of the case against them. Nothing should be inferred from an individual's non-attendance or not speaking, however the fact that they didn't attend or speak should be recorded and reported.

When setting up an interview under caution, a letter should be sent inviting the person, or an authorised representative in the case of a company (see below), to attend an interview under caution at an appropriate venue. Enough time must elapse between the individual being given notice of the purpose of the interview and the matters to be raised in it for them to consider the points raised and obtain proper legal representation.

If the suspect declines the opportunity to attend or the investigator does not conduct an interview under caution for any other reason, they will not be able to verbally ask the suspect for their representations.

A suspect is not obliged to accept the invitation and may therefore refuse to attend. If they do so, this can be brought to the court's attention if they plead guilty or are convicted at trial, as the extent to which they co-operated with the investigation is relevant at that stage. It is sensible to ensure that invitations are received by sending them using one of the Royal Mail's recorded delivery procedures.

If there is no response to the invitation to interview, it may be appropriate to attempt to write to the suspect again providing a final deadline for a response.

Cautions

When there are grounds to suspect that a person has committed an offence, they must be cautioned before any questions about it are put to them to ensure that the answers (or any failure to answer) are capable of being admissible in evidence in a prosecution.

The caution applies to each interview separately: if further questions need to be put to a person at a later time they should be cautioned again.

It is vital that, if an individual is suspected, no member of the investigation team should engage them in casual questioning about the case – particularly if it is still in a covert phase before any suspicions have been voiced. If the suspect is so engaged, albeit by chance or as a result of them 'fishing' for information, no direct questions of a routine nature should be put to them without benefit of caution. Great care must be taken in casual questioning as any answers may not be admissible.

An 'interview' is defined as the questioning of a person regarding their involvement or suspected involvement in a criminal offence or offences. Such an interview must always be carried out under caution. The caution is the familiar one to those who watch police dramas:

> You do not have to say anything but it may harm your defence if you do not mention when questioned something which you later rely on in court. Anything you do say may be given in evidence.

The investigator should ensure that the person understands the caution and should be prepared to explain what the caution means if the suspect is unclear. At the same time as the caution, the suspect should be told that:

- they are not under any form of arrest or compulsion to remain, and
- they may obtain legal advice.

The suspect's responses to questions put to them during an interview under caution may be used as evidence against them in any subsequent criminal proceedings. This is explained to the suspect by the caution. Evidence obtained during the interview can only be used against the person being questioned, it cannot be used in evidence against another person (for example, a co-defendant), although it may, of course, suggest additional lines of enquiry.

An interview under caution should always be tape-recorded (see below).

One important point to note. Generally, a specialist who has been appointed to act as an expert in any potential prosecution (or who is intended to fulfil that role) should not attend an interview under caution as this may compromise their independence. This may well rule out the lead investigating forensic accountant who may be required to present evidence as part of legal proceedings in their role as an expert witness. It could, however, involve another member of the team.

Records of interviews under caution

An accurate record must be made of every interview with a person suspected of an offence (i.e. every interview under caution). The record must state:

- the place of the interview
- the time it begins and ends
- the time the record is made (if different)
- any breaks in the interview, and
- the names of all those present.

Legal advice

Persons being interviewed in connection with offences have a right to consult privately with a solicitor. They can choose to do so in person or by telephone. The individual should be informed of this right when the interview is arranged and before the interview starts, and of course the suspect's legal adviser may be present at the interview.

Suspects who are under the age of 18 may require to be accompanied by a responsible adult. Normally this would be a lawyer but could also be a parent, guardian or social worker.

Conducting the interview

The interview should be conducted sitting down and as far as possible in comfort, with proper breaks for refreshment (normal meal breaks and at least 15 minutes every 2 hours). The interview should take place in an adequately heated, lit and ventilated room. Before the start of the interview, it is advisable to ensure that all persons present have switched off mobile telephones, pagers, etc., to avoid interruptions.

The interview should be conducted with the rights of the suspect in mind irrespective of the strength of feeling of the individuals conducting it. It may be that the conduct of an interview under caution is best carried out by a dispassionate professional as any unseemly or aggressive outbursts towards the suspect may invalidate any evidence uncovered.

The general do's and don't's of carrying out such interviews are:

Do

- Caution the suspect and make sure they understand their rights – to silence, to legal representation and to leave at any time.
- Be courteous and listen to them.
- Let them see and have time to read any papers referred to.
- Read and consider any papers the suspect brings and points they make.
- Take account of any special needs they have, for example, difficulties because of illness, disability or language.
- Make sure they understand what they are being asked.
- Check if they have any questions or points to raise before finishing the interview.

Don't

- Pressure or intimidate the suspect. The interviewer must not try to obtain answers by the use of oppression. Such an approach is likely to mean that any evidence obtained is inadmissible.
- Make any threats regarding prosecution, asset recovery or future action against the individual.
- Pressure them to make or sign any statement.

Ending the interview

The interview (or further interview) of a suspect must cease when all the questions considered relevant to obtaining accurate and reliable information about the offence have been put to the suspect. This includes allowing the suspect an opportunity to give an explanation and the asking of questions to test if the suspect's explanation is accurate and reliable, for example, to clear up ambiguities or clarify what the suspect said.

Audio-recorded interview under caution

The purpose of audio-recording an interview under caution is to ensure that the most accurate record possible can easily be made. Audibly recorded interviews are the best way to ensure that admissible evidence is collected from suspects who are interviewed. Interviews with suspects should therefore always be audio-recorded.

Interviewers shouild be aware of the provisions of PACE Code E on 'Audio-recording Interviews with Suspects'. If interviews with suspects are audio-recorded, the court may exclude evidence of the interview if a relevant provision of the Code has not been followed.

Code of Practice E provides for recording using any removable, physical audio-recording medium that can be played and copied. If a single deck/drive machine is used the copy of the master recording must be made in the suspect's presence and without the master recording leaving their sight. All tapes must be new and in sealed packaging before the interview commences.

Recording the interview

At the start of a tape-recorded interview, the interviewer should:

- give the place of interview
- the date and time, and
- introduce themselves.

All other persons present in the room should be asked to introduce themselves so that their voices may be identified on the tape.

The suspect should then be cautioned and told that they are free to leave. The suspect should be reminded of the right to seek legal advice if there is no solicitor present at the interview. Ensure that this is recorded on the tape so there is no question of any infringement of the suspect's rights.

If the suspect objects to the interview being recorded, the objection should be recorded on the tape and the recorder turned off.

At the end of the interview the suspect must be offered an opportunity to clarify anything that has been said or to add anything.

Non-tape-recorded interviews under caution – written record

If it becomes necessary to conduct an interview under caution that is not audio-recorded (e.g. where the suspect refuses to allow the interview to be taped), an accurate written record during the course of the interview must be made to reflect what was said.

The record should state:

- the place of the interview
- the time it began and ended
- the time the record was made (if different)
- any breaks in the interview
- the names of all those present
- the fact that a caution was given, and any further cautions or reminders, should be recorded, and
- the fact that the suspect was informed of the right to seek legal advice.

At the end of the interview, the interviewer should sign the record at the bottom of each page. The suspect should then read through the interview record and then sign each page to confirm their agreement that it is a correct and accurate record of the interview. Any alleged inaccuracies should be amended by the person interviewed, endorsed with a statement that the amendments accurately reflect the disagreement, and signed.

Where the person writes their own statement, it should begin:

> I make this statement of my own free will. I understand that I do not have to say anything but that it may harm my defence if I do not mention when questioned something which I later rely on in court. This statement may be given in evidence.

Admissibility

Any facts indicating a breach of a PACE Code will be considered by the court, which can make a ruling on the admissibility of the evidence. A breach of a PACE

Code may be evidence of oppression or may support a contention of unreliability by the defence. It may also lead to evidence of the confession being excluded as a matter of discretion under Sections 76 or 78 PACE or the common law.

Evidence has been excluded in the following situations:

- where the police made a note of an incriminating comment by the defendant but failed to show it to him or ask him to sign it
- where no appropriate adult was present on questioning a juvenile
- where the suspect was not cautioned, or
- where a person was not given an adequate opportunity to consult with a solicitor.

Interviews under PACE must be conducted with care and always with an eye to prosecution. The rights of the suspect must be preserved at all times and care taken with making a record of the meeting if it is to be used in court. Interviews should only ever be conducted under legal advice.

Court orders used in fraud investigations

Forensic accounting work is, in many ways, bound up with the law and forensic accountants will inevitably come into regular contact with lawyers in the course of their work.

Clearly, where fraud investigations are concerned, legal representation will be an essential component of any investigative effort and much of the work of the forensic accountant will be carried on in the context of legal advice.

Forensic accountants who become involved in dispute resolution, matrimonial work, compensation claims, consequential loss, asset tracing and similar work will inevitably be involved in some sort of legal process, be it preparing an expert witness report for the court or as part of a dispute resolution procedure.

Forensic accountants should therefore have a working knowledge of court procedure and general legal processes. The bases of the judicial systems in England and Wales and in Scotland, where they do things differently, should be clearly understood.

The other procedures which forensic accountants will meet are the granting of certain orders such as:

- 'Norwich Pharmacal' orders.
- Freezing orders.
- Search orders.

in connection with fraud investigations.

Before we look at the application of these orders to an investigation, one point should be made. Whilst these orders can be extremely useful when carrying out an investigation, applying for orders and going before a judge in chambers is an expensive process. They should not, therefore, be used speculatively, even if the court could be persuaded to grant one, and they should not be used where the sums involved in the investigation are relatively low as this would not be cost-efficient.

Where the client is determined or where cost is not a consideration these orders represent a formidable weapon in the investigator's armoury.

Norwich Pharmacal orders

A Norwich Pharmacal order, derived from the name of the case in which such an order was first granted (Norwich Pharmacal Co. v Customs and Excise Commissioners [1974] AC 133), is a court order that requires a respondent to disclose certain documents or information to the applicant. The respondent must be a party who is involved or mixed up in wrongdoing, whether innocently or not, but is unlikely to be a party to the potential proceedings. A Norwich Pharmacal order will only be granted where 'necessary' in the interests of justice. Orders are commonly used to identify the proper defendant to an action or to obtain information to plead a claim.

A Norwich Pharmacal order can be obtained pre-action, during the course of an action and post-judgment but cannot be obtained in support of foreign proceedings (S 25(7) of the Civil Jurisdiction and Judgments Act 1982).

This order is an exception to the general rule that only people who are actually named as parties to existing litigation are obliged to disclose documents and other materials relevant to the claims.

For example: if X sues Y for fraud, X can usually only obtain relevant documentation from Y. X cannot usually call for Z to provide documents, even though Z may have relevant or even key information. Z would normally only be obliged to produce this kind of information following a court order, so a Norwich Pharmacal order will be used to compel Z to reveal information.

Freezing orders

In serious cases the court can grant a 'Freezing order' or injunction (formerly known as a Mareva injunction) to stop a party from disposing of assets or removing them from the jurisdiction of the court pending resolution of a dispute.

Because of its severe nature a Freezing order, sometimes referred to as the 'nuclear option', will not be lightly granted and a condition attached to the grant of such an order is likely to be that the person who applied for it will pay the full costs of the person against whom it was made if it turns out to have been inappropriate. The courts will exercise caution in making such an order so the applicant must be sure of their ground before applying. Such an order will usually only be made where the applicant can show that there was at least a strong case that their claim would succeed at trial and that the refusal of the order would create a real risk that any judgment or award in their favour would remain unsatisfied.

Freezing orders can extend to assets held overseas and, in exceptional circumstances, foreign courts can be requested to assist by making a 'mirror order' freezing assets within their jurisdiction in support of the English proceedings. This can take some time however and the relevant assets may well have been moved again before such an order can be obtained.

In addition the court can order third parties, such as banks, to reveal details of assets and transactions involving those assets.

In certain circumstances where property has already been disposed of the courts can issue a so-called 'Unscrambling' order which would seek to put the parties back to an original position.

Clearly Freezing and Unscrambling orders require the involvement of a suitably experienced lawyer in making the application to the court.

Search and Seize orders

The courts have the power to issue a form of civil search warrant called a Search and Seize order. This type of order was previously developed by the courts and practitioners may have previously recognised it as an Anton Piller order – named after the case where the order was first granted (Anton Piller KG v Manufacturing Processes Limited [1976] Ch 55). Authority to grant a Search order is now contained in Section 7 of the Civil Procedure Act 1997 and Part 25 of the Civil Procedure Rules.

A Search and Seize order is a form of injunction which requires a party to permit entry to a property in order to conduct a search for, and if necessary to seize, evidence. Evidence could consist of, say, bank statements or company documents kept at a person's home and relevant to a fraud case or a situation where there is evidence that assets may have been fraudulently transferred.

These orders are usually applied for and obtained from the court without notice to the person who is intended to be the subject of the order to ensure that there is no prospect of evidence being removed or destroyed before the search can take place. However, a Search and Seize order can be issued in any case where the court is persuaded that the defendant is the sort of person who might destroy relevant evidence in their possession if the order is not made.

Strictly speaking, a Search order is not analogous to the search warrant used by the police because it does not directly empower the holder to enter or search premises. Instead, it requires the person in charge of the premises to let the holder in. In practice, however, the order has much the same effect as a magistrates' search warrant, since it is a contempt of court to refuse to let the holder in and the court can be petitioned in the event of any refusal.

The strategic way to use such orders in an investigation is to arrange for a legal representative to be at court with an application for a Search and Seize order. If a suspected fraudster is approached, after the order is granted, to admit investigators, say, to their home for the purpose of evidence gathering and refuses them entry the investigator should contact the legal representative who can then immediately apply to the court, in the person of a Judge in Chambers stating that the individual is in contempt for not letting them in and applying for an arrest warrant.

Nearly all Search orders will contain a provision forbidding the subject of the order to tip off others – apart from their lawyer – about the existence of the order. The person who has obtained the order should have put in place a means of telling whether others have been tipped off if this is a real possibility, for example in cases where a conspiracy is suspected. Where there is such a conspiracy simultaneous orders should be effected against the suspects, if possible. If the subject of the order is caught arranging for others to dispose of inconvenient evidence, they would risk prison for contempt of court.

Note that an individual cannot claim any right of non-incrimination by refusing to hand over suspect computers etc. Whilst, as we have seen, individuals have the right not to incriminate themselves this right does not extend to independent evidence such as that contained on a laptop. Failing to hand over such items puts them in breach of the order.

Only materials covered by the terms of the Search order may be removed from the property. If, however, such materials include items that exist only in computer readable form, then they will be required to give access to the computers with all necessary passwords to enable them to be searched. The search may only be conducted in the presence of the accused or someone who is their responsible representative.

These Search and Seize orders are often used in combination with Mareva-type Freezing orders. This can be a devastating combination when applied to a business or an individual trying to carry on a business as it not only freezes all their assets but forces them to reveal information, so it should be used with care. Such orders may also freeze assets of other members of the family if it is believed they were complicit in any fraud which can add further pressure on the accused.

Taxation issues

Fraud is not a victimless crime and will result in losses to business. Whether or not these losses can be recovered from the perpetrator will depend on whether or not there is anything left to recover, and whether the guilty party has any assets to claim against. It is possible to obtain judgment against a convicted fraudster and claim against them, making them bankrupt if necessary, so as to be able to claim against any property or other assets of value.

Alternatively the losses may be insured under a fidelity insurance policy and recovery made there, or it may be possible to claim against a third party, possibly a bank who acted negligently in opening a false bank account.

However, if neither of these is a viable option for complete recovery the remaining benefit is to claim any residual losses against taxation liabilities.

HM Revenue and Customs (HMRC) will require to be convinced that any losses claimed for are genuine. Any report made as a result of a forensic accounting investigation may well try to establish the quantum of losses and should identify the methods used by the fraudster to conceal their activities. This will form evidence to support a claim.

HMRC set out some key conditions for agreeing a claim for tax relief:

- The loss must not already have been claimed. Clearly if the fraudster has written off their depredations to the Income Account, albeit disguised as something else, relief against profits will already have been claimed so no further claim can be made. HMRC may well want to reassure themselves that any 'fictitious' entries are as a result of fraud so, again, the forensic accountant's report will be invaluable.
- If the fraud has been going on for more than six years and has not been charged against revenue, earlier losses may not be recoverable.
- The fraud must have been disclosed to the police and a prosecution sought.
- Frauds by directors may not be given any tax relief.

Any agreement with HMRC will undoubtedly involve negotiation and, where the claims for loss are substantial, an experienced tax practitioner should become involved.

One remaining area where practitioners can come into contact with the law is where investigations result in the forensic accountant having to prepare a report for the court and, perhaps, an appearance as an expert witness. This can be a difficult area and again there are procedures and protocols to be followed. We deal with these separately in Chapter 16.

Summary

- In order for a crime to be committed there has to be an act (*actus reus*) and an intention (*mens rea*).
- The law on fraud is primarily governed by the Fraud Act 2006.
- Fraud requires some form of deception which distinguishes it from simple theft.
- There are three primary offences: a general offence of fraud committed by false representation, by failing to disclose information or by abuse of position.
- There are some offences under the Theft Act 1968 relating to false accounting.
- The law of fraud is different in Scotland as it still maintains a system of common law, however the Proceeds of Crime Act and the Money Laundering Regulations do apply there.
- Cheating the public revenue is an offence used against VAT, tax and social security fraudsters.
- The Proceeds of Crime Act 2002 provided a mechanism for recovering criminal proceeds.
- It also introduced the offence of money laundering.
- Detailed rules as to how organisations must operate in connection with money laundering are set out in the Money Laundering Regulations 2007.
- There is legal protection for whistle-blowers to prevent them being victimised by employers.
- There is a new Bribery Act which consolidates the law on bribery and corruption in organisations. It places onerous responsibilities on directors to prevent corrupt acts by employees and agents.
- Companies who deal with US businesses or whose shares are quoted on a US stock exchange are liable under US law for corrupt acts.
- There is a prohibition on intercepting e-mails or other forms of electronic data
- There are several types of court order which can be used to obtain information from third parties, freeze assets and legitimise a search of private property.
- Fraud losses may be claimed against tax liabilities in certain circumstances.

Case study

Consider two situations:

1 The chief executive and financial director sign a Letter of Representation to the auditors and sign off the annual accounts of a listed PLC. They know of the existence of substantial contingent liabilities but make no mention of these, nor are they included in the annual accounts. Shortly after the accounts are published they exercise share options and both make substantial profits. Three months after the exercise of these options a substantial liability materialises and the company share price plummets. This was one of the contingent liabilities not mentioned to the auditors.

2 An accounting firm is carrying out a due diligence investigation into Target plc on behalf of their client, Predator plc, for the purpose of a potential acquisition. During the course of their investigations the directors of Target omit to point out that several of their best selling products contravene new environmental legislation and will have to be withdrawn from sale – with a seriously detrimental effect on the future results. The investigating accountants are not made aware of this and the

▶

executives of Predator plc don't spot it either. All other financial and operating issues are found to be correctly stated or represented. The directors of Target plc own shares in the company but do not retain their jobs as directors after the takeover.

Required

- Have any offences been committed under the Fraud Act 2006?
- If so what are they?
- What evidence would you need to support a prosecution?

Bibliography

Adams, S. (2007) Online communities face money laundering. www.telegraph.co.uk, 14 May.

Crown Prosecution Service (2006) *The Fraud Act 2006*. CPS, London.

Crown Prosecution Service (2007) *Proceeds of Crime Guidance – December 2007*. CPS, London.

Crown Prosecution Service (2008) *Theft Acts Incorporating the Charging Standard*. CPS, London.

General Council of the Bar (2008) *Proceeds of Crime Act 2002 Guidance*. Bar Council, London.

Grant Thornton (2009) *Anti-corruption and the Bribery Bill*. Grant Thornton UK LLP, London.

Guardian (2009) *Regulation of Investigatory Powers Act 2000*. www.guardian.co.uk.

Health and Safety Executive (2009) *Enforcement Guide – Collecting Witness Evidence*. H & SE, Bootle.

HMSO (1984) *Police and Criminal Evidence Act 1984*. HMSO, London.

HMSO (2000) *Regulation of Investigatory Powers Act 2000*. HMSO, London.

HMSO (2002) *Proceeds of Crime Act 2002*. HMSO, London.

HMSO (2006) *Fraud Act 2006*. HMSO, London.

HMSO (2007) *Money Laundering Regulations 2007*. HMSO, London.

HMSO (2010) *Bribery Act 2010*. HMSO, London.

Home Office (2007) *Asset Recovery Action Plan: A Consultative Document*. Home Office, London.

Home Office Guidance (1984) *Police and Criminal Evidence Act 1984 (PACE) and Accompanying Codes of Practice*. HMSO, London.

Hudson, A. (2009) *The Law of Finance*, 1st edn. Sweet and Maxwell (Thomson Reuters), London.

Jenkins, R. (2008) Solicitor took paralysed client's £1.2m payout. www.thetimes.co.uk, 8 April.

Leapman, B. (2007) Second Life world may be haven for terrorists. www.telegraph.co.uk, 13 May.

Mawby, D. (2007) *A Privilege Against Self-incrimination*. Shepherd & Weatherburn LLP, Edinburgh.

Martin, M. and Storey, T. (2010) *Unlocking Criminal Law*, 3rd edn. Hodder Education, London.

Murphy, P. (2005) *Murphy on Evidence,* 9th edn. Oxford University Press, Oxford.

Ormerod, D. (ed.) (2008), *Smith and Hogan Criminal Law,* 12th edn. Oxford University Press, Oxford.

Scottish Law Agents Society (2006) *POCA – Case in Point.* Scottish Law Agents Society, Glasgow.

Securities and Exchange Commission (2008) *Securities and Exchange Commission* v *Siemens Aktiengesellschaft, Civil Action No. 08 CV 02167 (D.D.C.).* Securities and Exchange Commission, Washington, DC.

Telegraph (2008) Solicitor stole £1.2m from quadriplegic client. www.telegraph.co.uk, 4 April.

Waugh, R. (2007) Sacked whistleblowers win £1m payout from council, *Yorkshire PostNews*, 14 August.

Western Mail (2009) Woman jailed for £70,000 theft. www.walesonline.co.uk, 31 January.

ZD Net (2005) Demon founder pleads guilty to email snooping. www.silicon.com, 15 September.

Websites

www.bbc.co.uk

www.cps.gov.uk

www.guardian.co.uk

www.hse.gov.uk/enforce

www.lexisnexis.com.uk

www.opsi.gov.uk

www.ps/copes@scotland.gsi.gov.uk

www.sec.gov/news/press

www.silicon.com/management

www.slas.co.uk

www.telegraph.co.uk

www.thetimes.co.uk

www.walesonline.co.uk

Part 2

THE ROLE OF THE ORGANISATION AND THE PSYCHOLOGY OF FRAUD

Chapter 4 The role of the organisation

Chapter 5 The psychology of fraud

Chapter 4

The role of the organisation

Chapter contents

- Introduction
- Corporate morality
- Ethics in business
- Corporate culture and the individual
- Individuals in organisations
- Groupthink
- Work-related behaviour
- Motivation and the role of corporate culture
- Socialisation
- Socialisation techniques
- Rationalising unethical behaviour
- Preventing rationalisation and socialisation of unethical behaviour
- Personal ethics

Learning objectives

After studying this chapter you should be able to:

- Appreciate the different forms of corporate culture
- Understand the concept of corporate morality
- Understand the role ethics plays in business activity
- Understand the influence of different types of corporate culture
- Understand the concept of groupthink
- Appreciate how corporate culture influences the actions of individuals
- Understand how individuals may be socialised into unethical behaviour
- Understand how individuals rationalise unethical behaviour
- Understand how to prevent this happening
- Have an appreciation of the conflict between personal ethical codes and dysfunctional behaviour

Introduction

In the first two chapters we looked at what might be best described as the formal structures of the organisation. The division between ownership and control, the increasing influence of good corporate governance practice and the refining of the roles of both internal and external auditors have created a framework for what we could loosely call good corporate behaviour.

However, these will not avail the company if the underlying ethos of the organisation is dysfunctional. As we have seen, the culture of an organisation – what we might describe as its value system or moral code – is often set by those at its pinnacle, namely the senior, most influential, even the most inspiring directors.

This has become known as 'tone at the top'. This phrase describes the influence that the controlling minds of the organisation, usually some or all of the directors, have on the culture of the organisation which influences the attitudes of the employees. As we will see, the ethics and mores of the organisation can have a significant bearing on the attitudes of employees towards what we describe as dysfunctional – that is unethical, corrupt or criminal – behaviour.

Anyone doubting this can see some not-so-shining examples by examining the corrosive effect on individual morality of Messrs Lay, Skilling and Fastow at Enron or the fear caused by the intimidation and deceit of Bernie Ebbers and Scott Sullivan at WorldCom, in the USA. These are well-documented cases and are admittedly the extreme edge of the spectrum, but they serve as examples of situations where powerful executives were able not only to enrich themselves but also to draw others into their sphere of influence and persuade them that the illegal or unethical actions they were taking were somehow justified.

Both Enron and WorldCom had all the trappings of corporate governance (see Chapter 1), they had non-executive directors, audit committees and even codes of practice for their staff to follow. What is of concern to the forensic accountant is the reality behind the façade – how the actual behaviour of managers and employees in companies differs from their published expressed values are and what the effect of that is on individual employees.

Why is this relevant to the forensic accountant? Because the greater the level of corruption and deceit within an organisation the greater the likelihood of theft and fraud, a likelihood which will pervade the entire entity and lead to losses both big and small. It is therefore the background in which an investigation might have to be conducted and forensic accountants should be able to recognise situations where, for example, staff are in fear of upper management, or feel able to lie to customers with impunity or steal from the company without worrying about being caught and punished. The warning signs are there.

Corporate morality

In the absence of unequivocal academic research in the UK it is not entirely clear whether any attempt by an employer to impose a greater set of moral values on employees than those required of them by the kind of society in which they live is doomed to failure. In Exhibit 4.1 we see that researchers in Australia discovered that the effect on employee behaviour of ethical codes was minimal: what influenced them the most, in practice, was the prevailing morality of society rather than of their workplace.

Exhibit 4.1 **Do codes of ethics work? Research in Australia**

Research carried out in Australia in 2000 revealed that there was no discernible associ-ation between the patterns of behaviour of employees and the approach of the organ-isation towards its ethical culture. It did not seem to matter whether the organisation had a strong ethical policy or not.

Instead researchers determined that the strongest ethical culture affecting em-ployee behaviour, in the organisations surveyed, came from an external shared source.

The researchers were not able to identify this external shared source but suggested it may range anywhere from the culture of office workers in large Australian corpora-tions generally via the common culture of the Australian community to a generalised contemporary world view.

What this means is that societal norms may have a greater influence on behaviour in the workplace than some form of 'company code'.

Whether or not this is an exclusively Australian phenomenon is unknown but that possibility should not be excluded given the Australian predilection for individual be-haviour and resistance to imposed regulations.

Source: Farrell, Cobbin and Farrell (2002)

Does this mean that ethical codes are doomed to failure? It may do. It may mean that people who live in a society which emphasises the cult of the individual at the expense of a collective morality have a weaker commitment to ethical behaviour than individuals who have been brought up to believe in the collective good.

There is evidence to indicate that in the absence of clear, strong leadership, codes of corporate ethics or values are seen by employees as nothing more than PR waffle or something for the HR department to disseminate and pontificate upon rather than as a practical, everyday code to operate by.

What is the relevance of this to forensic accounting? If the employees of the company have no functioning moral code of behaviour other than those set out by society as a whole, they will never adopt any of management's exhortations about 'doing the right thing', whatever that may be. They will tend to see themselves as separate from the organisation, owing no loyalty to it other than that which can be bought by a monthly salary.

Following this logic results in the conclusion that only the fear of being caught or their own personal morality will prevent employees from committing dysfunc-tional acts against the company such as:

- disloyalty – talking the company and its products down, discouraging prospec-tive employees
- inertia – moving at their own pace to process information or conduct business
- betrayal – disclosing confidential information about the company and its products
- corruption – accepting bribes or undue hospitality to favour particular suppliers or customers at the expense of others
- theft – of company assets, or
- fraud – theft covered up by deliberate manipulation of company records.

This, clearly, is not the case. Modern companies do not, or at least should not, operate in a climate of fear where 'ethical police' study every action. Most companies accept that societal norms should not be the only measure of business morality; instead they take the view that they have a responsibility to their employees and part of that responsibility is the elimination, wherever possible, of dysfunctional behaviour by establishing and disseminating a code of ethics and encouraging compliance with it.

There is some evidence to indicate that a degree of cynicism is present in employees and is directed towards statements of ethical values expressed by their employers which are at variance with the actual behaviour of those organisations. Clearly organisations which claim to have an idealistic set of moral values and then act inconsistently with them, or where those who purport to lead contravene their own code of ethics, will be unlikely to carry the workforce with them in a quest for moral correctness. Worse, they will set a shining example of bad behaviour which, logic says, is sooner or later bound to be followed by their subordinates.

Ethics in business

In 2007 the Institute of Business Ethics (IBE) carried out a survey entitled *Use of Codes of Ethics in Business*. This was the latest in a series of triennial surveys carried out by the Institute and, they report, it shows some significant changes from their previous survey in 2004.

The survey was sent to 200 companies listed in the FTSE 350 that were known to have an ethical policy or code. The usable response rate was 34 per cent (68 companies) and from this the IBE claimed they had sufficient data to be able to draw conclusions and evaluate trends.

The summary of results revealed the following:

- All the companies responding gave the main reason for having a code as guidance to staff.
- The IBE estimated that at least 85 per cent of FTSE 100 companies had an explicit ethics policy or code of ethics.
- Only 27 per cent of companies stated that the board of directors were taking direct responsibility for the ethical programme, which was broadly consistent with the findings of the 2004 survey. In 45 per cent of companies the company secretary or the legal department was responsible for ethical policy and codes of business ethics.
- Companies also saw codes as aids to safeguarding the company's reputation (85 per cent) and as a public statement of their ethical commitment (84 per cent): 81 per cent of the responses (as part of multiple answers) stated that companies saw ethical codes as a component of reducing operational risk.
- Seventy-one per cent of companies give ethics training to staff on the meaning and use of the code. This was up from 47 per cent in 2004.
- Electronic copies of codes were the preferred method of communication to staff, generally through use of the company intranet.
- Seventy-two per cent required compliance as part of the contract of employment and 52 per cent of companies had used the code in disciplinary proceedings.
- Eighty-two per cent took active steps to monitor the effectiveness of codes, up from 59 per cent in 2004.
- The most important ethical issue overall was safety and security, with concerns about the environment second. However, when these responses were analysed by industry both manufacturing industries and utilities placed bribery, corruption and facilitation payments first.

What does this admittedly limited survey tell us about attitudes to ethics in UK business?

The IBE states in the preamble to its results:

> There is evidence that boards of directors are more actively engaged in providing leadership in their companies on business ethics issues. It is one benefit of the new focus on governance issues and reputation risk management.

This is borne out by the survey finding that there were increases in the use of codes and in staff training, but there was no increase in the direct involvement of the board of directors and the use of codes was almost universally primarily for staff training, even if they had additional uses such as being part of risk management.

In 2005 the IBE carried out a survey into *Ethics at Work*. This was, they claimed, the first national survey of full-time workers on this topic. It was conducted through MORI so had some credibility as a statistically valid survey.

The results of this survey are even more interesting than those of the later one described above:

- About 80 per cent of the workforce felt positive about the ethical practices and standards at their workplace and felt that business was always or frequently conducted honestly.
- Sixty-six per cent thought their organisation lived up to its own standards on corporate responsibility.
- Sixty-eight per cent said everyone lies to the boss occasionally.
- Women were stricter in their ethical standards than men.
- Under 35's were likely to be less strict than older employees.
- One in five had personally observed behaviour by a colleague which violated the law or did not accord with their organisation's standard of behaviour.
- Of these half reported the misconduct to management.
- Twenty-five per cent of staff felt they would be branded as troublemakers if they reported any unethical or dishonest behaviour.
- Twenty-five per cent of employees said they had felt pressure to compromise their organisation's ethical standards.

The IBE go on to state: 'There is a clear gap between having a policy and all the staff knowing about it and conforming to it.'

There is a remarkable consistency about these percentages, although without access to the detail of the results this may be a specious conclusion, insofar as the survey reveals that:

- some 20 per cent of employees felt their employer did not conduct its business ethically, and
- some 25 per cent had observed unethical behaviour and the same percentage had come under pressure to compromise their standards.

Does this tell us that a fifth or so of UK business is, potentially, at best unethical and at worst corrupt? That is probably stretching things a little far but it does indicate that there may well be some organisations out there with codes of ethics but with, perhaps, a more flexible sense of morality than might be desirable. It also tells us that it is one thing to have a policy, and entirely another to expect it to act as a mechanism of social control within the organisation.

As expected, the survey also revealed that individuals working in the public sector had a much greater awareness of ethical issues and received more support than their colleagues in the private sector. The reason for this is likely to be cultural. The organisations in the public sector, for example, local authorities, the NHS, suppliers of social housing etc. are non-profit making and are concerned primarily with service delivery. They also have limited control over their income as they are funded through public revenue. There is no incentive for senior managers to distort results for personal gain and the prevailing ethical climate within the organisation serves to discourage individuals from committing fraud without a strong motive other than personal financial enrichment.

Corporate culture and the individual

Following on from considerations of attitudes of employees towards ethical policies, it is instructive to spend a little time looking at the attitude of employees to their workplace. As we will see from Chapter 10, part of the methodology of fraud investigation involves identifying employee links and subgroups, so an understanding of this kind of organisational psychology is directly relevant to the forensic accountant.

Another reason for looking at corporate culture is that the internal control environment – the attitude of individual employees towards internal checks and internal audit – coupled with their attitude towards theft and fraud can, as we will see, be determined by the prevailing culture of the organisation and of the subgroup within the organisation to which the individual employee belongs.

First, it is important to understand that the culture of an organisation exerts a strong but subtle pressure on an individual employee. Human beings generally feel the need to fit in with group norms, they tend to go along with 'the way we do things around here' because not doing so can lead to unpleasant personal consequences such as:

- social ostracism
- disfavour from more senior colleagues
- reduced promotion prospects, and
- gentle (or indeed not so gentle) pressure to leave both from colleagues and superiors.

Individual employees tend to identify most closely with colleagues in their immediate working environment. The larger the organisation the more distant other parts of it become one to another, and despite management's best endeavours to create corporate harmony and engender a feeling of oneness throughout the organisation, individual employees will naturally gravitate towards those they feel most secure and comfortable with – which will primarily be colleagues carrying out similar roles to themselves or working in the same subgroup.

However, these subgroups can cross organisational boundaries; thus accountants within an organisation will feel a kinship even if they work in physically disparate locations and may not, for example, associate with or feel close to sales or purchasing staff working in the same location. The reason for this is that they share a common culture based on training and the daily tasks they have to accomplish.

Secondly, it is a mistake to assume that organisations only have one style or culture. Different parts of an organisation, subsidiaries, divisions or departments can have their own subcultures within the overall tone of the organisation, established by local management.

Table 4.1 is a synthesis of several attempts to categorise cultural styles and is not based on any particular piece of research. It serves as an example of the variations

Table 4.1 Examples of corporate culture

Cultural approach	Symptoms
Anarchic (e.g. dot.com design-led organisation)	• Informal • Risk-taking • Individualistic – individuals held responsible for own actions • Charismatic leadership • Constant upheaval • High levels of drinking/socialisation • Consider themselves outside the norm/special cases • Rewards can be very high but also very volatile – emphasis on performance based rewards systems • Anti-bureaucratic • High level of commitment to work • Organisation is outward-looking and aggressive
Dictatorial (e.g. large family-owned company)	• Culture reflects values of dominant individual or group • Formalised structures with power in the hands of an individual or small group • Promotion difficult if not impossible but constant turnover of staff leaving • Blame culture – tendency to allocate blame for failures and mistakes to lowest-ranking employees • Limited amount of delegation – power remains in the hands of the dominant group so all decisions must be referred to the next level upward • Cautious and unwilling to take risks – the price of failure is high • Subculture of gossip and plotting – organisation is inward-looking and defensive • High levels of reward for employees with favoured status – rigid pay structures for others • Action outside group norms severely punished • Rejection of criticism originated from outside ruling group • Reluctance to change • Approach to risk erratic dependent on views of controlling individual/group • Can make erratic/illogical decisions
Bureaucratic (e.g. public sector body)	• Rules based • Rigid hierarchical structures • Delegated powers strictly determined – decisions outside delegated powers referred upwards and discussed with key decision makers • Rewards are time-based – pay rises determined by length of service rather than ability • Formal processes and procedures • Blame culture – tendency to allocate blame for failures and mistakes and to hide mistakes • Often high levels of individual skills confined in specific areas • Employees tend to be conformist and not totally financially motivated • Objective and impersonal – very senior management often faceless • Extremely risk averse

▶

Table 4.1 Continued

Cultural approach	Symptoms
Democratic (e.g. plc with strong corporate governance)	• Culture consensual – management attempt to persuade workforce of value of initiatives • High levels of explanation and transparency • High levels of delegation and individual initiative within overarching framework – powers fairly widely drawn • High levels of accountability – managers making serious errors are expected to fall on their swords • Senior management hold themselves accountable to stakeholders • High levels of loyalty to organisation • Some element of 'benevolent paternalism' – efforts by management to ensure workers feel valued • Co-operative ways of working • Blurring of boundaries in approaches to tasks • Rewards based on abilities and achievements • Risk averse – high levels of planning and consideration

it is possible to find either at an organisational level or at a sub-level within an individual entity. For the purpose of this exercise organisational cultures have been subdivided into four broad categories. Organisational psychologists and researchers will probably frown at the simplicity of these subdivisions but this is not a book on organisational theory – it is a book about forensic accounting and fraud!

It would be invidious or misleading to try to provide examples of each type of organisation so students should attempt to identify their own; however a suggestion is made of the type of organisation purely by way of illustration.

Following on from this broad subdivision, relating cultural styles to the control environment rapidly indicates where problem areas arise.

Table 4.2 sets out four possible cultural approaches, the management style most associated with that type of culture and the consequential risk factors which arise.

Clearly these are indicative rather than prescriptive but they do give some idea of how the work of the forensic accountant is affected by the nature and culture of the organisation. The culture of the organisation clearly influences the behaviour of individuals and research shows that this can result in individual dysfunctional behaviour or can reinforce patterns of behaviour among groups, which may seem acceptable within the bounds of the organisation but are, in fact, inappropriate in wider society.

The organisation is the context for individual actions and we will return to this analysis later in the chapter. Dysfunctional behaviour is, however, a personal thing – organisations don't commit frauds or corrupt people – people within organisations do. What we have to look at now is, given the organisational context, how does individual motivation fit in? From there we can go on to examine some organisational hot spot indicators or warning signs and consider how organisations can modify or improve their behaviour in order to eliminate, or at least minimise, the probability of this resulting in fraudulent behaviour, either by the individuals for themselves or by the individuals for the organisation.

Table 4.2 Corporate culture and risk factors

Cultural approach	Management style	Risk factors
Anarchic	• Incompetent • Confused and contradictory • Constant change for no obvious reason • High levels of in dividualistic behaviour • Blame culture • Flexible ethics driven by necessity rather than principle	• Low levels of control • High possibility of errors or mistakes going undetected • Low levels of consideration towards organisational assets • Attempts to cover mistakes through additional risk taking – which may make them even larger
Dictatorial	• Domineering • One-way communication • Employees undervalued • Imbalance of reward structures • Rewards not related to performance but to relationships • Perceived unfairness • Cultural values those of senior management	• Attitudes coloured by resentment – frauds may arise through employees wishing to challenge or 'get back' at the organisation • Overt observance of rules but possible covert behaviour • Rigid demarcation of management territories may give scope for fraud • Blame culture encourages the hiding of mistakes
Bureaucratic	• Slow • Conformist • Emphasis on collective decision making • Blame culture • Rigid conformance to plans and strategies • Discourages individual initiative • Homogeneous employees with similar cultural values • Rewards not linked to performance but to length of service	• High levels of conformism • Rules tend to be obeyed and rule breakers informed on • Security valued as key aspect of job role so risk is not considered acceptable • Highly bureaucratic systems make fraud difficult • Employees in remote locations may exploit rigidity of structures once removed from immediate supervision
Democratic	• Accountable • Decisions await consensus so can be slow to respond • Initiative fostered if of demonstrable benefit • Low level of risk taking • Rewards linked to performance • Culture geared around job satisfaction • High level of ethical values	• High levels of trust within organisation • Unscrupulous employees can exploit tendency to emphasise individual initiative and delegated responsibility • High levels of accountability reinforce tendency to hide mistakes and errors • Rewards based on performance encourage aggressive accounting practices to 'improve' results or hide losses

Individuals in organisations

Much has been written about the behaviour of people in organisations and the effect that being part of a larger whole has on them. This book is not the place to expound sociological theories of organisational behaviour, but aspects of it are relevant to the forensic accountant for two reasons:

- Forensic accountants engaged in designing accounting systems, or anti-fraud measures generally, need to know the areas at risk where misbehaviour by employees might be triggered. In this way it may be possible to design out the most likely areas where fraud and corruption might flourish.
- Through understanding a certain amount of corporate psychology forensic accountants can identify key risk areas when undertaking fraud investigations where a perpetrator is not obvious. These can range from identifying signs which indicate that executives may be up to no good to spotting departmental activities where the potential for fraud and corruption is greatest.

Clearly this can only be a brief overview of the basics. Interested students can read further in the books suggested in the bibliography at the end of the chapter.

We will look at two particular facets of organisational psychology:

- groupthink, and
- work-related behaviour.

Groupthink

Groupthink was a term coined by sociologist and journalist William H. Whyte in *Fortune* magazine in 1952. Whyte defined it thus:

> groupthink being a coinage – and, admittedly, a loaded one – a working definition is in order. We are not talking about mere instinctive conformity – it is, after all, a perennial failing of mankind. What we are talking about is a rationalized conformity – an open, articulate philosophy which holds that group values are not only expedient but right and good as well.

It was the work of psychologist Irving Janis in the 1970s which brought the concept to popular attention. Janis defined it as:

> a mode of thinking that people engage in when they are deeply involved in a cohesive in-group, when the members' strivings for unanimity override their motivation to realistically appraise alternative courses of action.

Janis looked at collective decision making in the context of group dynamics whereby a dominant leader influences the decision making of others, not in a hectoring or domineering fashion but in often inadvertent ways. In these cases subordinates are not afraid to speak their minds, nor is the leader averse to hearing what they have to say, but subtle constraints may prevent a member of the group from openly expressing doubt or criticism or even of thinking consistently in an independent way. So they are free to speak their minds, as long as doing so doesn't ripple the calm surface of the group's collective pond.

Janis predicated that groupthink is most likely to be present under two basic situations:

1 Where there are:
  - structural faults in the organisation leading to insulation of the decision-making group
  - a lack of a tradition of impartial leadership
  - a lack of norms requiring method in decision making and, perhaps most importantly, homogeneity of members' social background/attitudes/ideology.

This is the so-called 'golf club syndrome' where members of the group share similar social attitudes, come from similar backgrounds and have similar lifestyles. Behaviour considered to be outside group norms threatens to punish the perpetrator with the ultimate sanction – expulsion or rejection by the group. Part of the shock felt by many victims of Bernard Madoff was not simply that he had stolen their money but that he had defrauded fellow members of his exclusive Palm Beach Country Club who thought he was one of them.

2 Where the group is under actual or perceived pressure, i.e. where the group is faced with:
  - high stress from external threats with a low hope of any better solution than the leader's
  - low self-esteem temporarily induced by a history of recent failures that make members' inadequacies relevant
  - excessive difficulties in the decision-making process which lowers each member's sense of self-efficacy, or
  - moral dilemmas involving an apparent lack of feasible alternatives except ones that violate ethical standards.

Spotting groupthink

Janis identified symptoms that are indicative of groupthink. They are divided into three main types which are familiar features of many, but not all, cohesive groups.

1 Overestimation of the group:
  - Illusions of invulnerability – the illusion of the group somehow being invulnerable to dangers and risks that affect other people. This tends to encourage over-optimism and risk taking.
  - A belief in the inherent morality of the group. This results in members failing to acknowledge the consequences of their actions.
2 Closed-mindedness:
  - Collective rationalisation – concurrence among group members which assists in discounting warnings or other information which might cause members to reconsider their assumptions before recommitting to past policy decisions.
  - Stereotyped views of outsiders – defining them as ignorant, stupid, ill-informed, evil, etc. – which again aids in reinforcing group cohesion and assists in the process of collective rationalisation. This serves to demean outsiders so their views can be safely ignored or the effects of the group's actions on them minimised.

3 Pressures towards uniformity:

- Self-censorship of deviations from the apparent group consensus. Each member tends to minimise the importance of their own doubts and counterarguments.
- A shared illusion of unanimity concerning judgements conforming to the majority view. This partly results from self-censorship of doubts and the false assumption that silence means consent.
- Direct pressure on any member who expresses strong arguments against any of the group's stereotypes, illusions or commitments making clear that this type of dissent is contrary to what is expected of all loyal members. Members become reluctant to break group cohesion for fear of expulsion.
- The emergence of self-appointed 'mind guards' or 'gatekeepers' who protect the group from dissenting information which might shatter their shared complacency about the effectiveness and morality of their decisions. Thus the fearsome PA or assistant who supports the group and reinforces it without ever really being part of it.

When a group such as a board of directors displays these sorts of symptoms their decision-making process becomes ineffective. The group may begin to take decisions which may steer them away from an ethical course and, at an extreme level, lead to distortions of financial statements and even to corruption and plundering of the organisation.

But be careful! These situations are difficult to spot. Not every cohesive group is subject to groupthink, and circumstances may change over time as individuals within the group part company with it.

It is more likely to exist:

- where there is a strong or inspiring, but not overly dominant leader – an overtly dominant leader would tend to act dictatorially and would not act within the context of a group, except perhaps nominally. An ostensibly inspiring or strong leader, particularly in the absence of equally strong or effective subordinates, may create a situation where a small group of decision makers, headed by the leader, feels itself to be in charge and invulnerable, or
- in the absence of effective externalities such as strong non-executive directors, weak communication lines to and from the group, ineffective finance functions and compliant external auditors – in these cases the decisions of the group go un-challenged and, particularly if their initial decisions bring success, the group may start to become self-reinforcing and feel itself to be all-knowing and all-powerful.

It is now considered that symptoms of groupthink manifest themselves more fre-quently than was originally postulated by Janis. Indeed part of the Enron collapse can be attributed to a groupthink-style culture, inspired by Geoffrey Skilling, which set the tone and style of the business in the early years of its meteoric growth and which fostered a culture of constant success, at any price: no bad news and no excuses for failure.

Work-related behaviour

Work plays a significant part in most people's lives and consequently social scien-tists have, unsurprisingly, discovered a plethora of feelings, attitudes, responses and behaviours in the workplace. There are innumerable scholarly works of door-stopping size on the motivations and rationales for people's behaviour at work. In addition there are stunning numbers of 'how to' management books which provide instant, guaranteed solutions to managing those pesky workers and even peskier managers.

Because we are all human and exhibit the full array of human frailties under stress and because of our propensity for irrational behaviour and our often emotional and irrational reaction to events, it is horribly difficult for anyone to come up with a checklist of actions or signs which will:

- identify a fraudster
- guarantee ethical behaviour
- stop workplace pilfering, or
- manage workplace change.

in the way all the books say you are supposed to be able to do.

We will look at the psychology of fraud in Chapter 5 and will highlight some so-called 'red flags' or warning signs later in the book, but it is worth stating here and now that there is:

- no 'one best way' of preventing fraud or other forms of dysfunctional behaviour in organisations, and
- no way of identifying a potential fraudster easily from their actions or their appearance.

What we can say is that the study of workplace behaviour will provide clues, pointers or possibilities to areas or situations which can be identified within organisations where dysfunctional behaviour is more likely to happen than not. Any textbook or article which lists '10 Ways to Spot a Fraudster' is misleading, possibly dangerously so, for reasons we will explore later.

It is important to familiarise ourselves with some of the background to understanding employee behaviour before we look at the possible individual motives for the fraudster. There are, of course, career fraudsters, individuals who are serial fraudsters and repeat offenders but fortunately these people are, in the context of fraud within organisations, comparatively rare. Clearly some areas of fraud such as identity theft or external computer frauds are the province of criminal gangs, but these are not the people we are interested in. Most individuals who commit fraud in organisations are not intrinsically bad people and research into convicted fraudsters shows that they often offend for a first and only time.

Quite often they are good people who go bad. So why does this happen? We will look at individual motivation and the psychology of the individual in Chapter 5, but for now we will consider the effect that the organisation, or more accurately, the prevailing culture and values of the organisation, has on the individual employee. Note that here we are referring to the real culture that operates within the entity, not the expressed hopes of policies and procedures.

Let us begin at the beginning. Organisations employ people and people have to be managed; no one is born with a full array of management skills. Good managers may have personal qualities such as:

- good communication skills
- empathy
- the ability to motivate, and
- patience.

which distinguish them from bad or ineffective managers, but it can be argued that the approach they take or the organisational culture within which they operate is

Table 4.3 Management speak – what we say is not what we mean

Management concept	Perceived meaning
Self-actualisation	Being left to battle on by yourself
Empowered	Expected to carry out an unfeasibly large workload without resources
Lean management	Had their resources cut
Horizontal organisation	Not knowing who to report to
Sweating the assets	Working with outdated unreliable equipment

one which, consciously or unconsciously, is largely following precepts laid down by one or other of the leading management thinkers of the last forty years.

Management thinkers such as W. Edwards Deming, Peter Drucker, Tom Peters and, in the UK, Charles Handy, became stars of what has become an industry producing a veritable avalanche of management theory and motivational tomes, all designed to get the best out of the workforce and increase wealth and happiness for everyone. As this is not a textbook on management theory we'll go no further than that. As ever, interested students will find huge numbers of books on management theory to study, from the erudite and obscure to the, frankly, bizarre.

The point is that, in following the precepts of these management thinkers, managers with influence can create an environment where the individual employee can be left behind. All too often the euphemisms used by higher level management are perceived by those lower down the organisation as something completely different.

Whilst Table 4.3 might be slightly tongue in cheek, it serves to illustrate that the message transmitted by management may not be the one received by employees. Situations where individual employees feel that the latest management initiative doesn't take into account their needs, or where they feel imposed upon or ignored, can be fertile breeding grounds for a rather different form of entrepreneurial behaviour.

 ## Motivation and the role of corporate culture

Research has identified that by far the most common motivator for an individual to commit fraud is greed. The desire to have more than they can achieve legitimately appears to overwhelm certain individuals who then go on to commit crime. We will come back to individual motivations later in Chapter 5, but first let us examine the role of corporate culture in creating the climate where fraud and other forms of dysfunctional behaviour can flourish.

This question of influence is important as the prevailing culture of an organisation, its mores and values, does have a great effect on the putative fraudster. Whilst an ethical culture may not, by itself, stop the determined fraudster who has spotted an opportunity, the prevailing ethos in the organisation may serve to blunt the self-rationalisations they must engage in to justify their actions to themselves.

Similarly an organisation which couples a strong set of ethical values with a successful HR policy towards its employees – i.e. successful in the sense that they feel valued and rewarded by the organisation – has created a strong deterrent to the kind of dysfunctional behaviour which may result in fraud. We will look at the creation of such policies and some useful aspects of HR in Chapter 7. This may also serve to isolate the dysfunctional individual and reveal them as a person who stands out from the crowd for the wrong reasons.

Individuals in organisations often have less time to consider the ethics of any course of action than might be supposed. Within organisations there are a conflicting mass of:

- targets
- instructions
- routines
- timetables
- precedents, and
- pressures.

which can result in individuals making instant, expedient decisions which may not be particularly ethical or moral but which 'get the job done'.

Once this behaviour becomes acceptable it becomes institutionalised and the consequent rationalisations overwhelm the moral high ground.

Where unethical practice is accepted in organisations or, worse still, rewarded, the temptation to help oneself is reinforced. Thus a corporate culture which values 'winning' at any price may well, for example, encourage deviant behaviour in executives by rewarding them by results irrespective of how those results were achieved. For example this can create a climate where, say, bribery and corruption to obtain contracts is considered acceptable and normal. A corollary to such behaviour may be that, in such an organisation, executives might think it perfectly acceptable to inflate their expenses or even to invent fictitious officials to bribe whilst, in reality, transferring the money to themselves.

Forms of deviant behaviour such as:

- misrepresentations to customers
- misselling of financial products
- petty pilfering
- price fixing
- exploitation of staff – for example, use of part-time or immigrant workers on low wages
- breaches of Health and Safety legislation
- excessive remuneration packages for senior executives
- bribery and corruption
- abusing expense accounts, or
- abuse of product labelling rules

can come to be seen as normal because, within the organisation, this type of behaviour is seen as acceptable, or even praiseworthy. The employees who do this are otherwise quite normal, reasonable moral citizens who simply rationalise their unethical behaviour as being 'part of the game'.

As we will see later when we look at socialisation, those employees who are determined to cling to some form of higher moral values are not accepted as part of the team and can thus be isolated or even forced out. They feel uncomfortable with the prevailing ethos and, consequently, leave.

In some situations, where employees feel the level of dysfunctionality is actually harmful, they may become whistle-blowers and inform on colleagues or the organisation in the interests of maintaining a level of ethical standards. In some notable cases involving the NHS, employees finally reported dysfunctional behaviour by other employees, which appeared to be being tolerated both by them and by their immediate managers as routine, which, in reality, had turned into physical and mental abuse of vulnerable individuals.

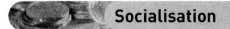
Socialisation

New individuals learn about the organisation they have joined and its culture through a number of socialisation processes. Clearly there are often formal induction procedures involving the dissemination of corporate literature including all the policies and mission statements. In ethical organisations subsequent socialisation processes reinforce the messages of ethical activity and the individual accepts the group norms of moral behaviour. However, in dysfunctional organisations the same is true of immoral behaviour – socialisation processes can perpetuate unethical or corrupt behaviour.

The processes act subtly to convince the individual that what they are doing is somehow ethical and right. The sense of values becomes distorted through processes of rationalisation, described later, reinforced by social interactions. One of the key considerations in the socialisation process involves the effect of working in groups or teams.

Group attractiveness

Researchers have identified that dysfunctional behaviour can exist among subgroups of employees such as teams or work groups, rather than being confined solely to certain individuals, although these might set the 'tone'.

Clearly some of what follows depends on the size of the organisation. The larger the organisation the more likely it is to contain groups and subgroups of employees who see themselves as part of, but at the same time separate from, the organisation as a whole.

On occasion these groups or subgroups establish a clear identity for themselves and create barriers between themselves and the rest of the organisation. This strengthens loyalty to the group within the framework of the organisation, or a part of the organisation, and creates barriers to entry into the group so that a new employee is only admitted gradually and is accepted only when the other members of the group are satisfied that the new member will abide by the group norms.

This can happen in divisions or subsidiaries which are remote from the centre and which have a degree of local autonomy. Managers strive to build a clear identity, maybe in the interests of 'team-building', which can serve to both increase group cohesion – the desired outcome – but which may also serve to set the group apart from the rest of the organisation if they don't feel part of the mainstream. Frauds in large organisations have frequently been found in subsidiaries or divisions which operate in this way as local management either strive to achieve unrealistic goals imposed upon them or decide to benefit themselves at the expense of what they perceive to be a rather faceless and indifferent organisation.

The processes of rationalisation and socialisation begin to work on the new individual who makes the effort to join the group. The alternative, for the new employee, can be isolation or even hostility as the group consciously or unconsciously seeks

> ### Exhibit 4.2   Socialisation at Arthur Andersen
>
> Former Andersen employees Barbara Ley Toffler and Jennifer Reingold looked at the
> fall of Arthur Andersen, the huge accounting firm which collapsed when their role
> in the Enron scandal was revealed, shortly to be followed by a similar problem at
> WorldCom. They said:
>
>> New recruits were socialised into believing that Arthur Andersen was a special
>> and exclusive organisation.
>>   Arthur Andersen offered something special: a way of life . . . getting a job
>> there meant making it. They all knew that their chances of making partner were
>> slim, and that they were in for a rigorous, exhausting few years as the grunts.
>> But there was a big fat brass ring at the end.
>
> In this way new recruits – or even more established employees – were less inclined to
> ask difficult questions or question dubious practices as this would undoubtedly nullify
> their chances of winning the brass ring.
>
> *Source:* Toffler and Reingold (2003)

to expel the member who doesn't fit. Research has shown that individuals are more
likely to be loyal to their immediate colleagues rather than to some concept of
corporate identity.

These groups can start to develop solutions to perceived or actual problems
which are outwith the codes of behaviour of the organisation as a whole. The more
desirable a group is to join the more readily individuals will be to surrender their
moral consciousness and accept rationalisations for actions which, outside work,
they would see as being unacceptable.

Ironically the emphasis on team-building and similar practices designed to create coherent identities can serve to emphasise these practices, which is not to say
that they should not be carried out, but that managers should be aware that if the
group norms become corrupted, such practices will tend to facilitate acceptance of
them rather than to counteract them.

Once the group norms are corrupted the process of socialisation works insidiously:

- Veterans act as role models for the dysfunctional behaviour and demonstrate
  acceptance of it.
- Newcomers are encouraged to affiliate with the veterans and develop behaviours
  which fit in with and please them.
- Newcomers have the rationalisations of dysfunctional behaviour reinforced by
  the group so that they begin to justify it to themselves and even to see it as being
  positive.
- Newcomers are encouraged to attribute any doubts they have to their own
  shortcomings, particularly naivety, so they are more susceptible to accepting
  dysfunctional behaviour as the norm.

Clearly the more senior the management demonstrating unethical or corrupt behaviour the greater the example shown to subordinates and the more readily it is
seen as being acceptable. Thus at Enron the roles of Geoffrey Skilling the CEO
and Kenneth Lay, the chairman, were seen as critical factors in developing the
dysfunctional culture which flourished there. Students are encouraged to read one

or more of the many books written, both by ex-employees of Enron and by former bankers and currency traders, which describe their acceptance of practices which, once they had left the fevered world of the office or trading desk, they wondered how they had ever accepted as being in any way normal.

The discontinuity between acceptable or encouraged behaviour at work and social norms and ethics outside work is rationalised by individuals by compartmentalising their lives – they become one person at work and another at home. In order to do this they frequently seek social support by associating with colleagues outside work or those in a similar situation. This reinforces the group norms and provides rationalisation and self-justification for their actions, so Enron employees socialised extensively with each other and bank traders related to other bank traders, all of which provided a framework for them to rationalise their actions which was often at the expense of personal relationships with individuals outside the group.

Socialisation techniques

Patterns of unethical behaviour can develop inside an organisation gradually and insidiously to such an extent that normal standards of ethics become distorted and the distortions become rationalised until employees feel that what they do is entirely justifiable. However, newcomers to the organisation have to be inducted into accepting these patterns of behaviour, and this is done through processes of socialisation.

Newcomers into organisations have to be socialised into the prevailing ethos or behaviour patterns of the entity they have just become part of. If they are not they will remain outsiders and may leave the organisation quite quickly if they find themselves, for whatever reason, unable to fit in with the prevailing ethos and are thereby excluded. They may even become a danger to existing employees who are engaging in dysfunctional behaviour by reporting to a third party, i.e. higher management, the auditors or a regulator, so it is important that they be socialised into the prevailing ethos as early as possible.

This may not be a conscious process. New employees are simply shown the processes and procedures and these are described as 'the way things are done around here' by an existing employee who is convinced that what they are doing is acceptable. Readers who wish to question these statements are referred to the books written by individuals who have worked for merchant banks, Enron, or as a chef in a busy kitchen where violence and abuse of low-level workers was endemic.

When they first become exposed to corrupt practices new employees often feel some sense of apprehension because of what psychologists call 'cognitive dissonance'. What this means is that in a dysfunctional entity the culture of the organisation, i.e. what are seen to be its behavioural norms, are at odds with the incoming individual's personal internal moral code and, perhaps, their experiences in other non-dysfunctional organisations. This creates an internal conflict between how they are expected to behave and what they instinctively feel is right.

Where the internal conflict is unsustainable the individual tends to leave the organisation, or seek relocation away from the dysfunctional area. Ironically this may serve to help perpetuate corrupt practices by weeding out those employees who might object to them or 'betray' them.

Research has uncovered some very powerful techniques whereby new individuals become socialised into tolerating dysfunctional or unethical behaviour.

Three techniques have been identified by researchers Anand, Ashforth and Joshi (2005). These are:

- co-optation
- incrementalism, and
- compromise.

Co-optation

In co-optation rewards are used to induce an attitude change towards dysfunctional behaviour. This sort of behaviour has been seen in the financial services industry where pension or savings policies from companies paying the highest commission were pushed at clients irrespective of whether or not they were suitable for their circumstances.

In extreme cases normal standards of business behaviour would be suspended simply because of the sheer size of fees available for co-operating in a dubious venture. One of the most notorious instances of this was Merrill Lynch's co-operation with an Enron earnings manipulation venture which involved Merrill Lynch purchasing three barges containing electricity generators floating off the coast of Nigeria. Enron booked the sale as income then subsequently bought the barges back and sold them on to a real buyer. Merrill Lynch trousered a substantial fee for engaging in the venture.

The prospect of reward in these situations often encourages individuals to resolve moral ambiguities which benefit them in some way, either financially or through enhanced prestige.

Incrementalism

In some organisations individuals are introduced gradually to corrupt acts. When the individual first meets instances of dysfunctional behaviour this creates a level of dissonance, as a consequence of which they tend to grasp at any rationalisations offered by their colleagues. Individuals gradually become immersed in corrupt behaviour to an extent that they would never have imagined themselves doing.

When the scale and extent of their behaviour is revealed or becomes apparent to them the individuals are often shocked and amazed that they could have engaged in such behaviour.

Compromise

Sometimes corrupt acts are carried out because individuals are seeking a solution to some problem or dilemma.

Exhibit 4.3 below gives an example of such a practice to illustrate the point that the individuals concerned could rationalise an immoral act as being the solution to a problem which, in a way, actually benefited their employer. In the example it could be argued that the used car dealership benefited through the payment of

---

Exhibit 4.3 **Spreading corruption: used car dealerships**

A study of used car dealerships in the USA discovered that dealers were paying bribes to sales staff in new car dealerships so they would get the best trade-in vehicles. If the used car dealers didn't get the good trade-in vehicles they would be sold on by the new car dealerships to other purchasers, which meant the used car dealers were cut off from the supply of quality used cars unless they paid the bribe.

In order to free up cash to pay these bribes the used car dealers often resorted to selling cars at an apparent undervalue – for example a £5,000 car would be invoiced and 'sold' officially at £4,500: £500 paid in cash by the purchaser could be used by the managers of the used car dealerships to pay the bribes. Thus the corruption spread.

Source: Anand, Ashforth and Joshi (2005)

---

bribes as, otherwise, they wouldn't get the quality vehicles. In such cases corruption becomes institutionalised as business practice.

This type of behaviour is frequently advanced as an excuse for the payment of bribes to secure contracts, i.e. that without such payments the work would not be forthcoming – 'that's just the way you do business here'.

Of course these methodologies are not mutually exclusive; indeed they may happen simultaneously and reinforce each other. New employees may be co-opted gently into the system through the identification of rewards: co-optation is encouraged as new employees are drawn in by tiny steps until finally employees are fully involved in the corrupt methods of working. Either they have abandoned most moral principles in the work environment or they consciously choose the unethical way over the other.

The point is that it is a matter of perceived choice. Unethical acts are more likely to be seen as justifiable if the individual perceives themselves to have a choice – the problem is that these are socialisation practices which often give only the *illusion* of choice and the changes from moral to immoral behaviour are subtle and appear to be not unreasonable.

 ## Rationalising unethical behaviour

This is an area which has not been given as much prominence by auditors and investigators as it might have been. Rationalisation and socialisation processes serve to reinforce each other. The dysfunctional employee recognises that the actions they are carrying out in order to retain presence in their group may not be socially acceptable outside work, and they must rationalise their actions to themselves in some way.

It is important to understand that corrupt individuals often do not see themselves as corrupt. Research into white-collar crime, which encompasses a rather wider spectrum of unethical behaviour than simple fraud, shows that individuals who are convicted of these crimes acknowledge the offence but go on to deny any criminal intent. They use a number of rationalising techniques which enable them to look at their unethical behaviour and justify it as normal business practice.

Table 4.4 Rationalising unethical behaviour

Strategy	Manifestation	Example
Denial of responsibility	Individuals claim they have little choice but to act unethically	• 'What could I do? I'm only a cog in the machine' • 'It's not my responsibility what they get up to in that department'
Denial of injury	Claims that what they did was a 'victimless crime', that no one was harmed so their actions are not corrupt	• 'It could have been worse' • 'Nobody died'
Acceptable	Individuals claim that unethical behaviour is normal in their particular industry	• 'Everybody does it' • 'You wouldn't get very far in this business if you weren't prepared to cut a few corners'
Denial of victim	The effect of the corrupt actions is seen as being the fault of the victim and not caused by the dysfunctional behaviour	• 'It's their own fault' • 'They chose to get involved' • 'They should have checked it out'
Appeal to higher loyalty	The actions are justified as they are part of a process with a much higher-order value	• 'I did what I did to help the company' • 'I did not report it because I am loyal to my boss and my colleagues'
Entitlement	Individuals justify immoral or illegal acts as being justified because they have 'earned' it due to unrewarded effort	• 'I'm entitled to this because of all the unpaid overtime I put in for this organisation' • 'They owe me a few perks – I work hard enough without anyone noticing'
Invidious comparison	The individuals compare themselves with others or attempt to rebut their accuser	• 'Others are worse than we are' • 'You don't have the right to criticise me'

Quite often in the course of a conversation, whether informally or in a formal setting such as a meeting, individuals will give away verbal clues which indicate their state of mind and which can provide pointers to the prevailing corporate culture. Apparently throw-away comments, such as those in Table 4.4, for example, can be a pointer for an investigator or auditor who cannot hope to fully understand the culture of an organisation they are not part of but who might be able to gain an insight into it through the actions of employees they come into contact with.

This attempt at understanding cannot but be an aid to their audit or investigation.

Gresham Sykes and David Matza, sociologists working on juvenile delinquency in the 1950s, established several forms of rationalisation which cropped up time and time again in their research. Their theory, which they called 'neutralisation' held that:

- people are always aware of their moral obligation to abide by the law, and
- they have the same moral obligation within themselves to avoid illegitimate acts.

Thus they reasoned that when a person did commit illegitimate acts, they must employ some sort of mechanism to silence the urge to follow these moral obligations. The theory was built upon four observations:

- Delinquents expressed guilt over their illegal acts.
- Delinquents frequently respected and admired honest, law-abiding individuals.
- A line was drawn between those whom they could victimise and those they could not.
- Delinquents were not immune to the demands of conformity.

This explained why individuals, other than those who might be described as full-time professional criminals, can drift between legitimate and illegitimate behaviours. As their own moral and ethical belief systems have not been replaced by a new, less stringent, code, they simply find a way of justifying dysfunctional behaviour so that it fits in with their personal standards of what they consider to be right or wrong. Later studies have postulated whether or not these rationalisations are used before or after the act, but for our purposes this is somewhat academic.

These types of rationalisation are used again and again by everyone from politicians to football hooligans, but inside an organisation they can be clues to the mindset of an individual and the culture within which they function. Research into this aspect of white-collar crime revealed that one way of doing this was for the criminal to distance themselves from the victim, and perpetrators of crime often adopted various distancing techniques such as:

- claiming their actions were caused by forces beyond the perpetrator's control – for example, some sort of need, real or perceived – 'I really needed the money'
- stating that anyone condemning the actions of the perpetrator was doing it out of spite as it was really not their fault – 'I don't know what came over me'
- the victim is demeaned or seen as stupid – 'serves them right'
- the victim is seen as somehow culpable – 'it's their own fault', or
- any loss or damage to the victim is minimised – 'well they're insured'.

Rationalisation in this way would serve to justify or explain the actions of the perpetrator to themselves, to assist them in coming to terms with their actions and to reconcile their criminal behaviour with their personal moral code or upbringing. This greatly eases the moral dilemma for those fraudsters who don't see themselves as criminals but who are aware of the immorality of their actions.

They seek to alleviate the pressure this places on their inner set of moral values by finding some form of rationale or justification for their actions. Over time commission of criminal acts becomes easier to live with and may even become almost routine. As criminologist Robert Cressey (1973) discovered, whilst the intial insurmountable problem was what prompted the commission of the fraud at first, as time progressed this was forgotten.

These neutralisation techniques are common in criminal gangs who engage in crimes such as identity theft or credit card fraud, where they badge their victims as being 'gullible fools', 'naive' or 'greedy' people who thus deserve to be ripped off.

Preventing rationalisation and socialisation of unethical behaviour

If dysfunctional behaviour becomes embedded in the organisation the effect can be catastrophic. Because rationalisation and socialisation processes are mutually reinforcing the effect of them can become entrenched and spread throughout the organisation. In consequence the organisation can lose the awareness of some of its practices being unethical and its internal checks and balances will fail to identify the dysfunctional behaviour which has become accepted as normal.

If and when this is pointed out by a third party the first response is denial. Frequently organisations will continue to carry on the dysfunctional behaviour or other behaviours which reinforce the original opinion. This can lead to loss of reputation, financial penalties or criminal prosecutions where the offences contravene the law. Managers must be aware of the propensity for such behaviours to become embodied in the organisation and should work actively to prevent it.

How can this be achieved if the behaviour is embedded in the very culture of the organisation? There are several key aspects which are crucial to this process:

- Lead from the front – senior management should set an example of honesty and openness.
- Train employees to:
  - question their actions – use examples such as the 'headline test', i.e. would they be happy if their actions became public knowledge?
  - recognise the use of euphemisms such as those quoted in Table 4.4 as part of the rationalisation process.
- Require internal audit or HR to review ethical policies and compliance with them as part of control procedures. Employees could be asked to certify that they have not been engaged in unethical or corrupt behaviour annually.
- Use performance evaluations to look at behaviour rather than simply outcomes. Many forms of performance evaluations are outcome-based – looking at the employees' ability to hit predetermined targets. The reliance on outcome-based performance appraisals is more likely to encourage unethical behaviour. This is true particularly where conditions are challenging and penalties for not hitting targets are severe. In such cases, if employees hit their targets the evaluator is often not tempted to question how the success has been achieved.
- Nurture an ethical environment within the organisation. This can require the establishment of ethical codes or practices and reinforcement of them by severely punishing breaches of the code. The code must not simply become a fig leaf sheltering bad practice – it must be real. The organisation must facilitate communication within the organisation, including whistle-blowing, and make it acceptable to question bad practice or unethical behaviour. Punishing whistle-blowers (Chapter 7) provides a rationalisation for not disclosing unethical practices and reinforces the group norms in situations where such behaviour flourishes.
- Review practices to ensure that dysfunctional behaviour has not been institutionalised. In large organisations, including those involved in the public sector where resources may be short, unethical practices may become the norm simply because they become the easy or most convenient way of achieving the desired outcome. Thus, for example, tendering procedures are bypassed or only paid lip

service to, safety concerns are ignored or rationalised away and accounts and budgets are manipulated to achieve desired or acceptable results.

- Introduce change agents or external reviewers. One of the ways of breaking down group bonds is to introduce change in such a way that it reformats ways of working and mixes up previously individual departments or subgroups. This often requires external input as insiders tend to be wedded to existing modes of operation. This must be handled carefully as change can produce uncertainty and is unsettling. Constant change can create resentment and barriers which go contrary to what management is trying to achieve and may, in fact, encourage the development of dysfunctional behaviour.

This, of course, is not a textbook on management theory and we will go no further than this. Hopefully this will give some indication for the forensic accountant when looking at organisations that the review starts with the ethos and culture not with the policies and procedures, which are often incidental to what is really happening.

Reviewing vulnerable high-risk areas within an organisation requires an understanding of behaviour and motivation, rather than a high level of accounting skills.

 ## Personal ethics

In her book *Trust and Honesty* (2006) Professor Tamar Frankel of Harvard University claims that deception has spread across the entire population and now affects not only corporate life but suppliers of healthcare, shoppers, applicants for jobs, students in examinations, journalists in their publications, competing athletes, scientists in research materials, politicians and even government employees. She claims that this is not confined to the USA but that deception and abuse of trust is a worldwide phenomenon.

She argues that, increasingly, individual personal morality is declining and that this is what underpins much of the deception and abuse of trust encountered in daily life.

When such deceptions are committed by significant figures in society such as high-profile businessmen, rock stars, film actors etc., they somehow validate the actions of lesser mortals like you and me. If this decline in personal morality is coupled with a failure of regulators to regulate and enforcers to enforce, the epidemic spreads.

It is against this background of an international decline in moral standards that the efforts of companies to create a corporate morality must be placed.

Clearly there is a general social disapproval of stealing and lying – these are not seen as desirable socially – for good reasons, and yet it transpires that, for example, employees who intellectually accept that it is wrong to take home company stationery, to surf the net on company time or to ring their relatives using the company phone nevertheless still do so. Thus the absolute morality which would prevent an individual from stealing someone's wallet containing £20 wouldn't stop them taking £20 worth of stationery home.

One survey, carried out in 2007 by online recruiter Fish4jobs, estimated that small-scale pilfering and office fraud cost UK business over £800m per year. Whilst this may not be the most statistically valid survey it does have similarities with some of the findings of the surveys carried out by the Institute of Business Ethics, referred to above, and is a good indicator of the scale of the problem.

According to the survey:

- Seventy-eight per cent of office workers have taken home stationery during the last year.
- Fifty-nine per cent put personal mail through the company post.
- Twenty per cent added £10 or more to expenses.
- Fifteen per cent inflated travel claims.
- Two per cent took a friend out for a meal and charged it to the company.
- Three per cent say they falsely claimed £50 or more back on an expenses claim.

Workers offer reasons for this behaviour:

- Eighty per cent of workers think their bosses regularly charge personal items to the company.
- Twenty per cent think that small 'fiddles' are an accepted part of company life – as long as they stay small.
- Twenty-nine per cent feel that getting a little back on expenses is acceptable because bosses often ask them for extras such as working late without pay.
- Sixty-seven per cent say taking home stationery is justified due to them having to make work calls from their personal mobile phone.

Here we can see examples of:

- The perception that the boss doesn't abide by the same rules which workers are expected to insofar as they are able to override procedures and controls. Note this may not be actually the case but the workers questioned perceived it to be, so the effect is the same.
- Workers getting their own back. They have to work late so they're getting a little unofficial 'reward'.
- It's part of corporate culture to use stationery and office equipment for personal gain.

These statistics illustrate the scale of the problem. Individuals distance themselves from the organisation and justify to themselves actions which, if carried out in another context, they might simply abhor. We assume that most individuals would not:

- steal £5 from a colleague or friend
- take a charity collection box, or
- shoplift from a department store

but are prepared to justify to themselves such 'small' things as minor pilfering of company stationery or use of computers and telephones for private purposes.

One study of workplace pilfering believed that at least some of it was 'hitting out at the boss, the company, the system or the state' and this may be true in some cases. Other researchers have identified it as a reaction to feelings of alienation at work, feelings that neither the company nor the boss actually care about you as an individual.

In most cases though experienced investigators say that the most common reason why people do this is because they can, because it's easy. Most small-scale theft occurs because it was simple to do and there appeared to be no prohibition against doing it – even where the individual's own internal moral code told them it was wrong.

This has nothing to do with need and everything to do with succumbing to temptation. It is interesting to note that one of the most common defences in cases of white-collar crime is the claim that upper management condoned it or that there was no clear policy in the organisation to distinguish right from wrong.

Of course there is a big difference at the individual level between minor pilfering and systematic embezzlement and, clearly, most individuals who 'acquire' things from their work would never contemplate larger-scale theft. However, the ease with which an individual under pressure, given the right opportunity, can turn small-scale pilfering into large-scale fraud is something all managers should consider.

Let us, for the moment, leave aside the morality of the serial fraudster and the morality of the individual who decides to actively defraud the organisation. What we are considering here are the attitudes of what we might describe as 'ordinary' individuals towards the organisations they work for.

Clearly, as we have seen above, corporate culture has some part to play. What is meant by that is the real culture of the part of the organisation in which the individual works, not the expectations of some form of imposed code generated by the HR department. However, that is not the only influencing factor, and personal ethics and personal feelings clearly have a part to play.

Research indicates that it is the interaction between:

- corporate culture
- personal feelings, and
- the level of corporate internal controls

which determines whether or not individuals will engage in anti-organisational acts such a pilfering, theft or sabotage.

Researchers are mostly of a consensus that such acts take place as:

- a form of rebellion – as a way of hitting out at the boss, the company, the system or the state, and/or
- as a challenge – to see if the individual can overcome the controls and restrictions placed upon them by the system, and/or
- where the culture of the organisation encourages such behaviour or has socialised employees into believing it is acceptable (see above).

We will return to these theories and look at personal motivation in more detail in Chapter 5, but for now we will simply note that where there is a dysfunction between a person's job and their ideas, attitudes and values they will adopt one of these strategies:

- Leave – resign or depart effectively withdrawing from the conflict.
- Breakdown – not resolve the conflict but struggle on in an increasingly dysfunctional way, subsequently becoming long-term sick or otherwise ineffective.
- Become alienated – this manifests itself in increased absenteeism, sabotage and 'fiddling'.

In the latter case it is important to recognise that often the motive isn't one of personal gain. The commission of a successful fraud or theft represents a triumph of the individual over the organisation. What the individual achieves by doing this is a demonstration of their creativity, a reassertion of their individualism in a conformist organisation.

Consequently in organisations where:

- the individual feels or is actively undervalued
- individuals feel or are isolated and unsupported

Exhibit 4.4   **Leeds City Council – revenge**

Steven Maw, a trusted accountant at West Yorkshire Passenger Transport Authority, a part of Leeds City Council, embezzled £870,000 by forging signatures and transferring monies out of the authority over a nine-year period. He hid the money in the accounts of a local church for which he was the treasurer. He was caught when he tried to buy a house in Scotland for £350,000 and the solicitors dealing with the purchase became suspicious of the source of the funds.

The court was told that Maw became aggrieved at his employers when they demanded the return of maternity pay paid to his wife after their baby had died when just a few hours old and required her to return to work. She became depressed and he became the only breadwinner for his large family.

Maw also felt unappreciated at work and aggrieved that his failure to qualify as a Chartered Accountant had hindered his promotion, despite his claims that he made vast sums of money for the Council.

He used the money to provide for his family and to pay bills, it was not spent on high living or excess.

The judge expressed surprise that the Council had apparently not noticed such large sums going missing over such a long period.

Source: Daily Mail (2007)

- relationships between parts of the organisation or between levels of management are dysfunctional, or
- individuals are engaged in monotonous, routine tasks with little opportunity to exercise some level of control or to assert their own individualism

they may well, if they don't leave or break down in some way, begin to act negatively and, if the opportunity arises, they are highly likely to collude or instigate theft or fraud even if their personal morality would, in other social situations, prevent them from acting in that way.

When asked why they started to commit fraud many individuals, apart from those who blatantly carried out their frauds for gain, were at a loss to come up with a convincing explanation – the problem was that, once they started, they couldn't stop.

Summary

- Organisations develop codes of behaviour through the use of policies and procedures.
- Personal morality may be determined by societal norms, not organisational factors.
- Small groups can become isolated and begin to feel infallible and invulnerable – this is known as groupthink.
- Poor management practice may isolate or alienate employees who will more readily accept dysfunctional behaviour.
- Dysfunctional behaviour in organisations may become normalised by management not asking too many questions.
- New employees can be socialised into dysfunctional behaviour.
- Those who do not accept group norms may leave or experience high levels of stress at work.

- Individuals engaging in dysfunctional behaviour develop techniques for rationalising it.
- These techniques may lead investigators to an appreciation of the real culture of the organisation.
- Employees may see dysfunctional behaviour as a challenge, a form of revenge or simply to relieve boredom.

Case study

You are an internal auditor working for the group Internal Audit Department of Megablast plc. You have been carrying out the review of one of the divisions, Meltwater, which sells to a wide range of retailers. Megablast's head office is based in Manchester but Meltwater is based in London. It has a number of branches in the Midlands and south. The division has developed a strong brand identity with its customers, many of whom are not aware that it is owned by Megablast.

Meltwater has its own senior management and this is the first internal audit visit for three years. It has been reporting increasing profits in a fiercely competitive market and costs are in line with budgets. There is thus a tendency for Head Office senior management to let them get on with it and not to interfere with what looks like a very successful business.

You have been at the offices of Meltwater for a day and this is your second day. Last night you had dinner with the financial controller who let slip that the next quarter's results would be even better than the last quarter's and that all of the executives in Meltwater were well on their way to earning a substantial bonus, perhaps even bigger than those for the last two years. You were not aware of the executive bonus scheme.

You decide to look at the sales side of the business in detail .One of the audit tests you have carried out is to check the sales staffs' expenses. Cross-checking the expenses claimed with diaries and visit reports, it soon became apparent that some staff were claiming and receiving travelling expenses for visiting customers when these members of staff were actually in the office.

You raise the matter with the sales manager. He explains that this is a practice he monitors carefully to ensure that the staff can obtain the money necessary to fit extras such as alarm systems and sat navs to the company cars they drive. He claims this is not for personal gain but is because the company refuses to pay for these items so he lets the staff do this 'unofficially'. It appears that the cars supplied to sales staff have very basic specifications, and compare badly with those supplied to similar staff in other companies and other divisions of Megablast.

In addition you query the policy which allows sales staff to vary the prices of goods from the official price lists and to grant 'special discounts' to selected customers. The sales manager said sales staff had very close relationships with customers and that this had always been the practice. Sales staff conferred with each other so they knew what prices were being offered to which customers. It was all designed to get customers to place bigger orders than they otherwise would. He did not interfere with the sales staff making deals but did 'keep an eye on things'.

The sales manager understood the concern you expressed about these irregularities and undertook to bring the practices to an end. However, he was most concerned that you did not include the matter in your report, as it could prejudice his prospects of promotion.

Required

- Comment on the management style of Meltwater and its relationship to Megablast.
- What issues have been raised in the running of the sales department? Will you accept or reject the sales manager's assurances and correction of the situation?

Bibliography

Albrecht, W.S. (1984) *Deterring Fraud – The Internal Auditor's Perspective.* Institute of Internal Auditors Research Foundation, Maitland, FL.

Anand, V., Ashforth, B.E. and Joshi, M. (2005) Business as usual: the acceptance and perpetuation of corruption in organisations. *Academy of Management Executive,* 19, 4, 9–23.

Berle, A. and Means, G. (1932) *The Modern Corporation and Private Property* (revised edition 1991). Transaction Publishers, Piscataway, NJ.

Cressey, D.R. (1973) *Other People's Money – A Study in the Social Psychology of Embezzlement.* Patterson Smith, Montclair, NJ.

Daily Mail (2007) Grieving father took revenge by stealing £875,000. www.dailymail.co.uk, 9 October.

Farrell, B.J., Cobbin, D.M. and Farrell, H.M. (2002) Can codes of ethics really produce consistent behaviours? *Journal of Managerial Psychology,* 17, 6, 468–490.

Frankel, T. (2006) *Trust and Honesty.* Oxford University Press, Oxford.

French, R., Raynor, C., Rees, G. and Rumbles, S. (forthcoming) *Organisational Behaviour.* John Wiley & Sons, Chichester.

Furnham, A. (2005) *The Psychology of Behaviour at Work.* Pyschology Press, Hove.

Institute of Business Ethics (2005) *Ethics at Work.* Institute of Business Ethics, London.

Institute of Business Ethics (2007) *Use of Codes of Ethics in Business.* Institute of Business Ethics, London.

Janis, I. (1972) *Groupthink,* 2nd edn. Houghton Miflin, Boston, MA.

Mars, G. (1984) *Cheats at Work – An Anthropology of Workplace Crime.* Allen & Unwin, London.

McLean, B. and Elkind, P. (2004) *The Smartest Guys in the Room.* Penguin, London.

Solomon, J. (2007) *Corporate Governance and Accountability.* John Wiley & Sons, Chichester.

Sykes, G.M. and Matza, D. (1957) Techniques of neutralisation: a theory of delinquency. *American Sociological Review,* 22, 664–670.

Toffler, B.L. and Reingold, J. (2003) *Final Accounting – Pride, Ambition, Greed and the Fall of Arthur Andersen.* Broadway Books, New York.

Whyte, W. (1952) Groupthink. *Fortune,* March.

Websites

www.aic.gov.au
www.bbc.co.uk
www.businessguardian.co.uk
www.criminology.fsu/crimtheory
www.dailymail.co.uk
www.ethics.iit.edu

www.fbi.gov

www.foresight.gov.uk

www.ibe.org.uk/codesofconduct.html

www.jstor.org/view

www.lexisnexis.com/uk/legal

www.money.cnn.com

www.psychnet-uk.com/dsm_iv

www.qestia.com

Chapter 5

The psychology of fraud

Chapter contents

Learning objectives

After studying this chapter you should be able to:

- Understand what is meant by the term 'red flag'
- Understand red flags in the context of employee behaviour
- Develop an understanding of the fraudster profile derived from research
- Consider the explanations of fraudsters for their actions
- Understand the criminological research into the motivation of the solo fraudster
- Understand the condition known as narcissism
- Appreciate why a theoretical understanding is important in fraud investigations

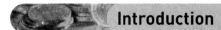

Introduction

In this chapter we are going to step into the complex and sometimes murky world of criminology, the sociology of crime, seeking the reasons why people do what they do based on their interactions with others.

We saw in Chapter 4 that individuals within organisations can be socialised into dysfunctional behaviour and that they will adopt a range of rationalisations to justify their actions to themselves. That chapter was concerned with dysfunctional behaviour as, perhaps, a group activity, or at least with behaviour condoned if not encouraged by the group. In Chapter 4 we discussed the socialisation of individuals within organisations into dysfunctional acts and established that where, broadly, there is considerable peer group pressure, individuals can become subsumed into the group. Much of this chapter does not apply in those situations.

In this chapter we are concentrating on the individual in situations where dysfunctional behaviour is not accepted or condoned, and is very much contrary to group norms. Here we are considering the motivations of the solo fraudster, the individual who acts alone in committing criminal acts of fraud against the organisation they work for and against what appears to be the prevailing ethos within the entity.

This chapter is confined to the embezzler. We don't consider the director or manager who distorts the accounts of an organisation in order to improve its share price or to trigger bonus payments. This is dealt with separately in Chapter 12. It may be that some of the motivations outlined here in connection with the individual fraudster acting against the organisation also apply in situations where fraud is committed by the organisation as a result of the activities of corrupt directors, but no specific reference will be made to this in this chapter.

It is important to establish at the outset that generally, people who engage in fraudulent behaviour are not necessarily people for whom a life of crime is predestined, nor are they always forced into it by desperation or poverty. People with good jobs, nice houses and loving spouses commit fraud for reasons which, at the time, seem to them perfectly justified. Some fraudsters are of course career criminals and we will see in these pages examples of individuals who have committed fraud more than once, but the vast majority of fraudsters are first-time offenders and, once their sentence is over, will never engage in such acts again – even where they may have the opportunity to do so.

However, it is equally important to realise that people who do commit fraud are determined and tough – they have to be to carry on their nefarious activities for any length of time. They understand that what they have done is a crime, even if this feeling may dissipate if the fraud continues for a long time or they leave the organisation with their crime undetected. As we saw in Chapter 4, the acceptance by the individual of their crime is often contrary to their internal moral code and this can create a dissonance within them which may eventually manifest itself in stress, depression or irrational behaviour at work.

However, other individuals are able to tolerate high levels of dissonance for some time and may never display the slightest hint of irrational behaviour or stress. There are many cases of fraudsters who have been able to hide their inner feelings so well for years that colleagues are surprised when their crimes are uncovered.

Reviewing the exploits of convicted fraudsters who have carried on their activities over a period of years indicates that:

- they are autonomous individuals capable of working alone
- they are intelligent individuals with skills which enable them to appreciate and circumvent internal controls
- they are good at telling lies, particularly to the auditors
- they are mentally tough – they meet their colleagues every day and continue to work in an area where they are committing crime without betraying themselves, and
- their defences often only crumble once they have been exposed.

Crime is committed by individuals. Generally speaking, organised professional criminal gangs aside, it is not a team game, but even if it were, each member of the team is an individual capable of making choices.

In this chapter we will look at the psychological theories which seek to explain why individuals commit fraudulent acts and what might lie behind the actions of fraudsters and those who would seek to enrich themselves illegally through deception and unethical behaviour. There is no one answer and, indeed, there may be no definitive answer at all. However, a basic understanding of some of the underlying psychological concepts is a useful tool in the forensic accountant's toolbox and may assist them in highlighting vulnerable areas of the business and, in reviewing patterns of behaviour, indicating the presence of possibly dysfunctional individuals.

A word of warning. Engaging in amateur psychology, whilst fascinating, is, if acted upon precipitately, extremely dangerous and should be avoided at all costs. The forensic investigator should not be distracted from evidence-based conclusions simply because the behaviour of an individual fits some sort of checklist of 'The ten ways to spot a fraudster' so beloved of many articles and textbooks.

When an individual is caught out and revealed as an embezzler the reaction among friends and colleagues is often shock and amazement. We are constantly surprised at the capacity of others to commit illegal and immoral acts – yet should we be? Are the signs there if only we could read them? We will look at the so-called 'red flags' of fraud and consider the reasons why these may not be as useful as some textbooks and articles would have you believe.

The psychology of fraud is not the story of the professional criminal, by and large. Although there are some serial fraudsters out there – and some of their stories are told in this book – most individuals who transgress do it only once. Leo Tolstoy put it well when he wrote 'the seeds of crime are in each of us', calling attention to the possibility that all of us are capable of committing crime at some level and in some degree given sufficient motivation and pressure. Who among us has not taken a pencil home from work or used the Internet at work for looking up private matters?

A considerable proportion of total fraud is, of course, practised by professionals, criminal gangs who use identity theft, stolen credit cards, computer hacking and similarly blatant techniques to appropriate money and goods for themselves. This chapter is not concerned with them; they are criminals and the province of the criminologist who studies burglars and car thieves. The individuals we are concerned with here are the so-called 'good guys' the senior managers like Paul Hopes (see Exhibit 5.1) who turn to fraud to give themselves another life, the civil servant who starts to embezzle because they are bored and angry with their employer, the executive directors who deliberately distort the financial statements and mislead

> ### Exhibit 5.1 — Fraud example – the quiet man in the purchasing department
>
> A 58-year-old accountant, Paul Hopes, pleaded guilty to embezzling £3.7m from retailer Toys 'Я' Us over a two-year period.
>
> Hopes had worked for the company for twenty-three years and lived quietly with his wife and two children in a modest house in Reading. However, he had a secret life of five star hotels, call girls and fast cars. He spent over half a million pounds on food, drink and entertainment, reputedly giving thousands of pounds to call girls and a Bentley to one he had become infatuated with. There is no suggestion his wife and family knew anything about his illicit activities.
>
> Hopes was the purchase ledger manager at the head office in Maidenhead and apparently carried out the fraud using bogus invoices and arranging for payment into a bank account he controlled.
>
> One of his colleagues said 'We just knew him as Paul from finance. He was a quiet, likeable chap. He just didn't strike you as that kind of person . . . getting arrested is the one memorable thing I can remember him doing'.
>
> *Source:* Marlow and Watts (2009)

the auditors in order to make their financial statements look better – ordinary people who, for their own reasons, turn to crime.

Why do they do these things?
What makes good people go bad?

Red flags

Any accountant who has spent any time with auditors or has read any of the literature on frauds will be familiar with a list of so-called 'red flags', often described as the classic indicators of fraudulent activity.

In the early days of the motor car in Britain, at a time when most personal transport was centred around the horse or people didn't have personal transport and walked, the law stated that this new-fangled machine had to be preceded at a distance of some 100 yards by a man with a red flag. This gave pedestrians and riders advanced notice of the horrors of the internal combustion engine and slowed the vehicle down to the pace of a brisk walk. The term red flag has thus become a synonym for any sort of warning or indicator that 'here is something to look out for'.

There are innumerable articles written about fraud in the accountancy and business press, usually with a title like 'How to recognise fraud in your organisation', and many of them contain this list of aspects of individual behaviour meant to arouse suspicion. Many textbooks on auditing and fraud also include them as a guide for investigators, as if they were some infallible guide to detecting the perpetrator.

According to these red flags the popular image of the lone embezzler is of a quiet little man who:

- gets on with his job and is a model employee
- is a good timekeeper, often in work early and stays late

- doesn't really talk to anyone or is polite but not familiar
- never takes a holiday, and
- never lets anyone else 'interfere' with what he's doing.

However, this profile is likely to be far from the truth. Research carried out, notably by accounting firm KPMG in their *Profile of a Fraudster* (2007), shows that the typical fraudster is much more likely to be a middle-aged senior male manager with experience and authority, rather than the stereotypical secretive, nervous loner. In many documented fraud cases the actions of the perpetrator came as a revelation to their colleagues and friends and only with hindsight did a couple of these so-called red flags appear to exist. In many cases the individuals were high-profile senior people in positions of trust, appeared to be ordinary individuals who didn't display any strange territorial propensities and took very nice holidays with their families.

Red flags and cognitive dissonance

Although this list of red flags may have become something of a cliché, that does not mean that there isn't any truth behind them, and it is a brave forensic accountant or internal auditor who ignores these warning signs completely and for very good psychological reasons.

The classic red flags for spotting suspicious behaviour in individuals are:

- Unwillingness to take holidays or breaks.
- Sudden changes in previous behaviour patterns.
- Increasingly erratic behaviour including irritability and shortness of temper.
- Increasing levels of complaints about superiors or the organisation.
- Increasing tendency to blame others.
- Evasive behaviour, e.g. unwillingness to look people in the eye.

Some of these aspects of behaviour are understandable when considered from a psychological perspective. The individual committing fraud is likely to be under stress either through:

- fear of discovery and its consequences, or
- because they are experiencing cognitive dissonance.

The inner conflicts which arise because of their problem manifest themselves through these symptoms.

As we saw in Chapter 3, the term 'cognitive dissonance' is used to describe the feeling of discomfort that results from holding two conflicting beliefs. When there is a discrepancy between beliefs or behaviours, something must change in order to eliminate or reduce the dissonance. In cases of fraud the conflict is between the inbuilt moral sense individuals have and the knowledge that what they are doing is illegal and very much against their sense of ethics. Fraudsters have been known to express relief that they have been caught because it brings their inner conflict to an end, even though it brings with it other problems not least the prospect of imprisonment and disgrace.

The key point, and one that must be emphasised, is that the actual red flag is a notable *change* in behaviour, not a consistent pattern of behaviour. Remember that some people are naturally quiet, secretive or antisocial – this does not mean they are fraudsters! They may not be the most popular employees but they could be the hardest working and most productive and so show up their more gregarious colleagues who are spending too much time at the coffee machine, thus creating resentment which manifests itself as suspicion.

Research into patterns of behaviour, based on anecdotal evidence from convicted fraudsters, indicates that most people begin their fraudulent activity after they have been working for the organisation for a while, so a 'normal' behaviour pattern is often quite well established. What the indicators are endeavouring to show is that a change in behaviour may be indicative of the commencement of fraudulent activity on the part of an individual and a consequent increase in stress levels. This increase in stress, the theory goes, manifests itself through behavioural change but, of course, behavioural change in an individual can be brought about for many reasons other than guilt or stress related to criminal activity; domestic pressures, job stress and illness can all contribute to a person exhibiting different behaviour from that previously displayed.

These indicators are useful only insofar as they represent certain conditions which might be associated with the likelihood or possibility of fraud but, as we have seen, they are far from infallible. They should be treated with great care by investigators. Some commentators go so far as to say that paying too much attention to these so-called warning signs can act as inhibitors on auditors who may be prevented from looking for other indicators of fraud if the red flags aren't present in individual behaviour. There is a temptation to assume that individuals who are acting normally are behaving normally.

The indicators should be read in the context of what research, which we referred to briefly above, has revealed concerning the behaviour of individuals who have committed fraud.

Employees who commit fraud

In 1907, sociologist E.A. Ross, writing about white-collar crime in general (including the excesses of industrialists and political leaders), put it colourfully:

> the villain most in need of curbing is the respectable, exemplary, trusted personage who, strategically placed at the focus of a spider web of fiduciary relations is able, from his office chair, to pick a thousand pockets, poison a thousand sick, pollute a thousand minds or imperil a thousand lives.

Perhaps a little excessive, but his key point resonates over 100 years later. An exemplary trusted person involved in financial dealings fits very well with modern research into the profile of the typical fraudster.

International accounting firm KPMG in their *Profile of a Fraudster*, based on their experience of fraud investigations carried out by the firm, extrapolated the details of 360 cases across Europe. Based on their findings they describe the profile of a typical fraudster thus:

- Seventy per cent of fraudsters were between the ages of 36 and 55 years old.
- Eighty-five per cent of perpetrators were male.
- In 68 per cent of profiles the perpetrator acted independently.

- In 89 per cent of profiles the fraudsters were employees committing fraudulent acts against their own employer, 20 per cent involved complicity with an external perpetrator, resulting in the conclusion that in only 11 per cent of all profiles the companies were attacked purely by externals.
- Sixty per cent of all fraudsters were members of senior management (including board members). An additional 26 per cent of profiles involve management-level people, bringing the total to 86 per cent of profiles involving management.
- In 36 per cent of cases the perpetrator had worked for the company for between two and five years before committing the fraud; in 22 per cent of cases the perpetrator worked for the organisation for more than 10 years. In only 13 per cent of cases had the perpetrator worked for the organisation for less than two years.
- The internal fraudster works most often for the finance department, followed by operations/sales or as the CEO.

KPMG found that greed and opportunity (which when taken together account for 73 per cent of profiles) were the overriding motivations for fraud. In more than half the profiles no prior suspicion existed, but in 21 per cent of profiles the companies did not act, even though there was prior suspicion.

Perpetrators were able to commit fraud primarily by exploiting weak internal controls, in 49 per cent of profiles, and were mainly detected by whistle-blowers or management reviews (46 per cent).

This profile matches data collected as part of research carried out in 2003 into fraud offenders in Australia and New Zealand by the Australian Institute of Criminology and Price WaterhouseCoopers. Researchers investigated 155 serious fraud cases and came up with a profile of the typical fraudster as being:

- male
- aged in their mid-40s
- educated to secondary level with some having professional qualifications
- company directors or involved in accounting duties and having relatively stable employment
- no prior criminal record, and
- acting alone in the commission of the offence.

Whilst this may give us some sort of general profile, what we need to look at are the forces which can turn a responsible, respectable, middle-aged manager or executive into an embezzler or someone who sets out to deceive investors, bankers and staff by deliberately falsifying their organisation's financial position.

Fraud research

There are two significant problems with researching behaviour and motivations by asking convicted criminals about their crimes:

- Such surveys only include information about the perpetrators who have been caught. These are the criminals who have made the wrong decisions or made mistakes and have thus been caught, so are their conclusions valid?
- Participants may present a distorted view of their decision-making patterns – for example burglars interviewed in prison often engage in 'rational reconstructions'

of the criminal event. Research evidence has shown that incarcerated burglars tend to reinterpret past behaviour to reflect an overly rational portrait of their crimes. They often describe how crimes should occur and not how they actually happened.

The biggest problem in relying on these types of populations for research purposes is that the experiences of captured and confined offenders may not be representative of the larger population of offenders. Their arrest and conviction are prima facie evidence that they have been unsuccessful and, therefore, they may differ in important ways from offenders who did not get caught. Clearly it can be argued that these people made ineffective decisions and are therefore atypical of offenders generally. However, criminological researchers, who have based a lot of their work on confined felons, for obvious reasons, conclude that to suggest that the people who have been apprehended differ significantly in their motivations and behaviour to commit the crime in the first place from so far undetected criminals seems unlikely.

Despite these and similar misgivings about interviewing offenders who are incarcerated or at the least known to criminal justice agencies, there is little hard evidence that these offenders think, act or report information differently from active offenders contacted independently of criminal justice sources. It cannot be denied that the interview setting, i.e. interviews taking place in jail, can colour a narrative or that interviews with a researcher are not different from what might be said elsewhere, yet offenders appear to report similar patterns of behaviour, regardless of how they were originally contacted or where they are interviewed.

Assuming therefore that the samples taken are representative of the offender population in total, i.e. the sum of detected and so far undetected fraudsters, there are some other aspects of the research which should also be taken into consideration.

- They are self-selecting – for example, only those fraudsters willing to be interviewed are included in these surveys.
- Establishing motivations can be difficult as quantitative surveys require data to be categorised in a certain way – so 'greed', for example, may well cover a multitude of more complex rationales.

Convicted fraudsters in their own words

With those caveats it is interesting to hear the words of convicted fraudsters – they do shed light on the attitudes and motivations which resulted in their actions. Research carried out by Professor Martin Gill of the University of Leicester (2005), on behalf of independent risk consultants Protoviti, examined the case histories of 16 convicted offenders and carried out face-to-face interviews with them over a period of months.

He identified these common factors between them – all of which fit the profile suggested by KPMG:

- All the offenders were male.
- They ranged in age between 24 and 62.
- Their jobs ranged from junior administrator to director – most were in senior or semi-autonomous positions.

- All were educated, some to degree level and some with a professional qualification.
- Reasons for offending included greed and debt, boredom, lack of life structure, temporary insanity and in one case blackmail.

Interviews with these offenders revealed some interesting views:

- Some interviewees claimed that a corrupt industry or company structure facilitated their offending. This applied particularly in the construction industry, which was considered to be riddled with corrupt practices, and in the brewing industry which, by its nature, handles a lot of cash, including cash payments for loans and mortgages.
- Some felt poorly treated by their employers, either through low pay or inadequate recognition, but mainly because they felt unsupported by either senior management or the organisation itself.
- Committing the offences was easy because of weak systems and/or a lack of fraud prevention strategies.
- Because the position of trust they were in gave them the autonomy and lack of visibility to commit the offences it enabled them to feel they wouldn't be detected.
- Most offenders had acquired the knowledge and skills they needed in the normal course of employment.
- The audit function (whether this was an internal or external audit function is not made clear) was rarely perceived as a threat although it did actually detect some frauds and contributed to the identification of some offenders. Analysis of detected frauds indicates that internal audit is considerably more effective that external audit in detecting fraud (Chapter 2).
- Whatever their initial reason for committing the offence, most continued do it because they enjoyed the benefits of having money.

Once caught some offenders admitted they were relieved it was over but others were shocked. In addition to having to repay the money taken, which resulted in them having to cash-in pension schemes and sell homes, they received what they considered to be long prison sentences. No one said they would commit the offences again.

Professor Gill accepts that his study is more than likely to suffer from the problems of revisionism – that convicted criminals tell lies in order to put themselves in a favourable light or to paint themselves as innocent victims – so some of the comments quoted here should be read in that light.

The group of fraudsters interviewed, as Professor Gill accepts, may well be a significantly biased group, insofar as it may include the most flamboyant, narcissistic offenders who may have completely different motives and methods from their more circumspect, silent convicted colleagues not anxious to discuss their crime. The group also does not include any women but there is no indication that Professor Gill deliberately chose to exclude them – there may not be any who fitted the criteria or, at least, none wishing to talk.

The interviews were semi-structured so the participants could develop any particular theme and were not confined within a strict methodology or timetable. It was made clear that the interviews were confidential and no names would be recorded so there was no need to lie. The interviewees were not required to answer any question they didn't wish to, which again took away any reason to lie, and were given the chance to ask any questions before the interview started to allay any disquiet they may have felt. Wherever possible information given was compared with other sources such as newspaper reports etc., although these were acknowledged as not being authoritative.

As most of the offenders had admitted their crime it was likely that they would be relatively forthright. Two of the offenders had not admitted guilt, and one charged with conspiracy still firmly believed in his innocence despite his conviction. The interviewees were of high status and committed their frauds in various ways.

The key individuals were:

William – senior manager convicted of conspiracy to defraud his company of £25m – he claims he is an innocent scapegoat of powerful executives.

Eric – owner/manager property developer who defrauded the business of which he was the majority shareholder.

Robert – defrauded employers of £65,000 by faking payouts on insurance claims. He kept the payments below the authorisation limit of £750, paying friends and sharing the proceeds; he circumvented internal checks and knew the audit procedures.

Geoffrey – a senior manager who defrauded the company of £400,000 by setting himself up as an independent contractor and signing off his own invoices. There were no internally regulated financial systems.

Alan – a sales director defrauded the company of £140,000. He knew he would be caught but didn't care, he had previously been convicted of cheque and credit card fraud and had run into debt.

Peter – worked as a quantity surveyor and is a serial offender. He defrauded his employers of £900,000 by setting up false companies and paying himself.

George – a communications manager with a signing authority of £75,000. He stole £250,000 in a two-month period but cannot account for his motivation as he really didn't need the money. The fraud was uncovered by his successor.

Jeremy – operated a private company in tandem with his duties for a parent company. He stole £240,000 by claiming the salaries and expenses of staff who had left and altering payrolls and work rosters for staff who were working for his company, not their employers. He was solely responsible for the management of the financial systems of his private company and the work carried out for the parent company.

A not untypical range of fraudsters.

In response to questions on motivation they said:

> when the opportunity presented itself to take the money I did. I was in a mad spending frenzy . . . I got used to having the money
>
> (Geoffrey)
>
> I just did not have enough money to do the things I wanted to do
>
> (Robert)

Those two individuals admitted that doing what they did was motivated primarily by greed.

Other motivations cited in the report include:

- Boredom and lack of structure to life ('the main reason was boredom and being stuck in a rut' – Alan).

- The search for status ('the reason I committed the offences was basically the will to want to succeed and being seen to do so and to be successful in the eyes of those around me' – Peter).
- Temporarily unbalanced ('I had been under a lot of pressure . . . high-level job . . . company experiencing turmoil . . . was not well supported . . . opportunity presented itself ' – George).
- Organisational cultures and structures ('feelings of being neglected and isolation. There was no formal appraisal system. We just got letters saying we were doing a good job. No formal reviews were done. There were no formal systems in place to recognise the needs of managers' – Jeremy).

Their views concerning the effectiveness of company procedures, particularly of the weak HR procedures encountered by so many, and the role, or lack of it, of the audit function are instructive. In the cases quoted in the report the fraudsters were able to identify:

- a weakness in the systems, because no proper controls were instigated:

> there appeared to be no coherent sales or purchase ledger or IT systems
>
> it was easy to set up a situation whereby I instructed accounts payable to set up an account, and present an invoice which would be sent by BACS straight to my account as a sole trader; no one questioned the invoices
>
> (Peter)

- a lapse in controls because they were not enforced:

> the purchase order systems were not enforced. Some suppliers would ask for a purchase order number but most did not
>
> (Geoffrey)
>
> third-party claims were collected loosely within case files so if a file was checked then it could always be argued that the information had fallen out
>
> (Robert)

- a weakness in controls caused by inexperienced or uncommitted finance staff or poor systems:

> the finance department was staffed by temporary staff and overseen by one accountant
>
> (Geoffrey)
>
> the company accounts systems were so antiquated it would take nine months to get paid . . . we at the sharp end needed to act quickly and our agents needed the money . . . I tried to ensure that all agencies that issued had a slush fund which we could top up
>
> (George)

- active complicity in doubtful practice by employers which they exploited for their own ends:

> this was the dirty end of the business – no one wanted to know
>
> (Gregory)
>
> it was not official practice but it was accepted as the way things were done; other executives did the same thing
>
> (Geoffrey)

Their comments about auditors are equally scathing:

> auditors have no experience of business. They're just people who know about figures but not business practice
>
> (William)
>
> audits were no problem. You have to remember how powerful I was. I knew the audits were no problem. I knew what they looked for
>
> (George)
>
> accountants can only work on the figures they have got, audit the same. Auditors came to see me and I just lied to them and gave them false pieces of paper and that was that. The checking process was abysmal. I was not worried because I have twenty years' experience of auditors . . . the lack of attention to detail, the lack of knowledge in auditing and accounting . . . there was no interrogation from audit and that was good for me
>
> (Eric)

Another revealing comment came from an individual we will call Grant who addressed an ICAEW conference on fraud in 2007. He had received cash payments amounting to £1.5m from customers in return for writing off their debts. He had faced redundancy five times in eight years and felt betrayed. His comment was 'I was confident the company would not find out. They didn't have the mechanisms for discovering it.'

He was caught out incidentally in another investigation by the police: the company had not detected him.

Exhibit 5.2   The unassuming bookkeeper – Sharon Hibbert

Unassuming middle-aged mother of two Sharon Hibbert was just the £15,000-a-year bookkeeper at a seafood company, while her husband ran a tiny haulage business.

But the truth was that the £29,000 Audi TT coupé in which she drove to work every morning and all the other trappings of their luxury lifestyle were funded by fraud. Over a seven-year period, the 50-year-old had stolen more than £1 million from the business where she was a trusted and respected employee.

Mrs Hibbert was bookkeeper and company secretary at BHJ UK Seafood in Hull and began pocketing cash in 1998. Soon afterwards she and her husband Peter, who made just £14,000 a year from his haulage business, started moving up in the world dramatically.

After improving their home near Beverley, East Yorkshire, including building a koi carp pond in the garden, they bought a riverside apartment now worth £112,000. The pair then moved into a £280,000 country home in the nearby village of Old Ellerby boasting garaging for five cars, grand stables and a two-acre paddock.

One neighbour said:

> We were told they had won the Lottery. We had no reason to believe she had done anything wrong. They seemed a very nice couple. At one point they ran out of space on the drive for all the toys. There was a yellow convertible sports car in the garage, two motorcycles and a great big six-wheel caravan. They spent thousands landscaping the back garden. It is one giant pond. They tried to buy more land because they wanted to extend.

The neighbour added 'I used to see her go to work near the dock in her personalised Audi TT and wonder how she got away with it. I'll never know how her bosses swallowed it.'

Mrs Hibbert was sent to prison for four years and her husband for three.

Source: Tozer (2006)

The psychology of fraud

Many criminologists hold that crime cannot be divorced from the society within which it flourishes and, consequently, many of the causes of crime can be attributed primarily to sociological factors such as upbringing and interpersonal relationships. Others take the view that it is solely the motivation of the individual which is the relevant factor, that ultimately we all act alone and it is this which determines whether or not individuals will be tempted into criminal acts.

Serious research into the motivations underlying what is generally known as 'white-collar crime' didn't really begin until 1939 with the work of Edwin Sutherland. Since then there has been some extensive research which we will summarise here in an attempt to shed light on the inner workings of the fraudsters mind. Students who wish to read further will find sources in the bibliography at the end of the chapter.

The work of Edwin Sutherland

In 1939 American criminologist Edwin Sutherland published a seminal work called *White Collar Crime* (1949). Until then the causes of crime were more or less considered to lie with the so-called 'lower orders', mostly working-class individuals made criminal by want and deprivation or through poverty and ignorance. In those days it was commonly accepted, at least in the USA, that the middle and upper classes did not commit crime. That they were somehow above such sordid behaviour, or so society would like to have believed.

Early criminological theories broadly held that criminal behaviour was inherent – that some people were genetically predisposed to criminality. The extreme end of these theories led to biological theories of the causes of criminal behaviour such as that propounded by Cesare Lambroso in the seventeenth century, who postulated that you could detect a criminal by the shape of his head. Surprisingly this preposterous notion took a long time to fade; as late as 1939 anthropologist Ernest Hooten in the USA was measuring criminals in an attempt to identify anthropomorphic indicators of potential criminality.

Whilst Hooten was wielding his tape measure in vain one of his fiercest critics, Edwin R. Sutherland, was beginning to reshape the landscape of criminology.

Sutherland took a different view to the prevailing wisdom that crime was poverty based and very much a lower or working-class activity, or, alternatively, linked to race, gender, age or, as we have seen, to biology. He started looking at the interactions and patterns of learning between individuals in groups and he developed a theory which he called 'differential association'.

The theory of differential association postulated that behaviour is learned through a process of communication within intimate personal groups. These groups teach what Sutherland called 'definitions' (which included skills, motivations, attitudes, and rationalisations) either favourable or unfavourable to the violation of the law. Criminal behaviour results, said Sutherland, when an individual is exposed to an excess of definitions favourable to the violation of the law over those definitions which are unfavourable; in other words the tendency of the group would be to break the law.

Sutherland examined four types of crime committed by large corporations:

- false advertising
- restraint of trade
- unfair labour practices, and
- patent, copyright, and trademark infringements.

He uncovered 980 violations of these laws among the 70 businesses that he studied (an average of 14 per company). Ninety per cent of the corporations were habitual offenders, with four or more violations. Sutherland relied on differential association theory to explain these crimes, arguing that young executives learn definitions favourable to the violation of the law through the routines of business practice. They were socialised into crime (Chapter 4). As these crimes were committed by middle-class businessmen this, of course, at the time directly contradicted the notion that crime was a working-class activity.

Sutherland considered this type of crime a greater threat to society than street crime because it promoted a cynicism and distrust of basic social institutions. It had, he said, a corrosive effect on the attitudes of managers of corporations to society as a whole, to the environment in which they conducted business, to their customers and to their employees. He called it 'white-collar crime' and defined it as 'a crime committed by a person of respectability and high social status in the course of his occupation'.

He advanced the theory:

> that persons of the upper socio-economic class engage in much criminal behaviour; that this criminal behaviour differs from the criminal behaviour of the lower socio-economic class principally in the administrative procedures that are used in dealing with the offenders and that variations in administrative procedures are not significant from the point of view of causation of crime.

Controversially, Sutherland drew attention to activities not normally included within the scope of conventional criminology at the time, namely crimes committed by so-called 'respectable people'.

Using his theory of differential association we can postulate that dishonest employees will corrupt honest employees if that is the prevailing culture of the social grouping in the workplace. We have seen in Chapter 4 how employees can be socialised into dysfunctional behaviour and modern research tends to bear out Sutherland's theories, in principle, even if they may not be as supportive of the mechanisms by which he felt individuals are influenced. This theory of differential association would, of course, work the other way insofar as a prevailing culture of ethical behaviour would, on this basis, inhibit the commission of dishonest acts.

The importance of Edwin Sutherland to our consideration of the psychology of the fraudster lies not so much in his theories – which are significant, *but* only really insofar as they relate to the behaviour of individuals within groups – but in the fact that he opened up a whole new field of criminology. His work was to be built on by others but he was the first – the father of the discovery of white-collar crime.

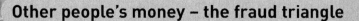

Other people's money – the fraud triangle

Although Sutherland is credited with inventing the term 'white-collar crime' and, as it were, starting the criminological ball rolling in the direction of crime committed by so-called respectable people, it was American sociologist Donald Cressey who began to look at the motivations of the solo embezzler.

In his classic 1953 text *Other People's Money: A Study in the Social Psychology of Embezzlement*, Cressey set out the path to embezzlement for the first time in a book which, although its principles have been embellished or enhanced through the work of others, has fundamentally stood more or less unchallenged since he wrote it.

Cressey called these solo embezzlers 'trust violators' simply because that is what they were, individuals who had betrayed the trust of employers and colleagues by taking money, goods or information which was not theirs to have and using it for their own purposes. What fascinated him was the hidden driver that prompted this breach of trust. What made someone who was not a criminal commit such an egregious act?

Cressey's view was that:

> trusted persons become trust violators when they conceive of themselves as having a financial problem which is non shareable, are aware this problem can be secretly resolved by violation of the position of financial trust and are able to apply to their own conduct verbalisations which enable them to adjust their conceptions of themselves as trusted persons with their conceptions of themselves as users of the entrusted funds or property.

His theory was that individuals who become trapped in fraud do so because they have a perceived need which they feel they can't share. Note that this may not be:

- an actual need, or
- something which an outsider would necessarily recognise as a need.

Rather it is what seems at the time to be an insurmountable problem so powerful that the only way to deal with it, as the individual sees it, is a course of action that will compel them to overcome their fears, inhibitions and personal morality to such an extent that they will see the commission of fraud to be a solution rather than a problem.

Among these motivating factors Cressey cited:

- an inability to pay debts, which might be particularly relevant to someone in a position of trust who might be expected to behave in a certain way
- an effort to regain a loss of status representing a personal failure, perhaps caused by bad planning or wrong decisions
- a wish to associate with individuals of a higher social standing but which can't be afforded at present income levels – which is, of course, basically greed but it stems from an inability to renounce the aspiration to be part of a desired group rather than greed represented, say, by a desire to spend money on high living and call girls, or
- resenting the position in the organisation the individual occupies, involving feelings of being overworked, under-appreciated or under-rewarded.

Figure 5.1 The fraud triangle

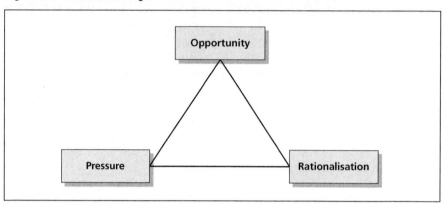

These motivations will recur in subsequent theories which we will look at later. Cressey created a fraud model which included three aspects:

- pressure – the perceived need
- opportunity – to relieve the organisation of its assets, and
- rationalisation – justifying the action internally.

This has become universally recognised as the 'fraud triangle' (Figure 5.1).

Cressey identified that embezzlers rationalised their actions to themselves before they acted, but that once they had begun a regular fraud their rationalisation was often abandoned as time went on. His view became, essentially, that once they had overcome their initial inhibitions such people didn't really view their actions as criminal at all, seeing them instead as being in some way justified and perhaps even forced upon them by outside circumstances (see Chapter 4).

 ## After Cressey

The latter part of the twentieth century saw a move away from Sutherland and Cressey's deterministic theories of crime towards the idea of crime as a choice. It has to be said that, whilst Cressey's work was seen as seminal in the study of fraud, and his development of the 'fraud triangle' is now universal, his theories of motivation centred around the idea of a 'trust violator' with an 'unshareable problem' are not now universally accepted.

Derek Cornish and Ronald Clarke, writing in 1986 in *The Reasoning Criminal*, developed a different hypothesis based on the idea of crime as a rational choice. They named the reasoning process the 'rational choice perspective'. It begins with:

> the assumption that offenders seek to benefit themselves by their criminal behaviour; that this involves the making of decisions and of choices, however rudimentary on occasions these processes may be; and that these processes exhibit a measure of rationality albeit constrained by the limits of time and ability and the availability of relevant information.

It takes the view that crime is a purposive behaviour designed to satisfy an individual's needs and that the rational element within it makes decisions as to how to satisfy those needs on the basis of a rational consideration of all elements involved in the decision. This has its roots in seventeenth-century ideas of Utilitarianism, whose greatest proponent in this country was Jeremy Bentham. Utilitarianism postulated the basis of decision making as being man as machine, a rational calculator who made decisions purely on the basis of 'pain or pleasure', i.e. avoiding pain and maximising pleasure.

The theory goes something like this – white-collar criminals are more rational than street criminals because:

- they are not, generally, in dire need because they are in employment
- they are not, generally, under the influence of drink or drugs
- there is no peer group pressure among males
- they live in a world which promotes rational decision making and planning, or
- they are generally older and more capable of mature reflection.

Consequently the need to commit a criminal act is not driven by desperation or absolute necessity but through a rational choice.

The theory advances the hypothesis that the putative criminal will weigh the balance of risk and reward before committing a criminal act and it is the weighting individuals give to each side of the scale that lies at the heart of this theory.

- On the one hand, the potential rewards – to satisfy the desire, or need, for more money which will bring with it a better life, more toys, a bigger house, more beautiful women, more fun in a brighter sun.
- On the other hand, the risk of getting caught – humiliation, name in the paper, bringing disgrace to the family or even loss of spouse and family, being shunned by friends, loss of employment, pension, possibly a jail sentence.

The flaw in this reasoning is that the rational choice perspective (Figure 5.2) assumes just that – that crime is a rational choice. It was soon pointed out that the theory ignores any element of the spontaneous, irrational, opportunistic or simply poorly thought through aspects of much crime – including fraud. The fact that so many fraudsters are caught because what they did was foolish and doomed to failure at the outset indicates that whilst, for some, commission of fraudulent acts may be the result of careful planning and consideration, for many it is the result of them seizing an opportunity and ignoring or minimising the downside risks of getting caught to an almost reckless extent.

Figure 5.2 The rational choice perspective

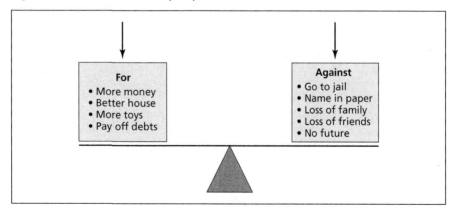

The problem is that there is no such thing as a universal answer to the question as to why someone commits fraud. The search for a universal answer is to deny the plurality of the nature of the individual; people have the annoying propensity to respond differently at different times to what would appear to be the same stimulus. Individuals who appear to be pillars of the community leading a placid and ordered life may suddenly become enraged by some action of their employer and take revenge by defrauding them of large amounts of money. Conversely poorly paid individuals work for years in charities with virtually non-existent financial controls handling significant amounts of cash, and will faithfully account for every penny.

Building on the work of Cressey, researcher W. Steve Albrecht (1984), who was primarily looking at internal audit, identified nine motivations for fraud which, whilst essentially identifying many of the same types of motivation as Cressey, included some additional factors:

- the fraudster who had a desire to 'beat the system'
- who saw the opportunity as a challenge, and
- those who adopted a kind of 'wheeler dealer', more insouciant, approach to fraud which had hitherto gone unrecognised.

Albrecht identified that perpetrators who were trying to beat the system committed larger frauds and bought high status assets (houses, cars, yachts, etc.), whereas those feeling inadequately rewarded, for example, committed smaller frauds.

One important sociological caveat to the work of Cressey is that much of his research was done in the 1950s. Albrecht was writing in the 1980s when societal norms had perhaps changed from the more rigid set of values embodied by the immediate post-war generation to a more individualistic attitude to relationships with other members of society in the relatively prosperous 80s, following the so-called '60s revolution' which broke down a lot of structural barriers in society.

This aspect of individuality was reinforced by research into employee theft carried out by Richard C. Hollinger and John P. Clark in 1983, building on the research into motivation carried out by Sutherland in the 1930s. This was the appearance of the fraudster who appeared to have no social conscience about the fraud they were perpetrating.

Hollinger and Clark recognised the motivations for fraud first outlined by Cressey and Albrecht – the perceived need postulated by Cressey and the 'beat the system' style motivations added by Albrecht – and added a new dimension, that of the culture of the organisation within which the fraudster operates. This ties in well with the socialisation of new employees into fraud outlined in Chapter 4.

Hollinger and Clark's research identified instances where:

- unscrupulous peers in an organisation tempted the innocent into fraud
- individuals were tempted when faced with opportunities to divert cash or disguise the theft of valuable stock and supervisory controls were weak or the organisation 'won't miss it'
- dissatisfaction with a job, caused by boredom or lack of interest or prospects, stimulated the desire to either 'get back' at the organisation as some form of revenge, and
- individuals could add excitement to their day by beating the system.

They also identified some key issues which are relevant not only to organisations in business but particularly to the charity sector and small business:

- employees felt more relaxed about committing frauds in organisations with weak formal controls and no clearly defined fraud policy, or
- employees felt that stealing from an organisation was somehow morally justifiable and represented additional remuneration or a 'perk' of the job.

Here the individual motivation may well be greed but the element of rationalisation in Cressey's fraud triangle was made easier by the prevailing organisational norms or peer pressure.

Researchers have recognised that financial motivations such as greed do not explain all forms of fraud. White-collar crime is not motivated solely by financial gain, nor is it solely explained by Albrecht's 'beat the system'-type rationales. Sociologist Ezra Stotland (1977) listed, in addition to the basic desire for money (greed):

- the threat of loss
- a sense of superiority
- ego
- power
- peer group pressure, and
- benefits to the victim

as motives for white-collar crime and went on to say:

> sometimes individuals' motivation for crime may have originally been relative deprivation, greed, threat to continued goal attainment, and so forth. However, as they found themselves successful in this crime they began to gain some secondary delight in the knowledge that they were fooling the world, that they were showing their superiority to others.

This may well be part of the explanation for complex, long-term frauds and computer fraud where specialist skills are required.

The Bondsman's Hypothesis and the Auditors' Assumption

There are however a couple of non-academic theories which we should also consider. These are rather raffishly known as:

- the Bondsman's Hypothesis, and
- the Auditors' Assumption.

In both of these the psychology of the individual is not important – there is no identification of need or desire for revenge, simply a moral failing. The Bondsman's Hypothesis comes, obviously, from the USA where bondsmen or bonding companies put up bail for individuals charged with crime.

The theory holds, based on the experiences of veteran bail bondsmen, that a violation of trust is not necessarily the result of one of Cressey's non-shareable problems or, for that matter, any of the other psychological theories post-Cressey identified above, but is based simply on the individual's desire for the good life over the routine and conventional. It has been described as 'babes, booze and bets' – those sins of the flesh which tempt the embezzler to unfasten the seatbelt of moral behaviour, rip off their tie and pile in. Clearly in our more egalitarian world the phraseology isn't as appropriate as it once was when most fraudsters were men, but the principle is probably sound. The case of Paul Hopes, cited above, may well be an example of the Bondsman's Hypothesis in action – we may never know.

The Bondsman's Hypothesis holds that the sweet life has a greater allure for some people than can be satisfied through the rewards of their legitimate career – so they must have more. Each person has a level of resistance to these attractions so not everyone succumbs. In recent studies carried out by KPMG most fraudsters cite simple greed as their main motivation. Whether individual psychology has changed in the last 20 years, as unlimited credit and 'shop 'til you drop' became modes of acceptable behaviour, we will leave the reader to meditate upon.

The Auditors' Assumption is based on Leo Tolstoy's assertion – 'the seeds of crime are in each of us'. It too is based on morality not psychology: the auditor believes that the potential for embezzlement is in each of us and that it is a function of the meeting of two variables – desire and opportunity. The desire is, in accordance with the Bondsman's Hypothesis, greed and it is the opportunity which the auditor is trying to stifle.

This, of course, largely echoes Cressey's fraud triangle. The difference is that here there is no unshareable problem which leads a good person down the path of crime and no tortuous rationalisation process. What there is here is the individual's desire to acquire things they could not normally afford and the simple opportunity which presents itself for them to do so – so they take it.

In most cases of documented fraud the primary motivation has been desire for material wealth – simple greed – and when the opportunity presents itself the fraud is committed. The desire for the good life is, in some cases, stronger than a simple opportunity for theft so the fraudster creates elaborate or ingenious schemes to obtain what they need, that which will satisfy them. This is not to say that it happens immediately. Individuals may go through a tortuous process of indecision or self-justification before the intensity of desire and their perception of the opportunity overcomes their moral and ethical scruples.

Some people resist for a long time before they succumb; for others the desire creates the opportunity. Where greed is a strong motivator, individuals may be more ready to seize or even invent the fraud opportunity. Fraudsters such as Michael Fielding (p. 148), or Sharon Hibbert (p. 138), both of whom were in a position of trust and were relatively unsupervised, plunged wholeheartedly into massive frauds against their employers as soon as the opportunity was realised and spent the money on good living and nice things.

There is a danger of confusing motivation with a retrospective justification of the act of fraud by the fraudster, and anyone attempting to analyse the motives of embezzlers has to take care not to conflate the two. As we saw in Chapter 4, in situations where the organisation itself is dysfunctional, rationalisation and socialisation techniques can be used to present corrupt or unethical behaviour as being reasonable or somehow justifiable in the circumstances, and those caught will often seek to justify their actions retrospectively and deny the fact that what they have been doing is wrong or that they are criminals. The ethical values they hold as members of society have been subsumed or suppressed by the rationalisations they have either absorbed as part of the organisational culture or have devised for themselves, so that their actions can be justified to themselves in some way.

Narcissism

One of the more curious by-products of the theories which try to explain fraudulent behaviour is that of narcissism. Full clinical narcissism is a DSM IV Cluster B personality disorder as catalogued in the *Diagnostic and Statistical Manual of Mental Disorders IV* (1994) developed by the American Psychiatric Association. We are not concerned here with the full spectrum of the disorder, merely how it manifests itself in business and its connection with fraud.

Typically narcissists:

- have a grandiose sense of self-importance
- are preoccupied with fantasies of unlimited success and power
- believe they are 'special' or 'unique' and can only be understood by other special or unique people
- require excessive admiration
- have a strong sense of entitlement, are envious of others or believe others are envious of them
- take advantage of others to achieve their own goals
- lack empathy and are contemptuous of others
- are very sensitive to criticism but are extremely critical of other people, and
- are arrogant or haughty.

First of all it should be pointed out that full spectrum narcissists are rare, studies are few and the cause is disputed. Narcissists by inclination don't take kindly to being studied or questioned, and there is a school of thought which disputes it is a disorder at all. However, for our purposes it will serve to illustrate the behaviour of a certain type of individual.

Occasionally individuals emerge who are or appear to be:

- very driven
- 'big personalities'
- able to gather a group of individuals around them who are quite deferential to the leader
- obsessed with enhancing their power and control, and
- endowed with limitless confidence and ambition.

Quite often they become very high achievers indeed. They are often very entrepreneurial and prepared to take huge risks because of their internal sense of infallibility and they frequently succeed spectacularly. However, their behaviour often contains the seeds of their own downfall. They make enemies, they run foul of the law or, more frequently, their overweening sense of self-belief makes them take one step too far and their empire crumbles.

Often it transpires that what they built was always a flimsy structure constructed for short-term personal satisfaction rather than something based upon the desire to build a long-term business empire. For them there is always the deal too far! Because of their propensity to take risks and their general attitude towards other people and societal norms (which don't apply to them) they are also capable of perpetrating quite egregious frauds.

Several extremely successful individuals have exhibited narcissistic behavioural tendencies, although it is of course impossible to describe them as clinical narcissists in the absence of clinical evidence.

Examples of such behaviour are:

- Leonora Helmsley – American hotelier who famously said 'only the little people pay taxes'.
- Robert Maxwell – owner of Maxwell Communications Corporation who defrauded the Mirror Group Newspapers pension fund to prop up his ailing empire. Described as a 'bully' who ignored his fellow directors and did not respond well to criticism.
- Christopher Skase – Australian entrepreneur who had 'a ferocious sense of the rightness of what he was doing' and was 'very impatient with criticism' (Prior 1994). His empire collapsed, he fled to Spain and resisted extradition on fraud charges involving A$1.5bn.

Clearly these are extreme cases, but they serve to make the point that individuals within organisations – who may be in positions of authority and who display many traits which reward them well such as ruthlessness, drive, ambition and a capacity for risk taking – may also be individuals who will also tolerate unethical and fraudulent behaviour providing it serves their purposes.

| Exhibit 5.4 | The greedy solicitor who wanted to be loved – Michael Fielding |

Using his 'immense intellectual capacity' to hoodwink his partners solicitor Michael Fielding was able to clear massive debts, fund a palatial London home and buy a luxury hideaway in Florida.

He also funnelled substantial sums abroad to feather his own nest for the time when discovery became inevitable; altogether he pocketed more than £5.8 million.

When one of his victims finally realised what he had been doing and wrote to his firm in 2001, Fielding intercepted the letter and left it, with a letter of farewell, on his boss's chair.

In it, he confessed to his three-year crime spree and spoke of his deep sorrow and shame for his betrayal of trust. He fled to America with his wife and spent years spending the money. Police tracked him down and in June he returned to Britain of his own accord. He was jailed for eight years.

The defence maintained that Fielding turned to crime after finding himself in an 'awful financial pickle' when his own law firm collapsed with massive debts, including £12 million owed to the Royal Bank of Scotland.

The prosecution said that Fielding joined the law firm Lawrence Graham in 1996 and less than a year later began stealing. The picture that eventually emerged showed 'repeated and systematic use of client accounts funds for his personal benefit'.

The prosecution added: 'He had a love of clothes and it seems an expensive taste in jewellery as well as an extremely valuable property in London.' The court was told that boxes of emeralds were found in his possession.

Fielding, who faces a £20 million bankruptcy order in America, had caused huge problems for his employers. Apart from the financial losses of up to £1 million not covered by insurance, their reputation had suffered.

In mitigation the defence barrister told the court that his client had once been an extremely highly regarded lawyer. 'A need to be loved might provide some clue as to why he got himself into the pickle he did, being too generous with his own money before he resorted to using others'.'

Source: Gibb (2005)

Crime and punishment

As far back as the 1930s Sutherland identified the fact that many corporations had committed criminal violations which had effectively gone unpunished. The perception grew and to some extent persists to this day that white-collar crime is not a serious crime at all. The seriousness of crime was measured by how the state viewed it – measured by how assiduously it was pursued and how seriously it was punished.

White-collar crime was generally perceived as being somewhat less heinous than say burglary or other forms of street crime. The average length of sentence up to 2005 for frauds prosecuted by the Serious Fraud Office was only three years, although some were accompanied by recovery orders under the Proceeds of Crime Act, 2002.

Anecdotal evidence from fraudsters cited in a couple of studies (see above) indicated that the risk of getting caught did not weigh seriously on the minds of those who committed fraud, and the possibility of imprisonment was not a serious consideration at the time they made their decision. The overwhelming conclusion, from anecdotal and other evidence, is that deterrence through the possibility of capture and punishment is not seen as an effective prophylactic against fraud.

This view that white-collar crime is not a serious crime may well be changing. The huge sentences handed out to convicted fraudsters in the USA, in particular the 26 years given to Geoffrey Skilling of Enron, the 25 years to Bernie Ebbers of WorldCom and the stunning 150 years to Bernard Madoff for his egregious Ponzi scheme may be being reflected in sentencing policy here in the UK. The point is, however, that for increased sentencing to be any form of deterrent and to assume a greater weighting on the 'No' side of the rational choice perspective it is the criminal or potential criminal who has to appreciate it, not simply finance professionals and lawyers.

Why does it matter?

Fraud is a complex issue and, as we have seen, there is no simple path – no one right way. Motivations abound but perhaps it is worth being reductive in the interests of clarity in attempting to pull it together. We have looked at various theories:

- criminal activity as learned behaviour (Sutherland) – which may be true of habitual fraudsters
- embezzlers with a non-shareable problem which tempts them into fraud given the opportunity (Cressey)
- 'beat the system' or challenge motivations (Albrecht)
- peer pressure, 'beat the system' or revenge frauds (Hollinger and Clarke)
- power and ego (Stotland)
- greed (Bondsman's Hypothesis)
- its in all of us (Auditors' Assumption), and
- narcissism.

Statistics taken from KPMG's *Profile of a Fraudster* tell us that greed and opportunity are indicated to be the overriding motivations for fraud, and the increasing prevalence of fraud in business raises many questions:

- Has society been corrupted by the emphasis on the rights of the individual and the desire for increased wealth, material possessions and the 'celebrity lifestyle' to such an extent that moral and ethical behaviour is seen as somewhat old-fashioned?
- Are we, as a society, too unwilling to investigate unless the facts are overwhelming in case we trample upon the rights of the individual or somehow offend their sensibilities?
- Are we, as individuals, too trusting and too willing to accept superficial explanations because it prevents us from facing an unpleasant truth – that one or more of our colleagues may be corrupt?

Why does it matter? In one way it doesn't – the fact that someone steals is sufficient unto itself – catch them, strengthen the controls, reinforce the policy or whatever it takes to minimise the opportunity of a repetition and move on.

In other ways it matters very much.

The focus must not be on post hoc rationale but on strategies for fraud prevention; on building control over potential fraudulent behaviour into the system rather than trusting to detection after the event. So how do we go about constructing such an approach?

Cressey took the view that, as this unshareable problem was a primary motive what was needed were:

- company programmes designed to eliminate the number of non-shareable problems among employees, and
- educational programmes designed to emphasise the nature of the verbalisations of trust violators by making it difficult for trust violators to see themselves as borrowers rather than thieves.

By contrast the bondsman and the auditor both take the view that no amount of educational programmes or ethical training will eliminate the desire of individuals for the temptations of the good life: all that can be done is to minimise the opportunity through sturdy internal control mechanisms. The emphasis is then on control and supervision – and an ear to the office gossip.

The prevailing theories of the motives underlying crime, that of it being some sort of rational choice, have coloured the attitude of the controlling authorities towards crime and punishment. If the cause is seen as deprivation then improve the lot of the poor, if it is gang-related break up the gangs, if it is problem-based then introduce counselling.

Fundamentally all the theories share one common thread – that of opportunity. If the criminal has no opportunity they have three choices:

- Leave and find an organisation where more opportunities exist.
- Give up and resign themselves to not having what they want or sharing their problem.
- Create an opportunity – which might result in a complex fraud or collusion.

The harder the fraudster has to work, the more complex the scheme or the more people involved in it, the greater the chance of detection and exposure. These are autonomous individuals capable of working alone and taking risks. They are intelligent and mentally robust – after all they visit the scene of the crime every day! It needs all the skills of forensic accountancy to catch them.

This is the area for the forensic accountant – defensive strategies to deny opportunity and detective skills to expose the criminal, and that is what we are going to look at next.

Summary

- There are so-called 'red flags' which are supposed to indicate fraudulent behaviour.
- Fraud research indicates that fraudsters are not antisocial loners but are more likely to be experienced senior managers.
- All fraudsters experience inner conflicts which may cause behavioural change.
- Sutherland was the first criminologist to postulate the idea of white-collar crime.
- Donald Cressey devised the fraud triangle of motive, opportunity and rationalisation.
- He held that fraudsters had a hidden perceived need which could only be satisfied by fraud.
- Later theories held that crime is a rational choice.
- The Bondman's Hypothesis holds that crime is a desire to break out of conformity and enjoy the good life.
- The Auditor's Assumption is that crime is in all of us.
- Narcissists can be leaders whose overriding desire for success and adulation can turn them to crime.

Case study

Mathew Arnold is 46 and is a contracts manager of Megabuild plc, a construction company based in Leeds, specialising in large construction projects such as office blocks, bridges, roads etc.

The company both employs workers and co-ordinates the employment of subcontractors on various contracts. Mathew's job is to select suitable subcontractors for a given contract – negotiate terms with them and produce all the documentation in connection with the contract. He also oversees the procurement of materials for the contract according to schedules produced by the design and engineering departments.

Mathew has a staff of eight including two assistant managers who liaise directly with the subcontractors and suppliers. Much of Mathew's role is problem solving and he spends a lot of time travelling to various sites and to visit subcontractors. He is very computer literate and spends a lot of evenings in hotel rooms on his own.

With the travelling Mathew often works very long days and often has to travel on Sundays for Monday morning meetings. This has contributed to the recent breakdown of his marriage and, because of what his ex-wife called aggressive behaviour, the fact that monthly contact with his children has to be supervised by a social worker. He also has nine points on his driving licence because of speeding convictions. If he loses his licence he will lose his job as he will no longer be able to carry it out. He is overweight and suffers from high blood pressure.

He carries out a lot of work by himself and simply reports the results to the Production Director Alison Blake. They meet intermittently so he can update her on progress or if there is a problem that needs her input.

Under the accounting rules either Mathew or his assistants can set up accounts for new suppliers and subcontractors on the system. They have to complete a form NS 27 for new suppliers or Sub4 for a new subcontractor. If Mathew's assistants want to set up a new supplier he has to countersign the form.

Mathew is currently supervising a contract to build a bypass around a town in Surrey and a bridge renovation contract near Newcastle.

Required

- What are the warning signs here?
- What could be done to minimise them?

Bibliography

Albrecht, W.S. (1984) *Deterring Fraud – The Internal Auditor's Perspective.* Institute of Internal Auditors Research Foundation, Maitland, FL.

American Psychiatric Association (1994) *Diagnostic and Statistical Manual of Mental Disorders IV.* American Psychiatric Association, Washington, DC.

Associated Press (1989) Maid testifies Helmsley denied paying taxes. *New York Times*, 12 July.

Bentham, J. (1789) *An Introduction to the Principles of Morals and Legislation.* Dover Publications, Mineola, NY.

Benson, M.L. (1985) Denying the guilty mind: accounting for involvement in a white-collar crime. *Criminology*, 23, 4, 583–608.

Cherbonneau, M. and Copes, H. (2006) Drive it like you stole it – auto theft and the illusion of normalcy. *British Journal of Criminology*, 46, 2, 193–211.

Clarke, R. and Felson, M. (2004) *Routine Activity and Rational Choice.* Transaction Publishers, Piscataway, NJ.

Cohen, L.E. and Felson, M. (1979) Social change and crime rate trends: a routine activity approach. *American Sociological Review*, 44, 4, 588–608.

Coleman, J.W. (1995) Motivation and Opportunity: understanding the causes of white-collar crime. In G. Geis, R. Meier and L. Salinger (eds). *White Collar Crime.* Free Press, New York.

Cornish, D. and Clarke, R.V. (1986) *The Reasoning Criminal.* Springer-Verlag, New York.

Cressey, D.R. (1953/1973) *Other People's Money – A Study in the Social Psychology of Embezzlement.* Patterson Smith, Montclair NJ.

Duffield, G. and Grabowsky, P. (2001) *The Psychology of Fraud.* Australian Institute of Criminology, Canberra.

Felson, M. and Clarke, R.V. (1998) *Opportunity Makes the Thief.* Home Office, London.

Geis, R.F., Meier, R. and Salinger, L.M. (eds) (1994) *White-collar Crime – Classic and Contemporary Views.* Free Press, New York.

Gibb, F. (2005) Solicitor lived the high life on £6m of his client's cash. www.thetimes.co.uk, 4 November.

Gill, M. (2005) *Learning from Fraudsters.* Protoviti, London.

Goldstraw, J., Smith, R.G. and Sakurai, Y. (2005) *Gender and Serious Fraud in Australia and New Zealand.* Australian Institute of Criminology, Canberra.

Hollinger, R.C. and Clark, J.P. (1983) *Theft by Employees.* Lexington Books, Lexington, KT.

Kelly, J. (2007) *The Strange Allure of Robert Maxwell.* www.bbc.co.uk, London.

KPMG (2007) *Profile of a Fraudster Survey.* KPMG, London.

Marlow, B. and Watts, R. (2009) Quiet Paul from accounts in secret life of fast cars and call girls. www.thetimes.co.uk, 29 November.

Nettler, G. (1974) Embezzlement without problems. *British Journal of Criminology*, 14, 70–77.

Ormerod, D. (ed.) (2008) *Smith and Hogan Criminal Law*, 12th edn. Oxford, Oxford University Press.

Prior, T. (1994) *Christopher Skase – Beyond the Mirage.* Wilkinson Books, San Francisco, CA.

Ross, E.A. (1907) *Sin and Society.* Houghton Miflin, Boston, MA.

Stotland, E. (1977) White-collar criminals. *Journal of Social Issues,* 33, 4, 179–196.

Sutherland, E.H. (1949) *White-collar Crime.* Holt Rinehart and Winston, New York.

Tozer J. (2006) Prison sentence for bookkeeper who stole £1m from food firm. www.dailymail.co.uk, 28 July.

Wells, J.T. (2004) *Corporate Fraud Handbook – Prevention and Detection.* John Wiley and Sons, Hoboken, NJ.

Wright, Richard A. (2004) *Edwin H. Sutherland – Encyclopedia of Criminology.* Routledge, New York.

Websites

http://www.jstor.org/view

www.aic.gov.au

www.bbc.co.uk

www.criminology.fsu/crimtheory

www.dailymail.co.uk

www.iia.org.uk

www.kpmg.co.uk

www.nytimes.com

www.psych.org

www.qestia.com

www.routledge-ny.com/ref/criminology/sutherland.html

www.thetimes.co.uk

Part 3

FRAUD RISK MANAGEMENT

Chapter 6

Defining and identifying fraud

Chapter contents

- Introduction
- Frauds committed by employees
- Financial statement fraud
- Building fraud defences
- The framework approach
- Inherent risk
- Aspects of accounting
- Fraud taxonomy – employee fraud
- Fraud taxonomy – financial statement fraud

Learning objectives

After reading this chapter you should be able to:

- Understand a working definition of fraud
- Appreciate the framework approach to building defences against fraud
- Understand the bases of evaluating inherent risk
- Understand the key accounting issues relating to fraud
- Develop a taxonomy of fraud
- Be able to identify the indicators of employee and financial statement fraud and their key features
- Understand the risk factors around fraud or corrupt behaviour at the organisational and the systems level

Introduction

Having looked at the legal background and some of the psychology of fraud it is time now to look at its practical manifestations.

The first thing we need to do is define precisely what we mean by fraud. Chapter 2 gave us the legal definition but that doesn't go very far in terms of its specific manifestations in the day-to-day life of an organisation. We need to look at the practical aspects of fraud in more detail so, in this chapter, we will seek to outline the practical process of fraud risk management which will lead us on to looking at some of the basic principles of fraud prevention. The student should note that, as this book is primarily about frauds within and by organisations and the role of the forensic accountant in advising the organisation and catching those who would seek to do it harm, we are *not* going to deal with:

- frauds against individuals such as identity theft or credit card fraud, or
- frauds by individuals outside organisations such as false insurance or compensation claims; however, we look at the forensic accountant's role in insurance and compensation work in Part 5.

We will look at Ponzi-type deceptions as these are, essentially, a fraud committed by an individual using an organisation of some sort. These frauds straddle the divide and are of some interest to the forensic accountant.

The Association of Certified Fraud Examiners (ACFE), based in the USA, has produced what it calls The Uniform Occupational Fraud Classification, otherwise known as the 'Fraud Tree', which is reproduced in Figure 6.1. The fraud tree is an attempt to arrive at a fraud taxonomy, to classify frauds by type and we have included it because it is so well-known and so universally quoted, that it would be remiss to omit it.

The problem with it, in UK terms, is that:

- It uses terminology which may be familiar to accountants in the USA but which means little in the UK. For example we do not talk about 'compensation' meaning 'pay' , we use the term 'supplier' not 'vendor', we don't, generally, talk about 'registers' we use the term 'till'.
- It includes certain types of fraud, in particular cheque frauds, which are significant in the USA but which have increasingly limited applicability in the UK. Electronic banking, electronic funds transfer and 'chip and pin' are far more prevalent in the UK than in the USA. Most employees, for example, in the UK are paid by bank transfer so many of the payroll frauds mentioned in the fraud tree are very difficult if not impossible here, as we will see in Chapter 11.

Rather than use the fraud tree we are going to classify frauds into two types:

- frauds committed by employees such as embezzlement or theft of assets, and
- financial statement or management fraud – frauds committed by the organisation in misrepresenting itself, founded on the actions of senior management.

It is important to realise that whatever view society has about fraud and whatever the opinions of convicted fraudsters may be, fraud is not a victimless crime.

The value involved in cases of fraud and deception, including fake investment schemes and deception frauds brought before the courts in the first half of 2009,

Figure 6.1 The fraud tree

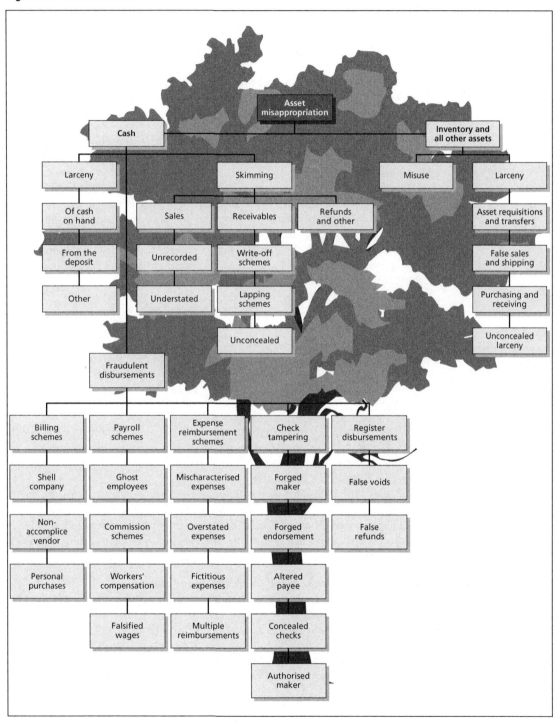

Source: Association of Certified Fraud Examiners, USA. 'The uniform occupational fraud classification' (ACFE website).

according to accountants KPMG, was in excess of £600m. This has to be paid for by someone. What this means in reality, away from cold statistics, is that:

- someone suffers irreplaceable loss
- someone or some organisation suffers a breach of trust which may take some time to heal
- the government is defrauded of taxpayer's money
- insurance companies suffer losses and put up premiums, or
- companies can be driven to the edge of bankruptcy

all so that the embezzler can enjoy the fruits of their deception. The figure of £600m is only known fraud – how much is out there that hasn't yet been revealed is, of course, unknown.

Frauds by individuals can seriously damage the organisation they work for. The frauds committed by a single individual can drain the organisation of cash, in some cases forcing it to borrow money, and in more than one case practically bringing the organisation down completely. The cost to an organisation's reputation, particularly where the fraud has been committed by someone with a respected position such as solicitor Michael Fielding (Chapter 5), can also do incalculable damage.

Frauds committed by employees

These can be categorised as frauds committed against the organisation or as occupational frauds.

This type of fraud is perpetrated by employees, or quasi-employees such as contractors. It may or may not involve collusion, two or more people working together, and it is the most common type of fraud, in one of its many guises, the forensic investigator will encounter.

It includes embezzlement or fraudulent behaviour connected with all major aspects of an organisation's day-to-day activities. It can include anything a company believes to be of benefit to it including not just physical assets such as inventories, cash, fixed assets and income streams but more intangible assets such as:

- trade secrets, e.g. research and development information
- product information – including recipes and specifications
- new product information
- employee information
- customer lists
- customer information – credit card details, etc., or
- tenders and prices submitted for bids.

Theft or disclosure of these may well involve bribery and corruption of employees and managers. We will look at the main types of employee frauds in more detail and the key indicators of such frauds later.

Financial statement fraud

This type of fraud we can, broadly, categorise as fraud committed *by* the organisation – or more precisely, its management. This type of fraud is perpetrated by senior management and consists of deliberate and systematic misstatement of financial information.

It involves:

- manipulation, including falsification or alteration, of financial records and supporting documents in order to deceive users of that financial information
- deliberate omission of information from financial statements, or
- intentional misapplication of accounting principles in order to deceive.

Such frauds include:

- deliberate misstatement of accounts in order to, say, artificially influence a share price or save tax
- concealment of transactions in cases of money laundering, or
- bribery and corruption.

Building fraud defences

To build fraud defences it is necessary to define what is being defended and what it is being defended against. Accordingly it is important that there is an attempt to define and classify the types of fraud likely to be met and what the key indicators might be that fraud is being perpetrated within a given organisation.

There are three key points to consider before we go any further:

1 Fraud takes different forms in different organisations. It would be tedious, if not actually impossible, in this book to attempt to try to identify and list every single sort of fraud in every possible combination of circumstances. The approach taken is to encourage organisations to create a fraud taxonomy of their own by identifying any vulnerable areas in their own organisation through a process of fraud risk assessment and analysing identified fraud risks, so that they can start building their defensive plans or carrying out investigations with maximum benefit to themselves and maximum disadvantage to the perpetrators.

2 Fraudsters are very creative and will come up with new variants on old themes, driven by the exigencies of the structure they are operating within and the opportunities which present themselves. Management should use the risk assessment process to think the unthinkable and to be as creative as the fraudster. Management should accept the possibility, however unwelcome it may be, that fraud in their organisation is likely to occur at some level and in some way. They must start by accepting this and try to identify and isolate vulnerable areas so that appropriate action can be taken. In this way opportunities for the fraudster are reduced – they can never be eliminated entirely.

3 By adopting a systematic approach in determining what types of frauds would be most likely in particular areas of the organisation some order and discipline

can be brought to what might otherwise be an unstructured or unco-ordinated approach to fraud prevention and detection.

Forensic accountants can and should be involved in every stage of the process by:

- using their experience and knowledge to identify fraud hotspots which might escape the untrained executive
- giving advice on how to build defensive systems to minimise the likelihood of fraud, or
- monitoring and controlling the process of fraud risk assessment (Chapter 7) so that it is carried out in a systematic manner and to ensure that all areas of the organisation are considered.

The forensic accountant is a valuable resource in this situation and can save the organisation much time and effort in carrying out fraud risk-assessment processes.

The framework approach

Now we have classified fraud into two main types we should be able to look at some specific types of fraud within the broad categories and consider how to combat them. Generally, however, the preferred course of action is to take a framework approach to fraud defence. The reason for this is straightforward enough. As we have said it is neither practical nor possible to identify every type of fraud which might arise in an organisation and then to build fraud-specific defences against them. Instead what are needed are efficient, effective and cost-beneficial anti-fraud approaches which can be tailored by management to their particular organisation, its culture, management information systems, internal control environment and reporting structure.

Let us consider some initial aspects which management and forensic accountants need to examine when establishing anti-fraud strategies. They require the organisation to take a fairly broad view of itself initially and to make an honest appraisal of its strengths and weaknesses. At this point we might be expected to produce some form of checklist but, as these are anathema to a framework approach, we will simply look at guidelines and definitions.

Inherent risk

Anyone familiar with audit planning or risk-assessment processes will recognise the term 'inherent risk'. Before the issue of the revised ISA 200, inherent risk was defined as the risk derived from the entity itself, its nature, activities, its management and the business environment in which it operates.

These now are classified for audit purposes as types of business risk, but we have retained the term 'inherent risk' as we feel it is a more accurate division of risk between what might be termed the broader-based general risks at the entity or organisational level and the detailed control risks at the accounting level. For all intents and purposes inherent risk is synonymous with business risk, but use of that term helps to avoid confusion.

Before we delve into the detail of accounting processes and internal control environments we need to take a wide angle look at the organisation, to look at it in its entirety as a functioning entity and ask some key questions about its essential nature.

The questions to ask are:

1 What is the nature of the organisation?
2 What element of control do individuals within the organisation have?
3 What external factors might influence the organisation's management?
4 What is the nature of the industry in which the organisation operates?

Of these the first is probably the hardest to answer, as the nature of an organisation is inevitably an amalgam of many factors including:

- its size
- its recent growth, whether organic or by acquisition
- the way it conducts business
- the experience and competence and attitudes of its senior management
- its ethical culture, policies and approach to staff
- the demographics of its staff
- attitude to training and development, and
- the approach to and efficiency of its communications with its employees.

By taking a broad approach to these questions it may be possible to decide, at an early stage, where the greatest level of fraud risk is likely to develop and where anti-fraud effort may need to be focused (Figure 6.2).

Let us consider some of these questions in more detail.

1 What is the nature of the organisation?

This encompasses a multitude of issues, some of which we have already looked at, and some of which we will consider in the following chapters. At this point we will merely flag up the key aspects that can be included in this catch-all heading.

Figure 6.2 Factors affecting the propensity for fraud in the organisation

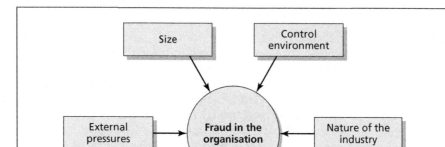

As we saw in Chapter 4, the culture of the organisation can have a significant influence on:

- the attitudes of its senior management towards its employees, which may encourage dysfunctional behaviour on their part, and
- the attitudes of the employees towards the organisation for which they work.

In turn this cultural aspect is often influenced by physical constraints such as:

- the size of the organisation overall
- whether it has grown organically or by acquisition
- the diversity of its locations
- the diversity of the products and services it sells
- its management structure, including the level of autonomy given to line management, or
- the ethical culture of the organisation.

Table 6.1 shows some examples of different types of organisation. This is meant to be illustrative and readers may feel that their organisation doesn't fit neatly into one of these categories. This may be so, but it is important to bear in mind that it is the essential underlying nature of the organisation which is to be considered, not how it appears to the outside world and not how senior management may think it appears to employees. For example, an organisation which may appear to be a paragon of good practice to the outside world may hide a culture which management fondly believes to be competitive and stimulating for their employees but which is in reality one of bullying and fear.

It is necessary for the forensic accountant analysing the strengths and weaknesses of organisations to peer beneath the surface and to discover what is really going on.

So these are illustrative examples, and no doubt a student of management theory will scoff at their simplicity, but for our purposes they will suffice.

The difference in the level of control over fraud is not directly correlated with size, except in the first instance. Small organisations are vulnerable to fraud not simply because of the lack of staff to institute strong internal controls but also because of the levels of trust placed in individuals and the amount of access they have.

It is the nature of the organisation which matters. For example a strictly controlled organisation with stout anti-fraud policies and a powerful HR department will be a lot less vulnerable to fraud than one where a great deal of trust and responsibility is placed on the shoulders of individuals. Into this should be factored the ethical culture of the organisation. This has a great bearing on the propensity for fraud to succeed because, as we saw in Chapter 4, a strong ethical culture can be a deterrent against fraudulent activity even in an organisation where the levels of control are not strong and individuals are trusted to behave ethically and honestly.

The nature of the organisation is also influenced by its development. For example if it has grown through acquisition the organisation may be an amalgam of different cultures drawn together as organisations merge. The organisation may be attempting to integrate staff into a common policy and way of working. This frequently results in change which is unsettling and which can breed uncertainty and foster dysfunctional behaviour. There may also be resentment on the part of some staff if they perceive themselves to be unfairly treated or ignored, which can also be a stimulus to fraud.

Table 6.1 Organisational types and the internal control environment

Type	Key features	Opportunity for fraud
Small- to medium-sized family company, partnership or charitable body	High level of involvement by owner/managers who exercise a great deal of control. Management style may be autocratic whilst masquerading as paternal. It may be difficult for employees to criticise or challenge owner–managers. Owner–managers may feel some sense of infallibility if the business is successful and are reluctant to change what appears to be them to be a successful approach. Owner–managers have a very high level of influence and power in the organisation so there are, generally, few constraints over their actions. A great deal of trust is placed in the company accountant or treasurer, who often has access to all the records and to the bank account. Accounting functions are usually limited to the provision of basic financial and costing information. Owner–managers tend to confine themselves to operational issues and have limited financial awareness. The internal control environment is generally weak and relies on individuals and trust.	Fraud by misappropriating cash is relatively easy to carry out – but also very easy to detect once the existence of fraud is realised. Theft of assets may be possible due to the absence of controls but the owner–manager's involvement may detect this rather more quickly than theft of cash. Any form of meaningful audit is extremely difficult due to the absence of controls. Management fraud is a strong possibility as the owner–manager and accountant, who may work closely, can collude to present a more optimistic view of the financial position than is actually the case. Owner–managers may pay personal expenses through the business and under-declare benefits – tax fraud.
A customer-facing, fast-response, highly technologically based business, managed by results, often involved in contract work, retail activity or creative media	Low-control environment as administration and systems, other than those directly relating to selling, are seen as an overhead and given low priority. The internal control environment may be quite strong within the financial and costing systems but opportunities exist outside these systems for fraud 'Horizontal' organisation structures may lead to loss of internal control as employees may report to more than one manager for different tasks. Emphasis on individuality within the organisation may lead to difficulties in enforcing policies and procedures.	Controls over transactions tend to be reasonably effective so misappropriating cash or assets may be quite difficult except for very senior individuals with appropriate access. Theft of portable assets such as laptops, Blackberries etc. may be relatively easy if use of these is uncontrolled. Supplier fraud including kickbacks, stock manipulation and expenses frauds etc. are often relatively easy to carry out. Expenses fraud by employees, particularly where claims often go unchallenged, may be relatively easy.

▶

Table 6.1 Continued

Type	Key features	Opportunity for fraud
A hierarchical, vertically integrated tightly controlled organisation with defined procedures and extensive supervisory and management control	The illusion of control, i.e. the impression that internal controls are effective when in fact they are not, can be quite strong. Organisations tend to have policies and procedures fostering a culture of ethical behaviour which can serve to mitigate or nullify fraudulent impulses on the part of individuals. The internal control environment is strong and the culture of the organisation mitigates against unethical activity. Fraud is confined to areas where individuals are trusted and relatively unsupervised or unchecked.	Fraud here is difficult (although not impossible) but will probably be confined to quite specific instances where opportunity presents itself and the fraudster has a strong motivation. Frauds tend to appear in obscure corners of the organisation or where an individual is trusted to an unrealistic extent. Individuals are able to commit frauds because they are trusted by the organisation and the possibility of them committing dysfunctional acts is not considered to be likely so they are perceived as low risk.

The demographics of the workforce may also be significant. For example:

- Women are statistically less likely to commit fraud than men.
- Younger people have a greater sense of individuality and less sense of a common morality than older people.

This is not to say that the best staff demographic is to employ exclusively old women, but the make-up of the workforce and the management is important.

Key factors also include the organisation's policies on training of staff and management and the efficiency and effectiveness of communications within the organisation – which we will look at later.

2 What element of control do individuals within the organisation have?

Fraud involves some element of control on the part of the perpetrator because, clearly, if they misappropriate assets, whether cash, goods or information, they have to be able to conceal that misappropriation. Consequently the embezzler must be able to:

- have control over the maintenance of some sort of accounting record or access to a record from which accounting numbers are derived
- authorise transactions of some sort
- sign and have the signature accepted, or
- issue instructions for certain courses of action and have the actions carried out.

Fraud takes place in the context of organisational activity and opportunities for fraud lie only within those areas of activity. A potential perpetrator is not faced with an unlimited range of opportunities and an infinite way of covering up the crime. Opportunities for fraud are circumscribed by the organisation, its systems, its culture and the business environment in which it operates.

For example it is said that 'brown envelope' bribery is endemic in the construction industry and that cash frauds are endemic in many leisure industries because there are opportunities and motivations within those industries for those practices to persist, but bribery is probably not common within merchant banks and cash fraud is probably not common within stationery wholesalers – they have their own particular frauds!

Within any organisation there can be a surprising number of people who may have some element of control over accounting records connected to assets. These include:

- counter staff in retail establishments who handle customer cash or returned goods
- any staff who issue receipts for or record cash collection
- individuals who work in inventory control
- managers with autonomy over a sales outlet who complete returns to a head office
- managers or staff who have control over more than one aspect of a transaction such as approving orders to and invoices from suppliers they have approved
- individuals dealing with casual employees or part-time employees paid in cash, for example, gang masters, supervisors or wages staff, and
- accountant/bookkeepers in small organisations and charities who have access to methods of payment or who deal in cash collection.

The point about control here is that where an individual, whether an employee or a senior manager, has unfettered control, i.e. where they are the sole originator and there is no other mechanism within the organisation to check the veracity of their actions, the organisation is vulnerable to fraud and deception.

Frauds committed by management tend to differ from those committed by employees. Remember that according to research, which we looked at in detail in Chapter 5, the individuals most likely to carry out frauds within an organisation are:

- male
- middle to senior management
- who have been part of the organisation for more than two years, and
- who are presented with opportunities, caused by poor controls or inadequate supervision, which
- coincides with their motivation to do so.

The combination of a motivated individual and an opportunity will result in a fraud which the offender will subsequently rationalise.

Managers engaged in fraudulent activity may attempt to use their position and authority to:

- Bully, intimidate or cajole employees to connive in frauds, particularly where fraudulent financial reporting is concerned or to disguise fraudulent transactions such as the payment or receipt of bribes, money laundering activities or similarly dubious events. They can take the lead in rationalising dysfunctional behaviour or in socialising employees into unethical work patterns, disguising it as 'the way we do things' (Chapter 4).
- Involve third parties or 'middle men' to aid them in diverting funds or in setting up bogus organisations whereby funds are paid to them by the organisation when the right documents, which they cause to be authorised, are submitted.
- Bypass, overrule or avoid internal controls. Frequently, as their frauds are not basically transactional, the internal accounting control system does not extend

to them and the accounting systems work automatically to process what is perceived to be properly approved documentation. A good many management frauds are effectively 'off the books', i.e. they do not involve any entries in the accounting records other than mechanically processing what are ostensibly genuine transactions.

Employees, on the other hand, tend to:

- Commit transaction-related frauds, disguising thefts by falsifying accounting records, e.g. falsifying expenses, amending stock or sales records, etc.
- Falsify records to disguise bribery and corruption involving middle and line or operating management. This would differ from a senior management bribery fraud where the individual would receive a 'pay off' for, say, awarding a contract or buying from a particular supplier and no entries would appear in the organisation's records.
- Influence dysfunctional or unethical behaviour in new or easily dominated employees and thus encourage or 'legitimise' this behaviour as normal business practice (Chapter 4).
- Be restricted by internal controls or by the nature of their employment. Except in very small organisations or those with lax or limited internal controls, opportunities for diverting income streams or theft of assets are limited. Employee fraud is therefore, theoretically, much less difficult to prevent and detect unless it is of a relatively minor or incidental nature.
- Collude so that one single person cannot easily be identified, for example a group of cashiers who each steal from tills in a random way so no pattern can be established by analysis.

To protect itself the organisation has to have internal control mechanisms which ensure, broadly, either that the work of any one individual is checked by another or that no individual has control over all aspects of a transaction. Where these principles of control break down is where fraud can flourish. We will look at principles of internal control later.

3 What external factors might influence the organisation's management?

External factors can have a great bearing on frauds. Clearly this is true of individual motivation, as we have already seen, but financial statement fraud in particular is generally a response to actual or perceived external pressures, such as:

- pressure from banks or investors to meet profit targets
- pressure to maintain a share price – particularly if part of management's remuneration is in the form of share options
- disguising poor performance to preserve jobs (including those of the executive directors)
- evading regulatory requirements such as environmental controls or legal reporting requirements
- meeting bonus trigger points, or
- obtaining credit from suppliers.

Looking at the big classic frauds of recent years it is clear that, for example, the management of Enron falsified so many accounting returns mainly to keep up the share price which, of course, benefited the perpetrators themselves although that was not it would seem, at least initially, the primary purpose. The primary motivation, it appears, was to keep Enron as a shining example of a well-managed, innovative top US company so the directors could bask in reflected glory. The same is true of the WorldCom fraud where the directors, principally the chairman Bernie Ebbers and chief financial officer Scott Sullivan, falsified accounts to help avert a share price fall.

Clearly there are interrelationships between these three factors. Frauds committed by directors in falsifying financial statements, for example, can lead to directors and managers receiving rewards to which they are simply not entitled such as bonuses, share options etc.

4 What is the nature of the industry in which the organisation operates?

Certain industries, as we will see later, have a propensity by their very nature to be vulnerable to fraud.

For example:

- The construction industry is susceptible to bribery and corruption involving surveyors, contracts managers and suppliers. It has also seen regulatory action in connection with price fixing cartels.
- The licensing trade is susceptible to theft of cash and inventory.
- The catering industry is vulnerable to corruption of cooking and waiting staff to use favoured suppliers.
- Retail clothing is susceptible to theft of inventory.
- Financial advisory, legal services and investment banking are areas for insider trading and money laundering.

Clearly not every company in these sectors is automatically a hotbed of fraud and corruption but some industries, by their nature, seem to attract individuals who see opportunities, because of the nature of business dealings within those industries, to indulge in dysfunctional activities. An awareness of this is something the forensic accountant should have at the back of their mind when evaluating an organisation's propensity for fraudulent activity.

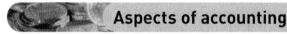

Aspects of accounting

Most accounting systems, because they have to record basically the same things in order to be able to provide the information for a standardised set of financial accounts, function in more or less the same way. They may have costing or executive information systems bolted on or integrated into them, they may have books of account called different things or subdivided in different ways, but:

- They all obey the rules of double entry. This means that if a fraudster removes an asset, be that cash or stock, from the system they have to account for it – thus creating what is known as a 'consequential debit'.
- They all must record information which enables accountants to prepare sets of financial accounts which comply with the Companies Act. In essence, they have to control, as a minimum:
  - cash and bank transactions, including payroll

- sales and receivables (debtors)
- purchases and payables (creditors)
- inventories (stock) and work in progress.
- They must conform to S386 of the Companies Act 2006 insofar as they must comprise what the Act defines as 'adequate accounting records'. External auditors will include this in their checking work. Destruction or deliberate hiding of records will set alarm bells ringing with the auditors and deliberately inadequate record keeping will prompt investigation and a recommendation for improvement.

These rules, together with:

- the requirements of the VAT legislation for even quite small businesses to keep proper records to record turnover and purchases, and
- the availability of cheap and reasonably reliable and effective accounting software

have compelled even relatively small organisations to maintain usable accounting records. The need for financial information has led to the development of complex information systems in larger organisations which can be used by the forensic accountant in fraud detection, as we will see in Chapter 13. What the growth and increased sophistication of information systems has done is to concentrate fraud into areas where individuals have authority and autonomy, i.e. those in a senior position of trust or has increasingly resulted in frauds becoming a group effort where internal controls are defeated through collusion.

In addition, legislation designed to prevent one form of criminal activity, and the general paranoia of official bodies around anything connected with possible terrorist or organised criminal activity, has greatly aided the forensic accountant in recent years.

For example, because of the Money Laundering Regulations 2007 it is very difficult now (or should be) for an individual to open a UK bank account without proof of identity which in most cases would have to be a passport accompanied by some form of utility bill to evidence address.

The average fraudster does not have ready access to the criminal underworld so this is, in most cases, extremely difficult for them if the bank's staff are operating the 'know your client' procedures properly. This, prima facie, makes supplier fraud more difficult because to carry it through successfully, the fraudster has to open a bank account in a business name and overcome the bank's own checking procedures – which, of course, is far from impossible but does create an additional hoop for the would-be fraudster to have to jump through. The ever creative fraudster however defeats this by using the Internet to set up an off-shore company, for example, in the British Virgin Islands, and uses a UK bank as a conduit to that company.

Consider payroll fraud, where the inclusion of 'ghost workers' was once a particular fraud of choice. Today individuals in employment have a wealth of records relating to their tax affairs administered through the PAYE system which are required by HM Revenue and Customs. Documents include P45's , P60's End of Year Returns etc. which are computerised and cross-checked by their computers against benefit information and information supplied by other employers. This requires the payroll fraudster to falsify HMRC documents and to have some form of mechanism for receiving the fake salary where employees are paid through the Bankers Automatic Clearance System (BACS).

Payroll frauds either tend to be restricted to leaving those employees who have left the company on the payroll and simply changing the banking details in the master file so that salaries are paid into the perpetrator's bank account, or confined to casual employees paid in cash, such as those recruited though gang masters or subcontractors. Internal audit procedures should detect this type of fraud more easily than they would detect 'invisible' workers.

The combination of the difficulty of opening bank accounts and the documentation required in respect of employees has greatly reduced the likelihood of some what might be described as old-fashioned, frauds beloved of some auditing textbooks but, of course, fraud is an ever-fertile field to plough.

Because most fraudsters, particularly in larger organisations, know about the accounting systems, internal controls and regular audits the wise fraudster may not attempt to steal anything from within the system unless they are in a position of sufficient authority to override the controls. If we look at the examples of the methods adopted by fraudsters quoted in Chapter 5, virtually all of them were aware of the internal controls and the audit routines and were able to defeat them relatively easily for some years.

Thus in larger organisations with extensive control mechanisms the wise fraudster will act on the margins of the accounting systems, obtaining the benefit from their fraud before any entries are made within it, thus presenting the accounting system with a fait accompli. In smaller organisations where the fraudster may have a lot of autonomy there may be no real controls so they are free to carry on embezzling.

An example of this type of fraud is the one known as 'skimming', where a proportion of income is diverted before being recorded in the books. The best examples of this are in the licensing trade where much of the sales income is received in cash. Intelligent diversion of a consistent proportion of takings before they are recorded in the records is very difficult for the forensic accountant to detect, particularly as, if it is done on a consistent percentage basis, the gross profit margin will look consistent, if a little low compared with similar businesses. The intelligent fraudster can blame the low margin on price promotions, incompetent staff, till malfunctions, poor stocktaking etc.

This is the most difficult type of fraud for the forensic accountant to have to deal with – accordingly it is important, as will be shown later, that defensive systems leave as little room as possible for the creative fraudster.

Set against the improvements in accounting records brought about by computerisation is the relatively easy availability of desktop publishing which enables the fraudster to produce realistic-looking documents, invoices, letterheads etc., in order to facilitate their deceptions.

At this point it would be useful to delineate some specific frauds we are going to look at in detail. As stated above we have categorised frauds into two types:

1 Employee fraud/misappropriation of assets.
2 Financial statement fraud.

We will look at the characteristics of these frauds and, in the following chapters, give some indications of investigative approaches to detecting and gathering evidence in connection with such frauds.

Fraud taxonomy – employee fraud

This is by far the largest category of frauds. It is thus the one most frequently perpetrated by employees and the one the forensic accountant working as investigator is most likely to come across.

Table 6.2 is an overview of some of the main features of common employee frauds. It cannot hope to be comprehensive but does cover the most common frauds typically encountered and is based on real-life examples of detected frauds. Extremely cunning undetected fraud types are, of course, not mentioned, nor are frauds which may be peculiar to particular uncommon business types.

Table 6.2 Key indicators of fraud

Category	Features	Key indicators
Purchasing/supplier fraud	Creation of fictitious supplier (usually by senior manager)	Use of Post Office Box address for supplier
		Lack of contact data, e.g. phone number
		Sequential invoice numbers from vendor
		Invoices prepared using Word or Excel
		Address matching employee's address
		Lack of supporting documentation
		Prices charged are significantly higher than comparable goods from another supplier without any commercial reason or significant product differentiation
		Lack of detail on invoice or unintelligible descriptions
		Invoices for services only
		Invoices for round sum amounts
		No or incorrect VAT number
		Supplier is paid more quickly than other vendors
		Vendor dealt with entirely by one individual who authorised account set-up and authorises invoices
	Bid fixing – bidders obtain inside information in return for bribe or kickback	Specifications can only be met by one supplier because of abnormal terms or prices
		Regular or well-known suppliers not asked to tender
		Pre-qualified suppliers
		Supplier size not in proportion to size of contract, i.e. small supplier/big contract
		Unusual location for supplier, i.e. not local
		Tenders accepted after closing date

Table 6.2 Continued

Category	Features	Key indicators
		Poor or weak controls over tendering procedures including lack of confidentiality and poor security of submitted tenders
		High level of 'extras' to contract accepted by company
		Changes to specification or price after contract awarded
		Large number of invoices from supplier below approval threshold authorised by specific individual
		Weak segregation of duties between assigning contracts or nominating suppliers and authorising invoices
	Bribery of employee	Close relationship (possibly involving personal friendships or social connections) between supplier and employee
		Weak segregation of duties between approval of suppliers and authorisation of invoices
		Supplier receives more favourable terms than usual, i.e. higher level of discount, shorter payment period
		Lack of quotation process for purchases – orders go automatically to same supplier even if cheaper alternatives are found
		Change of lifestyle by employee
Sales frauds	Cash theft (i.e. theft of cash receipts from customers and/or cheques *after* being entered into company records)	'Split' receipts (teeming and lading)
		Bank reconciliations not prepared or consistently incorrect
		Bank reconciliations include adjusting entries
		Unusual or inappropriate level of write-offs to bad debt accounts
		Excessive and illogical transfers between sales ledger accounts
		Amounts written off against provisions to which they don't relate
		Changes in employee lifestyle
		Employee displaying red flag behaviour patterns (Chapter 5)
	Invoicing frauds	Certain customers receive higher than average discounts
		'Special prices' for certain customers
		Accounts handled by manager – one particular staff member using non-standard procedures and/or documentation

▶

Table 6.2 Continued

Category	Features	Key indicators
		'On account' deliveries written off
		High level of customer complaints re substandard or inferior quality goods
		Unexpected loss of customers
		Inconsistent patterns of business
Expenses frauds	Fictitious nominal ledger expense or cost code used as a cover for withdrawals of cash or cheque payments for 'services' without going through purchase ledger system	No actual supply of services
		Cost of supposed services excessive or not budgeted
		Suppliers do not exist when contacted or addresses are virtual offices
	Claiming excessive expenses for business trips	Lack of clear policy and instructions on what is reimbursable and what isn't
		Expense refunds made in cash not by bank transfer
		Altered, amended or incomplete receipts
		Submission of photocopied documents rather than originals
		Altered or amended claims after being authorised (Expenses claims altered or amended by cashier after authorisation to pocket difference)
		Fictitious receipts created on word processor
		Expense claims from different periods including receipts with consecutive numbers (indicative of obtaining or stealing blank receipts)
	Fictitious or overstated petty cash payments	Regular cash disbursements not evidenced by vouchers or of an unusual nature
Cash/bank fraud	Skimming (theft of cash takings or sales receipts before entry into accounting records)	Lower than expected levels of income
		Actual profits less than budget
		Gross margins less than forecast
		Sales volumes × selling price not equal to reported turnover
		Excessive 'no sale' or void transactions on tills
		Excessive levels of refunds for 'returned' goods
		Inventory movements not in accordance with reported sales, i.e. more inventory sold than sales indicate
Payroll fraud	Fictitious employees	Numbers of casual workers paid in cash with limited documentation
		Use of 'gang-masters' who pay casual workers

Table 6.2 Continued

Category	Features	Key indicators
	Employees retained on payroll after leaving	High turnover of lower level employees who are inadequately covered by HR systems
		Weak HR systems not monitoring employees leaving
		Poor communication between HR department and payroll department
		Access to employee master file to amend bank details after employee has left rather than to delete them from payroll
		Failure to confirm employee details with line managers on a regular basis
		Employees paid in cash when most are paid by BACS
		Lack of documentation for employees either from HMRC or internal documents
	Excessive payments to colluding employee	Payment of employee at higher rate than grade or job would warrant
		Employee paid at higher rate than those of equivalent grade
		Failure to confirm pay scales with line managers
Inventory fraud	Theft of inventory (stock) and subsequent concealment	Unexplained differences between book and physical inventory
		Unexplained alterations to inventory records or valuations
		Inventory purported to be in unusual or inaccessible places
		Poor controls over sales of scrap or waste
		Unusual number of credit notes at period ends or stock-take dates
		Inventory lines with long turnover periods or abnormally large holdings of stock
		Inventory turnover in specific locations inconsistent with general level of inventory turnover
		Poor GP % or fluctuations in margin
		Delivery drivers driving part-loaded vehicles, asking for routes to be amended or asking for same route
		Deliveries received or made at unusual times of day
		Poor monitoring of inventory losses and infrequent counts
		Weak goods inwards and despatch procedures

▶

Table 6.2 Continued

Category	Features	Key indicators
		Poor segregation of duties between buying, warehousing, goods inward and accounting
		Poor control over returns and incorrect deliveries
		Weak stock-taking procedures
		Failure to follow up customer complaints re short or substandard deliveries or delays in delivery
Theft of sensitive information	Loss of customer information: • Customer lists • Customer information – credit card details etc. • Tenders and prices submitted for bids	Continuing loss of business to one particular competitor Customers approached directly by competitors with precisely targeted offers Theft from customer credit cards
Theft of trade secrets	• Loss of trade secrets, e.g. research and development information • Product information including recipes and specifications • New product information • Employee information	Competitors launch similar products within short time of own launch 'Spoiler' marketing campaigns prior to product launch Key employees approached directly by competitors with targeted job offers Employee red flags as above

This list is an indication of the range and variety of frauds determined and committed fraudsters can undertake. It is intended to include the most frequently cited frauds, but there is no end to the ingenuity of the embezzler. Take, for example, the activities of Cathryn Wiles (Exhibit 6.1) a finance officer at Blackpool Council who invented an entire children's home which she used as a cost code for 'expenses' and cost payments. The payments to a children's home through the financial

---

Exhibit 6.1   Fraud example – the Cherrywood affair

Cathryn Wiles, a finance officer at Blackpool Council, diverted £617,000 of taxpayers money into her own accounts over a five-year period.

She did it by inventing a fictitious children's home she called 'Cherrywood'. Payments were made ostensibly for staff caring for children in care but the money was actually used to buy an expensive car, holidays and extending her home.

She had begun defrauding the council to pay for an extension to her home, and as the initial thefts were not detected she created the fictitious children's home and extended her fraud. Initially sums were in the region of £3,000 but as time went on they got larger and she was embezzling sums in excess of £30,000.

Payments were made into the same account her wages were paid into.

She was jailed for two years and eight months. Very little of the money has been recovered.

Blackpool Council has launched an enquiry.

Source: Narain (2009)

accounts were, presumably, not correlated with the activities of social services within the council.

The awareness by the fraudster of the processes and procedures within the organisation, what is checked and what isn't, creates the opportunity for corrupt behaviour. Add to that a suitable motivation and the result is often fraud.

 ## Fraud taxonomy – financial statement fraud

This type of fraud represents a deliberate misrepresentation of accounting information. It may involve alterations to underlying accounting records or simply the creation of completely fictitious statements which bear no relationship to actual transactions or results. Clearly this most frequently involves overstatement of revenues and/or understatement of costs and this type of behaviour by senior management has featured heavily in the classic frauds of recent years including Enron, WorldCom and Parmalat.

Senior managers, in which we include all directors but also senior non-board managers, have an inbuilt advantage over the run of the mill employee embezzler as they often have the ability to override controls and to authorise transactions which subvert the internal control systems.

However, one key feature of such misrepresentations is that they invariably involve collusion. It is extremely difficult for one board member, even if it is the financial director, to so distort the numbers that a significant advantage is achieved by that distortion whilst at the same time convincing their colleagues of the truth of such numbers in the face of any other evidence they may have. Consequently all the major frauds of recent years have involved collusion, even though this may not have extended to the entire board.

Because managers collude together to perpetrate such deceptions, forensic investigators can be faced with a united front of executive directors all telling identical stories. They have the capacity to forge documents, backdate authorisations and generally muddy the waters so that gathering evidence for a legal case is rendered extremely difficult.

Table 6.3 (p. 178) shows the main types of financial statement fraud.

Table 6.4 (p. 179) lists the key features of such frauds.

Frauds which involve activities outside the financial systems are perhaps the most difficult to detect, but they run a close second to frauds perpetrated by management, often senior management. These, they may argue, may be perceived to be primarily for the benefit of the organisation, insofar as results are 'improved'. This may have the incidental benefit of triggering bonus payments or stock options etc. to the benefit of those very managers, but their rationale – how they justify such unethical behaviour to each other – is that they are doing it to benefit the business and not themselves.

Most accountants will instantly spot that many of these actions are 'one time' only – or at best short term. For example, moving costs into Year 2 from Year 1 or overvaluing stock at the end of Year 1 might solve a perceived problem for Year 1 – but creates problems for Year 2.

This is to fail to understand the thinking of managers who are involved in 'faking' accounts. Experience shows that directors and senior managers are, generally, extremely optimistic individuals and are often content simply to buy time either to

Table 6.3 Types of financial statement fraud

Type	Features	Key indicators
Financial	Overstatement of assets	Overvalued inventories
		Lack of provisions for probable losses
		Weak estimates of fair value of impaired assets
		Concealed liabilities
		False asset revaluations
	Overstatement of revenues	Accelerated revenue recognition contrary to UK GAAP (timing differences)
		Heavy billing close to year end followed by higher than usual level of returns and consequent credit notes (channel stuffing)
		Large number of transactions of related businesses, partnerships or joint ventures with no apparent economic purpose
		Large numbers of transactions with overseas subsidiaries in countries with weak reporting regimes
		Concealed or understated expenses or costs
		Fictitious revenues
		Moving costs or liabilities to subsidiaries audited by other firms than group auditors
		Changes in earning per share (EPS) debt/equity ratios not supported by economic factors
	Suppression of liabilities	Timing differences – delayed billing by suppliers
		Moving costs between periods
		Weak cut off procedures
		Suppression of costs – simple omission
Non-financial	Forged or false documentation	Lies on CV
		Faked or false qualifications
		Misleading or incorrect disclosure of non-financial information which may influence share price

enable them to 'sort it out' or to escape and leave the problems for their successor to deal with. Their attitudes, in these cases, tend to be on the lines of:

- We are where we are – we have to deal with what is in front of us now not worry about next year – we'll deal with that when it happens.
- This year's actual bonus is worth more than a possible bonus next year – we may not be here next year.
- We have a year to solve these problems.
- Things will get better – we will make enough money to cover the deferred costs/loss of income, etc.
- The auditors aren't the problem – if we tell our story with enough conviction and give them some paper to put in their file they'll go along with it.

Building on the basic fraud characteristics identified in this chapter we now need to link prevention strategies with some basic principles of fraud detection, and this forms the basis of the next chapter.

Table 6.4 Financial statement frauds – key features

Indicator	Features
Accounting anomalies	Irregular patterns of profits and/or income not borne out by nature of trade
Rapid growth or growth at a time when industrial sector as a whole is declining	Apparent growth at a time when the sector is under competitive pressure or growth which cannot be accounted for by valid commercial operations or actions
Rapid growth in activity not matched by cash increase	The business could be overtrading or some of the 'growth' may be fictitious Cash flow not matched by reported growth in activity
Fraud in decentralised or autonomous business units	Local management have local power and are not subject to direct main board overview or distanced from corporate culture
Centralised control systems which are not designed to address local operating conditions	Divisions, subsidiaries or branches not subject to full centralised control, e.g. not subject to regular internal audit or which account to head office by submission of returns etc. which are not checked or audited in detail on a regular basis
Apparent belief that any fraud discovered would not result in prosecution	Previously detected instances of fraud, corruption, misuse of funds etc. only punished by loss of employment or demotion

 **Summary**

- ACFE have classified frauds using a fraud tree but this includes a lot of American terminology not appropriate in the UK.
- Frauds have been divided into two types: those committed by individuals and frauds committed by the organisation.
- Accountants KPMG estimate fraud brought before the courts in the first half of 2009 at £600m.
- Fraud can cause serious damage to the running of the organisation and its reputation.
- Frauds committed by individuals include theft of cash and assets but also theft of confidential information and trade secrets.
- Frauds committed by the organisation mainly consist of misrepresenting the financial position of the organisation.
- Defences against fraud should be based on a framework approach incorporating several features. Fraud is too complex to build specific defences.
- Fraud defence starts with an assessment of inherent risk.
- From an accounting perspective all frauds have common features.
- Improvement in financial record keeping has reduced the risk of fraud in many areas, particularly payroll.
- It is possible to create a taxonomy of fraud which will help to focus anti-fraud activity.

Case study

Treaclemine Ltd is a family company owned jointly by Mr and Mrs Treacle. After ten years of trading they decided they needed expertise to help them expand the business so they hired Jack Spratt as CFO. What they needed was someone with the financial expertise they didn't have. The expansion began, and Mr and Mrs Treacle did whatever was needed to finance it. They refinanced their house, liquidated retirement accounts, and sold company shares to Jack Spratt so he owned 20 per cent of the business.

However, no matter how much money they put into the company, there never seemed to be enough. Sales were higher than ever, they hired more staff and the customer base expanded, but cash balances always remained low. The company occasionally went up against its overdraft limit. Mr and Mrs Treacle questioned Jack about the fact that the company never seemed to get ahead in spite of booming sales, and he calmed their fears by saying that cash flow was positive and the surplus cash generated by increased sales was fuelling expansion by funding increased receivables and inventory.

After Jack Spratt had been in place for about two years Mr and Mrs Treacle had a meeting with the auditors after the annual audit. Mr Spratt was on holiday and did not attend the meeting. The auditors were concerned about the company's trading position as a going concern. They pointed out that the projections produced by Jack Spratt were very optimistic and were unlikely to be achieved. They felt that, rather than the company doing well, unless the cash flow problems were resolved within the next few weeks, the company would have to go into administration as it would simply be unable to pay its debts.

They also pointed out some problems they had had during the audit. They felt Mr Spratt had too much control over the finances of the business and was able to override internal controls. He had got rid of the previous bookkeeper and appointed his wife, who, he claimed, was a qualified accountant, in his place. He had also removed one of the sales managers, hinting that they had been involved in fraud although there was no evidence of this.

They had had difficulty getting information out of Mr Spratt about several bank transfers. His wife claimed she knew nothing about them and that Mr Spratt was the only one with the information.

He regularly made financial decisions without consulting Mr and Mrs Treacle who trusted him to manage the cash flow. For example he rearranged the bank mandates so he could transfer money between accounts without Mr and Mrs Treacle being involved. He negotiated overdraft facilities directly with the bank.

The management information produced by Mr Spratt was extremely limited. The auditors were able to show that, in many cases, the figures he had produced to several board meetings did not bear any resemblance to the underlying records.

The auditors suggested that Mr Spratt may not be being totally honest with them and suggested that a specialist forensic investigator be brought in to review his activities.

Required

- What are the fraud risks in this company?
- What should Mr and Mrs Treacle do now?

Bibliography Association of Certified Fraud Examiners (1996) *Fraud Tree*. Association of Certified Fraud Examiners, Austin, TX.

Golden, T., Skalak, S. and Clayton, M. (2006) *A Guide to Forensic Accounting Investigation*. John Wiley, Hoboken, NJ.

Hopwood, W.S., Leiner, J.L. and Young, G. (2008) *Forensic Accounting.* McGraw-Hill, New York.

Huntington, I. and Davies, D. (1994) *Fraud Watch – A Guide for Business.* ICAEW, London.

Jeter, L. (2004) *Disconnected – Deceit and Betrayal at WorldCom.* John Wiley, Hoboken, NJ.

McLean, B. and Elkind, P. (2004) *The Smartest Guys in the Room.* Penguin, Harmondsworth.

Millichamp, A. and Taylor, J.R. (2008) *Auditing.* Cengage, London.

Narain, J. (2009) Jail: Council executive who stole £617,000 of public money for fake children's home. www.dailymail.co.uk, 13 March.

Penney, J. (2002) *Corporate Fraud – Prevention and Detection.* Tolley, London.

Silverstone, H. and Sheetz, M. (2007) *Forensic Accounting and Fraud Investigation for Non-experts.* John Wiley, Hoboken, NJ.

Singleton, T., Singleton, A., Bologna, G.J. and Lindquist, R.J. (2006) *Fraud Auditing and Forensic Accounting.* John Wiley, Hoboken, NJ.

Wells, J.T. (2004) *Corporate Fraud Handbook – Prevention and Detection.* John Wiley, Hoboken, NJ.

Websites

www.acfe.com/resources

www.dailymail.co.uk

Chapter 7

Fraud risk management

Chapter contents

- Introduction
- Defending the organisation
- General principles of risk management
- Organisation-wide approaches to risk management
- Fraud risk management
- Fraud risk management approaches
- Develop a fraud policy
- Fraud defence – the next steps

Learning objectives

After studying this chapter you should be able to:

- Understand the framework approach to building defences against fraudulent behaviour
- Understand the general principles of business risk management
- Understand the principles underlying institution-wide approaches to risk management comprising COSO and ERM
- Appreciate the importance of a systematic approach to fraud prevention
- Develop specific anti-fraud policies
- Understand the components of a fraud response plan and be able to develop one
- Appreciate the importance of having a nominated anti-fraud champion and the benefits of training
- Understand the framework for developing a practical anti-fraud programme

Introduction

In Chapter 6 we looked at the inherent risk of fraud and considered why the forensic accountant should take a broad overview of the organisation, its activities, management, culture and the business environment within which it operates order to develop an overview of the fraud risk potential within it.

The process of risk management is part of good corporate governance (Chapter 1) and it is the responsibility of the directors or senior management to consider risk in the context of the organisation and to take steps to minimise any adverse effects of identified risks to the assets or operation of the entity. This process should be reported to stakeholders as part of annual reporting. This book is only concerned with fraud risk management, but the wider scope of management's responsibilities for good corporate governance should not be forgotten.

We need now to turn to the practicalities of fraud risk management within the organisation.

Fraud is a business risk and combating risk requires a systematic and considered approach. In one way it can be treated similarly to any other business risk – the risk posed by competitors say, or the risk of fire, but in other ways fraud is a unique phenomenon. It is something organisations will stress that they are trying to actively discourage but, ironically, often end up almost encouraging through poor or inconsiderate management, lax controls or weak audit processes. Fraud happens whilst those who are supposed to guard against it, directors and auditors, are either looking the other way or not looking at all.

The best way to combat the possibility of fraud arising in the organisation is therefore to have some sound risk management policies and practices which take into account:

- the propensity of individuals to commit fraud
- the possibilities and probabilities of fraud in areas of the business, and
- identified weaknesses in both organisational and system controls

which will, hopefully, stimulate the institution through the organisation of policies and control procedures designed to prevent fraud.

In this chapter we will look at the basic principles of risk management as it relates to fraud and also at the types of policies and procedures managers can institute to minimise the possibility of it happening. No system is foolproof – all that can be done is to make the corporate ship as secure as possible so that the precious cargo of assets and cash that people have worked so hard to earn does not fall into the hands of pirates.

Defending the organisation

The strategy we are going to adopt as the basis or framework for our approach to fraud risk management in the organisation is fairly generic but its components will serve as pegs on which to hang more detailed procedures.

An effective, business-driven, fraud risk management approach encompasses activities and controls that have three objectives:

1 **Prevent** Reduce the risk of fraud and misconduct from occurring.
2 **Detect** Discover fraud and misconduct when it occurs.
3 **Respond** Take corrective action and remedy the harm caused by the fraud or misconduct.

In this chapter and Chapter 8 we will examine the first part of this strategy – prevention. The other components, detection and response, will be dealt with in Part 4.

As part of fraud prevention the challenge for organisations is to:

- Incorporate risk assessments, codes of conduct, and whistle-blower mechanisms into corporate objectives.
- Create a wide-ranging programme that manages and integrates fraud prevention, detection and response efforts.
- Understand all of the various control frameworks within the organisation and criteria that apply to them. This is wider than the internal control framework which encompasses the financial system and covers all aspects of an organisation's activities including, for example, HR policies and practices, purchasing and supply etc. Many of the aspects of the organisation that need to be considered lie outside the financial system.

Our aim, therefore, is to outline a general defensive strategy for fraud prevention based on:

- A comprehensive risk-assessment process covering all of the organisation's activities.
- The development of codes of conduct and related standards for all employees, including directors and senior managers. This includes clearly defined policies on such matters as fraud, whistle-blowing and computer misuse.
- Employee and third-party due diligence. This includes screening employees who might have access to sensitive data, and in addition, the screening of contractors and third parties.
- Communication and training – including communicating policies to employees.
- Specific fraud risk controls over IT applications – including matters such as making employees aware of the need for IT security, how to deal with such matters as phishing e-mails and what to do if they spot what they think may be a suspicious transaction.

In this chapter we will consider strategic aspects of fraud prevention and then, in Chapter 8, we will expand these principles and show how they can be applied in practice. First, however, we will look at some of the basic principles of risk management generally and at how these can be incorporated into the organisation so that they become intrinsic to the organisation and naturally dovetail with corporate objectives.

General principles of risk management

This is not a book about business risk management so we won't be looking at this topic in detail. Fortunately, however, the principles behind it are relatively straightforward. Readers who wish to enhance their knowledge of risk management practice will only have the problem of deciding which of the dozens of books on this topic they wish to read.

All organisations face risk in the course of their activities. Even public sector bodies whose role is to serve a community and who do not, generally, face much in the way of commercial risk have to deal with risk in, for example, compliance with rules and procedures, reputational risk if things go wrong or financial risk if its budgets are overspent; a charity may face risks around income generation, inability to carry out its activities through lack of volunteers or through a failure to comply with the many rules around the activities they can carry out. In short even the most innocent and non-commercial organisations cannot escape some degree of risk.

Commercial organisations are surrounded by risk. Most have a good idea of what these are and have developed strategies to deal with them. Some of the main categories such organisations may face are shown in Table 7.1.

One of the fundamental principles of risk management is that awareness of risk and approaches to dealing with it should be intrinsic to the organisation. We saw in Chapter 1 that risk management is part of good corporate governance and that it is therefore the responsibility of the directors to ensure that risks which may

Table 7.1 Business risk

Risk	Description
Strategic	Board makes wrong strategic decisions, i.e. growth through acquisition not organic growth – see Royal Bank of Scotland plc and acquisition of ABN Amro Bank NV; Vodophone Airtouch acquisition of Mannesman AG
Reputational	Bad practice, adverse publicity or catastrophic events affect the organisation's reputation to such an extent that confidence in it is lost. In extreme cases the organisation can be so damaged it ceases to exist, e.g. Ratner's jewellery chain, pensions misselling
Operational	Organisation has insufficient assets, personnel, finance or expertise to carry out its operations effectively, e.g. requirements for allowing 'internationally active' banks to calculate regulatory capital under Basel II using their own internal models for calculating operational risk capital charges – a more qualitative approach to the management of operational risk
Market	Market changes are not reflected in changes in the organisation, e.g. new competitors enter the market, or the market changes due to changes in technology or consumer preference, e.g. music downloads versus purchase of CDs – effect on HMV group and Zami (formerly Virgin Megastores) In finance changes to a market can be caused by manipulation of the market or failure to understand underlying conditions, e.g. trading in derivative instruments based on so-called sub-prime mortgages ultimately resulted in the collapse of Lehman Brothers
Technology	New technology makes existing processes or materials obsolete or inefficient, e.g. the increase in Internet shopping and banking affecting high street shops and the number of bank branches, the development of word processors drastically affected the typewriter manufacturing industry; increased risk of malware and hacking attacks on computer systems
Environmental risk	Risks arising from environmental issues including failure to comply with environmental legislation or claims arising against the organisation from environmental (including Health and Safety) issues, e.g. claims for compensation for illness caused by working with asbestos; Shell asked to pay £830m in compensation for oil pollution in Nigerian delta
Compliance	Failure to comply with applicable rules, regulations and statutes, e.g. failure to submit correct VAT returns, failure to report money laundering activities
Financial	Risks arising from poor or misleading financial management – includes interest rate and foreign exchange risks and, of course, the risk of fraud, e.g. miscalculations by Long Term Capital Management, Enron

affect the organisation are recognised and an appropriate strategy devised for dealing with them.

Risk management should thus be embedded within the organisation rather than being seen as some sort of 'bolt-on' annual exercise basically carried out by internal audit. Everyone in the organisation should not only have an awareness of risk including, of course, fraud but should also be able to contribute towards the organisation's approach to dealing with it.

There are organisation-wide approaches to risk management which seek to do just that in a formal way, and we will look at these briefly here before looking in more detail at specific aspects of the approach to fraud risk management in particular.

 ## Organisation-wide approaches to risk management

There are several formal approaches to integrating risk management into the operations of the organisations. These, essentially, cover the same ground and work in the same way, by involving employees at all levels and by formalising communications links so that system weaknesses and potential fraud risk areas can be identified and reported, allowing appropriate action can be taken.

Through the use of an integrated approach risk-management activities can be allied to organisational strategic objectives and to management goals, so that the implementation of, say, anti-fraud measures is seen as part of the organisation's normal activity and not as some sort of necessary evil internal audit function to which managers and staff only pay lip service.

Two of the best known organisation-based approaches are:

- control and risk self-assessment, and
- enterprise risk management.

We are not going to consider these in great detail but will outline the principles here for information. We will look at the detailed application of internal controls in Chapter 8.

Control and risk self-assessment

Control and risk self-assessment (CRSA) was devised as a method for implementing risk-management strategies identified by an organisation known as COSO, the Committee of Sponsoring Organisations of the Treadway Commission. This is a private-sector organisation, based in the USA, which is dedicated to providing business executives with guidance on corporate management issues, among which is the approach to dealing with risk. It developed an organisational internal control model against which businesses could evaluate their own risk. The COSO internal control framework consists of five interrelated components and, according to COSO, these provide an effective framework for describing and analysing the internal control system implemented in an organisation.

COSO takes the view that all the components of an internal control system are interrelated. Table 7.2 details the COSO view of an integrated internal control system.

Without going into too much detail, which is not appropriate here, the COSO principles can be implemented by using CRSA.

Table 7.2 COSO principles of internal control – components of an internal control system

Control environment	The control environment sets the tone of an organisation, its culture and values. It is the context within which the other components of internal control operate. Control environment factors include the integrity and ethical values of the organisation, management's operating style and the processes for managing and developing people in the organisation. The control environment is established by senior management.
Risk-assessment processes	The identification and analysis of relevant risks to the achievement of assigned objectives. Risk assessment is a prerequisite for determining how the risks should be managed.
Control activities and procedures	Control activities are the policies and procedures that inform employees of their actions and duties in connection with the control and management of financial and other systems. These include the actions necessary to deal with identified risks.
	Control procedures are those components of an internal control system which deal with the day-to-day routine procedures designed to ensure that the risk of error or serious misstatement in the financial system going undetected is minimised. We will look at these in detail later.
Information and communication	Information and communication is relevent both externally, i.e. communication with stakeholders, and internally, i.e. communication between managers and employees. Information must flow efficiently and effectively in and out of an organisation and also throughout it. This means that communication is seen as a two-way process.
Monitoring	Internal control systems need to be monitored continually, a process that assesses the quality of the system's performance over time. This requires a process of continuous improvement involving employees at all levels in the organisation which is not confined to internal or external audit or management review.

CRSA is an empowering process by which management and staff at all levels in the organisation collectively evaluate internal control systems and business risks under the guidance of a facilitator who could be an auditor, or indeed a forensic accountant. CRSA can be used to gather relevant information about risks and controls and to forge greater collaboration between internal audit, management and staff.

CRSA provides a framework and tools for management and employees to:

- identify and prioritise their business objectives
- assess and manage high-risk areas of business processes
- self-evaluate the adequacy of controls
- develop risk treatment action plans, and
- ensure that the identification, recognition and evaluation of business objectives and risks are consistent across all levels of the organisation.

CRSA takes a similar approach to risk-based issues, including fraud, as management initiatives such as total quality management (TQM) or enterprise risk management (ERM) insofar as it requires all employees to become involved in the process.

There are six aspects of CRSA:

1 Improving auditee participation by involving staff at all levels of the organisation so as to build upon and enhance the normal audit process.
2 Initiating control awareness seminars.
3 The use of control questionnaires by management as a framework for evaluating risk and controls.

4 Self-certification by managers of the effectiveness of controls.
5 Systematic and open-minded evaluation of risk and controls through workshops and focus meetings.
6 Management and staff assume total responsibility for control design implementation and review.

Whilst much of this may seem simple good practice and common sense, CRSA can be adopted as a formal methodology which encourages staff at all levels to think about control issues, and this goes a long way towards creating a climate within the organisation where corrupt behaviour does not flourish.

CRSA aims to integrate risk-management practices and culture into the way staff undertake their jobs, and the way that business units achieve their objectives. The successful implementation of CRSA has a number of specific benefits:

- It directly involves the staff in risk assessment and control evaluation activities, and thereby assists in creating a partnership approach between them and the audit function.
- It allows a better allocation of scarce audit resources by involving the staff in the risk assessment and control evaluation process. Audit resources can thus be concentrated into specific target areas.
- It educates management and employees in risk management and control evaluation processes.
- It assists in aligning business unit objectives with corporate goals.
- It fosters a sense of 'ownership' of risks and controls.
- It builds teamwork in addressing risks.
- It improves communication within business units and across the organisation.
- It provides a mechanism for raising the awareness of management and staff with regard to the effect that 'soft' controls such as organisational values, ethical standards competence and leadership styles can have on the overall health of the corporate control system.

However, CRSA has its limitations:

- It is primarily a technique for risk assessment and organisational improvement so it will not of itself detect fraud. Its aim is to improve risk assessment and internal control by involving management and staff in the process which will, hopefully, restrict or reduce opportunities for and the inclination to commit acts of dysfunctional behaviour.
- One important consideration is that of management style and the culture of the organisation. If a particular style of management discourages innovation and collaboration and does not foster discussion and criticism, participants in the process may not be honest in terms of risk disclosure, may not trust each other and so not work effectively as a team. A blame culture can lead to recriminations and an organisation which measures promotional worth by setting employees against each other competitively will not be able to create the right atmosphere of openness and trust which will make the process work.
- Workshops facilitated by senior managers may inhibit free and open discussion where participants do not have confidence in the process. Similarly senior management that is not committed to the CRSA approach may dismiss the findings of a focus group or workshop which comprised only employees more junior than themselves.

- It is important that the head of internal audit backs the process and provides facilitators of appropriate ability and expertise both to encourage the process to flourish and to convince sceptics that it has value.

In addition organisations considering CRSA should note:

- Difficulties may be experienced in attempting to introduce new management practices, techniques or concepts to an organisation.
- The CRSA process involves initial and continuous investment and its cost/benefit ratio is not easy to determine.
- Some of the major obstacles/restraints/pitfalls to the conducting of CRSA exercises are:
  - lack of top management support
  - lack of facilitators who lack the skills and experience in facilitation, consensus oriented techniques and the knowledge of the theory and application of controls, and
  - lack of knowledge by facilitators of the systems under review.
- There is often an underestimation of the time, investment, learning or planning necessary to mount a successful workshop or series of workshops.
- If the initial focus is too narrow it can limit the potential of the CRSA exercise; conversely starting off with a huge first project may cause the process to fail before any progress is achieved.

At first the process should consist of attainable steps which are capable of being measured by some form of key performance indicator. The proven benefits should be used to convince sceptics that the process is worthwhile so it can be applied in areas of the organisation where benefits may be less easily measured.

Enterprise risk management

Enterprise risk management (ERM) is a process which is promoted as a risk-management option and shares many similarities with the CRSA process described above, and for that reason we will not describe it in detail. As ever interested students will find a wealth of books on the topic. There are many definitions of ERM but one that will suit our purpose comes from COSO:

> a process, effected by an entity's board of directors, management and other personnel, applied in strategy setting and across the enterprise, designed to identify potential events that may affect the entity, and manage risk to be within its risk appetite, to provide reasonable assurance regarding the achievement of entity objectives.

ERM is an ongoing process involving individuals at every level of the organisation which looks at risk across the organisation. It is designed to identify potential events which, if they occur, will affect the entity and to manage risks so that they are contained within what the organisation considers to be acceptable levels. The idea behind an enterprise-wide approach is that, in this way, risks which affect different parts of the organisation can be assessed and evaluated collectively, thus reducing surprises.

The process is designed to evaluate the various possible responses to identified risks and to select the most appropriate. By co-ordinating risk responses and focusing management effort resources can be used to best advantage and losses minimised, thus facilitating the achievement of objectives.

However, all this is not as complex as it might appear. The Institute of Chartered Accountants in England and Wales (ICAEW) takes the view that ERM is not a new technique, and that the idea of integrating risk management across the organisation and of embedding risk management in the culture is central to all risk-management processes.

The two approaches outlined above are mechanisms for integrating risk-management approaches into the everyday life of the organisation. We must now consider some basic principles so that students will develop a sound understanding of the principles of risk management before we move on to the more detailed practical implementations. Those specifically relevant to IT systems are considered in Chapter 9.

Having looked at the types of risk an organisation faces and strategic approaches to managing risk we will confine our considerations to one type of risk only – the financial risk of fraud.

For the purpose of setting the context for what follows it is necessary, first, to look at the principles which underlie the organisational approach to fraud risk.

 ## Fraud risk management

In order to deal with the specific risk of fraud it will be necessary to carry out a specific fraud risk analysis. A preliminary review of the organisation itself and the systems and subsystems within it will indicate areas where investigation may prove fruitful and some form of matrix analysis may prove useful (Chapter 10). However, this can be a very complex and time-consuming process so is probably only suitable to the process of an investigation.

Much of this work should, of course, have already been carried out by internal or external auditors who should have identified the key risk factors within the organisation where these exist.

Key risk factors

Key risk factors from an organisational perspective are:

- lack of any form of ethical code or corporate standard of what constitutes moral behaviour
- management who prepare an ethical code which they ignore or promote corporate values but don't abide by them and set a poor example
- management apathy towards internal control issues
- poor communication between senior management and employees with the result that:
  - management decisions go unexplained
  - management cannot communicate its codes of values effectively, or
  - management can't listen to feedback from line managers or employees
- management that pays scant regard to the internal control environment – seeing it as 'red tape' or 'layers of bureaucracy' so they maintain systems which contain little in the way of segregation of duties or supervision
- a culture of not paying attention to internal rules and processes which are not enforced

- organisational structures which leave parts of the organisation outside the main-stream and away from routine overview, e.g. autonomous subsidiaries
- a situation where one company has been acquired by another, larger, organisation which is beginning to subsume the culture of the smaller organisation thus creating change and uncertainty
- having no redress or mechanism to deal with employees who say they feel they have been treated wrongly or unfairly or who feel unappreciated
- lack of training on fraud matters specifically but also generally
- line managers who ignore comments from employees who feel they have been passed over for promotion, or who complain they are not rewarded as well as colleagues who don't seem to work as hard as they do, or
- having no anti-fraud champion or, indeed, any individual promoting an anti-fraud culture.

Systems risk factors

In a specific systems context risk factors will include:

- lack of segregation of duties
- lack of supervision
- lack of authorisation controls
- poor communications between management and staff
- lack of awareness of ethical and other policies
- rapid turnover of employees
- constant 'fire-fighting' or crisis
- lack of access to information
- weak or antiquated accounting systems resulting in poor analysis
- poor audit trails
- poor physical controls resulting in inappropriate access to computer systems or inventories
- inadequate training of employees, and
- lack of competent staff – particularly in supervisory or audit roles.

Clearly good auditing, both internal and external, should over time have highlighted systems weaknesses and closed down a lot of the opportunities for fraud, even those which exist in small organisations with fewer employees from which to establish a proper system of internal control. Most of these principles are well known and it would be a poor auditor who did not identify a major systems weakness caused by weak authorisation controls or poor segregation of duties – and yet frauds continue to happen.

Fraud targets

Frauds against the organisation where assets are misappropriated by employees generally do not happen within the mainstream systems. In the absence of collusion, which we will consider later, frauds take place either:

- at the higher levels of management where the very managers perpetrating the fraud have also a key internal control or have sufficient influence to subvert it easily, or
- at the 'edges' of the system where seemingly innocuous transactions can be handled by a trusted employee.

This is one of the reasons why external auditors may not find fraud – simply because the fraudster is either not operating in an area material to their audit or are relying on management who may be lying to them.

Typical fraud targets, apart from the obvious ones of cash and inventory, will be more peripheral items, such as:

- incurring extra telephone/Internet costs to the business without permission, i.e. use of office facilities to carry out personal tasks, e.g. telephone, photocopying, computer time etc. – this is by far the biggest cost to the majority of businesses
- employee time – assigning subordinates to non-work-related activities
- data files – customer identification and/or bank details
- giving discounts or free goods/services to people that are not entitled
- stealing stationery such as pens, paper and envelopes
- stealing equipment ranging from staplers to cameras to computer hardware
- copying information files for personal use or for selling to third parties
- copying computer software for personal use or for selling to third parties
- stealing customer lists
- theft of trade secrets or intellectual property
- producing false orders and taking the goods
- false employees, or
- false suppliers.

Some of these apparent frauds are clearly not much more than simple theft and would be prosecuted accordingly but they all fall within the ambit of this book for our purposes.

This sort of preliminary work by investigators, considering reports, analysing relationships and considering areas of weakness, may well save time and cost in the long run. This need not be a lengthy process; indeed it may take place to some extent whilst detailed checking work is underway. Vulnerable areas can perhaps be identified relatively quickly, as can key relationships, but investigators should take time to consider all aspects of vulnerability and all aspects of relationships before finally closing the file, as the story they have been given initially may be far from complete.

 ## Fraud risk management approaches

When dealing with any sort of business risk there are basically four options. This is known as the 'TARA' approach to risk management. Students will find other mnemonics in risk-management textbooks but they all work in basically the same way.

The TARA approach is:

1 *Transfer the risk* – put the risk on to someone else – for example, an insurance company. For example, with respect to fraud, organisations should carry insurance, known as fidelity insurance, in respect either of specific individuals or of all management and staff. Its purpose is to enable the organisation to recover losses caused by dishonest behaviour. This may be expensive – it would depend on how big a risk the insurers consider the organisation to be – but instituting the types of control measures described in this book would undoubtedly help to keep premiums down. Claims under fidelity insurance policies often involve a forensic accountant in quantifying the losses and reporting to the insurers.

2 *Accept the risk* – it may be that after suitable review, investigation, analysis and consideration the organisation considers the risk of fraud is so low that they are prepared to accept it. This is known as residual risk, i.e. the level of risk an organisation is prepared to accept and live with. In this case losses due to fraud will be accepted and no specific measures, other than internal accounting controls, will be instituted.

This may be acceptable to management, but experience shows that most organisations are susceptible to some form of fraud or theft somewhere. To claim that the organisation has such powerful control mechanisms that fraud would only be at a very low level or that any serious attempt at fraud would be instantly detected is tantamount to hubris and, as in all the best tragedies, that sort of behaviour is invariably punished. Remember that all fraudsters have 'first go' advantage and often display a greater level of ingenuity or deceit than those charged with designing and monitoring controls and systems.

3 *Reduce the risk* – the business should take action to reduce the risk to as low a level as is feasible given the level of resource the organisation is able to commit. This is the option of choice for most organisations and is the subject of this section of the book.

4 *Avoid the risk* – the fourth option is to avoid risk by not engaging in activities which may be risky, but unfortunately fraud and corruption is not within the organisation's control so this strategy, which is of limited use at the best of times, is of no use here.

As we have seen, management has the responsibility, as part of good corporate governance, of instituting procedures to manage risk. What follows is a six-step programme designed to identify and evaluate the impact of fraud and corruption on the organisation.

The six steps are:

1 Assess the organisation and identify areas vulnerable to risk.
2 Assess the possible scale of risk.
3 Understand the processes and develop a methodology for dealing with identified risks.
4 Allocate responsibilities and resources to deal with identified risks.
5 Carry out monitoring and audit procedures.
6 Review the process and refine the strategy.

We will look at each of these steps in detail.

1 Assess the organisation and identify areas vulnerable to risk

This should include not just the more obvious areas such as fixed assets, inventories and cash but operational areas such as procurement, wages, invoicing and billing. The review should also consider all aspects of any particular risk, so in the case of fraud risk it should include not simply theft of assets but also such matters as the corruption of employees by outsiders, risk of employees paying bribes and the exposure to management fraud in terms of deliberate misrepresentation of financial statements.

Clearly there are some obvious areas which don't require forensic accountancy training to identify as vulnerable. These include:

- cash transactions – involving tills or cash collections by representatives or agents

- stock with easy illicit resale value – food, tobacco, alcohol, electrical/electronic goods, car parts, clothes, petrol, red diesel, etc., and
- assets which can easily be stolen, e.g. laptops and computer stores

but the assessment should also include other areas which may not be so obvious. For example:

- How rigorous are internal controls within purchasing procedures? Can purchasing managers both authorise new supplier accounts and approve invoices?
- Is there a tender procedure for awarding contracts? Who runs it? Who wins the tenders? Is it always the same contractors?
- Can low-paid clerks agree price discounts with customers?
- How often do managers check the names of staff on the payroll? Is the HR function separate from the payment of wages?

And think the unthinkable:

- What pressures are on senior management including executive directors?
- Could there be sufficient pressure to make them respond by falsifying or misstating the accounts?
- Are the activities of management at branches, subsidiaries and associates monitored adequately from the centre? Do we know what they are doing, how much discretion they have over budgets and management accounts and how they exercise it?

'Frauds' in the appendices contains a stunningly long list of possible frauds which could be perpetrated in an organisation, not all of which may be likely but any of which might be possible in a given organisation.

Remember that a fraudster has to be successful only in one small area, management has to watch everything. The key to successful evaluation is identifying these areas of opportunity for the fraudster which can be closed down or monitored closely. Fraud may not be stopped entirely in this way but the activity can be made much more difficult and the chances of detection are increased – which is the main objective.

2 Assess the possible scale of risk

The risks identified can be then evaluated and awarded some form of weighting. The weighting should take account of the imminence or likelihood of the risk materialising to the possible detriment of the organisation and the effect on the organisation if it does materialise.

The weightings can be as simple as high, medium or low or use some more complex mathematical approach.

One thing must be made clear and that is, irrespective of the approach used, there is always a considerable level of subjectivity in the assessment of the impact of risk and its effect on the organisation. This is because the act of assessment calls for an exercise of judgement and some intelligent estimation. It is not necessarily important to be precise in connection with fraud risk – the key point about assessing the likely impact is to identify the areas where immediate action may need to be taken and to distinguish them from areas where little or no action is needed immediately.

This would include not simply losses due to fraud but more intangible risks such as the risk to the organisation's reputation should a fraud or other form of dysfunctional behaviour become public knowledge. Clearly, for example, if the organisation is a listed company which encounters a major fraud it has to make a public disclosure which may have an adverse effect on the share price and the attitude of potential investors.

The effects on the organisation can be quantified in many ways but often a simple matrix is used. This can then simulate the operational strategy by determining which risks are addressed first and which might be safely ignored for the time being.

An example of such a matrix is given in Figure 7.1. Clearly this is the simplest possible version shown for purpose of illustration, in reality this can be made as complex as is deemed necessary. However, over-complication can lead to confusion so adopting the most easily understandable approach is advised – particularly if the matrix is to be used when briefing staff or management.

For students, examples of risk assessment matrices from public bodies can often be found on the Internet.

In the case of fraudulent or corrupt behaviour, attempting to quantify the risk is probably a futile exercise insofar as an ingenious fraudster, operating over several years, can get away with considerably more money than the organisation might expect. Frequently after a fraud has been detected and its full extent is revealed the result comes as a complete shock to managers. Often the full extent of the fraudster's depredations are not fully calculated as even the fraudster loses track of precisely how much they have stolen.

Even in organisations with a strong control environment, rigorous accounting procedures and a high level of compliance fraudsters can amass considerably more wealth at the organisation's expense than an academic calculation might indicate. The reason is that generally, fraudsters start off in a small way and their thefts increase over time. The longer the fraud goes on, particularly after the first anniversary, the more likely the fraudster is to increase the average size of their individual fraudulent transactions.

This was apparently true of both Stephen Maw at Leeds City Council (Chapter 4) who stole £870,000 over nine years, and Julie Wall who stole £557,000 from North

Figure 7.1 Risk assessment matrix

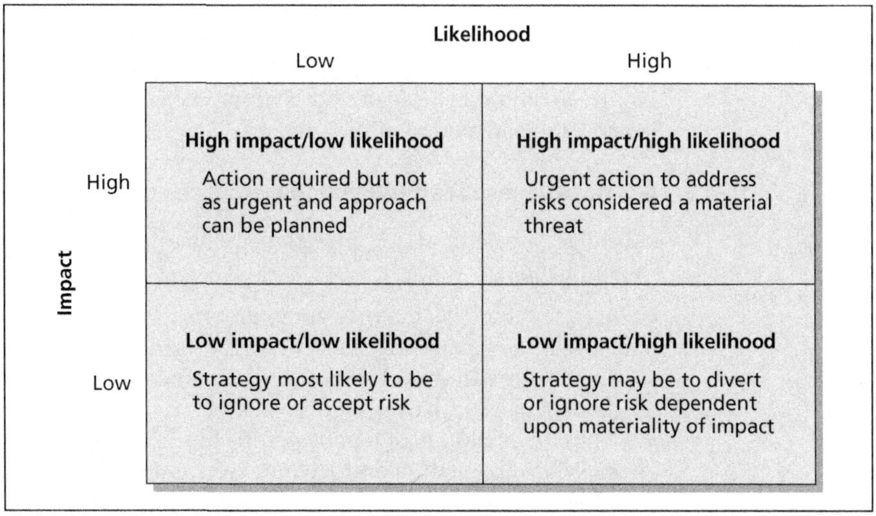

Kesteven Council in Lincolnshire (Chapter 11) over about nine years in organisational environments where internal control and internal audit procedures are generally strong. These employees were trusted: they were able to keep up their activities for a long time and build up gradually.

3 Understand the processes and develop a methodology for dealing with identified risks

The fundamental point to be understood is that fraud risk management must be tackled in an orderly and structured way (Figure 7.2). As we have seen, simply relying on internal audit or, worse, an annual audit by the external auditors will not deter the fraudster and will make detection difficult, if not impossible.

The organisational response must be holistic. This means that the whole of the organisation, its activities, processes and people must be included in the evaluation and everyone must be included, from the CEO to the car park attendant.

The first step in the fraud risk-management process is for the management to declare their intentions by developing and circulating appropriate policies. These policies should include:

- a fraud policy
- a whistle-blowing policy, and
- a prosecution policy.

It is axiomatic that all employees, including the directors, should abide by the policies and that any transgression is punished appropriately.

Once we have policies the next steps are to develop a systematised response to implementing anti-fraud measures. We will look at these in detail later in this chapter, but briefly they are:

- Appoint a champion.
- Develop a fraud response plan.
- Set up a fraud response team.
- Implement fraud awareness training.
- Develop and implement thorough HR policies.
- Consider the impact on the reputation of the organisation.
- Document and understand internal control procedures.

The risk-management approach should be documented and the plan communicated to all responsible parties. The document should be the responsibility of a risk group or committee headed by a champion charged with responsibility for ensuring the implementation of the strategy.

4 Allocate responsibilities and resources to deal with identified risks

Where responsibilities are allocated resources should be made available. These might include:

- strengthening the internal audit process through increased resources or enabling and empowering the department through increased access to all aspects of the organisation and by ensuring that the response of senior management to internal audit initiatives is positive
- provision of additional reporting software to enable the management to receive timely, comprehensive and accurate reports about all aspects of the performance of the organisation

Figure 7.2 Risk management process

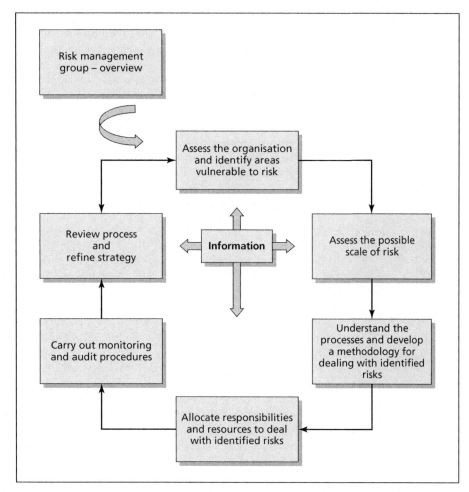

- changes to internal processes where these are defined as being weak or vulnerable, and
- recruitment of specialised staff, particularly in IT.

It is a mistake for management to acknowledge the possibility or probability of risk whilst, at the same time, denying the resources to deal with it. The caveat to this, of course, is that dealing with the risk, and all the ramifications that flow from it, is cheaper than allowing the risk to crystallise. However, it is rarely a suitable option to tacitly acknowledge fraud and turn a blind eye to it. As readers should be aware by now the damage to the organisation may not only be a financial cost but also in other, less tangible areas such as:

- poor staff morale
- loss of ethical employees, and
- potential damage to the organisation's reputation.

These are costs which cannot be easily quantified but which may be the most expensive of all in the long term.

5 Carry out monitoring and audit procedures

This is usually left to the audit function but, in reality, stems from the responsibility of all staff to foster a moral and ethical culture within the organisation such that defrauding it is seen as anti-social and perverse. This has to be led and maintained by senior management.

We have looked elsewhere in this book at the role of external and internal audit (Part 1) and management should use these resources appropriately. Only the smallest organisations can rely on internal controls functioning effectively without some form of internal audit presence as the annual external audit visit is insufficient to constitute an effective monitoring function.

Management should also use their internal management information systems to generate reports which will highlight anomalies to be followed up and investigated.

6 Review the process and refine the strategy

All processes should be subject to review and monitoring and fraud risk management is no different. As we have seen above, formal approaches such as COSO or ERM compel this process of constant review, but even organisations which don't go so far as to embrace a formal system could or should make fraud risk management review the responsibility of an audit committee or another committee of the board comprising non-executive directors.

The results of internal audit processes and ancillary activities such as a whistle-blowing hotline should be collated and reported appropriately. Changes in the organisation require changes to the strategy.

By implementing, resourcing and monitoring an organisation-wide approach to fraud risk management the entity is taking steps to protect itself, none of which are likely to have a detrimental effect on the function and operation of its internal processes and most of which will bring positive benefits in terms of improved reporting and management's knowledge of the organisation.

We can now look at some of these actions in more detail, starting with the development of anti-fraud policies.

Develop a fraud policy

The first principle when dealing with fraud is *prevention is better than detection*.

For this reason a good deal of any fraud prevention strategy is predicated upon the creation of a strong anti-fraud environment within the organisation.

As we saw in Chapter 4 many employees can demonstrate an ambivalent morality in the workplace, exacerbated by management attitudes. Where there is a culture of paying lip service to policies and where serious breaches go unpunished or, where there is no individual championing an anti-fraud culture, the organisation can suffer from extensive low-level petty fraud or even higher level serious fraud.

Management in many organisations is, no doubt, fully aware that the use of company resources for private purposes is generally officially frowned on but unofficially tolerated so, in practice, organisations turn a blind eye to:

- employees making personal phone calls
- photocopying amounts of personal documents

- using the Internet for private purposes during working hours
- taking company equipment such as laptops home in contravention of security policies
- submitting expenses claims not fully evidenced by documentation, or
- encouraging close friendships with suppliers or customers in the interest of 'good business relations'.

The reason is that, firstly, such relatively small amounts of 'unofficial' activity would doubtless cost more to police than the activity costs the organisation and, secondly, no organisation would want to lose the goodwill of its employees by engendering a culture based on the fear of reprisals or punishment for taking home an office pencil.

However, consider the following:

- Public sector bodies such as local authorities, hospitals, NHS Trusts, housing associations etc. are funded by public money which has to be accounted for.
- If it is acceptable to surf the Internet where is the line drawn as to what it is acceptable to access – online holiday companies or shopping websites might be acceptable but what about employees using social networking sites like Facebook or MySpace, online gaming or E-bay?
- If an organisation has 50 employees and each one steals as little as £10 worth of goods each week for 48 weeks, that costs the organisation £24,000 per year. This is a loss of profit so this would have to be grossed up to give the revenue that would be needed to be generated to replace it. If we estimate a gross margin of 30 per cent, this loss represents £80,000 worth of sales income.

As we have seen, no anti-fraud initiative will succeed without the framework of a strong corporate governance structure (Chapter 1). This requires a lead from the directors who will set both the organisation's tone and its attitude towards specific instances of what is considered unacceptable and what is considered acceptable moral and ethical behaviour by *all* employees of the business, including its directors and senior managers.

Consequently the first line of defence is the stated position of the organisation led by the directors and senior management. The organisation should make it certain, beyond doubt, where it stands with regard to unethical acts by its employees including senior staff and directors. Accordingly, when instituting anti-fraud policies, the first steps to consider are:

- The moral climate of the organisation – does it tolerate low-level pilfering or use of company assets for private purposes?
- Does the management lead in its attitude to unethical behaviour?
- Are the HR policies strong enough to identify and deal with staff who may feel alienated and ill-disposed towards the organisation and who may not abide by the policies?

There are many and various recommendations as to what sort of policies organisations should institute. Clearly providing detailed sample policies for all aspects of the organisation are well outside the scope of this book but we will suggest wording for some specific fraud policies pertinent to the subject.

It has been advocated, by some authorities, mostly those based in the USA, that the organisation's ethical stance should be included in any mission statement used by the organisation to state its objectives, approach and values. In the UK mission statements have often been derided as being rather vain posturings usually incorporating unfortunate clichés such as 'world class', 'delighting the customer' and offering 'solutions' but properly written they can be a clear statement of intentions and values.

A mission statement which clearly states the organisation's commitment to ethical principles and an intolerance of fraudulent and corrupt behaviour makes its case from the outset, and inclusion of a declaration of corporate values in a mission statement should be seriously considered.

Whether or not the organisation has a mission statement they should develop some specific policies for all employees. These should include an:

- anti-fraud policy
- whistle-blowing policy, and
- prosecution policy

each of which we will look at in detail.

Fraud policy

This is a policy which every employee should have as part of their staff handbook. Staff should have this as part of their contract of employment and they should be reminded about the policy on a regular basis. It should cover business ethics and fraud with explanations about acceptable behaviour in circumstances where there is a high risk of unethical behaviour taking place.

A sample fraud policy is shown in Exhibit 7.1.

A key part of reinforcing commitment to the policy is an annual reminder. All new staff should be given and acknowledge receipt of a copy of the fraud policy on commencing work. Existing staff should be sent it both on paper, by e-mail and through any corporate reporting mechanisms such as a company newspaper or bulletin.

The policy should be brief and easy to understand so that staff of all levels of competence can appreciate its contents. Staff who are blind, for example, should be provided with the policy in an acceptable format, either Braille or audio.

It may also be appropriate for some staff, if not all, to sign an annual declaration that they have read and understood the policy and will abide by its contents.

The policy should include:

- A statement of the commitment of the organisation to ethical and moral values.
- The role and attitude of the board to fraud and illegal behaviour.
- Who the policy applies to – if possible it should be made to apply to those the company deals with as well as its own staff.
- What actions are defined as fraudulent, i.e. include bribery and corruption, deliberate misrepresentation etc. as well as theft.
- The board's policy towards fraud and the actions it intends to take where instances of fraudulent or corrupt behaviour are discovered.

This policy may well be backed up by standing orders, instructions and disciplinary procedures. Employees throughout the organisation should be no doubt that the policy is going to be enforced and that it is not simply there as an appendix to the staff handbook.

Exhibit 7.1 Fraud policy statement: a sample

The following example of an anti-fraud policy statement should be used as a guide only. The content of your anti-fraud policy will depend upon the nature, size and complexity of your business.

Policy statement

(*Organisation name*) is committed to the prevention of fraud and the promotion of an anti-fraud culture. (*Organisation name*) operates a zero-tolerance attitude to fraud and requires staff to act honestly and with integrity at all times, and to report all reasonable suspicions of fraud.

(*Organisation name*) will investigate all instances of actual, attempted and suspected fraud committed by staff, consultants, suppliers and other third parties and will seek to recover funds and assets lost through fraud. Perpetrators will be subject to disciplinary and/or legal action.

This policy is endorsed and supported by the Board of Directors and Chief Executive Officer.

Definition of fraud

The term 'fraud' is commonly used to describe the use of deception to deprive, disadvantage or cause loss to another person or party. This can include theft, the misuse of funds or other resources as well as more complicated crimes such as false accounting and the supply of false information.

Examples include: (*Insert fraud examples – see Chapters 11 & 12*).

Individuals can be prosecuted under the Fraud Act 2006 if they make a false representation, fail to disclose information or abuse their position.

(*Organisation name*) has established procedures to encourage staff to report actual, attempted or suspected fraud and/or other forms of illegal activity without fear of reprisal.

Key responsibilities

The Directors of (*Organisation name*) are responsible for:

- Developing, implementing and maintaining adequate systems of internal control to prevent and detect fraud.
- Regularly reviewing (*Organisation name's*) anti-fraud policy statement and compliance to ensure it remains effective and relevant to the needs of the business.
- Investigating all allegations of fraud and commencing disciplinary and/or legal action where appropriate.
- Reporting to the Board of Directors on all aspects of fraud risk management.

Managers are responsible for:

- Familiarising themselves with the types of fraud and dishonesty that might occur within their business units.
- Monitoring compliance with internal controls and agreed policies and procedures.
- Notifying their Director (or other specified person) of any indications of fraudulent activity.

Staff are responsible for:

- Ensuring that (*Organisation name's*) reputation and assets are protected against fraud.
- Reporting known or suspected fraud.
- Assisting in the investigation of suspected fraud.

Reporting suspicions

Staff must report concerns about actual, attempted or suspected fraud to their line manager or (*alternative name*). Alternatively, staff can call the 24-hour whistle blowing hotline on (*Hotline number*).

Staff should not attempt to investigate any fraud themselves.

The Public Interest Disclosure Act 1998 protects employees who raise concerns about certain matters of public interest in good faith. Staff can obtain free independent advice from the charity Public Concern at Work on 020 3117 2520 or 020 7404 6609.

A copy of the *Whistle-blowing Policy* can be found on the intranet or can be obtained from (*location*).

Fraud response plan

(*Organisation name*) has established guidelines for senior managers on the immediate actions to be taken in the event of a fraud being discovered or suspected within their business unit. It covers reporting and recording requirements, securing evidence and preventing further losses, and the investigation process.

A copy of the *Fraud Response Plan* can be found on the intranet or can be obtained from (*location*).

Source: Fraud Advisory Panel

The policy should be supported by procedures for fraud response and investigation, which we look at later, and additional guidance as appropriate. Where necessary staff should be given training in understanding and recognising fraud and what to do if they encounter or suspect it.

Whistle-blowing policy

Whistle-blowing and internal 'tip-offs' are a major source of information about frauds in the organisation and the organisation should introduce processes to facilitate these and to make the process as non-threatening and straightforward as possible.

The organisation should set up and communicate to employees a whistle-blowing policy to encourage the flow of information. Clearly care has to be taken that this does not encourage malicious reporting, but any protections against this must not be so draconian that they discourage speculative reports which may lead to the exposure of dysfunctional behaviour.

Organisations must be aware of and comply with the provisions of the Public Interest Disclosure Act 1998 (PIDA). Note that under PIDA there is no statutory requirement for organisations to introduce a whistle-blowing policy although good practice in corporate governance codes in the UK does state that, if possible, a whistle-blowing policy should be instituted.

There are some specific instances where whistle-blowing policies are required:

- Listed companies subject to the Combined Code are obliged to have whistle-blowing arrangements or explain why they do not.
- Public bodies, which are assessed regularly, are expected to have a policy in place as part of the external audit and review of local authorities and NHS bodies.
- Companies subject to 'Sarbox' (Chapter 3) are also required to have whistle-blowing arrangements.

The nature of the whistle-blowing arrangements will be determined by an organisation's size, structure, culture, nature of the risks that it faces and the legal framework in which it operates.

One of the best methods for reporting fraud is a confidential 24/7 hotline, whether internal or operated by an external provider. However, no arrangement will work unless management creates the appropriate environment of honesty and trust to encourage individuals to come forward without fear. Clear channels of communication from employees to management are essential in creating an environment that encourages fraud prevention and detection.

This will avoid embarrassing revelations appearing on Internet sites or in the press.

Establishing effective reporting mechanisms is one of the key elements of a fraud prevention programme and can have a positive impact on fraud detection. Many frauds are known or suspected by people who are not involved. The challenge for management is to encourage these innocent people to speak out and to demonstrate that it is very much in their own interest to do so. Research has shown that although about one in four employees are aware of misconduct in the workplace, over half of those people fail to report it for various reasons, but mainly a mixture of fear and loyalty.

These include:

- loyalty to working groups or family
- the concept of not 'grassing' on colleagues

- disinterest – employees disassociate from the organisation and feel it is the organisation's problem
- unacknowledged admiration for someone 'getting away with it'
- fear of persecution by the organisation
- fear of being shunned by colleagues if the individual's role is revealed, and
- suspicion rather than proof.

The organisation's anti-fraud culture and reporting processes can be a major influence on the whistle-blower, as it is often fear of reprisals that has a major effect on them and results in potential informants remaining silent. Unfortunately there have been one or two well-publicised cases where whistle-blowers have been harried by management or have lost their jobs (see p. 73) and, in one well-known case, their professional qualification. These cases have doubtless reinforced the inclination of employees not to seek trouble and to keep their heads below the parapet.

As we have seen, research (Chapter 5) indicates that fraud is often committed by fairly senior managers which naturally worsens the situation for the whistle-blower as the alleged perpetrator might be, say, their line manager. Senior management's challenge is to convince staff that:

- combating fraud is the responsibility of everyone
- no one, no matter how senior, is exempt from exposure and its consequences, and
- the future health of the organisation and potentially their future employment could be at risk from fraud if it is allowed to damage the organisation.

The policy (see Exhibit 7.2) should contain statements to the effect that:

- Whistle-blowing is not a complaint – the aim of whistle-blowing is to report wrongdoing not to air workplace grievances.
- Arrangements for disclosure can be made that bypass line management.
- An employee has a right to confidentiality.
- Any helpline or other process is completely confidential. One good way of doing this is for it to be operated by a third party which then reports concerns to the appropriate level of management.
- The policy should explain the circumstances in which concerns can be raised with a body external to the organisation such as a regulator rather than to the management. This may be, for example, where the unethical behaviour is being carried out by the directors or senior management and either there is no alternative reporting line such as an audit committee (Chapter 1) or the process is not perceived to be trustworthy or secure.
- Persecution of or exposure of a whistle-blower or malicious reporting should be a disciplinary offence – possibly classed as gross misconduct rendering the perpetrator open to dismissal.

The practical arrangements made should reflect the policy.

Some organisations dislike the term whistle-blowing and prefer to use euphemisms such as 'speaking out' or 'raising concerns' – it matters not.

Whilst confidentiality should be guaranteed, anonymity is a different issue. Anonymous reports over an internal hotline can make allegations difficult to substantiate and investigate so individuals making a report should be encouraged to give their name. This, of course, will require a leap of faith by them so using internal hotlines and designated officers may not be enough to convince employees that they will be safeguarded.

Legal advice should be sought when setting up a hotline as, in some circumstances there are technical issues involving EU data protection rules and the 'Sarbox' legislation has problems with anonymous reporting which there is no need to expand on here.

Prosecution policy

The company should have a policy of referring detected frauds to the police for prosecution. This policy should be communicated to all staff as part of the fraud policy.

Exhibit 7.2 **Sample whistle-blowing policy**

Introduction
This whistle-blowing policy has been introduced in response to the Public Interest Disclosure Act 1998 and provides a procedure which enables employees to raise concerns about what is happening at work, particularly where those concerns relate to unlawful conduct, financial malpractice or dangers to the public or the environment. The object of this policy is to ensure that concerns are raised and dealt with at an early stage and in an appropriate manner.

This organisation is committed to its whistle-blowing policy. If an employee raises a genuine concern under this policy, he or she will not be at risk of losing their job, nor will they suffer any form of detriment as a result. As long as the employee is acting in good faith and in accordance with this policy, it does not matter if they are mistaken.

How the whistle-blowing policy differs from the grievance procedure
This policy does not apply to raising grievances about an employee's personal situation. These types of concern are covered by the organisation's grievance procedure. The whistle-blowing policy is primarily concerned with where the interests of others or of this organisation itself are at risk. It may be difficult to decide whether a particular concern should be raised under the whistle-blowing policy or under the grievance procedure or under both. If an employee has any doubt as to the correct route to follow, this organisation encourages the concern to be raised under this policy and will decide how the concern should be dealt with.

Protecting the employee
This organisation will not tolerate harassment or victimisation of anyone raising a genuine concern under the whistle-blowing policy. If an employee requests that their identity be protected, all possible steps will be taken to prevent the employee's identity becoming known. If the situation arises where it is not possible to resolve the concern without revealing the employee's identity (e.g. if the employee's evidence is needed in court), the best way to proceed with the matter will be discussed with the employee. Employees should be aware that, by reporting matters anonymously, it will be more difficult for the organisation to investigate them, to protect the employee and to give the employee feedback. Accordingly, while the organisation will consider anonymous reports, this policy does not cover matters raised anonymously.

How the matter will be handled
Once an employee has informed the organisation of his or her concern, the concerns will be examined and the organisation will assess what action should be taken. This

▶

may involve an internal enquiry or a more formal investigation. The employee will be told who is handling the matter, how they can contact him/her and whether any further assistance may be needed. If the employee has any personal interest in the matter, this should be declared by the employee at the outset. If the employee's concern falls more properly within the grievance procedure, then they will be advised of this.

How to raise a concern internally

Step 1

If an employee has a concern about malpractice, he or she should consider raising it initially with their line manager. This may be done orally or in writing. An employee should specify from the outset if they wish the matter to be treated in confidence so that appropriate arrangements can be made. Alternatively, employees can call the 24-hour whistle-blowing telephone hotline. This service is strictly confidential and callers will not be asked to give their name if they do not want to.

Step 2

If these channels have been followed and the employee still has concerns, or an employee feels that they are unable to raise a particular matter with their line manager, for whatever reason, they should raise the matter with their head of department, the head of human resources or the head of internal audit.

Independent advice

If an employee is unsure whether to use this procedure or wants independent advice at any stage, they may contact the independent charity Public Concern at Work on 020 7404 6609. Their lawyers can give free confidential advice at any stage about how to raise a concern about serious malpractice at work. An employee can, of course, also seek advice from a lawyer of their own choice at their own expense.

External contacts

It is intended that this policy should give employees the reassurance they need to raise concerns internally. However, this organisation recognises that there may be circumstances where employees should properly report matters to outside bodies, such as regulators or the police. If an employee is unsure as to whether this is appropriate and does not feel able to discuss the matter internally, Public Concern at Work will be able to give advice on such an option and on the circumstances in which an employee should contact an outside body rather than raise the matter internally.

Matters raised maliciously

Employees who are found to maliciously raise a matter that they know to be untrue will be subject to the disciplinary policy.

Source: CIMA (2008)

Clearly there is a question of materiality and complexity here. The authorities will not, in reality, be interested in prosecuting minor frauds simply because the sheer volume of paperwork involved in bringing a case to court has to be balanced against the result from the prosecuting authority's (e.g. the police, or the CPS, or the Procurator Fiscal in Scotland) point of view. However, this reality should not prevent the policy being stated as being one of automatic referral to the relevant authority.

The fact that a small fraud may go unprosecuted should not be seen as carte blanche for employees to feel that they can get away with small frauds or minor offences without serious punishment. The anti-fraud policy should make it quite clear that the organisation takes fraud seriously so that any detected fraud, theft or corrupt act, not limited by size, will be treated as a disciplinary offence which will result in the dismissal of the employee, i.e. it will constitute gross misconduct.

Employees should be left in no doubt that any subsequent request for references will indicate the facts of the dismissal – within accepted procedures and without libelling the former employee.

Now we have considered the policies the next steps are to reinforce the policies within the organisation and to consider the mechanism for responding to fraud.

Fraud defence – the next steps

As we looked at earlier, once appropriate policies are in place the organisation needs to carry through a programme of action which, if necessary, will educate and inform employees about fraud and will set the framework for dealing with fraud or other unethical acts.

All of what follows will require expenditure, which may not be easy to justify immediately in cost–benefit terms as the benefits are not easily measured. One of the problems identified with fraud defence is that, of course, if defensive processes are successful – nothing happens. There are no frauds! It then becomes increasingly difficult for anti-fraud champions to justify expenditure on staff training or increased levels of audit or control in the face of this negative. Management may thus be reluctant to see this as a success, attributing the absence of fraud to the honesty of the staff, the efficiency of audit or the defences in the IT systems, particularly when resources may be under pressure, so the temptation is to reduce expenditure on anti-fraud measures. This could prove to be a costly mistake.

However, research carried out by the Institute of Business Ethics in 2007 showed that companies which had ethical policies and which implemented them:

- produced turnover ratios 18 per cent higher than those without a similar commitment, and
- had an average return on capital employed (ROCE) ratio 50 per cent higher than those without ethical policies.

so there is some empirical evidence that carrying out business ethically improves the bottom line.

The key steps, which we referred to above, are:

- Appoint a champion.
- Develop a fraud response plan.
- Set up a fraud response team.
- Implement fraud awareness training.
- Develop and implement thorough HR policies.
- Consider the impact on the reputation of the organisation.
- Document and understand internal control procedures.

We will now look at these in more detail.

Appoint a champion

Fraud is a business risk and should be taken seriously and, as we have seen, the possibility of fraud and corruption should form part of routine business risk-assessment processes. The organisation should thus have a nominated individual who is responsible for:

- promoting ethical values and an anti-fraud culture in the organisation
- co-ordinating all fraud risk matters and ensuring risk assessments are carried out
- ensuring that momentum is maintained and that anti-fraud procedures are not simply a one-off paper exercise
- preparing the fraud response plan and setting up the fraud response team, and
- being the point of contact between the fraud response team and the board in the case of an investigation.

In the event of a fraud investigation this person will also be responsible for mobilising in-house resources and, in conjunction with a representative from the public relations department or an outside PR consultant, controlling the flow of information from the investigation to the staff and the outside world as necessary.

The anti-fraud champion clearly has to be a trusted individual so, for this reason, and for the reason that the whole anti-fraud exercise is multidisciplinary and cross-department, the optimum person to carry out the overview function is probably someone without fixed line responsibility.

It should not be anyone from the finance team directly, for obvious reasons, mainly because they may be conflicted. Consideration could be given to involving the head of internal audit but similar circumstances may prevent this so this type of activity could form part of the duties of someone holding a specific post such as an ethics officer or the company secretary (where this is not the finance director) who would liaise with an audit committee aided, perhaps, by technical advice from a forensic accountant. The board may feel that a director should be responsible, in which case a non-executive director such as the chair of the audit committee should take on the role and it should become an audit committee function. Whoever it is must have sufficient status within the organisation to be able to request the resources needed and whose reports will be treated with respect.

If the audit committee takes on the role of anti-fraud champion care will have to be taken that they do not become involved in executive decision making so much of their practical activity will necessarily have to be delegated to the executive.

Develop a fraud response plan

Part of the risk-assessment process would be to set up and keep under review a fraud response plan. The purpose of the fraud response plan is to ensure that, where fraud is suspected, the requisite actions are taken in the right way by the right people. Its aim is to prevent piecemeal, ad hoc investigations being carried out by untrained staff and to avoid inappropriate responses which might ruin an investigation before it has really started.

The development, monitoring and implementation of the plan should be the responsibility of the anti-fraud champion and it should only become operational when and where indications of fraud are revealed either though whistle-blowing or audit.

The fraud response plan should cover:

- the definition of fraud, i.e. what will come under the aegis of the fraud response team
- reference to other relevant policies, e.g. the fraud and whistle-blowing policies

- who to report to if fraud is suspected – this should be a director, unless, of course, they are a suspect
- what the form the response will take
- liaison with external bodies, e.g. legal representation and forensic accountants and the Economic Crime Unit of the police
- keeping the organisation informed, and
- forensic readiness procedures related to IT systems and designed to preserve digital evidence (Chapter 9).

The plan should include details of the composition of a fraud response team. Many organisations have policies which will attempt to keep the investigation internal and, in this way, they feel they can control the investigation and the impact of any disclosures on the staff and on the reputation of the organisation. However, this policy is only appropriate if the requisite skills are available and it should be considered carefully in the light of the size and complexity of the situation.

The requirements of an investigation and the legal considerations arising from it, including any possible prosecution, are likely to require, at the very least, that a forensic accountant and an external legal adviser will be needed.

Set up a fraud response team

Clearly if the fraud is likely to be fairly straightforward and relatively small investigating it in-house is a perfectly acceptable choice. The skills of internal audit, the IT department and any other in-house expertise such as the in-house legal team, can be brought to bear and the only outside consultation might be with the organisation's legal advisers and, perhaps, the Economic Crime Unit. However, what starts out as a relatively minor fraud may escalate, and if it does the response must escalate also.

In the case of frauds which, or potentially:

- are large and/or complex
- are high profile
- involve a senior member of staff or a director, or
- involve overseas transactions or possible collusion with other external organisations

the policy of dealing with it in-house may be counter productive and even result in the perpetrator being allowed to escape, a criminal prosecution being nullified and the possibility of recovery thwarted through bad practice and an inexperienced investigation.

Large and complex frauds require:

- specialised investigation skills
- co-ordination between investigators and the legal team in the serving of legal orders on suspects and asset tracing capability
- specialised forensic IT skills
- advice in connection with HR issues in criminal proceedings, and
- advice in dealing with the regulatory authorities.

It is important that business continuity is protected and managers and directors are not deflected by becoming involved in fraud investigations. The reputation of the organisation may need managing if the disclosures are likely to be embarrassing and the relevant regulatory authorities, such as the listing authority, may need to be informed.

For these and for other reasons which will become apparent as this book progresses it is felt preferable that the fraud response team's investigatory work is led by a specialist forensic accountant, with assistance as required from the internal audit function and in-house IT personnel, unless the fraud is relatively minor and the opportunity of a successful prosecution and recovery of the sums involved is relatively straightforward.

The team should include:

- an independent forensic accountant
- an advising legal representative familiar with fraud investigations
- the head of legal services of the organisation
- the head of public relations of the organisation
- the human resources director of the organisation
- investigating accountants from external advisers and internal audit, and
- a senior member of the IT department and an expert in the IT systems – this may be an external consultant.

The team should solicit the services of the internal audit and IT functions of the client, assuming these are considered to be uncorrupted. These will be able to bring their in-house knowledge and expertise to bear as appropriate, however they may not be privy to the full workings of the fraud response team and the complete investigation.

Members of the team may need some specific training on how to deal with incidents of suspected fraud. In particular they should be instructed in key legal issues such as the collection and preservation of evidence, both documentary and IT-based, and the process of a forensic investigation.

The point of contact between the fraud response team and the board should be the anti-fraud champion referred to earlier or the audit committee, as appropriate.

Institute fraud awareness training

Fraud awareness training should be available to key members of staff particularly in areas where risk assessments have identified fraud as being a strong possibility. The objective of this training is to raise both technical awareness and the profile of fraud within the organisation.

It may be, of course, that actual or potential fraudsters attend the training, but this should not be seen as a reason not to carry it out. The point is to drive home the organisation's attitude and response to fraud, which may well deter the individual before they are tempted or may suggest to determined fraudsters that they find easier pickings elsewhere.

The training is not to be designed to teach people how to commit fraud, they will work that out for themselves, it is to teach responsible employees:

- what constitutes fraud
- how to recognise fraudulent behaviour, and

- how to respond if they feel they have detected or suspect fraudulent or corrupt activity.

This has to be tempered with reason – the objective is not to generate a lot of leads or to stimulate malicious reporting, it is simply to raise awareness.

It should include consideration of:

- corporate culture and ethics
- the various anti-fraud and whistle-blower policies
- the audit approach – why it is necessary and how it works in principle
- why there is a need for internal controls
- the HR and disciplinary process, and
- IT processes and procedures, particularly where a forensic readiness programme is in operation (Chapter 9).

Training can be carried out formally in groups or through written media such as posters, newsletters, company intranet etc. The key is to develop a sustained campaign using various media, but without overkill. The objective is to avoid the employees becoming bored, seeing the reminders as routine and devaluing the message. In dysfunctional organisations (Chapter 4) this type of training may be used to attempt to nullify the cynical effects of veterans who try to corrupt new employees into supporting and sustaining unethical behaviour.

If frauds are detected and dealt with the facts should be communicated to all staff through the appropriate media. The uncovering of a fraud can be very shocking, especially to staff who worked with the alleged perpetrator, and the dissemination of information internally should be handled with the same kind of tact and sensitivity as is the dissemination externally to stakeholders, regulators and the public.

Develop and implement thorough HR policies

One of the surprising things about fraudsters is that many of the most egregious serial fraudsters have somehow evaded HR checking policies and got jobs where they are placed in a position to carry out fraud.

In many cases subsequent investigations have identified weak or non-existent HR policies which have resulted in the employment of individuals who have a previous history of fraud. Often HR managers have been reluctant to include unproven allegations, unproven in the sense of being tried in a court of law, in a reference for obvious reasons, and may well provide a bland, innocuous reference to the new employer, being satisfied with having removed the perpetrator from the organisation and thus passing any problems to the next employer.

This is bad practice: it may not be universal but it does go on and partially explains why serial fraudsters continue to be employed. The other reason why this happens is that fraudsters forge references which are not adequately taken up by new employers.

We look in more detail at the part active HR policies play in fraud defence in Chapter 8.

Consider the impact on the reputation of the organisation

Organisations should not be deterred by the thought of adverse publicity arising from fraud affecting the image or attitude of stakeholders to the organisation. A determination to observe a code of ethical behaviour should be seen as a positive quality and this point should be made when any disclosure has to be made either to the press or the regulatory authorities.

As detailed above, one of the members of the fraud response team should be the head of public relations and it is their job to ensure that any resultant publicity stresses the positive aspects of rooting out unethical behaviour.

Document and understand internal control procedures

It is axiomatic that the audit function, either internal or external, should have documented the internal control procedures and activities of the organisation. This will undoubtedly take the form of flow charts and systems manuals and forms part of the audit documentation.

These records must be maintained as accurately as possible and must be up to date. They form an aid to the investigation team in both identifying weaknesses and in identifying relationships which may be relevant to discovering the extent of any fraud.

As part of its routine review the question of documentation should be considered regularly and be reviewed by the anti-fraud champion in conjunction with the head of internal audit or the external audit partner.

In the next chapter we look at the principles of internal control and those very procedures.

 **Summary**

- Fraud risk management should be approached in a systematic manner.
- The basic strategy starts with prevention, followed by detection and response.
- Prevention is better than detection.
- There are formal approaches to risk management including CRSA and ERM. Both of these approaches require participation at all levels in the organisation and a positive approach by management.
- Specific fraud risks within the organisation should be indentified.
- Management are responsible for identifying and dealing with fraud risk.
- System risks and fraud targets need to be identified.
- The general principles of risk management are based on TARA: Transfer, Accept, Reduce, Avoid.
- The organisation should develop a methodology for dealing with fraud risk.
- This includes appointing a fraud champion, process review and staff training among other initiatives.
- The organisation should develop strong and clear anti-fraud policies.
- The organisation should develop policies and procedures to facilitate whistle-blowing.
- The management should develop a fraud response plan.
- Anti-fraud activity requires good HR policies.
- All policies and processes within the organisation should be fully documented and made available to staff.

Case study

Megablast plc is an international company trading in consumer and industrial electronics with operations in the UK, France, Germany and Holland, manufacturing plants in Cambodia and Indonesia and a large retail operation Ozblast, in Australia.

Megablast was formed by the merger of two smaller companies, Towngate Electronics Ltd which was sited in various locations in the north of England and Scotland, and Massive Makers plc based in the south of England and France in 1984. In the years since the merger the company has grown into a massive multinational with a turnover in excess of £2bn and reported profits in 2009 of £324m. The history of the merger is reflected in the fact that Megablast still operates from several sites which broadly reflect the sites operated by the old companies.

Staff from the various sites have formed teams which play each other in a company-wide sports league. They are known as the Towngate Mob and the Makers Massive and they play competitively with each other and other works teams in their various areas. The directors award an annual trophy for the winning team.

There is an audit committee comprising four of the non-executive directors. None of the directors have any formal accountancy qualifications.

There is an internal audit function headed by Peter Packer who is qualified ACCA. He has three qualified auditors and seven trainees in the internal audit department which is based in a small office in Slough.

Unknown to the rest of the board the CEO, Simon Chirpy-Herbert and financial director Denise Bobbit have developed a very close personal relationship.

Sales director Nigel Weasley is reviewing the results of his latest sales report:

- The sales launch of their new product the MJQ 478 has been, generally, a disaster. It was designed to replace two older products the JS 96 and the BMR 42 but has failed to live up to its specifications and has proved expensive. Sales have dropped 84 per cent. The JS 96 and the BMR 42 represent 32 per cent of Megablast's turnover.
- Another product the Doubleswitch has had to be withdrawn as it no longer meets EC regulations and most of the industry is buying a Chinese-made replacement. The Doubleswitch was approximately 5 per cent of turnover – no replacement is available.
- There is a report that Ozblast has suffered a downturn because of a weakening in the Australian economy. Sales are down 22 per cent but expenses are up 18 per cent so the net profit has declined dramatically.

Financial director Denise Bobbit is also reviewing her board papers. Highlights are:

- The group is within 5 per cent of its finance limits overall – the financing of the group is due to be renegotiated next month.
- The financial position of Ozblast has deteriorated markedly – the overdraft has increased 70 per cent in the last year.
- One of the UK subsidiaries, Fartown Components Ltd, has produced a surprisingly good result. It is based in Wales, in an area of high unemployment, and its results up to last quarter have shown a steady decline. A new managing director was appointed with a brief to turn the company around or close it down and the results have immediately improved.
- Research and development costs are increasing rapidly as the company desperately searches for new products. They have gone up 154 per cent in the last year.
- Sales overall are down due to the failure of the MJQ 478.
- The external audit for 2008 has been completed. The accounts have been finalised and no problems have been reported. The result of that is that all the directors will receive a substantial bonus for reaching a profit target. She has noticed that some of the figures had changed from her final draft figures, The auditors, in a note to

▶

her, explained that changes were made late following a meeting between the audit partner and Simon. The auditors have recently been awarded a substantial assignment to review the group's internal reporting systems. Denise wasn't involved in that decision.

- The bonus for the current year is dependent on the group achieving last year's profit plus 5 per cent.
- Each subsidiary company, except Ozblast, has a similar bonus scheme for its local management. The directors of Ozblast complained to the board that they had not received any bonus but their complaint was ignored. The recent results indicate that the company is in a downturn.
- Denise is puzzled by the some Ozblast information which shows that some individual product margins have declined following a change in supplier to a new company, that expenses for services provided such as professional fees appear to have increased considerably, wages costs have gone up which Ozblast management explained is due increased use of contract labour. Denise feels a little uneasy about some of the Ozblast numbers.

Simon Chirpy-Herbert has asked for her help in 'reviewing' the figures before the board meeting. She is not quite sure what this means.

Required

Review the scenario and list the key points regarding:

- Megablast's management style and culture
- How Simon Chirpy-Herbert might be looking to report future results
- What's happening at Ozblast
- What's happening at Fartown

Bibliography Chartered Institute of Management Accountants (CIMA) (2008) *Fraud Risk Management – A Guide to Good Practice*. CIMA, London.

COSO (1992) *Internal Control – Integrated Framework*. COSO, Alamonte Springs, FL.

COSO (2004) *Enterprise Risk Management – Integrated Framework*. COSO, Alamonte Springs, FL.

Fraud Advisory Panel (2006) *Sample Fraud Policy Statements*. Fraud Advisory Panel, London.

Golden, T., Skalak, S. and Clayton, M. (2006) *A Guide to Forensic Accounting Investigation*. John Wiley, Hoboken, NJ.

Hopwood, W.S., Leiner, J.L. and Young, G. (2008) *Forensic Accounting*. McGraw-Hill, New York.

Huntington, I. and Davies, D. (1994) *Fraud Watch – A Guide for Business*. ICAEW, London.

ICAEW (2002) *Risk Management for SMEs*. ICAEW, London.

Kaplan (2009) *Management Accounting – Risk and Control Strategy*. Kaplan Publishing, London.

KPMG (2006) *Fraud Risk Management – Developing a Strategy for Prevention, Detection and Response*. KPMG International LLP, Zurich.

Millichamp, A. and Taylor, J.R. (2008) *Auditing*. Cengage, London.

Moxey, P. (2003) *CRSA – A Powerful Tool to Prevent Another Enron?* ACCA, London.

Penney, J. (2002) *Corporate Fraud: Prevention and Detection*. Tolley, London.

Silverstone, H. and Sheetz, M. (2007) *Forensic Accounting and Fraud Investigation for Non-experts*. John Wiley, Hoboken, NJ.

Singleton, T., Singleton, A., Bologna, G.J. and Lindquist, R.J. (2006) *Fraud Auditing and Forensic Accounting*. John Wiley, Hoboken, NJ.

Wells, J.T. (2004) *Corporate Fraud Handbook – Prevention and Detection*. John Wiley, Hoboken, NJ.

Websites

www.cimaglobal.org

www.coso.org

www.dailymail.co.uk

www.fraudadvisorypanel.org

www.fvs.aicpa.org/resources

www.icaew.com

Chapter 8

Internal control

Chapter contents

- Introduction
- Internal control
- The control environment
- Monitoring of controls
- Employee and third-party due diligence

Learning objectives

After studying this chapter you should be able to:

- Understand the basic principles of internal control
- Understand the controls within an internal control system
- Appreciate the establishment of key controls to meet control objectives
- Understand the process of monitoring controls
- Understand the importance of pre-employment checks
- Incorporate the principles of risk management into the IT environment
- Evaluate IT systems using a formal methodology
- Establish a process for preserving digital evidence and responding to major incidents
- Consider the advantages and disadvantages of data storage using the Internet

Introduction

The principles of sound corporate governance require the directors to institute a proper system of internal control. Directors also have a statutory duty to act in the way they consider best promotes the success of the company for the benefit of the members as a whole (CA 2006, S172) and this statutory duty places on them the requirement to preserve the assets of the company. This, in turn, reinforces the requirement for them to establish and maintain a positive internal control environment, which of course includes sound internal control activities and procedures and the risk assessment process we have already looked at in Chapter 7.

We now move on to a more detailed explanation of specific internal control activities and procedures which should exist to monitor and control both day-to-day transaction processing and the security of assets so as to create a strong internal control environment. It is this internal control structure which is the foundation for detailed anti-fraud measures. Figure 8.1 outlines the relationship between the control environment and underlying activities.

Before we consider internal controls generally we had best establish a working definition and, for this purpose, we will adopt the definition of internal control established by the Auditing Practices Board (APB) (2009):

> The process designed, implemented and maintained by those charged with governance, management and other personnel, to provide reasonable assurance about the achievement of an entity's objectives with regard to reliability of financial reporting, effectiveness and efficiency of operations, and compliance with applicable laws and regulations. The term 'controls' refers to any aspects of one or more of the components of internal control.

Figure 8.1 Internal control

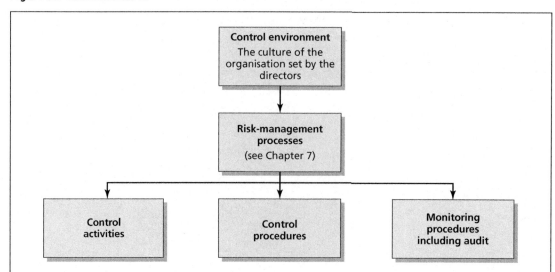

In other words internal controls are there to prevent, discover or eliminate the possibility of material, i.e. significant, errors or misstatements so that financial information is reliable, operations run smoothly and the law is complied with. Parts of this definition have echoes in statements made by The Committee of Sponsoring Organisations of the Treadway Commission (COSO), already encountered in Chapter 7, which developed guidance on what they call integrated control frameworks.

COSO has pronounced views on the usefulness of internal control and it is illuminating to quote from the executive summary to *Internal Control – Integrated Framework*:

> Senior executives have long sought ways to better control the enterprises they run. Internal controls are put in place to keep the company on course towards profitability, goals and achievement of its mission, and to minimize surprises along the way. They enable management to deal with rapidly changing economic and competitive environments, shifting customer demands and priorities, and restructuring for future growth. Internal controls promote efficiency, reduce risk of asset loss, and help ensure the reliability of financial statements and compliance with laws and regulations.
>
> Because internal control serves many important purposes, there are increasing calls for better internal control systems and report cards on them. Internal control is looked upon more and more as a solution to a variety of potential problems.

Included in that statement are the words 'reduce risk of asset loss' and it is that aspect of internal control we will concentrate on here. We have looked at the principles of integrated control frameworks devised under COSO, as implemented through a process known as control risk self-assessment (CRSA) in Chapter 7.

Good systems reinforce good behaviour; however, as COSO is at pains to point out:

- Internal control is not a panacea.
- Internal control cannot ensure success.
- Internal control will not turn an inherently poor manager or department into a good one.
- It cannot, by itself, respond to changing factors that are beyond management's control, e.g. increased competition.
- There is no such thing as 100 per cent effective internal control.

Whilst a sound system of internal control, integrated or not, can undoubtedly benefit an organisation in many ways we are only interested in one aspect of it, that of asset preservation and the prevention of dysfunctional behaviour among employees, in other words the prevention of fraud and corruption.

We looked at the principles of fraud risk management at the organisational level in Chapter 7 so it is now appropriate to look at the practical aspects of internal control in more detail. In this chapter we will look at this from the point of view of controlling transactions and assets, but principally the day-to-day activities of processing entries through the records and the principles that exist to ensure they are recorded properly.

Key to assessing system risk is to have the internal control systems and the operation of the management information system properly evaluated. This is normally the role of audit.

External auditors will concentrate primarily on those controls which relate to the financial system and the control of assets and liabilities as well as some of the controls involved in the risk-management processes of the organisation. Internal audit will also pay attention to financial controls but, in addition, may also be asked to review other internal controls including those used for management and operational purposes. For example, a company may have controls designed to prevent excessive use of materials in production, or controls designed to make operations efficient, such as an airline's automated controls to maintain flight schedules. These are not directly relevant to a financial statement audit but will be relevant to operational review and will thus come within the scope of internal audit.

This is not a manual of auditing so we will say no more about how they do this. However, it is instructive to students who are not familiar with audit practices to explain what the key components of an internal control system are.

 ## Internal control

Central to an effective system of internal control is a structured approach which:

- Identifies control objectives – these describe main objectives of the controls instituted to ensure financial reporting is reliable. Control objectives are designed to ensure such things as:
  - wages are only paid to bona fide employees
  - all cash sales are properly recorded, and
  - all purchases are made from approved suppliers.

  Once the control objectives within a system are identified the next step is to identify the risks relating to that activity.
- Identifies the possible risks surrounding an internal control – risks here are the probability that the outcome of a series of events may be other than what was expected. For example in the case of cash sales the risk is that instead of all the sales being recorded properly, some of the takings are skimmed off before they are recorded.

  Internal control activities need to be adequate to mitigate the risk. What this means is that, in order to know whether the control activities are robust enough, risks have to be assessed at the level of the transactions and not simply at an organisational level as we looked at in Chapter 6.
- Identifies all activities for which controls are required – controls are thus designed to ensure the integrity of accounting records and should be sufficiently robust to deal with the identified risks.

Any system of accounting and record keeping, in whatever type and size of organisation, will not succeed in detecting errors or misstatements without a range of internal control procedures and activities being built in to it. The purpose of these internal controls is:

- to ensure transactions are executed in accordance with proper authorisation
- to ensure all transactions are promptly recorded in the financial records
  - at the correct amount
  - in the right accounts, and
  - in the correct accounting period

  so as to permit preparation of financial statements in accordance with relevant legislation and accounting standards

- to ensure access to assets or information is permitted only in accordance with proper authorisation
- to ensure recorded assets are compared with the existing assets at reasonable intervals and appropriate action is taken with regard to any differences, and
- to ensure errors and irregularities are avoided or are discovered.

Clearly smaller and less complex organisations will operate with smaller and less complex systems; they may not, for example, have detailed written procedures, or formal risk assessment policies. In owner-managed businesses, for example, the owner–manager may well be directly involved in internal control matters which, in larger organisations, would be the responsibility of accountants, managers or internal auditors. Conversely they may place a good deal of trust in a single book-keeper or accountant thus ensuring there is no element of internal control at all.

Within larger organisations there will be many and various controls of different aspects of the organisation's activities, which we will look at in detail. There will also be an audit function.

The level of controls is influenced by:

- the size of the business
- its nature, including its ownership and how it is organised
- how diverse and complex its operations are
- the legal and regulatory framework it operates within
- the nature and complexity of the financial and management systems, and
- the level of materiality or significance of the transactions being controlled.

Let us look at the components of an internal control system in more detail.

The control environment

This comprises the attitudes, awareness and actions of the directors and senior managers of the organisation. It is, in effect, the culture of the organisation insofar as it relates to internal control and is part of the corporate governance framework (Chapter 1).

It includes:

- the fostering and communication of a culture of honesty and ethical behaviour throughout the organisation
- a commitment to competence – to training and maintaining the appropriate levels of skill and knowledge within the organisation
- management's philosophy and operating style, their approach to risk and attitudes towards correct financial reporting
- the organisational structure
- the involvement of non-executive directors in the audit process, and
- human resource policies – recruitment, training, evaluation, promotion and rewarding of staff.

Before we move on to specific aspects of internal control we need to be clear on what it is we are dealing with. We need to define what we mean by

- the management information system
- internal controls, and
- control procedures.

The management information system

Internal controls exist within the management information system (MIS). This system includes:

- the classes of transaction in the organisation's operations which are significant to the financial systems
- the procedures, both IT and manual, which are used to record those transactions
- the related accounting records, whether electronic or manual and the supporting information used to initiate, record, process and report transactions
- how the systems work, and
- the processes by which the organisation prepares its financial and operating statements.

Consequently the management information system, for our purposes, includes any components, add-ons or additional processes derived from or attached to the basic transaction processing systems, so the MIS includes costing systems as well as budgeting, forecasting and planning systems.

We will look specifically at IT aspects of the MIS later in this chapter and will deal with computer-based investigations in Chapter 13.

Control activities

These are the policies and procedures that help ensure that management directives are carried out, for example that necessary actions are taken to address the risks that threaten achievement of the organisation's objectives.

In an anti-fraud context these would include the anti-fraud policies set out in Chapter 7.

Control procedures

Examples of specific control procedures are:

- segregation of duties
- organisational controls
- authorisation and approval
- physical controls
- supervision
- personnel
- arithmetical procedures, and
- management controls.

You can remember these through the mnemonic SOAPSPAM.

These specific types of control procedure are well known to auditors: for the non-audit-trained reader this is what they are in more detail:

Segregation of duties

- This is the most important single control procedure and is the key to good system design. What it means is that *no one person should be responsible for the recording and processing of a complete transaction.*
- The involvement of several people reduces the risk of intentional manipulation or accidental error and increases the element of checking of work.

For example, let us look at a simple purchasing transaction for, say, lubricating oil. The transaction is split into its components each of which is handled by a separate individual or group:

- initiation (for example, the works foreman decides the firm needs more lubricating oil)
- authorisation (the works manager approves the purchase)
- execution (the buying department order the oil)
- receipt (on arrival the oil is taken in by the goods-in section who check to see it has been ordered is of appropriate quality and undamaged). They pass it on with appropriate goods-in documentation to
- the stores department who include it in the inventory records
- recording (the arrival of the oil is documented by the goods inward section and the invoice from the supplier is compared with the original order and goods-in note by the accounts department, and recorded by them in the books), and
- authorisation (the invoice is approved for payment by the appropriate manager)
- payment (the invoice is paid by the cashiers department).

Another example is the area of sales where initiation is by a sales executive, authorisation by credit control and the sales manager, execution is by the finished goods warehouse staff who physically send the goods, custody is transferred from the warehouse staff to the transport department, and the transaction is recorded by the goods outward section, the invoicing section and the accounts department. Table 8.1 describes the process.

Organisational controls

All organisations should have a family tree-type diagram which illustrates the internal layers of responsibility of management and staff. This is true even of horizontal, customer-facing organisations which presumably comprise more than one layer of management and staff.

The plan of the organisation structure should:

- Define and allocate responsibilities – every function should be in the charge of a specified person who might be called the responsible official. Thus the administration of the accounts department should be entrusted to a particular person who is then responsible (and hence answerable) for that function.

Table 8.1 Segregation of duties – sales and receivables

Transaction	Documentation	Handled by
Customer order	Customer order form	Sales department staff
Goods despatched to customer	Despatch note	Despatch department staff
Invoice to customer	Sales invoice	Accounts department – sales processing
Goods returned from customer	Goods returned note	Goods inward staff
Credit to customer for goods returned	Credit note	Accounts department – sales processing
Monies received from customer	Remittance advice	Cashiers department
Debt collection	Aged debtor report	Credit control

Each part of the sales cycle is handled by different departments and, often, different individuals within those departments so that no one person has control of a transaction from start to finish.

In smaller companies with less staff this aspect is reduced with a concomitant reduction in control.

- Identify lines of reporting both upwards and downwards through the organisation, and where appropriate, across it as well.

In all cases the delegation of authority and responsibility should be clearly specified. Employees should always know the precise powers delegated to them, the extent of their authority and to whom they should report.

Two examples:

- Responsibility for approving the purchase of items of plant may be retained by the directors for items over £X and within the competence of the works manager for a budgeted amount agreed by the board up to a total less than this.
- Responsibility for the correct operation of internal controls may be delegated by the board to specific management personnel and to the internal audit department.

Authorisation and approval

All transactions should require authorisation or approval by an appropriate person. The limits to these authorisations should be specified. Examples of such procedures are:

- All credit sales must be approved by the credit control department.
- All overtime must be approved by the factory manager.
- All individual office stationery purchases may be approved by the office manager up to a limit of £X. Higher levels of purchasing must be approved by the chief accountant.

Remembering the principle of segregation of duties outlined earlier, it should not for example be the case that the individual who has authority to, say, set up a new suppliers account in the purchase ledger is also responsible for authorising invoices from that supplier and approving payment to them.

That opens the door to a particular kind of fraud – the creation of a fictitious supplier. Auditors and investigators should always, when reviewing use of authorisations and authorities as system controls, also look at what else those individuals are allowed to do and how they do it.

Physical controls

These are such things as physical custody of assets and they involve procedures designed to limit access to assets and systems to authorised personnel only. These controls are especially important in the case of valuable, portable, exchangeable or desirable assets. Examples of physical controls are:

- use of passes to restrict access to a warehouse
- locks or keypads on doors
- use of passwords to restrict access to particular computer files, and
- hierarchical menus for computer operators.

Supervision

All actions by all levels of staff should be supervised. The responsibility for supervision should be clearly laid down and communicated to the person being supervised and to their supervisor at whatever level that may be.

Personnel

Procedures should be designed to ensure that personnel operating a system are competent and motivated to carry out the tasks assigned to them, as the proper functioning of a system depends upon the competence and integrity of the operating personnel.

Measures include:

- appropriate levels of remuneration concomitant with responsibilities
- promotion and career development prospects
- selection of people with appropriate personal characteristics
- staff training, and
- assignment of staff to tasks of the right level of competence to suit their abilities. This includes management.

Personnel controls should also encompass thorough vetting procedures for employees, including:

- interviews exploring the background of employees and concentrating on any apparent gaps in the CV
- the taking up of references for all new employees
- development of appropriate policies, as outlined above, and
- training initiatives to reinforce the anti-fraud message.

We look at the operation of these particular controls in more detail below.

Arithmetical procedures

These are the controls in the recording function which check that the transactions are all included and that they are correctly recorded and accurately processed.

Procedures include checking the arithmetical accuracy of the records, the maintenance and checking of totals, reconciliations, control accounts, trial balances and accounting for documents (sometimes known as sequence checks or continuity checks). Examples include:

- bank reconciliations
- control accounts
- reconciliations of suppliers statements with purchase ledger accounts, and
- checking the calculations on purchase invoices.

Management controls

These are controls exercised by management which are outside and over and above the day-to-day routine of the system. They include such things as:

- overall supervisory controls
- review of management accounts
- comparisons with budgets, and
- control of internal audit and any other special review procedures.

Examples are:

- Senior management must be aware of day-to-day activities and be seen by staff to be so. Glaring failures of control (for example, inventory thefts, excess inventory and unnecessary overtime) will become apparent and staff will not be motivated to perform well.

- Management accounts should be designed to summarise performance in detail. Any anomalies (for example, cost overruns, higher than budgeted wastage levels) should become apparent and should be investigated thoroughly.
- Budgeting and variance analysis is a management tool which should prevent or at least detect departure from management's intended plans.

An important principle of internal control is that if a control procedure is not evidenced it cannot be proved to have been performed. This means that there should be some form of evidence somewhere in the system which evidences the operation of the control. Individuals performing control activities should evidence their checking by means of signatures, initials, rubber stamps, etc. For example, if invoice calculations have to be checked, the checker could initial, for instance, some kind of posting slip attached to the invoice to indicate that this check has been carried out.

It is these controls and the evidence for them which can help either eliminate areas where a forensic investigator can be satisfied that the control system is functioning and turn their attentions elsewhere, or identify a possible perpetrator through a process of elimination.

Monitoring of controls

Management is responsible for maintaining and monitoring the systems of internal control, so they should establish suitable monitoring procedures. These are likely to include:

- internal and external audit
- management review – where senior managers perform audit-type tests on selected parts of the system, and
- analysis of the results by applying analytical procedures to, say, monthly management accounts and identifying anomalies or areas for investigation.

Internal audit, provided it is a truly independent, well-staffed and well-resourced objective function within the organisation, is a significant component of the internal control system and can represent a significant deterrent to dysfunctional behaviour.

It should have complete knowledge of the activities of the organisation and could, at least in theory, be a conduit for whistle-blowing and gossip. As they are part of the organisation they could be less likely to be seen as outsiders or 'police', although it must be said this is not universally true. As their remit is much wider than that of external audit they are routinely involved in reviewing areas of operation which lie outside the scope of a purely financial audit (Chapter 2) and this has two advantages:

1 They develop a knowledge of the operational aspects of the organisation and an understanding of the processes within it which is far wider than it would be if they concentrated solely on the financial systems.
2 They have the opportunity to observe the origination procedures from which the routine transaction processing derives. In this way they are able to ensure that controls exist outside the outside systems.

For example if part of their work involves consideration of value for money (VFM)-type initiatives they may look, for example, at procurement activities. This, in turn, may cause them to investigate tendering procedures or the awarding of supplier contracts, matters which are outside the remit of the external auditor. This may result in the detection of incidences of corrupt practices or managerial fraud simply because internal audit considered operational issues rather than simply the operation of financial controls.

Analysis of fraud detection success shows the significant part internal audit plays as detectors of fraud and as guardians of the organisation's assets.

Employee and third-party due diligence

We make no apologies for including here checks which, on the face of it, belong more fully to a human resources publication. The reason for including this information here is twofold:

- It informs the forensic accountant of basic principles of pre-employment checking so that they may advise clients who are perhaps not as fully aware as they might be of these important preventative measures.
- There have been several high-profile cases of individuals with previous convictions for fraud who have nevertheless been able to obtain jobs and repeat their offence (see Exhibit 8.1). Where fraud is suspected the investigator should review pre-employment screening techniques. As part of the investigation a review of CVs and employment histories may reveal information which escaped the interviewers and which might lead to a possible perpetrator being shortlisted.

It is not realistically possible to screen existing employees unless they are in an occupation which involves them working with children or vulnerable adults, where a Criminal Records Bureau (CRB) check is mandatory. Unless the requirement for the employee to produce a recent CRB check is part of the contract of employment it is highly unlikely that attempting this would be worthwhile for two simple reasons:

- It would not really go very far in preventing fraud. As we have seen, individuals who have previously had no criminal involvement may turn to crime for their own motives. They will not have a previous criminal record so checking would be futile.
- Requiring employees to undertake this would spread distrust among the existing workforce which would be more likely to damage any anti-fraud initiatives than to promote them.

Consequently we feel that any HR anti-fraud measures should be confined to pre-employment checking.

An important preventative part of the anti-fraud strategy is to ensure that prospective new employees are thoroughly checked before being taken on. There have been several instances of fraud where the perpetrator had previous convictions and had produced forged or false references which the employer had failed to check properly. The case of Sharon Bridgewater (Exhibit 8.1) is a good example of an occasion where some simple pre-employment checks would have revealed the extent of her nefarious deeds at a previous employer.

Exhibit 8.1   Sharon Bridgewater – serial fraudster

Sharon Bridgewater, 36, the finance director of a marketing agency, presided over redundancies as she siphoned off more than £2 million to fund extraordinary spending sprees on everything from vintage wines to top-range sports cars. Described as 'a female Walter Mitty' fantasist, she pleaded guilty to 16 counts of theft at Southwark Crown Court in London.

Police said that Bridgewater 'lived the lifestyle of a footballer's wife' over a period of years, investing £100,000 on a kitchen that was lauded in a glossy magazine and spending up to £2,200 at a time on dining out, including at Gordon Ramsay's restaurant at Claridge's.

She also bought a villa in Spain and a buy-to-let portfolio in the UK including a £650,000 converted barn in Essex, while her own home was kitted out with a £90,000 'entertainment system'.

The court was told that Bridgewater's first 'betrayal of trust' came in 1996 when, as accounts manager at the Surrey computer hardware firm Dyna-Five, she stole £25,000 disguised as payments to suppliers and HM Revenue and Customs.

The 'lapsed accountancy student' was then exposed as her boss checked the company's accounts and she pleaded guilty to eight false accounting offences before being sentenced to 150 hours' community service.

Later, however, having kept secret her conviction for fraud by pretending the community service was charity work, she managed to gain the job of financial director at the marketing firm Hicklin Slade and Partners based in Bloomsbury, central London.

Between August 1999 and May 2005, Bridgewater swindled millions from the firm, and continued to steal from it even as financial problems forced it to lay off its staff, spending £100,000 on the birthday of her boyfriend, who described himself as a 'kept man' and a 'house husband'. Bridgewater was present at meetings at which it was decided that staff should be made redundant.

After stealing £2 million from Hicklin Slade and Partners, she resigned and moved on to create an Internet banking facility into which she channelled £55,000 from a small radio station, Universal Sound Principles, which she persuaded to use the service.

Meanwhile Hicklin Slade and Partners called in auditors to look into their 'parlous financial state', and Bridgewater was exposed again. Initially she tried to lie her way out of the situation, blaming colleagues, one of whom was arrested. Bridgewater was sentenced to five years in jail and would be barred from being a company director for 12 years.

Source: Times Online (2007)

The more senior the position and the more sensitive the role the greater should be the depth of screening. Employees who, for example, might have access to sensitive data or information should be carefully checked to ensure that they are bona fide and can be trusted. In exceptional cases this may involve the use of specialist agencies to check the background and history of prospective employees.

Pre-employment checks

The types of pre-employment checks are set out in Table 8.2.

There are a variety of sources of information available relating to pre-employment checks and there are a number of investigatory firms which specialise in this type of work. International checks can also be made as one reason often given by job applicants, in order to explain an embarrassing two- or three-year gap in the CV, is

Table 8.2 Pre-employment checks

Check	Source/approach
Identity checks	Confirm with valid photo-identity documents e.g. passport, drivers licence etc. For non-UK nationals there should be confirmation that there is a valid right to work in the UK
Address	Written confirmation of address, e.g. utility bills Can be validated against the electoral roll Ensure this confirmation covers a long period, e.g. five years
Employment history	Previous 5–10 years Previous employers should be contacted – with permission – to confirm key details such as period of employment, salary, position held etc.
Academic/professional qualifications	Validated with original certificates – copies should not be accepted
Gap verifications	Check gaps in employment against passport stamps where the individual claims they were abroad travelling
Character references	References can be taken up from non-employment sources. The qualifications and status of the person giving the reference should be confirmed
Directorships/directors' due diligence	Confirm with details on file at Companies House – ascertain whether the applicant holds any current or previous directorships or any disqualified directorships Also, as appropriate, carry out searches against the Financial Service Authority's (FSA) Individual Register and Prohibited Persons Register
Credit history	Check against the register of County Court Judgements (Decrees in Scotland) Credit information listed at the applicant's current and previous addresses including County Court Judgments (CCJs), bankruptcies etc. Take up a credit history report from a credit reference agency
Criminal history	Note that spent convictions do not have to be disclosed
Public information	Many individuals now have their own entry on Facebook or similar networking site or they may maintain a blog or individual website. An Internet search or access to the individual's Facebook-type entry may be very revealing

'working abroad'. If the job is sufficiently sensitive the details of this overseas employment should be checked.

Note that it may be a good idea to carry out a second reference check on a new employee after, say, six months of employment have elapsed. The reason for this is that should an employee leave their previous employment suddenly, say as a result of disciplinary action or by way of precipitate resignation, the facts may not have filtered through to the previous employer's HR department before the initial reference was given and also, after a lapse of time, new information or views about the employee may become available.

The Centre for the Protection of National Infrastructure (CPNI) produces a *Good Practice Guide on Pre-employment Screening* (1984) which contains checklists and useful information of sources of data. If in doubt legal advice should be sought.

Contractors and subcontractors

The use of subcontractors can be a significant aspect of business activity and, where this is the case, the probity and integrity of the contractor is important. This is not about the quality of work performed, it is about the possibility that the contractor will seek to commit fraud by:

- bribery and corruption of purchasing or contract awarding managers, or
- over-invoicing or submission of costs for work not carried out.

In these cases permission may have to be sought from the individual or company to approach bankers, previous customers etc. There are some industry bodies which licence businesses to an appropriate standard, for example the Construction Licencing Executive in Scotland, but many so-called qualifying bodies are simple membership-only organisations with less than stringent requirements for accreditation.

Common sense procedures should be observed such as checking out claimed qualifications and membership of appropriate qualifying bodies and, of course, the status of the qualifying body itself. Key aspects to consider would be, for example, whether the qualifying body has any sort of inspection and enforcement regime to monitor the standards of its members. Contractors claiming membership of bodies to which they are not, in fact, accredited are an obvious danger sign.

Other checks might include reviewing the financial accounts of subcontractors but these may have little value if they are unaudited. If the contractor appears to be under financial pressure this is also a warning sign of potentially fraudulent behaviour.

Testimonials from previous customers are likely to be of more value but may still be too vague to be of use and will be unlikely to mention, at least officially or in writing, any examples of dysfunctional behaviour by the contractor.

Interviews

Don't forget the interview is also part of the process.

As well as providing an opportunity to discuss the candidate's suitability for employment, an interview will play an integral part of the pre-employment screening process because:

- it encourages applicants to be honest
- it allows the employer to find out missing information which is relevant to the pre-employment process and to probe candidates about their responses or for additional information, and
- interviews provide a good opportunity to add to the overall assessment of the applicant's reliability and integrity.

Rehabilitation of offenders

There is a particular point regarding applicants with previous criminal convictions which the forensic accountant should be aware of.

The Rehabilitation of Offenders Act (ROA) 1974 and the Rehabilitation of Offenders (Northern Ireland) Order 1978, establish that a criminal conviction becomes spent if an offender remains free of further convictions for a specified period. The length of the rehabilitation period depends on the sentence given, not the offence committed.

The Act therefore provides the individual with protection from the unfair disclosure of criminal records data, for example to prospective employers, because the individual is classified as having been successfully rehabilitated of the offence in question. Note however that for prison sentences in excess of two-and-a-half years the conviction is *never* regarded as spent.

Under the ROA a person is not normally required to disclose spent convictions when applying for a job except for applications for specific posts. Having spent convictions, or failing to disclose them, are not normally grounds for exclusion from employment, however the ROA states that it is reasonable for employers to ask individuals for details of any unspent criminal convictions.

Consequently, where an individual is to be employed in a position where they have access to company records and sensitive company data, the application form should include a question on unspent convictions.

Summary

- Internal control comprises the fraud environment within which are detailed control policies and activities.
- These can be formalised or not. Formal systems such as COSO are not a panacea for bad practice or weak management.
- Controls exist within the management information system. Controls have specific objectives.
- Control activities can be divided into eight types delineated by the mnemonic SOAPSPAM.
- In addition to accounting controls there should be strong HR policies and procedures for employees and contractors.
- HR procedures should include pre-employment screening.
- Previously convicted offenders may not have to disclose spent convictions so gaps on CVs should be followed up.

Case study

You have recently been appointed as financial controller to Bolington Group plc, a retailer which operates a chain of DIY stores in out of town outlets and smaller shop-based premises in the High Street. They have about 12 large megastores and 32 shop-based premises throughout the country.

All the stores, large or small, operate on much the same basis. All stores are run by a manager and all are self-accounting. Each store submits a daily return by computer to the head office in Todmorden which consolidates the results to produce weekly sales returns for management. The larger stores employ a bookkeeper but, in the smaller stores, the manager is responsible for completing the return.

There is no centralised inventory system. Managers are responsible for ordering goods as and when required. These can be ordered through head office using approved national suppliers but there is also a system whereby managers can order from local suppliers. Bolington believes that this gives managers flexibility to respond to local demand and to take advantage of local price deals. Managers complete an order form for what they need, which is not pre-numbered, and send a copy to head office. The order form should include prices and quantities and be signed by the manager as authorisation.

All stores operate a perpetual inventory count which should agree with the inventory records maintained in store. The inventory records are downloaded to head office monthly for management accounts purposes.

▶

All purchase invoices are paid by head office. If the invoice from the supplier matches the signed order it is checked for arithmetical accuracy and passed for payment. No other checks are performed on it.

Store managers are responsible for bankings and send a return to head office confirming sums banked. This should accord with the daily sales returns overall.

All staff are paid by head office. Managers receive a fixed salary with an annual bonus for exceeding a sales level in store. Other staff are paid for hours worked at an agreed rate. Managers authorise overtime worked.

Required

- What internal control risks can be identified within Bolington?
- How would you set about minimising these risks?

Bibliography

Auditing Practices Board (2009) *Glossary of Terms*. APB, London.

Chartered Institute of Management Accountants (CIMA) (2008) *Fraud Risk Management – A Guide to Good Practice*. CIMA, London.

COSO (1992) *Internal Control – Integrated Framework*. COSO, Altamonte Springs, FL.

CPNI (2008) *A Good Practice Guide on Employment Screening*, 2nd edn. Centre for the Protection of National Infrastructure, London.

Gill, M. (2005) *Learning from Fraudsters*. Protoviti, London.

Golden, T., Skalak, S. and Clayton, M. (2006) *A Guide to Forensic Accounting Investigation*. John Wiley, Hoboken, NJ.

HMSO (2006) *Companies Act 2006*. HMSO, London.

Hillison, W., Pacini, C. and Sinason, S. (1999) The internal auditor as fraud buster. *Managerial Auditing Journal*, 14, 7, 351–363.

Hopwood, W.S., Leiner, J.L. and Young, G. (2008) *Forensic Accounting*. McGraw-Hill, New York.

Huntington, I. and Davies, D. (1994) *Fraud Watch – A Guide for Business*. ICAEW, London.

ICAEW (2002) *Risk Management for SMEs*. ICAEW, London.

ICAEW (2003) *Fraud – Meeting the Challenge though External Audit*. ICAEW, London.

KPMG (2006) *Fraud Risk Management Developing a Strategy for Prevention, Detection and Response*. KPMG LLP, Zurich.

Millichamp, A. and Taylor, J.R. (2008) *Auditing*. Cengage, London.

Penney, J. (2002) *Corporate Fraud – Prevention and Detection*. Tolley, London.

Singleton, T., Singleton, A., Bologna, G.J. and Lindquist, R.J. (2006) *Fraud Auditing and Forensic Accounting*. John Wiley, Hoboken, NJ.

Wells, J.T. (2004) *Corporate Fraud Handbook – Prevention and Detection*. John Wiley, Hoboken, NJ.

Times Online (2007) Female finance chief who stole for life of luxury is jailed. www.thetimes.co.uk, 26 October.

Turnbull, N. (1999) *Internal Control – Guidance for Directors on the Combined Code*. FRC, London.

Websites

www.cimaglobal.com

www.coso.org

www.cpni.gov.uk/docs

www.crb.homeoffice.gov.uk

www.frc.org.uk/apb

www.icaew.co.uk

www.iia.org.uk

www.thetimes.co.uk

Chapter 9

Risk management and IT systems

Chapter contents

- Introduction
- Assessing IT system risks
- Formal approaches to risk management
- Specific approaches to protecting IT systems
- Forensic readiness
- Cloud computing

Learning objectives

After studying this chapter you should be able to:

- Understand the risk management problems specific to IT systems
- Appreciate the different forms of attack computer systems may be subject to
- Understand the process of assessing system risks
- Consider the use of formal approaches to risk management comprising CobiT and ISO 27000
- Understand the development and content of an acceptable user policy
- Understand management approach to system risks including the role of internal audit
- Consider areas of vulnerability outside the IT system
- Summarise the actions to be taken by management to reinforce good practice in the organisation
- Understand the policy of forensic readiness for preserving digital evidence in the event of an incident

Introduction

It may be a masterly statement of the blindingly obvious to say that business systems come under attack from two fronts:

- internally from disgruntled employees or those wanting to commit frauds, and
- externally through malware (malicious software such as viruses, worms and trojans) attacks.

We look at external attacks in Chapter 13, here we will concentrate on internal attempts to compromise the systems from the point of view of internal control.

A survey carried out in 2008 by the British Chambers of Commerce of about 4000 generally small- to medium-sized enterprises (SMEs) revealed some startling and, perhaps, not so startling statistics.

Among the not so startling statistics were:

- Ninety-four per cent of businesses had suffered from spam e-mail during the past 12 months.
- Thirty-one per cent claimed to have been the victim of phishing attempts.
- Twenty-three per cent had suffered from spyware infection.
- Nineteen per cent had experienced equipment failure or data loss following virus infection.
- Eleven per cent of businesses had experienced credit card fraud.
- Eight per cent had had laptop or desktop computers stolen.

They reported in detail by sector:

- Spyware infection and phishing attempts affected proportionally more businesses with fewer than 50 staff, with a turnover less than £1 million, and those working from home.
- Proportionally more of those in marketing and media (37 per cent) and professional services (36 per cent) had been affected by phishing attempts than other business sectors, possibly because of their greater propensity to use e-mail in the daily course of their work.
- Proportionally more of those in transport, distribution and storage (28 per cent) and manufacturing (26 per cent) had been affected by equipment failure or loss of data following virus infection.
- Theft of PCs and laptops affected a greater proportion of large businesses, those based in
  - business or retail parks
  - industrial estates/areas
  - the transport, distribution and storage sector, and
  - the public and voluntary services sector.

- Credit card fraud was a greater problem for those with a turnover of £5 million or more and those in retail and wholesale and the hotel and restaurant sectors.

The more startling statistics were these. Remember that this was a survey of smaller businesses but, as 98 per cent of UK businesses employ less than 50 people, the results are significant:

- Four-fifths of businesses used anti-virus software to help combat computer-related incidents and 77 per cent used spam filtering software.

- Worryingly, only 74 per cent routinely backed-up their business data – presumably the remaining 26 per cent trusted to luck; 70 per cent stored their data off-site.
- Only 63 per cent had installed a software-based firewall and 51 per cent a hardware firewall.
- Despite the best endeavours of the audit profession only 40 per cent had developed a strong password policy and only 21 per cent had compiled an asset inventory.

Clearly larger organisations, typically those with 50 plus staff and a turnover of £1 million or more, appeared to have greater resources to be able to deal with computer-related incidents. Significantly more of these organisations:

- routinely backed-up their data
- installed hardware firewalls
- developed strong password policies
- compiled an asset inventory
- had a formal written security plan
- employed an IT manager or IT supplier responsible for security
- use pc/server/laptop locks and security devices
- encrypted data, or
- used security markings.

In 2007 a DTI password survey of over 1800 adults found that just over one third recorded their password by writing it down or storing it on their computer! Nearly two-thirds never changed their password and about 20 per cent used the same password for both non-banking websites and their online bank.

A survey carried out by PriceWaterhouseCoopers on behalf of the (then) Department for Business Education and Regulatory Reform in 2008 showed that, whilst security and attitudes to security had generally improved considerably in the two years since their last survey, there were still some problems:

- Ten per cent of websites that accepted payments did not encrypt them.
- Twenty-one per cent of companies spent less than 1 per cent of their IT budget on information security.
- Thirty-five per cent had no controls over staff use of instant messaging (Hotmail).
- Fifty-two per cent did not carry out any formal security risk assessment.
- Sixty-seven per cent did nothing to prevent confidential data leaving on USB sticks etc.
- Seventy-eight per cent of companies that had computers stolen did not encrypt hard disks.
- Eighty-four per cent of companies did not scan outgoing e-mail for confidential data.

The report went on to note that, in some businesses, there was a clear gap between the good intentions of senior management and the actions actually taken. A third of companies that believed they gave a high or very high priority to security didn't have a security policy.

Case studies of system intrusions in the USA reveal that, on some occasions, hackers have taken low-level jobs with the target organisation and have used their role to discover system passwords, log-ons etc. The person who delivers internal post, the office cleaner, the temporary filing clerk could be individuals who can use their access to the office to observe and record employees using their access to the system. Once a system access password is discovered the hacker has a means of access past the firewall and in.

The report illustrated part of the problem by quoting a security officer at a retail bank who commented that information security had senior management's ear but middle management, who were responsible for implementation, were much less convinced of its worth.

Assessing IT system risks

We looked at the general approach to risk management in Chapter 7. As with all attempts to identify risk and to begin to deal with identified threats, the key to assessing risk is to adopt a systematic approach to evaluation.

The methodology for dealing with risk within IT systems is:

- identify the assets
- review the operation
- define the use of resources
- define access to systems
- secure software
- know exactly what software is running
- rehearse the response, and
- analyse the cause.

We look at each aspect of this below.

Identify the assets

First, organisations need to identify what data, systems and subsystems the organisation has and make an inventory of them. Hardware assets, particularly portable ones such as laptops and Blackberries, should also be identified and tagged. Loss of hardware can also mean loss of software and data.

From this the level of risk can be identified based on the sensitivity and value of the data. For example, a bank might consider customer identification data to be the most critical, whilst a research organisation might want to protect sensitive product development information.

The object of this is to determine how much protection each part of the organisation warrants and who might be responsible for protecting it.

Review the operation

The next step is to review the people, processes and technologies, including internal suppliers and partners.

This will include factoring in any problems identified through the risk assessments. For example, if sensitive systems are deliberately crashed through, say, a denial of service attack is there a back-up plan or a recovery methodology which will limit the damage to the organisation?

The organisation should also take due consideration of individuals who have access, or potential access, to sensitive data. Through its HR systems the organisation should not only validate the background of new starters thoroughly, but also ensure that basic security steps, such as the deletion of system passwords for leavers, are taken.

Define the use of resources

All organisations should have policies both as to what constitutes appropriate use of computer resources and key security issues. These will include such matters as remote access and what employees should and shouldn't be doing on their systems. This covers such things as Internet access, e-mail protocols etc.

It is important that organisations explain the rationale for rules, prohibitions and limitations to minimise the risk of employees ignoring them.

Define access to systems

Certain technologies, firewalls, authentification and authorisation and encryption need to be configured to reflect the decisions made as to who has access to which systems.

These should be monitored regularly through the use of regular audits, computer-assisted audit techniques, monitoring and intrusion detection tools.

Secure software

Insist that all software supplied by outside vendors is warranted free from unauthorised code. If it is developed in-house then developers should follow secure developing and testing practices.

Know exactly what software is running

Organisations need to keep track of which versions of software are running on their equipment and what patches and versions are installed. Every modification should be documented so that if security is breached there will be current records to determine when and where the hacker struck.

Procedures should be in place to ensure that IT professionals can add patches and updates as soon as these are available.

Rehearse the response

Have procedures in place which will guard against knee jerk or irrational responses in the case of an attack. This will enable the organisation to estimate how long it would take to diagnose problems or restore damaged systems.

Where fraud is suspected great care must be taken to preserve any evidence trail and nothing should be done without expert consultation.

Analyse the cause

Whenever a security breach is found the cause of the breach should be traced back to its origins. Lessons should be learned and systems controls and procedures amended or strengthened accordingly.

Formal approaches to risk management

It is outside the scope of this book to look in detail at IT systems. However, the forensic accountant should be aware of the existence of formal structured approaches to computer systems control and documentation so as to understand the principles behind them if a client is adopting one of these approaches and, perhaps, to include one of these approaches in any recommendations if they are not.

For organisations subject to the Sarbanes–Oxley (Sarbox) reporting requirements a formal structured approach to internal control is of great assistance when complying with the certification requirements.

We will look at two formal systematised approaches to maintaining a computerised system and assessing and dealing with system risk:

- CobiT, and
- ISO 27001.

CobiT

Control objectives for information and related technology (CobiT) is a governance and control framework created by the Information Systems Audit and Control Association (ISACA) and the IT Governance Institute. It is designed to provide managers, auditors and IT users with a set of generally accepted measures, indicators, processes and best practices to assist them in maximising the benefits derived through the use of information technology and in developing appropriate IT governance and control in a company.

CobiT starts by grouping IT processes into four broad groups:

- plan and organise
- acquire and implement
- deliver and support, and
- monitor and evaluate.

The content is split into 34 IT processes, which are summarised below. Each process is then split into subsections and described in detail. It is not appropriate to include all elements of CobiT here, but students can easily obtain full details from various publications or, of course, the Internet.

This summary of processes includes:

- High-level control objectives including:
  - summary of goals, and
  - a process description summarising the process objectives.
- Detailed control objectives of the process – this includes a total of 214 detailed control objectives divided amongst the 34 high-level processes.
- Management guidelines – includes:
  - process inputs
  - RACI (responsible, accountable, consulted and informed) chart (Table 9.1), and
  - goals.

Table 9.1 An RACI example

Item/description	Actions for pursuing strategy RACI (Responsible/Accountable/Consulted/Informed)								
	Name	Name	Name	Name	Name	Name	Name	Name	Name
Develop strategy: Establish approach Set priorities Develop action plan Completed strategy	I	C	I	R	I	I	I	C	C
Establish core team: Define purpose Define time commitments Define roles and responsibilities Identify necessary skills Identify technical support resources Identify core team members Core team established	C	I	R	C	I	I	I	C	C
Establish extended team: Define purpose Define time commitments Define roles and responsibilities Identify necessary skills Identify technical support resources Identify extended team members Extended team established	I	R	I	I	I	I	I	I	I
Pilot and validate policies and standards: Introduce policies and standards Develop communication plan Identify initial business audience Schedule information sessions Travel arrangements Publish standards and policies	C	C	I	I	I	I	R	I	C
Improve policies, standards and processes: Gather feedback Analyse feedback Modify/change policies and standards Update library Communicate changes Provide training as needed	I	I	C	I	R	C	C	I	I

Table 9.1 is an example of an RACI chart. Each individual listed across the top of the table (Name) has a designated task in connection with each component of the project. They are to be:

- Responsible (R) – for carrying out the task.
- Accountable (A) – for the success of the task.
- Consulted (C) – about the task where necessary.
- Informed (I) – as to the progress or otherwise of the task.

Each individual's role in the project is indicated by the relevant letter in the box opposite the task, under their name. Each person will of course have several roles in connection with the project as a whole but one task in connection with each separate component.

Clearly an individual can have more than one role in each component; they could be, for example, Responsible and Accountable for delivering it, but the example shows how a team's role can be divided up and tasks allocated according to relevant strengths and skills.

Use of such a tool as an RACI chart has three main advantages:

1 Each component of a project has to be analysed into tasks and work allocated. This forces managers into a planning phase and is designed to prevent important considerations being forgotten or inadequately dealt with, for example, by being delegated to an unskilled person.
2 Every component of the task has to be dealt with and reported on.
3 Each individual in the team knows their role and what they have to do – dates can be added to the chart as required.

Audit firms already use some form of RACI chart when audit planning and forensic investigators may find it useful when planning assignments.

As can be seen from this brief overview CobiT is a comprehensive framework for managing IT processes. It takes into account the different needs of managers, users and auditors which, because it is formalised, has the advantage of ensuring that everyone involved is appropriately tasked and knows where they stand, what their responsibilities are and what they have to do.

The control objectives are supported by audit guidelines which enable auditors and managers to review specific IT processes against these in order to help assure management where controls are sufficient, or to advise management where processes need to be improved.

The IT processes within each of those categories are as follows.

Plan and organise

The IT processes are split into separate components. These require managers to:

- define their strategy
- define what processes they have and the progression of those systems
- identify the processes
- communicate the strategy, and
- manage issues such as the IT invesment, quality and risk.

Within CobiT these processes are defined as shown in Table 9.2.

Table 9.2 Plan and organise – high-level IT processes

PO1	Define a strategic IT Plan and direction
PO2	Define the information architecture
PO3	Determine technological direction
PO4	Define the IT processes, organisation and relationships
PO5	Manage the IT investment
PO6	Communicate management aims and direction
PO7	Manage IT human resources
PO8	Manage quality
PO9	Assess and manage IT risks
PO10	Manage projects

Acquire and implement

The acquire and implement processes cover such issues as:

- identifying IT requirements
- acquiring the technology and
- implementing it within the company's current business processes, and
- the development of a maintenance plan.

Table 9.3 lists the IT processes contained in the acquire and implement domain.

Table 9.3 Acquire and implement – high-level IT processes

AI1	Identify automated solutions
AI2	Acquire and maintain application software
AI3	Acquire and maintain technology Infrastructure
AI4	Enable operation and use
AI5	Procure IT resources

Deliver and support

The deliver and support domain focuses on the delivery aspects of the information technology. It covers areas such as the execution of the applications within the IT system and its results, as well as, the support processes that enable the effective and efficient execution of these IT systems. These support processes include security issues and training.

Table 9.4 Deliver and support – high-level IT processes

DS1	Define and manage service levels
DS2	Manage third-party services
DS3	Manage performance and capacity
DS4	Ensure continuous service
DS5	Ensure systems security
DS6	Identify and allocate costs
DS7	Educate and train users
DS8	Manage service desk and incidents
DS9	Manage the configuration
DS10	Manage problems
DS11	Manage data
DS12	Manage the physical environment
DS13	Manage operations

Monitor and evaluate

The monitor and evaluate domain deals with a company's strategy in assessing the needs of the company and whether or not the current IT system still meets the objectives for which it was designed and the controls necessary to comply with regulatory requirements. Monitoring also covers the issue of an independent assessment of the effectiveness of IT system in its ability to meet business objectives and the company's control processes by internal and external auditors (Table 9.5).

Table 9.5 Monitor and evaluate – high-level IT processes

ME1	Monitor and evaluate IT processes
ME2	Monitor and evaluate internal control
ME3	Ensure regulatory compliance
ME4	Provide IT governance

ISO/IEC 27001

ISO/IEC 27001 is the only auditable international standard which defines the requirements for an information security management system (ISMS). The standard is designed to ensure the selection of adequate and proportionate security controls.

ISO/IEC 27001 is the formal set of specifications against which organisations may seek independent certification of their ISMS. The standard covers all types of organisations – commercial enterprises, government agencies and non-profit organisations – and all sizes from micro-businesses to multinationals.

It specifies requirements for the:

- initial establishment
- implementation
- monitoring and review, and
- maintenance and improvement.

of an overall management and control framework for managing an organisation's information security risks. It does not set out specific information security controls but stops at the level of the management system – it is a framework, not a recipe.

Bringing information security under management control is seen as a prerequisite for what they describe as sustainable, directed and continuous improvement. An ISO/IEC 27001 ISMS therefore incorporates several Plan Do Check Act (PDCA) cycles (see below) designed to facilitate process improvement.

For example, information security controls are not merely specified and implemented as a one-off activity but are continually reviewed and adjusted to take account of changes in the security threats, vulnerabilities and impacts of information security failures, using review and improvement activities specified within the management system.

ISO/IEC 27001 is intended to be suitable for several different types of use, including:

- formulating security requirements and objectives
- use within organisations as a way to ensure that security risks are managed cost-effectively
- compliance monitoring
- use as a process framework for the implementation and management of controls to ensure that the specific security objectives of an organisation are met
- identification and clarification of existing information security management processes and the development and identification of new ones to meet new threats
- use by the management to determine the status of information security management activities

- use by the internal and external auditors of organisations to demonstrate the information security policies, directives and standards adopted by an organisation and determine the degree of compliance with those policies, directives and standards
- use by organisations to provide relevant information about information security policies, directives, standards and procedures to trading partners and other organisations that they interact with for operational or commercial reasons
- implementation of a business enabling information security, and
- use by organisations to provide relevant information about information security to customers.

The information security controls from ISO/IEC 27002 are noted in an appendix (annex) to ISO/IEC 27001, rather like a menu. Organisations adopting ISO/IEC 27001 are free to choose whichever specific information security controls are applicable to their particular information security situations, drawing on those listed in the menu and potentially supplementing them with other *à la carte* options (sometimes known as extended control sets).

As with ISO/IEC 27002, the key to selecting applicable controls is to undertake a comprehensive assessment of the organisation's information security risks, which is one vital part of the ISMS.

As mentioned above, the essential basis of the standard is based on the Plan–Do–Check–Act cycle:

- Plan = define requirements, assess risks, decide which controls are applicable.
- Do = implement and operate the ISMS.
- Check = monitor and review the ISMS.
- Act = maintain and continuously improve the ISMS. The standard also specifies certain specific documents that are required and must be controlled, and states that records must be generated and controlled to prove the operation of the ISMS (e.g. certification for audit purposes).

As with all forms of quality improvement process, it must be led from the top or it will fail. Management must demonstrate their commitment to the ISMS, principally by allocating adequate resources to implement and operate it. Management should also formally review the suitability, adequacy and effectiveness of the ISMS at least once a year, assessing opportunities for improvement and the need for any changes.

Internal audit has a part to play insofar as part of the process is that of conducting periodic internal audits to ensure the ISMS incorporates adequate controls which operate effectively.

As with the more familiar quality standard, ISO 9001, the intention is that the organisation must continually improve the ISMS by assessing and, where necessary, making changes to ensure its suitability and effectiveness, addressing non-conformance or non-compliance issues, reporting them and, where possible, preventing recurrence.

Both CobiT and ISO 27001 are formal systems which can assist the organisation both in developing good practice and in raising awareness of security and control issues. Whilst they undoubtedly increase costs and can seem bureaucratic and time-consuming, they do have one overriding advantage which is that they compel management to pay attention to control issues and IT policies and, by preventing them from delegating and forgetting, ensure that proper attention is paid to IT security.

Specific approaches to protecting IT systems

Much of the basis of fraud prevention lies in a proper identification of risk. We have looked at the general principles of risk management and formal approaches to evaluating and dealing with risk. Here we look at some specific applications of the risk analysis process as it applies to IT systems and procedures.

There are three basic aspects to consider:

1 Policies and procedures.
2 Areas of vulnerability.
3 Actions to be taken in the event of a crime being committed or attempted.

Policies and procedures

It is a keystone of fraud prevention that proper policies and procedures should be in place to inform employees and others who come into contact with the organisation, such as contractors, suppliers or even customers, of the organisation's attitude to fraud and its approach to fraud prevention. Part of the process of risk management is for the organisation to evaluate its policies and procedures in relation to its IT systems. The organisation should develop an 'acceptable user policy' which will deal with such things as:

- the confidentiality of data
- the requirement for vigilance and for reporting suspect communications and breaches of security
- whistle-blowing policies (see Chapter 7)
- prohibitions on sharing passwords
- restrictions on Internet access and prohibitions on opening e-mails with attachments from unknown or doubtful sources
- use of computers for private purposes, and
- the disciplinary action to be taken for breaches of protocols.

In addition such a policy should make it a disciplinary offence for an employee to:

- try to access a system for which they have no permission
- steal someone's password and pass it on to a third party
- disclose or share passwords between employees
- use computers for private purposes – this could include a ban on accessing social networking sites such as Facebook, Bebo, MySpace and Twitter whereby it is possible, in certain circumstances, to bypass computer system protections
- copy software, or
- copy any data recorded on the system which is defined by the organisation as sensitive or confidential. A blanket prohibition may suffice but the policies must deal with situations where staff are permitted to take data home, for example, so they can work on it out of hours. The limits of this should be clearly defined.

Examples of acceptable user policies are included in the appendices.

The organisation should state categorically that it will investigate and report any instances of cyber crime to the police or other authorities and will assist in any investigation and, further, it should indicate that it will act to recover the value of assets or pursue a claim for damages against a cybercriminal or accomplice.

Details should be given of actions to be taken and, more importantly, *not* to be taken if a crime is uncovered.

Areas of vulnerability

As we saw earlier when considering the risk review framework, as part of its risk review procedures the directors or senior management should carry out a comprehensive risk review of all areas of vulnerability.

With regard to the possibilities of external hacking-type attacks these should include:

- Evaluation of the skills of employees with regard to computer technology.
- Consideration of how the organisation interacts with both the Internet and itself in terms of any intranets, etc.
- Evaluation of the controls which currently exist to address the risks of external attacks. This will include data back-up strategies, data recovery and disaster planning.
- Consideration of how often controls are reviewed and the procedures adopted in the cases where reorganisation has taken place or will take place.
- Evaluation of the software currently used as protection – its age and how frequently it is updated.
- Consideration of recent examples of cyber crime published in the media and whether the methods used would work against the organisation.
- Ensure that whistle-blowing hotlines etc. are known to staff and whether staff have faith in the process, i.e. that management will actually listen and whether or not their details will remain confidential (see Chapter 7).
- Consider how sensitive data such as passwords could be obtained by external means such as bribery and corruption.
- Consider the morale of staff and any disaffection among employees who may have left the organisation – ensure they can no longer access any systems after they have left.
- The organisation should consider the use of formal risk management processes such as CobiT or ISO 27000.
- A policy of forensic readiness (see below) should be instituted to deal with incidents of computer misuse or external threat.

Actions to be taken

These will include making good on policy statements such as reporting crimes to the police, forensic investigation and legal action against identified perpetrators.

The organisation should ask its current advisers, including external auditors, to identify whether or not they have the technical skills to investigate and advise on computer crime risks and defensive approaches. If they have not, the organisation should consider approaching a specialist organisation. Before the event is better than after!

As outlined above, most malware is introduced into organisational systems because individuals open innocent-looking e-mails, or access fake websites, which then open the door for the trojan or worm to be introduced into the system.

This is one area where, as we have seen, good defence is based on education and information – warning employees of suspicious e-mails, telling them to delete them unopened and constantly reminding them that requests for confidential information don't come through e-mail.

In addition to developing effective policies and staff training programmes there are some simple fixes which can be implemented to help minimise potential damage. These include:

- Develop and enforce a computer use policy including limitations on Internet access and prohibitions on certain sites where file sharing is common.
- All staff leaving employment must have their passwords and e-mail addresses disabled from the time of leaving.
- Information education and training of staff. Many attacks succeed because they get unwitting help from staff. Constant review of threats, information about suspicious e-mails circulating in the system, pop-up warnings from network managers, education about what to do if you find something suspicious all help.
- Denying staff the capability to load application software on to corporate hardware – this is to be done by IT staff only.
- Ensure that all operating system software is up to date.
- Install anti-virus software and download updates automatically when available.
- Install intrusion detection software and firewalls.
- E-mails and files should be scanned as they are downloaded into the network.

The network servers should incorporate software to scan e-mails and detect suspicious-seeming attachments about which they can then warn users. Technological change proceeds apace in that world – as fast as hackers devise a new form of attack software companies devise patches and fixes to defeat them – so keeping the anti-virus software up to date is vital.

Forensic readiness

In 2005 the National Infrastructure Security Co-Ordination Centre (NISCC) issued a technical note on what it called forensic readiness. The stated purpose of forensic readiness is to enable the organisation to maximise its potential to use digital evidence whilst minimising the costs of an investigation and consequent disruption to its operations.

Forensic accountants should be aware that whilst organisations can use formal systems methodologies such as CobiT and ISO 27000 to document and control their IT systems, the computer-based defences installed to protect the system from external attack – firewalls, passwords, data encryption and the like – can be breached from the inside by either ignorance or malice. Evidence to deal with system breaches, including loss of data or damage to systems, may be required as part of disciplinary proceedings or prosecution. Forensic readiness is an organisational approach to ensuring it is not lost or corrupted inadvertently.

Having a strong forensic readiness policy has two key advantages:

- First, if an organisation demonstrates that it has a strong forensic readiness policy and, moreover, is determined to use it to track and detect system abusers, this will have a deterrent effect on potential fraudsters.

- Second, the development and training required to implement the policy will raise awareness, among users, of potential threats to the system so that hopefully, for example, the suspicious e-mail is not just blithely opened, thus importing the trojan or virus, but is spotted, quarantined and dealt with.

In general the areas where digital evidence can be applied include:

- reducing the impact from computer-related crime
- dealing effectively with court orders to release data
- demonstrating compliance with regulatory or legal constraints
- producing evidence to support company disciplinary issues
- supporting contractual and commercial agreements, and
- proving the impact of a crime or dispute.

It is important to recognise that this is not a stand-alone solution; it is part of the overall risk assessment and business continuity planning processes and should be part of the risk-management processes of the organisation.

Clearly the evidence collection requirement is moderated by a cost–benefit analysis of how much the required evidence will cost to collect and what benefit it provides. The critical question for a successful forensic readiness policy is what can be performed cost-effectively. By considering these issues in advance and choosing storage options, auditing tools, investigation tools and appropriate procedures it is possible for an organisation to reduce the costs of future forensic investigations.

The NISCC Forensic Readiness programme follows ten steps which describe the key activities in implementing a forensic readiness programme:

1 Define the business scenarios that require digital evidence.
2 Identify available sources and different types of potential evidence.
3 Determine the evidence collection requirement.
4 Establish a capability for securely gathering legally admissible evidence to meet the requirement.
5 Establish a policy for secure storage and handling of potential evidence.
6 Ensure monitoring is targeted to detect and deter major incidents.
7 Specify circumstances when escalation to a full formal investigation (which may use the digital evidence) should be launched.
8 Train staff in incident awareness, so that all those involved understand their role in the digital evidence process and the legal sensitivities of evidence.
9 Document the evidence-based case describing the incident and its impact.
10 Ensure legal review to facilitate action in response to the incident.

We look at these steps in more detail below.

1 Define the business scenarios that require digital evidence

As we saw in Chapter 7, part of the process of defending the organisation is identifying vulnerable areas. The first step is therefore a comprehensive risk assessment:

- What is the threat to the business and what parts are vulnerable?
- What are the potential impacts on the business?

In assessing these scenarios, this step provides an indication of the likely benefits of being able to use digital evidence. If the identified risks, and the potential benefits of forensic readiness, suggest a good return on investment is achievable, then an organisation needs to consider what evidence to gather for the various risk scenarios.

2 Identify available sources and different types of potential evidence

What sources of potential evidence are they and where are they? How is data generated, stored, audited and retrieved, how long is data retained? Is there use of instant messaging which bypasses corporate e-mail servers? This may require software for intruder detection and for real-time monitoring of staff activities. This latter proposal may bring problems in terms of rights to privacy or human rights and needs careful thought and legal advice before implementation.

Some basic questions need to be asked about possible evidence sources to include:

- Where is data generated?
- What format is it in?
- How long is it stored for?
- How is it currently controlled, secured and managed?
- Who has access to the data?
- How much is produced?
- Is it archived? If so where and for how long?
- How much is reviewed?
- What additional evidence sources could be enabled?
- Who is responsible for this data?
- Who is the formal owner of the data?
- How could it be made available to an investigation?
- What business processes does it relate to?
- Does it contain personal information?

E-mail is an obvious example of a potentially rich source of evidence that needs careful consideration in terms of storage, archiving and auditing and retrieval. This is not the only means of communication used over the Internet, there is also:

- instant messaging,
- web-based e-mail that bypasses corporate e-mail servers
- chat rooms
- newsgroups, and
- voice over the Internet (Skype).

Each of these may need preserving and archiving.

The range of possible evidence sources includes:

- equipment such as routers, firewalls, servers, client terminals, laptops, embedded devices, etc.
- application software such as accounting packages, etc., for preserving evidence of fraud
- HR software for employee records and activities (for example, in case of identity theft), system and management files, etc.
- monitoring software such as intrusion detection software, packet sniffers, keyboard loggers, content checkers, etc.
- general logs such as access logs, printer logs, web traffic, internal network logs, Internet traffic, database transactions, commercial transactions, etc., and
- other sources such as: CCTV, door access records, phone logs, telephone data, etc.
- back-ups and archives.

3 Determine the evidence collection requirement

Once steps 1 and 2 are completed techniques can be adopted for the collection and retention of data which may constitute evidence of a crime. This is sometimes known as metadata, i.e. data about data. At its simplest it is data which serves to describe or contextualise raw data which can then be retrieved and used as part of the evidence trail. Companies should develop systems to ensure that there is a chain of forensic computer evidence linking cause and effect which is, primarily, based on systems logs of varying types.

For example, where there is evidence of suspect transactions from the accounting system it may be very useful for the investigator to know when those entries were made and who logged on to the system to make them. Metadata which identifies that, say, suspect journal entries were made by the alleged perpetrator logging on in the midst of a Sunday afternoon or when they had claimed to be on holiday could constitute evidence leading to a conviction.

4 Establish a capability for securely gathering legally admissible evidence to meet the requirement

The organisation knows the totality of evidence available and has decided which can be collected and retained in order to address identified risks. The problem is to collect it without interfering with business processes and, more importantly, interfering with employee rights.

With the evidence requirement understood, the next step is to ensure that it is collected from the relevant sources and that it is preserved as an authentic record.

At this stage legal advice is required to ensure that the evidence can be gathered legally and the evidence requirement can be met in the manner planned. For example, does it involve monitoring personal e-mails, the use of personal data, or 'fishing trips' on employee activities? There are some human rights issues here which will have to be addressed.

In the UK the Information Commissioner has stated:

- monitoring should be targeted at specific problems
- it should only be gathered for defined purposes and nothing more, and
- staff should be told what monitoring is happening except in exceptional circumstances.

5 Establish a policy for secure storage and handling of potential evidence

This could be in the form of data files maintained electronically at a remote location away from the main servers or on storage devices such as disks or memory sticks. It is important that procedures be adopted which ensure that the integrity of the evidence is preserved, i.e. that it cannot be lost or tampered with prior to being used in a legal case. This is the so-called chain of evidence and the PACE procedures should be borne in mind here (Chapter 3).

The use of an internal standard such as BS ISO/IEC 27001 (see above) is one approach. This specifies requirements for establishing, implementing, operating, monitoring, reviewing, maintaining and improving a documented information security management system (ISMS) within the context of the organisation's overall business risks. It specifies requirements for the implementation of security controls customised to the needs of individual organisations.

Physical security of data such as back-up files or on central log servers is important from the data protection point of view, and also for secure evidence storage. As well as preventative measures such as secure rooms with swipe card access it is also prudent to have records of who has access to the general location and who has access to the actual machines containing evidence.

Any evidence or paperwork associated with a specific investigation should be given added security by, for example, storing in a safe. Additional security of logs can also be achieved through the use of write once read many (WORM) storage media. This will provide access to archived data but present it being accidentally – or deliberately – overwritten.

6 Ensure monitoring is targeted to detect and deter major incidents

In addition to gathering evidence for possible later use in court, evidence sources can be monitored to detect threatening incidents in a timely manner. This is directly analogous to intrusion detection systems (IDS), extended beyond network attack to a wide range of behaviours that may have implications for the organisation. It is all very well collecting the evidence; this step is about making sure it can be used in the process of detection. By monitoring sources of evidence we can look for the triggers that mean something suspicious may be happening.

The critical question in this step is 'When should an organisation be suspicious'? A suspicious event has to be related to business risk and not couched in technical terms. Thus the onus is on managers to explain to those monitoring the data what they want to prevent and thus the sort of behaviour that IDS might be used to detect. This could be captured in a 'suspicion policy' that helps the various monitoring and auditing staff understand:

- what triggers should provoke suspicion
- who to report the suspicion to
- whether heightened monitoring is required, and
- whether any additional security measures should be taken as a precaution.

Any form of monitoring should produce a proportion of false positives, i.e. an event which looks suspicious but when investigated turns out not to be. The sensitivity of triggers can be varied as long as:

- the overall false positive rate does not become so high that suspicious events cannot be properly reviewed, i.e. so many are triggered that reviewers are overwhelmed, and
- false positives are generated so frequently that they become treated as routine events and are effectively ignored or discarded by reviewers. A form of complacency can set in so that when a genuine event occurs the signs are missed as they are buried in the routine traffic being ignored.

Varying triggers also guards against the risk from someone who knows what the threshold on a particular event is and makes sure any events or transactions they wish to hide are beneath it.

7 Specify circumstances when escalation to a full formal investigation (which may use the digital evidence) should be launched

If a suspicious event is detected it needs to be investigated, and in each case the full chain of evidence routine must be initiated to preserve evidence in case the event does turn out to have criminal intent. A policy should be in place to escalate those involved with an incident and what level of decision making is required so that the organisation's response can be put in place as quickly and efficiently as possible – in other words, at what point is the fraud response team informed?

The decision as to whether to escalate the situation will depend on any indications that a major business impact is likely or that a full investigation may be required where digital evidence may be needed. The decision criteria should be captured in an escalation policy that makes it clear when a suspicious event becomes a confirmed incident. At this point an investigation should be launched and policy should indicate who the points of contact are (potentially available on a 24/7 basis) and who else needs to be involved.

As with steps 3 and 6, above, the network and IT security managers and the non-IT managers need to understand each other's position:

- What level of certainty or level of risk is appropriate for an escalation?
- What strength of case is required to proceed?

For example, is the unsupported word of a whistle-blower enough? How much supporting hard evidence indications would be likely to be needed at this preliminary stage in order to trigger a wider investigation?

This decision should have been made at the point at which the organisation developed its fraud response plan (Chapter 7) and reference has to be made to that to ensure that the organisation is following its own procedures.

A preliminary business impact assessment should be made based on whether any of the following are present:

- evidence of a reportable crime
- evidence of internal fraud, theft, other loss
- estimate of possible damages (a threshold may induce an escalation trigger, i.e. anything potentially in excess of £X automatically becomes a confirmed incident)
- potential for embarrassment, reputation loss (brief the PR department!)
- any immediate impact on customers, partners or profitability
- whether recovery plans have been enacted or are required, or
- whether the incident is reportable under a compliance regime – e.g. to the UK Stock Exchange (UK Listing Authority) if the incident is material and is likely to affect reported results of a listed company, the Charity Commissioners or the Financial Services Authority.

8 Train staff in incident awareness, so that all those involved understand their role in the digital evidence process and the legal sensitivities of evidence

Forensic readiness is not confined to the computer department. Line managers, HR departments, PR departments and system administrators may all need specialist training to ensure that nothing is done to compromise the necessary data collection, or cast doubt upon its validity in any future criminal action.

There will be some issues relevant to all staff if they become involved in an incident. The following groups will require more specialised awareness training:

- the fraud response team
- corporate HR department where individuals are suspected of fraudulent or corrupt activity
- corporate PR department (to manage any public information about the incident)

- 'owners' of business processes or data
- line management, profit centre managers
- corporate security
- system administrators
- IT management
- legal advisers, and
- senior management (potentially up to board level).

At all times those involved should act according to 'need to know' principles. They should be particularly aware whether any staff, such as whistle-blowers and investigators, need to be protected from possible retaliation by keeping their names and their involvement confidential (Chapter 7).

Training may also be required to enable in-house staff and external consultants to understand how the relationships and necessary communications between them work.

9 Document the evidence-based case describing the incident and its impact

A case file documenting the incident and its ramifications is an important part of the process, not simply as a support for a legal case, insurance claim or disciplinary proceedings, but also to identify what happened to ensure there are no repetitions and that any loopholes are closed.

At this point reference should be made to the legalities of evidence collection, including the PACE rules (Chapter 3). Credibility is provided by both evidence and a logical argument.

The purpose of this step is to produce a policy that describes how an evidence-based case should be assembled. A case file may be required for a number of reasons:

- to provide a basis for interaction with legal advisers and law enforcement
- to support a report to a regulatory body
- to support an insurance claim
- to justify disciplinary action
- to provide feedback on how such an incident can be avoided in future
- to provide a record in case of a similar event in the future (it supports the corporate memory so that even if there are changes in personnel it will still be possible to understand what has happened), and
- to provide further evidence if required in the future, for example, if no action is deemed necessary at this point but further developments occur.

10 Ensure legal review to facilitate action in response to the incident

Legal advice is needed in order to review the strength of evidence in a criminal case and in order to avoid compromising proceedings by premature or foolish action. Legal advisers need to have knowledge of the law in the area of cyber crime. They may also have to be able to deal with a case which covers several jurisdictions.

At certain points during the collating of the cyber-crime case file it will be necessary to review the case from a legal standpoint and get legal advice on any follow-up actions. Legal advisers should be able to advise on the strength of the case and suggest whether additional measures should be taken; for example, if the evidence is weak is it necessary to catch an internal suspect red-handed by monitoring their activity and seizing their PC?

Any progression to a formal action will need to be justified, cost-effective and assessed as likely to end in the company's favour. Although the actual decision of how to proceed will clearly be post-incident, considerable legal preparation is required in readiness.

Legal advisers should be trained and experienced in the appropriate cyberlaws and evidence admissibility issues. They need to be prepared to act on an incident, pursuant to the digital evidence that has been gathered and the case may span legal jurisdictions, e.g. states in the USA, member states in the EU.

Advice from legal advisers will include:

- any liabilities from the incident and how they can be managed
- finding and prosecuting/punishing (internal versus external culprits)
- legal and regulatory constraints on what action can be taken
- reputation protection and PR issues
- when/if to advise partners, customers and investors
- how to deal with employees
- resolving commercial disputes, and
- any additional measures required.

Forensic readiness is complementary to, and an enhancement of, many existing information security activities. It should be part of an information security risk assessment to determine the possible disputes and crimes that may give rise to a need for electronic evidence. It is closely related to incident response and business continuity, to ensure that evidence found in an investigation is preserved and the continuity of evidence maintained. It is part of security monitoring to detect or deter disputes that have a potentially major business impact.

Forensic readiness procedures need to be incorporated into security training and into specific staff training.

 ## Cloud computing

One of the newest developments in the IT world is the growth of so-called cloud computing.

Organisations devolve their data processing and storage to, basically, the Internet. They use Internet-based providers to host their applications thus reducing their investment in hardware and removing the problems of data storage, upgrades and personnel issues from the organisation. In principle, providing the organisation controls system access, the question of security is solved as no-one really knows where the data is stored. It is, in fact, spread around various Internet providers and may not even be in the same country as the organisation.

The thought that precious applications and data storage are removed from the immediate control of the organisation may fill traditional accountants and auditors with horror, but advocates of cloud computing claim that, on the contrary, system security is increased by virtue of this very remoteness. They claim that if the organisation has got its security right at its end the data will automatically be secure as it is disbursed across the Internet.

However, computer security specialists are growing increasingly concerned that security may not be as tight as imagined. Several key issues have been identified as causes for concern:

- Access – data processed outside the enterprise brings with it an inherent level of risk, because outsourced services bypass the controls active within in-house IT processing systems. It may be difficult to establish who is actively managing the data, and thus who has privileged access rights to it.
- Compliance – customers are ultimately responsible for the security and integrity of their own data, even when it is held by a service provider. A local service provider can be subject to audit and security certifications but there is no requirement for cloud-computing providers to provide this level of access.
- Location – users may not know exactly where their data is hosted. Providers may indicate they are storing in specific locations or jurisdictions but may not, in fact, do so unless this is contractual.
- Data segregation – data in the cloud is typically in a shared environment alongside data from other customers. Encryption is one solution but if data is wrongly encrypted it can become unusable or complicate accessibility.
- Recovery – a cloud provider should have disaster recovery procedures and should have back-up and duplication procedures.
- Investigative support – investigating inappropriate or illegal activity may be impossible in cloud computing. Cloud services are especially difficult to investigate, because logging and data for multiple customers may be co-located and may also be spread across an ever-changing set of hosts and data centres. Computer analysts Gartner state:

> If you cannot get a contractual commitment to support specific forms of investigation, along with evidence that the vendor has already successfully supported such activities, then your only safe assumption is that investigation and discovery requests will be impossible.

- Long-term viability – because cloud computing organisations are generally enormous, for example, Google or Amazon, it is unlikely that they will collapse or be acquired by another, larger, company. In the event this did happen any contractual arrangements made should ensure the customer could recover their data.

Clearly the aspect of cloud computing which interests the forensic accountant specifically is the ability to investigate data, in order to carry out interrogation procedures on it (Chapter 13). If this is not possible or is, at best, extremely difficult investigators will have to factor this into their planning.

Summary

- Surveys have revealed a lack of awareness if IT security, particularly with SMEs.
- Larger companies tended to have more resources and be more aware of IT risks.
- IT system risks should be assessed methodically, including assessing what software is running and who has access to it.
- Hardware assets should also be identified.
- There are formal approaches to IT risk management, among them CobiT and BS27001.

- An acceptable user policy should be in place and communicated to staff.
- A policy of forensic readiness is useful to preserve digital information in the event of an attack.
- Cloud computing, where data is stored on the Internet, presents particular problems of data security.

Case study

Your specialist internal audit team looking at your company's IT systems has reported to you. Your company is an international Internet-based retailer selling to customers around the world who use their home computers to place orders.

Your IT auditor has noticed that, on several occasions, transactions were completed and goods were despatched but there was no record of funds having been received. The transactions appeared genuine to the point at which the order was approved and instructions given to the despatch department and the payment seemed to have been processed but then was apparently deleted from the system together with the record of the sale. The IT auditor discovered this by running a comparison check between deliveries and recorded sales and discovered that more deliveries were made than sales recorded. There does not appear to be any pattern to these incidents.

One anomaly also reported was an increase in orders from Russia, where the credit cards used were subsequently blocked by the credit card company. The goods had already been despatched before notification was received. It is believed that genuine cards had been cloned by criminals and it was several weeks before the cardholders reported the anomalies.

In addition the IT auditor has reported that the last upgrade to the anti-virus software was 18 months ago. The latest request for new anti-virus software was vetoed by the finance director on the grounds of cost. So far no cyberattacks had been reported so the director felt vindicated by the decision.

Analysis of credits issued revealed that there was an unusually high incidence of credit refunds arising from a location based in Germany. This was still under investigation.

Required

- Discuss the internal control risks faced by this organisation.
- What steps could management take to mitigate these risks?

Bibliography

Austin, R.D. and Darby, C. (2003) The myth of secure computing. *Harvard Business Review*, 81, 6, 320.

British Chambers of Commerce (2008) *The Invisible Crime – A Business Survey*. BCC, London.

British Standards Institute (2005) *ISOIEC27001*. BSI, London.

Brodkin, J. (2008) *Gartner – Seven Cloud Computing Security Risks*. Infoworld, www.infoworld.com, 2 July.

Chartered Institute of Management Accountants (CIMA) (2008) *Fraud Risk Management – A Guide to Good Practice*. CIMA, London.

Coderre, D. (2009) *Computer-aided Fraud – Prevention and Detection*. John Wiley, Hoboken, NJ.

Department for Business Enterprise and Regulatory Reform (2008) *Information Security Breaches Survey*. Department for Business Innovation and Skills, London.

Golden, T., Skalak, S. and Clayton, M. (2006) *A Guide to Forensic Accounting Investigation.* John Wiley, Hoboken, NJ.

Hopwood, W.S., Leiner, J.L. and Young, G. (2008) *Forensic Accounting.* McGraw-Hill, New York.

Huntington, I. and Davies, D. (1994) *Fraud Watch – A Guide for Business.* ICAEW, London.

ICAEW (2002) *Risk Management for SMEs.* ICAEW, London.

ICAEW (2003) *Fraud – Meeting the Challenge through External Audit.* ICAEW, London.

Information Systems Audit and Control Association: *CobiT Overview.* ISACA, Rolling Meadows, IL.

IT Governance Institute (2006) *Information Security Governance Guidance for Boards of Directors and Executive Management*, 2nd edn. IT Governance Institute, Rolling Meadows, IL.

KPMG (2006) *Fraud Risk Management Developing a Strategy for Prevention, Detection, and Response.* KPMG LLP, Zurich.

Millichamp, A. and Taylor, J.R. (2008) *Auditing.* Cengage, London.

National Computing Centre (2010) *CobiT – A Practical Toolkit for IT Governance.* NCC Ltd, Manchester.

National Infrastructure Security Co-ordination Centre (QinetiQ) (2005) *An Introduction to Forensic Readiness Planning.* NISCC, London.

Singleton, T., Singleton, A., Bologna, G.J. and Lindquist, R.J. (2006) *Fraud Auditing and Forensic Accounting.* John Wiley, Hoboken, NJ.

Wells, J.T. (2004) *Corporate Fraud Handbook – Prevention and Detection.* John Wiley, Hoboken, NJ.

Websites

www.britishchambers.org.uk

www.bsi-global.com

www.cimaglobal.com

www.coso.org

www.crb.homeoffice.gov.uk

www.frc.org.uk/apb

www.hbr.org

www.icaew.co.uk

www.iia.org.uk

www.infoworld.com

www.isaca.org

www.itgovernance.co.uk

www.ncc.co.uk

www.statistics.gov.uk/ukbusiness

www.thetimes.co.uk

Part 4

CARRYING OUT A FRAUD INVESTIGATION

Chapter 10

The approach to investigation

Chapter contents

Learning objectives

After studying this chapter you should be able to:

- Understand the decision that has to be made with regard to which organisation would carry out an investigation
- Recognise the purpose of the investigation
- Understand the need for a Letter of Engagement and to whom it is addressed, with particular emphasis on the question of legal privilege
- Appreciate the composition of the investigation team and the rationale for the inclusion of each individual
- Understand the planning process
- Understand the position with regard to a criminal prosecution and involvement of the police
- Understand the process of analysing pertinent relationships

Introduction

Forensic accountants are called in to investigate a fraud or a possible fraud in, basically, two situations:

1 A fraud has been uncovered by, say, an internal or external audit or management review and the management wish to employ specialists to gather the evidence in such a way that it will support a prosecution or, at the least, be able to defend a claim for unfair or constructive dismissal. Investigators may be called in to maximise the possibility of a successful recovery action against the perpetrators.
2 Fraud is alleged, perhaps by a whistle-blower, or preliminary indications of something unusual have been uncovered by audit procedures, but nothing is provable or yet certain.

We will look at these two situations separately as they involve different approaches and considerations.

A possible or probable fraud has been discovered

In the first case the alleged perpetrator may already have been suspended pending investigation and, for all intents and purposes, the existence of something serious having happened in an area of the business or gossip about the suspension of a colleague is common knowledge within the organisation. The office rumour mill is in full swing and the arrival of serious people in grey suits is expected hourly. In this case the arrival of forensic accountants and their subsequent investigation work will be likely to be accepted by the management and staff who may be only too willing to co-operate depending, of course, on the exact circumstances of the case and the relative popularity of both the accused and the accusers.

In this case management's options are:

1 to ask their existing audit firm to do the investigation, using a separate team to that of the audit staff, or
2 to employ another firm's specialists.

Management's thought processes would be likely to focus on the conflict of interest that the audit firm could be faced with if invited to carry out a fraud investigation. That conflict of interest is this: if the routine financial audit found nothing wrong, uncovering a material fraud subsequent to the audit, especially if the discovery date is reasonably close to the date the auditors signed off the latest set of financial statements, might leave the audit firm open to possible legal action for recovery. This might be the case if it is revealed that the fraud was something that routine audit procedures, properly carried out, ought to have alerted the auditors to in accordance with ISA 240, 'The auditor's responsibilities relating to fraud in an audit of financial statements' and ISA 330, 'The auditor's responses to assessed risks'. The situation is compounded if it is discovered that the fraud has continued for some years.

Consequently the audit firm has the dilemma that its own investigation may drop it deeper into a nasty negligence case. Whilst auditors are bound by their ethical code to do the best for their clients this could, understandably, place them in some difficulty.

It could result in them looking to emphasise areas of the investigation in which they had no audit presence and to minimise the impact of areas where they might conceivably have been found wanting.

It would be impossible for the audit firm to use the same personnel to investigate the possibility of a material fraud simply because, apart from any considerations of possible conflict, audit managers and partners will have built up relationships with the very people they might now be being called upon to investigate. This could lead to practical difficulties in carrying out their work and, in particular, the conduct of any fraud interviews. This situation would tend to negate the counter-argument, often trotted out, that the audit firm is familiar with the organisation's personnel, processes and procedures which would save time and, accordingly, cost.

In addition there may be some doubt as to their capability to carry out such an investigation as it would be likely to require specialised skills, e.g. the securing of evidence and the interviewing of witnesses and suspects which auditors may not possess.

In the end the organisation may simply feel that it would like another firm with the appropriate skills and experience to take a fresh look at the situation unblinkered and unbiased by any previous experience. This is usually the safest course of action. However there are situations where it is felt that it might be appropriate for the auditors to carry out the work, for example where there is potential for a material tax claim for the funds defrauded and it is sensible and practical for the forensic team and the tax investigations team to be from the same firm.

It should also be noted that the decision may be taken out of management's hands where a claim is likely to be made under any policy of insurance. The insurers may well insist on any investigation being carried out by an experienced forensic accountant and a properly constituted fraud response team.

A fraud is suspected but has not been discovered

In the second scenario outlined above, where a possible fraud is suspected but not yet established, the decision to be taken by management will involve other considerations apart from the relative merits of different firms or a desire to demonstrate the independence of the investigating team from the audit.

The key considerations here will be:

- Specialised forensic investigators are expensive and, if nothing is found, a considerable amount of money might have been wasted. Should the auditors investigate first to see if fraud is a possibility?
- As we have seen, the auditors know the company and the personnel involved. This will save time and may lead to the unmasking of any culprits rather more quickly than might otherwise be the case but there are objections to this – this very familiarity could be a hindrance to the perception of an independent investigation.
- The arrival of the auditors is a routine event and wouldn't cause any surprise among the managers and staff. The arrival of strangers will set the office rumour mill off at full speed, which might result in any as yet unidentified fraudster attempting to cover their tracks, possibly by destroying records or simply absenting themselves under a pretext such as illness. It may well cause uncertainty and unrest among staff which senior managers would have to deal with either by

exposing the real reasons for the presence of the investigators or by inventing some pretext. It may be, of course, that much of the investigation work can be done off-site using information extracted from the organisation's information systems outside normal office hours, but the presence of strangers will become apparent at some point.

- The reports may be the result of whistle-blowing in which case there may be a procedure to be followed. The report is malicious or mistaken, but either way the facts must be investigated. A fraud response plan (Chapter 7) may already be in place to cover just such an eventuality.
- If individuals are suspected but nothing is proven against them the legalities of their position with regard to relevant employment law, possible disciplinary procedures and their legal rights must be considered. This may require specialised input, not least from the legal team but also from an experienced investigator.

In this case the management has to decide how they are going to approach the investigation and what they are going to say to explain to the staff the presence of these strangers in their midst.

Clearly any consideration of the work to be carried out and the amount of planning and organisational work involved will depend on the circumstances of each case. Both these scenarios present their own problems and require planning and pre-investigation work. For the purposes of this chapter we will adopt the view that the investigators will be carrying out a substantial assignment requiring extensive investigation.

In some circumstances, as we have seen, it may not be conclusive at the initial stage that fraud has been committed, let alone which part of the organisation might be affected. On the other hand culpability may be obvious even if the extent of any fraud is yet to be fully established. What is important is that the investigators isolate areas which might prove to be fruitful in terms of the investigation such that a result can be achieved at the lowest appropriate cost and inconvenience to the client. This requires a process.

 ## Before the investigation commences

Whatever decision the management make the investigating accountants should be different from any audit team who have attended the client previously and should come free from preconceived ideas about the client and its personnel.

The most important point to make and one which must be clearly understood from the beginning is that the role of the investigator here is *not* to establish guilt or innocence – it is to establish the facts about what has happened, to investigate and to report the facts uncovered by their investigation in an impartial, objective manner.

The task is to establish:

- What has happened – the who, what, where, when and why of the case.
- If a fraud has been committed who committed it, who knew about it and just as importantly, who was not involved?
- Over what period the fraud was committed.
- How it was committed and what controls were circumvented.

- How much money or other reward was involved?
- What the best way is of getting the money back?
- What are the relevant issues? In particular what is to be done with any culpable individuals identified as a result of the investigation?
- What the insurance position is. Does the company carry fidelity insurance such that frauds by specified individuals or staff generally are covered? If so, have the terms of the policy been adhered to so that any losses may be recovered?
- Whether the insurance policy requires the organisation to conduct the investigation in a certain way and whether it requires the police's Economic Crime Unit to be notified.

Once the decision has been made to call in forensic accountants to report on the nature and extent of any fraud, the investigation has to be placed on a formal footing so the respective parties know where they stand.

In some cases investigating accountants may be appointed by outside bodies such as company insurers or regulators or, in the case of public sector bodies, government agencies such as the Comptroller and Auditor General or bodies such as the Law Society in respect of aberrant legal firms.

 ## Letter of Engagement

In every case where a firm is appointed to carry out an investigation a Letter of Engagement is required. This forms the basis of the contract between the client and the firm and is a legally binding agreement.

There are professional rules for accountancy firms regulated by recognised supervisory bodies which are outside the scope of this book. Firms which are not regulated in this way but which offer forensic investigation services should use forms of contract which will include similar clauses.

The International Standard on Related Services (ISRS) 4400 'Engagements to perform agreed-upon procedures regarding financial information' published by the International Auditing and Assurance Standards Board (IAASB) sets out the minimum content of a letter of engagement which, suitably adapted, could be used in these circumstances. The agreed-upon procedures here are the techniques used in forensic investigation and the financial information comprises the books, records and allied material and the financial statements where appropriate.

The Letter of Engagement should include, as a minimum:

- The nature of the engagement including the fact that the procedures performed will not constitute an audit or a review and that accordingly no assurance will be expressed.
- The stated purpose for the engagement which should be as widely drawn as is compatible with achieving the objective.
- The scope of the investigation and any possible identification of the financial information to which the agreed-upon procedures will be applied.
- The nature, timing and extent of the procedures to be applied which again should be quite widely drawn.
- Perhaps an indicator of the possible level of fees depending on the extent of procedures required. At the very least the basis of charging should be stated.
- The anticipated form of the final report of factual findings.

- Limitations on any distribution of the report of factual findings. Where such limitation would be in conflict with any legal requirements the forensic accountants should not accept the engagement. It should include a statement that the distribution of the report of factual findings would be restricted to the specified parties who have agreed to the procedures to be performed.

A key consideration here is the question of legal privilege. It may be preferable for the instructions to come from a legal firm rather than from the client directly where legal action is contemplated. The report of the investigators is thus addressed to them and not to the client. It is outside the scope of this book to discuss the detailed questions of legal privilege but it is advisable to consult lawyers before signing a Letter of Engagement commissioning an investigation.

 ## Setting up the investigating team

The work involved in an investigation, particularly if:

- the organisation is a large one and/or geographically diverse
- the fraud is long lasting, and
- the perpetrator has been adept at concealing their activities or where they have sown disorder or confusion to cover their tracks

is likely to be time-consuming and difficult.

Unless the perpetrator is identified at an early stage and falls weeping on the investigator's shoulder, ready to co-operate and identify all their nefarious deeds, the team is likely to be faced with sifting a number of fraudulent transactions from a huge number of genuine ones. Even where the alleged perpetrator confesses, they may be minimising their actions in the hope that all may not be discovered or may genuinely have underestimated just what they have done. In cases where the directors have misrepresented the financial statements there may be easily identifiable blocks of transactions which can be isolated and tabulated but in other cases of deception false transactions will mingle with genuine ones and, in the absence of co-operation from the suspect(s), it will be up to the investigators to prove their case.

Clearly to review every single possible transaction will be unrealistic, uneconomic and unviable so the planning process will need to identify the skills the team will need to accomplish the task successfully.

We looked at the composition of an in-house fraud response team in Chapter 7 and this would be very much the basis for an in-house response where the organisation feels competent to tackle any investigation without involving outside experts.

In practice, where the team mainly comprises external experts, the constitution of it will be slightly different but elements will be common to both.

The team is likely to include:

- *A lead investigator* to decide on strategy and tactics and to carry responsibility for the final report.
- *A manager* to co-ordinate the team members and their work.
- *Assistants* depending on the size of the task to carry out the detailed digging.
- *A member of the management team* probably at director level, possibly a senior non-executive director who will have an oversight role and facilitate meetings etc. with senior executives and non-executive directors as appropriate.

- *A computer forensic specialist and assistants* to deal with computer-based evidence and the investigation of computer hardware.
- *A legal representative* from an external firm acting in a consultancy capacity. It may be that the legal firm involved is the body to whom the report is addressed in order to secure legal privilege of the contents of the report and to limit enforced disclosure. It may be that the end product of the investigation is an action for recovery rather than a criminal prosecution and this should always be borne in mind.
- *An HR liaison* person to deal with issues relating to the staff of the organisation.
- If necessary, individuals with specialised skills such as surveillance also drawn from an outside agency.

Planning the work to be performed

The forensic accountants should plan the work so that an effective engagement will be performed; they must also document the planning process. There has to be a plan otherwise the investigation could waste time and resources.

Every investigation is different and but there are some basic constants which an investigation team should have.

The key planning points are:

1 Everyone in the team should know their role. They may have carried out investigations before and be used to working with each other in which case the team will gel together naturally. If they have been assembled from scratch it will be the role of the lead investigator and the manager to ensure that each member of the investigation team:
   - Has no connection with the target of the investigation such that findings may be compromised by accusations of complicity or such that a member of the team could face a conflict of interest.
   - Has the appropriate skills and knowledge to carry out the work. This may include a professional qualification such as membership of ACFE, in-house training on investigation work, experience and a reputation for diligent and thorough working practices.
   - Knows where they fit into the team – i.e. who they report to and who will be supervising their work.
   - Understands the methods of documenting findings including recording, indexing and document identification. In a fraud investigation preservation of original documents and detailed recording of how they were obtained, when they were obtained and how they have been preserved may be crucial to a successful prosecution.
   - Knows what not to do – in particular when dealing with such items as the suspected perpetrator's computer, Blackberry or PDA and mobile phone.
   - Understands the organisation, its structure and its internal controls and understands the role of the internal audit department, if any, in the investigation and any involvement with external auditors.
   - Understands the need for confidentiality and is aware of who knows about the investigation and, most importantly, who does not. If there is a 'cover story' they should be advised of it and understand it thoroughly.

2 Staff have to be allocated and work performed. There may well be a deadline – there is invariably urgency. The nature of the assignments do not permit leisurely planning so often the planning is swift and the plan amended as the assignment progresses: nevertheless the senior investigator responsible for the assignment must be able to demonstrate a process rather than a random series of actions. Every assignment is different so there are no specific planning rules, but the detailed planning process has to include, among other matters:

- identification of the scope of the work to be performed
- budget and timing
- staff requirements
- allocation of work between members of the investigation team
- supervision and review procedures
- arrangements for informing management and staff at the client as to the real or ostensible reason for the investigation. The investigation team should be advised of who, at the client, knows about the investigation if its true nature has not been revealed
- arrangements for documenting the work carried out
  - the findings of investigatory work
  - the conclusions arising from those findings
- arrangements for preserving physical evidence, i.e. documents etc.
- computer forensics and instructions regarding the client's computer equipment and software
- liaison with legal advisers
- arrangements for reporting to management
- liaison with Economic Crime Unit as required. This may not be advisable, for reasons we will refer to later, until after the detailed investigation work has been completed, or
- disclosures to HM Revenue and Customs in connection with any tax claim.

Investigators may find tools such as the RACI chart (Chapter 9) helpful in planning and documenting tasks.

Investigators should document matters which are important in providing evidence to support the report of factual findings, and evidence that the engagement was carried out in accordance with the terms of the engagement. They should carry out the procedures agreed upon and use the evidence obtained as the basis for the report of factual findings.

Investigation work – general points

This book has within it techniques and tactics for carrying out investigations into frauds, and specific reference should be made to those chapters when considering specific areas of investigation. However, some general points can be made applicable to all investigation assignments.

First, it is unlikely that a team will be asked to investigate on the basis that they have to investigate the whole organisation. The suspicions which caused the investigation to be triggered will serve, at least in the first instance, to point the team at a specific area within the organisation on which to focus their attention. It may be, of course, that the scope of the work will be extended as the investigation proceeds but at first there will be likely to be a target area or individual on which to concentrate.

In any case pre-investigation planning will be able to assist the team. This phase of the work will involve:

- A review of the personnel of the organisation, their responsibilities, roles and the extent of their authority. This may include a matrix matching their authority against internal controls and a social network diagram which may explain their links within the organisation.
- A review of the internal controls of the organisation including internal audit reports and management letters from the external auditors. These may include a review of system flowcharts and process flow diagrams (Chapter 8). The investigator can, at this stage, apply their own creative thinking to how they would overcome the system – a question which, of course, the fraudster has already answered! Identifying a breach of controls may well lead to a perpetrator – or at least narrow down the field.
- Meetings with internal auditors as appropriate. It may be that the suspicion was raised by internal audit and their help can be invaluable in saving time and effort simply because of their knowledge of the systems, the controls and the individual members of staff. If they have not been involved care has to be taken in dealing with them as they will have contact with the staff at the company.
- Discussions with external auditors may have to take place in the knowledge that the external auditors may feel somewhat defensive and in fear of legal action. They may well be trying to obtain details of the findings of the investigation or indications as to which areas are being looked at so they can review their own procedures in the light of what has happened.
- Analytical review (Chapter 12) of financial and management accounts. This can be important to identify areas where an embezzler may have tried to hide the consequential debits arising from their diversion of funds and is of significance in cases of deliberate misrepresentation of the financial statements.

Most of this work can be done off-site and away from the enquiring eyes of staff at the client's premises, as can much of the detailed investigation work where this is based on data extracted from the client's MIS.

Preliminary work and the information which triggered the investigation will result in the team looking at specific areas of the business.

The lead investigator

The lead investigator should have established a programme of work or, at least, an initial programme to review the suspect areas and to identify the perpetrators of any fraud discovered. If the fraud has already been revealed it may be that the work is simply to:

- establish the extent of it and its scope
- ensure that it has been confined, and
- gather the evidence for the prosecution and/or dismissal of the perpetrator.

Activities must be co-ordinated with the client. It may be, for example, that investigations are conducted out of normal working hours or at weekends when the office staff are not present.

Liaison with legal advisers is vital at every stage and they should be kept informed of progress as the investigation proceeds. It may be necessary to obtain court orders, such as Norwich Pharmacal orders or freezing orders (Chapter 3), so as to obtain information from, say, bank accounts or to freeze assets. In addition lawyers will be able to advise on the rights of individuals accused of any crime and matters such as the proper preservation of evidence.

The lead investigator is also responsible for ensuring computer forensic investigators have proper access to whatever they need to do. This may involve them taking away suspect machines for forensic examination but, at the very least, it will require that they have clear access to the computer systems, programs and data. It may be that e-mails, diaries and notes which are held on a central server will constitute evidence or may point to the activities of a perpetrator and the complicity of others. Forensic IT investigators will need full access to any servers and the information they contain.

The lead investigator must constantly review the progress of the investigation against the original information which triggered it and the results of any pre-investigation work. If nothing is being achieved the scope and direction of the work may have to be changed.

Investigations are fluid, and leading one requires attention to detail and an appreciation of the wider picture.

Criminal prosecution

The question of any police involvement must be reviewed. There are some instances, principally with respect to money laundering offences under the Proceeds of Crime Act 2002, where there is no choice but to make a report to the Serious Organised Crime Agency (Chapter 3), but where the investigation report is covered by legal privilege there is no instant obligation to make a report to the Economic Crime Unit. As fraud is a statutory offence in England, Wales and Northern Ireland the police, or more accurately the Crown Prosecution Service, have the jurisdiction to prosecute on the basis of what they call a 'relevant' event having been committed (see Chapter 3) if they discover it. Clearly if they know nothing about it prosecution is unlikely.

In practice it will, subject to legal considerations, be the client's decision as to whether the police should be informed. Anecdotal evidence indicates that police involvement, at least in the early stages of an investigation, could result in a certain amount of loss of control as investigating officers may want to establish their rights over the proceedings which can become a hindrance. In general, experience indicates that complex frauds may not proceed to prosecution because of their very complexity before a jury of lay people – open and shut cases are to be preferred!

It should also be pointed out that the police will not assist in recovering the money extracted by the fraudster.

Any discussions with the Economic Crime Unit should take place at a relatively early stage of the investigation, once the size and shape of the fraud is becoming apparent. The reason for this is straightforward enough, it is so that such matters as:

- preservation of evidence
- interviewing suspects
- sufficiency of evidence

- case preparation, and
- management of police expectations as to what work will be done and by whom.

need to resolved at an early stage and members of the investigation team need to be aware of what is needed. If necessary a separate document called a Memorandum of Understanding can be prepared so that all parties understand their roles.

The police have extremely wide powers to obtain evidence but these can only be used in the context of an investigation. Police powers cannot be used to provide evidence for the organisation's own team and any private legal action for recovery. If the matter is not to involve the police then other ways must be found to gather evidence.

Even if a prosecution is not contemplated at an early stage it is often best to be prudent. For example, in order to ensure that vital evidence is preserved, procedures such as digital imaging of computer records may be best carried out by a specialised external provider. They can assist the investigation but would also be able to provide a copy for the police should a prosecution subsequently become a realistic possibility. It is too late to contemplate prosecution if evidence has been allowed to become contaminated and the chain of evidence lost (Chapter 3).

Unless the value of the fraud exceeds £1 million or has an international or public interest dimension, in which case the Serious Fraud Office (SFO) will become involved, the local police authority will take the prosecution forward in conjunction with the Crown Prosecution Service.

As far as the client is concerned either the decision to prosecute has to be made at an early stage or, more usually, the investigation carried out by the forensic accountancy team is done on the basis that prosecution is likely. Consequently any investigation into fraud, where prosecution is possible, should follow the rules under the Police and Criminal Evidence Act 1984 with regard to the collection and preservation of evidence and the rights of suspects being interviewed (Chapter 3).

Legal involvement

In any investigation some form of legal involvement is vital. This can be in the form of an in-house lawyer but it is more usual to use a specialist legal expert with experience of forensic investigation. This is mainly because investigators need advice as matters progress but is also because a fraud investigation may well require the rapid obtaining of Court Orders to freeze assets, for example.

Civil investigations should be conducted using legal privilege as much as possible so that, if nothing is found, the results do not have to be disclosed at a later date. This requires the involvement of an external legal firm.

Lawyers will also be able to work with the investigators not only in giving advice as required but in the preparation and use of the various orders which can be used to gather information and prevent the disposal of assets. We consider these in detail elsewhere (Chapter 3) but generally these orders are:

- so-called 'Norwich Pharmacal' orders to obtain information from innocent third parties such as banks
- freezing orders to prevent the transfer of assets, and
- search orders to obtain information from private addresses.

As stated elsewhere these procedures are expensive and need to be handled with care so proper legal representation is vital.

 **Fraud reporting**

We will look at reports in more detail in Chapter 16 as part of the forensic accountant's experience as an expert witness. Even if the investigator is unlikely to be called to give evidence their report will, at some level, form part of any case. If the Economic Crime Unit takes the case over they will present evidence on their own behalf, some of which may have been extracted by the forensic investigator. If the claim is a civil one, for restitution or in pursuit of disciplinary proceedings, the report may well be a substantial part of the case.

Suffice to say at this point that any report made as a result of a forensic investigation should:

- Be in accordance with the instructions initially given by the client in the Letter of Engagement and in any subsequent instructions
- Contain full details of the work carried out and the subsequent findings of the investigation. This includes details of:
  - How the fraud was committed.
  - If a perpetrator has not been clearly identified indicators as to the key aspects of the individual which would be needed to have committed the fraud, i.e. their role, status, access to information etc. This may have to be done, in the absence of absolute proof, without naming any specific individual.
  - How much was involved or as close an indication as possible.
  - What reparations may be made by recovery from insurance or from perpetrator.
- Make recommendations arising from the work carried out including:
  - How could the fraud have been avoided?
  - How may it be avoided in the future?
  - What breakdowns in internal control or absence of effective controls were discovered?
  - How these may be rectified.

Remember also that the investigators are not required to make any judgements as to the guilt or innocence of any individuals identified in the report – they are there to establish what happened, to record facts and to draw conclusions based on those facts.

Forensic accountants must avoid the trap of drafting a report in such a way that it veers away from conclusions based on facts and draws conclusions which may be hypothetical or inferred. It is important that any conclusions drawn are based on the results of the investigation and are supported by sufficient, appropriate and reliable evidence.

Any assumptions or subjective statements must be clearly identified and separated from those supported by hard evidence. It may be difficult to draw unambiguous conclusions. Frauds may be complex, evidence may have been destroyed either deliberately or inadvertently and it is always possible that such conclusions as can be drawn are to be based on a balance of probabilities rather than definitive evidence. If this is the case it should be clearly stated in the report even though the client may ultimately be unsatisfied with it, having paid a no doubt substantial fee for the investigation!

Investigators should preserve their working papers after the investigation is concluded. It has been suggested that two years is an optimum time for retention of records but prudence would dictate that perhaps six years might be a more suitable period. If an offender is dismissed and sins again, evidence of earlier wrongdoing may be useful in any subsequent prosecution for an offence. There may be extensive retention requirements limits in connection with civil recovery cases and legal advice should be obtained in these situations.

Detailed investigation work

We have looked at the beginning and end of an investigation. We should now look at the all-important bit in the middle – the investigation work. (Investigatory procedures using computer-based techniques are dealt with separately in Chapter 13.)

Pre-investigation work

If a perpetrator has already been identified and a fraud uncovered the investigators may need to do little more than carry out procedures to establish the facts, clarify the scope and scale of the fraud and assemble evidence for a prosecution or to support a dismissal. Preliminary investigative work may be a minimum, but there should always be a consideration of audit reports and policies if only for the purposes of commenting on their effectiveness in any final report and in recommending procedural improvements to the client.

A preliminary stage in the investigation is to carry out a desk review of relevant procedures and reports together with the findings of any form of audit or internal control review. Investigators should also carry out preliminary work based on known or identified relationships in order to identify areas of weakness which may be hidden from conventional flowcharting procedures or which could indicate the requirement for there to be collusion in perpetrating a fraud. If a perpetrator has been identified it may be possible to identify accomplices, if any, through the use of matrices and relationship diagrams.

Risk management procedures

Most organisations of any size, as we saw in Chapter 7, carry out some form of risk assessment process. Much of this may be of little immediate value to the investigator – for example a reputation risk assessment arising from the possible use by a supplier of child labour in Vietnam is of little help in detecting fraud in a plant in Solihull – but the areas around compliance, bribery and corruption and procurement may well be of more than passing interest.

Investigators should review those procedures which may affect them but, more importantly, should review:

- the work carried out by whoever wrote the procedures in establishing current practice, i.e. what the organisation does now, and
- any work carried out by external or internal audit or local management in monitoring or reviewing these procedures and any reports they have written, particularly if a review has been carried out by an external agency other than the external auditors.

Internal control reviews

Chapter 8 discussed the main principles of internal control, and any investigator with a background in auditing will have immediately understood the significance of the key elements of internal control procedures and activities.

The investigator should have available flowcharts and system descriptions of the key control activities and the checks and balances within the system. If not available from the client these should be available from the external auditors who are required under IAS 315, 'Identifying and assessing risks of a material misstatement through understanding the entity and its environment', to document the system in such a way as to identify key controls and evaluate their effectiveness.

The auditor's management letters and any other reports will also serve as a source of information.

The work and reports of internal audit could be invaluable as these may well include information not recorded by the external auditors. As we saw in Chapter 2, internal audit looks into many more areas of the organisation than do the external auditors so their reports are likely to be of more use if only to enable the investigator to eliminate areas where fraud is unlikely to have taken place.

The problem with the documentation is that it probably doesn't tell the whole story. Many frauds bypass the internal control systems completely or insert documents into the system which have all the hallmarks of genuine documents. They may carry the right authorisations, relate to suppliers or customers who have been approved or individuals seemingly correctly employed simply because the perpetrator of the fraud is a key part of the internal control system, i.e. the fraud is being perpetrated by those who have signing authority.

Many frauds such as bribes and kickbacks relate to external activities which cannot be detected by conventional audit procedures. In practice, as we will see, these are extremely difficult to detect and are easier to stop than prove.

Matrices and relationship diagrams

One of the keys to unravelling complex frauds is to understand relationships. As with internal control reviews this is often best done by using diagrammatic representations of:

- areas over which individuals have authority and influence
- relationships within the organisation, known as social networks, and
- relationships between companies and other entities within a complex group, particularly where some may be situated overseas.

The use of network analysis tools can reveal patterns within the organisation which hitherto have remained obscured. This is because they have developed organically and are not formal relationships, so are not documented, or because they are not considered relevant to a financial or operational structure.

Information can be obtained locally from:

- staff lists and locations
- job descriptions and task requirements
- informal discussions with managers and staff
- e-mail monitoring
- questionnaires
- social activities networks (firms football team, darts league, etc.)

- office gossip, and
- surveillance.

or indeed any source which might be useful in identifying the formal and, perhaps more importantly, informal networks which can influence relationships within the organisation.

In addition there are database searches which can be done which might also yield information about activities and relationships, for example:

- Companies House searches
- Property Register (Land Registry) search
- Yacht register
- Internet search, for example, facebook 'friends', blogs and personal websites, and
- DVLA search.

Where there is dysfunctional activity in the organisation, network analysis may indicate areas of interest to the investigator outside the mainstream control and audit information they already have.

Matrices

One simple but effective tool to highlight relationships is the matrix. This indicates the relationship individuals may have with certain processes, activities, roles or positions.

It is important to realise that these 'activities' are not confined to work but also include out of work social links and relationships. The latter will vary from casual friendships to more profound relationships. They will include links such as playing for the same football team, going fishing together, being related or married etc. All bonds other than purely superficial friendships are significant.

For example, Table 10.1 illustrates the relationship named individuals may have with activities. The individuals are named on the left and the activities identified are across the top.

Table 10.1 Matrix of activities

	Activities					
	A	B	C	D	E	F
Fred		X	X		X	
Sue		X				
Joe			X			X
Bill	X				X	
Anna	X			X		X

Bill and Anna are involved in activity A and Anna is also involved in activity F with Joe. Fred also has links with Joe, through activity C and Bill through activity E and so on.

So far so good – it doesn't really tell us any more than we might already know. What we now have to do is identify the real relationships between the individuals and we do this by using the information in the matrix and converting it into a diagram showing the relationship between the individuals. This is known as a link diagram. Table 10.2 is a link diagram showing the relationships between the people in Table 10.1:

Table 10.2 Matrix and link diagram of relationships

	Fred	*Sue*	*Joe*	*Bill*	*Anna*
Fred		X	X	X	
Sue	X				
Joe	X				X
Bill	X				X
Anna			X	X	

In Table 10.2 we look at the relationships each individual has with the others in their department or within the organisation. The activities shown in Table 10.1 have been discarded here as what we are interested in is the relationships, but of course the information in Table 10.1 is useful for mapping access to information or possible collusion.

Here we can represent the relationships between the individuals in what is known as a link diagram, as shown in Figure 10.1.

Although this looks very confusing, and can be where dozens of people are involved, we can establish some links:

(a) Fred has direct relationships with everyone directly apart from Anna – maybe they work for him. Joe has a relationship with Fred and Anna but no direct relationship with Sue or Bill.

(b) Anna has a direct relationship with Joe and Bill but no connection with Fred or Sue except via the others.

A review of the matrix in Table 10.1 and this link diagram reveals that Anna and Fred together have some connection with every activity in the system, however the link diagram indicates no connection between them. There is a link via Joe or Bill, so on the face of it the principle of segregation of duties appears to work. However, if a direct link can be established between Anna and Fred investigators would have to consider the possibility of collusion between them undermining all the internal controls.

These types of diagram can be used to chart relationships within the organisation – and even external to the entity where this might be relevant.

Social networks

Matrices and link diagrams are useful in identifying networks with organisations but give no hint of the relative strength of the relationships. For example in Figure 10.1

Figure 10.1 Relationship or link diagram

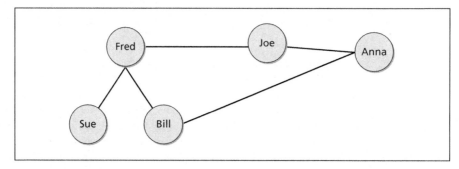

Fred and Joe may have a strong relationship because they are of equal status in the organisation, sit on a committee together and perhaps even socialise, whereas the relationship between Fred and Bill may be very much one way, for example, Fred may be Bill's superior.

This might or might not be relevant to the investigator who may only be looking for links, but if collusion is suspected the nature of the relationship could be of key importance.

Collusion may arise because (using the examples in Figure 10.1):

- Fred, Bill and Anna work together to circumvent controls and process fraudulent transactions for their mutual benefit.
- Fred either orders Bill to process something with Anna which Bill knows or suspects is fraudulent or convinces Bill that fraudulent transactions are in fact genuine, thus hiding Fred's fraudulent activities behind Bill.

Social networking techniques can expand the basic link diagram by including elements of the strength of the relationship and the direction of communication in a revised form of matrix and related link diagram.

Social networking is a complex subject and incorporates some techniques, including mathematical approaches, which are way beyond the scope of this book and, indeed, the mathematical abilities of the author. The techniques described here are very much a cursory approach and interested students should read further.

Here is another matrix and link diagram, this time including some idea of the nature of the relationships. Table 10.3 enhances our initial view of the network. We have replaced the X's in the original matrix with 1's or 0's because the relationships shown here are binary in the sense that they either exist or they don't. Clearly there is subjectivity in deciding how strong a relationship is, which is where this technique is vulnerable to criticism, but if a reasonable approach is taken and the criteria for determining the strength of relationships are decided and clearly expressed, this technique can prove to be extremely useful.

Table 10.3 Matrix and related link diagram

	Fred	*Sue*	*Joe*	*Bill*	*Anna*
Fred	0	1	1	1	0
Sue	1	0	0	0	0
Joe	1	0	0	0	1
Bill	1	0	0	0	1
Anna	0	0	1	1	0

Modelling the direction of relationships is also possible. In Figure 10.2 we have used a connector which describes the flow of communication either one-way → or two-way ↔.

Fred talks to Sue, Bill and Joe but only Fred and Joe have what might be described as a two-way relationship. Anna has a two-way relationship with Joe and, surprisingly with Bill. This latter relationship may be as a result of an informal, non-work-based relationship, e.g. they are both keen birdwatchers or perform amateur dramatics in the same company.

Figure 10.2 Communication flows

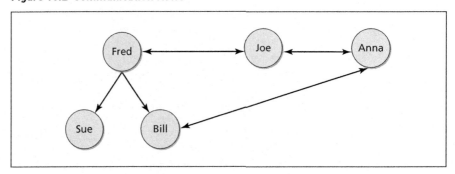

What we need to do now is to add an indication of the strength of the relationship and we can do this by simply adding a weighting to the communication link. We have used part of the diagram in Figure 10.2 to illustrate this. This may be important to investigators where it is necessary to determine the key personnel in a conspiracy or establish the significance of the interaction between the parties.

In Figure 10.3 although Anna appears to have similar relationship with Joe and Bill investigations show that, in fact, she contacts Bill twice as often as she does Joe. By combining weightings and the closeness of the relationships, values can be attributed to each connection in the network.

In a complex organisation this may result in a lot of lines (called 'edges') and connections (called 'nodes'). A diagrammatic representation such as this will indicate the strength of an individual's relationships within the organisation, which can be indicative of their real power.

Of course there may be perfectly innocent explanations for all of these connections and weightings, so not too much should be made of them until investigations in other areas may render them more significant. Initially this is background information unless a conspiracy is suspected, in which case, of course, such matrices and link diagrams can become highly significant.

Research indicates that individuals who are well connected in organisations generally have greater access to information, have a greater reach among their peers and consequently a greater ability to influence and sometimes direct aspects of the organisation's movement.

Figure 10.3 A weighted link diagram

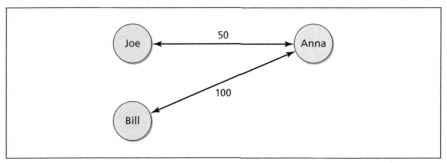

Figure 10.4 Gatekeepers

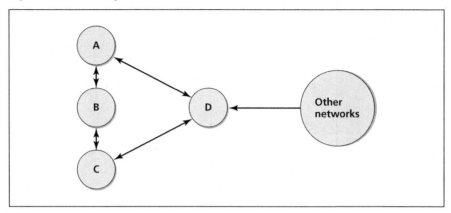

This type of analysis can also identify so-called 'gatekeepers', who channel access to individuals and the flow of information, and also highlight individuals who link differing parts of the organisation together.

These are illustrated diagrammatically in Figure 10.4.

In this situation D has a relationship with A, B and C and but acts as gatekeeper between them and other networks. D has a considerable amount of power as communications are channelled through them.

Note this may not be the proverbial dragon at the gate of the executive suite protecting the directors from the great unwashed in the rest of the organisation, but it may be a departmental manager who prevents their team from being accessible to other networks within the organisation. In this way they can hold the power themselves by deliberately restricting the access of their teams to wider networks. In this way the gatekeeper can control the flow of information and alter or amend it so as to present different versions of events to different parts of the organisation. Only if the gatekeeper is circumvented may the truth behind their actions, which may turn out to be fraudulent, be revealed.

We can also link networks together and show how they communicate. Figure 10.5, for example, could represent individuals within two departments or subsidiaries within an organisation. These types of diagram are also used to chart the relationships between companies and other bodies within a complex group.

Figure 10.5 illustrates how individuals can link disparate networks. In this case there are two networks: A–D and F–I and the link between them is E. The two networks do not communicate directly with each other. In this case E has power as E controls the information between two networks. Thus E may be able to bypass internal controls within each network or play one network against the other by simply restricting, amending or allocating information.

The significance of each individual within the overall structure can be established by counting the number of connections they have. In Figure 10.5 E is the most significant by virtue of position, but both A and F have links with the other network as well as extensive links within their own networks and are also therefore highly significant.

Figure 10.5 Network links

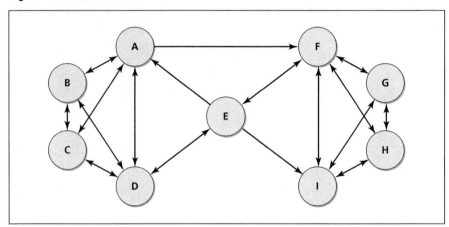

Cliques and subgroups

Figures 10.4 and 10.5 can also be illustrations of cliques and subgroups within the organisation.

Referring back to Figure 10.4 a subgroup or clique comprising A, B and C may exist with D being their face to the world. Thus a small department, say the stores department, may operate virtually autonomously as their only link to the rest of the organisation is D, who may be their supervisor or manager. Thus D can control A, B and C who have no means of verifying the validity of any instructions or requests given to them. In Figure 10.5 B, C, G and H have no interactions outside their own groups whereas the other individuals have some level of interaction between groups.

As stated earlier it is possible to weight these interactions and, of course, the direction of the information flow should always be noted. For example, in Figure 10.5, although I appears to be part of the action, their relationship with E is only one-way so they have less involvement than does A who has a direct link with F in the adjacent network.

Clearly this is a simplified version of a more complex reality. However, it does serve to indicate how relationships can be represented in a way which may draw out some of the realities of power and control within an organisation and highlight relationships which 'family tree'-type charts cannot begin to express.

In practice computer software can be used to gather information and to map networks and some of these tools can be found online and are free. More sophisticated programs are available but users should not get too drawn into this situation. Investigators are there to catch fraudsters, not carry out social or organisational research, so simplicity is the key until something more complex is required.

At this point, having perhaps ascertained links between possible perpetrators, we need to move on to specific approaches to fraud detection and examination of organisation systems and transactions. It is necessary to establish what has happened and for how long, so a detailed examination of transactions is the next step.

Summary

- There are two possible scenarios an investigator can be faced with: either a fraud has been discovered or fraud is suspected and the investigation is covert.
- Management must decide who is to carry out the work and if the external auditors are to be involved.
- The primary task of the investigator is to establish what has happened.
- A Letter of Engagement should be agreed between the client and the investigators.
- The investigation team will be multidisciplinary and will be led by an experienced investigator.
- The team will include a lawyer, an HR person and a PR person to manage the media as well as specialist IT staff.
- The work must be carefully planned.
- If a criminal prosecution is envisaged care must be taken to involve the Economic Crime Unit at a suitable point and in preservation of evidence.
- Fraud reports must be carefully drafted as they may be part of a legal action.
- The use of matrices and link diagrams can identify relationships and possible collusion.

Case study

You are head of the UK Compliance Team at Megablast plc which is listed on the London Stock Exchange. Megablast plc is a manufacturer of luxury cars with engineering and manufacturing centres in the UK and dealerships internationally. It has subsidiaries in the US, Japan, Germany and Switzerland. Megablast plc works with suppliers in the UK and abroad.

As head of the UK Compliance Team you report to the board of directors, lead the Compliance Team in the UK and also manage the compliance officers in your subsidiary companies overseas.

The company has a whistle-blower hotline which all employees and other stakeholders are encouraged to call if they want to report anything suspicious. The hotline is operated by an external provider 24 hours a day and they provide first-line assessment with native language speakers for each of your geographies.

At 9.30a.m. Friday morning, you receive a high-priority report that a member of the procurement team in the UK, William Blower, has reported suspicions about the UK Procurement Director, John Bung. Blower says that it has seemed for quite a while that John Bung has had particularly close relationships with some of the suppliers to Megablast plc. He says that his concerns were increased when he happened to see an e-mail from John Bung to a major company parts supplier which said:

> Thank you for the great day at the races last week. I very much enjoyed it and discussing how we can make business more profitable for each other. We need to make sure that we each get the most out of working for these big organisations, especially for ourselves. I look forward to continuing our discussions next time we meet off premises.

Your external hotline provider has instructions to immediately report to you any allegations concerning senior executives, including the UK Procurement Director. Your interest is raised by the content of the e-mail and you consider how you should handle this matter.

▶

A confidential conversation with William Blower reveals no concrete evidence but Blower indicates that John Bung appears to live a lavish lifestyle, takes many exotic holidays and treats the procurement staff to expensive dinners and drinks at least once a month. Blower also reveals that Bung is the exclusive handler for several large vendors and no one else is permitted to contact them. Your review of Bung's personnel file indicated that Bung earns a salary of £55,000 per annum. Based on your conversation with Blower and your review of Blower's personnel file, there is nothing to suggest he has a personal motive against Bung.

After meeting Blower, you and the head of HR both believe the allegations warrant further consideration. The head of HR is keen to interview John Bung, but you recall that there is a policy within the company to convene the fraud response committee when a situation arises like this. You therefore remind the head of HR of this and agree to convene the fraud response committee although she still wants to carry out the interview as soon as possible. Between you and the head of HR, you manage to gather the finance director, head of internal audit and the head of legal with you in a private meeting room and you discuss the options available to you.

Required

- Discuss the options open to the company at this time
- Should John Bung be confronted with the evidence so far?
- What other considerations should be borne in mind arising out of this situation?
- What course of action would be best?

Bibliography

Auditing Practices Board (2009) ISA 240 *The Auditor's Responsibilities Relating to Fraud in an Audit of Financial Statements*. Auditing Practices Board, London.

Auditing Practices Board (2009) ISA 330 *The Auditor's Responses to Assessed Risks*. Auditing Practices Board, London.

Chartered Institute of Management Accountants (CIMA) (2008) *Fraud Risk Management – A Guide to Good Practice*. CIMA, London.

Gill, M. (2005) *Learning from Fraudsters*. Protoviti, London.

Golden, T., Skalak, S. and Clayton, M. (2006) *A Guide to Forensic Accounting Investigation*. John Wiley, Hoboken, NJ.

Hopwood, W.S., Leiner, J.L. and Young, G. (2008) *Forensic Accounting*. McGraw-Hill, New York.

HMSO (2002) *Proceeds of Crime Act 2002*. HMSO, London.

Huntington, I. and Davies, D. (1994) *Fraud Watch – A Guide for Business*. ICAEW, London.

International Auditing and Assurance Standards Board: *The International Standard on Related Services (ISRS) 4400 Engagements to Perform Agreed upon Procedures Regarding Financial Information*. IAASB, New York.

Martin Kenney and Co. (2003) Link analysis in fraud investigations. International Law Office, www.internationallawoffice.com.

Penney, J. (2002) *Corporate Fraud – Prevention and Detection*. Tolley, London.

Silverstone, H. and Sheetz, M. (2007) *Forensic Accounting and Fraud Investigation for Non-experts*. John Wiley, Hoboken, NJ.

Singleton, T., Singleton, A., Bologna, G.J. and Lindquist, R.J. (2006) *Fraud Auditing and Forensic Accounting.* John Wiley, Hoboken, NJ.

Wells, J.T. (2004) *Corporate Fraud Handbook – Prevention and Detection.* John Wiley, Hoboken, NJ.

Websites

www.cimaglobal.org

www.dailymail.co.uk

www.fraudadvisorypanel.org

www.fvs.aicpa.org/resources

www.icaew.com

www.ifac.org/iaasb

www.internationallawoffice.com

Chapter 11

Investigating frauds against the organisation

Chapter contents

- Introduction
- Evidence gathering
- Specific types of fraud and approaches to detection
- Billing schemes – fictitious suppliers
- Sales fraud and cash theft
- Expenses fraud
- Inventory theft
- Payroll fraud
- Collusion with customers – corruption

Learning objectives

After studying this chapter you should be able to:

- Understand the principles of evidence gathering
- Recognise the salient features of different types of fraud against the organisation
- Understand detection methods for uncovering these types of fraud

Introduction

The business of the forensic accountant is one of evidence gathering to establish what has happened, to prove a crime or to make a case. This involves them in the use of a range of techniques which, if employed judiciously, will result in the accumulation of facts which may serve to support a criminal case, or the removal of corrupt directors or managers from the organisation.

In this chapter we look at the practical techniques which can be used by forensic investigators to gather their evidence. It does not cover IT-based approaches – these involve specialised techniques and approaches which are worthy of their own chapter, so see Chapter 13 for those.

Most of these approaches should be familiar to anyone who has an audit background but, whilst the techniques may be familiar, the approach is not. Those who don't have an audit background will find sufficient explanation in these pages to enable them to apply these approaches to their own particular circumstances. Detecting fraud is rarely straightforward which is why so many go undetected for so long. It is difficult because fraudsters cover their tracks and because there is a tendency for people to think well of their colleagues and to find it difficult to accept that they are dishonest.

However, if there is one message to be learned it is this – no one in the accounting or reporting function (including auditors both internal and external) should be complacent about the honesty and integrity of their colleagues, and that includes the senior management of the organisation (see Exhibit 11.1).

In earlier chapters we looked at some of the motivations of individuals who are not professional criminals. We looked at the so-called 'fraud triangle' (Chapter 5) where we identified the three key factors:

- motive or pressure
- opportunity, and
- justification/rationale.

Recapping some of the motives or pressures which often motivate the misappropriation of assets we have established that these comprise principally:

- greed
- the need to be seen to be successful
- debt
- unexpected need for money
- addictions drugs, alcohol, gambling
- sexual liaisons – the cost of maintaining relationships
- work-based pressures, for example, low pay, grievance or revenge
- dissatisfaction or boredom
- challenge to 'beat the system', and
- peer pressure due to socialisation.

Research indicates that frauds frequently start off as small-scale misappropriations and grow over time until they become too obvious to conceal, the perpetrator gets careless, the auditors detect them or a colleague turns them in. This is one of the reasons why suppression of small-scale frauds should be encouraged before the

| Exhibit 11.1 | Fraud example – the 'spineless' accountant |

Andrew Weatherall, a director of accountancy firm KPMG, was concerned that his wife would suffer when her previous partner reduced maintenance payments. Accordingly he supplemented his six-figure salary, inflating expenses by altering bills, creating false invoices, submitting multiple claims for legitimate expenses and claiming holidays as business trips.

This amounted to about £15,000 per month which he used to buy his wife expensive gifts and holidays. He claimed £480,000 worth of travel expenses of which £243,000 was supported by false documents.

When questioned he claimed it was a mistake but subsequently confessed. At his trial the judge described the fraud as 'systematic and determined and premeditated'. The judge described Mr Weatherall as 'a man who threw away his principles and took a weak and self-indulgent approach to financial and personal problems. It was a spineless approach to these problems.'

Mr Weatherall was sentenced to four years in jail. His wife is, allegedly, standing by him.

Source: Hough (2009)

small ones turn into big ones and why the creation of an ethical culture is so important in preventing low-level fraud and unethical behaviour.

Evidence gathering

In the event a crime is uncovered there is the question of gathering the evidence. The absence of properly preserved evidence not only makes criminal prosecutions more difficult but can lead to firms failing to get proper redress in the civil courts for recovery, being unable to make proper insurance claims or putting their best case forward to HMRC.

As the investigation proceeds every step along the way must be carefully documented and any findings carefully preserved. It is important that all the evidence collected remains unambiguously preserved and that the so-called 'chain of evidence' is not lost or broken. This requires specific documentary procedures which we looked at in Chapter 3.

With regard to computer-sourced evidence there are some very specific rules and procedures which *must* be observed. We dealt with this in Chapter 8 as part of forensic readiness and we will look at it again in Chapter 13 dealing with computer-based investigative techniques.

It cannot be emphasised too strongly that poor working practices in connection with evidence collection and preservation have ruined more than one investigation. The rule is *If you don't know what you are doing – do nothing until the expert arrives!*

Investigators need procedures to identify and preserve, in particular, digital evidence including e-mails and web transactions and they also need to have an understanding of some of the associated legal problems such as admissibility and privacy.

What is needed is an approach to fraud investigation which does not compound the problem.

Sources of evidence

Evidence of a crime, if it exists, will be in several locations:

- within the organisation's own records and systems
- in the suspect's work location – office or workstation, and
- at the suspect's home or a private address.

often contained in electronic media such as laptops, PCs or personal devices such as a Blackberry.

In addition it should not be forgotten that a large amount of information may be in the minds of colleagues and other staff. Obtaining evidence from each source requires a different approach.

Searching company premises and investigating servers is not difficult and much can be done behind the scenes before it is necessary to confront any suspects. Interviewing staff and colleagues is a way of unlocking information they have, and they may be willing and able to make formal statements concerning particular transactions or events which have a bearing on the case.

However, problems arise when dealing with company information which has been stored on private devices such as home PCs, personal laptops, memory sticks or devices such as Blackberries. These are the personal property of the employee and cannot be seized by the investigators without an appropriate Court Order (Chapter 3). In the absence of such an order disclosure of the contents of privately owned electronic devices is purely in the hands of the employee. For obvious reasons they may be unwilling to disclose these contents and may well seek to destroy or delete them.

If the organisation has clear policies on the storage of company data on private electronic devices it may be possible to prove a breach of such policies which could form the basis of disciplinary proceedings. This may be sufficent to remove the individual from the premises, but they are able to take any privately owned equipment with them, which can be quite galling for investigators!

Let us suppose that a senior manager is suspected of perpetrating some kind of fraud on the company. At this stage the company has done all it can to gather evidence from its own systems and records. What remains is to gather evidence which may be in the possession of the suspect at their work location.

At this point any investigation, however covert up to now, suddenly becomes overt and the effects of that have to be dealt with. These will have both HR and legal implications and may have a PR impact too if news leaks out to local media.

In the suspect's office there will undoubtedly be a computer, either a PC or a thin terminal. If the company is operating on what has come to be known as a 'thin client' basis where all the processing and storage is carried out on the main server and what is on the manager's desk is what used to be called a 'dumb terminal', the company can easily interrogate the server directly and gather any relevant information they need without entering the suspect's office, but if the information is held on a PC it has to be taken.

We will look at the approach to doing that later; first there is a legal question to be resolved.

Suppose on the suspect's desk there is a Blackberry and several memory sticks which do not belong to the company but which may belong to the individual. Further, suppose a laptop is discovered which is clearly the private possession of the suspect. The investigators are faced with the dilemma outlined above – so how to proceed?

Let us deal with the memory sticks first. Part of the answer here depends on the policies the company has in place. If there is a policy on storage of company data and that policy contains within it a prohibition on bringing into work any form of personal storage device then it may be reasonable for the investigators to take the memory sticks and examine them for company data even if the sticks belong to the employee. If the investigations they have made to date provide more than sufficient grounds to indicate a crime may have been committed the memory sticks could probably be investigated with impunity.

If they contain company data then the individual will be in breach of company policy and the organisation may be able to suspend them pending the outcome of the investigation which would get them neatly out of the way whilst the evidence-gathering phase proceeds.

The Blackberry is more problematical and the laptop even more so. Accessing them without permission would be likely to mean that the company falls foul of the Computer Misuse Act 1990 through unauthorised access. At this point the company may try to obtain a Court Order to search the private PC and Blackberry, as it would be useful to have this to hand *before* entering the suspect's office. However, in practice, this is would be unlikely to be granted as a judge would need to be convinced that there was sufficient evidence of a crime and that the personal equipment was critical to it before granting such an order. If the employee is in breach of company policies on storage of electronic data, e.g. by using a personal device, this could act as some form of leverage against them to persuade them to disclose the contents of their laptop or Blackberry by threatening them with suspension and subsequent dismissal. This may not, of course, prove to be a sufficiently big incentive to persuade the individual to tell all!

It may be of course that the suspect is known to work at home on company data and has a laptop at home. In this case and, perhaps, in the case of personal property on company premises, the best course of action would be to ask the suspect for a right of access to the devices both at home and in their possession at work. It may be possible to obtain a Search and Seize Order (Chapter 3) to facilitate entry to their home to search for documents and to investigate the contents of any personal computers or other electronic storage media.

The problem here is the lapse of time between confronting the employee and obtaining any order, assuming they volunteer nothing.

If the information is given voluntarily or obtained as a result of an order the company will be able to image the files from any private personal computer and to use any information gained as evidence – providing it has been properly gathered. We will look at this in Chapter 12. Evidence collected in this way can, of course, lend support to a prosecution and to internal disciplinary processes where court action is not contemplated but an action for unfair dismissal is to be avoided.

 ## Specific types of fraud and approaches to detection

Here we will look at specific types of fraud and how the forensic accountant can set about uncovering them. Specifically we will look at:

- billing schemes – fictitious suppliers
- cash theft
- collusion with customers – corruption
- expenses fraud
- inventory theft, and
- payroll fraud

Billing schemes – fictitious suppliers

One of the methods commonly used by managers in a position of authority is a supplier or 'vendor' fraud. To carry this through successfully the manager must be in a position to:

- set up an approved supplier
- direct purchases to that supplier, and
- approve orders or invoices from that supplier.

Here the manager sets up a company or business, ostensibly as an independent supplier to the organisation they work for, obviously without the knowledge of their employer or colleagues. Let's call it Fraudco. Fraudco may have an accommodation address, or in the case of foolish managers their home address, and a telephone number which is either connected to an answering machine or is answered by a messaging service.

The manager then authenticates his business as an approved supplier. Two options are then open to the manager:

- The manager then simply invoices the company for fictitious supplies from Fraudco – usually of services (thus avoiding goods inwards procedures), for example, consultancy or advisory services, valuation fees, surveyors costs etc. The manager authorises the invoices and passes them through the normal purchases system, *or*
- The manager is in a position to route genuine suppliers through Fraudco. The genuine supplier invoices Fraudco with the cost of the goods supplied, whatever they may be, and Fraudco then adds on a margin and invoices the manager's employer. The manager then pockets the margin made in Fraudco. This may be easier in industries such as construction where payments to subcontractors are made without deduction of tax or are outside the scope of VAT.

This latter course is a difficult fraud to pull off for obvious reasons and there probably has to be some element of collusion between someone in the supplying company and the manager (see Exhibit 11.2). The transactions would undoubtedly give rise to questions from a genuine supplier unless:

- the purchasing company is in a dominant position in the market, or
- the supplier is in a very competitive industry and fears to lose the business to a rival; thus they may be persuaded to go along with this unusual arrangement.

The beauty of this type of fraud from the manager's point of view is that, because the authority of the manager is unquestioned, the staff see nothing wrong, after all this is part of the manager's normal role. Once the supplier is set up all the manager has to do is to feed invoices into the system and they will, in due course, be paid.

Organisations apply the concept of materiality (Chapter 2) to their own procedures, particularly with regard to authorisation levels. It is common to set hierarchical limits so that, for example, Assistant Manager A can authorise transactions of up to £1,000, Manager B up to £5,000, Regional Manager C up to £25,000 and Director D up to £100,000. The consequence of this is to encourage the fraudster to limit the size of individual fraudulent transactions so that they are unlikely to appear in view of either the auditor or a superior manager. Manager B, therefore, who may be running a supplier fraud, will take care to keep individual invoices below

---

Exhibit 11.2 **Example – Pete's fraud**

'Pete' committed fraud in the construction industry by, basically, setting up his own company and, in collaboration with others, paying himself money he was not entitled to – twice. His justification was that bribery and corruption are endemic in the industry and he was simply joining in the culture. He was discovered by an auditor following up a minor irregularity.

When questioned 'Pete' said 'the reason I committed the offences was basically the will to want to succeed and being seen to do so and to be successful in eyes of those around me'.

Source: Gill (2005)

£4,999. The total of the embezzlement may be considerably greater than £5,000, but its components are not.

The result of this is that the authorisation by Manager B of his own invoices appears to comply with the organisation's internal procedures, at least in one regard. Similarly, unless the false invoices are unfortunate enough to be selected for a sample test by the auditors, the transactions may be below the audit radar and will not be considered. External audit is extremely unlikely to detect this type of fraud as they are looking for examples of controls and procedures in action and all the internal control procedures are being complied with, it is simply that the transactions themselves are fraudulent.

Internal audit may well detect this kind of fraud if they are able to carry out any form of analysis of purchases and payment patterns, if they detect that approved supplier procedures have not been carried out or if they receive a tip-off, however many cases of supplier fraud have been perpetrated for some years before being detected.

There is, however one snag for the embezzling manager and that is the opening of a bank account. Clearly they cannot expect their employer to send payment to their home address in their own name. Accommodation addresses are easily found as there are many organisations who will act as a mailbox address for correspondence, but banking the proceeds is more difficult. The fraudster has to set up a business bank account. To do this they have two options:

1 To meet the 'know your client' procedures set up by a UK bank under the Money Laundering Regulations. If they wish to use a UK limited company name they will have to produce a Certificate of Incorporation to the bank and provide a host of other details about directors etc., so they will need to set up a genuine company and tell a story to the bank. If they wish to set up some form of unincorporated business, again they will have to invent documentation to create the illusion of a genuine trading entity.

2 To set up an overseas company in a jurisdiction where reporting requirements are particularly lax and where reports are not made to the UK tax authorities. The British Virgin Islands (BVI) is a popular choice; companies can be set up relatively easily using the Internet and banking arrangements route monies from the UK to the BVI or a country of choice. Disclosure in countries such as the BVI is minimal and providing the local rules are complied with the company can proceed unmolested by the authorities. This has to be set up with a little care, of

course, to avoid any transfers of funds triggering a report under the Money Laundering Regulations (Chapter 3). There is also the propensity of the UK government to make deals with the tax authorities, as they have recently done with Dominica, Grenada, Belize and Lichtenstein, to disclose details of funds held overseas by UK residents.

None of this is a hugely insurmountable problem to the determined fraudster, but the longer the paper trail the greater the possibility of discovery. This kind of fraud is certainly not spontaneous – it has to be carefully planned which will help make the case against the fraudster should the fraud be uncovered.

Indicators of this type of fraud are:

- use of PO Box-type virtual office addresses
- lack of details on documentation, for example, phone/fax numbers
- use of invoices generated by word processor
- sequential invoice numbers from 'supplier'
- addresses matching or close to employee's address
- bills for services rather than goods
- invoices with similar names to existing genuine suppliers
- use of round numbers
- incorrect or missing VAT number
- irregular folds – folded to fit a pocket not an envelope or invoice not folded
- vendor gets paid more quickly than others, and
- vendor's invoices authorised by other than usual manager.

Detection

These frauds most often come to light through whistle-blowers or tip-offs, either by a member of staff concerned about what appears to be irregular practice by the manager or unusual expenditure patterns authorised from that source.

In the absence of those there are some audit-style procedures which can be used. These combine a mixture of IT-based approaches and basic audit techniques such as analytical review or straightforward substantive testing. We look at IT-based approaches in more detail in Chapter 13.

The basic approaches include:

IT-based approaches

- An IT sort of purchase transactions by supplier, payments, amount and invoice number – check for sequential numbers, regular invoicing, regular amounts, etc.
- Examine metadata (Chapter 13) which will provide details of the time when transactions were processed. Look for time stamps for transactions processed outside normal hours, at the weekend, etc. Search the data for patterns of entries processed outside normal hours, for example, entries consistently processed in early morning or late at night.
- Check computer access records for log-ins on terminals used for routine processing by persons other than the normal operators.
- Cross-check dates of data processed when suspected individuals were supposed to be on holiday or away from the location.

- Check for invoices from same supplier charged to different cost codes as the perpetrator seeks to spread the load.
- Cross-reference employees addresses with supplier addresses.
- Cheques/payments made out to a variant on the invoice name, i.e. not including word 'Ltd'.
- Review suppliers added by individuals responsible for authorisation of invoices or orders.
- Search for suppliers with similar names but separate purchase ledger accounts – quite often the perpetrator will choose a name similar to an existing supplier to further confuse the issue.
- Check the VAT number (see below).

Audit-based approaches

- Expenses billed by the supplier are charged to a cost code which then exceeds budget.
- Expenses are authorised by a budget holder who also authorised the set-up of the supplier – review new suppliers accounts and authorisation routines and procedures.
- Analyse charges in the largest expense accounts – fraudulent costs are often hidden in the biggest accounts.
- Examine original documentation from suspect suppliers – look for signs of 'home-made' invoices.
- Look for unusual or non-routine payment instructions, i.e. supplier paid more frequently than is usual or where payments are made in a non-routine way, for example, by cheque when other suppliers are paid by direct credit transfer. Cheques can be altered – credit transfers can't.
- Review reconciliations of suspense accounts and bank accounts.
- Look for an unusual number of journals.
- Examine accounts which are not commonly reviewed by auditors and are not large accounts such as 'Other Receivables' or 'Other Payables'.

Checking a VAT number

There are two ways to check a VAT number. One way is to ring HMRC who will tell you if the number is genuine but nothing more. The other way is the fun way: which is this.

All VAT numbers contain two check digits at the end of the number which are related to the other numbers. To check lots of these requires some automation but it is not a difficult process using a spreadsheet package.

The methodology is this:

1 List the first seven digits of the VAT registration number vertically.
2 Multiply each digit by a number from 8 to 2.
3 Add the sum of the multiplications.
4 Deduct a constant (97) from that total as many times as is necessary to arrive at a negative number.
5 The negative number should be the same as the last two digits of the VAT registration number if it is valid.

Example

The VAT registration number is shown as 429 0642 31 but the invoice looks home-made.

Calculate:

$4 \times 8 = 32$
$2 \times 7 = 14$
$9 \times 6 = 54$
$0 \times 5 = 0$
$6 \times 4 = 24$
$4 \times 3 = 12$
$2 \times 2 = 4$

Total $= 140$

Subtract the constant

$140 - 97 = 43 - 97 = -54$

The last two digits of the number should be 54 not 31 so the number is false.

This will not, of course, detect a genuine number being used fraudulently!

Sales fraud and cash theft

Wherever there is cash there is the strong possibility that someone will be tempted and try to steal it. Simple theft does not involve any form of deception because simply grabbing the money and running away or, worse, not running away, is a straightforward enough crime and the perpetrator is usually easily identified.

The object of this kind of internal cash theft, as with any other crime, is not to get caught, so the embezzler's intention is to conceal the crime or to commit it in such a way that suspicion falls away from them on to another, innocent, person. This is an in-house crime.

Despite its essential simplicity cash theft actually takes many forms and there are some classic types which fraud investigators should be aware of. The first is an old favourite which turns up in all the auditing textbooks, and occasionally in real life, known as teeming and lading. From there we will look at theft of cash from takings and associated thefts of inventory.

Teeming and lading

Much is made in old auditing textbooks of the old fashioned fraud of 'teeming and lading', also known as 'Robbing Peter to Pay Paul'.

In this type of fraud the fraudster steals a receipt from a sales credit customer, by altering a cheque or pocketing a cash payment where this happens.

The problem now is that, let's call them Customer A, think they have paid their account but the sales ledger shows they have not. To cover up this deficiency when another customer pays, let's call them Customer B, the fraudster does not credit Customer B's account with the full amount but splits it, allocating part to Customer A and part to Customer B. If the fraudster then steals another amount they have to keep on splitting receipts and allocating amounts to customer accounts to cover the deficiency caused by their theft (see Exhibit 11.3).

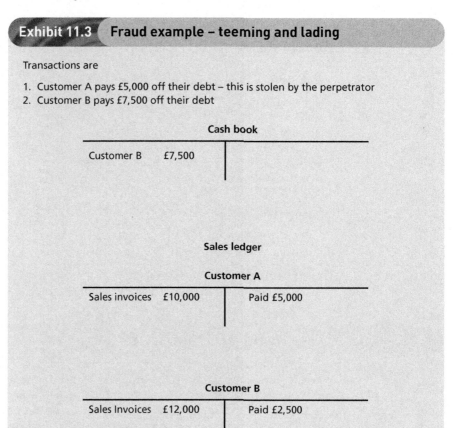

Exhibit 11.3   Fraud example – teeming and lading

Transactions are

1. Customer A pays £5,000 off their debt – this is stolen by the perpetrator
2. Customer B pays £7,500 off their debt

Cash book

Customer B	£7,500	

Sales ledger

Customer A

Sales invoices	£10,000	Paid £5,000	

Customer B

Sales Invoices	£12,000	Paid £2,500	

Notes

- The first payment from Customer A is stolen by the employee so doesn't enter the bookkeeping system
- The second payment from Customer B is split between A and B
- The employee must keep doing this now to cover the initial and successive thefts

Imagine the problems the fraudster has in keeping track of all this where they have taken several receipts from customers. Most of them have to keep some form of record of what they've done simply so they can keep track of it all which, of course, ultimately serves to convict them. The strain on the individual can be quite intense and these frauds do not generally last long. The perpetrator can never go on holiday, have time off sick or let anyone else have access to the ledger or their careful allocation of receipts could become totally unravelled.

The problem is that most customers now receive monthly statements so the fraudster has to intercept these where the records of receipts don't match the customer's payments and the embezzler also has to alter cheques or steal incoming cash, which can become noticeable. Such frauds can be quickly spotted by alert auditors because of the split receipts where the entries in the sales ledger don't match the entries in the cash book.

Useful tools in the fraudster's armoury in this case are the credit note and the bad debt write-off. To reduce the constant problem of splitting receipts so as to keep reducing the balance on a customer's account why not simply issue a false credit note and write the sales invoices off that way? Alternatively the offending indebtedness could simply be written off with a journal entry either as a bad debt or as some sort of 'mis-posting'.

This is why many fraudsters use the payables system rather than stealing receipts. The process is exactly the same as that described above but in this case the fraudster diverts a payment to a supplier into their own bank account and then splits subsequent payments when entering them in the records to disguise the theft. The payables system can be more difficult to audit than the receivables system and there are more opportunities for the fraudster to affect ledger balances by inventing discounts, refunds and credits, which helps when juggling payments, than with the sales system. In this way discrepancies can be covered up more easily and the difficult month end statement problem disappears. Many companies reconcile suppliers' statements with payables ledger balances but by diverting payments close to the month end the fraudster can claim these as a reconciling item and cover the discrepancy during the next month (Exhibit 11.4).

This type of fraud may still persist in small organisations with basic systems and, above all, a lack of segregation of duties whereby the person in charge of writing up the sales records also has access to receipts from customers and can make sure the customer never sees a statement of their account.

Exhibit 11.4 **Avoiding the month end payables reconciliation problem**

	Statement from A Supplier		£	
2 Mar	Invoice	23879		2000
5 Mar	Invoice	34185		4000
20 Mar	Receipt	5910		(2500)
22 Mar	Invoice	38915		6000
31 Mar Amount due				__9500__

Payables ledger – A Supplier		
7 Mar	Invoice	2000
12 Mar	Invoice	4000
18 Mar	Payment	(2500)
30 Mar	Invoice	6000
31 Mar	Payment	(5000)
Balance		__4500__

The discrepancy between the balances is explained because of the payment on 31 Mar. In fact this has been diverted to the fraudster's bank account but will not be queried because it is a reconciling item. The payment on 18 March is genuine – suppliers have to be paid – but may have been earmarked for another supplier in the cash book. The fraudster now has a month to divert monies from elsewhere to pay this supplier and not pay another. As long as the payables ledger is not sent to the supplier, and the balances can be reconciled, differences in timing and the nature of the entry can be concealed or successfully explained by the fraudster.

> ### Exhibit 11.5 Cash fraud and the Elvis lady
>
> A council cashier stole more than half a million pounds in car-parking fees to fund her Elvis Presley obsession. For nine years bosses at North Kesteven District Council failed to detect the thefts and regarded her as a 'mild and modest' employee. But in fact she was taking up to £10,000 a month and using it to buy Elvis Presley records and memorabilia – paying up to £3,500 pounds for a rare record from Japan.
>
> Julie Wall, 46, of Sleaford spent almost every penny on Elvis memorabilia after secretly helping herself to a fortune for almost a decade. Wall, who lived with her parents, also bought hundreds of CDs, DVDs, videos and signed mementoes during visits to record fairs, auctions and sessions on eBay.
>
> Wall, a council employee for 30 years, had the job of counting coins from cashboxes sited at the authority's eight car parks in Sleaford. She repeatedly held back hundreds of pounds from each box and then exchanged the coins for notes used in other council transactions. Over a nine year period she was estimated to have stolen £557,327.11.
>
> She was sentenced to three years in prison after admitting two charges of theft.
>
> Wall's collection – now worth an estimated £548,000 – has since been seized by police and it is expected to be used to recompense the council's losses.
>
> *Source:* Britten (2005)

In larger organisations this should be impossible for the reason mentioned above, that most sales ledger staff don't have physical access to receipts from customers, neither do they enter receipts into the sales ledger, and most customers get a monthly statement which would rapidly show up unusual splitting of amounts they have paid and a non-conformity of dates.

In a larger organisation any fraud of this nature ought to be extremely short term and easily detected as basic internal control procedures will prevent it occurring. However, it should be noted that the author has anecdotal evidence from forensic investigators that such frauds lasted in one organisation for five years and in another for ten! (See, for example, Exhibit 11.5.)

Other forms of cash theft

There are other kinds of cash theft which are much more common. These include:

- thefts from tills
- giving away free goods or under-pricing
- thefts from cash customers requiring receipts, and
- skimming credit or debit card details and selling them on.

Thefts from tills, also known as retail leakage, primarily arise as a result of employees failing to ring sales into the till or under-ringing. This can be a particular problem in places such as busy pubs or clubs or petrol stations late at night where the customer is not let into the shop area for security reasons.

In addition to straightforward cash theft, the theft of goods or selling them cheaply to friends or other members of staff (known as 'sweethearting') is a relatively common occurrence in badly controlled retail premises.

Detection methods

Frauds of this nature can be detected by:

- Horizontal analysis of receipts or bankings to establish a pattern. Clearly this has to be based on a period of honest sales or bankings in order to establish a basic pattern from which variations can be detected.
- Analytical review – for example, takings by till by shift.
- Measuring takings by till in a multi-till operation – look for any tills consistently lower than others.
- Confirming the number of tills supposedly in operation – managers have been known to introduce their own tills.
- Consistently 'lost' internal till registers, etc. – the perpetrators destroy or cause to be lost any internal records in the tills where these comprise an internal roll.
- Till records 'No Sales' where till is opened without a sale going through – or tills can only be opened by a supervisor or manager with a code. Instances of this can then be monitored.
- Falsification of cashing up sheets by managers – these can be connected to stock discrepancies.
- Personal cheques in cash drawer – to cover a discovered shortfall ('I was just cashing a cheque').
- Amounts in NCR (no carbon required) receipt books not aligned with printed spaces, i.e. the top copy given to the customer has not been carboned through to the office copies due to the perpetrator inserting a piece of cardboard between the top copy and the ones below – and a false receipt entered being written on a piece of blank paper – it is difficult to get the alignment exact.
- Surprise cash counts.
- Use of marked notes.
- Observe ringing-in/cash collection procedures or under-ringing through the use of dummy customers or CCTV.
- Use of other employee's log-on to disguise perpetrator.
- Excessive refunds – use IT data-mining techniques to monitor refunds to customers.

Fraud prevention

Defensive measures here include:

- CCTV monitoring tills.
- Pricing at 99p, i.e £4.99 instead of £5.00 – most customers wait for 1p change thus forcing the cashier to ring the sale into the till.
- Prevention of cashiers from ringing in 'No Sale' or giving cash refunds from the till without authorisation or a special key or code.
- Use of secret shoppers and marked notes.
- Surprise cash counts of tills.
- Removal of excess notes – usually a £50 float is enough so notes should be regularly removed from tills – this prevents staff from collecting what they have stolen at the end of the shift.
- Use of bar codes and EPOS systems.
- Ringing of amounts into tills visible to the customer.

These kinds of thefts are likely to be prevalent wherever there is cash and individually may not amount to very much. However, cumulatively, the effect can be considerable over time. Once any weaknesses in the system become known unscrupulous staff will take advantage of them so that theft becomes endemic in the organisation.

Many workers will rationalise what they do as being justified because:

- they are, or are under the impression that they are, low paid either objectively or in comparison with others
- it is some sort of perk of the job
- it relieves boredom or is a challenge to the organisation which they may perceive has no interest in them as individuals
- of resentment at what they see as profligate consumption by managers or directors, or
- they are only going to do it 'just this once' and pay it back.

Research indicates that individuals consider embezzling from an organisation to be less of a crime than burglary or simple theft: only when they are caught do the full implications of what they have done strike home. They consider that it is something of a victimless crime if they steal what they consider to be relatively small amounts from a large organisation, but fraud is never a victimless crime – someone has to pay for losses caused through theft.

Prevention based on appeals to a moral sense or some form of ethical code does not appear to be strong enough to overcome the temptation of an open cash drawer, so defensive measures based on strong internal controls are the best policy where cash or easily sold inventory is concerned.

 ## Expenses fraud

One of the most common forms of fraud in organisations is expenses fraud, overstating business expenses so as to recuperate more than was legitimately spent. This is indeed often so prevalent that it is not considered to be fraud at all, merely as some sort of 'perk' or compensation for having to do excessive travelling or having to stay away from home and family. The sums involved, except in a few spectacular cases such as that of Andrew Weatherall (Exhibit 11.1) are relatively small in the context of the whole organisation so employees consider padding or inflating the expenses to be something of a game, almost to be expected.

Common forms of expenses fraud are:

- Inflating expenses, e.g. mileage claims, altering receipts, submitting fictitious receipts, etc.
- Claiming for more expensive forms of travel than those actually taken, i.e. taxi fares when the bus was actually used.
- Claiming for expenses paid by others, e.g. claiming for a hotel bill actually paid by a client.
- Claiming for the same expense more than once using duplicate vouchers.
- Mischaracterising expenses – claiming for items the organisation refuses to pay for by stating them as something else, i.e. claiming personal travel or meals as business expenses (see Exhibit 11.6).

These types of fraud are very difficult to counter. Moreover they are most commonly committed, for obvious reasons, by managers and directors which can serve to discourage thorough checking and rigorous scrutiny.

However, there are some steps that can be taken to counter expenses fraud:

- Have an expenses policy which is clearly expressed and make all employees aware of the rules.
- Expenses should be reimbursed at set rates where practicable.
- Major expenses, for example, hotels, flights etc., should be booked and paid for centrally.
- Use of company credit cards should be restricted and use confined mostly to emergencies or unavoidable situations where the employee cannot pay.
- All expense claims must be authorised. If claims are to exceed a certain limit prior approval might be needed.
- Directors' claims should be authorised by the CEO and those of the CEO by the chairman.
- All expenses to be accompanied by receipts where possible. Receipts should be scrutinised for alteration or amendment or dates which are at variance from the dates of claim.
- Mileage claims must be checked for reasonableness (AA Routefinder) prior to payment.
- Expenses should be analysed against expected costs and employees in similar roles should have cost comparison made.
- Internal audit to carry out random sample checks on expense claims.
- 'Big spenders' should have claims analysed and audited by internal audit regularly.
- Claims for hotel expenses, meals, etc. should be compared with work diaries, etc.

It is now possible to automate expenses reimbursement which serves both to reduce processing costs and provide management with information about expenses claims. However, expense claims are and probably will remain a favourite source of illicit income for otherwise respectable people and the main approach is more likely to be one of deterrence than elimination.

Exhibit 11.6 The MEP and expenses

MEP Tom Wise was jailed for two years after spending £39,000 of taxpayer's money on fine wines and even an old car.

A former MEP who fiddled £39,000 of expenses was jailed for two years. Tom Wise, 61, who represented UKIP before becoming an independent, spent 13 months channelling the money into a bank account he secretly controlled.

He pretended the £3,000 'secretarial assistance allowance' he received every month was for his researcher Lindsay Jenkins, 62, but London's Southwark Crown Court heard he spent most of it on a love of fine wine, clearing credit card debts, buying a car and funding party political activities.

The court heard that, but for the discovery, Wise – thought to be the first British politician to be jailed for fiddling expenses – could have pocketed up to £180,000.

Like all MEPs, Wise became entitled to various allowances given by the European Parliament which were intended to assist him in discharging his work, both for the European Parliament and for the particular committee he sat on, the Culture, Media and Sport Committee. One of the allowances he was entitled to was the secretarial assistance allowance. Just a few months after starting his new job, Wise handed in two documents to support his application for the payment, which was governed by European Parliamentary rules forbidding staff wages going to MEPs.

▶

'The application was for £3,000 per month to be paid out by the European Parliament for the period October 1 2004 to September 30 2009, a potential total over the five years of £180,000.' Wise pretended the money would be paid directly to his assistant Mrs Jenkins, however the payments were made directly to a bank account controlled exclusively by Mr Wise.

Out of the money he received, Mrs Jenkins was paid £500 a month for work it was now accepted she had carried out.

Police eventually found he had blown £3,500 of taxpayers' cash on 19 cases of fine wine, used £6,800 clearing credit card bills and squandered £6,400 on a second-hand Peugeot 206.

Source: Bingham (2009)

Inventory theft

There are number of different types of fraud or theft involving inventories, ranging from straightforward theft or misappropriation of company assets to more complex schemes involving some level of inventory theft and concealment.

The main forms of inventory fraud comprise:

- theft of inventory
- set-aside
- delivery fraud
- falsification of goods inwards documentation
- theft of returns or scrap
- false returns, and
- own goods.

Looking at the individual types of fraud individually:

Theft of inventory

Straightforward theft of goods is probably the most common form of inventory theft and probably doesn't constitute fraud at all insofar as attempts to conceal it are rudimentary at best or even non-existent.

One of the anomalies with this kind of behaviour is that acts of theft are often observed by co-workers and:

- Are not recognised as theft as the employee is trusted and colleagues cannot accept they would do something dishonest.
- The individual is able to intimidate colleagues into keeping quiet.
- Colleagues tacitly support the thief as it is a way of striking back at an unpopular company – they are effectively aiding the theft either actively or passively.
- There is no mechanism to report the thief anonymously, for example, no whistle-blowing hotline.
- There is an unwillingness to report thefts as individuals believe in an unwritten code of solidarity and not being a 'grass'.

Of course there is also the possibility that all the employees in that area are involved!

Thefts are often more than an employee nervously smuggling items out under a large jacket; they can be on a larger scale and often quite well organised. Often trusted employees are given keys and codes to enable them to access company premises out of hours and this time can be used to appropriate goods and other assets without being seen by colleagues. In one case senior managers from a computer chips manufacturing company sidestepped the possibility of being caught removing goods from the premises by simply posting stolen chips to an accommodation address to be sold on at a later date.

There are many and various ways of committing stock frauds but most of them are variations on a theme. The main methodologies include:

- Set-aside: goods are set aside from a delivery and left in the despatch area. If the short delivery is noticed goods can be sent on later or the shortage blamed on the carrier. The set-aside goods can then be taken away and sold. Often short deliveries are ascribed to a variety of errors including picking errors, miscounting, carriage or even fraud at the customer end so instances are not always followed up.
- Delivery fraud: delivery drivers collude with goods-receiving staff to sign for a full load when only a part load is received. The remaining inventory was sold and the proceeds shared. In the cases of bulk loads part can be unloaded at an interim location before deliveries are made to customers. Unless customers have weigh-in facilities they cannot estimate the amount delivered accurately.
- Falsification of goods inward documents: the goods inwards staff falsify the entries of Goods Received Notes (GRN). On of the problems of stealing from a delivery is that the documentation, if properly completed, will show the full amount going into stock and the invoice will be for the full quantity delivered. Consequently the goods inwards records need to show that the full delivery never went into stock, so cannot have been misappropriated, whilst the record going to the accounts department needs to match the invoice.

  Suppose a delivery is for 500 units, from which the receiving staff misappropriate 50. The copy of the GRN sent to accounts to be matched to the purchase invoice needs to show 500, but the copy from which the stock records are written up shows 450. This involves judicious use of cardboard inserted between the leaves of NCR documents. A variation on this theme is to classify part of the incoming shipment as 'damaged' or not of appropriate quality and issue a Returns Note to cover the so-called shortfall, but the goods are never actually returned to the supplier.
- Theft of returns or scrap: this is one of the more obvious frauds, particularly where valuable metals or other goods are concerned. Success in this kind of fraud usually involves collusion with an employee of the receiving depot who is responsible for weighing-in or counting the scrap. The actual amount delivered is under-weighed or miscounted and a proportion is appropriated for the thieves to sell. The excess scrap is sold privately and the two of them share the proceeds.

  Goods returned as damaged or faulty may be taken by the employees as the customer has had due credit and, often, the company does not follow up what happens to returned goods. These items can either be repaired by the employees, perhaps using stolen parts, and sold on or sold as damaged.
- False returns: one of the major problems retailers face, particularly in the clothing sector is that of refunds being given for 'returned' goods. In many cases the goods returned have, in fact, been stolen either from the shop giving the return or from another branch. In some cases the shop assistants collude with the shoplifters to give refunds without proper evidence of an initial purchase. Alternatively goods may be 'sold' by the shop assistant to an accomplice but no payment is made, the assistant rings up a 'no sale'.

- Own goods: this is a fraud committed in bars and restaurants where the staff substitute their own goods for company items. For example, the bar staff buy their own cheap vodka from a discount supplier and decant it into an empty bottle of a more expensive brand which they then sell at full price. Proceeds of sale can then be removed from the till. The advantage of this type of theft is that it does not affect stock levels or gross profit margins, it is as if the perpetrators were running their own business inside their employer's business.

Fraud indicators

Clearly one of the major indicators of inventory theft is simply that items are consistently physically missing when the inventory records indicate that there should be some present. Such anomalies could be the result of mistakes in the records, such as:

- miscoding items in the stock records so the items are wrongly classified
- incorrectly completed Delivery or Goods Received Notes
- time delays in inputting deliveries into inventory or sales of goods
- items stored in the wrong location
- items wrongly packaged so the contents are different from the labels on any packaging, or
- increasing customer complaints.

However, with:

- use of electronic point of sale (EPOS) systems
- barcodes and readers
- examination of the contents of a delivery for quality and condition (which would reveal packaging problems), and
- computerised warehouse systems which control locations and goods inwards and outwards procedures

these types of errors should be minimal – particularly in retail premises. If the underlying systems and controls appear to be good, consistent stock shortages are indicators of pilferage.

Other indicators include:

- stock turnover at particular locations inconsistent with the general level
- lower than expected margins or margins different from the levels in similar locations
- deliveries made at unusual times of the day
- delivery drivers making part deliveries, asking for routes to be amended or insisting on delivering to particular locations
- poor or inadequate monitoring of stock losses
- weak goods inwards and despatch procedures
- poor segregation of duties between buying, warehousing, goods inward and accounting
- irregular or inefficient physical inventory counts or large test count differences
- inadequate follow-up of customer complaints especially concerning substandard products, incomplete deliveries or delays in delivery
- unexplained alterations to stock records, and

- Stock purported to be stored in unusual or inaccessible places or away from the main storage areas without commercial reason.

Detection methods

Detection methods for these kinds of fraud include:

- basic security, including CCTV, to monitor after hours activity
- restricted access to keys and codes – stores areas and areas containing small, easily portable assets to be secured and monitored
- analytical review of inventory transactions including:
  - stock turnover ratio by location
  - gross margin analysis by product or location
  - analysis of returns or stock write-offs
  - stock adjustment journals
  - items which have a high level of purchases but low usage or issue
  - inventory items unused in period
  - actual inventory use to budget, and
  - inventory balances written off or written down in the period.

Payroll fraud

You can tell the age of an accountant when they can remember the days when workers were paid mostly in cash and it was common to see queues of workers collecting pay packets stuffed with notes and coins. Of course in some industries and with some categories of employees this is still prevalent, but by far the majority now are paid by automated credit transfer directly into their bank accounts.

This change, coupled with:

- the difficulties of opening bank accounts under the 'know your client' rules, and
- the documentation required for HM Revenue and Customs for employees has cut the ground from under many a would-be payroll fraudster.

The classic forms of payroll frauds are:

- adding 'ghost' workers to the payroll
- falsification of overtime hours
- falsification of commission or other payments
- not removing workers from the payroll who have left employment
- 'outsourcing' employees where workers are classed as 'self-employed' when they are not – this is primarily tax fraud, and
- casual staff – use of illegal workers or workers with little or no documentation.

These were considerably easier when workers were paid in cash and the documentation required to process a payroll was considerably less than it is now.

For example the question of adding 'ghost' workers is complicated by the growth in HR procedures in the form of:

- contracts of employment
- starter's and leaver's forms

- authorities for deductions, and
- authorised pay rates.

not to mention the Coding Notices and other PAYE forms issued by HMRC for individuals, such as end of year P60 forms and Employers Declarations. All this bureaucracy makes this a task fraught with danger for the would-be embezzler. This is not to mention the creation of timekeeping records if they are hourly paid or on flexitime or a salary record if they are monthly paid – then there's the pension scheme and deductions – it makes it all very difficult.

Much easier therefore to fail to remove someone who was a genuine employee but who has now left employment from the payroll. An individual with appropriate access merely has to access the master file in the payroll system and change the former employee's bank details for their own. In this way the automatic BACS payment system will credit their account, if the employee is salaried there is no need to alter any other details. If there is a constant turnover of employees the fraudster can simply keep swapping departed employees so that they are removed from the payroll eventually.

Falsification of overtime hours and commission payments generally involves collusion with either a supervisor who can authorise overtime or a sales person who calculates commission. If clocking in isn't supervised in any way or timekeeping records are not authorised by a supervisor there may be some scope for paying a genuine worker more than they are entitled to, but in most cases, organisations have well-controlled procedures for controlling employee hours worked where these are variable – if for no other reason than the risks around payroll are fairly obvious even to the uninitiated.

It is not particularly difficult to control any payroll system adopting the principles of good internal control. Procedures for authorising overtime or commission payments, good procedures for starters and leavers, involving, as a minimum:

- a separate HR department to control starters and leavers
- rotation of duties within the payroll department
- restricting access to master file data
- use of approved payroll software, and
- verification and authorisation of rates, individuals and amounts by managers.

should basically restrict the opportunities for fraud by raising the risks to unacceptable levels.

Detection procedures

If there is suspicion of a payroll fraud, detection procedures would include:

- Check documentation from third parties i.e. HMRC/pension funds for all employees ensuring that the information has been received directly from the authority and not via any third party. Ensure these are original documents.
- Confirm all employees exist.
- Reconcile numbers and categories of employees with the HR database – look for names appearing on the payroll after known termination date.
- Analytical review:
  - payroll costs against budget
  - numbers of employees over time and period, and
  - average payments made.

- Analyse payroll for employees with large pay increases during an accounting period.
- Compare pay rates of workers with similar jobs – identify any anomalous rates – it may be that a person in the wages office is in collusion with another worker to overpay them, the two then splitting the overpayment.
- Check for employees with no deductions on payroll, i.e. those on low pay. This avoids necessity of accounting for tax deductions etc. with HMRC.
- Similarly review and confirm identities of part-time hourly paid workers, e.g. cleaners. Review internal controls re authorisation of pay and actual payment procedures.
- Identify any workers paid by cash or cheque outside the mainstream and observe a payout. Confirm the identity of these workers, validate the reason for non-standard payments and check their postal address is not the same as another employee and not a PO Box or accommodation address.
- Search for duplicate National Insurance numbers or bank accounts.

Casual workers

The points made above about the ease of controlling payrolls and identifying frauds rapidly do not, of course, apply where there are numbers of part-time or casual workers paid in cash.

Examples of this are low-paid workers such as cleaners, washers up or portering staff in the hotel and catering industry, pickers in the fruit and vegetable industry and students including overseas students.

There are, of course, a host of rules around part-time workers' rights, tax procedures etc. and many organisations obey them and treat part-time and casual staff wages with the same rigour as for full-time staff. For example for non-UK nationals they will require proof of identity, copies of passports or identity cards, visas etc. and will observe all the HMRC rules on deduction of PAYE and NIC from payments made. In these situations the opportunities for payroll fraud are minimised and the fraudster has limited opportunities.

Exhibit 11.7   Payroll fraud in the NHS

A hospital manager was jailed for four years yesterday for defrauding the National Health Service of almost £600,000.

In the largest ever NHS payroll scam, Joy Henry, 47, created 'ghost' employees and paid them weekly salaries before taking a substantial cut for herself.

To cover her tracks, she deleted the phantom shifts from the payroll system after the wages had been paid to the bogus workers, Southwark Crown Court heard. Henry, who split the cash with her then boyfriend, was working as head of the in-house recruitment agency at King's College Hospital NHS Trust when she committed the fraud between October 2000 and May 2003.

The prosecution alleged she put 10 people on the payroll system and paid them £580,000 even though they had never set foot into the hospital. In return they kept a third of the amount that passed through their bank accounts. Altogether Henry and her boyfriend, Joseph Oduguwa, are thought to have received £313,000.

▶

> The court heard that Henry, who pleaded guilty to conspiracy to defraud, used most of the stolen money to fund a life of luxury, including a top-of-the-range Audi convertible she bought for cash, a number of holidays in her native Nigeria and numerous first-class breaks to America.
>
> The court heard that the fraud was discovered by chance when a colleague noticed that large wage bills of up to £3,000 a week were being paid out.
>
> *Source:* Martin (2006)

However, in many industries these rules are not obeyed and even companies with an otherwise impeccable record can become inadvertently involved in illegal payments to casual workers. In the rather shadowy world of casual often foreign, sometimes illegal, workers, including asylum seekers and refugees, working at the very lowest levels of the hotel and catering industry or agriculture and fisheries this is an endemic problem.

In some cases the use of illegal immigrants or other workers is found in the supply chain where suppliers are put under price and delivery pressure by large customers. The temptation to employ illegal workers who cannot complain and who can thus be underpaid and overworked may be difficult to resist and there have been several cases in recent years, particularly in the clothing industry where these types of 'sweat shop' conditions have been uncovered. Clearly the supplier is mostly at fault but it may be that the customer, engaged in supply chain management, is more culpable than they are prepared to admit. The penalties for employing illegal workers are enormous, with fines of up to £10,000 per worker, so the risks to the company engaging in this kind of deception are high. This activity represents a fraud on HMRC, deceiving the UK Border Agency and is most often a fraud committed by management.

The main opportunity for fraud occurs where workers are paid in cash and operate off-site so their pay packets are given to them by a supervisor or manager. It is a relatively simple matter for the supervisor, gang master or manager to recruit a genuine worker and simply keep them on the payroll after they have left – collecting the pay packets and forging a 'signature' to confirm receipt. This solves the problem of having to create an identity for a 'ghost worker' (see Exhibit 11.7).

Short of a physical inspection of workers this is hard to detect, particularly where staff turnover is high. The corrupt manager or supervisor simply chooses a different worker to be kept on after they have left from time to time so that it doesn't look as though there is one very reliable worker who is always working a full week!

Even if the presence of the worker is demanded it is relatively easy for the supervisor or manager to claim that they didn't come in to work and appear to have left that day or the day before, or to intimidate a new illegal worker to impersonate one of the existing ones for the purposes of the inspection. Clearly employers will endeavour to obtain copies of identity documents where possible but these may well be forged or, in the case of refugees or illegal immigrants, non-existent.

There is also the possibility of a form of money laundering of cash where workers repay accidentally overpaid so-called 'accommodation allowances' in cash which are then refunded by a generous management, thus washing the money through workers payments.

Detection methods

Detection is very difficult where the turnover of workers is high or their identities can be fairly dubious. There are a few procedures which could be carried out:

- Observe payout to casual workers covertly, if possible on more than one occasion.
- Wages payout to be carried out by other than the supervisor or manager.
- Talk to casual staff – confirm existence of workers in a given period and track what happens to them. Often workers are intimidated by gang masters or supervisors who use threats such as loss of employment or trouble with the authorities to cover up instances of fraud and corruption.
- Follow up instances where pay packets not collected – trace the individuals concerned to a home address.
- All workers to sign for wages – review signatures for consistency.
- Go and find workers at any given random point – verify names and addresses, i.e. visit workplaces when they are supposed to be working and identify them all.
- Analytical review – costs/average per employee/turnover of staff, etc.

 ## Collusion with customers – corruption

We have looked at the legal issues surrounding bribery and corruption in Chapter 3 and the impact of the new legislation. Individuals in positions of authority or in control of information are often able to abuse that position and to betray the trust of their employers, thereby enriching themselves and, in many ways, impoverishing their employer.

We have already looked at dysfunctional organisations in Chapter 4 and seen how managers and employees can be socialised into unethical behaviour (see Exhibit 11.8) to the extent that the types of activity such as the giving of bribes to obtain contracts or information becomes socially acceptable within the organisation. However, it is a different matter when the unethical behaviour consists of outsiders bribing or corrupting the organisation's own staff.

Within the ethical organisation the giving or receiving of corrupt inducements is considered immoral without question, but where organisations are morally ambivalent about such payments, where perhaps 'oiling the wheels' is seen as acceptable practice, where does this leave the corruptee – the director, manager or member of staff who is paid to betray trade secrets such as:

- designs or new product specifications
- tender prices on behalf of rival bidders
- customer information such as contact details, product purchased etc.
- the secrets of processes, recipes and formulae for products, or
- samples of products or materials for competitors to study

or to simply take advantage of their position to:

- write off debts from customers
- sell goods at a 'special' discount
- buy goods from one source which may not be the cheapest or of the appropriate quality, or

- write off stock or other assets such as vehicles or plant and dispose of them to a co-conspirator merchant at a reduced price, who is then able to sell the goods for a full price

in return for a secret payment?

Bribery and corruption can take many forms. Payments can consist of:

- cash and cash equivalents, e.g. luxury goods such as designer clothes or accessories, consumer goods such as cars, boats, household goods etc or property overseas or in the UK
- entertainment – excessive corporate hospitality from event tickets to holidays
- sponsorship of causes or donations to charities – the employees' causes are supported in return for secrets or help
- facilitation payments – small payments made to grease the wheels of transactions and make them progress more quickly, or
- commissions on irregular transactions or excessive commissions paid to organisations for favours.

In time corrupt practices can be rationalised either by the individuals or the group of individuals concerned or as part of corporate culture; for example, deliberate over-billing by professionals such as accountants or lawyers is seen as valid in some scenarios and is rationalised as justifiable due to special time pressure or complexity.

'[People who have engaged in corrupt acts] excuse their actions to themselves as non-criminal, justified or part of a situation which they cannot control' was how Toby Bishop, President of ACFE, put it and research supports his view insofar as people who engage in corruption tend not to see themselves as corrupt. They acknowledge their actions as aberrant but refuse to accept they are criminal and justify them as normal and acceptable business behaviour.

Prevention and detection

The one advantage the company has in these situations is that staff who have access to confidential information are being trusted by their employer and are therefore likely to be treated differently from less trusted individuals.

This trust brings with it responsibilities and the likelihood is that employees privy to confidential or commercially sensitive information may have to expect

---

Exhibit 11.8   Fraud example – copier wars

A copier manufacturer announced discounts as high as 50 per cent and encouraged sales staff to pass the discounts on to customers. Instead sales staff approached customers with the original price list. They then informed the customer that lower prices could be negotiated but that this would lose the sales staff their commission.

The customers, happy to get the lower prices, issued compensatory payments to the sales staff for the 'lost' commission.

New sales staff had to be socialised into this process. Customers were hesitant at first but gradually became part of the process.

The rationale was that everybody won because the company got a sale, the customer got a low price and the sales staff got the commission they felt they deserved.

Source: Mars (1994)

certain restrictions on their behaviour which other employees may not have to cope with. Among such restrictions may be agreement to submit to searches, liability to disclose new relationships, monitoring of e-mails etc., matters which employees generally might consider unreasonable may have to become routine where trade secrets are involved.

These should be recorded as part of the contract of employment and acceptance by the employee must be obtained in writing.

Preventative measures to protect sensitive information

In cases where secrets are betrayed, detection at the time of the offence, or even shortly after it, is virtually impossible. The most a company can do is take preventative measures. Among these are:

- Ensure individuals who have access to confidential trade information are well rewarded so they are not tempted by the need for additional funds.
- Have a strong, clearly worded and easily understood anti-corruption policy. The organisation Transparency International has several templates for different sizes of organisation which can be used as a basis for such a policy. This must be reinforced through individual staff contract of employment terms (Chapter 7).
- Senior management should 'walk the talk', i.e. not be seen to be in receipt of excessive corporate hospitality or to mix socially with suppliers or advisors on a regular basis. This must include their families as well as themselves.
- Managers should be aware of staff behaviour. Where the behaviour of an individual changes this may be an indicator that something is wrong. For example:
  - staff who suddenly become more secretive or less forthcoming may have something to hide, or
  - staff whose lifestyle changes as a result of a 'legacy' or 'lottery win' may be displaying illicitly acquired wealth – something they may know is foolish but can't resist.
  Be careful however: the change in behaviour may be genuine, domestic strife or a genuine legacy from a deceased relative can cause people to behave differently. Believe the explanation but check it – discreetly.
- Maintain good staff relations and monitor staff behaviour for signs of stress. The reason for this is to ensure that, if the staff develop some form of unfulfilled need, e.g. the need to meet debts, an addiction to drugs or alcohol or a perceived desire to live an expensive lifestyle, then there is every opportunity to detect the signs at an early stage.
- Ensure lines of communication, in particular a whistle-blowing hotline, are available and can be used by staff without fear of reprisal (Chapter 7).
- If possible ensure that no one member of staff has access to all the confidential information in a given area. This may not be possible in certain circumstances but if it is then the management should also be aware of attempts by staff to obtain information to which they are not entitled.
- If possible rotate staff in and out of sensitive areas so that the information and access they do have can go out of date before they can reveal it.
- Change access codes and passwords frequently – use physical controls to deny access to sensitive areas to unauthorised personnel.
- Monitor staff relationships where possible – staff striking up relationships within the organisation should be discouraged to avoid any compromise of security and

segregation of duties and, clearly, staff striking up relationships with others in rival firms should be considered a warning sign. Clearly there are issues involving the rights of individuals here and these matters have to be handled sensitively but, as previously stated, employees operating in areas where they are privy to confidential and sensitive information may have to be subject to restrictions to their behaviour or lifestyle, and these must be made with their agreement as part of their contract of service. Enforcing a confidentiality clause through the courts after the event may satisfy the desire for revenge and act as a possible deterrent to others but will not repair the damage done.

- Monitor activities external to the business for indicators that there may be a spy in the camp. For example:
  - the loss of contracts to a particular rival more frequently than might be expected
  - 'spoiler' marketing campaigns run just before new product launches
  - rival products of a similar specification marketed suspiciously quickly after product launch, or
  - customers contacted by rival firms with targeted offers might be an indication that trade secrets have been revealed.

In these cases all that can be done is basic detective work, analysing what has taken place, how it might have happened, what information would have been necessary for the competitor or rival to achieve what they did and try to isolate who might have had access to the requisite information.

This may, unfortunately, lead to much suspicion but little conclusive evidence. Where the corruption takes the form of:

- the writing-off of debts
- the selling of assets at an undervalue, or
- discounting prices

accounting controls or forensic procedures are likely to have considerably more impact.

Systems-based approaches to detection

In larger organisations with a comprehensive MIS able to sort and analyse data some of these processes may involve the use of IT-based methods akin to those we look at later. However, whatever the size of the organisation, the principles remain the same. Whilst prevention of corruption, whether large scale or at a comparatively low level, is by far the strategy of choice there are some detection methods management or investigators can use to identify areas of unusual activity which may indicate corrupt activity.

The main systems-based approaches to identifying possible corrupt acts are:

- Analysis of frequency and size of credit notes and bad debt write-offs.
- Carry out a risk assessment of the relevant systems, including a form of link analysis (Chapter 10) to identify individuals with appropriate authority levels and possibilities for collusion.
- Analysis of frequency and size of asset sales.
- Identification of responsibility for authorising inventory write-offs and asset sales.

- Identifying non-standard pricing arrangements and analysing rationale.
- Analysis of discounts given to customers, particularly 'special' or non-routine discounts or allowances.
- Comparison of prices of identical goods sold to different customers.
- Comparison of prices paid for purchased items from selected suppliers with alternative suppliers not on approved supplier lists.
- Consideration of all new suppliers added to approved supplier lists where an existing long-term supplier has been removed.
- Analysis of timing of payments to suppliers – especially non-standard payments, i.e. weekly when everyone else is paid monthly.
- Investigation of any transactions involving larger than usual amounts of cash, i.e. cash disbursements or receipts in excess of petty cash levels – this, of course, where the trade does not normally involve cash.
- Review of accounts where transaction processes are handled directly by managers or directors without passing through the routine internal control procedures.
- Analysis of items billed to the organisation as fees, commissions, etc. – these could be bribes to individuals passed on to the organisation in another form. These may well be debited to large accounts where they can be hidden, for example, materials purchasing, site costs, etc.

Clearly some of these tests are cumbersome, time-consuming and difficult in practice and would only be used where there is a strong suspicion of some sort of favouritism or special treatment which is not justified by any commercial purpose. Wherever possible the principles of good internal control should be followed (Chapter 8) and, in particular, the principle of segregation of duties should be followed so that no one individual has the authority which would make it worth the while of an outside organisation to corrupt them.

This chapter has concentrated on frauds against the organisation committed by individuals either singly or together. Now we move to the next type of fraud: that of fraud committed by the organisation, or more precisely, its management.

Summary

- Motivations have been outlined in an earlier chapter but greed is the most common.
- It is crucial that evidence discovered is properly recorded and retained so as not to lose the chain of evidence.
- Sources of evidence may include client records and the perpetrators' personal records.
- Typical frauds involve billing schemes – fictitious suppliers, sales frauds and cash theft, payroll fraud, expenses fraud and collusion with customers and suppliers.
- Each has their own fraud indicators.
- There is a way of checking a VAT number – or you can just ring HMRC!
- Teeming and lading is a complex sales fraud but is easily detected.
- Skimming tills is common where there is a lot of cash.
- Common payroll frauds involve casual workers or not removing leavers from the payroll and changing bank details.
- Expenses fraud is very common but usually at a low level.
- Inventory fraud involves theft and concealment.
- Collusion with customers is very hard to detect and very costly.

Case study

You are the auditor of Betta Builders Ltd, a building company specialising in renovation work. It sells mainly to private clients seeking to renovate properties either for themselves or as an investment. It employs about 50 people most of whom are skilled workers specialising in plumbing, electrical, plastering, carpentry, glazing etc.

Sales revenue has grown by over 30 per cent in the last two years.

The company is managed by two directors, Sid Clump and Joe Maxie. Sid manages the financial and legal side of the business whilst Joe deals with the operational activities, including work scheduling, agreeing quotes with sales staff and all procurement. The two directors have mutual respect and trust each other and so do not check each other's work.

The company has an annual external audit but there is no internal audit function. There is a job costing system recording costs of materials allocated to contracts but other costs are not charged to individual contracts.

The system cannot therefore establish whether any individual contract is profitable and can only produce an aggregate income statement. One consequence of this is that the actual time taken to complete a job has to be very similar to the estimated time to avoid losses due to overruns – however there is no monitoring of time variances.

The company has managed to achieve a targeted gross mark-up of 25 per cent for the last few years.

Two staff are employed to prepare quotes for customers based on estimated labour and material costs plus 25 per cent. All quotes are reviewed by Joe before they are sent to customers. Ten per cent of the sales price is due when the job starts and 90 per cent when the job is completed.

Unknown to you, and to Sid, some time ago Joe lost a lot of money on foolish investments and was close to bankruptcy. He hid this from Sid and devised a way of extracting extra money from the company. He added 10 per cent to each quote which used more than three trades (plastering, plumbing etc.) thereby raising the gross mark up to 37.5 per cent in such cases. He then submitted an invoice for the 10 per cent additional charge in the name of a fictitious supplier of small tools and consumables. Sid would then code the invoice to variable overheads in the accounting system. Sid had set up a false business name and address and opened a bank account in that business's name. As Joe was solely responsible for buying materials he could time the submission of invoices to the completion of each job.

Joe has a very close relationship with some of the suppliers. Building supplies is a very competitive market and Betta Builders is always being approached by suppliers to do business with them. Sid, who claims to know nothing of the building trade, passes these on to Joe to deal with.

You are in the process of completing the audit of Betta Builders and an analytical review has pulled out the rise in variable costs. You decide to investigate.

Required

- What steps can you take to establish the validity of the variable costs?
- What questions might you ask the directors about the increase in variable costs?
- What other concerns might you have about Joe Maxie?
- What steps would you suggest taking in the event you discovered some unexplained anomalies in the costs?

Bibliography

Bingham, J. (2009) Disgraced ex UKIP MP Tom Wise jailed for two years for expenses fraud. www.telegraph.co.uk, 11 October.

Britten, N. (2005) Car parks cashier stole £1/2m to fund Elvis obsession. www.telegraph.co.uk, 21 October.

Chartered Institute of Management Accountants (CIMA) (2008) *Fraud Risk Management – A Guide to Good Practice.* CIMA, London.

Gill, M. (2005) *Learning from Fraudsters.* Protoviti, London.

Golden, T., Skalak, S. and Clayton, M. (2006) *A Guide to Forensic Accounting Investigation.* John Wiley, Hoboken, NJ.

Hanneman, R. (2005) *Introduction to Social Network Methods.* University of California, Riverside, CA.

HMSO (2002) *Proceeds of Crime Act 2002.* HMSO, London.

Hopwood, W.S., Leiner, J.L. and Young, G. (2008) *Forensic Accounting.* McGraw-Hill, New York.

Hough, A. (2009) KPMG accountant jailed for £555,000 expenses fiddle that paid for 'wife's lifestyle'. www.telegraph.co.uk, 16 September.

Huntington, I. and Davies, D. (1994) *Fraud Watch – A Guide for Business.* ICAEW, London.

International Auditing and Assurance Standards Board. *The International Standard on Related Services (ISRS) 4400 Engagements to Perform Agreed upon Procedures Regarding Financial Information.* IAASB, New York.

Mars, G. (1994) *Cheats at Work – An Anthropology of Workplace Crime.* Allen & Unwin, London.

Martin, N. (2006) NHS wages fraudster is jailed for four years. www.telegraph.co.uk, 25 February.

Penney, J. (2002) *Corporate Fraud – Prevention and Detection.* Tolley, London.

Silverstone, H. and Sheetz, M. (2007) *Forensic Accounting and Fraud Investigation for Non-experts.* John Wiley, Hoboken, NJ.

Singleton, T., Singleton, A., Bologna, G.J. and Lindquist, R.J. (2006) *Fraud Auditing and Forensic Accounting.* John Wiley, Hoboken, NJ.

Wells, J.T. (2004) *Corporate Fraud Handbook – Prevention and Detection.* John Wiley, Hoboken, NJ.

Websites

www.cimaglobal.org

www.faculty.ucr.edu/hanneman/

www.fraudadvisorypanel.org

www.fvs.aicpa.org/resources

www.icaew.com

www.ifac.org/iaasb

www.opsi.gov.uk/acts

www.telegraph.co.uk

Chapter 12

Management fraud

Chapter contents

Learning objectives

After studying this chapter you should be able to:

- Identify warning signs of financial statement manipulation
- Understand the methods used by managers to falsify accounts
- Understand the processes used by forensic investigators to detect these manipulations
- Appreciate the use of analytical procedures and the limitations of their application
- Understand the use of specific analysis techniques such as Beneish Ratios and Benford's Law

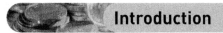

Introduction

Many of the most egregious frauds of the twenty-first century have been committed by management, in most cases very senior management. The names Enron, WorldCom and Parmalat shine like beacons in the history of fraud and set a standard that other would-be fraudsters can, we hope, only wonder at and not try to emulate.

This, of course, is nothing new. Over the decades, senior management, company owners and promoters have created illusions using fraudulent accounts and false promises in financial documents such as prospectuses to cheat the unwary and line their own pockets. There is a long and dishonourable roll call of names in the UK from share pusher Horatio Bottomley in the nineteenth century via Robert Maxwell and insurance fraudster Peter Clowes of Barlow Clowes in the twentieth to the management of Independent Insurance (Exhibit 12.1) in the twenty-first to name but a few of the more well-known culprits.

These are frauds committed by senior managers, including directors, which principally involve deliberate misrepresentation of financial information either for personal gain or to prevent some event such as the forcing of the organisation into administration or special measures.

In Chapter 5 we looked at the psychological theories of motivation for individual fraud and highlighted the 'fraud triangle' first postulated by Robert Cressey. This is fine for individuals but management fraud, as we will see, is a collective activity. Except in the very rarest cases, where one individual has absolute control, including over the financial reporting, such blatant misrepresentation of the financial statements requires co-operation and collusion between individuals involved at the highest level in the organisation.

Exhibit 12.1 Management fraud – Independent Insurance

When Independent Insurance published its accounts for 2000 its market value was in excess of £900 million, its assets were over £300 million and profit for the year £22 million. The outlook was declared 'positive'. Within months of publication the business collapsed and trading in its shares suspended. Over a thousand jobs were lost and thousands of shareholders lost their investments. Over £366 million had to be paid out from an industry compensation fund to policy holders.

What had come to light were the deliberate actions of three executives: chief executive Michael Bright, the deputy director and the finance director withheld insurance claims data from the company's actuaries. Additionally the chief executive together with the finance director made incomplete disclosure of some of the 'bad' agreements with the company's re-insurers. These actions made the company look more financially robust than it was.

The SFO and City of London Police investigation culminated in a defended trial in 2007. The prosecution case amounted to 30,000 pages, nearly 240 witness statements and 1,500 documents were shown to the jury. The defendants were accused of conspiring to defraud the directors, employees, shareholders, policy holders and others with an interest in knowing the company's financial state. It was not that their actions brought the company down; instead they masked the company's troubled performance. The resulting guilty verdicts brought prison terms for all three defendants of between seven and three years plus bans from being company directors for up to 12 years.

Source: Serious Fraud Office (2008)

Figure 12.1 The management fraud diamond

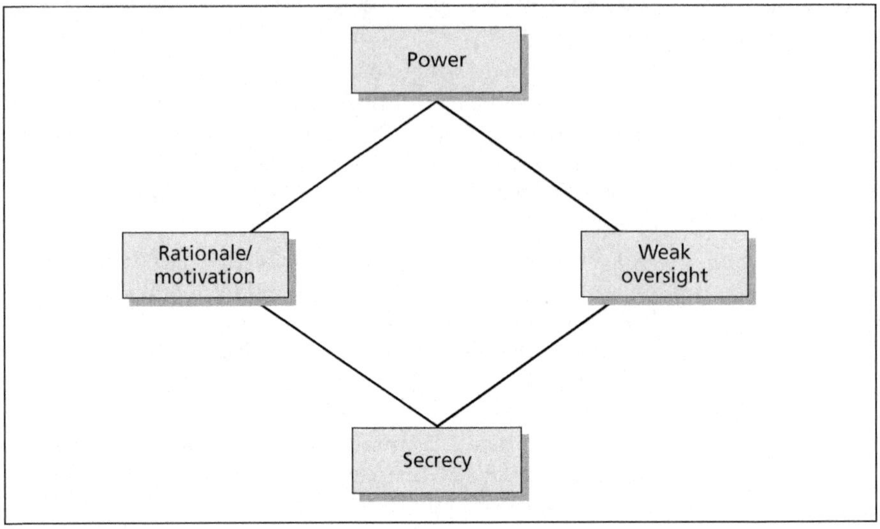

Figure 12.1 sets out a variant on the fraud triangle which we can call the 'fraud diamond', relating specifically to management fraud.

In this we see the required elements which go to make up such a fraud on the organisation:

- Power – to make decisions, to overrule objections and to influence others.
- Rationale or motivation – the reason why this is necessary. This is not necessarily the same type of individual motivation which spurs on the lone fraudster, although individual greed may well be an influence in some cases.
- Weak oversight – internal controls can be circumvented, internal audit deflected and external audit either deliberately misled or cajoled into accepting dubious practices. Colleagues who become aware of such practices refuse to face up to challenging them without concrete evidence, which is rarely forthcoming.
- Secrecy – this is a conspiracy. Everything to do with it must be kept quiet and the details confined to a very small group who share the responsibility.

Research into these types of fraud highlights their common factors:

- Collusion either deliberately or by omission with colleagues or co-directors.
- A willingness of colleagues and co-directors to turn a blind eye to unethical behaviour or to refuse to acknowledge it.
- An unwillingness to challenge the perpetrator.
- A policy of weak corporate governance within the organisation.
- A lack of understanding of certain aspects of operational activities.
- Poor or ineffective external audit.
- Deliberate misrepresentation to the auditors.

On the face of it, the more senior the individuals are who perpetrate these types of frauds the more easily, in many ways, they are able to accomplish what they set out to do. They have access to all the information, they can give instructions to staff which may be followed without challenge and they are in a position to circumvent many of the controls designed to prevent just such behaviour. On the other hand they are extremely visible and their actions rarely go unnoticed by staff and colleagues. They are the responsible officials in the organisation and their actions are likely to be scrutinised by the auditors.

However, as we will see, management frauds are far from uncommon and many persist for some years before being uncovered. In this chapter we will look at:

- financial statement schemes
- bribery and corruption
- false investment (Ponzi) schemes, and
- VAT fraud, also known as carousel fraud.

With regard to the last two categories we will look at VAT fraud briefly (this really usually involves the creation of a business purely to defraud HM Revenue and Customs), and we will look at the salient features of investment frauds, in particular so-called Ponzi schemes, so they can be recognised for what they are.

 ## Financial statement schemes

Financial statement schemes involve deliberate manipulation of financial statements in order to show a financial position which is either better or worse than the 'true and fair' view required by the external auditors before they sign them off.

Manipulation of financial statements was a key feature of the spectacular frauds in the USA such as Enron and WorldCom and is also of course, almost by definition, a requirement of those frauds known as 'Ponzi schemes' whereby the aim is to attract new recruits to the scheme with new capital so earlier investors can keep receiving a 'dividend', thus perpetuating the scheme. Lies about the financial health of the organisation are essential to such schemes.

Europe is not without its spectacular frauds. The Parmalat scandal, said to involve frauds of between €10bn–14bn, involved the use of various offshore subsidiaries and false bank accounts and resulted in the elaborate misrepresentation of financial information on a truly colossal scale.

In the UK there have been several considerably smaller but nonetheless indicative instances of financial statement fraud. These often involved the local management of devolved subsidiaries or divisions where they were away from the mainstream internal control mechanisms operated from the centre but, occasionally, these financial statement schemes were driven from the very top of the organisation.

Why do senior executives engage in such practices? There are several reasons:

- Having to meet previously announced profit forecasts.
- Internal pressures on management to meet profit or income targets – this can often arise in devolved subsidiaries or divisions with a high level of local control and limited overview from the centre.
- Maintaining the share price – this may be connected to the ownership of share options by directors.

Exhibit 12.2   **Fraud example – Parmalat**

One example of the methods used in the Parmalat fraud was a multi-step process whereby the illusion of revenue was created whilst at the same time removing debt from the books.

It went like this:

- Parmalat issued a false invoice to an offshore shell company – one they used after 1999 was called Bonlat. This created a receivable for a fictitious debt.
- At the same time it created a discounted bill of exchange which represented the subsidiary's repayment of that debt – its obligation to Parmalat.
- It then sold the discounted bill to a bank, giving the bank the right to be paid on the invoice. As the shell company, Bonlat, had no cash or revenue Parmalat loaned it the money to pay the bank.
- It recorded this as an investment in a subsidiary rather than as a loan.
- Finally at the end of the accounting period it assigned the credit and the liability on the invoice of the consolidated subsidiary to an unconsolidated subsidiary.

Parmalat then recorded the transaction as an asset because it had an amount owed to it by an unconsolidated subsidiary. It is alleged that in this way Parmalat was able to obtain loans from banks and record them as assets, thus overvaluing the business massively.

Source: United States District Court Southern District of New York: in re Parmalat securities litigation.

- Hiding indicators of going concern problems in order to maintain financing.
- Raising finance secured on inventories or assets (which may not exist).
- Reduction of profits to save tax or avoid the payment of dividends.
- Hiding profits for a 'rainy day'.
- Achieving an 'earn out' target after a sale of the business where sale proceeds are dependent upon achieving profit targets.

Readers may be wondering why directors and managers engage in these types of fraudulent manipulation of the financial statements. After all does this not necessarily involve a conspiracy of many, thus increasing the likelihood of it breaking down. Are the accounts not audited annually thus rendering the possibility of discovery more likely? How then can they succeed in anything other than the short term?

The short answer, as far as we know, is that generally they don't succeed for more than a few years, although the Parmalat manipulations (Exhibit 12.2) may have been going for more than ten years and the accounts manipulations at Enron went on for at least eight years before it crashed. Clearly there may be organisations out there that have successfully manipulated their accounts for years and which have never been unmasked, but frankly this is unlikely.

Sometimes the conspiracies do break down and the duplicity is revealed. The most famous instances of this are whistle-blowers Cynthia Cooper at WorldCom and Sherron Watkins at Enron, both of whom were relatively lowly employees in comparison with the individuals perpetrating the fraud. In most cases the conspiracy is confined to a few individuals. In the Greencore case illustrated in Exhibit 12.3 only three executives were involved and in the Transtec case (Exhibit 12.3) only the group financial director and another director were indicted: the group chief executive was acquitted.

Exhibit 12.3 **Fraud examples – frauds by directors**

Greencore

The UK's largest sandwich maker, Greencore, discovered accounting irregularities amounting to £15.8m in its mineral water Strathlomond premises in Scotland. Deliberate concealment of expenses and other costs affected the financial statements for the years 2006, 2007 and 2008.

Three senior managers who supervised a former financial controller were sacked when the fraud was uncovered.

Source: Herman (2008)

Transtec

The company was a supplier to the Ford Motor Company and agreed compensation to Ford amounting to $18m following a claim by Ford for compensation from Transtec for the supply of defective cylinder heads for their Ford Explorer vehicle. A payment schedule was agreed and payments made but instead of these being expensed they were capitalised as 'tooling' and then written off as obsolete. The outstanding amounts of the claims unpaid were not included as liabilities, whether contingent (at the time compensation was being negotiated) or actual (once the schedule of compensation was agreed).

Source: SFO (2006)

External audit

As we saw in Chapter 5 the external auditors are not, generally, considered by the perpetrators to be a concern. Analysis of past cases sadly indicates that external auditors tend to accept the evidence they are looking for when it is presented to them. The International Standard on Auditing (ISA) 580, 'Written representations', permits external auditors to obtain written representations from management as audit evidence that they have fulfilled their statutory responsibility to prepare 'true and fair' financial statements:

> The auditor shall request management to provide a written representation that it has fulfilled its responsibility for the preparation of the financial statements in accordance with the applicable financial reporting framework, including where relevant their fair presentation, as set out in the terms of the audit engagement.

Of course, if the directors were deliberately misrepresenting the financial statements, falsifying a letter to the auditors would be child's play.

ISA 580 goes on to say:

> Although written representations provide necessary audit evidence, they do not provide sufficient appropriate audit evidence on their own about any of the matters with which they deal. Furthermore, the fact that management has provided reliable written representations does not affect the nature or extent of other audit evidence that the auditor obtains about the fulfilment of management's responsibilities, or about specific assertions.

In other words auditors must look at the totality of their evidence before forming an opinion, including any representations made to them by the management. With auditors increasingly adopting risk-based approaches to validation of financial statements it is feared that, despite the best advice from the Auditing Practices Board, many firms of auditors are signing off accounts without the sufficiency of reliable evidence required to properly substantiate their audit opinion. In practice they are playing the odds that all will be well – which, in the vast majority of cases, it is.

So with some judicious forgery and the suppression of key documents coupled with a confident front and a large amount of bluffing and lying, the conspirators can be home and dry. One example of this is the auditor's apparent acceptance of the existence of a bank account purporting to amount to €3.9 billion owned by the Parmalat subsidiary Bonlat in the Bank of America in the Cayman Islands which subsequently proved to be fictitious (Exhibit 12.5). It is not known how the auditors verified this asset on Bonlat's Statement of Financial Position, but they must have done so because they signed off the accounts. Forgery, bluster and perhaps the unwillingness of auditors to accept the unthinkable, that what they were presented with were lies on a massive scale, enabled the directors to perpetuate a continuing fraud over many years until, inevitably, the house of cards they had created came tumbling down.

Internal audit

Internal audit is a bigger problem for the management fraudster, particularly if they are a truly independent function. It was an internal audit enquiry which undid the Welsh Slate directors (see Exhibit 12.4) and press reports indicate that internal audit also revealed the fraud at Greencore (see Exhibit 12.3).

The problem that managers and directors have with regard to internal audit is this. If the company adopts the key corporate governance principles as advocated by the Turnbull Report (Chapter 1) and as required by the Combined Code it will have an internal audit function which financial managers cannot control directly. Instead the internal audit function will be able to set its own agenda and report to the audit committee: the financial director will have little or no direct control over it. Consequently internal audit, with its intimate knowledge of the organisation, may well query financial information which purports to be in accordance with the underlying records but isn't. Consequently internal audit will have to be deflected or the cover-up will have to be a very good one if it is to succeed in the long term.

No fraudulent manipulation of results can take place without the involvement of the senior financial officers in the organisation, i.e. the financial director or financial controller depending on the structure and status of the organisation. A group-wide fraud on a Parmalat scale for example requires the full co-operation of the financial director of the group; a fraud at a subsidiary, such as the Greencore case, requires input from the local financial controller and the manipulation of the financial statements of a smaller company requires the involvement of the company accountant and financial director because, if for no other reason, they are the only ones who actually know how to do it.

Exhibit 12.4 Fraud example – Welsh Slate

Three managers of Welsh Slate company were jailed for a swindle that saw sales figures inflated with more than £10 million of false invoices. Former managing director Christopher Law, 53, was sentenced to two-and-a-half years.

McAlpine discovered the fraud after sending an internal audit team to investigate why outstanding debts on the false invoices were not being collected.

Customer letters were created to give the impression that payments were in the pipeline, while delivery notes and transport invoices for non-existent consignments were forged, the SFO said. The forged invoices were photocopied from genuine documents with the original details blanked out and substituted with false amounts. The court heard an example of the deception included showing auditors a stockpile of crates of roofing slates – only the outer ones were full while those on the inside were empty.

False cash payments to cover the invoices were created as were credit notes to cancel older debts and to avoid auditors examining them. About 54 per cent of the debt supposedly owed to the company was a complete fiction.

The prosecution said the three had not committed the fraud to make money, but simply to convince their bosses the Welsh outfit was well managed. He said the slate industry in North Wales was a source of pride for the whole region and had an 'emotional importance disproportionate to its size'.

Defending Law, John Rees QC said the managing director had acted under the weight of impossible targets set by the parent firm. He said Law had grown up in the South Wales mining community of Bryn, Neath Port Talbot, and witnessed at first hand the industry's collapse. Law was trying to save the slate business from suffering the same fate as mining, he said.

The SFO told the court that many of the firm's employees, taking their lead from the top, knew of and played an active part in the fraud in order to remain in well-paid jobs.

Mr Rees said Law believed his actions amounted to 'the wrong way of doing the right thing'.

Source: Devine (2009)

Indicators of financial statement manipulation

There are several key indicators that forensic accountants can use to flag up possible cases of manipulation of accounts:

- Recurring negative cash flows from operations which show paper profits. The movement of cash can be calculated from accounts or by simple observation of the growth in borrowings.
- Unusual profits above industry average or by a minority of business units.
- Rapid growth against market trend.
- Significant transactions with related parties, especially those audited by other parties or in another jurisdiction.
- Unusual or complex transactions at the end of a reporting period.
- Significant sales to entities whose substance and ownership are unknown.
- Disproportionate increases in the values of inventories and receivables year on year.
- Better or worse than expected results by a subsidiary or division which is sited away from centralised financial control.

- Subsidiaries or divisions with highly autonomous local management where interventions from the main (i.e. holding company) board directors or internal audit reviews are resisted or unreasonably delayed.
- Unusual or unexplained increases in the book value of assets (current and non-current).
- Unusual trends or relationships of assets to other parts of accounts, e.g. constant increases in debtor days ratio, change in ratio of debtors to sales.
- Violations of GAAP in recording assets as expenses.

Clearly these instances are unusual and equally clearly they can be quite difficult to detect. Internal audit may well detect anomalies in bookkeeping by using routine audit procedures, but in the absence of these how might these kinds of fraud be detected?

Detection methods

Investigations by internal audit, using routine audit testing procedures have, in the past, uncovered frauds because the underlying records either:

- do not support the financial statement at all, or
- have been altered or suppressed in such a way that the alterations are noticeable.

For example:

1 A company sells a service on the basis of a two-year contract which promises payment monthly over the two years as and when the service is supplied. The directors book the whole of the income as earned in year 1 to make the income look better and to meet a target. A simple reading of the contract reveals what they have done.
2 Maintenance and repair expenses are capitalised as non-current assets to improve profitability. Substantive testing by the auditors of additions to non-current assets reveals the misstatement.
3 A significant level of sales is invoiced in the last month of the accounting period. During the following month credit notes are raised to cancel the sales. A review of transactions after the end of the accounting period, a routine audit procedure, will raise suspicions of over-invoicing.
4 The organisation raises finance, in particular forms of bridging or short-term finance, secured by the lender on the values of non-current assets such as inventories or receivables. These values have to be manipulated by management to ensure that the value of the lender's security is within any possible banking covenants in relation to the amount of lending, e.g. the value of inventories and receivables to be not less than twice the outstanding amount on the bank's loan.

Where documents have been altered or destroyed, controls evidently overridden or certain transactions kept away from the main financial systems, the auditors' suspicions should be aroused and they should investigate further. However, in the absence of detailed audit review how can such frauds be uncovered without examination of the underlying records?

Detection methods initially centre on analytical review procedures which, if manipulation of results is present, should generate indications of where manipulation is taking place and what form it takes.

Before carrying out extensive analytical review procedures the investigator must undertake some preparatory work in order to form a proper understanding of the organisation and the expected outcomes from the review. Without some indication of what they might expect to find it would be difficult to identify an anomaly. The analysis of the numbers, whichever technique is adopted, will not have the level of meaning that it should have if the investigator has no understanding of the trading circumstances of the business or organisation, its history, the industry in which it operates, its competitors, etc.

The investigators must get to know the organisation and consider three key factors:

1 The degree to which those in authority in the organisation have reason to commit management fraud.
2 The degree to which conditions allow management fraud to be committed.
3 The extent to which those in authority have an attitude or set of ethical values that would facilitate their commission of fraud.

In doing so they will have to review detailed environmental and business factors such as:

- The present condition and future prospects of the industry of which the client is a part, including the competition.
- Underlying economic factors which may affect the performance or results of the organisation.
- The past history and the present condition and future prospects of the client itself.
- The organisation's strategic objectives and goals.
- Its historical performance.
- Performance of competitors.
- Previous announcements made for the last three years in the case of listed companies.
- The organisation's:
  - products and services
  - important customers
  - key suppliers, and
  - details of significant contracts.
- The management and key personnel of the organisation and any recent changes including their systems of reward, current and previous levels, etc.
- Expected budgetary performance and historical performance against forecasts.
- Any publicity, gossip, innuendo or allegations against or about the organisation whether admitted or denied by the organisation. A Google search of the organisation on the Internet may reveal a great deal of non-financial information and comment in the trade press or relevant websites. Internet gossip tends to be rather more unrestrained than printed media which should also be reviewed.
- Review of social networking sites such as Facebook, MySpace, Bebo, etc., where directors or senior employees may have posted personal information.
- The products and manufacturing and trading processes of the client and any recent changes.
- The locations of all the client's operations.
- Any difficulties encountered by the client in:
  - manufacturing
  - trading

- expanding or contracting the business
- labour relations, or
- financing the continuing operations.
- Any problems in accounting or in internal control systems reported by the internal or external auditors.
- Any problems in accounting measurement, e.g. in inventory valuation or income recognition, which might have a bearing on the figures.

The objective of this understanding is to enable the investigator to:

- develop an expectation of results
- define what is unusual or what will constitute a deviation from an expected result
- be aware of how financial information is assembled, and
- engage in discussions with management and staff.

Let's look at these points in more detail.

Develop an expectation of results

Knowledge of the circumstances of the business can be the context within which fluctuations in numbers and ratios can be explained.

For example, a sudden reduction in gross profit percentage might be as a result of a known price war resulting in a forced reduction in selling prices. The drop may then not appear to be anomalous – but should still be checked! Consistency with prior years or regular increases year on year may be anomalous in turbulent times and may be an indicator of fraudulent reporting. This is typical of Ponzi schemes. If the expectation on management to meet budgeted results is matched by achievement then the results tend not to be questioned. However, it may be that their achievement was through fraudulent reporting rather than genuine trading.

Define what is unusual or what will constitute a deviation from an expected result

This is inevitably related to the materiality of the figure being reviewed and its importance to the financial statements.

For example, a small percentage variation in a large balance can result in a significant difference. The investigator should be aware of the risk of the balance being misstated, including the level of internal control which affects its potential for misstatement. The investigator must also be aware of parts of the organisation which may not be consolidated but with which the business has significant trading relationships – perhaps on non-standard terms – such as joint ventures or partnerships.

These may have a valid commercial function but may also be used as a vehicle for manipulating the results through the issue of false documents such as loan notes, bills of exchange or fictitious invoices.

Be aware of how financial information is assembled

When carrying out the analysis work disaggregation of results is likely to provide more information to the investigator than analysing the organisation as a whole or in major parts. However, it should be recognised that fraudulent entries may not go through the accounting records so the investigator must ensure that the parts being analysed also constitute the whole.

For example, carrying out analysis work on the results of subsidiaries and divisions is all very well providing these are reconciled to the final consolidated accounts: fraudulent entries may have been slipped in disguised as consolidation adjustments or last-minute changes.

Engage in discussions with management and staff

Investigation of differences will entail discussion with management, if only to record their responses. Investigators should also obtain information from managers or staff not concerned with financial reporting. For example fluctuations in sales revenue can be discussed with sales staff or customer liaison as the fluctuation could be commercially valid. This type of investigation can also provide information about customers and suppliers which might be relevant to an understanding of the numbers.

Review complex areas of accounting

Some aspects of accounting may be complex and difficult to be absolutely confident about, for example the valuation of long-term work in progress in construction companies. Whilst there are accounting rules regarding the taking of profits and the recognition of losses there remains a degree of subjective opinion in the process of valuation, in particular the percentage completion of contracts. This particular area may also suffer from an endemic problem of corruption where surveyors certify higher or lower values of completed work than is true in return for a bribe. Investigators must establish as much independent evidence as is possible to support any contention of deliberate manipulation of the figures and may well wish to bring in their own expert to review the position. Where the organisation is engaged in complex or specialised activities it is even more important that the investigator becomes as familiar as possible with the organisation's activities and discovers as much as is feasible about the underlying principles on which the accounts are based. Consultation with independent experts may be the only answer in very difficult cases.

Analytical review procedures

The use of analytical review, or ratio analysis as it is sometimes known, is a powerful tool in the investigator's armoury. Auditors have known for some time about the effectiveness of analytical review as part of the audit process, indeed ISA 520, 'Analytical Procedures', requires auditors to use analytical techniques as part of the audit planning process, as a method of testing and as part of the overall review process at the end of the audit.

The purpose of analytical procedures is to help in telling the story of the financial statements, prepared by the directors, to gather evidence to show that the relationships between the numbers in the accounts are reasonable and logical and bear out what is known from other sources about the events of the accounting period.

Using analytical procedures as an investigatory tool has the same goal – to determine whether or not the financial statements tell a coherent story and whether or not some of the numbers may have been manipulated to 'window dress' the figures.

However, a word of warning. These techniques should be used judiciously as part of an overall investigation; they are not a substitute for other investigative techniques detailed elsewhere. These analytical procedures are designed to highlight possible areas for investigation and to add to the evidence. The investigator must avoid the danger of 'paralysis by analysis' where so many analytical procedures are carried out that the true issues become obscured.

There are some simple and some not so simple techniques which can be used to highlight possible problem areas and we will look at these in detail. It may be that some of these are not techniques normally used by auditors but, be that as it may, these are the approaches which are likely to assist the investigator the most by drawing attention to problem areas in the financial statements.

There are three important caveats when using analytical procedures:

- All the information used must be reliable. Analytical procedures are the analysis of relationships and are commonly used to indicate trends over time. The results for one period in isolation, in themselves, are meaningless until they are compared with other periods or benchmark numbers from a reliable source. The point is that the comparison numbers have to be reliable; if all the numbers used are false the test will reveal nothing specific except perhaps a series of confusing variances. For example if accounts for year 4 are considered to be dubious they can be compared with accounts for years 1–3 and variances noted. However, if the directors have manipulated the figures for each of years 1–4 the tests have no validity.
- Analytical procedures raise questions but they rarely provide answers. Indicators thrown up using these techniques must be followed through and investigated in detail and, where possible, explanations received for the apparent anomalies.
- Disaggregating the numbers into divisions, subsidiaries or regions may be much more successful than looking at the entity as a whole as anomalies may be confined to one area of the business under local control. Detection could be masked if analysis was carried out on an organisation-wide basis.

Horizontal and vertical analysis of financial reports

Arranging the financial statements for a series of accounting periods, be they annual financial statements or monthly management accounts, is a way of identifying trends.

There are two types of analysis to be performed – horizontal and vertical. Note that these are not mutually exclusive, the object is to perform both types of analysis as they reveal different facets of the accounts.

In horizontal analysis, as shown in Figure 12.2, the financial statements for several accounting periods are set out in horizontal format and the movement period on period is identified.

What the investigator is looking for are unusual or anomalous movements which might indicate a manipulation. Clearly the effects of economic factors such as inflation or interest rates which might affect the organisation over time will have to be factored in to these calculations.

For example the investigator will be looking for increases between periods in one set of numbers which are not matched by concomitant increases in related numbers, e.g. if income has increased by 20 per cent but allied costs such as cost of sales or selling costs have only increased by less than 10 per cent this would call for an investigation of both these sets of numbers as increases in income would be expected to drive increases in costs.

Table 12.1 shows the format of horizontal analysis.

Vertical analysis of results is based on the proportion that selected costs are of a base figure – usually income. These can be compared year on year to indicate any illogical or unusual changes which are not explained by known trading patterns.

Table 12.2 shows the format of vertical analysis.

Investigators should be aware that

- The source of the figures must be homogeneous. For example, if the business has grown by acquisition over a period of years the business in year 7 may be radically different from the business in year 1. In this case the numbers must be disaggregated in order to provide a valid comparison.
- There may be sound business reasons for variances and differences form one period to another. For example, gross profit percentages may have changed as a result of market conditions rather than because of falsification of inventory figures but the changes would indicate an area for further investigation. Investigators should be aware of the patterns of trading and have an idea of what the analysis should reveal before the work is carried out.

Table 12.1 Horizontal analysis

	2007	2008	% Change	2009	% Change
Income statement					
Turnover	257,000	286,000	11	294,000	3
Cost of sales	224,000	255,000	14	258,000	1
Gross profit	33,000	31,000	−6	36,000	16
Administration costs	9,000	8,000	−11	10,000	25
Selling and marketing costs	11,000	12,000	9	15,000	25
Interest	3,000	2,000	−33	1,500	−25
Taxation	2,000	3,000	50	0	−100
Net profit	8,000	6,000	−25	9,500	
Balance sheet					
Cash and bank	7,000	4,000	−43	1,500	−63
Inventories	12,000	14,000	17	18,000	29
Receivables	9,000	11,000	22	15,000	36
Total current assets	28,000	29,000	4	34,500	19
Non current assets	167,000	172,000	3	168,000	−2
Total assets	**195,000**	**201,000**		**202,500**	1
Payables	22,000	24,000	9	29,000	21
Other current liabilities	2,000	2,000	0	1,100	−45
Loans	15,000	13,000	−13	9,000	−31
Share capital and reserves	156,000	162,000	4	163,400	1
Total liabilities and share capital	**195,000**	**201,000**	3	**202,500**	1

Note: figures have been rounded for presentation purposes.

Table 12.2 Vertical analysis

	2009	%	2008	%	2007	%
Income statement						
Turnover	294,000	100	286,000	100	257,000	100
Cost of sales	258,000	88	255,000	89	224,000	87
Gross profit	36,000	12	31,000	11	33,000	13
Administration costs	10,000	3	8,000	3	9,000	4
Selling and marketing costs	15,000	5	12,000	4	11,000	4
Interest	1,500	1	2,000	1	3,000	1
Taxation	0	0	3,000	1	2,000	1
Net profit	9,500	3	6,000	2	8,000	3
Balance sheet						
Cash and bank	1,500	1	4,000	2	7,000	4
Inventories	18,000	9	14,000	7	12,000	6
Receivables	15,000	7	11,000	5	9,000	5
Total current assets	34,500		29,000		28,000	
Non-current assets	168,000	83	172,000	86	167,000	85
Total assets	202,500	100	201,000	100	195,000	100
Payables	29,000	14	24,000	12	22,000	11
Other current liabilities	1,100	1	2,000	1	2,000	1
Loans	9,000	4	13,000	6	15,000	8
Share capital and reserves	163,400	81	162,000	81	156,000	80
Total liabilities and share capital	202,500	100	201,000	100	195,000	100

Note: figures have been rounded for presentation purposes.

- Figures can be compared by business unit, by region over time. This will enable the investigator to identify trends and fluctuations which may be seasonal and normal for the type of activity. On the other hand sudden increases in income in the month before a reporting period end may look anomalous.

Disaggregating the numbers will be more successful than looking at the entity as a whole. Figures can be compared, for example:

- by business unit
- by activity
- over time, and
- by region.

to enable the investigator to identify trends and fluctuations. Of course these may be a natural part of the trading pattern, for example seasonal fluctuations; on the other hand sudden movements prior to the end of a reporting period may be grounds for suspicion, particularly as the scale of movements may not be consistent, i.e. the corrupt management may need to make big 'adjustments' one quarter to meet a profit target, but a smaller one in the next quarter so the 'adjustments' are not as large.

Ratio analysis

This is a form of analysis where the various forms of business ratio are calculated for the financial statements of the current and preceding periods. This technique would involve some elements of horizontal analysis as, again, the investigator is looking for trends over time which may be anomalous or unusual.

There are some points to note:

- As with horizontal and vertical analysis ratio analysis is best be carried out on particular segments of the organisation, for example, the branch at Walsall or the paint division or the subsidiary in France. They can also be used on individual account areas such as creditors or fixed asset depreciation.
- The investigator should have a working knowledge of the operational circumstances of the organisation and the likely effect on the accounts of its activities. This enables the identification of the trading or operational factors which are likely to have an effect on figures in the accounts. The investigator is then able to ascertain or assess the probable relationships with these factors and items and to predict the value of the figures in the light of these factors. The predicted value of the items can then be compared with the actual recorded amounts. For example, if the investigator knows that the organisation has been engaged in heavy discounting of product prices because it has been engaged in a trade war with its competitors a reduction in gross margin might be anticipated, and it might be possible to estimate the extent of such a reduction. If the actual margin falls by a larger value, or goes up, there may be grounds for further investigation. Based on this knowledge investigators should also consider the implications of predicted fluctuations that fail to occur.
- More analysis is not necessarily better analysis. A simple set of ratios well chosen will tell the story.
- The Association of Certified Fraud Examiners have identified several key ratios which may lead to the discovery of fraud which we will look at below.

Two things should be borne in mind:

- The ratios calculated will vary from industry to industry and organisation to organisation so it is the trend analysis which is important, not the size of the number calculated.
- If comparison is made between two years both sets of figures might have been manipulated so both might show consistent ratios. If possible comparisons should be made against a year which is known to be un-manipulated. Many of the ratios will not be affected by activity levels and changes in others could be partially explained by business activities. Unexplained movements should be investigated further.

Included in the ACFE recommended ratios are:

- current ratio
- quick ratio
- inventory turnover
- inventory days
- receivables turnover
- receivables days
- debt/equity (leverage or gearing)
- payables days

- gross profit margin, and
- net profit margin.

In addition to these more familiar ratios the ACFE also suggest the use of a rather sophisticated version of these known as Beneish ratios. We consider all of these below.

Current ratio	$\dfrac{\text{Current assets}}{\text{Current liabilities}}$

The current ratio measures the ability of the organisation to meet its immediate liabilities. It is a ratio of liquidity and a ratio greater than 1 indicates that liabilities can be covered through realisation of current assets. This ratio must be reviewed in relation to those ratios related to other elements of current assets and liabilities. As cash balances decline so will this ratio, whereas suppression of liabilities will improve it.

Ironically where a consequential debit arising as a result of fraud has been debited either against liability balances to disguise it or has been included as some sort of fictitious asset, the ratio will improve. This latter course of action is allegedly how the embezzlers in Parmalat disguised some of the losses they had created through their theft.

Quick ratio	$\dfrac{\text{Current assets} - \text{inventories}}{\text{Current liabilities}}$

This ratio is another liquidity ratio but this excludes inventories. The logic behind this is that, in a crisis, receivables and cash are more liquid than inventories which have to be sold and the cash collected before liabilities can be met. It measures the ability of the organisation to meet its current liabilities out of liquid resources. The same points relating to the current ratio apply here except that the effect of falsifying inventory numbers is, of course, removed.

Inventory turnover	$\dfrac{\text{Cost of goods sold}}{\text{Average inventory}}$

This represents the number of times the inventory is turned over in the period. This is important as money tied up in inventory is not able to be used for anything else so, broadly, the more frequently it is turned over (into receivables and cash) the better. Theft of inventory will tend to reduce closing inventory and increase cost of sales (from writing off missing inventory) so the ratio will increase. Artificial increases due to fraudulent closing inventory will tend to reduce the ratio. Substantial changes from period to period should be analysed to see if they relate to inventory fraud.

Inventory days	$\dfrac{\text{Closing inventory} \times 365}{\text{Cost of sales}}$

This represents the inventory turnover ratio expressed as days. The formula can also be written as:

$$\frac{365}{\text{Inventory turnover}}$$

In commercial terms this ratio is relevant because days in stock represents money tied up but also increases the risks of obsolescence, damage and storage costs. Significant changes in this ratio can indicate fictitious inventories as, of course, fictitious inventory never actually moves. Frequently a slowly increasing number of days, which looks anomalous compared to other ratios, may indicate that some inventory records have been falsified and don't represent real goods.

Receivables turnover	$\dfrac{\text{Credit sales}}{\text{Trade receivables}}$

This ratio measures how quickly receivables turnover, i.e. the speed of collection. Fictitious billing schemes will increase this ratio as the receivables will not be collected. It may also be the result of failing to write off bad or doubtful debts to maintain profit levels. The ratio can be reduced by writing off fictitious debts so the proportion of bad debt write-offs, including credit note issues, should also be investigated.

Receivables days	$\dfrac{\text{Trade receivables} \times 365}{\text{Credit sales}}$

This ratio records the number of days it takes the organisation, on average, to collect its trade debts. Again fictitious billing schemes will increase this ratio as the debts won't be collected and will, of course, have to be disguised or written off.

Debt/equity (leverage or gearing) ratio	$\dfrac{\text{Total debt}}{\text{Total equity}}$

This ratio represents the proportion of the business funded by debt compared with shareholders' equity. There are many variations on this ratio which tend to centre around the definition of debt so one basis should be adopted and used consistently. It can include all liabilities including trade payables and overdrafts. This ratio should be reviewed in conjunction with any increases in trade payables.

Payables days	$\dfrac{\text{Trade payables} \times 365}{\text{Cost of sales}}$

This represents the number of days the organisation takes to pay its trade payables. A reduction in this ratio, without a concomitant reduction in cash balances or receivables days (see above), may indicate that debits to trade payables represent non-cash transfers such as the write-off of expenses from the income statement to the balance sheet. In any case it would require investigation.

Gross profit margin	$\dfrac{\text{Gross profit} \times 100}{\text{Turnover}}$

This is one of the most useful ratios as it represents the profit made by the organisation from selling its goods and services excluding indirect costs. If the organisation's pricing structure and type of customer base remain consistent this margin should remain reasonably constant whatever the level of activity, i.e. if sales double the cost of sales should also rise proportionally so the margin will remain the same despite the increase in activity. Because it includes the levels of turnover and inventory, significant increases in this ratio may indicate fictitious sales (because there is no matching increase in direct costs) or increased inventory levels not matched by increases in costs of sales, i.e. fictitious inventory.

$$\text{Net profit margin} \quad \frac{\text{Profit before interest and tax}}{\text{Turnover}}$$

This represents the profit on business activities after taking account of expenses. The points made above concerning the gross profit margin apply equally to this ratio. In addition it may be affected by the transfer of revenue costs to the statement of assets and liabilities, as WorldCom did, by capitalising maintenance costs, thus increasing the ratio artificially.

 **Beneish ratios**

Professor Massod D. Beneish of Indiana State University in the USA investigated the extension of the use of analytical review in detecting fraud by considering the effect that manipulation of revenues or understatement of costs had on the appropriate asset accounts.

His theory, outlined in a paper in 1999, was based on the analysis of 74 companies. These were known manipulators identified through Securities and Exchange Commission (SEC) enforcement actions or news media reports. He refined the number of firms to include only those which had restated earnings at the request of auditors or as a result of an investigation. This is to eliminate firms who corrected errors made in quarterly filings or which traded in areas where comparison with a source of non-manipulated data could not be made. In Table 12.3 the results of firms which had restated their results following investigation or voluntarily are described as 'manipulators'.

The source of non-manipulated data was 1708 firms in Standard and Poor's COMPUSTAT database sorted by industry and year to match the accounts of known manipulators.

The results of this are shown below together with comparative results for super-manipulator Global Crossing.

Table 12.3 Comparison of results of Global Crossing with results of companies who (a) did not have to restate results (non-manipulators) and (b) those who did (manipulators)

Index type	Non-manipulators	Manipulators	Global Crossing
Days' sales in receivables index	1.031	1.465	3.436
Gross margin index	1.014	1.193	1.177
Asset quality index	1.039	1.254	1.170
Sales growth index	1.134	1.607	3.964
Total accruals to total assets	0.018	0.031	−0.069

Source: Beneish (1999) and Golden, Skalak and Clayton (2006)

Global Crossing was a telecoms company which filed for bankruptcy in January 2002. Data relating to the accounts for 1998 and 1999, which were prior to Global Crossing's collapse in 2002, have been included for comparison.

The key ratios are:

1 DSRI – days' sales in receivable index.
2 GMI – gross margin index.
3 AQI – asset quality index.
4 SGI – sales growth index.
5 TATA – total accruals to total assets.

These will be explained in detail later.

Interestingly, given the comparisons above, the alleged crime of Global Crossing was artificial inflation of revenues. The ratios for sales can be seen to be well out of line with those of non-manipulators.

Some of the ratios, particularly the DSRI and the GMI, are extensions of the simpler ratios described above, but some are markedly more complex.

The ratios are calculated in this way:

Days' sales in receivables index (DSRI)

$$\frac{\text{Trade debtors/sales} - \text{current year (t)}}{\text{Trade debtors/sales} - \text{previous year (t} - 1)}$$

This is the ratio of days' sales in receivables in the first year in which manipulation occurs (year t) to the prior year (year t − 1). What it is looking for is an imbalance between the two years caused by an artificial inflation of sales resulting in a concomitant increase in receivables – unpaid of course as they are not genuine. An increase in receivables could, of course, be caused by a change in the policy for extending credit to customers or a general economic downturn – which is easily confirmed. The most likely explanation, however, is the possibility of revenue inflation.

Gross margin index (GMI)

$$\frac{\text{Sales} - \text{Cost of sales/sales} - \text{current year (t)}}{\text{Sales} - \text{Cost of sales/sales} - \text{previous year (t} - 1)}$$

The GMI is the ratio of gross margin in t − 1 to the gross margin in year t. Deterioration in GMI is an indicator of deteriorating prospects for the firm and an indication of the possibility of earnings manipulation.

Asset quality index (AQI)

$$\frac{1 - (\text{Current assets} + \text{Net fixed assets})/\text{Total assets} - \text{current year (t)}}{1 - (\text{Current assets} + \text{Net fixed assets})/\text{Total assets} - \text{previous year (t} - 1)}$$

This is the ratio of non-current assets other than property, plant and equipment (PPE) to total assets and it measures the proportion of total assets for which future benefits are potentially less certain. If the AQI is greater than 1 it suggests that the firm has been deferring costs, effectively by capitalising them as an intangible asset. Of course changes in this ratio could be attributed to perfectly sound reasons such as the acquisition of purchased goodwill or the capitalisation of genuine development costs but this, again, is relatively easy to check. Firms can legitimately capitalise costs as part of the construction of tangible fixed assets but experience of fraudulent manipulation indicates that areas such as intangible assets, overstatement of inventories and reductions in debt provisions are the most common areas for the manipulator.

Sales growth index (SGI)

$$\frac{\text{Sales} - \text{current year (t)}}{\text{Sales} - \text{previous year (t} - 1)}$$

This reflects the possibility of their being a manipulation of earnings. Firms which are growing are more likely to commit fraud because their financial position and the need to maintain investor confidence requires a steady increase in earnings and puts pressure on managers to achieve targets. A high return from this index calculation should prompt investigators to consider earnings manipulation. In Table 12.3 the index for Global Crossing was 3.964 which was considerably greater than the average return for manipulators of 1.607.

Total accruals to total assets (TATA)

$$\frac{(\Delta\text{Current assets} - \Delta\text{cash}) - (\Delta\text{current liabilities} - \Delta\text{current portion of long-term debt} - \Delta\text{tax}) - \text{depreciation and amortisation}}{\text{Total assets}}$$

Total accruals to total assets is indicative of management's attempts to finance losses through discretionary use of an accruals policy where cash is decreasing. It measures the change in (Δ) current assets and liabilities between t and t − 1 excluding the changes in cash and tax balances and excluding depreciation and amortisation.

All the indices included in this section are indicative and should be treated with care. As usual they should not be looked at in isolation but in conjunction with other evidence and the investigators' knowledge of the organisation. Any significant variation from the ratios calculated by Beneish for non-manipulators, shown above, should be investigated. Some of them may be potential red flags, others may lead nowhere, but used as an analysis and planning tool they can be very powerful and lead investigators in the right direction.

Specific types of organisational fraud

Following the use of analytical review techniques comes consideration of specific types of organisational fraud.

Clearly some are simple. Both Enron and WorldCom, for example, as part of their accounts manipulation strategy, simply capitalised expense costs as assets and somehow convinced the external auditors that this accounting treatment was valid. This is unsubtle and requires little in the way of disguise, but should equally be somewhat easier to detect than a complex fraudulent billing scheme.

As outlined above, ratio analysis can lead the investigator into key areas for investigation, but once there it is necessary to recognise the signs of deliberate and systematic manipulation of transactions and balances.

We will look at two types of fraudulent manipulation:

- improper revenue recognition, and
- asset valuation – which includes consideration of inventory and receivables values and the improper capitalisation of revenue costs.

Improper revenue recognition

Improper recognition of revenues falls into two categories:

- premature recognition of genuine revenue streams, and
- fictitious revenues – false sales to false customers.

Clearly any investigation into possible overstatement of revenues will be conditioned by awareness of the types of inherent risk indicators mentioned earlier, such as:

- Pressure on management to meet targets, either internal performance measures such as budgets or external expectations of the market or the Stock Exchange, particularly at half year or year ends.
- Announcement already made or hints given of performance levels which actual results may not support.
- The existence of bonus or reward schemes triggered by thresholds of achievement (bigger sales = bigger profits – particularly if there are no awkward costs to worry about!).
- 'Earn out' deals based on profit targets where the new corporate structure has increased costs without increasing sales thus lowering the profits on which the earn out is based.
- To resolve an unexpected shortfall in sales, for example, following the loss of a major customer.

It is easy to underestimate the ability of management to carry through these practices. The auditor looking to test controls in the revenue transaction cycle or to verify year end debtor balances will be presented with what seem to be genuine documents evidenced at a senior level in the organisation. There have been several instances where companies, often subsidiaries based off-site, have inflated sales for some particular reason, whether it was to enable employees to reach some sort of target or simply in an attempt to show the subsidiary or division was performing better than it actually was. In most cases the fraudulent inflation of revenues has escaped the external auditors.

Traditional auditing textbooks make great play, in systems-based auditing, of the testing of controls in the sales/revenue cycle and the importance of good cut-off testing which is designed to identify instances of premature revenue recognition; however some of the techniques used by managers would not be detected by conventional testing. This particular type of accounting fraud featured heavily in the US cases of Enron and WorldCom, so audit firms were wise to raise the profile of the possibility of this type of fraud in their audit risk evaluations of their clients.

The fundamentals of the techniques employed to do this fall into two basic types:

- accelerating bona fide revenues so that, for example, the whole of the proceeds of a long-term contract are taken in year one instead of being amortised into revenue over a number of years, and
- what is colloquially known in the USA as 'channel stuffing' whereby, for example, a manufacturer makes a large delivery to a distributor on a sale or return basis and records the delivery as a sale.

Manipulation techniques for the investigator to watch out for include:

- Accelerating deliveries or holding open the books to include transactions which were more properly those of a later period.
- Overstating the percentage of completion on contracts in progress.
- Revenues from linked contractual arrangements are taken even though the specific service to which the arrangements relates may not have been delivered, e.g. support or maintenance fees for a period of years in connection with software supplies.
- Sales under sale or return or so-called 'bill and hold' arrangements where there is a transfer of title to goods to the customer but actual delivery is deferred – consequently the revenues are recognised as turnover and, if the manipulator is really cheeky, the goods can also be included in inventory.
- Recognition of sales where there is a right of return without taking account of the estimated value of returns.
- Recognising gross turnover as principal when really acting as agent.
- Understatement or disguising of allowances, discounts etc.
- Recognising as revenue transactions which are not normally classified as sales such as goods on consignment, sales with special conditions, goods shipped for trial or evaluation.
- Fictitious sales – falsification of inventories, shipping documents and invoices.

Detection

Detection techniques involve the use of analytical procedures (above), as well as some fundamental audit procedures.

Key indicators or this type of activity are:

- unusual sales patterns
- weak or ineffective cut-off procedures
- discrepancies in documentation between invoices and deliveries
- discrepancies between sales volumes and purchasing/production volumes
- revenues not in accordance with contracts
- large volumes of credit notes issued after the period end
- sales entries not within usual systems, i.e. 'special sales'
- long outstanding receivables
- irregularities in inventory levels or unexplained or unusual entries in inventory records
- transactions with unconsolidated third parties over which the organisation has control or a significant involvement
- involvement in partnerships or joint ventures audited by other firms and/or based overseas – particularly in countries with weak or non-existent disclosure requirements, and
- sales revenues not matched by cash generation.

Exhibit 12.5	Fraud example – Parmalat and the Bank of America balance

The questions began in December 2003 when Parmalat had difficulty making a €150m bond payment. The company, which had 36,000 employees, was supposed to have been sitting on €3.95bn in cash, so Italian bankers were puzzled by its predicament. Parmalat's founder, Calisto Tanzi, brushed bankers' concerns aside, saying the company had a bit of a liquidity problem.

Parmalat's problems quickly reached epic proportions after it made the extraordinary admission that the €3.9bn it thought it had in the bank did not exist. The money was supposedly in a Bank of America account held by Bonlat, a subsidiary based in the Cayman Islands.

Bank of America said there was no such account.

Parmalat's primary auditor was Deloitte & Touche, but the Milan branch of Grant Thornton dealt with some of the company's subsidiaries, including Bonlat. When Grant Thornton checked with Bank of America, the auditor received a letter on Bank of America letterhead confirming the existence of the account. However, Bank of America said the letter was forged.

Investigators have been trying to find out if the money ever existed in the first place. There are suspicions that company executives invented contracts that were shown to the banks in order to raise cash that was then used to cover up day-to-day losses.

'The money was there in the first place but it got lost along the way', a US analyst said. Some press reports say as much as €10bn has disappeared from the company's accounts.

Source: Tran and Jay (2004); copyright Guardian News & Media Ltd, 2004.

Asset misstatement

Asset misstatement includes a multitude of sins (see Exhibit 12.5). Basically the principles for the fraudster here are to:

- disguise losses due to misappropriation of assets by capitalisation
- inflate asset values so as to increase the value of the business, and
- capitalise costs more properly charged to revenue thus increasing profits and asset values.

Deliberate manipulation of the values of assets and their corresponding effect on the income statement include:

- Deliberate overvaluation of inventories including the value of work in progress.
- Not writing off obsolete, slow-moving or valueless inventories.
- Improper capitalisation of expenses as part of asset value, e.g. capitalisation of ongoing maintenance costs, inclusion of selling or marketing costs as part of asset values or capitalisation of interest costs on non-specific loans.
- Capitalisation of research expenditure.
- Classification of research expenditure as development costs or over-valuation of development expenditure based on non-existent products or over-optimistic returns from future products as yet undeveloped.
- Over-valuation of unlisted investments.

- Fictitious investments – held in remote locations or with mysterious third parties (e.g. balances in offshore banks) where direct verification is difficult or impossible due to local disclosure restrictions.
- Suppression of sales of investments. The idea is to report sales proceeds of investments as income but still uphold carrying value in accounts by suppressing sales documents.
- Reclassification of inter-company debt as receivables including transfers of debt from subsidiaries to non-consolidated entities.
- Misclassification of investments to avoid write-downs of value.
- Use of complex derivative instruments – upholding at a value in excess of the values of the underlying assets from which the instruments are derived.
- Over-valuation of complex financial instruments where there is no market or the market has collapsed.

Detection methods

Detection methods will include analytical procedures but also some traditional audit hard slog of checking the details of transactions. If manipulation has occurred one incidence may well lead rapidly on to another as fraudsters tend to be consistent and often creatures of habit – what works once will work again!

Detection methods include:

- Substantive audit-type procedures on all significant balance sheet items. All major asset acquisitions to be matched with invoice, insurance and title documentation.
- Examine all transactions involving sale and purchase of assets to and from associated or related ventures.
- Analytical review – examine reasons for changes in asset ratios over time.

Fraudulent inventory

Inventory is a key figure in the financial statements because of its effect on profit and asset values. Of course the fraudster cannot simply increase inventory year by year without increasing the overall size of the organisation, as progressive increases in stock values without increases in sales and costs of sales will appear ludicrous. It may be therefore that over-inflated inventory is also an indicator of revenue inflation.

Warning signs here are:

- The inclusion of inventory that cannot be physically verified for some reason.
- Problems with shipping, storage etc. documentation.
- Unusually large purchase orders for excessive quantities.
- Goods on sale or return schemes included in inventory.
- Reversals or alterations to book inventory records after the reporting period.
- Weak or non-existent cut-off procedures.
- Inter-company or inter-plant movement during stock counts.
- Falsifying shipping documents to show stock in transit.
- Changes in stock levels with no corresponding increase in creditors or accruals.
- Changes to reported gross profit margins not matched by individual transaction margins.

Detection methods centre around:

- Substantive audit-type procedures on inventory transactions. This will include sample checks on movement and pricing checks.
- Matching of inventory numbers per the accounting records with those shown in management and financial accounts.
- Review of the basis of valuation of work in progress.
- Examination of contract expenses for indicators of bribes – these will include:
  - round sum payments with no detailed documentation, often authorised by a senior manager or director
  - commissions for unspecified services
  - excessive expenses refunds poorly supported by documentation, and
  - fees unsupported by adequate documentation.
- Review of internal and external audit examination of inventory recording procedures.
- Examine all transactions involving sale and purchase of inventory and work in progress to and from associated or related ventures.
- Analytical review – examine reasons for changes in asset ratios over time.

Asset manipulation can be difficult in well-run organisations with a strong internal audit presence. Often entries are not put through the books so that frauds are 'off the books', i.e. either involve taking assets before they are recorded in the system or altering the final version of the financial statements so they do not accord with the underlying records.

Benford's Law

Benford's Law can be a powerful tool for the forensic accountant to use when analysing data sets in an attempt to isolate fraudulent transactions. Its use in fraud detection is to detect false entries, i.e. fictitious entries where the numbers have been invented by the perpetrator and do not derive from any real transactions. An example of their use is in the detection of fraudulent expenses claims where many of the numbers have been dreamed up by the fraudster who then forges documentation, or fails to submit any.

Briefly, the test is based on the number of times any particular digit might be expected to occur in a particular position in a set of numbers. As far as the forensic accountant is concerned this is an observable phenomenon which occurs when looking at data sets of numbers which have been derived from other numbers, i.e. numbers which have been multiplied, divided or raised to a power.

The rather complex mathematics of the proof of this is beyond the scope of this book (and certainly of its author) but one statement for the mathematically minded which will hold true is that combining distributions of unrelated numbers gives a distribution of distributions, which will tend to conform to Benford's Law.

The observations made by Frank Benford revealed that about 30 per cent of numbers had the figure 1 as the first digit, about 19 per cent had 2 and only 4.5 per cent

Exhibit 12.6   Benford's Law – an example of the normal curve

The proportion of first digits in any representative sample of a given set of numbers is shown below:

First digit	Proportion
1	0.31
2	0.18
3	0.13
4	0.09
5	0.08
6	0.07
7	0.06
8	0.05
9	0.04

When illustrated it gives a curve like this:

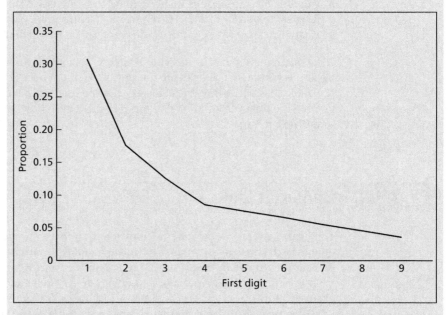

This can be repeated for second numbers, third numbers, etc., using data-mining software. Any deviation from this 'normal curve' is a warning sign that something may be amiss!

had 9 as a first digit. Without maths the logic of why this is so can be considered like this. Consider the assets of a business worth £1,000,000:

- to become £2,000,000 the business has to double in size
- to become worth £3,000,000 it only has to grow by 50 per cent, and
- to become worth £4,000,000 it has to grow by one third – and so on.

In short, the distance from 1 to 2 is considerably greater than that from 2 to 3 and much less than that between 8 and 9; consequently lower numbers are likely to be much more prevalent than higher numbers.

Clearly the forensic accountant will need the appropriate tool for the job but there is software available which will carry out the analysis.

Exhibit 12.7　Fraud example – the loan officer

During a bank audit the investigators analysed the first two digits of credit card balances written off as uncollectible.

The graph showed a large spike at 49.

An analysis of those amounts, i.e. from £480 to £499 and £4,800 to £4,999 showed that the spike was caused by amounts between £4,800 and £4,999.

The limit for approval of a write-off of a balance by a loan officer at one managerial level was £5,000 and it was quickly established that one person was responsible for the bulk of the write-offs. It turned out that the individual was involved with a circle of friends who applied for credit cards: when their balances approached the credit limit of £5,000, he wrote them off.

An example of the use of Benford's Law in an investigation is illustrated in Exhibit 12.7 (see also Table 12.4).

The first digit test is, in essence, a reasonableness test – it can be used to indicate areas of possible anomalies and direct the investigator's attention. Second and third digit tests can be used to refine the sample further.

However, caution must be exercised when applying this technique to sets of numbers. Not all data sets will conform to Benford's Law. Table 12.5 illustrates examples of situations where the application of Benford's Law would not be appropriate.

Some of these anomalies speak for themselves – where numbers are assigned by computer there is no test, price points and fixed selling prices will tend to produce peaks and throw out what look like anomalies, i.e. points on the curve which don't fit the graph, but the reasons for these should be fairly obvious.

Clearly Benford's Law can be a powerful tool but one which must be used with some circumspection. It can be quite easy to come up with an array of false positives

Table 12.4 When Benford's Law analysis is likely to be useful

Sets of numbers that result from mathematical combinations	Receivable amounts (Quantity × Price) Creditors (Number purchased × Price)
Transaction level data	Sales, expenses, disbursements
Large data sets	Full year's transactions
Accounts that appear to conform, i.e. when the mean of a set of numbers is greater than the median and the skewness is positive	Most sets of accounting numbers

Source: Durtschi, Hillison and Pacini (2004)

Table 12.5 When Benford analysis is unlikely to be useful

Assigned numbers	Invoice numbers, payment reference numbers etc.
Numbers influenced by psychology	Prices set at thresholds, e.g. £1.99 or ATM withdrawals
Accounts with large numbers of specific numbers	Accounts recording fixed payments, e.g. £100 refunds or parking fines
Accounts with built in maxima or minima	Asset accounts with a minimum spend amount
Where no transaction is recorded	Bribes, backhanders etc.

Source: Durtschi, Hillison and Pacini (2004)

(identifying a fraud when none is present) if the technique is used with inappropriate data sets.

Such an analysis may, of course, highlight system failures or operating problems but completely fail to detect fraudulent transactions. Research indicates that most data derived from combining numbers will be suitable and it is best if the whole data set is analysed, not just a sample.

Bribery and corruption

This subject could be worth a chapter of its own as it is becoming a major issue for UK companies operating overseas and with those connected in some way with US companies. However, we will look at it in the context of each aspect of bribery and corruption. Regulators are taking an increasingly dim view of bribery and corruption and several large companies have, in recent years, faced enquiries about possible corruption in international trading.

Even if it can be demonstrated that the company has not committed any illegal acts, the very fact of being subject to an enquiry results in:

- Increased reputational risk – this can have a serious effect on future business as companies with suspect reputations may not be invited to tender for large contracts even if nothing has been proven. Mud sticks.
- Costs and time involved in dealing with the information requests and accommodating the investigators. This can involve a lot of senior management time and legal costs.
- Disclosure of previously confidential details. Any reports made on behalf of public bodies may become public property. These may reveal details of methods and approaches which could be beneficial to competitors.

So far, in this book, we have looked at:

- the legal position (Chapter 3)
- dysfunctional organisations and how they influence the behaviour of employees (Chapter 4), and
- corruption of employees within the organisation (Chapter 6)

so now we need to look at bribery and corruption as a way of doing business, in other words corruption sanctioned either overtly or covertly by management.

The risks from bribery are a growing concern for both large and small companies which can be confronted with demands for bribes, faced with competitors acting corruptly or undermined by employees violating their codes of conduct. The increasing enforcement of foreign bribery laws, the imposition of record fines and the threat of criminal penalties for company directors and employees are giving enterprises pause for thought.

New pressures are coming from socially responsible investment funds and indices which are adding anti-bribery criteria to their screening procedures. In addition, development banks and export credit agencies are stepping up their due diligence and introducing debarment sanctions for companies engaging in corrupt behaviour. As a result, responsible companies understand the need to guard and promote their reputation for integrity and responsibility as stakeholders become less tolerant of lapses.

Exhibit 12.8   **Bribery and corruption – Mabey & Johnson**

In a landmark case, the steel bridge manufacturer Mabey & Johnson Ltd became the first company to be prosecuted in the UK for corrupt practices in overseas contracts and also for breaching a United Nations embargo on trade with Iraq.

Already under investigation for making payments during 2001/2002 to the Iraqi government relating to contracts to supply bridges bought by Iraq with revenue controlled by the UN under the 'oil-for-food' programme, Mabey & Johnson voluntarily reported to the SFO in 2008 that it had made corrupt payments to officials in Jamaica and Ghana on supply contracts with the governments in those countries.

The Iraq payments assisted the then Iraqi government under Saddam Hussein to bypass UN scrutiny and acquire funds that could be used for other than humanitarian or infrastructure development purposes. The corrupt payments in Jamaica and Ghana were required to ensure that the company would be awarded contracts.

In negotiations with the SFO, the current management of Mabey & Johnson admitted to not only the Jamaica and Ghana payments but also to similar practices in Bangladesh, Mozambique, Angola and Madagascar. The company agreed to plead guilty to the Jamaica and Ghana offences and to the UN sanctions busting and agreed that it would be subject to financial penalties and to an independent monitoring regime reporting to the SFO. In September 2009 Crown Court judge Lord Rivlin imposed fines, confiscation and costs on the company. Reparations are also to be paid by the company to the UN and to the governments of Jamaica and Ghana. In total the financial penalty amounts to around £6.6 million, including a fine of £3.5m.

Source: Serious Fraud Office (2008)

An essential element of corporate social responsibility is honest and transparent trading. Bribery and corruption create a disincentive to trade as well as uneven trading conditions that can damage economic systems and the individuals within them.

So, however entrenched bribery and corruption may appear, it is very important that high standards of business integrity are maintained. UK law makes it illegal to bribe foreign public or private officials or office-holders (Chapter 3). Any UK national or company can be prosecuted in the UK for this crime – even if no part of the offence took place in the UK. A company can also be held criminally liable if it can be shown to have authorised, directed or actively connived in an act of bribery by any of its overseas subsidiaries, by virtue of the laws of incitement and conspiracy. This would include, for example, directing a subsidiary to pay a bribe or providing the necessary funds to a subsidiary, knowing that they were to be used for a bribe (Exhibit 12.8).

There are a number of steps that can be taken to combat bribery and corruption by the organisation. The steps that follow are based on an anti-bribery programme methodology devised by Transparency International and reference should be made to their website for the complete programme.

The key features of a strong anti-bribery programme are:

- An organisation should develop a programme that articulates clearly and in reasonable detail values, policies and procedures to be used to prevent bribery from occurring in all activities under its effective control. The anti-bribery programme should be consistent with all laws relevant to countering bribery in all the jurisdictions in which the organisation transacts its business.

- The board of directors or equivalent body should commit to an anti-bribery policy and provide leadership, resources and active support for management's implementation of the programme. The chief executive officer is responsible for ensuring that the programme is carried out consistently with clear lines of authority.
- The organisation should develop the programme in consultation with employees, trade unions or other employee representative bodies. Compliance with the programme should be mandatory for employees and violations of the programme should be subject to disciplinary action.
- The policy should prohibit all forms of bribery whether they take place directly or through third parties, i.e. agents, contractors or representatives overseas or subsidiaries located outside UK jurisdiction.
- The policy should make it clear that no employee will suffer demotion, penalty, or other adverse consequences for refusing to pay bribes even if such refusal may result in the enterprise losing business.
- The organisation should establish and maintain an effective system of internal controls to counter bribery, comprising financial and organisational checks and balances over its accounting and record-keeping practices and other business processes related to the programme.
- The organisation should maintain, available for inspection, accurate books and records that properly and fairly document all financial transactions and should not maintain 'off-the-books' accounts.
- The enterprise should subject the internal control systems, in particular the accounting and record-keeping practices, to regular review and audit to provide management assurance on their design, implementation and effectiveness.
- The organisation should also contractually require its agents and other intermediaries to keep proper books and records available for inspection by the enterprise's auditors or investigating authorities.
- The organisation should be open about payments to political parties and charities and not use these as a pretext for bribery.
- 'Facilitation payments', i.e. small regular payments made to oil the wheels, are bribes and these should also be prohibited.
- The organisation should implement its programme and use its influence to encourage an equivalent programme in other business entities in which it has a significant investment or with which it has significant business relationships.
- The organisation should conduct a form of due diligence before entering into any joint venture or consortium and before appointing agents and other intermediaries.
- The enterprise should ensure that joint ventures and consortia over which it maintains effective control have programmes consistent with its own.
- All agreements with agents and other intermediaries should require prior approval of management. Agents and other intermediaries should contractually agree to comply with the enterprise's programme and be provided with appropriate advice and documentation explaining the obligation.
- Compensation paid to agents and other intermediaries should be appropriate and justifiable remuneration for legitimate services rendered.
- The organisation should conduct its procurement practices in a fair and transparent manner. It should avoid dealing with contractors and suppliers known or reasonably suspected to be paying bribes. It should undertake due diligence, as appropriate, in evaluating prospective contractors and suppliers to ensure that they have an effective anti-bribery programme.

- The organisation should make known its anti-bribery policies to contractors and suppliers. It should monitor significant contractors and suppliers as part of its regular review of relationships with them and have a contractual right of termination in the event that they pay bribes or act in a manner inconsistent with the enterprise's.

The Transparency International corruption perceptions index shows that, as one might expect, the most corrupt countries are also some of the poorest countries in the world, but other perhaps not so poor countries also feature quite highly on the list. Countries such as China, India, Argentina, Turkey and Brazil feature at the wrong end of the corruption index, yet some of these are vast potential markets which UK companies are competing to enter or develop.

Management may well take the view, rightly or wrongly, that having somewhat idealistic policies and regulation is all very well but the reality of international competition is that big bribery and corruption in some form or another always has been and always will be the way to do business. In some countries bribes may be extorted by corrupt officials where they have the power to grant permits or certificates or may be a voluntary act by the payer designed to put them one step ahead of the competition.

The problems may be compounded by weak inter-governmental co-operation, low levels of transparency and disclosure and local laws which are often vague, ill defined and poorly enforced within the contracting country. Whatever the cause, in the UK, this will be an illegal act and it may well be the task of the forensic investigator to attempt to uncover it.

The problems for the forensic investigator are twofold:

- Secrecy – senior management are aware of the legal position and the potential costs of being caught out. They should be only too aware that revelations that the organisation has committed corrupt acts may be very damaging in both personal and corporate terms. Clearly they will take steps to disguise such payments so that they are not accidentally revealed to auditors or even known to lower-level managers within the organisation.
- Complexity – some contracts, particularly for infrastructure developments or, say, in the armaments industry, will be complex and involve a number of contractors, subcontractors, even sub-subcontractors not to mention experts or advisers such as engineers, quantity surveyors, architects, geologists, lawyers etc. The UK company may be a subcontractor or a main contractor but on large projects may only be one of many.

The project structure may be as shown in Figure 12.2, which provides some idea as to the scale of the problem. Corruption could take place at many levels within the contract. It could be built into the contract price, it could come in the form of fees, commissions and discounts, pricing of materials or services, it could be at the level of a contracting government, local officials, service providers, power and water companies or at any point in the performance of the contract.

What the forensic investigator has to consider is:

- Where in the hierarchy does the organisation come, i.e. is it a main contractor or a sub-subcontractor?
- Who might be the recipient of any form of bribe or corrupt payment?
- How might such a payment be made?

The idea behind trying to identify these factors is to attempt to discover the payment method. The key point is this: however the bribe is paid funds have to leave

Figure 12.2 A complex international infrastructure project

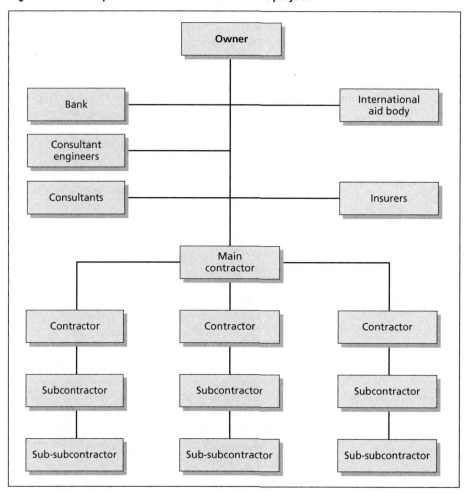

the paying company in some way either to reimburse an agent or third party, to fund some related party or bank account used for corrupt payments ('slush fund') or to pay off the corrupt official directly by transferring money to an overseas bank account.

Approaches must vary to fit the situation but key areas will be:

Ask the directors and senior managers about corrupt payments. Ask them to provide a Letter of Representation ratified by the board and minuted to the effect that no such payments have been made. This is designed to pressure directors into owning up.

Using whichever techniques are appropriate using IT searches (Chapter 13) to look for:

- transfers of funds to related parties with limited documentation
- transfers from related parties to overseas jurisdictions
- discounts, fees and commissions paid
- payments to overseas agents
- round sum payments

- pricing adjustments
- 'additional' fees or 'exceptional charges'
- transfers to overseas bank accounts in known tax havens
- transfers of funds with no obvious commercial purpose
- establishment of subsidiaries, partnerships or joint ventures in areas with limited disclosure requirements, and
- use of bank accounts with specific designations which are only used for a limited number of payments.

In addition, analytical review techniques could be used to look at contract costs, in particular payments to agents, consultants and subcontractors. These will be based on a comparison of the levels agreed to be paid in the original contract documentation with the levels or amounts actually paid.

Tracking such payments can be difficult and will require a thorough understanding of the documentation and the terms of the contract. The investigators should attempt to obtain the co-operation of the organisation wherever possible. Anecdotal evidence indicates that, once an investigation has commenced and management realise that corruption is suspected or has been discovered, co-operation is forthcoming in an attempt to mitigate penalties. This does not remove the requirement for investigators to carry out a full investigation to discover the scope and extent of what has happened. Management, after all, have broken the law and lied already so it is not beyond the bounds of possibility that they will continue to try to disguise the full extent of their corrupt activity.

 ## False investment (Ponzi) schemes

This is not strictly the area for the forensic accountant as they are quite often serious frauds which are investigated by the regulators. However, information on how to spot one is included here mainly for completeness as it is a form of management fraud. Ponzi schemes are named after Charles Ponzi who invented this particular fraud in the nineteenth century using International Postal Reply coupons, an unlikely idea nowadays but extremely relevant at the time.

In a classic Ponzi scheme, the promoters' promise to invest client money but instead use it for something else, usually themselves, create fictitious profits and when investors ask for their earnings or principal, they pay them with money from new investors. Ponzi schemes can keep going until someone becomes suspicious, there is an economic downturn and large numbers of investors wish to withdraw money or the promoter has extracted so much that there is not enough money left to pay investors and the scheme collapses.

No two Ponzi schemes are alike, which makes them hard to spot, except in retrospect. The standard 'if it looks too good to be true, it is', may not help here because Ponzi schemes don't always promise enormous returns. The profits don't have to be spectacularly large. Bernard Madoff's promised returns were not spectacular, but they we above market returns and, above all, they were consistent. In one instance Madoff investors were getting a 10 per cent return on investment whilst other forms of investment were paying as high as 30 per cent. However, Madoff continued to pay 10 per cent when the returns from other investments had collapsed.

There are several warning signs.

The scheme promises a minimum return, or steady returns

Any promise of a stated return, no matter how big or small, should be a warning because if the market goes up and down, most investments go up and down with it. A history of consistent returns regardless of market conditions should be treated with caution.

Scheme promises low risk

All investment involves some level of risk, particularly when the investor moves away from conventional investment sources such as regulated banks, building societies or pension/insurance-based schemes regulated by a body such as the Financial Services Authority. Any scheme which promises high(ish) rewards or consistent rewards coupled with a low level of risk is clearly something to be scrutinised closely. There is a direct correlation between risk and reward – the higher the reward sought, the greater the risk is likely to be.

The offer is pitched as something exclusive

Part of Madoff's appeal was his funds were pitched as something only available to somebody who was really somebody. He confined his activities to a particular social circle or recommendations from selected agents and even turned people down. This, of course, merely increased the attraction for a particular type of investor.

Pressure to act

In many cases potential investors are put under pressure to make quick decisions. They are told the offer is only open for a short space of time, or that the number of investors is limited. Legitimate investment opportunities are rarely very time-sensitive, the object of the fraudulent scheme is to get the investors signed up before they have time for reflection.

The offer comes from someone you know

Many Ponzi schemes do not advertise and rely on word of mouth to grow (Exhibit 12.9). Because the initial investors see the promised returns they become enthusiastic promoters of the scheme and tell their friends the good news. Alternatively schemes will be promoted within a relatively narrow circle or group so that word can spread quickly.

Pressure to reinvest

Sadly the history of Ponzi schemes shows a depressing tendency for investors who have made money and cashed out to reinvest. Clearly the thought pattern is that they have been successful once so surely it will be OK and they will continue to prosper. This aids the promoters of the scheme as they don't have to find new investors, just keep milking the old ones.

You can't explain what you're investing in

Frequently the promoters claim to have complex systems for 'beating the market' or arcane technology or some way of confounding the normal laws of probability. Any literature will be deliberately vague and opportunities for the promoters to

> ## Exhibit 12.9　Ponzi schemes – it can happen here
>
> Celebrities, sports stars and high-profile businessmen are among those duped into an alleged £80 million Ponzi scheme, that police claim was so convincing many of its victims cannot accept they have been scammed. London police suspect at least 600 people around the world have lost huge sums invested in an allegedly bogus high-yield fund.
>
> Clients of Business Consulting International (BCI), a Knightsbridge-based investment firm accused of running an £80 million Ponzi scheme, are being invited to public meetings by City of London Police to be told how their money was lost.
>
> They said it is one of the biggest Ponzi frauds ever detected in Britain. The alleged Ponzi scheme ran between 2007–08 and was marketed by word of mouth between friends and relatives, who were told that they could earn returns of between 6 and 13 per cent annually.
>
> Senior officers took the unusual step of holding a series of meetings at the City force's headquarters for hundreds of people embroiled in the alleged fraud, but investigators fear many savers caught up in the scheme are reluctant to accept their losses.
>
> Many of them were introduced by family members, friends and business associates they met at wealthy sports clubs and upmarket West End bars.
>
> Police said several alleged victims have already lost their homes, others have been declared bankrupt and some have attempted suicide. Two families lost huge sums of money they had saved from years of benefits to help pay for the long-term care of their disabled children.
>
> Officers remain in a desperate race to track down the missing money, some of which may be held in accounts in Dubai, the Cayman Islands and Thailand.
>
> They have seized assets worth about £1 million, including jewellery and watches, as well as £250,000 cash, but the finds are just a small portion of the alleged missing cash.
>
> *Source:* Moore (2009), O'Neill (2009)

explain their methods in detail will not be taken up. Information will be sparse and frequently companies involved will not file accounts or public documents.

There's no third party holding your money

In any legitimate investment, where the promoter is advertising a strategy of buying and selling shares, for example, a third party holds the actual sums invested and that party issues statements. Monies can be held in designated accounts and the investor can authorise its release as required. Handing over all the money to the promoter, whether or not they issue statements, denies that fundamental overview of activity which an independent deposit holder would have. Lack of transparency, statements or investment details is a clear sign something is wrong – legitimate companies have to account for the money they hold.

Clearly this idea is no good for the promoters as they want their hands on the money – it is not going to be invested.

You're investing in a market where interest rates are low, and the economy is rebounding from a fall

This creates an environment where promises of above normal returns will stimulate investment by people hoping to beat the market. This, again, is designed to attract investors with spare cash. If the scheme is marketed discreetly and confined to a particular clientele, and providing its claims are not too outrageous it will find a receptive group of investors prepared to take a risk. SFO officials are predicting a growth in the number of Ponzi schemes as interest rates remain low.

Carousel fraud

Carousel fraud, also known as missing trader intra-community (MTIC) fraud, is a particular sort of VAT fraud, often characterised by a circular chain of transactions, where the goods are moved about to create fictitious transactions which can end up back with the original perpetrator of the fraud. It characteristically involves high-value, high-volume goods such as mobile phones, computer chips and electronic goods such as MP3 players. Frequently, only the people at the ends of the chain are the actual fraudsters, using innocent intermediary dealers and wholesalers to perpetrate the fraud.

In its very simplest form, known as 'acquisition fraud', the fraudster brings goods into the UK from another EU country. This requires the fraudster to register for VAT. They then sell the goods to a UK business and properly charge VAT. The customer is entitled to reclaim that VAT as input tax but, before the output tax becomes payable on his VAT return, the fraudster absconds with the cash.

A more complicated form is the traditional carousel fraud. Goods are imported VAT-free but are not sold for consumption in the home market. The goods are sold through a series of companies, each liable to VAT, before being exported, possibly even back to the original seller.

In this type of fraud, the first link in the chain often goes missing without accounting for the VAT, simply keeping the VAT they have charged. The final link in the chain re-exports the goods and reclaims the VAT it has paid as input tax before disappearing. The government has suffered a net loss, having repaid VAT to the last link in the chain without having been paid it by the first link. This carousel can be perpetuated through several EU countries and losses to the Exchequers can mount quickly.

The scale of the problem is very large as these tend to be done on a massive scale. One estimate is that such frauds cost EU countries £74 billion per year.

Such frauds are usually outside the province of the forensic accountant and are investigated by government agencies, principally HMRC and the SFO. They are very difficult to anticipate as, up until the point the trader absconds all the paper work looks and is genuine. Many quite routine transactions will have precisely the same type of activity, and, indeed many quite legitimate traders may be involved in buying and selling on these goods.

The only suspicious activity lies in the nature of the goods, the size of the transactions and the fact that companies involved may not have a trading history, having been set up for the purposes of the fraud.

The EU Commision has recently changed the VAT rules in an attempt to beat such frauds. Under a reverse charge mechanism, the supplier does not charge VAT but it is accounted for by the customer who, if a fully taxable person, deducts this VAT at the same time. The need for an effective payment to the Treasury is therefore removed as well as the theoretical possibility to commit this type of fraud.

Ever-creative fraudsters have simply moved away from the types of goods affected by these new rules. In 2009 frauds involving EU Carbon Credits were detected, resulting an another change in the law exempting them from VAT, but this is outside the scope of this book.

In the next chapters we continue the process of fraud investigation by looking at the use of computers in the process of fraud detection.

Summary

- Directors and managers have been misrepresenting financial statements for many years in order to benefit themselves.
- These types of fraud often happen in divisions or subsidiaries remote from the centre.
- A combination of power, weak oversight and an appropriate rationale or motivation is required. Secrecy is a key component – this is known as the fraud diamond.
- There are key warning signs of the possibility of financial statement manipulation. These include pressure from external sources such as banks or creditors, heavily incentivised pay, or hiding excess profits or poor performance.
- External auditors should be alert to the possibility of fraudulent manipulation and be aware of warning signs.
- Internal audit is more familiar with company processes and is in a position to detect anomalies.
- Variations from expected performance or a predominance of unusual transactions, especially at the end of reporting periods, are warning signs.
- Analytical review is a useful audit tool.
- Reports can be analysed in various ways to throw out variations over a period of time.
- Beneish ratios are a particular type of ratio analysis designed to highlight anomalies between accounting periods.
- Specific types of fraud include improper revenue recognition, suppression of costs or manipulation of asset valuations.
- When applied Benford's Law will throw out instances of fictitious numbers in a given sample.
- Bribery and corruption is a serious issue for companies which must increasingly have policies and procedures in place to combat it.
- These must be made to apply to contractors and agents overseas as well as local staff.
- There are clear warning signs which indicate the presence of a possible Ponzi scheme.
- These are based around results and promises which are at variance with market conditions and a culture of secrecy from the investing organisation.
- Carousel fraud is normally tackled by government bodies as it is international and often on a very large scale.

Case study

You are the CEO of Mightybig Corporation plc (Mightybig) a company listed on the London Stock Exchange. Mightybig is an electronics manufacturing company with interests worldwide. It also has interests in pharmaceuticals and commodity trading.

You earn a salary of £500,000 but if the profits of the company were to exceed £800m for 2009 you stand to earn a bonus of £2.5 million. If they don't you get nothing. Other potentially big bonus earners include the financial, sales and production directors, who could also earn bonuses of £1 million each. In addition you

▶

all four have share options and an announcement of very big profits would cause a big rise in the share price.

On the board there are four non–executive directors who only attend meetings and rely on the papers the executive directors send them.

There is an internal audit function reporting to the audit committee which comprises three of the non-executive directors and the non-executive chairman. This committee reports to the main board of directors.

Management accounts for the year put the profit at £750 million so at least another £50 million needs to appear if the bonuses are to be triggered and the share price rise achieved.

You and your fellow directors really want that bonus.

You have a good relationship with the auditors and don't really think that they are very effective in their checking as the audit only takes about four weeks and is founded on a risk-based strategy. There is little or no substantive testing as the internal control systems are considered to be excellent.

Required

- How would you set about 'earning' your bonus?
- What would be the effect on the published financial statements?
- What considerations would the external auditors have to take into account and how would this affect their audit work?

Bibliography

Beneish, M. (1999) The detection of earnings manipulation. www.baur.edu.

Bolognia, J. and Lundquist, R. (1987) *Fraud Auditing and Forensic Accounting*. John Wiley, Hoboken, NJ.

Devine, D. (2009) Three former Welsh State managers jailed for fraud. www.walesonline.co.uk.

Durtschi, C., Hillison, W. and Pacini, C. (2004) The effective use of Benford's Law to assist in detecting fraud in accounting data. *Journal of Forensic Accounting*, V, 1, 17–34.

Golden, T.W., Skalak, S.L. and Clayton, M.M. (2006) *A Guide to Forensic Accounting Investigation*. PriceWaterhouse Coopers LLP/John Wiley, Hoboken, NJ.

Goundar, S. (2009) Carousel fraud costs HMRC £2bn in VAT revenues. *Accountancy Age*, 6 August.

Herman, M. (2008) Greencore sacks three over accounts fraud. www.times.co.uk, 25 June.

Hopwood, W.S., Leiner, J.L. and Young, G. (2008) *Forensic Accounting*. McGraw-Hill, New York.

Jordan, B. and Kelly, L. (2008) Perfecting the investigative process. *Chartered Accountants Journal*, 87, 3, 16–19.

Moore, M. (2009) Celebrities lose out in British Bernie Madoff Ponzi fraud. www.telegraph.co.uk, 19 July.

Negrini, M.J. and Mittermaier, L. (1997) The use of Benford's Law as an aid to analytical procedures in auditing. *A Journal of Practice & Theory*, 16, 2, 52–67.

O'Neill, S. (2009) Even as police investigate £80m Ponzi scheme some victims can't believe it. www.thetimes.co.uk, 20 July.

Reuters (2009) *How Carousel Fraud Works.* Thompson Reuters, London.

Scott, M. (2009) *Red Flags of Ponzi Schemes.* Association of Certified Fraud Examiners, Austin, TX.

Serious Fraud Office (2006) *Transtec plc.* Serious Fraud Office Press Room. London.

Serious Fraud Office (2008) *Historic Cases – Mabey & Johnson: Overseas Corruption.* SFO, London.

Serious Fraud Office (2008) *Historic Cases – Independent Insurance.* SFO, London.

Silverstone, H. and Sheetz, M. (2007) *Forensic Accounting and Fraud Investigation,* 2nd edn. John Wiley, Hoboken, NJ.

Tran, M. and Jay, A. (2004) Parmalat: all you need to know about the collapse of the Italian dairy giant. www.guardian.co.uk, 6 October.

Transparency International (2009) *Defence Against Corruption Project.* Transparency International UK, London.

United States District Court Southern District of New York: in re Parmalat securities litigation Master Docket number 04 MD 1653 (LAK).

Wells, Joseph T. (2001) Irrational ratios. *Journal of Accountancy,* August, 80–83.

Wells, Joseph T. (2004) *Corporate Fraud Handbook.* John Wiley, Hoboken, NJ.

Websites

www.accountancyage.com

www.acfe.com

www.business.timesonline.co.uk

www.emeraldinsight.com

www.hmrc.gov.uk

www.icaew.com/forensicaccounting

www.sfo.gov.uk

www.thetimes.co.uk

www.transparency.org.uk

www.telegraph.online

Chapter 13

The use of IT in fraud investigation

Learning objectives

After studying this chapter you should be able to:
- Identify external threats to IT systems including the use of viruses, worms and trojans and denial of service attacks
- Understand the risks from internal threats to MIS integrity
- Understand the principles of preserving digital evidence on suspect computers
- Develop an understanding of how data is stored
- Understand the principles of how data can be analysed for information to provide digital evidence
- Learn the difference between using IT to perform analyses of the data and the use of algorithms to generate fraud indicators
- Understand the importance of gathering non-financial evidence

Introduction

In this chapter we will concentrate first on defining what challenges the forensic investigator faces in dealing with various types of computer fraud, both external and internal, and we will look at how investigators use computer-based tools to find out what has happened and to gather the evidence they may need. Students should read this chapter in conjunction with Chapter 9 where we looked at computer risk management and forensic readiness.

It is not the function of this book to recommend software or to be a promoter for any particular software reseller. There are many and various packages on the market which will do what investigators wish with a greater or lesser degree of success. Of course some large accounting firms which carry out forensic investigations use bespoke software and what it can do and how it works is a closely guarded secret, but they also use proprietary software where this will generate the information they need.

The reality of forensic investigation is that the use of computer-based techniques will inevitably be a significant tool in the forensic investigators' toolbox, and investigators must be familiar with the basis of the techniques they will have to use in order to gather the evidence they need or to eliminate lines of enquiry. Organisations processing large volumes of data will not yield their secrets to the paper and pen; it is more likely that a combination of computer-assisted auditing techniques (CAATs) and specialised data mining software will reveal the diamonds hidden in the clay of the organisation's records.

The reader should be reassured that this chapter does not require any arcane skills of computing, nor, hopefully, does it teem with jargon.

The whole area of IT in forensic investigation is fraught with danger for two reasons. The first and main danger is contamination of evidence through inadvertent bad practice or poor training. The use of CAATs may well require the services of someone with a reasonable level of computer skills, whereas some are written to be idiot-proof and can be used by IT illiterate auditors. What is certainly not for idiots is forensic investigation of any hardware or software items which any suspected perpetrator may have been involved with. The key message here is:

IF IN DOUBT LEAVE IT ALONE!!

Some fraudsters have a level of sophistication in computing which may not be matched by their innocent colleagues. More than one investigation has been compromised or ended because an untrained person accesses a suspect machine whilst 'trying to help' whereupon:

- the hard drive promptly overwrites itself, or
- the access is carried out in such a way that the trail of evidence is lost.

The danger is that the 'chain of evidence' is broken and, as a consequence, the prosecution or action for recovery fails because the defence can allege that any computer-derived evidence has been compromised.

The defence in any subsequent legal action merely has to demonstrate that it was possible that some form of unauthorised access took place in the period between:

- the accused last using the machine, and
- the commencement of the forensic investigation

to be able to claim that their poor naive client was framed! Without proper evidence-based procedures any investigation can be severely compromised before it has properly begun, hence the relevance of the forensic readiness procedures detailed in Chapter 9.

The second danger is a legal one. Investigators must always be aware of the legal limits of what they are and are not allowed to do. Chapter 3 details the main provisions of the Regulation of Investigatory Powers Act which, for this purpose, relates to the interception of e-mails, and the Computer Misuse Act 1990 which could present a danger to the investigator if they access a computer which does not belong to them and which they have no permission to search.

Where the hardware and software belongs to the client this does not present a problem but where, say, a laptop belonging to the suspect is accessed without their permission the investigators could have committed an offence.

Computer crime taxonomy

Table 13.1 shows the most common types of computer-based fraud. For this purpose we are only looking at frauds against organisations – the question of frauds against individuals such as credit card cloning and identity theft are outside the province of this book and are covered perfectly adequately elsewhere.

In this book we will look in detail at the first category, alteration or theft of data files to hide fraud or to distort financial information, for the simple reason that whilst much computer-based crime is centred around malware, data theft and phishing, for example, these are not really the province of the forensic accountant.

Table 13.1 Computer crime taxonomy

Type of computer crime	Comprises

Alteration or theft of data files	• Changing data in order to:
	  • hide frauds, or
	  • distort financial information
	• Theft of information for sale to competitors

Unauthorised access to systems	This includes: • Attempts by external hackers to crack the computer security in order to steal data or information, such as customer identity details, or to compromise the system maliciously through the introduction of malware to damage a company's reputation • Denial of service attacks often accompanied by blackmail demands • Internal log-ons by unauthorised users in an attempt to view or copy information to which they are not entitled • So-called 'structured query language [SQL] injection' attacks where a hacker breaches the firewall and 'injects' software into a database programmed in SQL. This then searches for pin numbers, passwords or transaction records and passes them to external servers to sell on
Theft of time	Using a system for unauthorised purposes such as running an unauthorised business, shopping on E-bay etc.
Eavesdropping	Using packet sniffer tools to listen to traffic travelling between network computers to capture data
Software piracy	Copying and selling illegal copies of software

However, we will consider these as they can have serious ramifications for the client and the forensic accountant may well be called upon for advice.

We will look at computer fraud from the point of view of:

- external frauds – attacks from outside the organisation, and
- internal frauds – data manipulation and theft from inside.

External computer frauds

It could be argued that external computer frauds, which for this purpose are defined as assaults on the organisation from external sources, with or without inside help, are rather outside the scope of this book. However, forensic accountants should be familiar with what is after all one of the most pernicious problems which is currently exercising the minds of IT security managers everywhere.

The author's own organisation, Leeds Metropolitan University, has had its network defences tested many times and, whilst some of this might be attributed to computer studies students flexing their programming muscles, some of it has undoubtedly been far more serious attempts to defeat system security for some nefarious purpose.

It is now universally recognised that cyber crime is an international business run by criminal gangs. It has even escalated to government level. In 2008 during the conflict between Georgia and Russia concerted denial of service (DoS) attacks brought the Georgian web infrastructure down. The threat that terrorists pose to the World Wide Web is a real one. The effect would not necessarily be confined to individual users or organisations which might be affected, serious though this would be, it could result in such a loss of confidence that it might render the whole structure unusable.

Tackling such crime is a real problem and one which the forensic accountant should understand and appreciate.

Clearly this is a very technical area and the practicalities of dealing with computer security should be left to the experts. The aim here is to provide sufficient information to enable a basic understanding of the issues and approaches to the problems.

Modes of attack

External attempts to access confidential data fall into three basic categories:

1 Deceptions – where the perpetrators pretend to be what they are not, e.g. a bank or building society, and ask people to give up their details voluntarily.
2 Temptations – where individuals are asked to give up passwords and PINs in return for a supposed reward which of course never comes.
3 Attacks – computer hacking to get past firewalls to introduce malicious software, known as malware, into data or program files or to force organisations to pay up to prevent systems crashes caused by e-mail overload.

Deceptions

Examples of deceptions abound and it will be unusual for anyone who spends any time using e-mails not to have seen an example. These include:

- 'Phishing' e-mails where the gullible are asked to return confidential data such as passwords and ID confirmations to an address purporting to be a bank or regulatory authority. The usual approach is to pretend that the bank or building society is carrying out a 'security review' and would you (gullible person) kindly confirm your password, etc. by clicking on the enclosed link. The enclosed link will either lead to a fake website or, more worryingly, allow the system to download some form of computer virus or key logging software.

  Phishing emails are now a common method whereby malware is introduced into organisational systems. This malware takes the form of trojans, viruses or worms which do anything from:
    - simple malicious damage, wiping files, causing hardware to malfunction, etc., or
    - stealing confidential information and passing it back to the originator, to
    - recording key strokes, particularly at the log-on stage, thus revealing computer IDs and passwords which can subsequently be used to hack the system.
- Spoof websites purporting to be a bank or a genuine selling organisation. Respondents give credit card or password details which are then used by the spoofers to commit crime by emptying bank accounts or buying goods.

Temptations

Temptations play on three things – social engineering, human greed and that inner optimism which tells people 'it won't happen to me'.

Many people, when they see the possibility of a substantial return for very little effort, may feel a frisson of temptation. Fortunately the vast majority of us pass up the opportunity on the basis that if it seems too good to be true it probably is. However, a minority – enough to make the crime worthwhile – are eternally optimistic

---

Exhibit 13.1   Fraud example – the Swedish bank job

In January 2007 Swedish bank Nordea reported that it had lost approximately Kr 7-8m, about half a million pounds, due to a deliberately targeted electronic attack.

A phishing e-mail was sent to several of the bank's clients containing a trojan called haxdoor.ki. When the clients attempted to log on to their online banking service, using their confidential log-in information, the trojan harvested the information by directing the customers to a fake website, which, after the clients had entered their information, told them that the site was experiencing technical difficulties and to try again later. The criminals were then able to use the client information conveniently gifted to them to extract money from the customers' accounts.

The crime was believed to have been perpetrated by an organised Russian crime gang. The point to note is not just the technical ability displayed by the criminals, in using a tailor-made trojan to collect the data, but the level of planning and sophistication which went in to targeting and accessing the data.

Source: Espiner (2007)

and are prepared to take a risk. They respond to the approaches and, eventually, send money. They never see the promised return or their money again. Such frauds include:

- Online investment frauds where individuals set up fake investment opportunities or purport to sell shares in a company with a revolutionary new product – strangely people do send them money! Some of these are basic Ponzi-type schemes where an initial return is paid out to the first investors using money taken from later investors. Once enough victims have been attracted the promoters cash out and disappear. Some such schemes purport to raise money to promote a revolutionary, but of course phoney, product or service. Others take the form of online lotteries where many individuals buy tickets but few win.
- Advance fee frauds also known as Section 419 frauds named after the relevant section of the Nigerian Criminal Code – a popular crime largely instigated in West Africa. The instigator claims to be the possessor of millions of dollars which they are prepared to share with you but first they need your bank details so they can liberate the money – strangely these too work occasionally.

Exhibit 13.2   Fraud examples – advance fee fraud

Example one

Two Nigerians and a Frenchman were sentenced to prison for swindling people out of more than $1.2 million in a massive e-mail scam. The three men executed so-called advance fee frauds. Victims were told their help was needed distributing money for charity. In exchange, victims were promised they would get a commission that would go to the charity of their choice.

The victims were told they first needed to wire-transfer money for various fees. In some cases, victims were sent counterfeit cheques in order to the cover the fees, which bounced even though victims had already sent the money.

In one variation of the scam, people were sent an e-mail that purported to be from someone suffering from terminal throat cancer who needed help distributing $55 million in charity money. The victims were told they would get a 20 per cent commission that would go to a charity of their choice for their trouble.

To make the ruse seem more legitimate, the scammers sent photos of the supposed throat cancer victim, along with other fraudulent documents that ostensibly confirmed the $55 million.

Source: Kirk (2009)

Example two

Three men were sentenced at Southwark Crown Court for defrauding business loan applicants in the USA, Canada, Australia and New Zealand of downpayments made for phantom loans.

Operating from business premises in Brighton and in Darlington, the defendants conspired to defraud people overseas who responded to press advertisements for commercial loans. The fraudulent scheme required applicants to pay certain non-refundable advance fees to have their applications processed. However, no loans were forthcoming. Instead, further financial conditions would be imposed that proved impossible for the applicants to meet.

Consequently, the applicants would withdraw and thereby forgo their deposits.

Source: Serious Fraud Office (2003)

> ### Exhibit 13.3 Fraud example – TK Maxx
>
> Hackers stole credit and debit card details belonging to over 45 million customers of TK Maxx in an attack on the computer systems of the parent company TJX.
>
> Transaction details from January 2003 to June 2004 were accessed. TJX admitted that data was accessed from its systems in Watford, Hertfordshire and Massachusetts over an 18-month period from July 2005 to December 2006.
>
> The company confirmed information had been stolen from 45.6 million cards used in the UK and US between January and November 2003. However it did not know how many details were stolen from November 2003 to June 2004.
>
> It is the world's largest theft of credit card details. Two files from Britain were stolen and TJX may never know what was in those files.
>
> The company did, however, state that PIN numbers were not stolen as these were kept on a separate, encrypted, database. According to TK Maxx, about 75 per cent of the cards had either expired at the time of the theft, or the stolen information did not include the security code data contained on the card's magnetic strip.
>
> *Source:* Richards, Selb, and Brown (2007); Barrow (2007)

Attacks

Attacks on company network systems and the introduction of malware are perhaps the biggest e-crimes organisations face today. These attacks either involve the use of malicious software generically known as malware, which we can divide into viruses, trojans and worms, or direct attacks using spam in huge quantities (DoS attacks).

These attacks on systems security are designed to harvest data or, in the case of denial of service attacks, to encourage the victim to pay up to prevent it happening again – an old-fashioned protection racket with a cyber twist.

Viruses, worms and trojans

Table 13.2 summarises the salient features of the three most common types of hostile software. These are specifically designed to either damage computer systems or to obtain information from them which can be used by criminals to obtain money or goods or information of a confidential nature which they can then sell on.

The crimes are as old as civilisation – they are forms of burglary, theft and blackmail – the only difference is that these are perpetrated at a distance by extremely computer-literate individuals who do not have any face-to-face contact with the victims of their crime and can therefore react with complete ruthlessness in the commission of their crime. They can distance themselves from it (Chapter 4) and have the advantage of 'first go' so only extremely good defences and constant vigilance will keep them out.

Denial of service (DoS) attacks

A denial of service attack is one where an IP address (basically the numerical identifier of an individual computer on the Internet) is flooded with data to the extent that it becomes overloaded and ceases to function. Perpetrators use a chain of

Table 13.2 Computer malware

Virus	A computer virus is analogous to a human virus insofar as it has a range of effects from severe to mildly annoying. The virus will sit on the computer until the program is opened or run at which point it swings into action and starts to do what it was written to do.
	A virus cannot be spread without a human action to keep it going as they are almost always attached to an executable file (.exe), which means they can't infect the computer until the program is run or file is opened.
	People continue the spread of a computer virus, mostly unknowingly, by sharing infecting files or sending e-mails with (unwittingly one hopes) viruses as attachments.
	Virus effects can range from the mildly annoying to extremely destructive and they can cause severe damage to hardware or software.
	Anti-virus software should be updated constantly to deal with known viruses but new ones are constantly being invented.
Worm	A worm is similar to a virus. Worms spread from computer to computer, but unlike a virus, they can spread within a system or travel between systems without any human intervention. A worm takes advantage of file or information transport features on the system, which is what allows it to travel unaided.
	The biggest danger with a worm is its capability to replicate itself on the system, so rather than a computer sending out a single worm, as it would a single virus, it could potentially send out hundreds or thousands of copies of itself, with devastating effect.
	Due to the ability of a worm to replicate itself and its capability of travelling across networks the end result in most cases is that the worm consumes too much system memory (or network bandwidth), causing Web servers, network servers and individual computers to stop responding.
	Worms such as the Blaster Worm have been designed to tunnel into systems and allow malicious users to control computers remotely.
Trojan horse	A trojan horse may appear to be a piece of useful software but will damage a computer or network once installed and run on it. Users are tricked into installing the trojan because it comes disguised as legitimate software or files from a legitimate source, i.e. via an e-mail (see the section on phishing e-mails above). Trojans are often delivered through false e-mails.
	When a trojan is activated the results vary. Some are designed to be simply annoying by doing things like making characters fall off the screen or changing the desktop by adding silly desktop icons, others can cause serious damage by deleting files, destroying information or installing secret software which can reveal log-on information including passwords.
	Trojans are also known to create what is known as a 'back door' which will enable hackers to penetrate the system. Unlike viruses and worms, trojans do not reproduce by infecting other files, nor do they self-replicate.
Blended threat	A blended threat bundles some of the worst aspects of viruses, worms and trojans into one. Blended threats have the replicating capability of viruses and worms and the capacity of trojans to create a port into the system.
	They launch multiple attacks which could damage a local system and leave a back door. They use multiple modes of transport so they can replicate via e-mail, Internet relay chat (IRC) and file-sharing networks. They may damage several areas of a network at the same time by attacking, say registry, .exe and HTML files at the same time.
	Blended threats are considered extremely serious as they tend to be extremely destructive and can self-replicate.

slaved PCs known as 'bots' to create a 'botnet' which can then be used to launch the attack. The bots can be innocent home computers which, unknown to the users, have been hijacked to deliver data in the form of spam or e-mails to overwhelm the target.

DoS attacks are increasingly used by criminal gangs who attack businesses which rely on the Internet to trade such as online gaming or betting sites. The attack is

> ### Exhibit 13.4 Fraud example – denial of service attacks
>
> William Hill, Betdaq, Totalbet and UK betting all said they had been attacked or suffered extortion attempts prior to the Cheltenham Festival. The companies were threatened that further assaults would follow unless payment was made.
>
> The sites attacked are likely to show the characteristic pattern of increasing response times and then suddenly no response from the server as it gets overwhelmed. The attacks seem to be well co-ordinated as the servers being targeted are overwhelmed very quickly. Once attacked the websites can stay offline for hours. Gambling sites have been targeted because so many of the events they offer odds-on are time-limited.
>
> Attacks on betting sites have become increasingly commonplace since their first appearance three years ago. The latest spate follows reports last November of Eastern European crime syndicates using threats of computer hacking to extort pay-offs from online businesses in the UK.
>
> A spokesman for William Hill said 'We had and continue to have no intention of dealing with demands made by blackmailers.'
>
> *Source:* Out-Law.com (2004); Leyden (2004)

accompanied by a blackmail message to pay up or attacks will continue until the site has to be shut down. They have even been used against X-box Live players to force them out of online games and by activists (known as 'hacktivists') to attack environmental or political targets.

Dealing with viruses, worms and trojans requires an organisation-wide approach which will be quite likely to fail, to a greater or lesser degree, at some point. Networks are vulnerable and the bigger the network the more vulnerable it becomes, if for no other reason than the greater the number of users the more likely it is that a suspect e-mail will be opened or a password given away.

Even the best policies can be forgotten or ignored and the best system defensive tools may be thwarted by foolish or reckless behaviour by individuals who give in to temptation or even the simple spirit of enquiry – I wonder what happens if I click on this? Unfortunately constant vigilance and reinforcement of policies is the only way to deal with this problem, and human nature being what it is, those initiatives are bound to fail at some point. The organisation must be ready with its anti-malware tools and its diagnostics and should publish to its employees the effects of foolish behaviour and the cost to the organisation of rectifying it.

People who devise malware do so for two reasons:

1 For fun, because they can and to see if it works. They enjoy the anonymous notoriety of being the person who wrote the software which makes people's computers turn themselves off every hour on the hour for example. It's not dangerous – it's silly and annoying.

   Some individuals may do it because they enjoy doing damage for no reason – mindless vandalism appeals to them on some atavistic level so they write software which causes chaos and damage and, again, gain some perverse satisfaction from that.

2 For gain, for criminal purposes and, as might be imagined, this is by some distance the main reason why malware is circulated. It is done to obtain confidential data for use in crimes or to hold systems to ransom. This is now very much the province of organised crime.

These are ultimately more serious, because whilst system corruption can be annoying and cause delays and lost data it is rare for this to be a terminal event: good back-up procedures and anti-malware patches can usually sort the problem out in time. The theft of confidential information, however, can wreak damage which is not merely financial but reputational as well.

Before we look at defence remember:

- Attackers always have 'first go' advantage. There are, generally, no preliminary warnings – all of a sudden the network starts misbehaving or a DoS attack arrives out of the blue and starts to shut down all the Internet connections.
- Attacks come from anywhere. The Internet is truly global so attacks can be delivered well away from well-regulated and policed jurisdictions. The perpetrators, even if their attacks are defeated, may never be traced let alone brought to justice.

Attackers use distancing techniques to separate themselves from their targets. To them it is merely a game or an exercise in skill – they have no desire to empathise with the target or consider the problems they are causing. Hackers who have been caught generally show no remorse for their actions and, in some sections of society, may even be seen as heroes.

Computer-literate staff and technicians must recognise that most workers do not understand the computers they use every day and that if something goes wrong they ring the Helpdesk once the tried and tested remedial technique of switching it off and back on again fails to cure the problem! Consequently there is a first assumption by many people that if it's on the computer it must be OK. Many staff are slow to suspect an e-mail – after all they get dozens every day. The result, if staff are not vigilant and alert to what spam e-mails look like, for example, is a welcome door for the worm which, 24 hours later if not detected, will crash the system or worse.

Inside help

However, apart from the danger of employees blithely opening suspicious e-mails, there is another form of assistance that attackers get from inside the organisation. This takes the form of a corrupted current employee or a disgruntled former employee who takes away sensitive information. Research by computer consultants Ibas (now part of Kroll Associates) indicated that 65 per cent of British professionals admitted to stealing commercially sensitive information, including e-mail address books, sales presentations and technical product information.

In some cases staff who have left organisations find that their e-mail and passwords still function and they are able to access company information for some time after having left employment.

Several attempted frauds have used a combination of external attacks and inside information provided by corrupted staff.

The preventative strategy here is based on the human resource strategy detailed in Chapter 7 and ensuing that, wherever possible, all staff are treated with respect, made to feel part of the organisation and are adequately remunerated, particularly where they are tasked with guarding the enterprise. Once they have left, however, their access must be disabled instantly to ensure that they are no longer able to access the systems from outside.

Exhibit 13.5 **Inside help – attempted fraud at Sumitomo**

One of the most egregious examples of using inside help in recent years was the attempted fraud at Sumitomo bank in London.

The colourful gang of fraudsters, which included Soho sex-shop owner David Nash and 'Lord' Hugh Rodley (who bought his title), were let into the bank by a security supervisor after hours. They tampered with CCTV equipment and installed spy ware into the network connections which proceeded to record key strokes giving the gang logons, passwords and other sensitive data.

Their subsequent attempted transfer of amounts totalling £229m only failed because of errors in completing the technically complex transfer documents.

In this case an employee in a sensitive role was able to facilitate the attempt by the gang – a vulnerability which should be considered as part of any review of risks.

Source: Weaver and Bowcott (2009); Brown (2009)

Exhibit 13.5 illustrates another problem area for management and that is where low-paid staff such as cleaners, security guards etc. are bribed by criminals to facilitate access to company premises out of hours. There are stories in the USA of hackers who obtained temporary jobs in companies they were targeting as cleaners, maintenance persons or other 'invisible' workers and were able to watch individuals log on, or locate passwords which had been written down by staff. They only needed one password to get initial access and they were into the system. All staff have to be included in the risk assessment process, however lowly their role might be considered to be.

Internal computer frauds

Internal computer frauds are defined, for our purpose, as frauds committed by employees or individuals who have access to systems from inside the organisation as opposed to hackers who try to break into the system from the outside, with or without help. Here we are concerned with embezzlers who use computers to manipulate records to transfer funds or who steal goods or assets and then amend company records to disguise their crime, and with directors or senior managers who manipulate accounting records in a material way in order to distort financial statements.

As we saw in Chapter 11, in any investigation of a known or suspected crime the process is conducted in stages; no team of investigators will simply turn up and start work, there has to be a process of planning and evaluation. Clearly if the fraud has already been uncovered this may not be an unduly protracted process but where fraud is only suspected the process will be slower.

Where fraud is suspected one of the first tasks of the forensic investigator, as part of the planning process, will be to consider fraud hotspots. As we have seen the role of the investigator is to discover what has happened, and to do this all areas which might be vulnerable to fraud must be considered. Until investigators can be reasonably confident that they have uncovered the full extent of any wrongdoing it is not sufficient to consider one area in isolation or even to accept the word of a self-confessed fraudster that they limited their depredations to only one or two areas. They have no reason to maximise their culpability and may well seek to minimise their actions in the hope of leniency.

Accordingly a review of vulnerable areas or hotspots is an important part of the process. This may, of course, have already been carried out by management or internal audit as part of their risk management reviews, and if a formal system of risk management is in place the work of the forensic investigator may be considerably simplified.

Identifying fraud hotspots

For management purposes this is a straightforward identification of risk and quantification of the impact of the risk to the organisation. For the fraud investigator it is a process whereby the areas and consequently the potential perpetrators can be narrowed down. As a key management responsibility risk assessments should be part of the routine activities of the organisation and monitoring and evaluation of the risk-management process is one of the key responsibilities of the internal audit function.

Management should ensure that all areas of operation are reviewed regularly. If a framework such as control risk self-assessment (CRSA) (Chapter 7) has been adopted staff and line managers should be encouraged to be creative and to consider innovative ways of defrauding the organisation and using the IT system to do it and/or hide it.

It should always be borne in mind that, however sophisticated the systems, there is always the human factor. All systems rely on some form of human intervention and the most sophisticated system can be breached because someone uses a password that can easily be guessed ('password', 'letmein', name of boyfriend/girlfriend/ mother/cat, favourite footballer/pop star etc.) or someone doesn't follow procedure and an individual is allowed access to systems they should really have nothing to do with.

Human folly should never be discounted!

However, at a systems level there are two aspects to narrowing down the risk areas from the investigator's perspective:

- control weaknesses, and
- key fields.

Control weaknesses

The basic principles of good internal control were considered in Chapter 8. These are systems-based controls which apply to the operation of an IT function just as much as to, say, invoice processing and students should ensure that they are familiar with these principles which we have denominated with the mnemonic SOAPSPAM.

Investigators will review the IT systems to:

- Evaluate the efficiency and effectiveness of key controls.
- Review the actual operation of key controls in practice, if possible by reviewing the work of internal audit. They want to be sure that the controls in fact operate the way they are supposed to in theory.

- Consider who might be in a position to take advantage of a control weakness or an area without controls. This will incorporate a review of the position and status of senior managers and directors and will incorporate a consideration of any propensity to override controls or institute 'special arrangements'.
- Consider who might gain an advantage from a control which is not working properly or which could be bypassed by collusion or line management override.

This requires what the fraudster will undoubtedly have:

- a knowledge of the system, and
- the ability for some creative thinking.

Thinking the unthinkable is one of the key requirements of both good risk management and good investigatory practice, and everyone is included. Remember, according to the KPMG Fraud Profile (Chapter 5) many if not most frauds are committed by senior managers in a position of trust who have been with the organisation for some years and who may be the very people who might be part of the internal control structure.

Key fields approach

This is a micro view of frauds and looks at the data being entered. What the investigator or reviewer is asked to do is to consider the types of data being entered, which fields could be manipulated and who would benefit in consequence. This will be likely to require expert input from someone who knows the computer systems well and, it is suggested, the data operators themselves. Data entry operators often find ways of cutting corners, and finding things that the system will do which are unexpected – even by system designers.

It should be possible to identify:

- Who can enter, modify or delete data fields?
- Would any fraud require collusion with a data-entry operator?
- Why might this be done?
- Are there key controls that would prevent this from happening?
- What tests could be performed to identify a fraud?

Investigators might use an internal control evaluation questionnaire to determine the parameters of the system and the ability or otherwise of employees to circumvent controls. These can be standardised questions, to some extent, and are looking for the answer NO. If the answer to these types of question, the 'is it possible?' question, is YES there is a systems weakness of some sort. The seriousness or implications of the weakness would then have to be evaluated.

Table 13.3 shows some internal control evaluation questions and their implications for part of a sales and inventory system. Remember the perspective here is always fraud – there are many other control questions which could be asked concerning the administration of the sales system.

In short, risk managers and auditors should consider the possibilities of fraud being committed by, or in association with, individuals who have responsibility for direct input of information into the system.

By considering who inputs what and how far their privileges extend in terms of what data they can access and amend (i.e. what permissions they have on the system) it is possible to draw up a matrix of who might be involved or need to be

Table 13.3 Example – internal control evaluation questions – key fields – sales and inventory

Control question	Implication
Can operators dealing with sales alter terms of trade such as discount rates on prices?	In collusion with a customer sell goods at an under-value
Can operators processing sales invoices alter customer credit limits on the system?	Customers with poor payment histories can still get supplied in return for a kickback to the operator
Can operators processing payments alter destination bank details?	Payments to suppliers are diverted into another account controlled by the operator or accomplices
Can operators alter inventory quantities by amending delivery details so as to reduce the inventory balance shown on the system with fictitious under-deliveries or over-sales without any other control?	Inventories on the system appears to be nil whilst there is still a balance of stock which can then be stolen and sold
Is it possible for individuals to trade in their own right without any system monitoring controls showing an overall position?	One for the trading desks of finance houses, derivative and futures dealers and commodity brokers many of whom have been hit by traders running their own books without any overview. Nick Leeson at Barings ($1.3bn), Jerome Kerviel at Soc Gen (£3.7bn), John Rusnak at Allied Irish ($750m), Brian Hunter at Amaranath ($6.4bn) . . . the list goes on

Table 13.4 Control evaluation matrix – purchases

	Authorises suppliers and approves payments	Raises/ approves purchase orders	Matches orders to invoices	Enters invoices to purchase ledger	Reconciles suppliers' statements with purchase ledger	Approves payments	Processes payments
Manager Jim	X	X				X	
Mike		X	X				
Jane				X	X		
Susan							X

involved to commit a fraud. These are similar to the matrices and link diagrams we looked at in Chapter 10, but here we are concerned with system authority and access rather than relationships.

Table 13.4 is a theoretical example of a control evaluation matrix for a simple purchases system. Again the emphasis is on fraud – what we are looking for here are instances where the internal control principle of segregation of duties is being bypassed either through one person having too much authority or through possible collusion. These individuals have system access to be able to process or view the stated tasks and the authority to carry them out.

A simple matrix such as this could have highlighted the level of access enjoyed by Edward Bowe (see Exhibit 13.6) and raised a question as to why he needed such a level of access that he was able to both withdraw money and conceal the withdrawal and that of Joy Henry (Chapter 11) who was apparently able to create and arrange salary payments for fictitious employees entirely on her own.

In this simple matrix Manager Jim can approve suppliers and is also able to raise purchase orders as well as approving those raised by Mike. Jane is in control of

> ### Exhibit 13.6 Internal fraud – the garage man
>
> Edward Bowe was the company accountant for a Merseyside-based chain of garages called Leaders. A trusted senior employee, he had worked for the company for over a decade under the supervision of a financial director.
>
> He had access to the IT systems at work and also from home via the online service. He used that access to gradually withdraw £619,894 from his employer's account over five years. Bowe was responsible for paying into the bank account as well as for withdrawals. He altered the counterfoils of the paying-in book and siphoned off the balance. Forensic accountants were able to track the progress of his activities from his computer.
>
> Mr Bowe was described by the judge as a 'scoundrel and dishonest individual' who had stolen the cash because of 'pure greed'. Bowe was sentenced to four years' imprisonment.
>
> *Source:* Insider Media (2009); Motortrader (2003)

processing the invoices and of reconciling the purchase ledger with suppliers' statements. Susan pays suppliers on the basis of information supplied by Jane and Mike, i.e. that invoices are valid and that the purchase ledger account for a supplier reconciles to the supplier's statement.

Collusion between Jim and Jane gives them control of almost the entire purchasing function of the business. Jim can create fictitious suppliers and approve or raise orders, Jane processes the orders and they tell Susan it is OK to pay the supplier they have created. For them it solves the 'not going away' problem fraudsters have as one can cover for the other. They don't go away together as their collusion is a secret.

Jim's fraud is not compromised by any difficulty in data processing and Jane, who could not commit fraud on her own is now able to do so. Neither Mike nor Susan can commit purchasing fraud as they have incomplete access to documentation.

> ### Exhibit 13.7 Fraud example – the 'Robin Hood' bank manager
>
> A bank manager behaved like a latter day Robin Hood by channelling more than £7 million from the accounts of wealthy customers into the accounts of companies who were in trouble.
>
> Benedict Hancock (39), a Royal Bank of Scotland senior relationship manager, who had worked for RBS for 18 years, made no personal financial gain from transferring the money. He said he wanted the companies to do well for their sake rather than his.
>
> He looked after the affairs of around 40 corporate clients. When some of the firms needed extra cash to see them through difficult times he loaned them money from his richer customers by setting up a series of false accounts. If the customers queried the movement of funds he told them he had invested the money in Bank of England Bonds for them. He ensured that the accounts received the interest they were due.
>
> The 'loans' were revealed when one of his clients discovered their accounts was £5 million short.
>
> Two firms paid back the 'loans' but one was unable to and RBS wrote off the missing money.
>
> Hancock was sentenced to 18 months in prison.
>
> Mr Hancock's barrister said 'All of Mr Hancock's customers spoke very highly of him – he was dedicated to his job.'
>
> *Source:* Khan (2008)

Of course this is a simple example, but in practice a fraud of this nature might be very hard to detect in a routine audit because:

- all the documentation would seem legitimate
- invoice processing and payment are separate functions
- suppliers' statements are reconciled, and
- Jim is a senior manager.

All the controls look to be in place and functioning.

 ## Computer forensics and the preservation of evidence

Computer, or digital, forensics is concerned with the preservation of evidence on computers and other forms of storage device such as Blackberries, PDAs, mobile phones etc. It includes all forms of storage media from CD-ROM to memory stick as well as from less obvious sources such as Web pages.

One of the most important principles in computer fraud investigation is to ensure that the chain of custody remains unbroken, that is the clear progression of evidence from the scene of the crime to the court via the investigator. If the chain is broken the defence in any prosecution can argue that the evidence presented has been altered or tampered with in some way, or is not the responsibility of the accused at all.

In the UK forensic investigators should comply with the Association of Chief Police Officers (ACPO) guidelines. These are made up of four principles:

- Principle 1: No action taken by law enforcement agencies or their agents should change data held on a computer or storage media which may subsequently be relied upon in court.
- Principle 2: In exceptional circumstances, where a person finds it necessary to access original data held on a computer or on storage media, that person must be competent to do so and be able to give evidence explaining the relevance and the implications of their actions.
- Principle 3: An audit trail or other record of all processes applied to computer-based electronic evidence should be created and preserved. An independent third party should be able to examine those processes and achieve the same result.
- Principle 4: The person in charge of the investigation (the case officer) has overall responsibility for ensuring that the law and these principles are adhered to.

Computer-based electronic evidence is no different from text contained within a document: accordingly, the evidence is subject to the same rules and laws that apply to documentary evidence.

In presenting a case the onus is on the prosecution to show to the court that the evidence produced is no more and no less now than when it was first acquired by the investigator. Special care must be taken when handling computer evidence because most digital information is easily changed, and once changed it is usually impossible to detect that a change has taken place or to restore the data to its original state unless other measures have been taken.

A computer forensic specialist must be properly trained to perform the specific kind of investigation that is at hand.

In addition the computer tools that are used by the investigators must also be validated to ensure that the evidence cannot be said to have been corrupted by the tools used to extract it and analyse it. There are many computer tools used in these types of investigation, all of which must be used only by trained investigators with extensive computer knowledge. Amateur dabbling in digital computer forensic investigation is to be strongly discouraged!

Care also has to be taken when investigating computers and devices. Clearly permission must be received before any access is gained to these items. Where they belong to the organisation on whose behalf the investigation is taking place this does not present any problems, but where the machine or other device is the personal property of the suspect they are able to deny permission for investigators to access their machine.

In this case it may well be advisable to have a search order in place (see Chapter 3) to force compliance.

Evidence preservation

The ACPO guidelines state that in order to comply with the principles of computer-based electronic evidence, wherever practicable, an image (i.e. an exact duplicate) should be made of the entire target device, e.g. a hard drive. Partial or selective file copying may be considered as an alternative in certain circumstances, e.g. when the amount of data to be imaged makes this impracticable.

In a minority of cases it may not be possible to obtain an image using a recognised imaging device. In these circumstances, it may become necessary for the original machine to be accessed to recover the evidence. With this in mind, it is essential that a witness who is competent to give evidence to a court makes any such access. It is essential to show objectively to a court both continuity and integrity of evidence.

It is also necessary to demonstrate how evidence has been recovered, showing each process through which the evidence was obtained. The basic rule is that evidence should be preserved to such an extent that a third party is able to repeat the same process and arrive at the same result as that presented to a court.

Frequently the investigator does not have the luxury of examining intact files as attempts may have been made to delete incriminating data. In these cases experts must search for fragments of deleted files on the hard drive and attempt to restore what has been deleted.

In most cases it is inadvisable to log off or use the Windows 'shut down' procedures to turn off suspect computers where they have been left running in order to move them or work on them, as any volatile data, data stored in RAM will be lost if the computer is turned off.

If the computer has to be moved the best advice is:

- If the machine appears to be off move the mouse to see if it really is off or if it springs to life.
- Do not allow the user to close programs or shut down the machine.
- Allow any printing to finish – it may be relevant.
- Ask the user for any passwords.
- Check for Post It notes or scraps of paper which may contain user names or passwords.

- *Unplug the machine from the electricity supply* – do not shut it down using the close down procedures as this will delete temporary files.
- Follow any network cables and disconnect – any information on network servers can be accessed separately.
- Consider the benefits of photographing the machine and the surroundings, cabling and any labels.
- For laptops beware of opening the lid if it is closed. Some machines power up when the lid is lifted if it has been left in dormant mode. Instead remove the battery and any power cable.

The growing use of cryptographic storage has discouraged investigators from simply switching off machines as it may be that the only copy of the keys to decrypt the storage are in the computer and turning it off will cause that information to be lost.

Moving it should be resisted if possible until the forensic specialists have been able to access it.

Forensic investigators will use computer investigation tools to analyse the open drives and ports and to search for encrypted files. It is also possible to scan RAM and registry information to show recently accessed web-based and local e-mail sites and any log-in or password information.

One initial technique used by computer forensic investigators to demonstrate that evidence has been preserved is to take a cryptographic hash of an evidence file and to record that hash elsewhere so that it can be established, later, that the evidence has not been modified since the hash was calculated.

A cryptographic hash function is a procedure which takes an arbitrary block of *data* and returns a fixed-size *bit* string, the (cryptographic) hash value, such that an accidental or intentional change to the data will change the hash value.

The process of creating an exact duplicate of the original evidentiary media is often called imaging. Using a stand-alone hard-drive duplicator or software imaging tools and a write-blocker, the entire hard drive is completely duplicated. Clearly this must be done before any investigation of the data takes place. This is usually done at the sector level, making a bit-stream copy of every part of the user-accessible areas of the hard drive which can physically store data, rather than by duplicating the file system.

The original drive is then moved to secure storage to prevent tampering. During imaging of static data, a write protection device or application is normally used to prevent changes from accidentally being introduced to the evidence during imaging. At critical points throughout the analysis the media is verified again, using hashing, to ensure that the evidence is still in its original state. In some situations where criminal proceedings are not contemplated this step may be omitted due to the time required to perform it and, in that case, the quality of the evidence relies on the suitability of the process. Where criminal proceedings are likely it is essential that incorruptibility of the data can be demonstrated and the process of taking a cryptographic hash value is recommended.

Typical forensic analysis includes, among other things:

- a review of material such as metadata giving the timing and source of transactions, looking for unusual timings (weekends, evenings, etc.), transactions grouped around period ends or entries to unusual accounts
- reviewing the Windows registry for suspect information
- discovering and cracking passwords

- keyword searches for topics related to the crime
- extracting e-mails and Web site information for review
- data analysis, and
- data mining.

The use of computers in fraud detection is an interesting and fast-growing area and readers with an interest in it and knowledge of computing and mathematical applications will find it a rewarding study.

Using data analysis to detect fraud

The use of what have become known as computer-assisted audit techniques (CAATs) and the development of sophisticated data analysis software has greatly improved the investigator's chances of catching internal fraudsters.

One of the main problems investigators have to overcome is the sheer volume of data. Even if, in the example shown above in Table 13.4, Jim and his little team were processing 500 invoices a week, that produces in excess of 20,000 invoices in a year (allowing for holidays etc.) for the auditor to review, to which could be added allied documents such as purchase orders and goods received notes representing transactions of which only a relative few might be fraudulent. Of course the investigators could sit with the invoice files and look for those which Jim has obviously typed on Word using his home address and a fictitious VAT number and this may work, but the chances are it will not. It is certainly a useless approach for very large organisation processing hundreds of thousands or even millions of transactions per year.

The sheer volume of transactions processed by a credit card company such as MasterCard is unimaginable to anyone brought up on paper-based systems. All over the world in every currency, 24 hours a day, 7 days a week, 365 days a year they process huge numbers of transactions, a number of which are fraudulent. The systems they use to detect possible fraudulent transactions need to be, and are, very sophisticated. We will look at the principles behind these later.

Consider a clothing retailer with 200 shops. They lose stock through shoplifting – sometimes by third parties but also by staff, they lose money through fraudulent refunds or 'no sales' mostly committed by the staff in collusion with customers.

Here are some startling statistics:

- In Britain 1.6 million adults would contemplate shoplifting if they lost their jobs.
- 1.3 million said the rising cost of food would make them consider retail theft.
- 2.6 million admitted to shoplifting over the past 12 months – up 30 per cent on the previous year.
- Residents in the north-west were most likely to turn to theft, with 12 per cent admitting they have stolen in the past year. Wales and the West Country were least likely to steal, with 4 per cent admitting theft.

Source: G4S Security (2008)

Retailers cannot station a human auditor in every shop to check transactions – but what they can do is to have computerised auditors analysing transactions and highlighting areas for investigation. The use of data mining software has become a valuable tool in controlling stock losses and highlighting unusual or exceptional levels of refunds – which may or may not be fraudulent.

Exhibit 13.8	Examples – clothing retailers cut stock losses

Fraud at Peacocks

Retailer Peacocks identified 20 cases of internal fraud within the first six weeks of implementing specialist data mining software. Five cases of fraud identified by the software resulted in staff being dismissed within that period.

The software was used to highlight cases of fraudulent activity, including staff voiding genuine transactions and pocketing the cash from the till, illicit refunds and unauthorised staff discounts.

Source: Knights (2005)

Jaeger cuts stock losses

Clothing retailer Jaeger with 140 shops in the UK and Europe invested in a data mining application to help identify where it was losing money. The application is located centrally and interrogates data held on different systems throughout the business, including both the head office and the company's stores and concessions.

It uses a feed from the company's electronic point of sale (EPOS) system to spot potential fraud such as excessive discounting by a single member of staff. It also has time and attendance data feeding into it as well. The application generates exception reports. The audit team use their data mining application to generate exception reports as usual then they continue to use the application to ask more questions of the data so that they can understand whether the system is reporting a false positive or a genuine loss. One of the earliest discoveries was that theft by employees was only a small part of total losses at Jaeger.

Data mining is helping the clothing retailer to manage its stock, thereby reducing the need for markdowns when items go out of season and reducing the number of items that go missing altogether.

Source: Hadfield (2009)

Computer forensic investigation

As we have seen the size and complexity of modern IT systems and the difficulty in analysing large volumes of data predicate that a large part of the forensic investigator's work is based around the use of computerised techniques. It should be stressed at the outset that this book will not attempt to describe or provide a detailed methodology for the computer specialist, as much of the application of these techniques is highly technical and requires some detailed knowledge of IT processes. The aim of this section of the book is to provide, for the non-specialist:

- an understanding of the approach to computer forensics
- an explanation of some of the jargon used by forensic IT specialists
- examples of some of the approaches and methodologies where computers can be used successfully, and
- an overview of some of the disadvantages of computer-based approaches.

What follows is a little technical but it is important. The forensic investigator must understand, in principle, the limits of computer-based investigation and some of these limits are set by how the data is stored, what format it is stored in and what can be done with it. A forensic IT investigator may well try to explain to the lead investigator the limitations of any form of data search and the investigator should have at least a basic understanding of what they are talking about. Computer people are prone to using jargon and acronyms and it is incumbent upon lay people to grasp at least the fundamentals so that they have an understanding of the limits of what they may be trying to achieve.

The data problem

Before any form of investigative analysis can begin the investigator needs to have access to the relevant data, ensuring that the integrity of the data is maintained and taking due care to ensure it is not contaminated, assuming a target area has been identified. The steps involved in this process are relatively straightforward:

- Identify the objectives.
- Identify the data required.
- Define the parameters of the data – i.e. in what form is it required?

Before beginning any form of analysis there are some key questions:

- Is the data complete?
- Does it retain its integrity, i.e. has it been 'tampered with' either before it was asked for or during the process of obtaining it?
- Is it the original data or is it a copy of the original taken from another source, e.g. is this a head office version of the data or is it taken from the local office or subsidiary where the fraud is suspected?
- Is it relevant to what the investigation requires – i.e. does it cover the suspect period, does it contain too much extraneous information etc.

At this point it can be very useful to consult with a computer forensic specialist. The reason is simple.

Clearly we are assuming that the client has given full access rights to the system and that no-one on the IT staff is considered to be compromised by any possible fraud. The local experts will know if what is proposed to be accessed is the best source of information to meet the defined objective. Information may be held or categorised in many different ways within a system depending on the system architecture and the most obvious way may not necessarily be the best or most efficient way.

Sources of digital evidence

Evidence can be obtained from various locations and may be stored in several places such as:

- hard drives
- external hard drives
- network servers, and
- data transfer media such as memory sticks, CDs, floppy disks, etc.

In addition to text and number files such as Word or Excel, and transaction data, there will be:

- An Internet history – obtainable from temporary files, social networking sites, cookies etc.
- 'Favorites', shortcuts or recently accessed information recorded by Windows.
- E-mails – usually preserved on a separate e-mail server; e-mail applications also include diaries and calendars which can be a source of information.

- Network information – server logs (log-on/log-off), file access/deletion logs, remote access logs, Internet logs. These can be used as metadata (see later) to extract unusual data entry patterns. These logs must be preserved by investigators as network administrators often delete them regularly.
- Mobile phones, Blackberries, PDAs etc. – may include contact details, photographs, audio and video files.

Remember that, as well as transaction information, data for this purpose can include:

- Metadata – that is the information about the data/files, i.e. when the file or record was created, last accessed, last modified and last printed, showing dates and times, etc.
- Non-transaction data such as e-mails which have been sent or received by the suspects between each other or an external third party.

We will look at these separately – for now we will concentrate on transaction-type data.

Accessing data

Investigators will access data in two different ways:

- By running reports off the client's system – either standard form reports or especially requested bespoke reports using a report generator. Information may be able to be downloaded electronically into audit software to be interrogated.
- By capturing the data within the system, bypassing application software, and sorting it for use with audit software.

In any event the investigator will have to deal with the problems of accessing and imaging data without losing the audit trail or in any way corrupting the original data – thus giving the defence barrister an open goal to shoot at in court. If there is any indication that the process of the investigation may have compromised the data in any way the whole thing may fall because the accused can simply plead that they were not responsible for what was discovered.

Earlier in this chapter we dealt with the preservation of digital evidence, and readers are referred to the forensic readiness procedures described in Chapter 9. These procedures *must* be followed to the letter.

However, at this point investigators may simply be searching records or analysing data searching for possible patterns – they may not be in a position yet to call this evidence. Still it may become evidence, so strict evidence preservation procedures must be observed from the start of the investigation. This includes the use of write-blocker hardware and software to prevent the investigator's activities being written back to the system and contaminating the data, which could potentially become evidence to be relied upon in court.

Data transfer

Investigators may be faced with information from:

- mainframe legacy systems
- client/server systems

- mobile communication devices, or
- enterprise-wide applications integrating information from a variety of sources

working across different platforms.

The investigators will have to consider the possibilities arising from the data sources. Modern audit software is extremely flexible and able to cope with information from a variety of sources. Generalised audit software such as ACL and IDEA can analyse such data and carry out various forms of analysis of the data which greatly speeds up the investigator's task.

Data transfer can be accomplished in many ways, from the client's system to the investigator's including:

- zip disks
- CD ROM/DVD
- memory sticks
- wireless transfer
- network connection
- FTP (file transfer protocol)
- e-mail
- server back-up tapes, or
- hard disk drives.

Zip disks, CDs and memory sticks have many advantages as they are cheap, readily available and all PCs and laptops (but not Netbooks) can handle them. They are capable of holding gigabytes of data. Write once read often CDs can solve the data corruption problem as once written to the CD client data cannot subsequently be amended.

Connecting the investigator's PC to the network will require access rights and the data transfer may be slow depending on the bandwidth available and the baud rate (the rate at which data is transferred in terms of bits per second [bps]). File transfer protocols such as TCP/IP greatly speed up this process and virtually all modern systems now accommodate this.

Data can be transferred in an ASCII file format, although IBM systems use something called EBCDIC which is a more cumbersome sort of ASCII. This is a representation of characters by numbers and is useful as it transfers raw data without any sort of formatting such as tabs, bold or underlining. The advantage of an ASCII format is that any computer can understand it.

Information transferred via the Internet uses FTP software to access data from remote sites.

Mainframe tape is still used – particularly by bodies processing huge amounts of data, especially on IBM systems.

HM Revenue and Customs are known to use mainframe tapes as they apparently lost one in 2007 containing the details of 6500 pensioners. This was a back-up tape operating on an IBM system but was mislaid after being taken to another office. The Ministry of Defence have reportedly lost several laptops, memory sticks and disks containing data both encrypted and in clear. These incidents serve as a warning to anyone transferring sensitive data – control and security of data is paramount.

The main considerations, however it is carried out, are:

- The original files must not be corrupted or altered in any way because of the transfer.

- All of the information must be transferred completely, i.e. the transferred files must be identical to the files on the client's system.
- The transfer methodology must be secure as must the destination computer – the client's data is sensitive because it belongs to them irrespective of what the actual data comprises, so it must be kept confidential and access to it must be limited.
- If the data is to be used as evidence in criminal proceedings the chain of evidence must be unbroken. Access to the copied data must be controlled and logged so that there is no possibility of corruption or alteration of the data whilst it is in the investigator's custody. This applies also to any hardware which may be removed by the investigators for testing.

Data attributes and structures

Data comes in many shapes and sizes dependent upon the basis upon which it is stored.

The basic file types are:

- fixed length flat files
- variable length files
- delimited files
- multiple-record-type files
- relational files
- standard formats, and
- open database connectivity.

Fixed length flat files

The information for a given record is stored in one place in a file of a fixed length. The data is independent of all other records. An example of this might be a personnel record containing first and last names, address and telephone numbers. Because the location of each record can be calculated, access is fast.

Variable length files

As might be supposed the length of the file is dependent upon the amount of information stored in the location. This type of record can contain fixed and variable length portions. Variable length files must be scanned from the beginning in order to find a particular data element as the computer does not know where each record starts. A field separator records the end of each record.

Delimited files

This is a form of variable length file. The end of each field is marked by a field separator and the end of each record is marked with an end of record marker. The length of each field depends on the amount of data contained in it. Delimited files often use commas as separators – these are known as comma separated values (CSV) – but

Exhibit 13.9 Example – file structures

Flat file

012674	Harris	Joan	2745
371489	Dunbar	Lindsey	3960
237658	Bolington	Stuart	6127

Delimited file

012674, Harris, Joan, 2745
371489, Dunbar, Lindsey, 3960
237658, Bolington, Stuart, 6127

tabs and semi-colons are also used. A CSV file is a way to collect the data from any table so that it can be conveyed as input to another table-oriented application such as a relational database application. Microsoft Excel can read CSV files. A delimited file may have to be converted into a flat file before analysis can be made.

Exhibit 13.9 shows flat file and delimited file structures.

Multiple-record-type file

These files contain records which are of different lengths and, as might be guessed by its title, records which contain different information. For example a payables ledger in this format may contain details of the supplier (name, address, telephone, etc.) and details of what had been purchased from that supplier in another record.

Relational file system

This stores common information in one file and detailed information in other files. Data held within individual applications can be accessed by the entire system. The advantage relational data storage has over flat file storage is that, with flat files, every attribute of a record has to be entered which, of course, can lead to repetition of data and more voluminous files. With relational file storage the common information is stored and is located by means of a key field such as a number or a designated code.

Table 13.5 Multiple-record-type file

Record type				
1	Megablast Coatings	23 Main Street Anytown	Madchester	0123-456789
2	Metal oxide	3	£1256.00	23-6-09
2	Red ochre	0.5	£69.99	23-6-09
1	Bloomers	1 The Works	Tadchester	0123-987651
2	Topsoil	0.3	£751.00	08-07-09
2	Fertiliser	2	£864.10	08-07-09

Record type 1 contains information about the supplier.
Record type 2 contains information about purchases.

Key fields

Each database table must have a field, or a combination of fields, that contains a value which identifies each record in a unique way. For example, a customer number uniquely identifies each customer. This field or fields are called the *primary key* of the table.

The primary key serves two key purposes in a relational database management system (RDBMS).

- Because the value is unique, it ensures that there are no duplicate records in the database.
- The primary key is also used to establish table relationships and, thereby, connect the data in related records held in different tables. Records are stored in order by the primary key.

Clearly in order to be a primary key, the field must never be null. Null means there is a missing or unknown value. A null value is not the same as a zero or a blank. In a numeric field, a zero may be a real value. A primary key field is one where the values in that field are rarely (ideally never) changed.

There can, of course, be more than one primary key attached to each record. This is known as a multi-field or compound primary key but, to avoid complexity, it should contain as few fields as possible.

So the characteristics of a primary key field or fields are that its values:

- uniquely identify each record (no duplicate values)
- are never null
- rarely (if ever) change
- and the key includes as few fields as possible.

The primary key will then enable the investigator to locate any record irrespective of where it is stored in the database.

Open database connectivity (ODBC)

The aim of ODBC is to make it possible to access any data from any application, regardless of which database management system (DBMS) is handling the data. ODBC manages this by inserting a middle layer, called a database driver, between an application and the DBMS. The purpose of this layer is to translate the application's data queries into commands that the DBMS understands. For this to work, both the application and the DBMS must be ODBC-compliant – that is, the application must be capable of issuing ODBC commands and the DBMS must be capable of responding to them. PCs must have the relevant ODBC drivers installed on them in order to access the data.

Investigators need to understand the relevant database structures to see how information might be related so as to give the required information. Provided this is understood investigators can extract information from the various data tables and carry out the necessary analysis. The point is that accessing data is just that – data. Investigators must recreate the relationships using key fields (the markers identifying items of data) in order to set up the information in a format suitable for them to carry out their data analysis.

It is possible to export data from many applications into a .DBF format (which is used by standard database packages such as FoxPro and dBase or in spreadsheet formats such as Excel or Lotus 123) and this is a way of requesting data from client's systems. However, standard packages often have size limitations so investigators must be careful to ensure that they have all the records. This can be done by referring to control totals.

Extracting data

In most fraud investigations the investigator will extract the data from either the suspect's computer where it is stand-alone data or from the application software. From this they will build their own database of information which they can then interrogate. The most important aspect of this is that *the original data must remain intact, unaltered and unaffected by the process of copying or extraction.*

The investigator must take an image of the data from the client records and use that for the purpose of analysis. There is no combination of circumstances that would warrant carrying out a forensic investigation on the original data.

Clearly CAATs as part of a routine audit will use the original data but that is a completely different thing to a forensic investigation.

Care must be taken when extracting and recombining the data. Clearly the step that investigators take is, effectively, a form of processing of the data. The minute it is taken out of its original location something has happened to it. The comments regarding data security made above are pertinent here. Investigators must not prejudge what the data will, they hope, show nor must they make any attempt to influence or present data in a way which is anything other than totally objective.

The key issues here are:

- Improperly extracting source data – fields can be lost or data corrupted, data may be incomplete (e.g. deleted fields). Any investigation is therefore flawed or capable of being challenged on the grounds that the extraction process hasn't been carried out successfully and doesn't include all the data or the process of extraction has corrupted some of it.
- Misinterpreting the data – even if it is correctly extricated it may be presented in a form which is capable of misinterpretation. For example both debits and credits may be presented in such a way that they all appear to be debits. Care has to be taken with delineating the data and in reading it.

Deleted files

The data to be investigated has first to be loaded into the investigators' database and care has to be taken that all the records are transferred. This should include deleted files.

In most databases deleted files are not actually removed from the records until a specific event happens such as a purge, a reindexing or a reconfiguration of the database. Files which an operator deletes are generally 'marked for deletion' by the system which simply means that they are not printed out or displayed when the database is questioned, however the records still exist within the system.

For obvious reasons these transactions could be of great interest to the investigator; thus, when extracting the records for investigation, deleted files should come too. It may be, of course, that some of these files have been deleted or overwritten but it is surprising how often files which a perpetrator thought had safely vanished are resurrected by forensic computer specialists.

One of the areas where this 'marked for deletion' situation is extremely common is in e-mail storage where the system marks e-mails for deletion but does not, in fact actually remove them. Suspicious e-mails can thus be retrieved using specialist software and read by the investigators.

Data cleaning

Of course downloading an entire database full of transaction data is going to give the investigators a huge amount of stuff to look through – most of it irrelevant to what they want to do.

The process of data cleaning is designed to standardise the records so that anomalies stand out straight away.

Data cleaning will remove such things as headers and footers from files, commas and full stops, extraneous words and characters etc. Using long strings of characters to obtain matches is difficult and could result in an inordinate number of transactions. If the data is slimmed down to its essential components the matching process is made simpler.

However, this process comes with a major health warning! It must only be performed by experienced and skilled computer auditors – it is not for the amateur sleuth. In addition it represents an alteration to the clients base data so all cleaning operations must be carefully logged in order to maintain the chain of evidence. Tampering with data can introduce a ray of hope for the defence barrister and great care must be taken to ensure that whilst the format of the data may be abbreviated it has not, actually, been changed at all.

Many data analysis tools don't require this so it is not something this book will take further. Students interested are referred to specialised computer literature on this topic.

Data analysis

As we have already said, the great advantage of the use of computer-based techniques is the ability of investigators to apply them to large quantities of data.

The use of data extraction and analysis software enables investigators to carry out various techniques in order to:

- test out their initial hypotheses about any fraud and how it might have been committed
- apply scientific and mathematical techniques to data which will have validity in court as evidence

- revise and amend the tests and carry out further analyses depending upon the results of those tests, and
- document the results.

The usefulness of each technique varies depending upon the fraud being investigated. Clearly one single technique is rarely appropriate and a combination of techniques will have to be used in any particular situation. Therefore investigators should be familiar with a range of techniques so as to be able to apply them as the investigation requires. The most useful techniques are as follows.

Filters

A filter displays data in accordance with predefined criteria designed by the user.

The process involves the investigator interrogating a large population of data and drilling down into it in order to extract data with particular attributes. The display criteria can isolate specific transactions or groups or types of transaction thus enabling them to discover transactions which lie outside normal criteria or formal protocols. Exception reporting is a type of filter-based routine.

Display criteria can be single or combined using 'AND' and 'OR' expressions. The data location is specified using parentheses to allow multiple conditions to be processed.

Example

Expressions vary depending on what software package is used, but the basic structure of a filter looks like this:

```
Quantity > 0
Value < 100,000 or Quantity < 75
(Location = 'Bought' or Location = 'Nominal') AND Clerk = 'Taylor21'
```

This isolates the transactions in a range by value and quantity processed by a particular individual with the log in or staff number *Taylor21*.

This type of report is probably one of the most common tools used by the investigator. It can be used, for example, to extract:

- unusual journal entries such as those for large round sum amounts close to reporting period ends
- largest accounts by value or number of entries including suppliers and nominal ledger accounts
- payments to employees in excess of agreed rates
- payments to employees who have left the organisation, or
- payments made up to various approval limits authorised by specified individuals.

This is probably one of the easiest and most basic techniques yet one of the most effective. Clearly, as we have already stated, it is important that investigators fully understand how data is stored and what the capabilities of data extraction are before attempting data extraction using a filter.

The problem, for the investigator, lies in defining the criteria to be used before the reports are run. The danger is in setting the criteria in such a way that potentially fraudulent transactions are ignored or excluded, creating the illusion that all is well. Accordingly this type of search is usually carried out only after a certain amount of preliminary investigative groundwork has been carried out.

Often the results of a filter search will provide the hard evidence of fraudulent transactions which will crystallise suspicions of the fraudster's activities. Filter searches can be used for 'fishing expeditions' but in organisations with complex systems processing large volumes of data this may be akin to throwing a worm into Loch Ness in an attempt to catch the monster!

Gaps

The investigators can search for gaps in number sequences, for example, document numbers. The software looks for continuity and completeness. In addition, and perhaps more to the point, it can also uncover sequences where none might be suspected such as:

- missing transactions where there should be a consistent pattern, or
- a list of consecutive transactions where there shouldn't be any pattern.

This may reveal items such as:

- missing documents, for example, GRNs, sales orders, invoices, etc.
- gaps in cheque numbers, or
- missing bankings where revenues should be banked daily.

This software can also be used to look for sequences where none should exist, such as consecutive supplier invoice numbers from a particular supplier which could be an indication that the invoices are fictitious.

Recalculation/analysis

This is a technique, sometimes known as 'Expression/Equation' where investigators extract data from two different sources, combine it and either:

- match it against data stored in the system to see if the results are identical, or
- perform analytical review type techniques on it such as horizontal analysis or percentage calculations.

Investigators use this technique to build a model or paradigm against which they can match the real data. Clearly it is unlikely to be an exact match as there will always be differences between a theoretical calculated value and one that has built up organically over a period of time, but the object is simply to highlight an area for more detailed investigation – or to rule out areas which appear to be untainted by fraud or deception.

Clearly the exercise should not simply be a repetition of what the system is already doing. Data has to be taken from impeccable sources that differ from those the system is using to produce the numbers the investigator is trying to verify.

Examples are:

- Gross margin per product × volume sold: to match calculated GP against what has been reported or recorded. This is looking for under-recording or excessive allowances in retail outlets, e.g. where shop managers or staff are undercharging friends or conspiring to give refunds on previously stolen articles.
- Calculating Quantity × unit price fields: combined and matched against actual invoiced values or sales values charged to look for over- or under-invoicing frauds, e.g. particular customers undercharged where sales staff receive kickbacks.

Exhibit 13.10 **Example – recalculation/analysis**

A report could be formulated to calculate:

1. Opening inventory quantities + Purchase quantities − Issue quantities = inventory balances, then
2. Compare calculated inventory balances with reported values and throw out anomalies.

If the information is taken from the same source that the book stock ledger already uses the answers will be the same and there will be no anomalies! The investigator may find the lack of anomalies suspicious – until they think it through! However, if the same information can be obtained from different sources it may throw up the possibility of stock theft.

The problem is that the system may only store quantity information once and in one place so the test fails. However, use of creative thinking may reveal that the system, as well as entering quantity information into the inventory ledger, also records it into the costing system – so there are two sources after all. It may not be a perfect match but it may throw out a big enough discrepancy to stimulate further investigation.

- Gross pay + NIC + pension × no of employees = total salaries: looking for 'ghost workers' in the payroll system.
- Total quantity sold × price per product + opening debtors − closing debtors − credit notes = sales receipts: looking for cash theft.

Exhibit 13.10 shows a simple use of the recalculation function to look at inventory levels.

This type of technique can also be used to validate management reports or trading summaries.

Statistical analysis

Basic statistical analysis can provide a quick overview of data which enables investigators to focus on anomalous areas and direct their detailed testing. It may also give an indication of the levels of materiality involved.

It is used to provide information about numeric data fields including:

- mean, median and mode
- standard deviation
- range (highest/lowest values)
- highest value
- lowest value, or
- sum of absolute values.

This enables the investigator to highlight anomalies such as negatives in a revenue population or unusually high or low values. Again this process is simply a way of quickly making an overview of a large population (100 per cent sample) of data and drawing conclusions.

Transaction dates are a numerical field so by analysing dates transactions of interest could be identified. Information such as:

- latest and earliest dates of entry
- transactions outside chosen date range, or
- blank or invalid dates.

Exhibit 13.11 Example – stock manipulation

A routine internal audit CAATs program was run on an inventory goods inward field
The resulting printout looked like this:

	Number	Total items
All inward positive	12,384	638,415
All inward negative	123	−321
Totals	12,607	638,094
Abs. Value		638,736
Range		214
Std Dev		13.4
Highest 5	103 103 101 100 98	
Lowest 5	−6 −6 −5 −4 −4	

There were negative values in the goods inward field – which revealed an internal control software issue.

Upon investigation it was revealed that the warehouse manager had been disguising shortfalls in physical counts by amending the goods inward field. The system required all issues to be recharged to budget headings so this was the only field available for him to make 'adjustments'.

Investigation indicated some element of pilfering but the difference was primarily due to poor record keeping.

may well give the investigator a useful insight into what has happened. For example by extracting information about when dates and times transactions were entered into the records it might be possible to find cases where data was entered:

- at weekends
- during holiday periods, or
- early in the morning or late at night outside normal office hours.

Of course there could be innocent explanations such as staff working overtime to recover a backlog but it could also indicate that a fraudster was entering or amending data unobserved and thus, so they thought, unquestioned.

This kind of analysis can also be used to stratify data for sampling. Techniques such as monetary unit sampling require the total value of the population to be known before specifying the sampling interval.

Duplicates

The search for duplicate records is a useful technique. In many cases accounts processing software will not permit duplicate key fields such as invoice numbers or payment numbers, however if it does these must be searched for. What, of course, it does permit is duplicate addresses and names or, to be more accurate, names which are similar but not identical to one another. It may also permit duplicate items such as serial numbers or identification numbers as these may not be control fields, merely descriptors.

For example the investigator could search on key fields such as:

- supplier name
- supplier address, or
- supplier bank account number.

What the investigator is looking for here are:

- different suppliers with the same address
- supplier addresses matched to staff addresses extracted from the HR database
- same suppliers with different addresses
- same suppliers with different banking details
- same bank details – different suppliers
- variations on the name or address which might indicate different suppliers but which are, in fact, the same
- same address different suppliers
- duplicated vendors with duplicated invoices posted to different accounts, or
- duplicated invoices processed through the system.

This might indicate frauds such as:

- Multiple suppliers invoicing from the same address – which is a virtual accommodation address or the address of an employee.
- Suppliers invoicing twice for the same items either slight variations on their name, for example, Eezi-Clean Ltd and Eeezyclean Ltd – two invoices, two payments, one service.
- Electronic payments where the name of a genuine supplier has been used but the bank details are not genuine and are the fraudster's. The electronic transfer does not monitor names, merely sort codes and account numbers, but the payments will look genuine to someone approving the electronic transfer as part of internal control because they will recognise the supplier name but will not, of course, be able to verify the numbers.

Searches could also look for:

- Duplicate payments to suppliers where payments to one supplier are consistently duplicated. The fraud works when the clerk processing the payments asks for and subsequently diverts the refunded overpayment into their own pocket, which is often difficult in larger systems, or, more likely, shares the overpayment with the supplier.
- Duplicate names on a payroll with identical addresses and bank details. The fraudster has created fictitious employees (see Exhibit 11.7 re Joy Henry above) but retains their own address and bank details to enable them to stay in control and to collect the money.
- Duplicate bank details on the payroll but different names. Here an employee who has left the organisation is retained on the payroll but their bank account details in the masterfile are altered to that of the fraudulent employee.

This is a relatively straightforward test which can prove productive for the investigator.

Sorting and indexing

Again this is a relatively straightforward process where a large population of data is sorted. Often the investigator will load the data into their own database in order to carry out the sort. In these cases only part of the data is being looked at, for example:

- sorting by value may be looking for clusters of transactions around certain authority levels, or
- by date may be looking for high value transactions posted just before a period end.

Examples of sorts are:

- by value ascending or descending
- alphabetically, which could highlight anomalous names
- in date order – looking for transactions outside a given date range or clustered, and
- journal entries looking for round sum transfers.

This kind of sort may also highlight anomalies such as:

- dates which are very old – or future dates if the software permits these to be entered
- transaction values which are unexpectedly high or low for the records being sorted
- supplier names starting with blanks or unusual characters or unexpected supplier names
- inappropriate transactions in population, or
- blanks where input data would normally be expected – outside mandatory fields for data entry, i.e. descriptions of service rendered.

For example fraudsters often use large nominal accounts to hide fraudulent entries hoping that they will go unnoticed in the mass of data. It may be useful to search large accounts, e.g. raw material purchases-type accounts, or staff travel and subsistence to ascertain whether or not they include any unusual or non-standard items.

Sorting the data in these accounts by key fields such as supplier code or even size may well throw up anomalies which a simple inspection of the account as it stands historically would not reveal.

 ## Data mining

The techniques we have considered above are all valid investigatory processes but, increasingly, fraud detection is becoming reliant upon much more sophisticated processes. Electronic transaction processing has increased exponentially with

- the increased power of computing available
- the availability of credit in general and
- increased access to the Internet in particular.

This is a highly technical and complex area and this book can only provide a general overview of the principles and techniques involved. To fully understand this activity requires a level of computer knowledge which it is assumed the reader does not possess so only an outline of the main approaches is provided. As ever interested students are urged to read further and more widely.

There are two strategies where data mining techniques in fraud detection are involved.

1 Use of intelligent software to continually monitor transactions related to particular activities, individuals, accounts or organisations. This then throws out for

investigation what it considers to be anomalous or suspicious transactions. This is so-called 'pattern recognition' type software and it is used by banks, credit card and insurance companies and many online retailers, to interrogate the vast quantities of transactions they process every day.

2 Software which is used to interrogate large data sets, using mathematical or statistical base algorithms in order to carry out specific tasks.

We will look at these procedures in more detail shortly: however before we do, we should first consider how data is stored in a computer system.

Data storage

Clearly data storage is a critical component of the effectiveness of any investigation involving computer-based approaches. The method of data storage determines:

- the method of access
- the flexibility of use of the data, and
- the ease with which reports can be generated.

If data is stored in a rigid way, where the capability to generate reports is determined by the software, there is little the investigator can do but either plod through what information they can gather and supplement their report generation with a good deal of substantive testing or, perhaps, attempt to grab the raw data and reconfigure it into a more flexible format so that it can be interrogated electronically. This latter course is often difficult and there is always the danger that the data so gathered is incomplete or has been altered in some way.

Key to the use of arithmetical- or statistical-based investigatory tools is the basis on which data is stored. Some programs hard code transactions so they are stored in specific locations. So, for example, a purchase transaction is coded to a supplier code in the purchase ledger, to a nominal ledger expense code and to the purchase ledger control. They sit in computer files in those locations and will be extracted in a fixed format when the appropriate report is run. These are often PC-based small accounting-type systems but larger systems are often also configured in this way. Data can be extracted and tests performed on it, but it is inflexible and these systems are clearly not suitable for more sophisticated types of continuing fraud detection software.

Most modern systems use database software to store data in a more random way which is extracted via report generators. The great advantage of these systems is their flexibility and the fact that data storage isn't duplicated – the transaction details are only stored once. The data is recorded with identifying details establishing:

- What type of transaction it is – for example is it a currency value or a quantity?
- What it relates to – purchase, sale, expense, etc.
- Which accounts it relates to, i.e. purchase ledger, sales ledger.
- Other allied information, i.e. cost or inventory ledger information, date, relevant names, etc., even operator details.

The type of information related to the transaction is, effectively, tagged together but it is stored in a database format rather than being hard coded into separate ledger accounts. In this way the data can be sorted by any of the tags attached to it so, for example, the system could generate a report of all transactions in a given period with a given client within certain parameters, or a report of all transactions for a particular account on a particular day.

In short it is a much more flexible method of data storage and a boon to the forensic investigator.

Data warehousing

Data warehousing is a repository of data stored in such a way as to facilitate decision making, reporting and analysis.

The principle behind data warehousing is that information can flow from operational applications into what has become known as the 'decision support environment', which is a way of describing software designed to interrogate the transaction data so as to produce information in a way specified by the user, thereby eliminating extraneous information.

Application systems collect and store data to support routine business applications such as invoice processing, accounts, payroll etc. They provide the means for data entry, internal controls and a level of reporting but they are not always suited to some of the more sophisticated requirements of management, particularly in the area of strategic decision making or model building and forecasting. It was recognised that data needed to be extracted and stored in a way which would facilitate these kinds of managerial activity – hence data warehousing.

Data warehouse systems consist of layers, all of which are interconnected. These are:

- Operational database layer – this is the source data for the data warehouse – the operational systems.
- Data access layer – this is the interface between the operational and the reporting software. It contains tools to extract, transform and load the relevant information into the data warehouse.
- Metadata layer – this contains the data dictionaries. In database management systems (DBMS), a data dictionary is a file that defines the basic organisation of a database. It contains a list of all files in the database, the number of records in each file, and the names and types of each field. Most database management systems keep the data dictionary hidden from users to prevent them from accidentally destroying its contents.
- Data dictionaries do not contain any actual data from the database, only bookkeeping information for managing it. Without a data dictionary, however, a database management system cannot access data from the database.
- Information access layer – this is where the data is accessed for reports and analysis. It contains the reporting software.

Data warehousing is successful providing sufficient initial thought has been put into planning the system architecture and the process of extraction. There are some practical issues:

- Data warehouses rely on business systems to supply the raw data.
- Business systems tend to process large amounts of data and to carry a lot of extraneous detail necessary for them but not necessary from a data warehousing point of view.

- Business systems are designed to support operational functions so may not carry all the data required to enable satisfactory 'what-if'-type model building to be accomplished.

However, from the investigator's viewpoint data warehousing and data mining create opportunities to review huge data sets quickly so as to extract information which might indicate fraudulent activity – or even to identify a fraudster.

Two important points must be stressed from the outset:

1 This type of work is highly specialised and is only used where there are large data sets and a need for ongoing fraud detection. These are not, necessarily, appropriate tools for a one-off fraud investigation. These techniques in their entirety are used by such organisations as:
    - banks and credit card companies to detect ongoing frauds
    - large multiple retailers to monitor transactions at branches
    - insurance companies processing online applications for insurance and claims, and
    - e-commerce retailers in connection with card-not-present frauds.
2 These applications are expensive. They require skilled computer technicians and the appropriate hardware and software. In terms of a one-off investigation elements of some of these techniques may be appropriate but they are rarely applied to their fullest extent in that context.

It is important that forensic accountants are aware of the existence of these techniques so as to be able to make intelligent and informed decisions as to their use in the investigatory process. As ever, interested students who are computer literate can read further.

Data mining methodologies

We outlined above the use of two computer-based approaches to the detection of anomalous transactions:

- So-called 'intelligent software' which monitors patterns of behaviour and attempts to isolate anomalies or variations from the norm.
- Interrogation tools which can be used on a one-off basis using mathematical- or statistics-based detection techniques.

To illustrate the first approach, the use of intelligent software, we will look at the example of a credit card company. This will demonstrate how this type of software is used and will give the reader an indication of the cost and complexity of installing and using this type of approach to fraud detection.

Intelligent software – identifying credit card fraud

The advent of electronic banking and online retailing resulting in the ability to transfer funds using secure methods has brought about a revolution in consumer behaviour and with it increased opportunities for the fraudster.

The sheer number of transactions is fairly boggling. One source estimates that:

- Barclaycard carries out 350 million transactions a year in the United Kingdom alone.

- Royal Bank of Scotland carries over a billion transactions a year.

The problem that investigators have in large populations is twofold:

- The size and scale of the data is so enormous that the relatively straightforward types of audit analysis outlined above would still leave a tremendous number of dubious transactions which would need to be investigated.
- Fraud is better detected as it happens rather than retrospectively – the snag here is that the more the fraudster carries out the fraud, the more evidence there might be to be found and the more easily they should be detected, so detecting the first fraudulent transaction is very difficult if not impossible.

All investigatory techniques are based around the detection of anomalies whether they be single anomalous transactions or data entries, or whether they be clusters of transactions which don't fit a pattern. Of course statistical-based approaches alone will not provide a certainty that a fraud has been perpetrated, rather these techniques are designed to flag up areas of suspicion for further investigation.

For example banks and credit card companies use intelligent software to monitor movements on clients' accounts. Most people live their lives on a regular pattern, they buy petrol, they go shopping, they buy a season ticket, they travel up and down the UK and they use their bank card to pay for goods and services within a range of values and locations. If suddenly their account is charged with the purchase of a digital camera in Hong Kong this creates an anomaly and the software will flag it up as an item to be investigated.

The bank can contact the customer to discover whether or not they are actually in Hong Kong and if they have just bought a camera!

This type of transaction – the purchase of the camera in Hong Kong – has created what is known as a *suspicion score*. That transaction has created an exception to how the account would normally have been predicted to behave. What happens is that each record in the enormous database of bank transactions is imputed a suspicion score which is uprated as time progresses. These are then ranked and the accounts which generate the highest suspicion score are investigated.

One well-known activity that criminals with stolen cards engage in is to clone them and use them overseas to buy goods or to use them in CNP (card not present) frauds to buy goods, so a transaction which:

- breaks a normal pattern of behaviour, and
- involves a transaction in foreign currency of a particular size.

will raise an alarm. A sudden entry on to the account of a transaction in foreign currency is suspicious if there is no previous history of similar transactions on the account and so will be likely to raise the suspicion score for that account and trigger an enquiry.

One of the problems of course is that people don't always behave in an orderly way so this method often generates a lot of false positives – it may look like a fraudulent transaction but it isn't. The account may, of course, already contain fraudulent transactions, so the data the system is using as its baseline may be flawed.

However, the use of intelligent software is one way that organisations processing vast quantities of data can identify anomalous transactions for further scrutiny. Outside organisations such as banks, credit card or insurance companies, its use is comparatively rare as this type of technique is designed to detect apparent anomalies within a set of routine activities. In the commercial world of buying and selling, such patterns are less likely so the relevance of such software is less apparent; consequently the success it might bring in generating enquiries for investigation does not outweigh the costs of designing, installing and running it, which in the case of banks, of course, it does.

Use of mathematical or statistical algorithms

We looked earlier in this chapter at methodologies where the investigator extracts data then sorts and filters it in order to extract what might turn out to be suspicious transactions. Data mining techniques are applied to the entire database so that large data sets can be interrogated on a 100 per cent basis in a flexible format.

Data mining uses a great many advanced mathematical and statistics-based techniques and it is outside the scope of this book to explain in detail the concepts that underlie them. Instead we will look at examples where data mining has been used or could be used in fraud detection.

The tools which form a considerable portion of the armoury of the fraud detective are generally based on two principles:

- Probability-based tools (e.g. neural networks, decision trees) work from data populations to try to predict the probability of transactions being frauds based on observed criteria in existing populations.
- Statistical tools (e.g. link analysis, machine learning) are generally based upon comparing observed data with expected values. However, expected values can be derived in various ways which are outside the scope of this book, but it will be apparent that if the expected values are faulty or poorly observed the result will be a huge number of false positives.

Some tools (e.g. text mining) are used for digging and for extrapolating information from large data sets and thus simplifying the search. They are of great value in looking at non-numerical data sets such as e-mails where key word searches can prove fruitful.

The principle techniques used are:

- neural networks
- machine learning
- decision trees, and
- link analysis.

We look at these in more detail below.

Neural networks

These are software systems based on processes of learning and remembering. They have really come to the fore following the spread of much more powerful computers which can run neural network-type applications in a commercial context. They are used in:

- Classification – a methodology developed for discriminating between two things based on similarities, for example, a methodology for detecting fraudulent loan applications. The approach taken by the investigators is to develop a set of 'rules' based on the previous experience so that such applications share some common features. For example, they may determine that these 'rules' are:
  - applicants class themselves as self-employed so there are no verifiable salary details, merely an unaudited set of accounts

- applicants always state they own their own home but do not appear on the electoral roll
- multiple applications are submitted from different addresses but always quote the same mobile telephone number, and
- addresses match previously denied applications.

Any applications fitting one or more of these rules can be flagged for follow-up and investigation.

- Clustering – organising observations into groups with similar features. This can be used to detect collusion – for example cashiers colluding together to give refunds where they think one individual will be noticed. The software will detect clusters of refunds where one individual may not stand out.
- Prediction – this type of software generally has a predictive capability which can be used to create scenarios. One proprietary brand of software has a capability to explore a number of theoretical possibilities, while all the time the thought process is tracked on screen – in short a 'what-if' scenario builder.

Statistical approaches – machine learning

The approach here is entirely statistics- and probability-based and uses mathematical approaches based on 'IF/THEN' type rules. Students of statistics may be familiar with such concepts as CHAID (chi-square automatic interaction detection) or CART (classification and regression trees) and the decision tree. These form the basis of this kind of analysis, but we will not cover these in detail as they are specialised and outside the scope of this book.

Decision trees

These are something many readers will be familiar with if they have studied statistics and probability. They appear most frequently in project management but the principles can also be applied to situations where fraud has a high probability of occurring. Clearly this is predictive software and not strictly within our topic of fraud detection, but it can be a useful defensive tool.

The core technology of these decision tree tools are machine learning algorithms which automate the process of segmenting important features and ranges hidden in a database.

Basically these techniques are used to predict the probability of a crime. For example decision tree-type analysis can be used by retailers to discover situations in which fraudulent transactions are likely to increase – enabling them to take steps to reduce their loss.

The aim is to construct a model using the retrospective data to predict a class of new object from its description, i.e. a possibly fraudulent transaction or account. Some commentators state that if you monitor an account for long enough it is essentially certain to raise a suspicion flag above a threshold eventually, thus generating a large number of false positives all of which need to be investigated.

Figure 13.1 gives an example of how data mining techniques culminate in a decision tree used to illustrate the findings. It shows how data can be extracted to build a fraud profile and thus enable the retailer, in this case an online e-retailer, to focus resources in a cost-efficient and more effective way.

Figure 13.1 Data mining fraud detection

(a) Step 1:   Information is taken from the transaction database of an e-retailer over a period of time. The upper box indicates that out of 2315 transactions 230 (9.9 per cent) were fraudulent i.e. may have involved the use of lost or stolen cards. The data is analysed by price range.

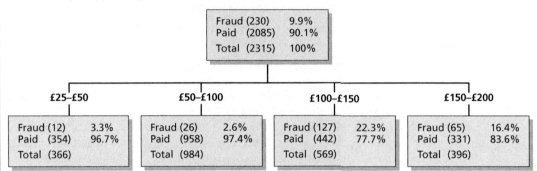

This indicates, perhaps unsurprisingly, that higher priced items are more vulnerable to fraud. This analysis will provide hard data about the price range of products which are the most vulnerable.

We can thus begin to build a 'rule' or model for detection of possible fraudulent transactions

Data mining software can go further to identify and quantify the risk profile. (Step 2)

(b) Step 2:   By analysing the data again for known fraudulent transactions a 'rule' can be generated, based on a probabilities. In the example below all the data in Step 1 was analysed and intelligent neural network software applied to it. This produced the following 'rule':

IF	PERCENT_AGE	25 – 30 is	63.00
AND	MEDIAN INCOME IS	<	20,000 ± 2,000
THEN	TRANSACTION IS		FRAUD
Rule probability			78.6%
This rule exists in			181 records

What this means is that where the age of the customer is between 25 and 30 and with a median income between £18,000 and £22,000 the probability of fraud is 78.6 per cent.

(c) Step 3:   What we can do now is analyse the same data in Step 1 but this time by product:

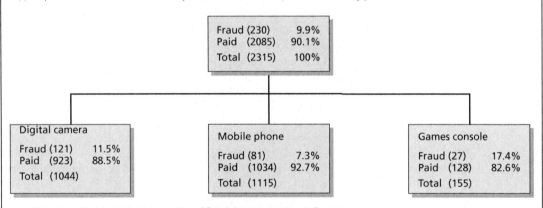

This shows that the highest proportion of fraudulent transactions is for games consoles

Using these steps the retailer can produce a fraud risk profile.

The highest probability of a fraudulent transaction is where the transaction is for a games console by someone in the age range 25–30 with a median income of between £18,000 and £22,000 per annum.

Accordingly the retailer can flag such transactions for investigation at the point of sale and develop routines for detection or prevention.

Lower level risks can be identified for other products and consumer profiles.

All of these processes can be carried out by intelligent software and are thus much less complex and time consuming than they may appear. However interpreting the output from such software requires the skills of someone familiar with it so it is likely to require the involvement of forensic computer specialists to analyse the data and create the rules and defensive routines.

This is clearly a simple example but it illustrates how these forms of analysis can be used by retailers, banks and credit companies to create risk profiles, generate suspicion scores and introduce checks and controls in order to reduce losses arising from fraud.

Link analysis

Link analysis is used to reveal underlying patterns hidden in large data sets. It is used in money laundering investigations and to detect fraud in the insurance and e-commerce sectors.

One important point is that, before this kind of operation is performed, there must be a complete understanding of the information contained in the data set and the data must, itself, be complete. One of the problems of using link analysis techniques is that transactional databases, i.e. those recording day-to-day information, may not be consistent in recording data, for example transactions with 'John Smith Ltd' may be recorded sometimes as 'John Smith Ltd', J. Smith Ltd', 'John Smith Limited' , 'Smith Ltd' or even just 'Smiths' depending on the context, the demands of data input, etc.

Consequently the data must be:

- Cleaned – to remove extraneous characters from the data stream, e.g. '£' from a field which will analyse the amount as a number not a monetary value or extraneous characters such as commas and full stops, %, <, >, @, etc and appellations such as Mr, Mrs, etc.
- Converted – to a standardised format – so dates need to be in a standard form dd/mm/yyyy so that all date fields are comparable. Similarly fields which represent currency, weight, distance, time must have a single uniform standard of conversion. This is because some of the algorithms used can only work with numeric fields so text may also have to be converted into some form of number.
- Concatenated – data can be combined into a single data object rather than being expressed in discrete fields. Contact details are often stored in fields with, for example:
  - first name
  - last name
  - street address
  - town, and
  - postcode, etc.

These can be combined into a single entity for the purposes of analysis.

Once the data has been prepared it can be processed in order to uncover correlations within it, so, for example, in money laundering cases link analysis can be used to link:

- home and business addresses
- bank accounts, and
- transaction identification numbers, etc.

and thus derive patterns involving individuals or groups which otherwise may not be apparent.

The major problem with link analysis is the amount of preparation needed. It is probably not as useful, in the general scheme of things, perhaps because of the time and effort required to prepare the data as say neural networks, outlined above, or software which uses statistical or machine learning algorithms in order to detect patterns and predict behaviour but can be extremely effective in cases where deep investigation of large volumes of data is required.

IT-based non-financial approaches to fraud detection

Fraud detection is not simply about analysing financial data. For example the ancient art of letter writing has been supplanted to large extent by e-mails. It is possible to extract an individual's e-mails from the e-mail server and read them. However, where there is no specific suspect or there may be a number of possible suspects the problem may be in reviewing a large quantity of text in order to attempt to identify a possible perpetrator. Some software will carry out sophisticated pattern matching based on linguistic patterns etc. but this is far outside the scope of what fraud investigators could use it for because these are approaches used by government agencies which are monitoring data traffic for terrorist activities or criminal gangs.

However, on a simpler level text miners can be applied to large quantities of unstructured text such as e-mails in order to detect key words or information which matches preset criteria. These techniques must be used circumspectly, for example, it is probably of little use asking a text miner to give you every instance where individuals use the word 'fraud' or 'backhander' because you are more likely to find that's the internal audit department discussing internal control than two members of staff planning a fraud!

What is needed are some key words which it may not be possible to decide upon until the investigation has uncovered a certain amount of information. Then it might be names, addresses, particular contract details or key words such as 'enjoyed' or 'hospitality' where corruption might be suspected.

If a key word or phrase is found text miners can gather together all documents containing that word or phrase and present a summary of it. Clearly this may generate a lot of false positives but it can also indicate links and connections which may not be immediately apparent from financial records. For example if two members of staff are colluding – say in connection with a contract fraud with an outside contractor – they may both e-mail the contractor but not each other: the link is the contractor. A text miner will bring out all e-mails with that contractor within a given time period for study.

The most common form of e-mail, using Microsoft Outlook, is usually handled through a central network server.

If an individual or group of individuals are under suspicion the appropriate action would be to:

- change the permissions on the server to prevent e-mails from being deleted, and
- extract relevant e-mails and read them.

If the investigators are faced with a huge volume of e-mails data mining software can be used to extract e-mails based on key word searches. Clearly the key words have to be relevant to the fraud – suspects are unlikely to mention 'bribes' or 'kickbacks' in their e-mails but may, as we have seen, make reference to entertainment for example. They may also use euphemisms such as 'commissions', 'fees', or 'facilitation payments'. A certain amount of creativity and ingenuity is required on the part of investigators to extract the nuggets of gold from the dross.

Where the suspect is using some form of Hotmail account no record will appear on the central server but traces are often left on the individual machine which can be extracted. Google Mail stores everything in short-term memory.

It may also be possible to track websites which have been accessed by individuals. These will be in the History but websites such as www.wayback.com can also be used to trace an archive of previously visited sites if the organisation has subscribed.

Summary

- Using IT in fraud investigations is fraught with danger of corrupting evidence. If in doubt *leave it alone.*
- Methods involve a variety of computer-aided auditing techniques (CAATs) and specialised techniques known as data mining.
- Computer crime can be analysed into specific types.
- External frauds can be described as deceptions, temptations and attacks.
- Deceptions and temptations encourage the unwary to send money under a false premise or log on to a fictitious site so as to download a virus or trojan.
- Attacks are usually accompanied by blackmail or extortion demands and are aimed at online businesses.
- Most common attempts to affect computers come from viruses, worms, trojans or a combination of these collectively known as malware.
- Attackers can sometimes be aided by inside information.
- An analysis of vulnerable areas in the organisation can reveal the potential fraud risk. A matrix is a good way of doing this.
- Preservation of evidence is crucial in computer investigations as it is easily lost through bad practice.
- Do not power down or log out suspect computers, unplug them from the mains.
- The ACPO guidelines set out the principles for the preservation of evidence.
- The sources of digital evidence should be identified.
- Data extraction or transfer must be handled extremely carefully and should only be carried out by an expert.
- Data is stored in many formats. Data warehousing makes data analysis easier.
- Forms of data analysis include filters, gap analysis, recalculations and forms of statistical analysis, duplicates and sorting and indexing.
- Data mining applies statistical techniques to data to search for patters or anomalies.
- Data mining techniques include link analysis, neural networks, machine learning and decision trees. This work is very specialised and has to be carried out by an expert.
- Much evidence can be gathered through non-financial investigations into such things as e-mails and websites.

Case study

You are the head of internal audit of Whoppa plc. You have recently had information via the whistle-blowing hotline that the purchasing director Jason Grasp has been receiving backhanders from suppliers for granting them preferred supplier status.

The informant tells you that Jason has received money in cash and also by direct transfer into a company he runs called Efficiency Experts Ltd. Suppliers then inflate the price they charge to Whoppa to get their money back.

Jason is also accused of receiving bribes from a number of overseas customers.

Your informant, who has retained their anonymity, also accuses the purchasing manager, Kylie Crumpet, of similar corrupt acts and alleges that she operates her own company and routes supplies through it to Whoppa. She inflates prices as she recharges these supplies and retains the mark-up for herself. The informant estimates that Whoppa is being overcharged by 10–15 per cent on most of the supplies it sources where Jason and Kylie are directly involved.

Both of them are also accused of putting through fictitious invoices. You recall having seen invoices from Efficiency Experts during one enquiry so it looks as though these allegations need to be investigated.

You carry out computer-based investigations which reveal information sufficient to, at least initially, give cause for concern that these allegations are true.

You visit Jason's office when you know he is away on business.

On his desk is his company computer. Also on his desk are several memory sticks which appear to belong to him.

Required

1 What do you do now? Outline the next steps of the investigation process in order to identify evidence of wrongdoing by Jason Grasp.
2 Identify any relevant legal or other issues. What particular problems may you encounter in this type of enquiry?
3 Kylie Crumpet is also suspected of a fraud. Identify what computer investigation procedures you or your team could carry out into the accounting or other records to gather evidence of any offences committed by Kylie Crumpet.

Bibliography

Andrade, L. and Firestone, W. (2006) *Foundations to Computer Forensics and Online Crime Investigations.* Outskirts Press, Parker, CO.

Austin, R. and Darby, C. (2003) The myth of secure computing. *Harvard Business Review,* 81, 6, 120–126.

Barnett, N. (2005) *Traces of Guilt.* Corgi Books, London.

Barrow, B. (2007) TK Maxx card hackers target 45m customers in 'biggest ever' heist. www.dailymail.co.uk, 31 March.

Bolognia, J. and Lundquist, R. (1987) *Fraud Auditing and Forensic Accounting.* John Wiley, Hoboken, NJ.

Bolton, R. and Hand, D. (2002) Statistical Fraud Detection: a Review. *Statistical Science,* 17, 3, 235–255.

British Chambers of Commerce (2004) *Setting Business Free from Crime.* British Chambers of Commerce, London.

Brown, D. (2009) Bogus peer Hugh Rodley tried to pull off world's biggest bank raid. www.thetimes.co.uk, 5 March.

Coderre, D. (2009a) *Internal Audit – Efficiency through Automation.* John Wiley, Hoboken, NJ.

Coderre, D. (2009b) *Computer Aided Fraud – Prevention and Detection.* John Wiley, Hoboken, NJ.

Espiner, T. (2007) Swedish bank hit by 'biggest ever' online heist. www.zdnet.co.uk/news, 27 January.

G4S Security (UK) (2008) *Fifth Annual Crime Survey.* G4S (UK), Carshalton.

Golden, T.W., Skalak, S.L. and Clayton, M.M. (2006) *A Guide to Forensic Accounting Investigation.* PriceWaterhouse Coopers LLP / John Wiley, Hoboken, NJ.

Hadfield, W. (2009) Jaeger uses data mining to reduce losses from crime. *Computer Weekly*, 23 February.

Hand, D.J. (2007) Mining personal banking data to detect fraud. In P. Brito, P. Bertrand, G. Cucumel and F. de Carvalho (eds), *Selected Contributions in Data Analysis and Classification.* Springer, Berlin.

Hand, D., Blunt, G., Kelly, M. and Adams, N. (2000) Data mining for fun and profit. *Statistical Science*, 15, 2, 111–131.

Hopwood, W.S., Leiner, J.L. and Young, G. (2008) *Forensic Accounting.* McGraw-Hill, New York.

Khan, U. (2008) 'Robin Hood' bank manager took £7m to give to poor. www.telegraph.co.uk, 17 September.

Insider Media (2009) Technology beating the villains. NewsCo Inside Limited, www.insidermedia.com.

Kirk, J. (2009) Three spammers sentenced in US for advance fee fraud. www.macworld.co.uk, 3 April.

Knights, M. (2005) Data mining software reveals fraudulent employee activity. *Computing*, 1 December.

Leyden, J. (2004) Online extortionists target Cheltenham: bookies attacked, cash demanded. www.theregister.co.uk, 17 March.

Mena, J. (2003) *Investigative Data Mining for Security and Criminal Detection.* Butterworth Heinemann, Burlington, MA.

Motortrader (2003) Four-year sentence for dealership embezzler. www.motortrader.com, 12 May.

Out-Law (2004) Online bookies facing blackmail threats. Pinsent Masons LLP, www.out-law.com, 18 March.

Parliamentary Office of Science and Technology (2006) *Computer Crime*, postnote October 2006, Number 271. Houses of Parliament, London.

Richards, J., Selb, C. and Brown, D. (2007) Millions are caught in great credit card heist. www.thetimes.co.uk, 30 March.

Seetharaman, A., Senthilvelmurugan, M. and Periyanayagam, R. (2004) Anatomy of computer accounting frauds. *Managerial Auditing Journal*, 19, 8, 1055–1072.

Serious Fraud Office (2003) Three sentenced in advance fee fraud. www.sfo.gov.uk, 27 June.

Silverstone, H. and Sheetz, M. (2007) *Forensic Accounting and Fraud Investigation*, 2nd edn. John Wiley, Hoboken, NJ.

Slapper, G. and Tombs, S. (1999) *Computer Crime*. Pearson, Harlow.

Vaassen, E., Meuwissen, R. and Schelleman, C. (2009) *Accounting Information Systems and Internal Control*. John Wiley & Sons, Chichester..

Weaver, M. and Bowcott, O. (2009) 'Lord of Fraud' jailed for eight years for attempted £229m bank theft. www.guardian.co.uk, 5 March.

Wells, Joseph, T. (2004) *Corporate Fraud Handbook*. John Wiley, Hoboken, NJ.

Websites

www.accountancyage.com

www.acfe.com

www.athens.ac.uk

www.britishchambers.org.uk

www.business.timesonline.co.uk

www.computing.co.uk

www.computerweekly.com

www.dailymail.co.uk

www.emeraldinsight.com

www.g4s.uk.com

www.guardian.co.uk

www.hbr.org

www.hmrc.gov.uk

www.icaew.com/forensicaccounting

www.insidermedia.com

www.justice.gov

www.macworld.co.uk

www.motortrader.com

www.out-law.com

www.parliament.uk/parliamentaryoffices/post

www.sfo.gov.uk

www.theregister.co.uk

www.wayback.com

www.thetimes.co.uk

www.zdnet.co.uk/news

Part 5

NON-FRAUD WORK

Chapter 14

Valuation of businesses and marital assets

Chapter contents

- Introduction
- Valuation of businesses
- The concept of value
- Bases of valuation
- Earnings-based valuations
- Yield-based valuations
- Matrimonial work – divorce and separation
- Tracing the marital assets
- Asset tracing

Learning objectives

After studying this chapter you should be able to:

- Understand the basic principles of the valuation of unlisted and unincorporated businesses
- Understand the issues relating to marital breakdown including the valuation and tracing of marital assets
- Develop an understanding of the board principles of assest tracing

Introduction

Forensic accountants are increasingly becoming involved with a range of activities not involving fraud and fraud prevention but which, nonetheless, still require them to use their full range of evidence gathering and analytical powers.

In this chapter we will look at the tricky business of valuation. Valuations are required for all sorts of reasons, including the sale or acquisition of a business or when couples who have built up a business split up and have to value the marital assets.

This latter situation is one becoming increasingly familiar to the forensic accountant as couples with substantial assets, whose relationship has come to the end of its road, become embroiled in legal proceedings and require their services. The objectivity and independence of the forensic accountant's report can serve to assist the court in coming to a decision. In Chapter 16 we will look, in detail, at another aspect of the role of the forensic accountant, that of the expert witness who may be called upon to provide evidence either as part of dispute resolution procedures or, of course, as part of fraud or employment proceedings.

In Chapter 15 we examine some rather more low-profile tasks the forensic accountant can be called upon to assist with, those situations involving claims. These can be claims made by the client, for recovery of losses or damages for personal injury or conversely defending claims made against the client under the Proceeds of Crime Act 2002 where they are being accused of benefiting from a 'criminal lifestyle'.

Valuation of businesses

Forensic accountants are often asked to form an opinion of the value of an unincorporated business or of the shares in a non-listed company. This can happen for several reasons:

- To price the business for sale or purchase as a going concern.
- For tax purposes – for example in connection with:
  - capital gains tax (CGT), including 31 March 1982 valuations for rebasing and indexation purposes
  - inheritance tax (IHT)
  - employee share schemes, including advice on market value under the Finance Act 2003 'restricted share' regime
  - goodwill valuations for partnerships and sole traders
  - group reorganisations and restructurings
  - stamp duty
  - employee benefit trusts, or
  - enterprise management incentive schemes.
- In legal proceedings in connection with:
  - compensatory damages where, for example, an interest in a business hasn't materialised or has proven to be not worth what was promised
  - to assist in reviewing the reasonableness of a claim for a quantum of damages
  - in cases where a valuer is being accused of negligence
  - management buy-outs, capital reconstructions or share buy-backs or where there is a possible oppression of minorities who appeal to the court

- valuation of a lost opportunity – where there has been an alleged market manipulation ('concert parties') or where an opportunity to acquire a business in a takeover battle has been thwarted through foul play, a valuation of the lost opportunity may be required by the court
- estate and trust cases where an independent fair value is required to avoid trustees or executors being accused of disposing of an interest in a business at an undervalue, or
- in divorce proceedings – valuation of the parties' assets where both have an interest in a partnership business or where one spouse has a claim against the assets of the other. We will look at this separately later.
- In connection with the introduction of new partners into a partnership or sole trading enterprise.
- As part of financing arrangements where a valuation of underlying security may be required.
- Actions under what was Section 459 Companies Act 1985 now S994 Companies Act 2006 – an application to the court in connection with actions by the directors of a company considered to be unfair and prejudicial to the rights of minority shareholders. A successful claim is likely to result in the court requiring a sale of the shareholder's interest.

The list goes on. Suffice to say the valuation work of the forensic accountant may form a substantial part of the decision-making process or, in the case of a dispute, may be a central plank of evidence in a legal case.

The valuation work has to be approached with the highest level of objectivity and competence. Valuations of unlisted securities are often difficult and it has been said that, given the same information, no two accountants will come up with the same valuation. Clearly any valuation of disputed assets often forms a substantial component of the case between parties which is to be settled by the court.

It is paramount that the process of valuation must not only be fair, it must be seen to be fair. All qualified accountants must abide by their ethical codes which stress integrity and objectivity as primary components of the independence the accountant must bring to their work. This is always an important aspect of the work of the accountant but it is probably true to say that it is even more important where dispute resolution is concerned, particularly where court proceedings may be involved.

The highest standards of professional behaviour must be maintained. Accountants may, indeed, come to different valuations of unlisted shares, but they should have arrived at their opinions honestly, competently and without bias.

Any element of bias or, dare it be said, ineptitude, in the estimation of value will be frowned upon by the court and may well result in the case presented failing and some element of criticism of the accountant, as witness, by the judge in the case. This will, of course, also displease the client.

There is the concern that the forensic accountant, in carrying out the process of valuation, may leave themselves open to accusations of negligence if they should value an asset which is subsequently sold for substantially more than that valuation. This would imply, assuming a relatively short length of time between the valuation and the subsequent sale, that the valuation has been inexpertly or even negligently prepared.

However, it is clear that, unless it can be clearly demonstrated that the original valuation had been negligently prepared, the court will not entertain a claim against the expert where the subsequent proceeds are within a range of possible valuations or where circumstances have changed which have influenced the ultimate sale proceeds. This reinforces the necessity for:

- all steps in the valuation to be fully documented
- all assumptions to be clearly outlined and justified, and
- the basis adopted to be explained fully to the client.

Where the valuation is going to be tested in court this process should be automatic as only a fool goes into court inadequately prepared and under-documented, but even where the forensic accountant is merely acting as adviser the documentary process must be as rigorous.

The concept of value

There is no objective standard which defines 'value'. A machine may be completely worthless in an objective marketplace yet have great sentimental value to its owner because, for example, it was the first piece of machinery they bought when setting up their factory. Sadly, of course, sentimental value cannot be measured in any currency so has to be discounted as a basis of valuation, although the emotions associated with something having sentimental value may compel the seller to drive a hard bargain when it comes to selling it.

How do we define value in terms of assets? They often have three values:

1 the original cost
2 the written down or depreciated value, and
3 the replacement value – what it would cost to replace it in the open market

so, to accountants, the concept of the 'value' of an asset varies with circumstance.

For example, in the case of a business which has collapsed, any assets may be worth written-down value or less as they are to be sold quickly at second-hand prices. The business itself may be worth virtually nothing unless there is some residual goodwill left in its name. For example when Woolworths collapsed the administrator was able to sell the name to an online retail operation separately from any sales of tangible assets such as the property.

In contrast someone selling a business as a going concern would look to maximise the value of the assets in order to get the best price and would also, clearly, be looking to maximise the value of any underlying goodwill inherent in the name and reputation of the business.

'Value' also has a relationship to the size of what is being sold. If an individual is selling, say, a 10 per cent share in a private company consideration has to be given as to what it is that is actually being sold:

- A less than 25 per cent share has some but not many rights. What is being sold is the interest of a non-influential minority shareholder.
- A shareholding of between 15 per cent and 50 per cent is also a minority share. However, a holder of 25 per cent or more of a company's share capital has certain rights under the Companies Act 2006 which, whilst not extensive, do give the holder certain powers such as the ability to block a special resolution. What is being sold is the interest of an influential minority shareholder.
- A shareholding of over 50 per cent is, of course, a majority shareholding.

All three of those types of holding can be valued on a different basis depending upon what size of holding is being sold. If the entire business is sold it is, of course, valued as a single entity.

These factors:

- the nature of the transaction, and
- the size of the holding being sold

have a direct bearing on the basis and size of valuation.

Such deals can be structured in many ways where companies are involved but two common approaches are:

- Purchase of the share capital of the target company by the new owners either as individuals or through a purchasing company, thus creating a mini group.
- Purchase of the assets of the target company or business by the acquirer but not any shares. In this case the acquirer can purchase the assets they really want and leave others, commonly receivables and cash, and perhaps some liabilities, behind in the target company which is then liquidated. This is a 'clean' acquisition by the acquirer and avoids problems with enforcing indemnities and warranties post-sale.

However the sale is structured the business valuer must be aware of the basis of the deal and the motives behind it as this may have an impact on the valuation itself.

Fair value

The concept of 'fair value' is one which currently exercises the mind of accountants to an extraordinarily significant degree and is one of the most difficult concepts to quantify. It is a phrase which often appears in legal agreements or in a company's articles of association when a 'fair value' is what has to be calculated by the accountants.

To illustrate the point let us consider a scenario:

A company is owned by three people A, B and C who have equal shares. The company is valued at £12 million so if the whole business is sold each should receive a one-third share, i.e. £4 million.

Supposing C wants to sell – there are three scenarios, discounting, for this purpose, any provisions requiring C to offer the shares to existing shareholders first.

Sale to a third party

C's minority holding, influential as it is, will have to be discounted because it is a minority holding. Let us assume a discount of 60 per cent – making C's shareholding worth £1.6m (£4m – (60 per cent × £4m)). If C sells to an outsider it is unlikely that C will receive any more than this as a minority shareholding in a private company is not a particularly attractive asset for an investor, even if it has some limited influence.

Sale equally to A and B

If C sells equally to A and B they will each have a 50 per cent shareholding and no-one will have overall control. C's share is probably still only worth £1.6m as it does not give either of the acquirers a significant advantage.

Sale to either A or B

However, if C sold to *either* A *or* B they would acquire a controlling interest – 67 per cent. The value of a controlling interest is much greater than that of a minority so would attract a lower discount, say 20 per cent. The valuation would still require some level of discount as, although a significant holding, it is still less than an absolute majority, i.e. 100 per cent. This could make C's share worth a lot more – up to, say, around £6.4m (£12,000,000 × 67 per cent less 20 per cent) – because of the benefit it would bring to the acquiring shareholder A or B.

So depending on the structure of any arrangement C makes to sell their shares C's shareholding is worth, on this basis, anywhere between £1.6m and £6.4m because it attributes some of the value acquired by the new majority shareholder (either A or B) to the seller, C.

In reality the actual value depends on:

- the overall value of the company being agreed, and
- the discount factors to be applied

which will be a matter for negotiation between the parties. It is here that the skill of the forensic accountant comes in.

Market value and assumptions

HM Revenue and Customs use the term 'market value' as the basis of valuing shares for tax purposes and the term 'market value' as defined in the relevant statute. The definition of market value for capital gains tax can be found in Section 272 of the Taxation of Chargeable Gains Act 1992, for inheritance tax it can be found in Section 160 of the Inheritance Tax Act 1984 and for stamp duty land tax in Section 118 of the Finance Act 2003.

These definitions are all very similar and broadly define market value as:

> The price which the property might reasonably be expected to fetch if sold in the open market at that time, but that price shall not be assumed to be reduced on the grounds that the whole property is to be placed on the market at one and the same time.

The current statutory definitions are similar to those used in earlier Acts and over the years the above definition has been examined by the courts in numerous cases. The case law was usefully summarised by the Court of Appeal in the case of *IRC v Gray (Executor of Lady Fox (Deceased)* in 1994. The case law established some important assumptions that must be made when arriving at the market value in accordance with the above definition.

These are:

- the sale is a hypothetical sale
- the vendor is a hypothetical, prudent and willing party to the transaction
- the purchaser is a hypothetical, prudent and willing party to the transaction (unless considered a 'special purchaser')
- for the purposes of the hypothetical sale, the vendor would divide the property to be valued into whatever natural lots would achieve the best overall price (this is the principle of 'prudent lotting')
- all preliminary arrangements necessary for the sale to take place have been carried out prior to the valuation date

- the property is offered for sale on the open market by whichever method of sale will achieve the best price
- there is adequate publicity or advertisement before the sale takes place so that it is brought to the attention of all likely purchasers, and
- the valuation should reflect the bid of any 'special purchaser' in the market (provided they are willing and able to purchase).

Using these assumptions the concept of 'fair' or 'market' value are contemporaneous and, for our purposes here, mean much the same thing. The point is that any valuation takes place in that hypothetical world of the perfect market between a willing buyer and a willing seller where all relevant information is known by both parties.

 ## Bases of valuation

The valuation of unlisted businesses is a peculiar art – it is certainly not a science – and requires the exercise of judgement and a sense of realism. There are many specialised tomes written on the art of valuing businesses and this book is no place for a detailed exposition of the techniques, however we will give an outline of the predominant approaches so that those unfamiliar with the principles, or who have forgotten them during the period since they took their examinations, can appreciate the basics.

The first principle in valuation is to be clear on what is being sold. For example, is it the equity of an unlisted company or is it all or part of the assets with no sale of shares?

Clear instructions are required so that the forensic accountant is informed of:

- the purpose for which the valuation is required, and
- the effective date of valuation.

Where valuations are being made in connection with legal proceedings the forensic accountant should be aware of relevant case law as this can give a guide as to the current thinking behind the valuation bases which the court is used to seeing and which it will find acceptable.

It may be that valuations are required to be made for different times in the life of a business because the precise date of any critical happening or the effect of any critical happening may not be established with certainty. It may be that the forensic accountant has to prepare a range of valuations and use the one that best fits the times the court has decided upon. This may be very significant where the valuation is based on the future flows of income or cash.

There are certain features of the process of valuing a business which are particularly relevant to the work of the forensic accountant and we will examine these in some detail to give the reader a working knowledge of the key aspects of each methodology.

First of all let us summarise the basic approaches.

Figure 14.1 summarises the basic approaches to the task of valuing businesses where the value cannot be easily obtained from an independent source, for example a Stock Exchange valuation of listed shares.

Figure 14.1 Valuation of unlisted businesses

Technique	Approach	Areas of difficulty
Assets-based valuations	This commonly involves valuing or revaluing the assets of the business (non-current assets including intangibles, inventories, current assets etc.), deducting the identified real liabilities, where a cash outflow is virtually certain, and calculating an amount for the goodwill in the business	Valuations of tangible assets and, in certain circumstances, inventories, commonly involve specialist valuers. Forensic accountants will have to be sure of the experience, qualifications and competence of any valuer The calculation of goodwill is often a contentious item. This is, broadly, the excess over net asset value that a buyer is prepared to pay for the business. This is an area forensic accountants are often involved with
Earnings-based valuations	Based on either multiples of profits or 'super-profits (profits in excess of a 'normal' rate of return or future maintainable earnings)	Forensic accountants become involved in both the calculation of the 'profits' to be multiplied and the multiplier
Discounted cash flow	Frequently used by private equity firms who buy for investment. It basically values the business based on the present value of future cash flows	Forensic accountants become involved in the cash flow calculations and the discount factor to be applied
Dividend yield	Used in connection with the valuation of small shareholdings in private companies	The rate of yield is a problem as in most private companies there is no continuous pattern of paying and there is often not a comparable listed business which can be used for comparison

The basic approaches we are going to consider here are:

- assets-based valuations
- earnings-based valuations
- discounted cash flow (DCF), and
- dividend yield.

We will look at each of these in turn in more detail.

Assets-based valuations

These are normally used when the whole entity is being sold. In this case what the purchaser is buying is the whole, or substantially the whole, of the business, either the whole or the major interest in the shares or the interests of partners or sole traders. In many cases an assets-based valuation is used where maintainable profits are not high or where the assets are the most attractive part of the business to the acquirer. Many business valuers prefer to look at future maintainable earnings as a basis of valuation, but assets-based valuations are still common.

The basis of valuation comprises:

- the market value of net assets (tangible and non-tangible assets and current assets minus liabilities), plus
- goodwill – based on the ability of the business to generate future profits because of its reputation, its position in the market, its trading record, etc.

We will look at these separately.

Tangible and intangible assets

Key issues are:

- Valuations of properties, plant and equipment. These are usually on an open market, existing use basis and valuations are usually made by specialist valuers. Sometimes other bases such as replacement cost or a 'forced sale' basis can be applied or some form of DCF calculation adopted but these tend to be out of the ordinary and would have to be agreed by negotiation between the parties.
- Collectibility of receivables (debtors) – in many cases the outgoing owners are left to collect any receivables if a business is being sold in its entirety thus leaving any bad debt risk with them.
- Liabilities – should include all liabilities which are likely to crystallise together with an estimate of any potential liabilities which are uncertain as to timing or amount, for example, contingent liabilities. The purchaser should be made aware of these so that suitable warranties and indemnities can be included in the sale and purchase agreement.
- Positive cash and bank balances may be retained by the vendor and not included in the sale of the entity as there is no point in the purchaser buying cash balances, particularly if they are borrowing money to do so.

The valuation should ignore book or written-down values, as these are an accountant's construct comprising cost value minus accumulated depreciation which is based on an estimate of the asset's 'useful life', but instead should look at the real underlying value.

Of particular interest here would be:

- Land and property shown in the accounts at an undervalue – the key point here is to consider any alternative uses to which the assets could be put, e.g. development of old industrial sites for leisure developments which could affect the valuation. Research or local knowledge could be important here if, for example, redevelopment plans are likely.
- Research and development expenditure – the future commercial value of any development expenditure or of any research which might ultimately result in a saleable product could be a key factor here. The basis of research and the status of both research and development projects should be reviewed as, again, there may be hidden value.
- The valuation of any current assets has to be considered and allowances and provisions to either reduce the value of uncollectible debts or to make allowance for additional costs not included in any financial statements should be included as appropriate. The position re any contingent liabilities or contingent assets will have to be considered and, if necessary, an estimate included in the valuation. However, these are more often covered by warranties and indemnities in the sale and purchase agreement unless the effect of any liability, should it crystallise, is likely to be so large as to make the business unviable.
- If the company is in trouble, i.e. there are going concern issues. Valuations of assets may have to be adjusted substantially downwards if a forced sale is anticipated.

Goodwill

The value of goodwill is always a difficult issue. It is often relatively easy to arrive at a valuation of net assets, but the value of goodwill is often a much more difficult business and is often the point of dispute between the parties.

The basis of valuation of goodwill may be important for tax purposes and, of course, it may be one of the most significant assets the business has to sell.

Sometimes it is simply an estimate or educated guess based on what any potential purchaser is prepared to pay for the business over and above the calculated value of its net assets, in other cases it is a careful calculation. However the figure is arrived at it is unlikely to be universally agreed between the parties at first instance and there will always be a certain amount of horse trading until a mutually agreeable number is arrived at.

The valuation of goodwill is, at least initially, often based on a multiple of sustainable profits generated by the business. The multiple is open to negotiation, although three years is often cited, as of course is the basis of calculation of the profits to be used. The points in the section on earnings-based valuations are therefore relevant here and anyone attempting to value goodwill as a separate item should refer to the principles described in that section.

 ## Earnings-based valuations

This type of valuation is often used when valuing:

- less than the whole of an entity
- goodwill (see above), or
- when entities have a level of tangible assets which is negligible in comparison with the totality of the underlying business.

For example businesses such as:

- solicitors or accountants practices
- news agencies
- insurance brokers
- medical and dental practices
- petrol stations, and
- hotels, pubs and off licences

may have a relatively low level of assets but may generate considerable income. In these cases the valuation is frequently based on their ability to generate turnover.

The methodology is relatively simple as the valuation is based on:

- a multiple of turnover adjusted for exceptional or non-recurring items, and
- the application of a discount factor which will form the basis for negotiations.

There are important non-financial factors to consider when valuing businesses, particularly smaller ones. These will affect the valuation but, again, are not capable of precise quantification and will form part of any negotiation between the parties. Examples of important points to consider here are:

- The name and reputation of the business – how much was vested in the individuals who owned the business rather than the business itself?
- Its potential to generate future income over and above its existing level of trade.
- Customer loyalty – will customers leave as a result of any change in ownership?

- Management and staff continuity – often managers and staff have relationships with key customers so will any existing staff leave with the outgoing owners or are there plans to reduce existing staff levels?
- The location of the business relative to other existing businesses of the acquirer.
- Relationships with suppliers – outgoing owners may have had special terms because of the length of the trading relationship which may not be available to a new owner.

Consequently the valuer will need to review the financial statements for a period of years to arrive at a suitable turnover figure. Commonly the turnover will be an average, or weighted average, over a period, say three years. When arriving at an average turnover number any exceptional one-off sales would have to be excluded as, of course, these would distort what is intended to be a base level of maintainable turnover.

Once the turnover figure has been agreed the next problem is to apply a factor or multiple to it. When arriving at a multiple the factors outlined above which may affect the business adversely must be taken into consideration. Students looking for guidance at this point as to what a suitable multiplier might be will be disappointed. Multiples can be as low as 1 or as high as 10, perhaps, depending upon the circumstances of the business outlined above, the ability of the seller to negotiate, the willingness of a buyer to buy, the market or any one of a dozen other factors which influence the price.

Other forms of earnings-based valuation are based on profit rather than turnover.

The price/earnings method – calculating future maintainable earnings

This basis is often used for the valuation of controlling interests and is frequently adopted as a realistic basis of valuation in both commercial and matrimonial disputes (see later).

This is a method of valuation which has been supported by the courts. It is particularly relevant to businesses with:

- a steady growth record
- future earnings potential, and
- a regular capital expenditure requirement.

The basic principle involves:

- assessing future maintainable earnings, and
- determining a multiplier or suitable rate of capitalisation known as the price/earnings (P/E) ratio.

Future maintainable earnings (i.e. profits) are the profits an investor would expect in an ongoing business, i.e. what they might 'earn' from the business in future years after all the costs of running it have been accounted for.

Although this is a forecast of the future, accountants will have to be guided by the past as this is all they have by way of facts on which to base their calculations. It requires a certain degree of skill and experience to establish the base level of maintainable profits. For example exceptional events such as one-off or special sales or exceptional, non-repeated costs need to be excluded from the calculations otherwise these will introduce distortions into the valuation.

What the forensic accountant is trying to establish is a 'steady state' of profit earning potential by the business. Clearly the past may be an unreliable guide, especially where profits have fluctuated, and part of the art of share valuations is to construct a case for what reasonably could be considered to be a base level of historical earnings from which can be derived an estimate of future maintainable earnings.

Points for the forensic accountant to consider when trying to establish a base level of earnings include:

- How dependent is the business on key customers or suppliers?
- Is the business dependent on new technology products or brand names – if so what would the effect be of a decline in their earning power?
- At what stage in the product life cycle are the business' core products and what is the current state of the industry in which it operates?
- What are the future plans for the business – have any key strategic decisions been made recently which may affect it in the longer term?
- Profits/losses arising from the sale of assets need to be excluded.
- Accounting policies need to be considered to ensure that they are in line with Generally Accepted Accounting Practice (GAAP).
- The effect of any operations that have been discontinued needs to be excluded from historical figures before any trends are projected.
- Conversely the effect of new or recently acquired operations or ventures needs to be considered for their future contribution to profits.
- Any non-trading income should be excluded, for example, royalties, interest, foreign exchange gains and losses.
- Any trading with related parties which is not at arm's length should be excluded.
- Any items relating to directors' expenditure must be excluded – although salary cost levels may need to be adjusted to reflect a reasonable level of management remuneration. This is important where what is being valued is a partnership. Partners do not draw salaries, they are remunerated by profit share and, accordingly, there is no charge against partnership profits for the time and abilities of the controlling management. Partnership profits may need to be adjusted for such a charge based on reasonable levels of remuneration and associated employee costs (such as NI and pension contributions). Many directors who are also shareholders in private companies may take remuneration in the form of dividends in order to reduce national insurance liabilities so this also has to be taken into consideration.
- Amortisation of non-cash items such as goodwill or capitalised development costs should be excluded.
- Interest paid, taxation and depreciation costs should also be excluded where the company being valued is a larger enterprise or is a takeover target – see the notes below.

Remuneration

As we will see later part of any settlement in matrimonial proceedings will take into account the earnings of each party as employees where this is appropriate. As we saw during the process of valuation of shares, where maintainable profits are being calculated, forensic accountants will review the level of directors' remuneration as part of the calculation.

However, where the disputed assets consist of a business which not only provides the value but also provides the income for the parties, establishing the appropriate level of remuneration can be problematical.

In private companies the level of remuneration may bear no relationship to the amount of work carried out by the directors or their competence in their role. Shareholder/directors may keep remuneration low to help increase profits; conversely they may take excessive amounts out in order to reward themselves for success. There may be no pattern from year to year, indeed it may be more influenced by the spending patterns of the individuals concerned than commercial considerations or tax planning. There may even be some form of self-created bonus scheme which may also create fluctuations in earnings.

In carrying out valuations forensic accountants will have to adjust the actual remuneration in the financial statements to what might be a comparable level of remuneration earned by the individuals if the company was managed and run by non-shareholders.

The question is – how is an appropriate level of remuneration set?

There are three basic approaches:

1 Review the levels of remuneration earned by individuals in a similar position in a listed company. Whilst it may not be appropriate for the directors of, say, a privately owned retail and distribution company to compare themselves with the chief executive officer of Tesco or Sainsbury's there may well be some form of comparison with a larger company where the information on directors' remuneration is publicly available.

2 There are many surveys of salaries and benefits which can be made use of. In addition Croner Reward publish an (expensive) survey of directors' rewards annually which would serve as a useful guide.

3 There is also a market rate – the rate at which someone would have to be paid to fill that role if the present incumbent was not there. This may require input from a specialist recruiter to advise the forensic accountant or it may just be possible, by reviewing advertisements in suitable journals, to estimate what a suitable salary package might be.

Establishing profits

When valuing larger enterprises many valuers take the view that the profits to be considered for capitalisation should be based on what they call EBITDA (earnings before interest, taxation, depreciation and amortisation) in which case taxation and depreciation should definitely be excluded from the definition of earnings. This is sometimes known as the *enterprise valuation method* and it is commonly used when valuing larger organisations or acquisition targets where the emphasis is on pre-tax maintainable earnings.

However, in valuing smaller private companies it can be argued that what many investors are actually interested in is distributable profits after tax. In this case it may be more appropriate to calculate maintainable pre-tax earnings and apply a notional average tax rate to them rather than the actual charge. This will smooth out any anomalies caused by fluctuations in tax rates or the effect of tax allowance claims exceeding depreciation. Deferred tax should be treated in the same way as taxation for this purpose.

Interest and financing costs are excluded in order to arrive at a valuation of the trading entity without any distortions caused by its underlying financial structure.

Establishing a multiplier

The next problem is to decide on the multiplier to be used. Clearly it may be possible to successfully identify the quantum of maintainable earnings taking into account the sort of adjustments listed above, which may well be agreed between valuers for opposing parties; however identifying a suitable multiplier may be considerably more subjective. Most textbooks or articles on business valuations tend to avoid the issue by advising the valuer to look at comparable listed companies or cases where transactions involving similar-sized private companies are involved in order to arrive at an appropriate multiplier.

In practice there are several problems with this:

- It is often quite difficult to find a comparable listed company – they tend to be much larger and perhaps more diverse. The businesses are unlikely to be exactly the same.
- Listed companies tend to be rather better controlled as they are required to have a much greater level of corporate governance (Chapter 1) than the average unlisted company. They are thus likely to be considered to be a much less risky investment by any potential investor so the multiple for a listed company would be lower than might be appropriate.
- Companies with strong management teams will have a higher P/E than those with weak management.
- High growth companies should command a higher P/E than those with lower growth.
- Companies with lower borrowings should also have a higher P/E than those extensively borrowed.
- Transactions involving the sale of private companies are often not publicised – or, at least, the basis of valuation isn't.
- Quoted P/Es of listed companies in the financial press only relate to the sale of a relatively small proportion of the share capital and so don't include any element of control.

However, the basis of valuations made for court purposes are a matter of public record and so could be used as a guideline for valuers. We look at these below in the section on matrimonial disputes.

Identifying a level based on a comparable listed company may be only a starting point and valuers of unlisted businesses have to take into account additional considerations, such as:

- the levels of business risk involved (the higher the risk the greater the return on investment required and consequently the lower the multiple)
- the size of the controlling holding involved (see above), and
- the cost of financing the acquisition.

Such considerations may be particularly pertinent when the asset being valued is an unincorporated entity or a share in one. As every schoolboy knows the great value of limited liability is just that, in the absence or personal guarantees to a bank, all an investor in a company can lose is their investment, whereas an investor in an unincorporated body may, potentially, lose everything.

The risk factor may therefore loom very large in the negotiations. Vendors will naturally seek to discount the risk factor but any business valuer would do well to do some background research into the market and the industry involved, both at a national level and locally. The value of background research cannot be underplayed. Accountants often confine themselves simply to the mechanics of valuation but an investigatory, forensic approach may well provide a much more sustainable argument for a particular multiplier than quoted precedent or comparable businesses.

Discounted cash flow method

This is a process with which most accountants will be familiar. The value of the business, based on the present value of its future cash flows, is discounted at a rate which takes into account the risk of the investment.

Because of the levels of uncertainty in forecasting this method is not common. It is, however, often used by private equity investors when looking at acquisition targets as a form of investment. In other words they are merely valuing their investment based on the rate of return it will bring them rather than as a long-term business opportunity. The comparison is often against other forms of investment, including such things as the returns from property investment, bond yields or interest rates. Table 14.1 (p. 416) gives an example of a DCF calculation.

Many of the same considerations shown above when we looked at maintainable earnings above, apply to DCF type calculations:

- The pattern of profits and any clues to future performance which can be derived from an examination of past results.
- The markets the company is presently operating in and the potential of those markets.
- Any economic or cultural factors which have influenced past earnings and may influence future earnings.
- Key strategic and operational decisions affecting the business.
- How reliable budget and cash flow projections are and whether the assumptions they are based on are feasible and realistic.

The skill here is, again, to obtain as much information as possible both about the business itself and its background and that of the industry it operates in. The problem of accurate forecasting is well known to most accountants and the temptation to take an optimistic view should be resisted.

The discount factor is another element of uncertainty. The discount rate relates to the opportunity costs borne by investors when buying into a company's assets or providing capital. The discount factor to be applied will take into account a risk free rate of interest as adjusted for both inflation and risk. In some cases the weighted average cost of capital (WACC) (see Table 14.2, p. 416) can be used which does have the advantage of being a less subjective basis of valuation thus reducing the potential for dispute, unless of course there are anomalies in the underlying business funding.

Valuations on this basis also assume a terminal or residual value. Clearly operating cash flows can only be reasonably accurately forecast for a relatively short period – say three years. At the end of that period the business will still have a significant value and it is that value which also has to be factored into the calculations.

Table 14.1 Discounted cash flow

	Year 1	Year 2	Year 3
Operating profit	110	125	140
Add depreciation and non-cash items	5	4	6
	115	129	146
Movement in working capital	10	−5	12
Capital expenditure			−50
Tax payment	−35	−37	−49
Net cash flow	**90**	**87**	**59**
Discount rate compound 10%	1.10%	1.21%	1.33%
Cash flow discount to present value	**82**	**72**	**44**
Total present value	**198**		

Assumptions: discount from year 1; residual value after year 3 to be calculated separately; discount factor to be applied to total present value.

Table 14.2 Weighted average cost of capital (WACC), Sweetiepie plc

Component	Market value	Proportion (%)	Individual cost* (%)	Weighted average
Ordinary shares	5m × £1.50 = 7,500,000	52	15	0.52 × 15% = 7.8
Preference shares	2m × 0.90 = 1,800,000	13	6	0.13 × 6% = 0.8
Loan	5,000,000	35	12	0.35 × 12% = 4.2
	Total 14,300,000			Total 12.8

The weighted average cost of capital is 12.8%.

*The individual cost is based on the rate of interest or dividend paid on the amount borrowed.

The terminal value reflects the value of all expected future cash flows beyond the explicit forecasting period. There are two ways of estimating a terminal value:

1 A calculation based on future maintainable earnings is carried out as described above and this is used as a residual value.
2 An assumption is made that the company's cash flow beyond the immediate forecast period will grow at a constant rate and an appropriate factor is applied based on the weighted average cost of capital.

 ## Yield-based valuations

This is appropriate to minority holdings in unlisted companies where there is little or no element of control and the investor is primarily interested in the return on their investment or dividend. It is thus difficult to extrapolate an appropriate rate of return from the previous history of the company, but not impossible.

The problem is that private companies often have no set dividend policy and generally make little attempt at using dividends to encourage or stimulate investment. Clearly, by their very nature, there is little point in private companies doing this. As explained above owner/directors often take remuneration in the form of dividends to reduce NIC liabilities, so the level of dividend can fluctuate dramatically from year to year.

However, many companies often have shareholders who are not directors, for example family members who do not take an active part in the company, but who rely on their investment in it as a source of income or who, the directors feel, should gain some reward for their continuing loyalty. As a consequence, in such cases, there may be an indicative level of dividend which could be a guide in a yield-based valuation.

There are two basic methods of approaching yield-type valuations.

The first one is to use a sustainable earnings-based valuation, as described above, and discount it heavily for a minority shareholding. The usual negotiations will apply when estimating an appropriate discount factor.

As we have seen the discount factor for a minority interest will be considerably greater than a discount for a majority or influential minority as, of course, a minority interest is basically an investment in expectation of a return rather than an investment with a view to influencing or controlling a business venture. In addition the small minority investor has no immediate exit route as there are usually restrictions on the right to transfer shares in a private company which would further tend to devalue any investment. As a result the discount factor to be applied will be extremely high, possibly as high as 90 per cent.

The second method is to look at:

- an average maintainable rate of dividend based on any historical rate of dividend paid to shareholders who are not active in the business, and
- apply an appropriate yield factor, taking into account the risks of investing in a private company. This would be considerably higher than, say, the yield from ordinary bonds or savings accounts.

and thus calculate a capital value from that. This is a relatively straightforward calculation, i.e. if the maintainable dividend per share is, say, £5 and the investor requires a yield of 11 per cent the price per share is £55.

As we stated at the beginning of this chapter, however a final value is arrived at, the process of arriving at it should be fully and clearly documented, if only to be able to deal with any enquiries from HMRC who might have their own ideas of what the value should be.

In a worst case scenario the valuer may have to justify their original valuation to a court, and without contemporaneous notes the basis could be made to look weak or informal thus rendering the valuer open to charges of negligence or poor practice.

Guidance on the valuation of interests in businesses has been given by the court in connection with matrimonial disputes, another area of increasing interest for the forensic accountant.

Matrimonial work – divorce and separation

In the majority of matrimonial cases the court has to make awards on the basis of a limited pool of assets and income and, consequently, the making of suitable provision for both parties and the needs of any children are relatively straightforward. However, where wealthy couples are concerned the situation is rather different, particularly where one of the principle assets is an interest in a business built up over the course of the marriage.

The entrepreneur who has built up a substantial business, which now comprises the bulk of their wealth and is the source of their ongoing income, is not now able to abandon their spouse in favour of a newer, younger model without the spouse's contribution to the growth of that business being recognised, even if the discarded spouse's part was to run the home and look after the kids while the empire was being built.

Prior to the case of *White* v *White* (2001) (1 AC 596), in 'clean break' cases one party could make a settlement on the other which was based, broadly, on income and housing needs. It was common for these needs to be annualised and converted into a lump sum under what was known as the 'Duxbury' formula based on actuarial tables known as Duxbury Tables.

A Duxbury calculation was an assessment of what level of lump sum a person would need in order to spend the rest of their life at a certain level of expenditure each year. The calculation presupposed that the lump sum would be invested, on receipt, at a specific rate of return for the remainder of the recipient's actuarial projected lifespan, and that the entire amount should have been spent by the time of the recipient's death.

Whilst this might be a big sum, this calculation often left one spouse with a considerably greater proportion of the joint wealth than the other, and the court has now held this to be unfair where both parties contributed to the success of the venture which created the wealth.

The decision in *White* v *White* ((2000) UKHL 54) (Exhibit 14.1) in 2000 resulted in a change away from an assessment based on need to a more equitable basis which recognised the contribution made to the growth of the couple's assets by both parties: this is where the forensic accountant comes in.

It is not unusual nowadays for divorcing couples with substantial assets to employ forensic accountants in the negotiations between the parties. Their involvement is often twofold:

- Valuing interests in businesses which provided the income for the family and which may comprise a substantial part of the joint wealth.
- Tracing assets which one party alleges the other may have hidden.

Exhibit 14.1 **Equitable split – *White* v *White***

In the *White* case the two parties, Mr and Mrs White, formed a farming partnership which was estimated to be worth £4 million. Both parties, through business work and domestic activity, had built up the business over the years.

When the marriage ended Mrs White was awarded £980,000 which was deemed sufficient to satisfy her needs regarding property and income.

However, it was pointed out that had she been treated as an equitable partner in the business she could have received much more. Eventually the House of Lords decided that her share, on an equitable basis, was worth £1.7 million – not quite half as Mr White's family had helped the two of them initially.

Source: UKHL (2000)

The family business

The *White* decision (Exhibit 14.1) represented a significant change in the law and a new direction for the courts. One consequence was to bring the share valuation expertise of the forensic accountant in valuing businesses more to the fore as the basis of apportionment is no longer income but tends to be assets based.

We looked at the valuation of businesses above and those principles, of course, hold true in divorce and separation cases as much as they do in the case of a simple sale and purchase. However, there is another facet of the valuation to consider which stems from the decision in White and that relates to the principle of equity.

This was explained by the judgement in another case, *McFarlane v McFarlane*, where the House of Lords ruled that the settlement should not simply cater for the wife's needs but also compensate her for her losses. In that case the wife had given up a successful career to bring up the couple's children and an element of the award was to compensate her for, effectively, the loss of her career or the potential for her to have a career.

At this point it is worth considering the words of Lord Nicholls in the McFarlane case:

> Valuations are often a matter of opinion on which experts differ. A thorough investigation into these differences can be extremely expensive and of doubtful utility . . . This is to misinterpret the exercise in which the court is engaged . . . a broad analysis, not a detailed accounting exercise.
>
> UKHL (2006)

He went on to say that valuations of private businesses 'are among the most fragile valuations that can be obtained'.

This can be shown by the robust approach of the judge in the *H v H* case shown in Exhibit 14.2.

Whilst a forensic accountant would be correct in observing the principles of share valuation set out above when making an initial assessment or claim, in divorce cases, as we have seen, the courts are undoubtedly looking for what they see as an equitable split and are not necessarily concerned with the technicalities of precise valuations.

In particular the courts are not particularly interested in the subtleties of minority v majority holdings or discounts for this and that, what they are looking for is a valuation of a business as an entity which appears fair and equitable and which the judge can then use as a basis for dividing up the assets between the parties. It is helpful therefore if forensic accountants advising each side take a view which is not too extreme in the first instance.

Consider the case of *H v H* shown in Exhibit 14.2. It is clear that, in that case, the respective forensic accountants were doing the best for their clients by arriving at valuations which might be said to be at opposite ends of the spectrum of possible values. The claimant went high, the defendant went low. This might have been helpful for the judgment, of course, as it identified where the middle ground was, but in other cases it may simply annoy the judge and lead to the imposition of a value which neither party is satisfied with.

Far better then for forensic accountants to try to agree a value pre-hearing and present the judge with a fait accompli. This is not to say that the judge will accept it, but it makes agreement more likely. Of course this is somewhat of an ideal position

Exhibit 14.2	The court's valuation of a business – the case of *H* v *H*

The thorny issue of business valuation was considered by Mr Justice Moylan in the case of *H* v *H* (2008) *EWHC 935*.

They were litigating over the capital value of a successful restaurant business, which had been owned by the husband long before this marriage (his second) had taken place, and in which he intended to continue to work.

In this case, the Judge clearly felt that from the outset the parties had adopted the most extreme of positions. The wife had asked for too much and the husband had offered too little. Both sides employed forensic accountants to value their interest.

Both accountants agreed that the valuation should be based on future maintainable earnings (FME) and the application of a multiplier to those earnings, in order to calculate the capital value of the business. The wife's accountant contended for FME of £856,000; the husband's, of £633,000. The wife's accountant applied a multiplier of 9; the husband's, a multiplier of 6. The parties then argued about the multiplier and about a number of other complex issues affecting the final figure. The judge considered them all, in the interests of fairness to both parties, but made it clear that he was not validating the exercise.

The Judge decided upon an FME of £725,000 and a multiplier of 6.5, which gave a net business valuation of £2.5 million. He found the husband's involvement of more than 33 years in the business as a relevant premarital contribution, and rejected the wife's application for equal division of capital.

Mr Justice Moylan expressly referred to fairness as the overriding principle. He assessed the wife's needs and, although both parties had argued for the wife to be given a clean break (the husband on the basis of an excessively low capital award, the wife on a near wipe-out of the husband's capital), found a clean break to be unachievable. He awarded the wife capital and continuing maintenance. Presumably, this satisfied neither party. After all, they had racked up joint legal costs of £400,000!

Source: Stowe (2008)

and, in real life, the intricacies of valuation are more likely to lead to some distance between the values but, by adopting the principles laid down in *H* v *H* and similar cases, forensic accountants may save the court time and their clients cost.

In the case of separation and divorce, in addition to their basic work on valuation, forensic accountants can also advise:

- on the best way of releasing funds from the business in order to meet liabilities under divorce or separation agreements
- on the sale of a business if it has to be realised to meet the capital requirements of the settlement, and
- in cases where funds need to be raised to meet the courts' requirements without disposing of the business.

In Scotland there is a broadly similar attitude towards matrimonial assets. Scotland operates a 'clean break' system and, consequently, the court will seek to ensure that both parties can get on with their lives without financial reliance on each other. Consequently lump sum settlements are the most common. Valuation issues for the forensic accountant in Scotland will thus be very similar to those of their colleagues in England and Wales.

Tracing the marital assets

In matrimonial work, as in so many other areas, the essential part of the forensic accountant's work is to establish, as nearly as possible the truth of the situation, i.e. to value what assets need valuing and to discover any assets that one party has attempted to conceal from the other so as to enable the court to make an appropriate decision.

We look at the general approach to asset tracing in more detail later, but these particular points are relevant when considering assets relating to marital disputes where they may have been moved suddenly when the split occurred, rather than as part of a systematic or planned deception or fraud.

In divorce cases each party has to submit what is formally called an 'Affidavit of Means' colloquially known as a 'Form E' from its technical name in the rules.

This 28-page form requires the parties to provide details of:

- capital assets, e.g. property, shares, bank accounts, etc.
- expensive personal assets, e.g. jewellery, cars, antiques, etc.
- liabilities, e.g. loans, mortgages overdrafts, etc.
- income from all sources including both earned and unearned, and
- future needs – what will be needed to support the individual and any children including accommodation requirements, need for a car, etc.

This provides the basic information the court needs to sort out the financial settlement between the parties.

Clearly in the case of very wealthy individuals concealment of assets and income is a great temptation. A recent survey by accountants Grant Thornton revealed that one-fifth of couples divorcing through the English and Welsh courts in 2007 tried to conceal assets or income from their spouse, a significant increase on the figure for 2006, when only 10 per cent of divorcing couples hid assets.

Of those concealing assets from their spouse, in the majority of cases (88 per cent) it was men that hid assets from their wives, up from 80 per cent in 2006, whereas only 2 per cent of women tried to conceal assets from their husbands, up from 0 per cent in 2006. In the remaining 10 per cent or so of instances, there was an equal split between men and women keeping assets or income under wraps.

They attributed this to:

- couples marrying later and thus being unwilling to lose wealth built up before the marriage, and
- the recent high-profile cases involving very wealthy individuals, particularly the Parlour case in which Mrs Parlour, ex-wife of former Arsenal footballer Ray Parlour, established a substantial claim on his future income which received a lot of media attention and may have served to encourage concealment.

Whatever the reasons it is, of course, unwise to conceal assets and income from the court, as lying to the court may involve a charge of perjury should the lies be revealed at a later date.

Solicitors, as officers of the court, are bound to report any instances of concealment they discover and should not be a party to concealment of assets from disclosure on Form E as failure to properly report to the court would be likely to be classed as fraud. Of course not all solicitors are so scrupulous, but the deceitful spouse may search in vain for a solicitor prepared to perjure themselves simply to save their client money.

Forensic accountants can be employed, where the case warrants, to search for assets and income which may be undeclared or which may have been moved out of the court's jurisdiction.

The information that each party has about the other is very important. Wives, if they have adopted a domestic role, for example, may not know much about the detailed workings of their husband's business, but they may recall conversations about overseas investments, may see documents relating to bank accounts, and may even be passive or active parties to tax avoidance (or evasion) strategies. The first port of call for the investigating forensic accountant is the client and their memory of past events plus any documentation they may have been able to get hold of.

Where there is a strong suspicion that assets have been deliberately concealed as part of a matrimonial dispute it is unlikely that solicitors will be involved, and even if they are they will be likely to plead client privilege in response to information requests. Accordingly, unless there is proof of criminal activity, i.e. completing a false declaration of Form E and deliberately hiding assets or income, obtaining information from the other party's solicitors or advisers will be virtually impossible. If proof becomes available, of course, this should be brought to the attention of the court. This is where the work of the forensic accountant could prove invaluable. Information obtained by illegal means is invalid and will not be recognised by the court.

The more obvious ways in which one party may seek to undervalue or disguise marital assets include:

- Failing to include or undervaluing antiques, artwork, hobby equipment and tools. These can be kept outside the marital home, for example, at work or hidden with friends or in undisclosed storage.
- Where there is property or cash overseas, use of overseas organisations such as a non-disclosing Lichtenstein-based *Anstalt* to dispose of the property and disburse the cash.
- Income that is unreported on tax returns and financial statements particularly where the business involved cash. Skimming cash by the owner may have been a useful (if illegal) tax evasion device in the past but this could result in a cash pile being accumulated which now forms part of the marital assets. This of course may be difficult to trace. The advantage to the skimmer, of course, is that it depresses the value of any business being valued and provides a handy little nest egg to be spent at leisure.
- Cash kept in the form of portable instruments such as travellers' cheques. These may be found by tracing bank account deposits and withdrawals.
- Cash invested in portable valuable assets such as gold, paintings, jewellery, stamps or coins which can be moved outside the jurisdiction of the court and the documentation for which may be extremely sketchy.
- A trust account set up in the name of a child, using the child's Social Security number.
- Investment in certificate 'bearer' municipal bonds or savings bonds. These do not appear on account statements.
- Collusion with an employer to delay bonuses, stock options, or salary increases until a time when the asset or income would be considered separate property.

- Creating a false obligation to a friend or an organisation, particulary one abroad in a low tax country, which has to be repaid.
- Expenses paid for a girlfriend or boyfriend, such as gifts, travel, rent, or tuition for college or classes which the party may be unwilling to disclose.
- A delay in signing long-term business contracts until after the divorce. Although this may seem like clever planning, if the intent is to lower the value of the business, it is considered to be hiding assets.
- Distorting the accounts of any businesses through delaying invoicing or increasing provisions for costs or against asset values such as inventories or receivables etc. so as to reduce the value for settlement purposes. This should be a futile gesture as forensic accountants will consider this possibility when examining the financial statements on behalf of the claimant for the purposes of valuing the asset.

More seriously, in cases where considerable wealth is involved, one party may attempt to conceal assets by moving them abroad. Clearly examination of bank statements, correspondence and e-mails may well uncover these attempts or, of course, the spouse could have prior knowledge of the existence of overseas assets.

Any indication of the presence of something like a company set up in a tax haven such as the British Virgin Islands should be treated with extreme suspicion and any transfers to it investigated. Where one party attempts to move assets overseas suddenly, particularly into so-called 'tax haven' countries or countries with restricted disclosure to the UK authorities, there are several considerations for the investigator.

Unless the assets comprise cash or valuables, literally taken out in suitcases, any transfer from a UK bank account will leave some sort of trail, at least initially. The point here, for the purposes of tracing the marital assets, is that it would not be necessary to find where the money ended up – only to establish that it had gone. In other words all the investigator has to do is identify the fact that, say, a large sum of money had been transferred out of a bank account to an unknown destination abroad: this would be enough for a prima facie case of concealment. The fact that the transferor then moved it through three other bank accounts into various other jurisdictions is irrelevant.

Money held in a bank account overseas, as opposed to being transferred to it at the time of the split, may be hard to find without recourse to legal action to force overseas banks to reveal details, actions which can be time-consuming and costly or, indeed, not work at all, dependent upon which countries are involved. Such overseas bank accounts can be funded by:

- mutual offset arrangements, e.g. where monies are paid into offshore accounts by an overseas person or organisation in return for some form of reciprocal arrangement in the UK
- arrangements whereby work done overseas is rewarded overseas and the monies are never repatriated to the UK or reported to the UK tax authorities, or
- fictitious loans made by false companies registered overeas and 'repaid' by funds remitted from the UK.

There may be some form of paper trail, particularly in the latter case, but often records are destroyed or concealed and, of course, one spouse may well have built up the overseas account without the knowledge of the other, for just such an eventuality as divorce.

Asset tracing

Asset tracing generally is a part of the forensic accountant's work which often derives from some other assignment they are involved in, as we have seen above in the case of matrimonial disputes. For example:

- a fraudster may have hidden assets in different bank accounts or overseas
- money launderers move funds constantly, and
- organisations may move assets out of the UK to evade tax.

The forensic accountant may be asked to trace hidden assets, whether they are deposits in undisclosed UK bank accounts or the illicit proceeds of criminal activity laundered through a number of organisations either held offshore or disguised as legitimate businesses.

Individuals engaged in criminal activity, in particular dealing in such crimes as drug dealing, prostitution or people trafficking, often generate large amounts of cash. As these people do not wish to live conventional lives they need to create a legitimate front to explain their lifestyles and they do this by setting up businesses through which they can launder the proceeds of their illicit activities. Such businesses traditionally deal in cash, or could legitimately deal in cash transactions, and sliding illegal receipts in amongst genuine activity 'washes' the illegal money, which is then able to be used legitimately by the proprietors of such businesses. These front organisations will pay tax and VAT in the usual way.

Typical of the kind of business ventures used to wash illicit funds are:

- restaurants
- bars
- shops/mini markets
- scrap metal dealerships
- travel agencies – useful for transferring funds overseas, and
- property.

The process of tracing is far from easy and can ultimately prove futile, but there is considerable scope for investigation which may produce results.

Clearly the first thing the investigating accountant needs is information. If funds have been moved through bank accounts there is always a trail – the difficulty is in following it to where the information is not immediately accessible. It is always assumed that, in the case of offshore banks in tax havens or deposits with Swiss bankers, information is not forthcoming but this is not necessarily the case – and the situation is changing.

In many cases individuals move money through a complex series of bank transactions but assets can be moved or concealed in a variety of ways:

- The use of shell companies or trusts to buy property or assets overseas. Companies can be incorporated in countries with low or non-existent reporting regimes. By judicious use of fraudulent documentation funds can be transferred to these companies and used to buy property overseas outside the jurisdiction of the UK courts. An example of this kind of organisation is the *Anstalt* – a trust-type organisation permitted under Lichtenstein law.
- Use of front companies and false loans – again companies are incorporated in countries with a high level of corporate secrecy. The company then makes a 'loan' to the fraudster which is repaid. The loan isn't real but the repayments are.

- Foreign bank transfers – there are countries where the banks make no enquiries as to the source of large deposits of currency. This is a great benefit to the fraudster who can move money out of the UK into such accounts and it becomes extremely difficult to trace the subsequent movement of those funds once they disappear into a bank with no currency disclosure rules. The money may not stay with the original transferee bank but may be moved into other jurisdictions. Companies in tax havens such as the British Virgin Islands can be formed using the Internet and are frequently used by fraudsters to overcome some of the restrictions placed on the opening of new accounts by UK banks (Chapter 15).
- The use of false invoices by import/export companies has proved to be a very effective way of integrating illicit proceeds back into the economy. This involves the overvaluation of entry documents to justify the funds later deposited in domestic banks and/or the value of funds received from exports. This can be a way of repatriating funds previously moved abroad.
- The use of 'parallel banking' procedures such as the hawala or chit systems may enable funds to be moved internationally without any cash effectively leaving the UK. This involves the use of brokers or middle men (and women) who will arrange for the mutual exchanges of funds. Such arrangements are extremely difficult, if not impossible, for the investigator to penetrate and large scale hawala-type dealings have to be investigated by government agencies with investigatory powers.

There is increasing pressure on so-called tax haven countries by the UK tax authorities to reveal information about deposits held by UK residents. The latest countries that have agreed to do this are Lichtenstein, Dominica, Grenada and Belize. Individuals with bank deposits in Lichtenstein, for example, will be forced to voluntarily disclose them to HMRC or face severe penalties should accounts be revealed subsequent to an amnesty period granted by HMRC to encourage such voluntary disclosure. Use of an *Anstalt*, for example, may help disguise invested funds but the *Anstalt* has to make an annual report to the Lichtenstein tax authorities who are now co-operating with HMRC so non-disclosure is unwise.

Asset tracing, whether in the course of a matrimonial dispute or not, is an interesting if perhaps mildly frustrating part or the forensic accountant's work. Valuation of businesses is something which recalls more traditional accounting skills as is the next aspect of the forensic accountant's work, that of dealing with claims.

Summary

- A growing part of the forensic accountant's work is advising on business valuations.
- These can be as part of acquisitions but also in connection with marital disputes.
- The basis of valuation will depend on the size of the holding being sold.
- An assets basis is normally appropriate for valuing majority holdings but for minorities some form of earnings basis is used.
- These can involve establishing a level of maintainable profits and applying a multiplier to them.
- These issues form the bases of disagreement between forensic accountants in dispute cases and the court will apply its own approach based on the needs of the parties and fairness.

- The criteria applied by the court have changed and forensic accountants should be aware of current case law as it applies to valuation of marital assets.
- Where one party has attempted to hide marital assets, forensic accountants may be involved in tracing them.
- This involves following the trail if assets have been transferred abroad or reviewing the underlying truth behind loan or expenses schemes where monies are transferred abroad.

Bibliography

Bloomfield, S. (2006) Divorce settlements B.A.C.K.L.A.S.H. *Independent*, 5 February.

Draper, N. (2009) *Selling a Practice in the Recession*. Draper Hinks, Southam.

Drury, C. (2004) *Management and Cost Accounting*. Thompson Learning, London.

High Court of Justice Family Division (2007) *H v H*. 2007 EWHC 459 (Fam).

HM Courts Service (2005) *Form E Financial Statement – Ancillary Relief*. HM Courts Service, London.

HM Revenue and Customs (nd) *Share and Assets Valuation*. HMRC, London.

Grant Thornton (2010) *One-fifth of Divorcing Couples Hide Assets from their Spouse*. Grant Thornton LLP, London.

IRC (1994) *IRC v Gray (Executor of Lady Fox, deceased)* 1994 STC 360.

Kapila, R. (2008) *The Forensic Accountant's Changing Role in Matrimonial Disputes*. Sim Kapila, London.

NIFA (2009) Credit crunch squeezes multipliers. *NIFA News*, Issue 20, NIFA, London.

Stowe, M. (2008) *Divorce, Hidden Assets and Suspected Fraud – What Can you Do?* Marilyn Stowe LLP, Harrogate.

Supreme Court of Judicature (2004) *Parlour v Parlour*. EWCA (Civ) 872.

Wood, F. (2008) *Business Accounting*, 2nd edn. Pearson, Harlow.

Wood, N. (2008) *Asset Tracing and Recovery – Tools of the Trade*. International Bar Association, London.

UKHL (2000) *White v White*. UKHL54 2000 3WLR 1571.

UKHL (2006) *McFarlane v McFarlane*. 2006 UKHL 24.

Valuation Office Agency (2006) *Inheritance Tax Manual – Practice Note 1: Valuations for Revenue Purposes*. Valuation Office Agency, London.

Websites

www.bailii.org/ew/cases

www.draperhinks.com

www.ewi.org.uk

www.familylawweek.co.uk

www.grant-thornton.co.uk/press_room

www.hmcourts-service.gov.uk

www.hmrc.gov.uk/sharesschemes

www.ibanet.org

www.marilynstowe.co.uk

www.parliament.uk

www.voa.gov.uk/instructions

Chapter 15

Claims

Chapter contents
- Introduction
- Consequential loss claims and damages for loss
- Personal injury and medical negligence claims
- Challenging confiscation orders

Learning objectives

After studying this chapter you should be able to:
- Develop an understanding of the forensic approach to consequential loss and damages claims
- Appreciate the role of the forensic accountant in medical negligence claims
- Understand the principles behind challenging Confiscation Orders made under the Proceeds of Crime Act 2002

Introduction

Some of these aspects of the forensic accountant's work have been the province of accountants for many years and are not new at all. The principles of establishing losses for consequential loss claims is a familiar one to many accountants in practice but they are worth looking at here, if for no other reason than many students of forensic accountancy who have not had the benefit of long years in a practising accountant's office will find something of value to think about, hopefully!

What is new to the practice of forensic accountancy is the increasing amount of work coming from challenges to Confiscation Orders made under the Proceeds of Crime Act 2002. As we saw in Chapter 3 the court has the power to grant such an order where individuals are living what is deemed to be a criminal lifestyle. These orders are brutal and make no distinction or allowance for families or spouses. The matrimonial home can be taken even if the poor spouse had no idea her hubby was a drug baron. However, it is possible for a defence to be mounted in order to save assets which might have been honourably acquired.

Forensic accountants may worry about the morality of this. The client is, of course, a convicted criminal, moreover a criminal convicted of a very serious crime – otherwise the Order could not be granted. Should accountants be trying to save the assets of such individuals – or do they deserve all they get? The answer is, of course, that the forensic accountant has to act objectively and with integrity. If someone has been unfairly treated, even if they are a convicted criminal, they are still entitled to the protection of the law. If the forensic accountant accepts the work they are bound to do it to the best of their ability, no matter what wrong the client has done and who they may have done it to.

Consequential loss claims and damages for loss

The term 'consequential loss' is well known in English law because claims under the heading of 'consequential loss' are, in reality, damages claims of a special nature. This is because they arise under some form of contract – be it a construction contract, a rental agreement or a contract of insurance.

In many cases consequential loss or loss of profits claims arise in connection with a contract of insurance where compensation is required as a result of some event, e.g. a fire, flood or other catastrophe. In the case of construction or other contracts restitution may be required as a result of a failure or negligent behaviour on the part of one of the parties resulting in a loss to the other. For example delays in completion of a building beyond an agreed point may affect the trading of the business which was supposed to move into that building on the agreed date – a fact which should have been in the minds of the parties to the contract when they signed it.

Because of the legal nature of such damages it is instructive to look at the definition in the leading case of *Hadley v Baxendale* in which the judge said:

> Where two parties have made a contract which one of them has broken, the damages which the other party ought to receive in respect of such breach of contract should be such as may fairly and reasonably be considered either:

> (1) arising naturally, i.e. according to the usual course of things from such breach of contract itself; or
>
> (2) such as may reasonably be supposed to have been in the contemplation of both parties at the time they made the contract as the probable result of the breach of it.
>
> Court of Exchequer (1854)

The test here is foreseeability insofar as any quantum of loss is not confined simply to the immediate damage but should also include restitution for all losses which might fairly and reasonably have been foreseen by the parties in respect of the event or failure which triggered the claim.

For example, suppose a business occupies a building which it rents from a landlord. The building burns down as a result of defective wiring which is the landlord's responsibility. The restitution is not simply the repairs to the building, the replacement of stock, fixtures and fittings of the business etc., it is the loss of profits caused by the inability of the business to trade and the costs of setting that business back on its feet again. These additional losses should have been 'in the contemplation' of the parties at the time the lease was signed, i.e. what if the building burns down and the business suffers?

Compensation thus takes two forms:

1 Restitution for losses which are a direct and natural consequence of the event or breach of contract, for example, the cost of remedying defects which are classed as direct losses.

2 Compensation for losses which do not arise from the natural course of events but which may be a consequence of it providing that was in the minds of the parties when the agreement was made. These are called indirect losses.

The term 'losses', in the context of indirect losses, can mean more than just the loss of potential profits. In fact, under English law, the courts have sometimes included loss of profits in the first category of direct losses. In a case involving the destruction of a chemical plant (*Deepak Fertilisers and Petrochemicals Corporation v ICI Chemicals & Polymers Ltd and Others*) the court found that reconstruction costs and loss of profits all arose as a direct result of the breach of contract or duty of care so were classed as direct losses.

The effect of this is that compensation payable under the second heading – indirect losses – may, of course, include loss of profits but could also include compensation for such things as:

- loss of market share
- loss of business opportunities etc.
- business interruption
- product liability
- claims for loss or liquidated damages from third parties, and
- fixed costs and overheads.

Forensic accountants may be involved in assembling such claims but, of course, may also be retained to refute them. Insurance companies and legal firms often retain forensic accountants to attempt to dismantle claims brought against their clients by litigators.

Typically, for example, in the case of business interruption, forensic accountants may be called in at an early stage to help assist in minimising losses. Even in difficult situations businesses should attempt to minimise their claim as much as reasonably possible. They simply cannot spend spend spend on the assumption that it will all be rolled into their claim and be refunded when the claim is settled.

In other cases forensic accountants may be involved in preparing a case as part of legal proceedings and may be required to act as expert witnesses.

By their nature no two claims will be the same and it is impossible to consider every type of case the forensic accountant may find themselves involved in, but we will look at some of the more common situations.

Loss of profits/business interruption claims

Where a loss of profits claim is concerned the forensic accountant must make an estimate of the losses arising as a result of the event or breach of contract. Clearly this process is driven by the requirements and conditions of any contract of insurance or other form of agreement under which the claim is being brought.

For example a contract of insurance may have specific requirements regarding the calculation of losses capable of being claimed under the policy: it may specify certain exclusions of costs or earnings which cannot form part of any claim.

Clearly these conditions must be complied with if the insurers are to accept the claim, so the starting point for the forensic accountant is the contract under which the claim is being brought.

When trying to establish the quantum of any claim the first port of call for the forensic accountant will, of course, be historical information which can be used as a basis for projections of what the business might have achieved. This will be in the form of accounts, budgets, financial records etc. The methodology used incorporates many of the same techniques used when calculating future maintainable earnings (Chapter 14) in connection with business valuations.

The process will involve:

- An analysis of sales, costs and overheads. These figures will have to be analysed carefully to remove unsustainable results, exceptional losses, one-off events, etc.
- Adjustments where aspects of the business have been discontinued or where new income streams were established.
- These then can be extrapolated to create a picture of what results the business might have achieved had it not been for whatever happened. The bases and assumptions under which projections are made must be carefully considered as it is these which will be most open to direct challenge. Most accountants will be able to come to an agreement on an analysis of historical data but the subjectivity of assumptions is another matter entirely.

  Factors to be considered include such matters as:
  - changes to the customer base – new customers, loss of old ones
  - changes to suppliers or terms and conditions of supply
  - changes in the market which could affect the marketability of products or services, e.g. competition, new technology, new products
  - the actions of competitors – including pricing issues, and
  - political and economic factors affecting the business.

- Changes in the operations of the business immediately prior to the event may be significant. For example the launch of a new product may indicate an increase in sales, closure or planned closure of a factory might indicate problem areas.

- Increased costs arising from the catastrophic event, e.g. hire of computer equipment, rental and storage costs etc. should also be considered. The forensic accountant's fees for preparing the claim may also be capable of being included in it.
- Savings made because of lower operational activity levels or fortuitous cost savings which the business is able to take advantage of as a result of the event, for example, not reopening a costly site and re-allocating the workforce, need to be factored in to the claim.

Once the claim has been calculated the bases and assumptions used must be clearly documented as these will form part of the negotiations which will undoubtedly ensue once the claim is submitted. Any discussions will not centre on the quantum of the numbers, it will be based on the underlying assumptions and suppositions. There is nothing wrong with adopting an optimistic view of these, however it should be pointed out that adopting an extreme view will result in time and cost to the client – the principle is *not* akin to haggling in a bazaar, it is aimed at arriving at an acceptable solution as quickly and painlessly as possible. After all the client has already suffered a loss – there is no need to make it any worse.

Damages

Parties to a contract may agree a set or calculated sum that would be paid by the defaulting one in the event of a breach of a contract. These are referred to as 'liquidated damages' due to the fact that a court is not required to quantify the losses sustained. In other words there is a formula within the contract which specifies how such damages are to be calculated in the event of some form of breach which triggers the relevant clause.

In order to be enforceable however such liquidated damages clauses may not be penal in nature. This was established in the case of *Dunlop Pneumatic Tyre Co Ltd* v *New Garage Co Ltd* where the court decided that a liquidated damages clause would be considered a penalty and unenforceable where the sum to be paid by the defendant was 'extravagant and unconscionable in amount in comparison with the greatest loss that could conceivably be provided to have followed from the breach'.

The sum of liquidated damages should be based on a pre-estimate of likely losses arising in the event of non-performance of their part of the contract by one of the parties to it. If it is not, or is excessive, it may be considered to be a penalty clause and therefore unenforceable at law. Where the situation is not clear forensic accountants may be asked to advise as to whether or not any damages clause within the contract may be considered to be excessive.

In deciding whether a liquidated damages clause is a penalty or not, the court will take into consideration:

- Does the contract itself refer to the clause as a liquidated damages clause or a penalty?
- Is the basis of calculation or the estimate of loss imprecise? In other words is the sum a genuine pre-estimate of the losses that would be sustained or is it disproportionate to the actual losses that could be sustained? Note, however that a stipulated amount is not considered necessarily disproportionate simply because it is notably greater than any actual loss that was sustained.
- Was there, at the time the contract was signed, an imbalance of bargaining power between the parties such that one party effectively dictated the terms of the contract to the other?

- There is a presumption that a clause will be a penalty when a single sum is payable on the occurrence of one or more breaches, some of which may be serious and others may be trifling.
- If it is difficult or impossible to pre-estimate the loss then the clause is less likely to be a penalty.

Generally, if the basis of calculation is acceptable, the courts are reluctant to upset such clauses where both parties had full freedom of contract to make the agreement between them in the first place. If however there is an element of oppressiveness in the contract or the sum is considered to be excessive the court may consider it disproportionate.

Any liquidated damages clause can be calculated with reference to a formula or time period.

In these cases the role of the forensic accountant may be twofold:

1 At the point the contract is drawn up to advise on the formula for the estimation of liquidated damages – in other words pre-estimating the loss.
2 In reviewing the calculation under the contract in the event a claim is made.

The key element in this is clearly the wording of the agreement or contract. Where the wording is ambiguous or capable of misinterpretation the basis on which the forensic accountants have made their calculations should be clearly stated and they must then be prepared to defend their work, if necessary, as part of legal proceedings brought to resolve any ambiguity.

Care should be taken as to the jurisdiction under which damages claims are to be calculated as other countries have different legal bases for looking at these sorts of claims.

Personal injury and medical negligence claims

Forensic accountants may be asked to advise on connection with personal injury claims where the claimant suffers a loss due to negligence, i.e. a loss which is attributable to the negligence of another person who owed a duty of care to the claimant. Typically these are medical negligence cases but they can also arise as a result of industrial injury or hazard caused by negligence in the workplace.

This area is, of course, mostly the province of lawyers and has received a bad press recently through legal firms being accused of 'ambulance chasing' and 'where there's a pain there's a claim' tactics by some unscrupulous firms. Despite this the losses suffered by claimants are very real and forensic accountants can contribute to ensuring that the financial calculations are on a sound footing and that all aspects of the financial claim have been included.

Before May 2007 forensic accountants were frequently called to advise in damages claims because of the uncertainty surrounding the court's approach to the quantum of such claims, what has been described as somewhat of a 'finger in the air' approach. Judges were able to exercise a considerable degree of discretion in the calculation of claims, other than fatal accident claims, where there was a prospect of a future loss of earnings as a result of the incident. Following the case of *Wells* v *Wells* (1999) the courts established that the basis of the award was to calculate a lump sum which, when invested as an annuity at 3 per cent per annum, would return sufficient to both compensate the victim for loss of earnings and to meet the costs of medical care. The awards took account of the victim's age, gender, type of occupation and level of economic activity.

In addition to the basic quantum of damages victims were able to claim so-called 'Smith & Manchester' awards which compensated them for possible damage to their competitive position in the labour market.

However, May 2007 saw the publication of the sixth edition of the Ogden Tables, actuarial tables for use in personal injury and fatal accident cases. The tables provide an aid for those assessing the lump sum appropriate as compensation for a continuing future pecuniary loss or consequential expense, such as care costs, in personal injury and fatal accident cases. The tables are prepared by the Government Actuary's Department.

These tables were based on much more recent research which established that the key factors which determined whether an individual remained in work until retirement age were:

- employment status
- disability, and
- educational attainment.

These provided a much more actuarial basis for calculating awards and, whilst adoption of these tables is not mandatory, the view is that the court would find it difficult to avoid using them.

The new Ogden 6 tables removed some of the vagaries of the 'Smith & Manchester' awards and has, consequently, had a major impact on the work of forensic accountants in connection with such claims. Much of the work now lies purely in the province of lawyers arguing about the applicability of the various multipliers and multiplicands to be used in the formulae.

However, it may be that there is still work to do in connection with claims involving the self-employed. The basis of the tables involves calculations based on past and future earnings. The basis of the calculations are, broadly, to apply a multiplier from one of the Ogden 6 tables to the claimant's present earnings and then to discount the total produced for their future earnings potential, again based on an appropriate multiplier from within the tables.

The forensic accountant could be called in to advise on what might be considered to be appropriate income levels. As we have seen elsewhere in this Part this would involve consideration of the pattern of earnings from the business, taking into account any exceptional or unusual items and confining the calculation to maintainable earnings.

The report should include considerations of:

- Reported earnings based on accounts – audited or not – and tax returns, etc.
- Income earned which has not been reported, i.e. cash sales concealed from HMRC. This of course may cause further repercussions if included in a claim – but they should be considered.
- Decisions about the business which might have been taken but for the accident or incident. These of course are easy for the claimant to state but less easy to prove. The court will not entertain wildly speculative claims or claims which are patently unfeasible but future plans which could have come to fruition should be considered.
- Budgets and projections based on reasonable assumptions.

The effect of the injury on the individual and their business and the resultant impact on future profits will have to be considered. Where the individual is the key driving force in the business and plays a significant part in its growth and development which, as a result of the accident, they are no longer able to do, the effect on the earnings of that business may well be substantial and this would have to be recognised by the court in the Ogden calculations.

Challenging confiscation orders

Under the Proceeds of Crime Act 2002 (Chapter 3) criminals in the UK who are enjoying what the law calls a 'criminal lifestyle' as a result of criminal activity may be subject to a Confiscation order. Under Section 75 a person has definitely a criminal lifestyle if the offence is one of a list of involving such crimes as:

- drug trafficking
- directing terrorism
- people trafficking
- money laundering
- arms trafficking
- counterfeiting
- intellectual property crimes (copyright infringement)
- pimping and brothel-keeping, and
- blackmail.

If convicted of one of these offences then the individual is deemed to have a criminal lifestyle so that any assets they have will be deemed to be derived from their criminal lifestyle and thus subject to confiscation.

The other way to be deemed to have a criminal lifestyle is if the conviction relates to general criminal conduct, i.e. that the individual is basically a full-time criminal, or particular criminal conduct relating to the offence for which they were convicted. If found to have a criminal lifestyle the prosecution can pursue the defendant for everything they have or it can be restricted to the benefit from the offence that the defendant has just been convicted of.

Contrary to the usual legal principle of criminal law in the UK, that an individual is innocent until proven guilty, in these cases the burden of proof lies with the defendant, in other words it is up to them to prove that the assets that they have were *not* gained as a result of criminal conduct. The court will make a presumption that such assets were gained as a result of a criminal lifestyle unless the individual can prove otherwise.

The problem with Confiscation orders made under the Act is that they are permanent. This means that if any residue of the order remains unsatisfied after the initial swoop by the authorities on known assets, any assets which the defendant subsequently acquires can also be subject to the order. So if, say, on release from prison the ex-criminal 'goes straight', gets a job and buys a house, this too can be confiscated under the order to meet any unsatisfied historic liability, plus interest.

The problem that a forensic accountant might well be faced with does not lie with identifying the assets acquired as a result of crime, that is the responsibility of the state, but in preventing assets being seized that should not be subject to the order. The work entails, in other words, defending the criminal's own property as opposed to someone else's property that they happen to be in possession of or which they acquired as a result of being a criminal as opposed to, say, being a solicitor.

The court, when trying to determine how much a defendant has benefited from crime, will not be restricted to the crime of which the accused has just been convicted but will instead 'assume' that the defendant has a criminal lifestyle and that all monies/property received in the previous six years derives from their general criminal conduct. The prosecution will attempt to list all the major transactions over the last six year period and invite the court to apply the assumption of criminality.

The lifestyle finding in itself is not the problem, that is a question of fact to be determined by the court, it is the assumptions that follow that is the concern of the forensic accountant.

There are two ways of avoiding the assumptions:

- First, the court cannot make the assumption if it is shown to be incorrect, so that if the defendant can show that a particular source of income was entirely legitimate then the assumption cannot be made that it wasn't. In that case the legitimate income is excluded from any calculation.
- Second, an assumption can be avoided if there would be a serious risk of injustice if the assumption were made. This could include so-called 'double-counting' where the Crown's calculations appear to include property considered more than once.

For example a defendant convicted of money laundering charge may well have had a legitimate income as, say, a solicitor or banker. If that is a fact and details of income can be accepted by the prosecution, rather than having to call witnesses, then it can be pointed out that it is beyond dispute that there was some legitimate income in an attempt at avoiding the statutory assumptions of criminality for six years. Further if it can be established that the defendant had a legitimate income or that their lifestyle could be explained by some other legitimate income stream, say gambling or being an amateur antique dealer, then those assertions also become part of the defence case.

Forensic accountants can use these admissions to quantify any income or assets acquired by legitimate means so as to exclude them for any confiscation order made after conviction.

The process to be adopted by the forensic accountant is, again, one of searching records to identify income streams and expenditures which could be legitimate.

The process can be based around:

- Taking early action – if the defendant is convicted and the crime is covered by the Act a claim may well follow, so getting hold of all the client's records as early as possible is a good start. The actual client will be the criminal's legal representative and any report will be made to them. This will maximise the possibility of legal privilege. If the appeal against the order is retrospective then all the information may well have to be obtained from the prosecution.
- Bank records are crucial so these must be taken into the possession of the client's lawyer as soon as possible. Similarly any accounting records etc. should also be secured.
- It is important to get a conference with the criminal as soon as possible. They may be unwilling to do this as they have just been convicted of a serious crime and may be facing a lengthy period of imprisonment, however the client's lawyer may well be able to persuade them to meet with the forensic accountant.

- If possible all the prosecution's legal papers and files should be obtained to see what they have and the basis of any claim made or about to be made.
- Delay paying any money over or liquidating any assets for as long as possible – it is far easier to pay over than to recover any overpayment.
- Where there are accounting records, for example where the criminal had a business, these may be incomplete. Much of the material handed to the forensic accountant may be irrelevant or inconsistent but it may be possible to demonstrate that the business generated profits or surpluses which could fund the purchase of assets, such as a house. Other records such as bank statements, cheque book stubs, paying in books, correspondence, diaries etc. may well indicate legitimacy.

Clearly if the individual is a career criminal and has no other activity this is a futile exercise and probably shouldn't be started, but where there is demonstrable income it is often worthwhile. The forensic accountant's fees may well be capable of being covered by Legal Aid if the individual has already had all their assets claimed. The work of the forensic accountant in these cases may well preserve some assets for those left behind so it is worth considering.

In the next chapter we look at the final aspect of the forensic accountant's work, that of acting as an expert witness.

Exhibit 15.1	Example – confiscation orders: beware the unguarded moment!

The accused admitted to the possession of Class A drugs under caution at a taped interview.

The arresting officer carried on what seemed to be a casual conversation after this admission wherein the accused admitted having been a drug addict for 15 years and having used heroin, marijuana and cocaine on a daily basis.

On the basis of this 'evidence' a confiscation order was made for £65,700 being the 'benefit' of an estimated £30 per day habit for 365 days for the previous six years.

The burden of proof then fell on the defendant to prove that he had a legitimate source of income to meet the cost of his habit.

Source: NIFA News (2007)

Summary

- Forensic accountants frequently become involved in determining amounts due under insurance policies for consequential loss.
- There may be conditions under which a claim has to be formulated.
- Claims can be brought for damages which were foreseeable at the time the contract was signed.
- Care has to be taken to distinguish a claim from a penalty which is not enforceable.
- The work in connection with personal injury and negligence claims has changed since the publication of the Ogden 6 tables although there may still be call for a forensic accountant in the case of self-employed individuals.

- Confiscation claims made under the Proceeds of Crime Act 2002 can be challenged to show that assets were not acquired as a result of criminal acts but through genuinely legitimate means.

Bibliography

Brown, C. (2007) *Ogden 6 – Swings & Roundabouts*. Barlow Lyde & Gilbert, London.

Clarke, J. (2008) *Contingency Rethink Sparks New Approach*. Clarke, J., Hardwicke Bldgs, London.

Court of Exchequer (1854) *Hedley* v *Baxendale*. 1854 9 Exch 341.

Deepak Fertilisers Petrochemicals Corporation v *ICT & Others* (1998) 2 Lloyd's Rep. 139.

Denton Wilde Sapte LLP (2008) *Consequences of 'Consequential Loss'*. Denton Wilde Sapte, London.

Dunlop Pneumatic Tyre Co Ltd v *New Garage Co* (1915) AC 79.

Furmston, M. (2008) *Cheshire, Fifoot and Furmston's Law of Contract*. Oxford University Press, Oxford.

HMSO (2002) *Proceeds of Crime Act 2002*. HMSO, London.

NIFA (2007) Forensic accountants in confiscation proceedings. *NIFA News*, issue 18.

Pearson, G. (2008) *Forensic Accounting in Insurance Claims*. Vantis, London.

Turner, C. (2007) *Unlocking Contract Law*. Hodder Education, London.

Wells v *Wells* (1999) 1AC 345.

Websites

www.bailii.org/ew/cases

www.blg.co.uk

www.nifa.co.uk/publication

www.opsi.gov.uk

www.vantisplc.com

Chapter 16

The forensic accountant as expert witness

Chapter contents

- Introduction
- Civil proceedings
- Criminal proceedings
- Duties of the expert witness
- Preparing the report
- Specific accounting issues in reporting

Learning objectives

After studying this chapter you should be able to:

- Understand the role of the accountant as an expert witness
- Appreciate the difference in approach between civil and criminal proceedings
- Appreciate the role of the expert witness in court proceedings
- Understand how to construct an expert witness report

 **Introduction**

Under the normal rules of evidence the opinion of a witness is not normally admissible: witnesses are to confine themselves to known facts and should not provide the court with the benefit of their view of the case before it. It is up to the court to come to a judgment on the matter and judges take great care in jury trials to avoid the risk of the jury being unduly influenced by the opinions of witnesses.

One exception to this rule is the expert who is called to advise the court on matters which the court lacks the competence to deal with itself, usually those of a technical nature such as medical, technical or scientific issues.

An expert is defined as an individual qualified by academic achievement or experience (or usually both). In fact the courts are generally less impressed by academic or professional qualifications than they are by relevant practical experience and may be persuaded to accept evidence from individuals with proven competence in a particular field but without formal qualifications, however, in most cases, experts called to testify are qualified by both experience and achievement.

Where either a criminal or civil legal action is contemplated the forensic accountant may well find themselves involved as an expert witness and a report, prepared by a forensic accountant under instruction, may well end up as part of proceedings.

The role of the expert is to advise the court. The expert is there to provide the facts around which the arguments might rage and partially on the basis of which a judgment is made. The facts of the expert's report may be unchallenged and unassailable or they may be subject to severe cross-examination in the course of proceedings.

It is important to appreciate the differences between civil and criminal proceedings as they are subject to different rules. The forensic accountant should clearly understand the various rules appropriate to each type of legal process which we will summarise here.

We will also look at reporting requirements. It is beyond the scope of this book to look at the principles of evidence in all its legal finery, or indeed to consider the minutiae of court proceedings. Instead we will concentrate on the principles expert witnesses must abide by, whatever they are called upon to do. There is one important point to make here.

This chapter only relates to situations where the forensic accountant is acting as an expert. In many criminal trials, say a fraud trial, much of the evidence for the prosecution may be derived from the work of the forensic accountant. However, that investigation report will probably have been written to the client's lawyer in an effort to maximise legal privilege and will be a recital of work done and discoveries made, it will, in short be a factual report of what happened. It will not be the report of an expert per se and this Part is not relevant to that kind of report.

However, in formulating a report it might be useful for the forensic accountant to be cognisant of the reporting requirements under the Criminal Procedure Rules and to use the format as a basic template.

At this point it may also be useful for the putative expert to point out the existence of the Expert Witness Institute (EWI) in London who maintain a database of experts and publish very useful information. Individuals who are called to give expert testimony would do well to consult their publications.

Forensic accountants approached to be expert witnesses will need clear instructions and a letter of engagement. The EWI publish pro forma documents and a

Code of Practice. Alternatively accountants will need to agree a letter under the provisions of The International Standard on Related Services (ISRS) 4400 *Engagements to perform agreed-upon procedures regarding financial information,* published by the International Auditing and Assurance Standards Board (IAASB) which sets out the minimum content of a letter of engagement which, suitably adapted, could be used in these circumstances.

The EWI also have model forms of report for both civil and criminal assignments which may prove useful to the reporting accountant.

This book concentrates on the requirements contained in the Rules, which are the minimum needed to satisfy the court.

Civil proceedings

The process of giving evidence in civil proceedings is determined by the Civil Procedure Rules 1998 Part 35 ('the Rules') as subsequently modified. Forensic accountants who may act for the court in civil proceedings should familiarise themselves with the Rules and the subsequent modifications. The latest modification is number 51. The Civil Justice Council has issued a protocol which sets out the procedures to be adopted and this should be studied closely.

The Rules state unequivocally that the expert evidence should be the independent product of the expert uninfluenced by the pressures of litigation. The role of the expert is to assist the court by providing objective, unbiased opinions on matters within their expertise. They should not assume the role of an advocate.

In preparing their report the expert should consider all material facts, including those which might detract from their opinions. Experts should make it clear:

- when a question or issue falls outside their area of expertise (see below), and
- when they are not able to reach a definite opinion, for example because they have insufficient information.

Both sides to a dispute may appoint their own expert and it is usual, but not mandatory, in such cases for the experts to meet prior to the proceedings. The purpose of such a meeting is to agree and to narrow down the contentious issues and in particular to identify:

- the extent of the agreement between them
- the points of and short reasons for any disagreement
- action, if any, which may be taken to resolve any outstanding points of disagreement, and
- any further material issues not raised and the extent to which these issues are agreed.

In some cases the court will consider whether to give permission for the parties to rely on evidence from a single joint expert. The court will take into account all the circumstances, in particular whether:

- it is proportionate to have separate experts for each party on a particular issue with reference to:
  - the amount in dispute
  - the importance to the parties, and
  - the complexity of the issue.

- the instruction of a single joint expert is likely to assist the parties and the court to resolve the issue more speedily and in a more cost-effective way than separately instructed experts
- questions put to a single joint expert may not conclusively deal with all issues that may require testing prior to trial in which case a single expert may not be appropriate.

The form and content of the report

The Rules lay down a minimum content of report and how it should be prepared. It is important to follow these rules as the court is used to seeing reports prepared on this basis and may reject as unsuitable some other form unless all these requirements are included. It goes without saying that the expert's report must be clearly and succinctly written and deal purely with the relevant issues.

However, authors of reports should be aware that their reports may well be read by persons who have little or no technical knowledge. Consequently it may be necessary to explain fundamental principles and concepts – even perhaps the basics of double entry bookkeeping – which if necessary may require the use of diagrams and examples.

At all costs the report must be free of jargon or unexplained abbreviations even if these are in familiar use within the profession. For example mention of 'UK GAAP', without explaining what it is, is likely to leave the lay person baffled and totally unappreciative of the no doubt significant point being made. Worse the use of such abbreviations and jargon may require the expert to come to court to explain their report, which may damage their credibility as a witness.

An expert's report should be addressed to the court and not to the party from whom the expert has received their instructions. The expert's report must:

- give details of the expert's qualifications
- give details of any literature or other material which has been relied on in making the report
- contain a statement setting out the substance of all facts and instructions which are material to the opinions expressed in the report or upon which those opinions are based
- make clear which of the facts stated in the report are within the expert's own knowledge, and
- say who carried out any examination, measurement, test or experiment which the expert has used for the report, give the qualifications of that person, and say whether or not the test or experiment has been carried out under the expert's supervision.
- where there is a range of opinion on the matters dealt with in the report:
  - summarise the range of opinions, and
  - give reasons for the expert's own opinion.
- contain a summary of the conclusions reached
- if the expert is not able to give an opinion without qualification, state the qualification.

In addition it must contain a statement that the expert:

- understands their duty to the court, and has complied with that duty, and
- is aware of the requirements of Part 35, the practice direction and the Protocol for Instruction of Experts to give Evidence in Civil Claims.

An expert's report must be verified by a statement of truth in the following form:

> I confirm that I have made clear which facts and matters referred to in this report are within my own knowledge and which are not. Those that are within my own knowledge I confirm to be true. The opinions I have expressed represent my true and complete professional opinions on the matters to which they refer.

Cross-examination of experts on the contents of their instructions will not be allowed unless the court permits it (or unless the party who gave the instructions consents). Before it gives permission the court must be satisfied that there are reasonable grounds to consider that the statement in the report of the substance of the instructions is inaccurate or incomplete. If the court is so satisfied, it will allow the cross-examination where it appears to be in the interests of justice.

Criminal proceedings

The process of giving evidence in criminal cases is determined by the Criminal Procedure Rules 2010 ('the Rules'). Here the court process in criminal cases is adversarial, which is the major difference in approach between civil and criminal proceedings. This means that in criminal cases, the expert is likely to be challenged, sometimes quite brutally, by the other side who will seek to undermine the credibility of the expert if that would be of value to their client.

The expert's evidence may well form a considerable part of, for example, the prosecution's case against a fraudster. If the defence can undermine the expert's conclusions by evincing credible innocent explanations for what appear to be fraudulent transactions, or highlight a break in the chain of evidence (see Chapter 3), the prosecution case may be considerably weakened.

The Rules specify again that it is the duty of the expert to help the court by giving an objective, unbiased opinion on matters within their expertise and this duty overrides any obligation to the person from whom they receive instructions or by whom they are paid.

There is also an obligation to inform all parties and the court if the expert's opinion changes from that contained in a report served as evidence or given in a statement.

Content of expert's report

The form and content of an expert's report in criminal proceedings is the same as that detailed above for civil proceedings. In other words it must contain all the information about the expert, the work they carried out and the conclusions they have drawn. It must be accompanied by the statement that the expert is aware of their duty to the court etc.

The expert must make the same declaration as any other witness: 'I believe that the facts stated in this witness statement are true.'

In cases where both sides produce experts the court may direct the experts to:

- discuss the expert issues in the proceedings, and
- prepare a statement for the court of the matters on which they agree and disagree, giving their reasons.

Except for that statement, the content of that discussion must not be referred to without the court's permission.

In criminal cases, where there is more than one defendant, they each may wish to produce their own expert. In complex fraud trials with multiple defendents this could cause confusion and delay but there is a procedure for this eventuality. Where more than one defendant wants to introduce expert evidence on an issue at trial, the court may direct that the evidence on that issue is to be given by one expert only. Where the co-defendants cannot agree who should be the expert, the court may:

- select the expert from a list prepared or identified by them, or
- direct that the expert be selected in such other manner as the court may direct.

It is important to understand that the court, whilst recognising the expert's qualifications in general, will be particularly interested in their competence in connection with the specific matters before the court. The court will focus upon the qualifications and experience of the expert in connection with the particular set of circumstances before it. Consequently, for example, in the question of a case which hinges on valuation of private company shares the court will be interested in the expert's experience and success in valuing shares rather than purely on their qualification as, say, a chartered accountant.

It is for the court to decide that the expert selected has the required qualifications and expertise. The court will not accept an expert's evidence uncritically – it will want to know how conclusions have been reached and the basis of the evidence used in reaching that conclusion or recommendation.

There is also a distinction between the competence of an expert and the credence granted to their evidence. It is unlikely that the court would refuse to accept the report of an expert at all but there is always the consideration of how much weight to attribute to its contents. If, for example, it contains evidence which otherwise would be inadmissible, e.g. hearsay or anecdotal evidence, the court may well take the view that the expert witness's evidence can be admitted but that objection can be made to the inadmissible portion which can then be ignored.

The expert must be provided with all the information relevant to the issue, but not anything that is outwith the question they are being asked to consider. It is not conducive to obtaining an expert's opinion to provide them with every file relevant to a particular case where they are being asked to comment on only one part of it. However, they must be provided with all the information necessary to prepare their report and to arrive at an independent and objective conclusion.

The expert should detail the information upon which they have relied in their report which will enable the court to ascertain whether or not their conclusions are based on all the known facts.

 ## Duties of the expert witness

The first and most important rule is that it is the duty of an expert to help the court on matters solely within their own area of expertise. This duty is paramount and overrides any obligation to the person from whom the expert has received instructions or by whom they are paid.

As can be seen there are two aspects to this overriding duty

- The expert must not stray out of their area of expertise.
- Their role is to help the court – not to venture an opinion or to embellish the facts in any way.

To do so is to firstly to run the risk of the validity of the evidence being challenged and secondly to, no doubt innocently, give incorrect evidence which may have repercussions on themselves both as expert witnesses and as professionals. It must be remembered that the court does not comprise experts, it comprises lawyers and lay persons acting as a jury. If an acknowledged and authoritative expert gives evidence on a complex subject there is every possibility that it will go unchallenged. In most cases this enables the court to establish a quantum of facts around which the case may turn, but if those facts are incorrect and the court is not equipped to recognise that fact the expert witness has failed in their duty, the judgment in the case may be flawed and result in a miscarriage of justice.

The most egregious case in recent years was that of Professor Sir Roy Meadow whose testimony in one case falsely convicted the defendant, Sally Clark, but whose testimony also went a long way to wrongly convict another defendant, Angela Canning – both of whom were later released on appeal (see Exhibit 16.1).

Exhibit 16.1 | **Example – when the expert gets it wrong: Professor Sir Roy Meadow**

Professor Sir Roy Meadow was an eminent, if not the most eminent, paediatrician of his day. He was called to give evidence in the criminal case against Sally Clark, accused of causing the death of her two children.

Professor Meadow gave a considerable amount of testimony, much of which was later challenged on medical grounds. One of the key areas of his testimony, and one which carried considerable weight with the jury who convicted Sally Clark, was nothing to do with medicine but was statistical.

Professor Meadow stated in court that the chances of their being two cases of sudden infant death syndrome (SIDS) in one family was 1 in 73 million – an analogy he reinforced by saying it was akin to winning the Grand National at odds of 80 to 1 in four successive years. This carried enormous weight with the jury – particularly as the defence never really challenged his sums.

Professor Meadow's evidence also helped to convict Angela Cannings, another mother who had lost two children to SIDS.

However, he was wrong. Professor Meadow had taken the established probability of their being one case of SIDS in a family of 1 in 8543 and squared it for two deaths. This, however, only has a statistical validity if both incidents are independent of each other – which of course they cannot be. The children had the same parents, lived in the same house etc.

Experts in statistics were outraged and the Royal Statistical Society even issued a press release stating that the claim by Professor Meadow had no statistical validity.

Sally Clark was imprisoned for three years before being released on appeal in 2003. Professor Meadow was struck off the General Medical Register but was reinstated by the Court of Appeal in 2006.

Sally Clark died of alcohol poisoning in March 2007 having, her family claimed, never been able to come to terms with her imprisonment after the death of her children.

Source: Freeman (2006); Rozenberg (2006); Telegraph (2007)

It should be pointed out that courts may well take the view that if one part of an expert's evidence is subsequently proven to be unsafe the whole of their evidence may well be treated as suspect.

In addition to what might be classed as the primary directive, expert witnesses should also bear in mind the following:

- Expert evidence should be the independent product of the expert uninfluenced by the pressures of litigation. The useful test of independence is that the expert should consider their report and be able to decide that they would have given the same advice irrespective of which party in any dispute had instructed them.
- It is taken as a given that the expert complies with the ethical code of whichever professional body they are accredited to.
- An expert should assist the court by providing objective, unbiased opinion on matters within their expertise, and should not assume the role of an advocate. They should not take it upon themselves to promote the view of the party instructing them either overtly through statements in the text or covertly by failing to include facts or background information which might appear detrimental to their case.
- Expert evidence should be restricted to that which is reasonably required to resolve the proceedings but the expert should consider *all* material facts, including those which might detract from their opinion.
- Care must be taken to ensure that all pertinent facts are included. In two headline cases forensic and medical evidence was withheld from the court. In the Sally Clark case (Exhibit 16.1) a Dr Williams stated 'it is not my practice to refer to additional results in my post mortem unless they are relevant to the cause of death'. Dr Williams had it forcefully pointed out to him that it was not up to him to decide what to disclose – he had to disclose everything. Dr Williams was found guilty of serious professional misconduct by the General Medical Council, subsequently struck off the (then) Home Office list of forensic pathologists and was banned from doing court work for three years. The consequences of getting it wrong can be very severe in terms of the witness's professional future.
- An expert should make it clear as soon as possible:
  - when a question or issue falls outside their expertise, and
  - when they are not able to reach a definite opinion, for example, because they have insufficient information.
- If, after producing a report, an expert changes their view on any material matter, such change of view should be communicated to all the parties without delay and, when appropriate, to the court.
- The expert must state if any conclusions are provisional or qualified in any way. The reasons for any provisional or qualified conclusion must be stated. If further information is required before a final unqualified conclusion is reached this should also be stated.

Preparing the report

In practice how does all this actually affect the forensic accountant preparing a report? Clearly the relevant reporting format rules outlined above must be borne in mind but, subject to that, what other considerations are important? Let us look at the basis of reporting in a civil case, where the forensic accountant is acting as an expert.

In civil cases the expression of opinion and the exercise of judgement may stretch the forensic accountant's skills in expressing an opinion which may well not be based on hard facts but on experience and – in some cases – little more than intuition. However, the report must be capable of standing up to scrutiny and criticism. The final report should be read through carefully and forensic accountants would be well advised to have any report which is to be used in legal proceedings reviewed:

- by another forensic accountant or experienced colleague, or
- by a legal representative

if the report is likely to be contentious or open to more than usually vigorous challenge.

Firms should operate their usual quality control and peer review procedures to ensure that:

- the final report complies in all respects with the instructions given
- that any conclusions can be substantiated, and
- it does not exhibit any bias or selectivity.

Key questions would be:

Is it in accordance with instructions?

The instructions themselves must be adeqate to cover the points at issue. Usually the instructions given are summarised in the report or the Letter of Engagement is included as an appendix to the report so the court can decide whether or not the forensic accountant has been properly instructed in the case.

The forensic accountant must ensure that:

- all matters on which they are instructed to report have been covered, and
- all matters have been given equal or appropriate weight in the report as matters which have been glossed over may well come under attack.

In areas where there is limited information it may not be possible to come to a conclusion or opinion, in which case this should be clearly stated.

It may be that some assumptions have to be made for the purpose of the report: if so these have to be stated as well as the rationale behind them. These assumptions may well change as further information becomes available.

Does the report express any views outside the expert's field of competence?

We have already considered the effect of this above with reference to the Sally Clark case but it bears repetition. Accountants, by virtue of their training, have a wide range of competencies and may feel that all accounting matters fall well within their competence.

However, there are certain areas where this competence should not be assumed and one of these is valuation. Clearly most accountants would recognise that they are not competent to value commercial property but what about the value of say, a brand, or capitalised development expenditure or goodwill? In these cases it may be appropriate to consider using an expert with a proven track record or credibility in such valuations where these are material to the exercise being performed.

Are all assumptions clearly stated?

Accountants' reports generally involve some level of assumptions. These are particularly significant in connection with valuations of businesses where the levels of future maintainable profits are being considered (see Chapter 14), and where the valuing accountant is concerned about the ability of the business to generate a level of profits. This involves assumptions about such matters as the market, the competition, the management of the business, its products etc.

The assumptions, of course, need to be clearly stated, but what is just as important is that the rationale for adopting those assumptions also needs to be explained in full and in a way that is clearly understandable to the court and, in criminal cases, to any jury who are unlikely to have much in the way of accounting experience.

It is likely that, if there is to be a challenge to the report, this will be one of the battlegrounds, so careful attention needs to be paid to the wording used as well as to the assumptions themselves. An invalid assumption may well discredit the report even if much of it is pertinent and useful to the court – where a partial challenge to an expert's report can be mounted successfully juries are all too ready to undervalue the evidence given in total.

Are the assumptions consistent?

The report should tell a consistent story. For example if a valuation report predicates an increase in turnover there should be a concomitent increase in variable costs. It may be, for example, that the report refers to an increase in activity levels – if so the question of increased staffing needs to be considered and with increased staffing may come increased supervision requirements etc. Where attention is drawn to figures in the body of the report these should be referenced in any appendices for the avoidance of doubt.

Any assumptions used, of course, have to be fully explained and justified. These may be open to challenge if they are seen as unrealistic or unfeasible.

Have copies of key documents been included?

Where the expert has relied on key documents these should be included as an Appendix to the report. For example the report may make reference to projections made by the directors and tabled at a board meeting. In that case a copy of the projections and the relevant minute should be included so the readers of the report can follow the reporting accountant's train of thought and logic.

Remember the object is to assist the court, so the report should not make reference to documents the court does not have or make unexplained jumps in calculations without evidencing, wherever possible, what has been done.

Is the background information correct?

This is a matter of recital of facts but may also include facts about which one party was unaware. Situations where there may be errors of fact, for example around dates, must be carefully checked.

There may be a temptation for reports to use background information selectively in support of a case or to omit key facts such as the loss of a contract or major customer. This must, of course be resisted. All facts relevant to the case must be included – even if they may be detrimental to one's own client.

There is often the temptation to mix fact and opinion. For example the reporting accountant may report a fact and then add additional wording, for example 'this shows that the company was well regarded in the industry' – a comment which is unsupported by facts.

Are the conclusions properly stated and consistent with the report?

The conclusions should flow from the report – indeed the wording of the report and the calculations contained in it are all leading up to the conclusions drawn and recommendations (if appropriate). Each step along the way must be carefully spelled out with facts and evidence, assumptions justified and calculations carefully explained for the innumerate.

Are the conclusions reasonable in the light of the information in the report and do they flow from the facts and inferences stated?

Clearly the conclusions drawn are the essence of the report. In most cases the recital of facts, the arguments and calculations in the report are there to support the conclusions.

As stated above the assumptions in the report may be challenged in the course of proceedings, but if those assumptions are considered reasonable and the conclusions flow from them the forensic accountant should stick to their guns and defend their views.

However, the conclusions should make sense holistically. It is no good developing a beautiful argument and devising elegant calculations to demonstrate that future maintainable earnings should be £200,000 per year when the most the business ever made in any one year previously was £100,000. The assumptions might look reasonable and the calculations may all be impeccable – but the conclusion, as a conclusion, doesn't hold water.

Does the report deal with any matters which might undermine the conclusions or opinion?

Only very rarely are all the facts of a case indisputable and all the assumptions unchallengeable. If this were a common occurrence there would be no need for barristers! The report will have to deal with areas which may well:

- contain uncertainties or unknowns about which assumptions have to be made or
- be a matter of judgement or opinion which may contradict the judgement, or opinion of another.

These instances should be recognised and acknowledged in the report and, to the extent possible, be dealt with.

An example of this is the multiple used in the valuation of a business on a maintainable profits basis. A forensic accountant acting for one party may legitimately take the view that the multiple should be six. Another forensic accountant may scoff at this as far too generous and estimate that it should be three. There is, of course, no right answer and it will be for the court to decide perhaps where the truth lies in that particular set of circumstances. However, it would be foolish not to acknowledge this type of uncertainty in the report so the multiple of six, say, should be justified and a reasoned argument set out as to why it is six and not three or another figure.

Are the appendices consistent and appropriate?

Classic errors in reporting include:

- A change in some detailed calculation in an appendix made at the last moment but the summary calculation in the body of the report remains unaltered.
- An appendix may be included – but not referred to in the report as a result of a last-minute change.
- Too many appendices may be included – reports are not judged by weight!

Suffice to say that all appendices should be considered for relevance, and cross references checked to ensure that they are consistent.

Specific accounting issues in reporting

Away from the generality of writing expert witness reports there are some specific accounting issues which have to be addressed. These are relatively routine matters for most accountants but need to be considered and anticipated in any report as, if not addressed, they are likely to result in questions from the lawyers.

What is the status of any financial information on which the report is based?

This is the first and most obvious question but it is nevertheless one which must be made clear in any report.

For example, if the report is relying on accounts:

- Are they final or draft?
- Audited or unaudited?
- Management accounts or financial accounts?
- If they are audited financial accounts are the auditors' reports unqualified?
- If they are unaudited management accounts what reliance can be placed upon them – has any work been done to validate the figures?
- How up to date are they? If the report is relying on audited accounts for two years and unaudited management accounts for the latest period what guarantee is there that the unaudited accounts are drawn up on a basis consistent with the audited accounts, i.e. adopting the same accounting policies, and that they include all material items – for example provisions and valuation adjustments?

What is the status of any internal audit department whose work is being relied upon?

If during the course of an investigation the work of an internal audit department is to be relied on the forensic accountant must reassure themselves that it is:

- Independent of executive influence – i.e. that the internal audit function does not report directly to or have its budget controlled by any of the executive directors, particularly the finance director. If there is any question that the work of internal audit can be directed and controlled by the executive it is not independent and should not be relied on.

- Does the head of internal audit (HIA) have status in the organisation? The status accorded the HIA is indicative of the status of internal audit. The HIA should be a senior officer of the business with budgetary and managerial control over the world of their department.
- Are internal audit report recommendations acted on? Again this is an indication of the status and respect accorded to internal audit. If they report independently – say to an audit committee – any recommendations they make should carry weight and should be considered by the executive. If they are routinely ignored the forensic accountant has an indicator of both the status of internal audit and, perhaps, the attitude of the executive towards internal control.
- Are the members of the internal audit department competent, qualified and receiving up-to-date training? Do they use up-to-date audit techniques and are they cognisant of relevant audit issues including fraud prevention and reporting?

Does the report take account of recent developments in the business?

Historical reporting is just that – a matter of past record. Businesses are fluid entities and variables change all the time. The report must take into account recent events including:

- Changes in the economic cycle – rapid economic downturns can have a serious detrimental effect on businesses, sometimes indirectly. For example a downturn in the economic cycle which results in a significant reduction in the retail sales volumes has a marked effect on suppliers. A downturn in new car sales has a detrimental effect on component suppliers.
- Loss of key staff. If a key member of staff, say a product designer or sales executive, were to leave to work for a competitor what effect would this have on the future of the business?
- Changes in the market – are there new entrants to the market, new products, former competitors leaving the market, etc.?
- At what stage in the product life cycle are the business's key products – are there proposals for new or revised products?

Have the accounts been accepted by HMRC and all liabilities agreed?

This is perhaps not so relevant for larger corporate businesses but could be of importance where unincorporated businesses or partnerships are concerned. Any issues raised by HMRC should be considered in the report.

Have all the calculations been checked for consistency, logic and accuracy?

This may seem an obvious point but all calculations, spreadsheets etc. should be reviewed and checked before the report is submitted. Common errors such as incorrect use of formulae in spreadsheets or inconsistencies between appendices and the report body can be detected by simple arithmetical checking. To submit a report with an arithmetical error devalues it.

Acting as an expert witness is an onerous responsibility and not to be taken lightly. If the author of any report has to justify it in person in court they must be prepared to withstand cross-examination by an experienced and trained barrister – a daunting prospect for anyone. Any report which is to be used in legal proceedings must be capable of withstanding such a challenge and the author must be familiar with it.

Having said that it is an area where real expertise can be demonstrated and the work of the forensic accountant shown at its best.

Summary

- The opinions of witnesses are not normally admissible as the court is the arbiter of the case.
- Expert witnesses are there to help the court on technical matters.
- There are specific rules under which the expert witness reports to the court.
- In criminal proceedings the process is adversarial and the report may be challenged.
- It is important that the expert does not stray out of their area of expertise.
- All relevant matters must be included in the report.
- The report must accord with the instructions given and must be consistent with established facts.
- Assumptions must be clearly stated and justified.
- Conclusions must be consistent with the report.
- It is important to establish the status of any accounts used.
- The report should take into account any recent changes.

Bibliography   Criminal Procedure Rules (2010) *Part 33 Expert Evidence*. Ministry of Justice, London.

Civil Procedure Rules (1998) *Part 35, 51st Update – Rules and Practice Directions*. Ministry of Justice, London.

Civil Justice Council (2005) *Protocol for the Instruction of Experts to give Evidence in Civil Claims*. Civil Justice Council, London.

Dyer, C. (2005) Pathologist in Sally Clark murder case is charged with witholding vital evidence. *British Medical Journal*, 330, 7490, 497.

Expert Witness Institute (2006) *Code of Practice for Experts*. Expert Witness Institute, London.

Fenny, I. (2006) *Expert Evidence*. Guildhall Chambers, Bristol.

Freeman, S. (2006) The mistake that cost Roy Meadow his reputation. www.thetimes.co.uk, 17 February.

Gibb, F. (2007) Grief stricken Sally Clark drank herself to death. www.times.co.uk, 8 November.

R v Clark (Sally) (No 2) (2003) *EWCA Crim 1020 (CA)*.

Regina v Maguire (1992) *1 Q.B. 936, 957D*.

Roberts, G. (2006) Disgraced Meadow reinstated by judge. *Independent on Sunday*, 18 February.

Rozenberg, J. (2006) Sir Roy Meadow, the flawed witness, wins GMC appeal. www.telegraph.co.uk, 18 February.

Telegraph (2007) Baby case solicitor Sally Clark found dead. www.telegraph.co.uk, 17 March.

Websites

www.bbc.co.uk

www.business.timesonline.co.uk

www.ewi.org.uk

www.independent.co.uk/news

www.justice.gov.uk

www.guildhallchambers.co.uk

www.lexisnexis.com

www.sallyclark.org.uk

www.telegraph.co.uk

www.thetimes.co.uk

www.ukpmc.ac.uk

Appendices

Sample acceptable use policy for the Internet

You may have in place content controls and filters to prevent inappropriate Internet use. An Internet acceptable use policy sets out your employees' responsibilities when using company Internet access in their day-to-day working activities.

Acceptable Internet use policy – sample template

Use of the Internet by employees of [business name] is permitted and encouraged where such use supports the goals and objectives of the business.

However, [business name] has a policy for the use of the Internet whereby employees must ensure that they:

- comply with current legislation
- use the Internet in an acceptable way, and
- do not create unnecessary business risk to the company by their misuse of the Internet.

Unacceptable behaviour

In particular the following is deemed unacceptable use or behaviour by employees:

- visiting Internet sites that contain obscene, hateful, pornographic or otherwise illegal material
- using the computer to perpetrate any form of fraud, or software, film or music piracy
- using the Internet to send offensive or harassing material to other users
- downloading commercial software or any copyrighted materials belonging to third parties, unless this download is covered or permitted under a commercial agreement or other such licence
- hacking into unauthorised areas
- publishing defamatory and/or knowingly false material about [business name], your colleagues and/or our customers on social networking sites, 'blogs' (online journals), 'wikis' and any online publishing format
- undertaking deliberate activities that waste staff effort or networked resources, and
- introducing any form of malicious software into the corporate network.

Company-owned information held on third-party websites

If you produce, collect and/or process business-related information in the course of your work, the information remains the property of [business name]. This includes such information stored on third-party websites such as webmail service providers and social networking sites, such as Facebook and LinkedIn.

Monitoring

[business name] accepts that the use of the Internet is a valuable business tool. However, misuse of this facility can have a negative impact upon employee productivity and the reputation of the business.

In addition, all of the company's Internet-related resources are provided for business purposes. Therefore, the company maintains the right to monitor the volume of Internet and network traffic, together with the Internet sites visited. The specific content of any transactions will not be monitored unless there is a suspicion of improper use.

Sanctions

Where it is believed that an employee has failed to comply with this policy, they will face the company's disciplinary procedure. If the employee is found to have breached the policy, they will face a disciplinary penalty ranging from a verbal warning to dismissal. The actual penalty applied will depend on factors such as the seriousness of the breach and the employee's disciplinary record. [These procedures will be specific to your business. They should reflect your normal operational and disciplinary processes. You should establish them from the outset and include them in your acceptable use policy.]

Agreement

All company employees, contractors or temporary staff who have been granted the right to use the company's Internet access are required to sign this agreement confirming their understanding and acceptance of this policy.

Source: www.businesslink.gov.uk, accessed July 2010; Crown copyright 2010.

Sample acceptable use policy – e-mail

An e-mail acceptable use policy sets out your employees' responsibilities when using e-mail in their day-to-day working activities.

Acceptable e-mail use policy – sample template

Use of e-mail by employees of [business name] is permitted and encouraged where such use supports the goals and objectives of the business.

However, [business name] has a policy for the use of e-mail whereby the employee must ensure that they:

- comply with current legislation
- use e-mail in an acceptable way, or
- do not create unnecessary business risk to the company by their misuse of the Internet.

Unacceptable behaviour

- Use of company communications systems to set up personal businesses or send chain letters.
- Forwarding of company confidential messages to external locations.
- Distributing, disseminating or storing images, text or materials that might be considered indecent, pornographic, obscene or illegal.
- Distributing, disseminating or storing images, text or materials that might be considered discriminatory, offensive or abusive, in that the context is a personal attack, sexist or racist, or might be considered as harassment.
- Accessing copyrighted information in a way that violates the copyright.
- Breaking into the company's or another organisation's system or unauthorised use of a password/mailbox.
- Broadcasting unsolicited personal views on social, political, religious or other non-business related matters.
- Transmitting unsolicited commercial or advertising material.
- Undertaking deliberate activities that waste staff effort or networked resources.
- Introducing any form of computer virus or malware into the corporate network.

Monitoring

[Business name] accepts that the use of e-mail is a valuable business tool. However, misuse of this facility can have a negative impact upon employee productivity and the reputation of the business.

In addition, all of the company's e-mail resources are provided for business purposes. Therefore, the company maintains the right to examine any systems and inspect any data recorded in those systems.

In order to ensure compliance with this policy, the company also reserves the right to use monitoring software in order to check upon the use and content of e-mails. Such monitoring is for legitimate purposes only and will be undertaken in accordance with a procedure agreed with employees.

Sanctions

Where it is believed that an employee has failed to comply with this policy, they will face the company's disciplinary procedure. If the employee is found to have breached the policy, they will face a disciplinary penalty ranging from a verbal warning to dismissal. The actual penalty applied will depend on factors such as the seriousness of the breach and the employee's disciplinary record. [These procedures will be specific to your business. They should reflect your normal operational and disciplinary processes. You should establish them from the outset and include them in your acceptable use policy.]

Agreement

All company employees, contractors or temporary staff who have been granted the right to use the company's email services are required to sign this agreement confirming their understanding and acceptance of this policy.

Source: www.businesslink.gov.uk, accessed July 2010; Crown copyright 2010.

Frauds

This appendix looks at common types of internal fraud and some of the methods through which they may be perpetrated.

Asset misappropriation

Cash

Theft of cash

- Stealing from petty cash.
- Taking money from the till.
- Skimming of cash before recording revenues or receivables (understating sales or receivables).
- Stealing incoming cash or cheques through an account set up to look like a bona fide payee.
- Teeming and lading.

False payment requests

- Employee creating false payment instruction with forged signatures and submitting it for processing.
- False e-mail payment request together with hard copy printout with forged approval signature.
- Taking advantage of the lack of time which typically occurs during book closing to get false invoices approved and paid.

Cheque fraud

- Theft of company cheques.
- Duplicating or counterfeiting of company cheques.
- Tampering with company cheques (payee/amount).
- Depositing a cheque into a third party account without authority.
- Cheque kiting (a fraud scheme using two deposit accounts to withdraw money illegally from the bank).
- Paying a cheque to the company knowing that insufficient funds are in the account to cover it.

Billing schemes

- Over-billing customers.
- Recording of false credits, rebates or refunds to customers.

- Pay and return schemes (where an employee creates an overpayment to a supplier and pockets the subsequent refund).
- Using fictitious suppliers or shell companies for false billing.

Misuse of accounts

- Wire transfer fraud (fraudulent transfers into bank accounts).
- Unrecorded sales or receivables.
- Employee account fraud (where an employee is also a customer and the employee makes unauthorised adjustments to their accounts).
- Writing false credit note to customers with details of an employee's personal bank account or of an account of a company controlled by the employee.
- Stealing passwords to payment systems and inputting series of payments to own account.

Non-cash

Inventory and fixed assets

- Theft of inventory.
- False write-offs and other debits to inventory.
- False sales of inventory.
- Theft of fixed assets, including computers and other IT-related assets.
- Theft or abuse of proprietary or confidential information (customer information, intellectual property, pricing schedules, business plans, etc.).
- Receiving free or below market value goods and services from suppliers.
- Unauthorised private use of company property.
- Employees trading for their own account.

Procurement

- Altering legitimate purchase orders.
- Falsifying documents to obtain authorisation for payment.
- Forging signatures on payment authorisations.
- Submitting for payment false invoices from fictitious or actual suppliers.
- Improper changes to supplier payment terms or other supplier details.
- Intercepting payments to suppliers.
- Sending fictitious or duplicate invoices to suppliers.
- Improper use of company credit cards.
- Marked up invoices from contracts awarded to supplier associated with an employee.
- Sale of critical bid information, contract details or other sensitive information.

Payroll

- Fictitious (or ghost) employees on the payroll.
- Falsifying work hours to achieve fraudulent overtime payments.
- Abuse of commission schemes.
- Not deleting leavers from payroll and amending bank details in master file.
- Improper changes in salary levels.
- Abuse of holiday leave or time off entitlements.

- Submitting inflated or false expense claims.
- Adding private expenses to legitimate expense claims.
- Applying for multiple reimbursements of the same expenses.
- False workers' compensation claims.
- Theft of employee contributions to benefit plans.

Fraudulent statements

Financial

Improper revenue recognition

- Holding the books open after the end of the accounting period.
- Inflation of sales figures which are credited out after the year end.
- Backdating agreements.
- Recording fictitious sales and shipping.
- Improper classification of revenues.
- Inappropriate estimates for returns, price adjustments and other concessions.
- Manipulation of rebates.
- Recognising revenue on disputed claims against customers.
- Recognising income on products shipped for trial or evaluation purposes.
- Improper recording of consignment or contingency sales.
- Over/underestimating percentage of work completed on long-term contracts.
- Incorrect inclusion of related party receivables.
- Side letter agreements (agreements made outside of formal contracts).
- Round tripping (practice whereby two companies buy and sell the same amount of a commodity at the same price at the same time. The trading lacks economic substance and results in overstated revenues).
- Bill and hold transactions (where the seller bills the customer for goods but does not ship the product until a later date).
- Early delivery of product/services (for example, partial shipments, soft sales, contracts with multiple deliverables, up front fees).
- Channel stuffing or trade loading (where a company inflates its sales figures by forcing more products through a distribution channel than the channel is capable of selling).

Misstatement of assets, liabilities and/or expenses

- Fictitious fixed assets.
- Overstating assets acquired through merger and acquisitions.
- Improper capitalisation of expenses as fixed assets (software development, research and development, start up costs, interest costs, advertising costs).
- Manipulation of fixed asset valuations.
- Schemes involving inappropriate depreciation or amortisation.
- Incorrect values attached to goodwill or other intangibles.
- Fictitious investments.
- Improper investment valuation (misclassification of investments, recording unrealised investments, declines in fair market value/overvaluation).
- Fictitious bank accounts.

- Inflating inventory quantity through inclusion of fictitious inventory.
- Improper valuation of inventory.
- Fraudulent or improper capitalisation of inventory.
- Manipulation of inventory counts.
- Accounts receivable schemes (for example, creating fictitious receivables or artificially inflating the value of receivables).
- Misstatement of prepayments and accruals.
- Understating loans and payables.
- Fraudulent management estimates for provisions, reserves, foreign currency translation, impairment, etc.
- Off balance sheet items.
- Delaying the recording of expenses to the next accounting period.

Other accounting misstatements

- Improper treatment of inter-company accounts.
- Non-clearance or improper clearance of suspense accounts.
- Misrepresentation of suspense accounts for fraudulent activity.
- Improper accounting for mergers, acquisitions, disposals and joint ventures.
- Manipulation of assumptions used for determining fair value of share-based payments.
- Improper or inadequate disclosures.
- Fictitious general ledger accounts.
- Journal entry fraud (using accounting journal entries to fraudulently adjust financial statements).
- Concealment of losses.

Non-financial

- Falsified employment credentials, for example, qualifications and references.
- Other fraudulent internal or external documents.

Corruption

Conflicts of interest

Kickbacks

- Kickbacks to employees by a supplier in return for the supplier receiving favourable treatment.
- Kickbacks to senior management in relation to the acquisition of a new business or disposal of part of the business.
- Employee sells company-owned property at less than market value to receive a kickback or to sell the property back to the company at a higher price in the future.
- Purchase of property at higher than market value in exchange for a kickback.
- Preferential treatment of customers in return for a kickback.

Personal interests

- Collusion with customers and/or suppliers.
- Favouring a supplier in which the employee has a financial interest.
- Employee setting up and using own consultancy for personal gain (conflicts with the company's interests).
- Employee hiring someone close to them over another more qualified applicant.
- Transfer of knowledge to a competitor by an employee who intends to joins the competitor's company.
- Misrepresentation by insiders with regard to a corporate merger, acquisition or investment.
- Insider trading (using business information not released to the public to gain profits from trading in the financial markets).

Bribery and extortion

Bribery

- Payment of agency/facilitation fees (or bribes) in order to secure a contract.
- Authorising orders to a particular supplier in return for bribes.
- Giving and accepting payments to favour or not favour other commercial transactions or relationships.
- Payments to government officials to obtain a benefit (for example, customs officials, tax inspectors).
- Anti-trust activities such as price fixing or bid rigging.
- Illegal political contributions.

Extortion

- Extortion (offering to keep someone from harm in exchange for money or other consideration).
- Denial of service attacks.
- Blackmail (offering to keep information confidential in return for money or other consideration).

Source: *Fraud Risk Management – A Guide to Good Practice*. CIMA, 2008. Copyright CIMA 2008.

Glossary

Advance fee fraud The fraudster collects fees in advance without ever intending to fulfil the agreement to provide services or products. These are also known as S419 frauds, a fraud scheme that now includes fax and e-mail versions of a letter from a supposed official in Nigeria or another country. The official has a large sum of money (often stated as $20–$30 million) to transfer out of the country. Due to exchange controls, the official asks for the victim's help with the transfer. All that is required to earn a hefty reward/commission is to furnish the official with your bank account number, and they will handle the rest. What actually happens is that the perpetrator depletes the victim's bank account.

Affiliate bidding A condition in purchasing when multiple bids are tendered for a contract from a single company under various names to give the appearance of competition.

Aggressive earnings management Accounting practices designed to maximise income, minimise costs and show the Statement of Financial Position at its maximum. Techniques used may be a very liberal interpretation of International Accounting Standards or fraudulent manipulation of the figures.

AVS (address verification system) The first security mechanism supported by credit-card issuers for card-not-present transactions. AVS validates the billing address information provided by the consumer against the billing address information that the issuer has on record for the account. Specifically, AVS checks the post code and the numeric part of the street address and returns a match/mismatch response.

Backdate To post a date on a document earlier than the actual creation date for purposes of deception.

Back door In computer fraud, an unauthorised entry point or weakness discovered by a hacker. Similar to a **Trapdoor**, except that back doors are usually pre-existing weaknesses.

Bait and switch In consumer fraud, advertising a low-cost item and then steering the customer to a higher-priced item when they come to buy, claiming the low-priced item was 'sold out'.

Bid rigging In purchasing, any scheme that gives the appearance of competitive bids but is actually not competitive because the participants establish the winner before submitting bids for the contract.

Bid rotation In purchasing, when bidders for contracts collude to distribute work among themselves by establishing which among them will win particular bids.

Boiler room operation A fraud scheme that attempts to sell worthless securities (or similar assets) over the telephone through high-pressure sales tactics. If the money is sent in or the credit card number given out, nothing of value is received.

Bribery To offer money in exchange for favoured treatment or to compel or influence some action. Official (government employee or elected official) bribery involves a promise for acting or withholding some official act. Official bribery (corruption) is unlawful in most cultures.

Commercial bribery is known as 'facilitation payments' in some cultures and is not a crime, although it often is against the organisation's policies and procedures.

Bucket shop A securities fraud scheme that pretends to buy and sell securities for customers, but actually never invests the money it receives. The scheme depends upon stock price manipulation or a continuously rising market to encourage more buyers than sellers. Also associated sometimes with the **Pump-and-dump** scheme.

Card trading There is a thriving market for compromised credit card-accounts, with trades taking place in clandestine chat rooms.

Chain of evidence In evidentiary matters, the record of possession from original discovery until production at trial. If the chain of evidence is broken or unclear, the evidence may be challenged as not the original or not in its original condition.

Collateral frauds Fraudulent representation of collateral for a loan that (1) does not exist, (2) is not owned by the loan applicant, and/or (3) is grossly over-valued.

Collude In the context of fraud, to act together for a fraudulent purpose.

Commercial bribery Giving and accepting payments to favour or not favour a commercial transaction or relationship. See also **Bribery** and **Corruption**.

Computer virus See **Virus**.

Conflict of interest An employee owes a duty to the employer to act in the interest of the employer (and no other) when carrying out duties as an employee. A conflict of interest exists when the employee has some personal kinship, friendship or financial interest in a transaction that may divide the employee's interests and put their duty to their employer in jeopardy.

Conspiracy Two or more persons come together for the purpose of committing a fraud.

Cooking the books Altering the official accounts to deceive. See also **Journal entry fraud**.

Corruption Bribery of a government official. See also **Commercial bribery**.

Cost of goods sold changes Unusual changes in cost of goods sold, as a percentage of sales may be an indicator of the theft of revenue or theft of finished goods inventory. See **Fictitious refunds scheme**.

Covert Hidden or secret, as in 'covert operations'.

Credit card readers Small electronic devices that can capture the information stored in the credit card's magnetic stripe. These devices are commonly used in restaurants or petrol stations and other retail locations where collusive employees have physical access to customer cards.

C V V (card verification value) A three- or four-digit numeric code that is printed, but not embossed, on the back or the front of credit cards issued in some countries. Card issuers use different names for this security feature. The CVV code is not recorded in the magnetic stripe of the card, which provides protection from skimmers.

Cyber crime Referring to frauds perpetrated on the Internet or through the use of computers.

Defalcation Another word for fraud, theft or other dishonest act relating to a position of trust in an organisation.

Denial of service attack A computer virus or computer program run to generate many thousands of requests to the central computer, thereby tying up the processor and denying legitimate requests of access.

Directory advertising schemes Fraudulent invoices claiming that the company is listed in a business directory and requesting payment. There may or may not be such a directory, and the directory may or may not ever be distributed or distributed as widely as claimed. What is certain is that no one ever ordered or authorised the directory advertisement.

Embezzlement Theft of money from an employer by an employee using false entries in accounting records to cover up the crime.

Employee account fraud When employees are also customers, they may make unauthorised adjustments to their accounts (including write-off).

Employer fraud Fraud committed by an employer who misrepresents the amount of payroll or classification of employees (for example, attempts to avoid a higher insurance risk modifier by transferring employees to a new business entity rated as a lower-risk category).

Expenses fraud Charging unauthorised or fictitious amounts on an expenses claim.

Exposure The potential for loss.

Extortion The offer to keep from harm in exchange for money or other consideration. The demand for restitution in exchange for not prosecuting a crime is a form of extortion.

False claims Claims for reimbursement by an employee or contractor for non-existent or inflated expenses. False claims can be for business expenses or personal expenses (such as medical). See **Padding expense accounts**.

False credentials Misrepresenting education or experience or professional certification to fraudulently obtain and hold employment.

Fictitious refunds scheme Preparing false documents of refunds to cover thefts of cash. A retail cashiering fraud.

Fictitious sales A scheme to record sales to fictitious customers or fictitious sales to existing customers at the end of one period and reversing the transactions at the beginning of the next period. The purpose of the scheme is to inflate sales to create false profit statements or earn unwarranted bonuses. Excessive credit notes or sales cancellations at the beginning of an accounting period can be an indicator of this fraud.

Fiduciary duty The acts necessary (usually of an authorised employee or agent) to carry out a responsibility to care for assets prudently.

Firewall A software program that protects direct access to a local area network by establishing a 'public' network in front of the 'trusted' network. The purpose of the program is to secure data and systems from hackers.

Forensic Suitable for use in a court proceeding.

Forensic investigation Examination of a business process for evidence of fraud.

Forgery Creation of false documents or altering existing documents, especially financial instruments or other authorisations.

Fraud (No real legal definition.) A theft, concealment and conversion to personal gain of another's money, physical assets, information, or time, involving a deception. When somebody knowingly lies to obtain benefit or advantage or to cause some benefit that is due to be denied. If there is no lie, there may be abuse but not fraud. Deceit or trickery (for example, intentional perversion of truth in order to induce another to part with something of value or to surrender all legal right), an act of deceiving or misrepresenting. A representation about a material fact, which is false and made intentionally, knowingly, or recklessly so, which is believed and acted upon by the victim to the victim's damage.

Fraud scenarios A method of developing mental models of possible frauds: 'thinking like a crook'.

Fraudster One who commits a fraud.

'Ghost' employees Fictitious employees on the payroll, for whom the supervisor or manager receives the extra salary.

Hacker A person who attacks another's computer and seeks to gain unauthorised access by hacking (breaking down) the computer's logical security.

Inflated inventory An indication of embezzlement or possible theft of inventory.

Influence peddling The offer by a government official to use their office to influence actions for a private party in return for something of value.

Informant A person, such as a co-worker or friend of the accused, used in the investigation of a fraud who may know something about the crime but is otherwise not involved.

Insider trading Using business information not released to the public to reap profits trading in the financial markets.

Inventory shrinkage Theft of physical inventory, especially in the retail trade.

Investigation A structured gathering of documentary evidence and testimony to solve a reported fraud.

IP-based geolocation The IP address of the consumer's browser can provide critical information for Internet fraud screening. IP geolocation technology can be used to identify with reasonable accuracy the geographic location of the consumer, even though most consumers connect to the Web via Internet service providers (ISPs) that assign a new IP address to each new connection and despite the fact that for some ISPs, all connections may appear to originate from the same IP address (typically through a proxy).

Journal entry fraud Using accounting journal entries to fraudulently adjust financial statements.

Key logging 'Key logging' devices or software (or spyware) may be used to record and sift every keystroke made on a personal computer.

Kickback A payment by a vendor to an employee at the request of the employee in order for the vendor to receive favourable treatment.

Kiting Using several bank accounts in different banks, making deposits and writing cheques against the accounts before the deposit cheques clear the banking system, creating a 'float' of money out of nothing more than the lag in time while cheques clear and post to their respective accounts.

Lifestyle changes A possible indicator of theft is the sudden change in lifestyle such as exhibiting more than usual wealth.

Lowballing Placing an unusually low bid to win the business, often with the intent to inflate the price later with extras or change orders. Can also indicate a defective request for proposal. Used to be common practice when competing for audit work.

Misappropriation A polite word for theft.

Monetising goods Fraudsters know that the Internet can provide safe and efficient ways to market stolen goods, and online auctions are one of their favourite channels. Fraudsters can auction merchandise that they already have stolen or, better yet, simply act as a broker and have the site ship the goods directly to the auction winner.

Negative databases Databases of prior fraud, called negative databases, are a simple defensive method against repeat offenders, and because most Internet fraud cases appear to be caused by repeat offenders, it is a useful tool. The first step is to build a negative database of confirmed fraudulent orders; the merchant can then compare elements in incoming orders to information in the prior-fraud database to see if a match exists.

Number generators Credit card number generators are easily downloadable from hacker sites. These programs produce lists of properly formatted, but randomly generated, credit card account numbers from hundreds of different issuing banks. Some of the numbers generated by the program, typically one in every ten, will match an active account.

Over-billing schemes Padding invoices with extraneous or fictitious items. Intentional duplicate billing, such as billing two parties for the same work is also an over-billing scheme.

Overt Open, not hidden. See **Covert**.

Padding expense accounts Adding extra expense items or inflating the value of legitimate expense items to obtain unwarranted reimbursements.

Padding overtime Adding extra hours to falsely inflate the payroll and earn unwarranted pay.

Pattern detectors Pattern detectors are designed to identify suspicious orders by analysing the linkage and timing of a series of orders. They too are rule-based systems, but they detect fraud by finding linkages among multiple orders as opposed to looking for patterns in a single order. In many instances, an individual order may not have any of the traits that would indicate the possibility of fraud. However, by relating an individual order to other orders placed over a relatively short period of time, merchants can detect fraud patterns. For example, some fraudsters now tend to place many small orders, often with different credit cards, instead of one large order that may be deemed suspicious by the merchant. In some cases, however, these orders are all placed under the same user account or have the same e-mail address or telephone number.

Perjury Lying under oath, in court appearances, or evidential documents.

Perpetrator The person who commits the fraud.

Personal identification number (PIN) A code used to access personal data or accounts.

Phishing An attempt to fraudulently acquire sensitive personal information, such as passwords and credit card details, by masquerading as a trustworthy person or business, such as the issuing entity itself, often by using electronic communication such as e-mail or instant messages. Fraudsters may also establish a website that has an appearance of a genuine corporation to be used in information-gathering and fraud.

Pilfering Theft, usually referring to theft of physical goods. In retail business, customer theft is known as shoplifting and employee theft is called pilfering. Occasionally used also with theft of cash, especially petty cash or for small thefts.

Ponzi scheme A fraud in which a high rate of return is promised on investments. The first few investors receive the high rate of return from part of the investments of later victims. At no time is any actual investment made.

Positive databases A positive database can be used to identify orders originating from trusted returning customers, which for some merchants my represent a significant percentage of incoming transactions. This approach is particularly easy for websites that allow customers to create a password-protected user account, which enables a relatively secure identification of previous customers. See also **Negative databases**.

Posting Entering transactions into books of account or between accounts in the financial records.

Pretence Also false pretence. To represent something to be what it is not.

Pump-and-dump Manipulating stock prices by artificially creating demand through rumour, high-pressure sales tactics, or multiple large orders. The price is 'pumped' upwards and then when other investors join the trend, the original investors 'dump' the stock in a rapid sell-off. See also **Bucket shop**.

Pyramid scheme A commercial version of the Ponzi scheme where the fraudster sells bogus distributorships, franchises or business opportunity plans to people who are in turn induced to do the same.

Reconciliation A process of comparing details with control totals, such as cheques paid during the month and deposits made that month with the change in bank balance at end of the month.

Red flags Symptoms and indicators (of fraud).

Restitution Restoring money or property to the victim of a fraud.

Risk scoring A risk-scoring system uses a statistical computer model to evaluate dozens of potential fraud indicators (gathered from the methodologies already described). It then produces an overall numerical score that indicates the likelihood of fraud for an individual transaction.

Rule-based systems While Internet merchants typically have limited history on an individual credit card, they do have detailed information, such as billing and shipping address details, IP address, e-mail address, and, most importantly, details about the type and quantity of products being ordered. Rule-based systems enable merchants to take advantage of this detailed data by setting up multiple order-evaluation screening criteria, each based on a number of order characteristics. For example, orders for an unusual number of the same product with a next day delivery request to a mail-drop address are likely to be fraudulent. A typically rule-based system enables a business user to rapidly deploy and maintain a large library of business rules that are evaluated in real time as an order is processed. When one or more of the rules are triggered, an order-disposition action is taken; typically, the order is flagged for manual approval and verification, or the order could be automatically declined.

Ruse A scheme that tries to make something appear as something else. Hiding the true meaning or acting out a lie. A subterfuge or pretence.

Salami In banking, a fraud that involves taking all of the 'round-down' fractional pence from periodic interest payments and crediting them to a single account. Thus each transaction has only a thin slice removed.

Shoplifting Customer theft from retail inventory.

Shorting In medical and merchandise frauds, delivering less prescription medicine or other goods than actually charged to the insurance company, government or other entity.

Short shipping Shipping less than the quantity shown on the invoice (or shipping nothing at all).

Shoulder surfing Observing someone using a PIN (personal identification number) by covertly looking over their shoulder, sometimes with the aid of binoculars or video camera with zoom lens.

Shrinkage See **Inventory shrinkage**.

Spyware Computer software that collects personal information about users without their informed consent, including benign collections such as tracking the websites a user visits and sending them to an advertising agency, and more malicious and potentially fraudulent attempts to intercept passwords, credit card numbers or other account numbers as a user enters them for other purposes. Spyware does not spread like a computer virus, but gets onto a computer system without the user being aware, either by piggybacking on a desirable piece of software, or by means of a **Trojan horse**.

Teeming and lading Stealing a customer payment and then using a subsequent customer payment to cover the previous customer's account. This requires splitting of customer receipts or posting to incorrect accounts and is often uncovered through issuing of monthly statements.

Theft Permanently depriving the owner of goods or cash.

Tone at the top The messages and actions of senior management in relation to fraud detection and deterrence.

Trapdoor In computer fraud, a means of unauthorised access to the computer operating system or files, usually placed by a hacker.

Trojan horse A type of computer program that remains inert (and possibly hidden) until activated by an external event such as a date. Used as viruses to disrupt or destroy computer operations, or used to open a **Trapdoor** for unauthorised access.

Unauthorised use Policies should be in place to determine what business resources may be used for personal business and at what times. Other use constitutes theft.

Under-ring To record less than the actual sales price. Usually refers to a cashier ringing a sale on a cash register. Under-rings may be a method used in skimming cash by the cashier, or they may be used to give unauthorised discounts to an accomplice.

Unethical Behaviour that does not meet community standards for right behaviour, but that does not violate any laws.

Uttering In Scotland, the crime of issuing a false document of making a false pretence.

Virus In computer operations, a program that is deliberately released into a system with the ability to replicate itself and spread by attaching unauthorised data to files. Viruses can be benign, just taking up disk storage space, or they may be destructive and actually destroy data or deny authorised access.

Voids In cashiering, ringing a 'void' to cancel a previous sale. Excessive voids may be a sign of till theft.

Whistle-blowing The act of an employee revealing suspected fraud (possibly involving senior management) to an outside third party or to a non-executive function such as the audit committee.

Index

Note: Page references in **bold** refer to terms in the Glossary

Printed in Great Britain
by Amazon

18599094R00289